MW01078724

Encyclopedia of HAIR

A CULTURAL HISTORY

VICTORIA SHERROW

GREENWOOD PRESS
Westport, Connecticut • London

Library of Congress Cataloging-in-Publication Data

Sherrow, Victoria.
Encyclopedia of hair : a cultural history / Victoria Sherrow.
p. cm.
Includes bibliographical references and index.
ISBN 0–313–33145–6 (alk. paper)
1. Hairdressing—History. 2. Hairdressing—Encyclopedias.
3. Hairstyles—History. 4. Hairstyles—Encyclopedias. I. Title.
TT957.S46 2006
391.5'09—dc22 2005020995

British Library Cataloguing in Publication Data is available.

Library of Congress Catalog Card Number: 2005020995
ISBN: 0–313–33145–6

First published in 2006

Greenwood Press, 88 Post Road West, Westport, CT 06881
An imprint of Greenwood Publishing Group, Inc.
www.greenwood.com

Printed in the United States of America

The paper used in this book complies with the Permanent Paper Standard issued by the National Information Standards Organization (Z39.48–1984).

10 9 8 7 6 5 4 3 2 1

Contents

List of Entries

Guide to Related Topics

CELEBRITY HAIR

Advertising
African Americans
Aniston, Jennifer
Baker, Josephine
Baldness, Voluntary
Ball, Lucille
Bara, Theda
Beards, Men's
Bow, Clara
Breck Girl
Brummell, Beau
Diana, Princess of Wales
Elizabeth I
Factor, Max
Fawcett, Farrah
Hair Colorants
Hairstyles, Twentieth-Century
Hamill, Dorothy
Harlow, Jean
Hepburn, Audrey
Kennedy, Jacqueline Bouvier
Lake, Veronica
Monroe, Marilyn
Mustache
"Mustache Gang"
Parker, Sarah Jessica
Pickford, Mary
Ponytail
Presley, Elvis Aaron
Sassoon, Vidal
Shampoo
Soul Patch
Temple, Shirley
Twiggy
Valentino, Rudolph

CONSUMER AND SAFETY ISSUES

Advertising
Aging and Hair
Allergic Reactions
Animal Testing
Barbers
Begoun, Paula
Folliculitis
Fragrance
Hair Colorants
Hair Straightening
Hair Transplant
Lake, Veronica
Laws and Regulations
Tonics, Hair

CONTESTS, AWARDS, AND COMPETITIONS

Competitions
Hairdressing
Salons, Hair and Beauty
World Beard and Moustache
Championship

CULTURES AND CUSTOMS

Africa
African Americans
Amish
Arabia, Ancient through Middle Ages
Byzantine Empire
Celts, Ancient
China
Comb

Coming of Age
Egypt, Ancient
Elizabethan Era
Flappers
French Revolution
Gibson Girl
Greece, Ancient
Hair Art
Hair Jewelry
Hippies
India
Japan
Latin America, Ancient Times to 1500s
Memento
Mesopotamia
Middle East
Monastic Styles
Mourning
Native Americans (North American)
Nuba
Punishment
Puritans
Regency
Religion and Hair
Renaissance Europe
Roman Empire
Salons, Hair and Beauty
Scalping
Shampoo
Shaving
Society of Friends (Quakers)
Vikings
Yoruba

DISEASES AND DISORDERS

Albinism
Allergic Reactions
Alopecia Areata
Dandruff
Folliculitis
Hair Analysis
Hair Loss
Hirsutism
Hypertrichosis
Lice, Head
Lice, Pubic
Pityriasis amiantacea
Psoriasis
Seborrheic Dermatitis
Tinea Capitus
Trichophagy
Trichotillomania

GROWTH AND PHYSICAL CHARACTERISTICS

Africa
Aging and Hair
Beards, Men's
Beards, Women's
Body Hair
Eyebrows
Eyelashes
Hair Color
Hair Loss
Hair Removal
Mustache
Pubic Hair
Sideburns
Soul Patch
Unibrow

HAIR AND THE ARTS

Factor, Max
Hair (the musical)
Hair Art
Hair Color
Hair Jewelry
Hairspray
Henna
Lady Godiva
Literature
Renaissance Europe
Superstitions

HAIR CARE BUSINESS

Advertising
Alberto-Culver Company
Begoun, Paula
Breck Girl
Clairol
Comb
Dial Corporation
Factor, Max
Hair Dryers
Hair Loss
Hair Straightening
Hair Transplant
Henkel Group
John Frieda Professional Hair Care, Inc.
John Paul Mitchell Systems
Johnson Products
L'Oreal
Malone, Annie Minerva Turnbo Pope
Marcel Wave
Michaeljohn
Natural Products
Procter & Gamble
Revlon
Salons, Hair and Beauty
Sassoon, Vidal
Shampoo
Styling Products
Styling Tools
Unilever
Zotos International, Inc.

HAIR CARE ENTREPRENEURS

Alberto-Culver Company
Clairol
Factor, Max
Gillette Company

HAIR CARE: TOOLS, PRODUCTS, AND METHODS

Africa
Alberto-Culver Company
Baldness, Voluntary
Barbers
Beards, Men's
Burma Shave
China
Comb
Dermatology
Eyebrows
Eyelashes
Factor, Max
Fragrance
Gillette Company
Hair Colorants
Hair Dryers
Hair Net
Hairpin
Hair Removal
Hairspray
Hair Straightening
Hair Transplant
Hair Weave
Harper, Martha Matilda
Headgear
Henna
India
Japan
John Frieda Professional Hair Care, Inc.
Gibson Girl
Kohl
Native Americans (North American)
Natural Products
Permanent (Permanent Wave)
Pompadour
Sassoon, Vidal
Shampoo
Styling Products
Styling Tools
Tonics, Hair
Trichology
Walker, Madam C. J.
Wigs and Hairpieces
Worthington, Charles
Zotos International, Inc.

HAIR COLORANTS

Hairdressing
Harper, Martha Matilda
John Frieda Professional Hair Care, Inc.
John Paul Mitchell Systems
Johnson, George Ellis
Johnson Products
Joyner, Marjorie Stewart
L'Oreal
Malone, Annie Minerva Turnbo Pope
Marcel Wave
Noda, Alice Sae Teshima
Overton, Anthony
Roffler, Edmond O.
Salons, Hair and Beauty
Sassoon, Vidal
Walker, Madam C. J.
Washington, Sarah Spencer

HAIRDRESSERS/HAIRSTYLISTS

Africa
African Americans
Alexandre of Paris
Barbers
Battelle, Kenneth
Dessange, Jacques
Eber, Jose
Fekkai, Frédéric
Harper, Martha Matilda
Hershberger, Sally
John Frieda Professional Hair Care, Inc.
John Paul Mitchell Systems
Kazan, Michel
Marcel Wave
Masters, George
Michaeljohn
Noda, Alice Sae Teshima
Normant, Serge
Ouidad
Roffler, Edmond O.
Salons, Beauty and Hair
Sassoon, Vidal
Wigs and Hairpieces
Worthington, Charles

HAIRSTYLES AND TRENDS

Afro
Arabia, Ancient through Middle Ages
Baldness, Voluntary
Bangs
Bara, Theda
Beards, Men's
Bob, The
Bouffant
Bow, Clara
Brummell, Beau
Buzz Cut
Byzantine Empire
Celts, Ancient
China
Cornrows
Crew Cut
Dredlocks
Egypt, Ancient
Elizabethan Era
Feathered Hairstyle
Flappers
Fontange
French Revolution
Gibson Girl
Greece, Ancient
Hair Colorants
Hairstyles, Twentieth-Century
Hair Weave
Harlow, Jean
Henna
India
Japan
Kennedy, Jacqueline Bouvier (Onassis)
Lake, Veronica
Latin America, Ancient Times to 1500s
Marcel Wave
Mesopotamia
Middle Ages
Middle East
Monastic Styles

Mourning
Mustache
Nuba
Parker, Sarah Jessica
Permanent (Permanent Wave)
Pompadour
Ponytail
Pubic Hair
Punk
Regency
Religion and Hair
Renaissance Europe
Roman Empire
Salons, Hair and Beauty
Sassoon, Vidal
Shaving
Sideburns
Temple, Shirley
Toupee
Victorian Era
Vikings
Water Wave
Yoruba

HISTORY

Advertising
Africa
African Americans
Afro
Arabia, Ancient through Middle Ages
Barbers
Beards, Men's
Beards, Women's
Breck Girl
Brummell, Beau
Celts, Ancient
Charm Schools
China
Cornrows
Dredlocks
Elizabethan Era
Flappers
Fragrance
French Revolution
Gibson Girl
Hair Art
Hair Colorants
Hairdressing
Hair Jewelry
Hair Loss
Hair Straightening
Hair Transplant
Hair Weave
Henna
India
Japan
Kohl
Latin America, Ancient Times to 1500s
Memento
Mesopotamia
Middle Ages
Military
Mourning
Mustache
"Mustache Gang"
Occupations
Politics and Hair
Pubic Hair
Punishment
Puritans
Regency
Renaissance Europe
Shampoo
Shaving
Sideburns
Superstitions
Tonics, Hair
Victorian Era
Vikings
Wigs and Hairpieces

ORGANIZATIONS

American Beauty Association
American Health and Beauty Aids Institute
Bald-Headed Men of America
Cosmetic, Toiletry, and Fragrance Association, The
Cosmetic Executive Women
Hairdressing
Locks of Love

ORNAMENTATION

Adornment, Ornamental
Adornment, Symbolic
Africa
Afro
Beards, Men's
Byzantine Empire
Celts, Ancient
China
Comb, Decorative
Comb, Liturgical
Egypt, Ancient
False Beard
Greece, Ancient
Hair Net
Hairstyles, Twentieth-Century
Headgear
Japan
Latin America, Ancient Times to 1500s
Mesopotamia
Middle Ages
Middle East
Renaissance Europe
Roman Empire
Victorian Era
Wigs and Hairpieces

SOCIAL AND LEGAL ISSUES

African Americans
Afro
Aging and Hair
Animal Testing
Beards, Men's
Bob, The
Body Hair
Dredlocks
Hair Analysis
Hair Color
Hair Net
Hair Removal
Hippies
Laws and Regulations
Locks of Love
Middle Ages
Mustache
Native Americans (North American)
Palmer, Joe
Politics and Hair
Pubic Hair
Religion and Hair
Shaving
Title VII
Wigs and Hairpieces

SPIRITUALITY/RELIGION

Amish
Beards, Men's
Coming of Age
Egypt, Ancient
Headgear
Laws and Regulations
Middle Ages
Middle East
Monastic Styles
Native Americans (North American)
Politics and Hair
Puritans
Religion and Hair
Society of Friends (Quakers)
Yoruba

Preface

The *Encyclopedia of Hair* looks at the history of hair through the ages, revealing certain common threads as well as many differences among cultures around the world. Ideas about what constitutes attractive, stylish, or appropriate hair have varied from place to place and from one historical era to the next. Certain styles have come and gone, while others reappear with variations. Men's and women's hairstyles have reflected ideas about age, gender, religious beliefs, occupation, politics, and other aspects of life. Hairstyling approaches also reflect practical considerations such as climate, occupation, economics, and the kinds of tools and materials that are available. Since the twentieth century, mass media and celebrities have played an increasingly influential role in determining hairstyle trends and fashions.

The focus of this book is on the care and appearance of the hair (both head and body) and on the social-historical, health-related, age-related, regulatory, and other non-utilitarian aspects of grooming hair and dealing with facial and body hair. The book does not offer advice for selecting and using hair products or give advice on personal grooming but does cover the history of some major products and techniques, as well as describe some of the leaders and leading companies in the hair care industry. In modern times, hair care has become a major industry as hair care services and products used to color, cleanse, condition, and style the hair reap annual sales measured in billions of dollars.

While an exhaustive account of hairstyling in every culture since prehistoric times is beyond the scope of this volume, the encyclopedia notes some significant sociological, psychological, political, legal, religious, and economic aspects relating to hair on the head and body. An introduction gives an overview of the book, as well as discusses the scientific aspects of hair composition and growth. The broad topics in the volume include: care and cleansing of hair and scalp; attitudes toward hair removal and practices in various cultures; hair arrangement and styling; business and commercial aspects; laws and legal matters; trends and trendsetters; organizations for hair care professionals; health and science; political importance; and spiritual/religious aspects. The *Encyclopedia of Hair* introduces readers to the diversity of various cultural perspectives but contains more detailed information about Western styles, particularly those in the United States, because American readers make up the primary audience for this volume.

Readers who wish to pursue the topics in this volume will find numerous references for further reading and an extensive bibliography including books, articles, and Web sites. Suggestions for further reading also appear at the end of entries, which are listed alphabetically. Some entries on broad topics (e.g., barbers, beards, hair colorants, wigs, and hairpieces) run several pages long. Within the entries themselves are cross-references, set in boldfaced type. Images are used to illustrate various topics as well as expand on the text. The encyclopedia also includes blind entries that will direct readers to entries on related topics. A subject index completes the book.

Material for the encyclopedia was gathered over a period of several years from various primary and secondary sources. Information about ancient times comes from cave paintings and archeological finds, including tombs and museum exhibits. Translations of works written by ancient historians in Rome, Greece, the Middle East, and other places provide fascinating glimpses of hair care practices and styles during earlier times. Likewise, historical material about hair and hairstyling can be found in letters, diaries, journals, biographies, autobiographies, and the works of anthropologists and other scientists, as well as travelers. The graphic arts and artifacts of various cultures provide still more information. Material about well-known people came from published interviews, autobiographies, and authoritative biographies.

This volume is written for people who wish to learn more about the social history and customs of different cultures, as well as the changing attitudes toward hair as a continuing focus of personal appearance. Students, librarians, teachers and professors, researchers, and general readers may find the information both useful and interesting.

Introduction

Throughout history, people have cared about their appearance and sought ways to personalize their looks or gain social rewards through grooming and self-adornment. Anthropologists believe that this desire to groom and beautify the body is an inherent part of being human.

Hair is a key aspect of appearance, one that is always on view unless it is purposely concealed, removed, or lost as a result of aging or disease. The act of grooming hair is common to certain fur-bearing animals, but, unlike other animals, human beings often cut, remove, or otherwise alter their hair. Also unlike fur-bearing animals, human hair is most obvious only on certain parts of the body: head, face, armpits, legs, and pubic region.

COMPOSITION AND GROWTH OF HAIR

Hair itself is a biological polymer, made up of about 10 percent water and more than 90 percent proteins, called keratins. Keratins in hair are fibrous types of protein held together by disulfide bonds, which are strong covalent bonds between two sulfhydryl groups. These chemical components and strong chemical bonds make hair a durable material. Hair that is sealed in a tomb or other container can last for thousands of years.

A hair consists of an inner cortex surrounded by a covering called the cuticle, which is made up of scale-shaped layers. Human hair cuticles typically have six to eight layers. Cortical cells contain numerous fibrils, separated by a softer material called the matrix. Each hair grows from a follicle, which contains at least one tiny oil-producing sebaceous gland. Healthy hairs end with a root nourished by tiny blood vessels called capillaries. The root of the hair is surrounded by a white-colored bulb, and when hair is pulled out by its root, this bulb remains attached.

The materials that make up a hair and give it color are produced inside the follicle. Human hair follicles operate independently rather than as a group. As a result, large numbers of hairs are not shed at once, as they are in some animals. Unless a disease process occurs, nearly all—about 90 percent—of a human's hair follicles will continually stay in the growing phase. During that growing phase, cells in the matrix produce keratin, as well as melanin, the substance that gives hair its color.

Hair follicles generally stay in the active stage for about three years or more before going into a degeneration phase that lasts about three weeks. Then comes a resting, or shedding, phase, which lasts for about three months. During this phase, the hair from that follicle drops out. A healthy follicle will then regenerate itself and begin a new cycle to produce hair.

The hair on the human head grows about one-half inch per month, and the average life span of a hair is between four to seven years. Hair growth occurs most rapidly in people aged fifteen to thirty and also tends to grow faster on women than men. The distribution of body hair also differs in men and women, and the amount of body hair varies from one ethnic group to another.

The number of hairs and texture vary among races and nationalities. Among people of European descent, people with natural red hair have the fewest number of hairs, followed by blond and then brunette. People of African descent usually have thicker hair than other groups. The average number of follicles on the scalp is about 100,000 to 150,000.

Human hair changes according to the environment and the ways in which it is arranged or chemically treated. A hairstyle will not remain in place if it gets wet, for example. Chemical treatments that rearrange the chemical bonds are required in order to create lasting styles or lasting changes in texture.

CHANGING FUNCTIONS OF HAIR ON HUMANS

Early humans had a great deal more hair distributed all over the body, but this changed through the millennia. For prehistoric humans, hair helped to protect the body from extreme temperatures and abrasions or other injuries. It also may have provided some camouflage. Over time, however, most of this hair diminished. As hair disappeared, the number of sweat glands on the body increased, which enabled people to stay cooler.

Scientists have concluded that there were important reasons for these changes. In *The Naked Ape* (Morris 1999, 99), zoologist Desmond Morris wrote, "If the hair has to go then clearly there must be a very powerful reason for abolishing it." Scientists note that as people began to wear animal skins, use fire for heat, and find more effective forms of shelter, hair was not needed as much to protect them from changing weather. Less hair also reduced the chance of parasites and made it easier to stay healthy, since a hairless body was easier to keep clean.

Scientists also say that the loss of hair may have served to increase sexual attraction and maintain relationships between males and females. Less body hair meant that sexual organs were more visible. Exposed skin also felt stronger sensations during sexual activity. As people began to hunt in groups and form communities, they shared their work and resources. This type of society worked better if men and women formed stable pair-bonds to rear their young and to minimize the competition among men for the same females. According to author Wendy Cooper, "Such a degree of cooperation could have been possible only if sexual rivalry was reduced to the minimum and the unprotected females could be left safe from the advances of other males" (Cooper 1971, 13).

As human lifestyles changed, the function of hair also changed so that it served more of a social and cultural role. Hair became a source of strong interest and even fascination, appearing in artwork, mythology, folklore, and magical and spiritual customs. Scientists attribute some of this interest to the fact that hair grows only on certain parts of the body and certain body hairs begin growing during puberty, a significant time in human development. In addition, hair continues to grow throughout a person's life, so it became a symbol of renewal and regeneration—even of life itself. Some cultures find it significant that the largest growth of hair occurs on the head, the uppermost part of the body. And since hair can be altered in many ways and still grow back, it offers people the chance to express their personal tastes and preferences.

A UNIVERSAL PURSUIT

Grooming, styling, adorning, and removing hair have been common practices in all societies since the beginning of recorded history. For example, two statuettes from the Ice Age, known as the Venus of Willendorf (thought to date back to 30,000–25,000 BCE) and the Venus of Brassempouy (30,000 BCE), show evidence of deliberate hairstyling. Through excavation and exploration, scientists have found pictures, artifacts, and writings dating back thousands of years, proving people around the world cared about the length, texture, color, growth, style, and loss of their hair.

To groom their hair, people have been willing to spend time, energy, and money, as well as endure lengthy and uncomfortable procedures. They have hunted down elusive reptiles or plants to obtain hair-care ingredients, plucked out masses of hair with clam shells, sat under hot machines wearing tightly wound metal rods, borne two-foot tall wigs on their heads, used chemicals that burned the scalp, and undergone surgical procedures, to name a few methods.

People have washed, combed, brushed, cut, colored, arranged, and decorated their hair in countless ways, ranging from simple to quite elaborate. The resulting styles have reflected spiritual beliefs, as well as social, political, and historical events, as well as the materials and technology that were available for styling hair. While prehistoric people may have chosen to dab colored mud on their hair and attach an ornamental bone or shell, their modern counterparts through the ages have worn perfumed oils, ivory combs, gold mesh snoods, powdered wigs, diamond hairclips, extensions, or purple wash-out paint.

The goals of hair-styling have varied, though some remain constant through time. Some of them include the desire for good luck or protection from evil spirits; attracting a mate; complying with cultural mores (or, conversely, showing nonconformity); fighting signs of aging; impressing other people; or revealing one's job or rank.

Hair can even be used to intimidate a military foe. The Roman historian Diodorus described the fearsome appearance of Celtic warriors in battle. These warriors used lime to bleach their hair to a startling white shade and then styled it back from the forehead for a mane-like effect. They combined this hairstyle with face paint in a vivid blue shade made from woad. The legendary Irish warrior Cu Chulainn supposedly dyed his hair three different shades and wore long, stiff points that were strong enough to pierce an apple (Powell 1958, 65). In other times, soldiers have worn distinctive mustaches or other facial hair to look more fearsome and assert their masculinity.

More often, hair styling served more common social functions. One predictable and longstanding function of hair was to identify people by gender, which was part of attracting a mate.

SOCIAL MEANINGS OF HAIR

Gender Differentiation

Throughout history, men's and women's hair styles often have been quite different, and both have varied with the changing fashions. Certain styles have been regarded as "feminine" while others were viewed as "masculine," which set the genders apart and enabled people to identify one another more easily. For thousands of years, in most cultures, women wore their hair longer than men's. This changed in the twentieth century in western cultures. At the turn of the twenty-first century, most men opt to wear short hair but they may also wear it longer. Women are free to cut theirs short, and both men and women can receive hair-care services at "unisex" hair salons.

During certain eras, women's hair was also bound and covered, especially after marriage. In *Rapunzel's Daughters* (2004), author Rose Weitz explains the origins of early Judeo-Christian attitudes toward women's hair that influenced hairstyles in western society:

> Pre-modern Christian theologians . . . believed that Eve, and all women after her, were inherently more susceptible than men to the passions of the flesh and the Devil's seductions. As a result, women posed constant dangers to men's souls, having the power to tempt men as Eve had tempted Adam. Meanwhile folktales told of mermaids and sirens, like the Lorelei, who enchanted and entrapped sailors by singing while combing their long tresses. (Weitz, 4)

For these kinds of reasons, throughout the Middle Ages, European women covered their hair. In the Middle East and parts of Asia, Muslim women covered their hair and continue to do so today. Covering the head is also a cultural or religious imperative for women in certain other places. Wedding customs reflect these ideas, since women covered their heads with a veil, which their husband uncovered during the ceremony. In some cultures, a married woman who revealed her hair in public was assumed to be an adulteress.

These attitudes found their way into laws, and in the United States, some states passed laws during colonial days or later stating that a woman's hair belonged to her husband. A wife was forbidden to cut her hair without her husband's permission.

Similarly, the idea that men's hair should be shorter than women's took hold in early Jewish and Christian societies. Religious leaders pointed to a letter that the apostle Paul wrote to the Corinthians, saying, "Does not nature itself teach you that for a man to wear long hair is degrading to him, but if a woman wears long hair it is her pride?" (Simon 2000, 16). During the Middle Ages, Roman Catholic leaders continued to urge men to cut their hair, as well as their beards.

From time to time, political conflicts arose over hairstyles. During the 1600s, men's hair became embroiled in religious and political conflicts as the Puritan "Roundheads" prided themselves on their own short hair and derided the Royalist men in England who wore long curls and wigs. During the French Revolution, simple hairstyles were a sign of the revolutionary while elaborate hair signaled a member of the aristocracy.

The practice of removing or keeping facial or body hair also has been related to gender. In certain cultures, women have been expected to remove all their body hair, or to remove it at certain times, such as marriage. Men's facial hair has been in and out of fashion, though some religious groups have consistently mandated beards for men. While men's facial hair is accepted as a sign of masculinity, women typically remove obvious hair on their chins, cheeks, or upper lip. During the twentieth century, the vast majority of women in western cultures also began shaving their legs.

In western societies, as capitalism advanced during the Middle Ages, religious control over daily life diminished. Men in western cultures had once gained more status and pride from a wife who appeared modest, with hair discreetly hidden. In a capitalistic culture, however, hairstyling and hair ornaments were among the visible signs of a man's wealth.

Social and economic forces continue to affect styles in hair to the present day, whereas in religion-based societies, hairstyles tend to reflect the group's beliefs. In societies where gender roles are strictly defined and/or women are regarded as subservient to men, women may still cover their hair or wear very simple, traditional styles.

In addition to conforming to customs that dictated "appropriate" styles for men and women, people also have chosen their hairstyles to enhance their appeal to the opposite sex. As the entries within this volume demonstrate, beauty ideals have varied throughout history, along with preferences for certain hair colors, lengths, and ornamentation. In general, however, well-groomed hair has been regarded as one sign that someone will make a healthy, industrious, and dependable mate.

Spiritual Customs

Just as religious beliefs play a role in designating certain hairstyles for each gender, they led to numerous customs regarding hair. Some of these customs involve sacrificing hair or wearing specific styles for religious ceremonies. The custom of sacrificing hair from the head or face in order to request favors from the gods can be found in ancient Greece and Rome, for example.

Other customs involve mourning. One common custom, dating back to ancient times, required mourners to leave their hair loose and unkempt as a sign of their grief. A person in mourning was presumed to be too distraught to devote time and attention to personal appearance. In Greece, some people shaved their heads and hung a lock of hair from the deceased on their door. Some cultures expected people to place their own hair in the tomb or vessel that contained the body of the dead.

One of the most dramatic mourning ceremonies involving hair takes place among aborigines who live in northwestern Australia. When a death occurs, people alternately prostrate themselves on the ground and then run a few steps while beating their heads with shells and stones, or, for men, sticks that have sharp flint on the ends. Their heads bleed from these blows as they lie upon the body of the deceased. Close relatives of the dead person keep his or her hair and may attach it to their own beard or hair after the burial.

Underlying many belief systems is the idea that hair has inherent power. In the Old Testament story about Samson and Delilah, Samson is heroic and powerful as long as he has his hair. He loses that power when Delilah tricks him and cuts it off. In the fairy tale of Rapunzel, the heroine gains power by lowering her long, healthy tresses so that her suitor can climb up and rescue her from the tower where she was imprisoned. Native Americans thought that enemies could make use of their hair if they got hold of it, so they burned stray or combed-out hairs. In some cultures, hair itself is sacred. Ancient Buddhist teachings held that hair was a gift from one's ancestors and should be cherished like other body parts. The Sikhs, a religious denomination in Asia, regard hair as sacred. Devout Sikhs are expected to leave their hair uncut throughout their lifetimes.

People may cherish locks of hair as a memento of loved ones who died. Hair remains in much the same condition over time so it can be a source of enduring memories of a loved one or of a certain stage of life, such as infancy.

Group Membership

In addition to signifying religious beliefs or identity, hairstyles may denote membership in other groups, including clans or tribes. It may reveal a person's occupation and marital or socioeconomic status. Certain hairstyles may also indicate age, stage of life, and/or state of health. Younger people typically have thicker, longer, and shinier hair. Maintaining such a look into old age requires the resources to buy certain products and accessories and time to spend on personal grooming.

People in different cultures have communicated their marital status through hair. Married women in many societies, including Japan and the Hopis of the American southwest, wore their hair up or in specific styles, depending on whether they were single or married. In Africa, certain ways of braiding the hair have shown whether a woman was yet married.

Hair also can indicate socioeconomic status. The ability to afford certain kinds of hair-care products, services, styling tools, and adornments may signal wealth and confer status on a person. Modern technology has blurred these distinctions somewhat as a variety of hair-care products and mass-produced materials became available in different price ranges and people gained access to tools and products they can use themselves.

Certain occupations have become known for their distinctive hair—or lack of it. Some people, such as Egyptian pharaohs, medieval monks, or chiefs among Native American tribes, have had distinctive and recognizable hairstyles. Slaves in many ancient cultures had their heads shaved, as did certain prisoners.

The idea of shaving the head as a sign of subordination, humiliation, or punishment persisted into modern times. After World War II, French women who had collaborated with Nazi soldiers were publicly humiliated when members of their communities shaved their heads. Since ancient times, victorious armies have shaved their conquered enemies bald in order to degrade them and leave a visible mark of their defeat. This practice continued into the twentieth century.

In other cases, people shave their heads to show that they have voluntarily joined a group. This happens when people enter Buddhist monasteries or certain military organizations. The loss of hair can indicate a separation from society or a commitment to put the welfare of a group above one's individual wishes.

MODERN ATTITUDES

In modern times, as in the past, hair continues to serve a psychological role in most people's lives and it provides a means of revealing cultural and social values. People use their hair for self-expression as well as a vehicle for gaining social acceptance.

While some religious or cultural groups maintain a traditional outlook on hair and hairstyles, including mandating gender-specific styles, most people in today's world base decisions about their hair on aesthetic preferences. During the 1960s, hair came to symbolize a certain freedom, and choosing one's style embodied feelings of individualism and personal identity. That same era marked an expanding awareness of other cultures, leading to a deeper appreciation of diversity in hairstyles and beauty ideals.

Since the early twentieth century, mass media have played an expanding role in shaping attitudes about beauty and appearance. That century also saw numerous innovations in hair-care products, which became a booming industry, along with the rapid growth of beauty and hair salons.

Before the late 1800s, American women had regarded hair care and beauty culture as private matters. Beauty historian Kathy Peiss describes how social and economic changes, including the expanding roles of women in the workplace, helped to change those attitudes:

> Commercial beautifying was generally considered as a "vulgarizing calling," a legacy of its ties to personal service and hands-on bodily care. This view changed as women's need for jobs grew more pressing in the late nineteenth century. Industry, immigration, and urban growth had transformed American economy and society. (Peiss 1998, 62)

In an industrialized world with mass communications, people's attitudes about hair and hairstyling are influenced by advertising and the visual and performing arts. Hairstyling decisions often are influenced by the hair-care industry and by celebrities. Billions of people now have access to the same images and commercial messages.

A BOOMING INDUSTRY

Beauty has become a commodity and the global hair care products and services businesses bring in billions of dollars each year. In 1995, Americans spent more than $4.5 billion on hair products. Divided into products and demographic sectors, this included $1.7 billion for shampoos, $1 billion for conditioners, $600 million for hair sprays, $500 million for gels and mousses, $1 billion for hair coloring, $100 million for men's hair products, and $125 million for home permanents and straightening products. Still more millions were spent on barbers and salon visits.

The black beauty industry is particularly robust. African Americans spend an estimated $325 million on hair care each year, and in Brazil the black hair-care market exceeds $2 billion. In Britain, this market accounts for about $50 million each year. South African women spend about $130 million a year on hair care. Today, in the United States, the hair-care industry employs hundreds of thousands of Americans who work as stylists, salon owners and managers, teachers in cosmetology schools, in merchandising, in product research and development, in manufacturing, and in distribution. A study commissioned in 2003 by the National Accrediting Commission of Cosmetology Arts and Sciences (NACCAS) found that the average income for a salon professional in the United States ranged from $30,000 to $50,000 a year.

Hair-care businesses thrive even in places where this kind of activity has been suppressed. For example, after the Taliban government fell in Afghanistan, more women began working as hairdressers. Before 2003, Afghan women who gave and received hair-care services did so secretly for fear of being arrested, and women were not allowed to show their faces in public. Hair and beauty care have been luxury items in this war-torn country, yet numerous women who need to earn a living or support families as widows found that these jobs offered them real economic opportunities. As of 2005, a beautician in the Afghan capital typically charged more to complete a hairstyle than a physician charged for a patient visit.

From the Stone Age to the Middle Ages to the Age of Reason and then the Space Age and Information Age, the preoccupation with hair continues. New technology gives people more tools to manipulate and alter their hair if they choose and may one day even find a way to prevent the hair loss that comes with aging. As long as humans care about their appearance, they will continue to use their hair as one visible way to express themselves and communicate a variety of social messages.

ADORNMENT, ORNAMENTAL

Throughout history, men and women in various cultures have worn hair ornaments. Cave paintings dating back to prehistoric times indicate that people added mud, clay, feathers, and bones to their hair and wore animal skins for ornamental reasons, as well as for warmth or protection. Hair ornaments have been found in ancient ruins, grave sites, paintings, pottery, and sculpture. They are worn for their aesthetic appeal, as well as to keep hair in place for stylistic or occupational reasons.

Ornaments range from simple to elaborate and come in various sizes, shapes, and designs. Often, especially in ancient times, the materials come from nature—flowers, leaves, feathers, shells, seeds, pearls, and gemstones. Feathers frequently appear on traditional **Native American** headgear, as do animal bones and skins. Modern ornaments may be wholly or partially synthetic, and most are made by machine rather than by hand.

It's believed that **hairpins** date back to prehistoric societies. They evolved from simple, one-pronged sticks made from natural materials, to simple or ornate, double-pronged U-shaped pins, to modern metal and plastic mass-produced hairpins.

Flowers and leaves are among the earliest known ornaments, and specific flowers were chosen based on a person's age or for special occasions. In **ancient Greece** and Rome, young women wore floral garlands. Hyacinths often adorned the hair of bridal attendants in Greece.

Men and women wore various kinds of hairpins, floral ornaments, and hair bands during the **Roman Empire** and in ancient Greece, Turkey, and **Egypt**. One type of hair band worn by Roman women was made from their own hair, or hair taken from slaves or other women.

Since ancient times, people in **Africa** have worn diverse ornaments made from feathers, shells, bone, wood, beads, coins, or cloth. These materials, as well as mud containing colorful ores, contribute to the overall hairstyle and also may signify a person's social rank, occupation, age, and other traits.

Women in ancient **Japan** wore kushi (combs) and kogai (long matching hairpins or sticks) made from abalone shells, wood, precious metals, ivory, and jade. Lacquerwork and mother-of-pearl are also popular for decorating hair ornaments in Asia.

European hair ornaments changed during the **Middle Ages**. Men wore pointed hoods with collars, and some medieval headgear featured rooster feathers. Married noblewomen typically wore a ring or cone-shaped hat and short veil;

for church, they wore hats or flat bonnets. Ribbons and gold threads were popular for social occasions, as were tiaras or headbands studded with gemstones or pearls. During the late Middle Ages, nets became more popular, as did snoods—airy, loose bags of handmade lace designed to hold the hair—and other cloth or net bags designed to contain the hair. Members of the lower classes wore simple, usually unadorned hairstyles.

As commerce and town life grew, prosperous Europeans spent more money on clothing and personal adornment. Clergymen expressed alarm, and some lawmakers tried to restrict behavior that they labeled as extravagant and vain. In 1485, the town council of Ratisbon (in Germany) passed an edict limiting the wives and daughters of prominent men to "2 pearl hair bands not to cost more than 12 florins, one tiara of gold set with pearls, not more than three veils costing 8 florins each" (Schaff 1997, vol. 6) [an unpaginated electronic work].

Last Horse wearing body paint and feathers in his hair. *Library of Congress*

During the Renaissance era, headdresses, tiaras, and other hair accessories became more ornate. Women of means decorated their hair with pearls, precious stones, ribbons, and veils, and some men also trimmed their hats with gems. Long gold or silver hairpins called bodkins were studded with diamonds, pearls, emeralds, and other gemstones. Women used cords or ribbons for a technique called lacing or taping, which bound their hair around the head. Lower- and middle-class women used simple cloth ribbons or cords, while wealthier women chose gold or silk laces.

To adorn their towering hairstyles and **wigs**, women in eighteenth-century France, England, and other countries added tall plumes, flowers, gemstones, ribbons, and an array of crafted objects, including replicas of ships. Plumes also appeared on men's headgear. In Spain and Latin cultures, women wore lace mantillas, often draped over a high comb, which might be simple or ornate.

During the **Regency** period, ornamental combs, diadems, and silk ribbons secured and adorned women's upswept hairstyles and buns. Bonnets, hats, or turbans were worn on social outings. Flowers, plumes, ribbons, pins, and decorative combs, often in romantic designs, were popular during Victorian days, when hair remained in upswept styles but with more curls and poufs than in the preceding era.

In Japan, **China**, and other Asian countries, combs remained popular, along with various hairpins and sticks crafted from tortoise, metal, wood, and other materials. Trimmings included mother-of-pearl, coral, seashell, and beads, for example. Flowers were used from ancient into modern times.

To adorn the **Gibson Girl** hairstyles of the early 1900s, women added flowers and combs to their soft, billowing **pompadours**. Some ornaments were engraved or made with seashells, pearls, or gemstones. Plumes and bandeaus trimmed with feathers and jewels were also worn. The Grecian band was made in different widths and materials, including velvet, satin, or silk, then left plain or trimmed.

> "The hair is the richest ornament of women."
>
> MARTIN LUTHER (1483–1546), German religious reformer

Fashion magazines offered advice about hairstyles and ornaments. An article in the March 1911 issue of *The Delineator* warned against too many ornaments:

> In combs, barrettes, bandeaux and other accessories there are many varieties, and a judicious selection is of no small importance in the general effect of the hairdressing. Too ornate or too numerous ones are in bad taste and detract from, rather than add to, the beauty of the coiffure. The large hairpins of shell with the tops inlaid with gold filigree or set with brilliants are very attractive and modest ornaments. Two or three of these may be used at the sides of the coiffure and prove of very effective service as well as a decoration.

Before World War I (1914–1918), most women had long hair, which was called their "crowning glory" and was a major focus of appearance. Wealthy women added lavish jewels, combs, feathers, and silk turbans to their coiffures. One of the most popular ornaments was the aigrette, which dated back to the 1600s. It was made from gold or silver, molded to look like an egret—a type of feather—and then enameled and/or trimmed with gemstones.

Practicality became important after 1910, as women cut their hair into a **bob**, and more women began entering the workplace, especially after 1920. Women still trimmed their hair with jeweled combs and pins, decorative bands, and other accessories, especially for dressy occasions.

During the early 1940s, longer waved hairstyles were again more common. Women working in war-related industries wore bandannas, nets, and other accessories to keep their hair out of their eyes and away from machinery. For social occasions, they donned festive turbans or snoods, as well as combs, decorative pins, or barrettes. Snoods made a comeback in the United States when actress Vivien Leigh wore them in her role as Scarlett O'Hara in the epic 1939 film, *Gone With the Wind.*

After the mid-1900s, hair accessories made use of new materials. Rubber bands, which became available in the mid-1800s when the process of vulcanization developed, were mass-produced in different colors and thicknesses. Plastic hairbands, combs, and barrettes were available in all price ranges. Headbands and barrettes were designed especially for young girls, and some took their designs from popular cartoon characters, fairy tales, or children's films.

For **African Americans**, the 1960s brought ornaments that showed ethnic pride and suited natural hairstyles. They included "**Afro** picks" made from wood or plastic, some featuring the black power symbol—a raised fist—on the ends.

By the twenty-first century, stores offered hair ornaments in an array of colors, styles, materials, and price ranges. They included hairbands, headbands, barrettes, decorated ponytail holders made from soft or rigid materials, clips, combs, and more. The 1980s brought "scrunchies"—stretch ponytail holders made from cloth over elastic bands. Glittery ornaments, including small sparkling beads made with Velcro, were popular, along with "claw" barrettes of different sizes and shapes that were used to secure ponytails and other upswept or partially upswept hairstyles.

See also: Adornment, Symbolic; Byzantine Empire; Comb, Decorative; Coming of Age; Elizabethan Era; Hairstyles, Twentieth-Century; India; Religion and Hair; Renaissance Europe; Victorian Era

Further Reading: Bornoff, Nicholas, et al. *Things Japanese* (2002); Bryer, Robin, *The History of Hair* (2003); Charles, Ann, and Roger DeAmfrasio, *The History of Hair* (1970); Corson, Richard, *Fashions in Hair: The First Five Thousand Years* (2000); Lester, Katherine Morris, and Bess Viola Oerke, *Accessories of Dress* (1940); Liversidge, Joan, *Everyday Life in the Roman Empire* (1976); Schaff, Philip, *History of the Christian Church* (1997); Turudich, Daniela, *1940s Hairstyles* (2001); Zdatny, Steven, *Hairstyles and Fashion* (1999).

ADORNMENT, SYMBOLIC

Hair may be adorned with objects that signify a person's status, rank, occupation, or achievements. One of the best known is the laurel wreath, a symbol of victory or achievement that originated in Greek mythology. In the myth, Daphne, daughter of the river god Peneus, had decided not to marry. After Apollo fell in love with Daphne, he pursued her as she fled into the woods. As he drew near, Daphne prayed to her father asking him to help her escape, and Peneus turned her into a laurel tree. Apollo declared that, from that day on, he would wear a wreath of laurel leaves on his head.

When the original Olympic games were held in 776 BCE in Athens, **Greece**, the winner of the race was crowned with an olive wreath (*cotinus*, or *kotinos*). Laurel wreaths crowned the winners at the Pythian Games held in Delphi during the sixth century BCE. They became a symbol of achievement not only in athletics but also in the arts, literature, government, education, and other pursuits.

In a similar tradition, ancient Romans awarded laurel wreaths to military leaders, heroes, and people who showed great patriotism. In both Greece and Rome, the kings, emperors, and other rulers wore a laurel wreath to show sovereignty. Julius Caesar declared the laurel wreath a symbol of the supreme ruler in 44 BCE, and during the Republican era of the **Roman Empire**, only one man was allowed to wear the "Laureate Corona," which designated his supreme status. These wreaths were made from gold and gemstones, not real leaves, and led to the modern crown. Centuries later, in 1804, Napoleon I donned a laurel wreath made of gold when he crowned himself emperor of France.

In honor of ancient traditions, Olympic medals contain a sprig of laurel in the design, and commemorative coins minted for the XXVIII Olympiad in Athens, Greece, in 2004 feature a stylized olive wreath. Winners of the events that year were crowned with wreaths made from olive branches.

In **China** and **Japan**, hair ornaments also held symbolic meanings. Ancient Japanese thought that certain ornaments, such as thin sticks, had the power to protect them from evil. Ancient Egyptians wore a golden lotus (either real flowers or lotuses made from gold, sometimes trimmed with malachite or other gems) for good luck.

Floral hair ornaments had specific meanings in different cultures. During ancient Grecian feasts, while they were dancing around the temple, young people in Athens wore crowns of roses as a sign of innocence. Since ancient times, the lily was a symbol of fertility, and Greek brides wore headpieces containing lilies and wheat (for abundance).

Because of these traditions, in early Christian days church officials regarded roses as a sign of paganism and some clerics banned people from wearing them. Later, the rose became acceptable again among Christians. For some **Native Americans**, the white rose traditionally symbolized security and joy; it was worn during wedding ceremonies.

The word "coronation" may have come from "carnation," since the Greeks put these flowers in their crowns. A Korean tradition holds that a young girl can tell her fortune by placing three carnations on her head and seeing how long each flower stays fresh.

See also: Adornment, Ornamental; Africa; Egypt, Ancient; Greece, Ancient; India; Latin America; Yoruba

Further Reading: Bornoff, Nicholas, et al., *Things Japanese* (2002); Haig, Diana Reid, *Walks Through Napoleon and Josephine's Paris* (2004); Heilmeyer, Marina, *The Language of Flowers: Symbols and Myths* (2001); Miller, Stephen G., *Ancient Greek Athletics* (2004); Scobie, G., et al., *The Meaning of Flowers* (1998); Swaddling, Judith, *The Ancient Olympic Games* (2000).

ADVERTISING

People in the hair care business use various forms of advertising to promote products, hair care tools, equipment, and services. Methods of advertising have changed dramatically through the years as new forms of communication developed and competition increased among companies. Since the 1800s, advertising methods have become far-reaching as mass media replaced word of mouth, local displays, and regional publications.

Nineteenth-Century Advertisements

In the United States during the 1800s, people who made and/or sold personal grooming products for the hair—mostly soaps, **hair tonics**, **combs**, and brushes—advertised

Hovey's Cocoa Glycerine for preserving and dressing the hair.
Library of Congress

them with posters, signs, banners, placards, business cards, display wagons, and billboards, as well as newspapers and other periodicals.

One of the earliest techniques for marketing products was the distribution of advertising cards, also called trade cards. During the 1840s, perfume manufacturers in New York City and other places distributed cards dipped in the scents they were selling. These cards identified the scent and the manufacturer and featured attractive designs with images of pretty girls, flowers, angels, and hearts.

The first American magazines did not contain advertising, but ads began to appear during the late 1870s. Advertisers recognized that female consumers were more likely to make the buying decisions for the household, so they began advertising in magazines devoted to women.

Hair tonics, soap, shaving razors, and personal grooming tools, including items that were used on the hair and scalp, were among the first products advertised in print media. Black-and-white ads for hair-cleansing products appeared in *The Pictorial Review, Saturday Evening Post, Good Housekeeping,* and *Ladies' Home Journal*, among other magazines. The ads usually were fairly simple and straightforward; some contained images of the product and/or people. Ad copy and images reflected the mores and values of the times, using language that reflected the consumers' sensibilities. Ads for some products, including certain hair tonics, made extravagant claims about the beneficial effects the user could expect.

The shampoo industry had yet to develop, and ads urged people to use various soaps to cleanse both the body and hair. An 1882 ad for Slidall's Soap dubbed it "The Soap for All Uses" and claimed it would clean not only the body and hair but also bathrooms, laundry, kitchens, babies, dogs, teeth (real and false), and the harness and carriage.

In 1882, innovative newspaper advertisements for a new brand called Ivory Soap said simply, "Ivory Soap—99 44/100th percent pure." Its makers—Procter &

Gamble—expanded that message by claiming that people should choose Ivory because it was more pleasant and effective than other soaps and so pure it would "float." Variations on that same ad were used for decades. A magazine ad in 1896, done in color, featured a fresh-faced "Ivory Girl."

The 1897 ads for Pear's soap, made in England, took a light-hearted approach with catchy slogans. The Pear's ads that appeared in magazines before Christmas show Santa Claus standing before a fireplace filling a stocking. A young boy sleeping nearby suddenly awakens and says, "Good morning, Santa! Have you used Pear's soap?"

Early 1900s

In the decades that followed, businesses put more money and effort into advertising, which became a lucrative profession. **Shampoo**, which was commercially available at the turn of the century, was among the most frequently advertised products.

Shampoo ads became a magazine fixture. For example, a 1914 ad for Canthrox Shampoo in *American Magazine* showed women at a camp using the shampoo to wash their hair in a lake. That same year, ads for Harmony Hair Beautifier and Shampoo in the *Saturday Evening Post* promoted both the product and the Rexall chain of stores that sold the Harmony line.

Beginning in the late 1800s, companies often connected their products with celebrities. Testimonials from society women, beauty experts, and actresses, as well as athletes, models, and well-known beauties, including British actress Lillie Langtry, were used to bolster claims. Along with pictures of these women, some ads contained their favorable comments about the product, while other ads claimed or implied that the celebrity used the product.

As the motion picture industry developed, more actresses endorsed various brands of shampoo. To promote its "Mulsified Cocoanut Oil for Shampooing," the Watkins Company used photos of actresses May Allison, Ethel Clayton, and Norma Talmadge in its 1918 ads. In 1947, actress Joan Leslie appeared in magazine ads for Procter & Gamble's Drene Shampoo. The color picture of Leslie, which appeared in *Good Housekeeping* magazine, came from her film *Repeat Performance* (1947). Celebrity endorsements have remained a constant in advertising hair care products.

As was true during the 1800s, early twentieth-century ads revealed cultural biases and stereotypes that favored the looks of white Europeans. Ads for bleaches, hair straighteners, and hair removal products targeted women of color or women whose features did not conform with the "beauty ideal" of fair skin, silky or softly waving hair, and the small-boned, delicate features typical of Northern Europeans. For example, as early as the mid-1800s, Crane & Co. offered a hair-straightening preparation that purported to reduce kinkiness. A similar product called Curl-I-Cure was marketed as a "remedy" for unwanted curls.

Some ads made big promises regarding the ways their shampoo would improve women's lives. A 1940 ad said that using Drene Shampoo would "reveal up to 33% More Lustre in Your Hair." During World War II, Drene ads claimed that using the shampoo would make hair easier to style, which was important to women working in wartime industries or serving in the military.

New Media and Methods

By the 1920s, ads could be heard on radio as well as seen in print media. The first grooming products advertised on radio were soaps, and soap companies sponsored most serial programs, which became known as "soap operas." Radio ads for Lustre-Crème Shampoo featured a song claiming that the shampoo would impart "three-way loveliness" by leaving hair fragrantly clean, manageable, and free of loose dandruff.

Advertising techniques encouraged people to identify with their products and with the people in the ads. They also warned consumers about the social risks of poor grooming. During the 1920s, sex in advertising became more obvious. Ads for grooming products often focused on how certain products could increase one's popularity and sexual desirability. A 1952 television ad showed a teenager preparing for an important date by washing her hair with Drene.

During the 1930s, television offered companies the chance to market products to millions of people in more dramatic and effective ways. By the early 1950s, millions of American households owned a television set. That number continued to grow and advertisers capitalized on this large audience.

Hair care products were staples on radio and television ads, which often featured models or actresses. A number of ads were sponsored by Colgate-Palmolive-Peet, which made Toni shampoo, Toni home **permanent** wave, and the popular "Halo" shampoo. Ads explained that Halo produced lather yet did not contain soap as an ingredient and that it "glorifies your hair" by leaving it clean. The radio jingle "Halo, Everybody, Halo" became one of the most popular advertising tunes in history. It debuted on July 4, 1944, on the "Theater of Romance" program. During the 1950s, television ads told consumers, "Halo reveals the hidden beauty of your hair." The legendary Frank Sinatra sang in one well-known television ad for Halo.

By the mid-twentieth century, hair product ads could be found on radio, television, and in numerous magazines that targeted women, men, and teenagers. Ads touted various shampoos, grooming creams, **hairspray**, styling products, permanent waves, hair color, and shaving products, among others. The hairspray market was especially lucrative during the late 1950s and early 1960s, along with home hair coloring products. After 1950, more ads appeared in full color and ad campaigns became increasingly sophisticated.

Famous Ad Campaigns

Some of the best-known ads in history feature hair care or shaving products. One long-running series of ads aired not over the radio or on television but on plain wooden signs posted along American highways: **Burma Shave**. Sales of this shaving cream rose dramatically after the company came up with the idea of writing catchy jingles on a series of signs that would be seen by passing motorists.

During the 1960s, the William Esty agency produced a sophisticated campaign for Noxzema Medicated Instant Shave Cream. In television ads, a man neatly shaves his face while Swedish model Gunilla Knutsen says, "Take it off, take it all off. The closer you shave, the more you need Noxzema." Another well-known Noxzema ad, in 1973, featured football great Joe Namath shaving. These ads aired during the Super Bowl and other programs.

For decades, young women with shining hair known as **Breck Girls** appeared in ads for Breck shampoo. Although some of these women were unknown or relatively unknown, the company began using more models and actresses after the 1950s.

A growing roster of famous women endorsed Lustre-Crème Shampoo, a cream formula shampoo that claimed it was so gentle that it "Never dries—it beautifies." Ads claimed that "the most beautiful hair in the world is kept at its loveliest . . . with Lustre-Crème Shampoo" and that using it would turn a woman into a "Dream Girl, a Lustre-Crème Girl." Manufactured by Colgate-Palmolive, Lustre-Crème was priced so that the average woman could buy it. The shampoo was billed as "Hollywood's favorite" and an array of blond, brunette, and red-haired actresses endorsed Lustre-Crème from the 1940s into the 1960s. In 1953, actress Marilyn Monroe, celebrated for her glamour and sex appeal, appeared in an ad that claimed "4 out of 5 top Hollywood stars" favored Lustre-Crème. Monroe is shown holding a bottle of the shampoo with a caption that reads, "Yes, I use Lustre-Crème Shampoo." Elizabeth Taylor was another "superstar" who appeared in Lustre-Crème ads. Others included Bonita Granville, Jane Wyman, Betty Hutton, Jeanne Crain, Doris Day, Loretta Young, Esther Williams, Barbara Stanwyck, Virginia Mayo, Shirley Jones, Natalie Wood, Joan Collins, Joan Crawford, Ava Gardner, Anne Baxter, Rita Hayworth, Grace Kelly, Betty Grable, Debbie Reynolds, Rhonda Fleming, Ruth Roman, Maureen O'Hara, Jane Russell, June Allyson, Arlene Dahl, Anne Baxter, Deborah Kerr, and Cyd Charisse. A famous 1956 ad featured photos of twenty-three actresses. During the 1960s, actress Sandra Dee, a favorite with teen audiences, appeared on television ads for the shampoo.

After the 1950s, full-color ads created by top ad agencies competed for customers in the rapidly growing market for hair color products. Hair coloring products had become more natural looking and easier to use, and the stigma against using these products was diminishing.

Famous ad campaigns for home hair coloring kits came from **Clairol** and **L'Oreal**. To introduce its Miss Clairol home hair coloring kit, Clairol launched a hugely successful campaign with memorable slogans. In 1956, advertising executive Shirley Polykoff of Foote, Cone, & Belding in New York City came up with the catch lines "Does she or doesn't she? Only her hairdresser knows for sure." After this ad appeared in *Life* magazine that fall, sales of Clairol's Hair Color Bath soared. When Clairol launched its revolutionary shampoo-in product Nice 'n Easy, Polykoff wrote "The closer he gets, the better you look." Later, she wrote these memorable lines for Lady Clairol cream bleach hair color: "Is it true blondes have more fun?" and "If I've only one life, let me live it as a blonde."

Polykoff recommended that the women in the Clairol ads should look like attractive, everyday people, not glamorous models in evening gowns. She aimed to make hair coloring more mainstream, since the practice once had been socially unacceptable and associated with women of "loose morals." To further demonstrate that respectable and married women colored their hair, Clairol ran ads featuring "mothers" with similarly blond-haired "daughters."

Large-scale, favorable publicity made Clairol products top sellers. From 1956 to 1962, the number of American women who colored their hair increased from 7 percent to 50 percent.

L'Oreal, a French beauty products company, launched ad campaigns to challenge Clairol's position in the American hair coloring market. A popular brand in Europe, L'Oreal claimed that its formulations were superior and more natural looking than those made by competitors. Designed to give L'Oreal products "prestige appeal," this text was written by Ilon Specht of the McCann Erickson agency in New York City:

> I use the most expensive hair color in the world. Preference, by L'Oreal. It's not that I care about money. It's that I care about my hair. It's not just the color. I expect great color. What's worth more to me is the way my hair feels. Smooth and silky but with body. It feels good against my neck. Actually, I don't mind spending more for L'Oreal. Because I'm worth it.

L'Oreal ads featured blond actress Meredith Baxter, known for her roles in television series, including *Family* and *Family Ties*. The memorable tag line, "I'm worth it," refers to the fact that Preference was priced slightly higher than similar brands.

Celebrity Endorsements

High-profile celebrities endorsed hair care products during the 1970s, a decade when healthy, natural looking hair was the goal. Olympic gold-medal figure skating champion **Dorothy Hamill** endorsed Clairol Short and Sassy conditioner and shampoo. Millions of people around the world had seen Hamill's performance in the Olympics, and many women and girls imitated her wedge haircut. Television and print ads for Short and Sassy showcased Hamill's glossy dark hair as she skimmed across the ice.

Actress **Farrah Fawcett** was a spokesperson for Wella Balsam shampoo and conditioner. Fawcett's thick, layered blond hair set a major style trend after she appeared on the hit series *Charlie's Angels*. Dark-haired Jaclyn Smith, Fawcett's costar on *Charlie's Angels* and a former Breck Girl, also endorsed Wella products.

Hair-color product ads continue to feature celebrities. Actresses Cybill Shepherd and Heather Locklear have endorsed L'Oreal's Preference. During the 1980s, Clairol hired actress Linda Evans to promote Ultress, an upscale brand designed to compete with Preference. In the mid-1990s, Julia Louis-Dreyfus, who costarred on the hit comedy series *Seinfeld*, appeared in ads for Clairol's Nice 'n Easy. In humorous ads, Louis-Dreyfus is shown riding in airplanes and buses, where she approaches women and tells them they will enjoy trying a different hair color. She then shampoos with Nice 'n Easy and dazzles other passengers with the quick, attractive results. Also during the 1990s, actress Andie MacDowell began endorsing L'Oreal's Excellence hair color, while **Sarah Jessica Parker**, star of the hit HBO series *Sex and the City*, endorsed Garnier Nutrisse. Parker is known for her sense of style and various hairstyles, including a "signature" hairstyle featuring long, loose curls on dark blond hair with highlights. Sales of Garnier Nutrisse increased more than 50 percent after Parker's ads began to air.

During the 1990s, Clairol presented another well-known ad campaign for its Herbal Essences shampoos and conditioners. Ads emphasize the flowers, herbs, and other natural ingredients and fragrances of the products. Commentators have pointed out the sensual messages and double-entendres in the ads. Consumers are encouraged to enjoy a "totally organic experience" and "have an affair with your hair." Women who use Herbal Essences are shown looking ecstatic, while they repeat the word "Yes!" to suggest that the effects are quite pleasurable, even thrilling.

A Vast Industry

By the twenty-first century, companies were spending billions of dollars a year to advertise shampoos, conditioners, hair colorants, and other hair care and shaving products. In 2001, Clairol spent more than $60 million to launch its new line of Renewal 5X hair care products. The top ten television advertisers of 2003 included several companies that make products for hair care and hair removal: Procter & Gamble (second to General Motors for the most money spent: $3.32 billion); Lever Brothers; Colgate-Palmolive; Bristol-Myers; and American Home Products.

Ads for hair care and hair-removal products are common in all forms of the media. Celebrity endorsements remain powerful advertising tools. Top models and other celebrities sign multimillion dollar contracts to represent products.

Companies have developed increasingly effective methods for analyzing consumers and specific consumer groups to sell products. Marketing research experts gather statistics about different sectors of the population in order to determine who buys what kinds of products and why.

Television Infomercials

Some hair products are promoted via television infomercials—special advertising programs that appear on regular television channels or on special shopping channels, such as Home Shopping Network and QVC. The infomercial emerged during the late twentieth century as an innovative and "personal" way to reach consumers by talking to them directly about a product. Lori Davis hair care products and **Jose Eber** hair extensions are among the products that began their sales campaigns through infomercials featuring Davis and Eber, along with celebrities who endorsed the products.

Some celebrities, including actresses Connie Stevens and Susan Lucci, have developed their own lines of hair care products to sell on television shopping networks. Hairdressers also market their hair care products on shopping networks.

Critics say that infomercials, as well as other ads, make claims that may be unsubstantiated, exaggerated, or false. They also speculate about whether the people who promote products in the ads actually use them.

See also: African Americans; Aging and Hair; Alberto-Culver Company; Begoun, Paula; Bob, The; Breck Girl; Burma Shave; Clairol; Eber, Jose; Hair Color; Hair Colorants; Hair Net; Hairspray; Permanent; Procter & Gamble Company; Sassoon, Vidal; Shampoo; Shaving; Styling Products; Styling Tools; Tonics, Hair; Walker, Madam C. J.; Wigs and Hairpieces

Further Reading: Allen, Margaret, *Selling Dreams* (1981); "Classic TV Ads," http://www.roadode.com/classic.htm; Cummings, Bart, "Polykoff Put Herself in User's Shoes," *Advertising Age*, October 1985, 48ff; Fox, Stephen, *The Mirror Makers: A History of American Advertising and Its Creators* (1984); Gross, Michael, *Model: The Ugly Business of Beautiful Women* (1995); Hamill, Dorothy, *Dorothy Hamill On and Off the Ice* (1983); Kuszynski, Alex, "Trading on Hollywood Magic," *New York Times*, January 30, 1998, C1, C4; Packard, Vance, *The Hidden Persuaders* (1957); Polykoff, Shirley, *Does She . . . or Doesn't She? And How She Did It* (1975); Tedlow, Richard S., *New and Improved: The Story of Mass Marketing in America* (1990); Watkins, Julian Lewis, *The 100 Greatest Advertisements, Who Did Them and What They Did* (1959).

AFRICA

For thousands of years, people living in Africa have devoted time and attention to styling their hair, and some traditional styles are still worn today. Ancient hieroglyphs, sculptures, and masks reveal intricate and varied hairstyles worn by people in different regions of this large continent. Hair coverings do not appear on ancient sculptures and drawings, which may mean that hair was supposed to be visible to other people.

Hairpins, beads, cowrie shells, colored cloth, flowers, and other objects have been used to adorn hair or symbolize particular stages of life or events. The Kwere of Tanzania made ornate hairpins. In Nigeria, the Ibo crafted wooden hair combs for grooming and styling their hair.

When they began to visit Africa, Europeans were impressed by the number and variety of African hairstyles. In his book, *Description and Historical Account of the Gold Kingdom of Guinea*, written in 1602, Dutch explorer Pieter de Marees provided a detailed description and drawings of sixteen distinct hairstyles he observed in that region.

Hair also had a special spiritual significance in Africa. Many African cultures saw the head as the center of control, communication, and identity in the body. Hair was regarded as a source of power that personified the individual and could be used for spiritual purposes or even to cast a spell. Since it rests on the highest point on the body, hair itself was a means to communicate with divine spirits and it was treated in ways that were thought to bring good luck or ward off evil. According to authors Ayana Byrd and Lori Tharps, "communication from the gods and spirits was thought to pass through the hair to get to the soul" (Byrd and Tharps 2002, 4–5). In the Cameroon, for example, medicine men attached hair to containers that held their healing potions in order to protect the potions and enhance their effectiveness.

Hair also has strong social and sexual connotations. Most societies regard long, thick, neatly styled hair on a young woman as a sign of health, respectability, and fertility—qualities that make them desirable mates. In traditional African cultures, both men and women groomed their hair, and unkempt hair was a sign of illness, mourning, or antisocial behavior.

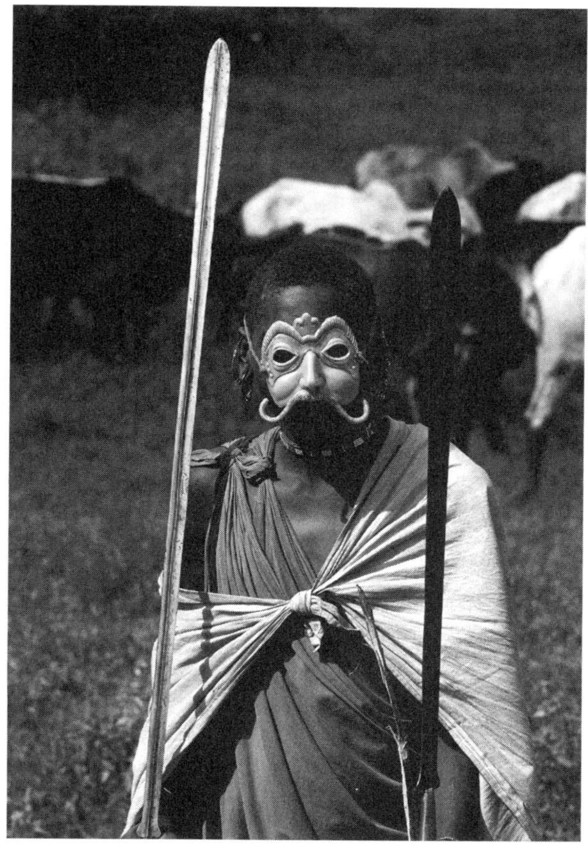

An African warrior.

Hair Types

Hair colors and textures vary throughout Africa. Hair varies from thin to thick and from nearly straight to softly curling (e.g., the Ashanti) to tight curls (e.g., the Mandingo). Scientists believe that the dense, curling hair texture most typical in Africa helps to shield the head from strong sunlight. About 75 percent of the dark-skinned people on this continent have hair labeled "kinky," while 15 percent have curly hair. Curly hair is found among Ethiopians, Nubians, Somalians, and others. Straight or wavy hair on black Africans is most often found in very humid regions and in forested areas of the Sahara and Sudan.

Most Africans have dark hair, usually black, but some have lighter hair in brown, blond, or red shades. Scientists think these light shades sometimes occur because of environmental factors or as a result of nutritional deprivation that prevents normal pigmentation.

Diverse Styles

Since ancient times, hairdressers have enjoyed a high status in traditional African cultures, and hair-grooming time was sociable. In most communities, including those in Ghana and Senegal, hairdressers work only with members of their own gender. Hairdressing, which might be done daily, involves cleansing, then combing, oiling, and styling into various braids, wraps, curls, twists, or other shapes, sometimes with decorative accessories.

Braiding remains one of the most common styling techniques in Africa. Certain braiding patterns are associated with religious occasions and other events in

Swahili women. *Library of Congress*

a person's life, as well as everyday styles. For some styles, braids are arranged in intricate designs around the head. Sections of hair might form geometric shapes, such as triangles or quadrangles, at regular intervals, or the rows might be curved.

Hair wrapping also produces complex designs. In some traditional hairstyles, women wrap a section of their hair from top to bottom with a thick thread and then arrange these sections around the face and head. Other wrapped styles, dating back centuries, are designed to stand upright from the head.

Styling aids from animal fats, plants, and minerals date back to ancient times. Palm oil was a favorite aid for conditioning and styling. In central Africa, women used a mixture of ochre and animal fat to hold their hair in long cylindrical shapes. Tavo—a combination of honey and animal fat—has long been used as a fixative for curled braids in the Malagasy Republic (formerly Madagascar). The Nubians developed a type of ironing comb they used to make rows of tight coils around the head.

Traditions and Rituals

Hair has been a part of customs and rituals designed to thwart evil spirits, bring good luck, or comfort those in mourning. Many customs relate to the head and hair of newborns or the dead. For example, during the naming ceremony that takes place seven or nine days after birth, the Yoruba may shave a baby's head to mark its passage from the spirit world into the world of the living. The shorn hair may be used in good luck charms or healing tonics. A dead person's head is shaved to mark the passage from this world to the next. Among the Akan of Ghana, however, women and men who are most closely related to a dead person shave their heads and bodies as a sign of respect. Certain groups use hairs from the deceased, or from their relatives, in the funeral rites.

Another custom, practiced in the Malagasy Republic (formerly Madagascar), dictated that widows shave their heads. Some women had their hair removed in such a way that it could be used as a wig after the mourning period ended. Women in some parts of West Africa were expected to stop grooming their hair when they were widowed in order to repel attention from other men, since people of both genders avoided someone with untidy hair.

Social Significance

African hairstyles have revealed a person's age, birthplace, clan membership, socioeconomic status, marital status, and occupation, among other things. For instance, Kuramo men of Nigeria could be recognized by their partially shaved heads, with just one tuft of hair on top. Among the Masai, women and children traditionally keep their heads shaved while male warriors wear long braids dyed with red clay. Community leaders wore the most elaborate hairstyles, and only the ruler wore a headdress. Crowns were made from leather, gold, beads, and fancy braids. Priests also have worn hairstyles that set them apart from other community members.

Young women may wear styles that show they are open to marriage, whereas married women's hairstyles show they are unavailable. Before marriage, Ibo girls in present-day Nigeria traditionally used clay, ground coal and palm oil to shape their hair into a horn-shape that bends toward their brows. Girls in Senegal may wear braids and whimsical styles, while married women have plainer, covered styles. In Kenya, young Turkana men spent hours getting elaborate hairstyles that show they have completed the initiation rites for adulthood. Among some ancient societies, African men wore their hair in a distinctive style when they were about to go to war. This signaled their families to prepare for a possible death.

In modern-day Africa, many groups have retained their traditional hairstyles. They include the Boro of Niger, the Ibo and Yoruba of Nigeria, the Mangboru of Zaire, the Samburu in East Sudan, and the Wolof of Senegal. In most African communities, hairstyles still differ for unmarried and married women and they change from childhood to adulthood.

See also: Adornment, Ornamental; African Americans; Comb; Coming of Age; Cornrows; Dredlocks; Hairdressing; Headgear; Religion and Hair; Styling Products; Styling Tools; Superstitions; Yoruba

Further Reading: Arnoldi, Mary Jo, and Christine M. Kreamer, *Crowning Achievements: Africans Art of Dressing the Head* (1995); Byrd, Ayana D., and Lori L. Tharps, *Hair Story: Untangling the Roots of Black Hair in America* (2002); Cordwell, Justine M., and Ronald A. Schwarz, eds., *The Anthropology of Clothing and Adornment* (1979); Davidson, Basil, *African Kingdoms* (1966); Fisher, Angela, *Africa Adorned* (1984); Persadsingh, Neil, *The Hair in Black Women* (2002); Sagay, Esi, *African Hairstyles: Styles of Yesterday and Today* (1983); Sieber, Ray, and Frank Herreman, *Hair in African Art and Culture* (2000).

AFRICAN AMERICANS

Grooming and hairdressing practices among African Americans have reflected their distinctive cultural heritage, the prevailing styles, pressure to conform to the larger society, and the emergence of trendsetters. African Americans have created or popularized styles that influenced trends in the United States and other countries.

Impact of Slavery

During the 1500s, Europeans began forcibly bringing people from **Africa**, mostly the western coast, to colonies in the Caribbean as a source of cheap labor. By the 1600s, Africans also were being brought to North America and the slave trade expanded. When slavery finally ended in the 1800s, about 20 million Africans, most of them between the ages of ten and twenty-four, had been kidnapped from their homelands and sold.

In addition to losing their freedom and their families, homes, and communities, Africans lost the symbols of their personal and group identity, including their hairstyles. They were further humiliated when slave traders shaved their heads, something that was done to African prisoners of war, as a sign that they were anonymous captives.

Most slaves did not have time to spend on their appearance or other personal activities. Southern plantation slaves worked seven days a week and usually lived in unhealthy slave quarters where head lice and ringworm were common scalp afflictions. In addition, they lacked soap and the combs and oils they had used to groom their hair in Africa. Since hairdressing was important in their native cultures, this was yet another form of cultural deprivation that African American slaves endured.

In addition, African Americans faced discrimination on every front, including negative attitudes about their appearance. In the colonies and later the United States, standards for "attractiveness" were based on white European looks—light skin tones and straight or gently waving hair, along with fine-boned, delicate features for women. To further dehumanize African people, whites sometimes referred to their hair as "wool," as though it belonged to animals rather than people.

Faced with these obstacles, scalp diseases, and hard labor in the hot sun, many male slaves shaved their heads or cut their hair short, wearing a hat outdoors. Women often used cast-off fabrics to make scarves or kerchiefs that covered their heads and gave some protection against the sun. Slaves who worked inside the home were expected to stay neat and clean. Male slaves sometimes wore wigs like their white masters or a hairstyle that resembled white styles, while female house slaves braided and plaited their hair. African women with long, wavy hair faced another threat: if a white mistress was jealous of a house slave, the mistress forced the slave to cut off her hair, making her less attractive.

During the early 1800s, new laws and practices meant that many slaves did not have to work on Sundays. This day was set aside for rest and religious observations, so on Sundays they would comb and style each other's hair, shave, and attend church. Women took off their kerchiefs and removed the cotton rolls that usually bound their hair all week to let their hair hang in curls around their necks and shoulders.

Slaves devised hair care tools, such as using wool carding tools to comb through tangles. Men used axle grease as both a dye and hair relaxer. Authors Byrd and Tharps note that cornmeal and kerosene were used to cleanse the hair and scalp. Butter, goose grease, and other kitchen fats were used to moisturize dry hair. Sometimes after applying the fat, women styled their hair into curls with a heated butter knife. Flooded with messages that straight hair was more attractive than tight curls, some African Americans, including slaves and freedmen, tried concoctions designed to relax their hair. One preparation, made from lye mixed with potatoes, could burn the skin if it touched the scalp. Other African Americans wore their hair in more natural styles. Among both whites and African Americans, however, people with lighter skin and straighter hair were considered more "attractive" and had access to better jobs than those with darker skin and more "African" features. Lighter-skinned blacks with straighter hair, along with white society, perpetuated the idea that tightly coiled or kinky hair was "bad" and was a "problem" that should be "fixed" if possible.

After slavery was abolished in the 1860s, some African Americans continued to straighten their hair not just to conform with mainstream styles but also to avoid the mistreatment and legal and social discrimination that came with being nonwhite. Some women of color, and a smaller number of African American men, lightened their hair with household bleaches.

By 1900, more commercial bleaches were being sold, along with products and tools designed to "fix" tightly curled hair. White-owned businesses dominated the hair care industry. African Americans were urged to use products that would make their hair straighter and smoother—and therefore more socially acceptable. Ads claimed that light, straight hair was "better" and "more attractive" than dark, curly, or kinky hair. Most hair straighteners and lightening products contained caustic chemicals, including laundry bleach. Creams and lotions, often combined with hot irons, were used to straighten hair. Men relied on pomades and other preparations to help them achieve the desired "look."

As the 1900s began, more African Americans entered the hair care business, often because they wanted to improve the health and growth of their own hair. In 1898, **Anthony Overton** founded his Hygienic Products Company, which sold saponified coconut shampoo and AIDA hair pomade, along with dozens of other grooming products. Madam Gold S. M. Young and **Sarah Spencer Washington** developed hair products as well as successful salon businesses.

During the early 1900s, **Annie Turnbo Malone** and **Madam C. J. Walker** created lucrative businesses. Through her Poro Company, Malone developed and sold a treatment product she called "Wonderful Hair Grower." Walker promoted the use of the hot comb as a safer and gentler method of grooming hair than the old-time hair tongs or "pullers." Her company sold affordable cleansing and conditioning products door-to-door, and then in drugstores.

Thousands of salespeople gained economic security working for the Poro and Walker companies. The founders invested time and money in the black community to promote education, health care, and other services. They organized their employees to carry out charitable activities.

African Americans also operated successful barbershops and beauty salons. They offered the usual cutting and styling services, as well as permanents and hair-straightening procedures.

Images in mass media, including the new motion picture industry, continued to promote white European beauty standards. Beauty contests were segregated by race, so African Americans began sponsoring their own events. The winners of these contests and the African Americans pictured in black magazines and newspapers tended to have straightened hair styled like women in mainstream "white society." Traditional African styles featuring braids and cornrows were associated with poor blacks living in rural areas.

Men straightened their hair, too, using mixtures called "conks" (short for congalene), which combined eggs, potatoes, and lye. Some people mixed their own conks and applied them at home, while other men had their hair straightened by a barber. Conks were used into the early 1960s.

Some black leaders and citizens rebelled against the pressure to conform. They criticized the widespread practice of hair straightening and said that African Americans should take pride in their natural looks and their heritage. Some also criticized companies that promoted white beauty standards or tried to convince people that kinky or very curly hair was unacceptable.

Changing Times

During the 1920s, more African Americans celebrated their coloring and distinctive features. **Josephine Baker** and other African American celebrities were admired for their beauty, style, and glamour. Singer/actress Lena Horne and actress Dorothy Dandridge were among the African American women who became famous during the 1930s and 1940s. Nonetheless, during those years African Americans frequently were relegated to small or stereotyped roles in film and theater. One persistent image in the films of those decades is a black maid or cook with her hair wrapped in a kerchief.

As the twentieth century continued, more African Americans entered the ethnic hair care industry in order to provide products that suited their hair textures. In 1931, E. F. Young, a former farmer from Mississippi, began selling his hair care and grooming products. The products, which he initially mixed over the kitchen stove, grew into the Young Manufacturing Company and provided jobs for fellow African Americans in his region. During the 1950s, **George E. Johnson**, founder of the successful **Johnson Products**, introduced Ultra-Wave and Ultra-Sheen, followed by the Afro-Sheen line of the 1960s.

By the 1960s, a movement to change negative attitudes and discriminatory practices swept through the nation. The slogan "Black Is Beautiful" is associated with the civil rights and black pride movements. People discussed how the dominant white society had propagated negative views about the appearance of nonwhites in order to enslave and oppress people of color. By denying the validity of black culture and promoting feelings of inferiority, the dominant culture could more easily control the behavior of minorities (Lakoff and Scherr 1984).

During this time, African Americans embraced their heritage and physical appearance, rejecting the idea that white standards were "better." Many women and men rejected straightening tools and chemicals and adopted a "natural" or "**Afro**" hairstyle. They wore traditional curled and twisted African styles with cornrows, braiding, hair wrapping, and **dredlocks** (sometimes called "dreads" or "locs"). African accessories, including beads and cloth wrappings and hair picks, were popular.

The black pride movement focused attention on the racist and stereotyped standards of appearance that were part of American culture. As attitudes changed, fashion and cosmetics advertisements became more diverse and featured more women and men from different ethnic groups.

Magazines played a key role in promoting African American models and products for people of color. In 1945, John H. Johnson, the founder of Johnson Publishing Company, launched *Ebony* magazine, which became the world's best-selling black magazine. It featured articles on beauty, fashion, health, and fitness, as well as articles on people, current events, history, sports, entertainment, and other topics. Johnson's company expanded to include Fashion Fair Cosmetics, Supreme Beauty Products, and the Ebony Fashion Fair, which remains a popular annual event.

Essence, which debuted in 1970, was another ground-breaking publication created by African Americans and geared to the interests of black women. Its fashion and beauty articles showcased black models and celebrities and provided a new forum for black designers, makeup artists, photographers, stylists, and writers. Lavish color photos and advertisements showed black women and men wearing exciting hairstyles and accessories.

More African Americans built successful hair care products businesses. In 1964, Edward and Bettiann Gardner cofounded Soft Sheen Products, which they had started by making products in the basement of their home in Chicago. Soft Sheen, which produced the Optimum and Care Free Curl brands, grew into a multimillion-dollar company, with sales in the United States, Canada, Caribbean, and West Africa. The Gardners and their four children operated the business and supported African American causes, including the arts.

As the twenty-first century began, however, large corporations were buying out black-owned hair care businesses. L'Oreal owned Johnson Products Inc., Soft Sheen, and Carson Products; Alberto-Culver had purchased Pro-Line.

More Style Choices

During and after the 1960s, more African American women wore traditional hairstyles or styles that blended African and modern American styles. Some of them featured cornrows—numerous small braids woven all over the head. African American celebrities, including actress Cicely Tyson, popularized the hairdo by wearing it at performances and public events such as the Academy Awards presentations. This style often complemented the texture of a black woman's hair and did not require the use of chemical hair straighteners and relaxers.

White women also wore cornrows, and the style became a fad in 1979 when a nineteen-year-old actress from California, Bo Derek, wore beaded cornrows for her starring role in the film "*10*." Derek's long blond cornrows received much attention and prompted more nonblack women to try this style. Tourists also enjoy trying the hairstyle when they vacationed on Caribbean islands where beaded cornrows are popular.

During the 1990s, Venus Williams and Serena Williams, sisters and tennis champions, sometimes wore cornrows adorned with colorful beads or other braided hairstyles, both on and off the courts. Tall and athletic, the Williams sisters have appeared in fashion and beauty magazines, endorsed athletic wear, and design their own lines of clothing as well as their tennis outfits.

Natural hairstyles worn to reveal the texture of unprocessed hair have become a source of pride and affirmation. According to *Essence* magazine, the last quarter of the twentieth century brought "the liberating freedom to wear hair kinky or straight, to wear cornrows or dredlocks (called 'locks'), weaves or wigs, to be braided or clean-shaven. Indeed, what we've come to understand and appreciate is that the real beauty of Black hair lies in its enormous versatility" (Edwards 1995).

New products also have been marketed for unstraightened hairstyles. A 1972 ad for the Afro Sheen line showed a well-dressed father and son wearing natural Afro hairstyles while admiring an African sculpture. The text, which included African words, described the grooming and conditioning properties of Afro-Sheen shampoo, conditioner, dressing cream, and hairspray.

After the 1960s, more African American male and female models were featured in prestige magazines, television ads, and high-fashion runway shows. Beverly Johnson was one of the first African American models to reach "supermodel" status. Many more would follow, including Iman, Naomi Campbell, Naomi Sims, Veronica Webb, and Tyra Banks. The first black Miss America was crowned in 1983—Vanessa Williams, now a well-known singer and actress. Another black woman, Suzette Charles, was first runner-up that same year. Debbye Turner won in 1990, followed by Marjorie Vincent in 1991. Likewise, in 2003 and again in 2004, African American women—Erika Harold and Ericka Dunlap—were crowned "Miss America."

More black actors achieved prominent roles on television and in feature films, as well as in ballet, opera, and theater. Diahann Carroll broke ground as a leading lady on Broadway, then as the star of her own television series, *Julia.* Carroll later appeared in a glamorous role on the hit television series *Dynasty*.

African Americans cited for their talents and looks include Billy Dee Williams, Denzel Washington, Will Smith, Taye Diggs, Derek Luke, Janet Jackson, Halle Barre, Jada Pinkett Smith, Thandie Newton, Lela Rochon, and Beyonce Knowles.

African American designers and hair stylists have influenced popular trends in fashion and beauty. Many trends originate in the black pop music world and in predominantly African American communities. Shaved heads on men became more popular after superstar basketball player Michael Jordan and other well-known African American athletes, musicians, and actors chose this look. Although conservative hairstyles for men have been the norm in the workplace, shaved heads and dredlocks can be seen in executive offices and other workplaces, such as hospitals. At the 2004 Summer Olympics, African American athletes wore myriad hairstyles, including cornrows, shaved heads, ponytails, short hair in curled or straight styles, long straight or curly styles, and different kinds of braids.

See also: Adornment, Ornamental; Africa; African Americans; Afro; American Health and Beauty Aids Institute; Baldness, Voluntary; Barbers; Cornrows; Hair Color; Hair Colorants; Hair Straightening; Hair Weave; Hairstyles, Twentieth-Century; Joyner, Marjorie Stewart; Laws and Regulations; Salons, Hair and Beauty; Styling Products; Styling Tools; Wigs and Hairpieces

Further Reading: Byrd, Ayana D., and Lori L. Tharps, *Hair Story: Untangling the Roots of Black Hair in America* (2002); Edwards, Audrey, ed., *Essence: 25 Years Celebrating Black Women* (1995); Gatewood, Willard B., *Aristocrats of Color: The Black Elite, 1880–1920* (1990); Lakoff, Robin Tomach, and Raquel L. Scherr, *Face Value: The Politics of Beauty* (1984); Miller, Melba, *The Black Is Beautiful Beauty Book* (1974); Peiss, Kathy, *Hope in a Jar* (1998); Rooks, Noliwe M., *Hair Raising: Beauty, Culture, and African American Women* (1996); Sterling, Dorothy, and Mary Helen Washington, *We Are Your Sisters* (1984).

AFRO

The Afro, from the word Afro-American, refers to a hairstyle featuring thick, tightly curled hair in a large, rounded shape. The style is well suited to the texture of Afro-Caribbean hair and usually is associated with **African Americans** as a natural way to wear their hair. Authors Ayana Byrd and Lori Tharps write that black women in South Africa wore styles resembling what became known as the "Afro" during the late 1950s and early 1960s. Their natural, unstraightened hairstyle was called a "bush." Non-Africans also have worn variations of the Afro.

Before the 1960s, some African Americans chose to wear more natural hairstyles—for example, the former slave and abolitionist author Frederick Douglass—but these people were in the minority. For centuries, most African Americans styled their hair to look like other men and women in the larger, predominantly white, society. These styles often required them to spend time and money on chemical straighteners and/or hot combs or irons and other products.

Afros became fashionable in the United States during the mid-1960s, when more African Americans let their hair grow longer and assume its natural shape. The Afro and related hairstyles showed racial pride and embraced a multicultural view about what looks attractive. Also, some African Americans disliked the process of straightening their hair and preferred styles that were easier to maintain. The Afro reflected changing hairstyles, since white males also were growing their hair longer. When men of any race with kinky or very curly hair grew long hair, it usually stood away from their scalp and held that shape. During the late 1960s, many celebrities, including members of the Jackson Five singing group, musician Miriam Makeba, actor Clarence Williams III, and actress Pam Grier, wore Afros.

Marsha Hunt, from the stage production of *Hair*, wearing the Afro style. *Photofest*

For some people, the Afro was a sign that someone was part of the black pride political movement. Angela Davis and Jesse Jackson were among the prominent political activists who wore Afros. Authors Byrd and Tharps link the hairstyle to a desire for "a strengthened Black world, one that encompassed politics, economics, art, literature, education, and a new aesthetic" (52, 2001). The phrase "black is beautiful" expressed these attitudes. Some people with Afros were protesting racial discrimination, the Vietnam War, and the "established order" in government and politics. An Afro represented freedom and independence from the older generation, as well as the limiting attitudes of white America.

The Afro became a fad among youth, especially students, political activists, musicians, and other performers. It spread to whites, including youths in Britain where it flourished during the late 1960s. Whites who had naturally curly or kinky hair could wear Afros, while others needed a permanent to obtain the look. White celebrities who wore some form of Afro include singer/actress Barbra Streisand, musician Art Garfunkel, *Today Show* movie critic Gene Shalit, and actor

Gabe Kaplan, who starred on the television series *Welcome Back, Kotter*. People with straight hair who did not want a permanent could buy Afro wigs in an array of colors, ranging from black to blond.

Many African American youths who adopted Afros were criticized by their parents and others, who said they looked messy and ill-groomed. On the other hand, African Americans who did not wear an Afro might be criticized by their peers for not being "black enough." Some African Americans with naturally straight hair felt pressure to use chemicals that would make it kinky. Hairdressers who worked with these clients developed processes for what they referred to as "turning straight hair nappy." During one television demonstration, hairstylist Nat Mathis styled a white woman's long, blond hair into an Afro.

Because it connoted change and political unrest, some white Americans found this hairstyle disturbing and even frightening. In the African country of Tanzania, the Afro was banned as a symbol of neocolonialism. And in the Caribbean, members of the Rastafarian movement chose not to adopt the Afro.

For some people, however, the Afro went beyond politics. Natural styles were easier to maintain than styles that required chemical straightening or other treatments that changed hair texture. Many people enjoyed the look and feel of "natural" styles.

The Afro had economic repercussions. As more people wore natural styles, hair-related businesses, including barbershops and beauty salons that catered to ethnic clients or made straightening products, lost business. Some hair care product companies adapted to changing tastes by making products and tools, such as Afro picks, for people who wore natural styles, or they created conditioning products designed for the Afro. Stylists also learned to style and trim the Afro, telling customers that professional care produced a neater, more attractive look.

By the 1970s, people no longer regarded the Afro as unusual or as a political statement, but rather a hairstyle choice among many others. Versions of the Afro become trendy from time to time. For example, in 2002, model Naomi Campbell wore an Afro hairstyle for the August issue of the British edition of *Vogue* magazine. Singer/actress Beyonce Knowles wore an Afro wig for her role in the Austin Powers film *Goldmember*.

See also: Adornment, Ornamental; Africa; African Americans; Hairdressing; Hair Straightening; Hairstyles, Twentieth-Century; Johnson, George Ellis; Johnson Products; Politics and Hair

Further Reading: Boston, Lloyd, *Men of Color: Fashion, History, Fundamentals* (1998); Byrd, Ayana D., and Lori L. Tharps, *Hair Story: Untangling the Roots of Black Hair in America* (2002); Edwards, Audrey, ed., *Essence: 25 Years Celebrating Black Women* (1995); Jones, Lois Libert, and John Henry Jones, *All About the Natural* (1971); Lakoff, Robin Tomach, and Raquel L. Scherr, *Face Value: The Politics of Beauty* (1984); Peiss, Kathy, *Hope in a Jar: The Making of America's Beauty Culture* (1998); White, Shane, and Graham J. White, *Stylin': African-American Expressive Culture from Its Beginnings to the Zoot Suit* (1998).

AGING AND HAIR

Since ancient times, people have sought to reduce the signs of aging on hair, which include changes in growth, color, texture, and density. Gray hair, thinning

> "Regrets are the natural property of gray hair."
>
> CHARLES DICKENS (1812–1870), British author

hair, and baldness are visible signs of aging, while a full head of thick, shiny hair is regarded as a sign of youth and vigor. Numerous products and hair care services target consumers who want to look younger. They include **hair colorants** for men and women, nutritional supplements, surgical **hair transplants**, salon extensions, **wigs and hairpieces**, and other products that could promote hair growth, limit hair loss, or improve hair texture.

Aging Process in Hair

Scientists have found that aging of the hair occurs not only with chronological aging but also because of genes and heredity, stress, nutritional state and overall health, lifestyle, and exposure to chemicals or the sun and other elements. As people age, their bodies produce smaller amounts of the hormones and enzymes that affect hair growth.

Aging hair follicles produce less melanin, the substance that gives hair its color, so the hair turns various shades of gray and white. This process can begin in a person's thirties or even earlier. The rate and amount of color loss depends upon heredity and other factors. In most cases, this process is gradual and begins at the temples and top of the head, spreading to other areas of the scalp. About 40 percent of all people have some gray hair by the time they reach their forties. People of Asian heritage tend to "go gray" at a later age than Caucasians.

Facial and body hair may also turn gray, but this usually happens at a slower rate than it does on the head. In some cases, hair in the armpits, chest, and pubic area does not turn gray.

With aging, hair also tends to become both finer and thinner. Hairs without pigment are thinner in diameter than pigmented hair. Hair also tends to grow more slowly, and some follicles stop producing hairs, which results in thinning. Men may notice hair loss in the form of male pattern baldness. Women also tend to lose hair in certain patterns, although hair loss is more uniform across the scalp.

As people age, their body hair also tends to become thinner, while individual hairs in these areas become coarser. Some women develop thicker facial hair, especially on the upper lip and chin area, as their levels of the hormone estrogen decline, making the "male" hormone testosterone more dominant. Older men may find that their eyebrows and the hairs around their ears and nose become thicker and coarser.

The Quest for Youth

Since ancient times, people have looked for ways to disguise thinning or missing hair and to color gray hair with various dyes. Wigs were one solution, and wigs sometimes became fashionable in a country because a ruler wore false hair to cover a balding head. People devised various **tonics**, ointments, and masques containing oils and other plant or mineral materials to remedy baldness. As societies became industrialized, new products to color gray hair or minimize hair loss came into the marketplace.

The desire to maintain a youthful appearance may be linked to the fear of death and unpleasant conditions associated with aging, such as health problems, loss of sexual potency, and diminishing mental and physical abilities. A youthful appearance often is associated with professional success and personal happiness.

Social attitudes and values, which differ from culture to culture, influence a person's desire to appear young. Some cultures esteem older members more than others. The United States, for example, is considered to be a "youth-based culture," while certain Asian cultures show greater respect for the elderly.

Gender also plays a role, since women traditionally are judged more on the basis of appearance than men are. Women are more likely than men to color gray hair, although the percentage of men who color their hair has risen steadily since the late twentieth century.

Products and Consumer Issues

Remedies for aging hair have become increasingly sophisticated. New preparations, treatments, and surgical techniques are available, and many people also turn to hormones, special foods, nutritional supplements, and exercising as ways to promote youth and vitality.

The beauty and toiletries industries now offer thousands of different products that purport to help people look younger. These include scalp treatments, hair dyes, wigs, and hairpieces. Salons offer anti-aging massages, coloring services for gray hair, and other treatments. Companies encourage people to buy nutritional supplements, herbs, tonics, lotions, creams, shampoos, conditioners, and other so-called "hair restoratives." People may also seek medical treatment in the form of hair transplants.

Controversy surrounds many products that claim to be "anti-aging" or to "grow hair." In 1987, the U.S. Food and Drug Administration (FDA) decided to examine some "anti-aging" claims. The FDA asked twenty-three prominent cosmetics manufacturers to verify advertising claims that their products contained "anti-aging and cellular replacement ingredients." If such ingredients were present, the FDA claimed this would require them to reclassify these substances as drugs rather than cosmetics. Since drugs must meet much stricter safety standards than cosmetics, any company that continued to make such claims would have to submit the product for FDA testing to determine its safety and effectiveness.

Scientists and critics of the cosmetics industry claim that most anti-aging claims are unfounded. They note that ads for anti-aging products referring to the results of "clinical studies" usually are based on studies commissioned by the company selling the product. The studies also may be designed in ways that "prove" the claims in the ads. Critics also question "before and after" pictures that portray people who supposedly used the product.

Social Attitudes

Social scientists who study attitudes about aging and appearance note that some cultures focus more on inner beauty than on outward appearance. A number of

Eastern cultures, for example, stress physical and mental harmony that people convey in their behavior and social interactions. They believe that people show their inner grace through movements, gestures, and facial expressions. In certain cultures, some features of aging are admired, or at least not considered unattractive. In India, for example, gray hair is considered to be pleasing.

Author Michelle Dominique Leigh has lived in Europe, Asia, Africa, and South and Central America and studied the way women in these regions deal with the effects of aging. She writes, "Using pure and natural ingredients and simple, empowering rituals, the women in traditional cultures whom I have known cultivate their beauty as they cultivate other aspects of their overall well-being—out of self-love and acceptance, not out of despair at the first signs of aging" (Leigh, 1996).

Other cultures promote the idea that a younger appearance is far better than an older one. Most images in American fashion and beauty magazines portray a young, physically "perfect" look at the "standard." Americans are inundated with articles, books, television programs, and ads promoting products and techniques to improve the appearance and reduce signs of aging.

Critics of this viewpoint also decry the double standard of aging. They claim that women who show signs of aging are more likely to be dismissed, ignored, or considered less attractive, while men with facial lines or gray hair may be described with positive words, such as "mature" and "distinguished." Women working in television and film complain that they lose jobs or cannot find many good roles after age forty. They also note that older actors may be paired with younger—sometimes much younger—women, while the reverse rarely happens. Changes are occurring, however, as people work to stay healthy and fit and popular magazines present more women over forty as sexy and attractive.

Scientists state that the "beauty ideal" for women emphasizes youthful features because these traits signify a fertile woman, and men are biologically programmed to seek a fertile mate. In contrast, men can father children at much later ages than women can conceive, and older men may be perceived as having more economic means to support a family. Marriages between older men and younger women once far outnumbered the reverse, but these statistics are changing, partly because women's earning power has increased in many societies.

Targeting Older Consumers

Since the 1980s, the beauty industry has been paying more attention to women over forty, fifty, and beyond. Companies recognized that an increasing number of "baby boomers"—people born between 1945 and 1961—were over forty, and these consumers have tremendous buying power.

More ads for hair care products have featured models and actresses over age forty, among them Linda Evans, Dayle Haddon, Andie MacDowell, Melanie Griffith, Julianne Moore, and Heather Locklear. Other popular female celebrities, such as Renee Russo, Tina Turner, Patti LaBelle, Joan Collins, Jaclyn Smith, Cheryl Tiegs, Christie Brinkley, Goldie Hawn, Demi Moore, and Salma Hayek express confidence about their looks and are viewed as proof that "older" women can be fit, attractive, and sexy. In 2004, Tiegs and Brinkley joined a group of women who donned swimsuits for a special anniversary photo celebrating the annual *Sports Illustrated* swimsuit issue.

As the number of people over age fifty continues to increase, companies offer older consumers new products created for aging hair. Since 2000, hair care companies have introduced serums and lotions that claim to give "mature hair" a younger texture and appearance. New fashion, beauty, and lifestyle magazines include beauty, health, and lifestyle articles for women over forty.

See also: Hair Weave; Hair Loss; Toupée

Further Reading: Banner, Lois W., *In Full Flower: Aging Women, Power, and Sexuality* (1993); Darling, Lynn, "Age, Beauty, and Truth," *New York Times*, January 23, 1994, sec. 9, 5; Friday, Nancy, *The Power of Beauty* (1996); Kinzer, Norma, *Put Down and Ripped Off: The American Woman and the Beauty Cult* (1977); Leigh, Michelle Dominique, "Ageless Beauty," *Natural Health*, July/August 1996, 80–82, 145; Leigh, Michelle Dominique, *The New Beauty: East-West Teachings in the Beauty of Body and Soul* (1995); Melamed, Elissa, *Mirror, Mirror: The Terror of Not Being Young* (1983); Sontag, Susan, "The Double Standard of Aging," *Saturday Review*, 23 September, 1972, 29–38.

ALBERTO-CULVER COMPANY

The Alberto-Culver Company, a multinational firm with sales of $2.8 billion in fiscal year 2003, manufactures and sells personal care products and household products in over 120 countries. The company's hair care brands include Alberto VO5 hair care products, St. Ives products for hair and skin, Consort men's hairsp-ray, and TRESemme. As of 2004, it was the seventh largest producer of hair care products in the United States. Its subsidiary, Sally Beauty, is the world's number 1 professional beauty supply distributor.

Alberto-Culver began as a hairdressing products business on the West Coast. Its first product, Alberto VO5 conditioning hairdressing cream, became popular with Hollywood stylists and then with retail customers. By 1958, it was the top-selling product of its kind in the United States, and it is still sold today.

In 1995, Chicago entrepreneur Leonard Lavin bought the company and moved its headquarters to Chicago, where Alberto-Culver focused on its VO5 hairdressing cream. Advertising, especially on popular television programs, boosted sales. The company changed the nature of television advertising in 1972 when it won the right to buy thirty-second spots instead of the traditional sixty-second commercials. Then, in 1983, Alberto-Culver pioneered the fifteen-second commercial. The company introduced a new product, Alberto European Styling Mousse for hair, to the United States.

In addition to its packaged products, the company makes and markets Sally Beauty Company products and is the world's largest seller of beauty supplies to the professional salon and barber markets. Through direct sales and 2,350 stores located in the United States, Canada, Germany, the UK, and **Japan**, Sally Beauty sells hair care products and styling appliances, as well as cosmetics, to professionals and consumers.

After purchasing Sally Beauty in 1969, Alberto-Culver developed a chain of 2,000 stores in the United States, Great Britain, Canada, Japan, and Germany. Through its Beauty Systems Group, the company has distributed its own Alberto-Culver brand and other brands, including Wella, Shiseido, and Redken, to the professional beauty markets before selling these three brands to other companies. Its Indola professional hair care company, which was sold to the **Henkel Group** in 2004, produces hair colorants that became the leading brand for salons in Europe, Israel, and Southeast Asia.

In 2000, Alberto-Culver bought Pro-Line, which then ranked as the third bestselling line of ethnic hair care products in the United States. Sales of these products, which are sold in countries around the world, reached $100 million in 2001.

Alberto-Culver has a large market-share in hair care styling products sold in Great Britain, Canada, and Latin America, where its skin care lines also sell well. The company supports charities, programs, and organizations that emphasize health care, education, child care, and women in the workplace.

See also: Advertising; Hair Colorants; Hairstyles, Twentieth-Century; Salons, Hair and Beauty; Styling Products

Further Reading: "About Us," http://www.alberto.com/aboutus.html; BusinessWeek Online "Company Profile: Alberto Culver," http://www.miami.com/mld/miamiherald/business/9220122.htm; "Henkel to Buy Indola Professional Hair Care Company from Alberto-Culver," *Cosmetics Design*, July 5, 2004, http://cosmeticsdesign.com/news/news-NG.asp?id=51946.

ALBINISM

Albinism, sometimes called hypopigmentation, refers to a genetic condition in which melanin, the substance that gives color to the hair and skin, is not produced or is produced in abnormally low quantities. The hair follicles of people with true albinism lack melanosomes, so the hair has little or no pigment; thus, it appears nearly white or very pale yellow. In people of color, the hair color may be a deeper shade of yellow. Likewise, people with albinism have unusually pale skin. In some cases, the iris of the eye also lacks color and can appear pink.

Albinism occurs in people of all races. About 5 people per 100,000 in the United States have some form of albinism. In oculocutaneous albinism, the normal growth and development of skin and hair are not affected. People who have a type of albinism called Griscelli Syndrome suffer from immunodeficiency problems that may require special medical treatment. Another type, Hermansky-Pudlak syndrome, entails diseases of the lung, kidney, and/or intestine and a tendency to bleed. With all types of albinism, people have eye problems, including sensitivity to light. In ocular albinism, only the eyes are affected by a lack of pigmentation.

Albinism has existed since ancient times and was noted in the writings of the Greeks and Romans. Some historians say that Noah, of the biblical flood story, may have been an albino. Because they look unusual and the cause of their condition was unknown years ago, people with albinism were thought to have supernatural powers, such as mind-reading ability, or were even accused of being witches. In some cultures, people with albinism have been ostracized. The first scientific paper on the subject was written in 1908 by Sir Archibald Garrod, and since then scientists have made new findings using techniques that evolved for genetic research.

During the 1800s, some people with albinism were featured in circus sideshows. American circus impresario Phineas T. Barnum employed a teenager named "Amos," the Martin sisters (Florence and Mary), and the Rudolph Lucasie family, from the Netherlands. Florence and Mary Martin, who appeared onstage in New York City at Barnum's Broadway American Museum, wore their long pale hair hanging down.

Well-known people born with albinism include the Reverend William Archibald Spooner (1884–1930), a scholar who taught divinity, history, and philosophy at England's Oxford University, where he also served as dean and then president. Modern-day celebrities with albinism include musicians Johnny and Edgar Winter, who perform blues, country, and Cajun music as the "Winter Brothers" and as solo artists and Yellowman (Winston Foster, b. 1956), an internationally known Jamaican reggae artist. Salif Keita, nicknamed the "Golden Voice of Mali," was born and raised in a West African culture that believed albinism was a sign of bad luck. He overcame this ostracism to pursue his musical career, blending the African and European traditions. Since 1984, Keita has lived in Paris, France.

Scientific research continues to reveal new information about the origins and transmission of albinism. In 2000, scientists at Jefferson Medical College in Philadelphia reported that they had used chimeraplasty, a type of gene therapy that repairs faulty genes, to turn the hair of albino mice to a darker color.

See also: Hair Colorants

Further Reading: Ashley, Julia, and Dennis L Cates, "Albinism: Educational Techniques for Parents and Teachers," *RE:view* 24, fall 1992, 127–133; Bolognia, J. L., and P. E. Shapiro, "Albinism and other Disorders of Hypopigmentation," in *Cutaneous Medicine and Surgery*, eds. K. A. Arndt, et al. (Boston: W. B. Saunders, 1996); Gribbin, August, "Five National Team Drafts Working Map of Human Genome," *Washington Times*, 26 June, 2000, 1; Landau, Elaine, *Living With Albinism* (1998); Waardenburg, P. J., *Remarkable Facts in Human Albinism and Leukism* (1970).

ALEXANDRE OF PARIS (1924–)

Alexandre of Paris (also known as Alexandre de Paris and Alexander of Paris) became one of the best-known and most influential hairstylists of the twentieth century. As a child growing up in Cannes in the south of France, Alexandre began working in the salon of his Italian grandmother.

From there, he progressed to working in the salon that the famous hairdresser Antoine of Paris operated in Cannes. One of Antoine's famous clients was the Duchess of Windsor (the former Wallis Warfield Simpson), and she was pleased with the way Alexandre styled her hair. As the duchess introduced the young hairdresser to some of her wealthy European and American friends, his reputation grew.

In 1952, Alexandre opened his first Paris salon. Within five years, he had attracted such a prestigious clientele that he could afford to open a luxurious new salon in one of the city's most fashionable neighborhoods. Alexandre was known for his classic and flattering hairstyles with touches of glamour. His men's salon in Paris also set trends for masculine hairstyles. Later, his shop in Paris became famous for its selection of fine handmade ornaments that were called "jewels for the hair."

Throughout the 1950s and 1960s, Alexandre attracted some of the world's most famous clients. After actress Grace Kelly married Prince Rainier of Monaco in 1957, she named Alexandre as her official hairdresser. Other well-known clients included the wife of the Aga Khan, Vicomtesse Jacqueline de Ribes, and actresses Elizabeth Taylor, **Audrey Hepburn**, Tippi Hedron, and Sophia Loren, among others.

Alexandre became better known to people in the United States when he created special hairstyles for First Lady **Jacqueline Kennedy** during the highly publicized visit she and President John F. Kennedy made to France in 1961. For the state dinner at the Palace of Versailles, Alexandre arranged Mrs. Kennedy's hair in a full, curved style meant to resemble a Fontange. It was further adorned with diamond clips from the famous jeweler Van Cleef & Arpels. Before her arrival, Mrs. Kennedy had sent Alexandre a lock of her hair so that he could make a matching dark brown hairpiece to incorporate in her upswept hairstyles.

Although Alexandre continued to work in his salons and train other stylists, after the early 1960s he spent much of his time traveling to see clients. During the spring and fall couture collections, Christian Dior, Yves Saint Laurent, Christian Lacroix, and Karl Lagerfeld, among other top designers, sought his services to style their models' hair.

In his honor, HairWorld awards its "Master Alexandre de Paris Trophy" to junior and student hairdressers who achieve the highest scores at its biennial events. The first Alexandre de Paris trophies were awarded at HairWorld 2002.

See also: Fontange; Hairdressing; Salons, Hair and Beauty

Further Reading: Carter, Ernestine, *The Changing World of Fashion* (1977); Flaherty, Tina Santi, *What Jackie Taught Us: Lessons from the Remarkable Life of Jacqueline Kennedy Onassis* (2004); Spoto, Donald, *Jacqueline Bouvier Kennedy Onassis: A Life* (2000); Winkler, Susan Swire, *The Paris Shopping Companion* (2002).

ALLERGIC REACTIONS

Consumers may suffer from allergic reactions—called contact dermatitis—caused by hair care products, both homemade and commercially prepared. Symptoms include a rash that may appear at the site of contact and also on other areas of the body. Other allergic symptoms include redness, weeping skin, swelling, and papules—small, solid raised areas on the skin.

Ingredients in a product also may cause problems that are not due to allergies—for example, when **shampoo**, hair color, or chemicals from a **permanent wave** get into the eyes, or when someone applies a product to an already irritated scalp. For that reason, labels warn users to avoid contact with sensitive eye tissues or broken skin. They instruct people to conduct a "patch test" before using certain products.

People have reported allergic reactions to oil of spearmint, certain fragrances, preservatives, and coal tar hair dyes. While some ingredients may cause allergic reactions in fairly large numbers of people, others affect a small minority.

Among hair care products, shampoos rarely cause a reaction because they are washed off after being on the hair for only a brief time. Rinse-out conditioners also rarely cause allergic reactions. Adverse reactions usually occur in connection with permanent waves, chemical hair straighteners, dyes, or bleaches. Most allergic reactions to hair color occur with procedures that involve two-part processing. The most likely culprit is the chemical paraphenylenediamine, or p-phenylenediamine. Another possible allergin is ammonium persulfate, which is found in some hair bleaches.

After **hair colorants**, the hair product most likely to cause a reaction is a permanent wave that contains glyceryl thioglycolate. These are usually three-part permanent waves, also known as acid perms. Another chemical found in permanent waves, cysteamine, occasionally causes an allergic reaction. An older version called a cold permanent wave, made with ammonium thioglycolate, seldom causes a reaction.

Allergic reactions to hair products usually are not life threatening but people may decide they need medical treatment. In a six-year survey (1977–1983), a task force organized by the American Academy of Dermatology found that an average of 210 reactions per year required medical care, per each million cosmetic items purchased. Most of these reactions resulted from skin care products, followed by hair products including dyes. People may be allergic to the ingredients in the coloring agent, to ingredients in the "developer" solution, or to both.

The task force found that the following ingredients were most likely to cause reactions: fragrance, preservatives, p-phenylenediamine, lanolin and its derivatives, glyceryl monothioglycolate, propylene glycol, toluenesulfonamide/formaldehyde resin, sunscreens and other ultraviolet light absorbers, and acrylate or methacrylate.

In a 1972 report, the President's National Commission on Product Safety estimated that about 60,000 Americans each year experienced symptoms of allergic reactions, including itching, rashes, **hair loss**, burns, sneezing, and watery eyes. Most people did not consult a physician unless their reaction was severe. The commission noted that many people are slow to realize that a product caused their symptoms, often because they have used the product before. People may suddenly react to a product they have used for years with no problems.

Some manufacturers have reformulated their products to reduce the chances of an allergic response. They omit certain fragrance ingredients and preservatives, two categories of ingredients that are often associated with allergic reactions. To help manufacturers, the International Fragrance Association has compiled a list of chemicals they suggest should either be avoided or used in limited amounts.

Companies also have conducted more tests to determine the likelihood of allergic reactions. One common method for testing products is the patch test. After placing a small amount of product on the skin, scientists watch for reactions over a period of time.

Consumers may now buy products that claim to be "hypo-allergenic," "allergy tested," and "fragrance free" ("Hypo" means "less than"). The words "hypoallergenic" do not guarantee that a product will never cause a reaction in anyone who uses it, but using hypoallergenic products may reduce that possibility.

The United States has no federal definitions and standards to govern the use of the term "hypoallergenic." During the 1970s, the Food and Drug Administration (FDA) proposed a regulation that would require manufacturers to back up claims that a product was "hypoallergenic," but a court struck down that regulation in 1978. In an article for its official publication, *FDA Consumer*, the FDA warned consumers that "there is no such thing as a 'nonallergenic' cosmetic—that is, one that can be guaranteed never to produce an allergic reaction" (Morrison, 1978).

To gather more information, the Cosmetic Ingredient Review (CIR) was set up in 1976 by the **Cosmetic, Toiletry, and Fragrance Association** (CTFA), in cooperation with the FDA and Consumer Federation of America. The CIR panel, which is made up of physicians, scientists and other experts, has evaluated studies and literature relating to product safety and the effects of thousands of ingredients used in cosmetics and hair care products.

As of 1980, however, there were still no legal standards governing the use of the word "hypoallergenic" on a label. Critics, including the American Medical Association's Committee on Cutaneous Health, said that the term "hypoallergenic" could be misleading.

The FDA continues to propose ways to give consumers more accurate information. It suggested that companies eliminate the terms "medically proven" or "clinically proven" from their labels and also ruled that companies could not make claims that imply an adverse reaction can never occur.

The FDA Division of Colors and Cosmetics deals with reports from physicians and individual consumers about the adverse effects of using a cosmetic or grooming product. If a product appears to cause reactions in a significant number of people, the FDA is authorized to remove it from the market.

The cause of an allergic reaction can be difficult to determine, because the average consumer uses at least seven different personal care/beauty products in a given day. Also, some individual ingredients are not specified on the label, since they fall under a larger heading such as "fragrance." With hair products, however, a consumer may be able to pinpoint which product caused a reaction by the process of elimination.

See also: Alopecia Areata; Folliculitis; Hair Straightening; Laws and Regulations

Further Reading: Bradbard, Laura, "On the Teen Scene: Cosmetics and Reality," *FDA Consumer*, May 1994, reprinted at http://www.cfsan.fda.gov/~dms/cos-teen.html; Morrison, Margaret, "Hypoallergenic Cosmetics," *FDA Consumer*, June 1974; Patlak, Margie, "Hair Dye Dilemmas," *FDA Consumer*, April 1993; Stehlin, Doris, "Cosmetic Allergies," *FDA Consumer*, November 1986, http://vm.cfsan.fda.gov/~dms/cos-224.html;

Stehlen, Dori, "Cosmetic Safety: More Complex Than at First Blush," *FDA Consumer*, November 1991, http://vm.cfsan.fda.gov/~dms/cos-807.html; Steinman, David, and Samuel S. Epstein, *The Safe Shopper's Bible* (1995); U.S. Food and Drug Administration (USFDA), Center for Food Safety and Applied Nutrition, Office of Cosmetics, "Hypoallergenic Cosmetics," December 19, 1994 (Revised October 18, 2000).

ALOPECIA AREATA

From Latin words that mean "fox's disease," alopecia areata is an inflammatory, non-scarring type of hair loss that can occur in men, women, and children. An estimated 2.5 million Americans suffer from alopecia areata, and about 1 percent of the U.S. population, including males and females, will be stricken with alopecia by age fifty. It can affect members of all ethnic and racial groups.

The hair loss may occur only in certain areas or it can affect the entire head (alopecia totalis). It may also cause overall thinning of the hair. A loss of all body hair is called alopecia universalis.

The causes of this condition, which has been observed since ancient times, are poorly understood. Currently, it is classified as an autoimmune disorder, meaning that the body's own immune system somehow "signals" the hair follicles to stop producing hair fiber. Some scientists believe that a major trauma or chronic mental, physical, or emotional stress can trigger alopecia. Viruses, poor thyroid functioning, and allergies also may play a role.

Although alopecia is not life threatening, it can cause serious emotional distress, especially for women who live in societies where hair is an important aspect of physical appearance.

Traumatic alopecia refers to hair loss resulting from outside causes, such as a person pulling out their own hair. It may also occur when chemicals are applied incorrectly to the head during hair-straightening and other procedures, or from an accident that injures the scalp and hair follicles.

Alopecia may spontaneously go into remission and the hair growth returns to normal. Statistics show that about 65 percent of people who experience patches of hair loss may have a spontaneous remission within six months to two years after the onset of alopecia. The age of onset is also a factor. People who begin to lose hair at an early age and have a history of allergies are less likely to go into remission.

Corticosteroids, such as prednisone, are the most common medical treatment for "patchy" alopecia. These may be taken orally or applied topically in the form of a cream or lotion. Sometimes they are injected into bald areas or injected systemically into the body.

Before and during the early 1900s, doctors thought that applying irritating agents—ammonia, mustard seed, or carbolic acid—to the scalp would restore hair growth. These substances are no longer considered effective, however. Some dermatologists use preparations made with anthralin, one of the few irritants that have been shown to be effective.

Other treatments for alopecia include ultraviolet light phototherapy and minoxidil, a chemical treatment in liquid form that is also used to minimize hair loss associated with aging.

See also: Allergic Reactions; Hair Loss; Trichotillomania

Further Reading: Ormsby, O. S., and H. Montgomery, *Diseases of the Skin*, 7th ed. (1948); Stark, Andrew, "What's Natural?" *Wilson Quarterly* 27 (Spring 2003): 1; Thompson, Wendy, et al., *Alopecia Areata: Understanding and Coping With Hair Loss* (2000).

AMERICAN BEAUTY ASSOCIATION

Based in Chicago, Illinois, the American Beauty Association (ABA) aims to serve as the "unified voice" of the professional salon industry. As of 2004, the ABA included more than 250 member firms in the United States. These members are manufacturers, manufacturer representatives, and associated firms, including hair, skin, and nail care companies.

The ABA was founded in 1985 when The National Beauty and Barber Manufacturers Association merged with The United Beauty Association. In its mission statement, as set forth on the ABA Web site, the association states that it was formed to expand, serve, and protect the interests of the professional salon industry. The ABA also has subgroups to meet the needs of different industry segments, including the Nail Manufacturers Council and Esthetics Manufacturers and Distributors Alliance.

The ABA holds educational conferences and other industry events for its members and advocates on their behalf in regard to laws and political issues that affect the salon industry. It also sponsors the ABBIES Awards Program, which was created in 1996 to honor creative marketing in product development, advertising, packaging, salon education, and public relations.

In 2003, hair care products and tools won ABBIES in the categories of "Best Marketing for In-Salon Use Products," "Best Marketing For New In-Salon Products Appliances/Sundries," "Best Marketing For New Salon Retail Products Hair Care Line," "Best Marketing For New Salon Retail Products Single Hair Care Product, "Best Marketing For New Salon Retail Products Appliances/Sundries," "Best Product Re-launch In-Salon-Use-Only Product," "Best Product Re-launch Salon Retail Product," and "Best Print Advertising in Salon Industry Publication Advertising Insert."

The ABA also raises funds for charitable causes, including the Pediatric AIDS Foundation and Breast Cancer Research Foundation.

See also: Salons, Hair and Beauty

Further Reading: The American Beauty Association: "ABBIES," "About the ABA," "Association News," "Events Calendar," http://www.abbies.org/.

AMERICAN HEALTH AND BEAUTY AIDS INSTITUTE

The American Health and Beauty Aids Institute (AHBAI) is an international organization of businesses in the ethnic beauty aids industry. According to the AHBAI Web site, this trade organization is made up of "Black-owned companies that manufacture ethnic hair care and beauty related products featuring the Proud Lady Symbol."

The AHBAI was founded in 1981 by ten African American business owners under the leadership of Chairman **George E. Johnson**, founder of **Johnson Products**, and Executive Director Lafayette Jones. Since then, it has grown from ten members to seventeen members and one hundred associate members. As of 2004, its symbol, called The Proud Lady, can be found on 3,500 products made around the world.

From the beginning, the AHBAI was a source of information for its members and it gave business owners access to industry trends and networking opportunities. In 1984, it began publishing *AHBAI News*. The first woman executive director, Geri Duncan Jones, was named in 1988.

AHBAI actively works with members of the black community on job, internship, training, and scholarship programs. In 1991, it founded The Fred Luster Sr. Scholarship Foundation to honor one of the AHBAI's founders, Fred Luster, who founded Luster Products Inc. Together with Eckerd Drugs, AHBAI raises money for the United Negro College Fund.

Its annual AHBAI Proud Lady Beauty Show in Chicago is the largest Midwest trade show focusing on African American cosmetologists, barbers, and nail technicians. The show, which debuted in 1989 with 5,000 in attendance, attracted more than 13,000 professionals in 2004. One popular feature at the show is the "World Fantasy" hairstyle competition.

See also: African Americans; Salons, Hair and Beauty

Further Reading: "About AHBAI," American Health and Beauty Aids Institute (AHBAI), http://www.ahbai.org; "AHBAI Milestones," http://proudlady.org/about/milestones.html.

AMISH

The Amish belong to a Christian religious sect that grew out of the Mennonite faith, which is rooted in the Anabaptist movement that began in Europe. The denomination officially formed in 1693 under their leader, a Swiss bishop named Jacob Amman. During the early 1700s, groups of Amish began settling in the Pennsylvania colony, where founder William Penn offered religious freedom to colonists. Today, Amish people live in twenty-two states and Canada.

Old Order Amish do not use electrical power or automobiles, and they regard "plain living" as a way to stay closer to God. Their strict religious beliefs and strong sense of family and community emphasize separation and independence from the outside world. Most of them work as farmers or craftspeople.

Members of the Amish community base their appearance on principles of modesty and simplicity. They wear plain clothing without zippers, buttons, or decorative trimmings. Likewise, they do not use professional hairstyling services, hair colorants, or electric razors. The Amish support their beliefs and practices with various texts in the Bible. The following are two examples, stating that women should cover their heads, especially in church: "For if a woman is not covered, let her also be shorn. But if it is shameful for a woman to be shorn or shaven, let her be covered" (1 Cor. 11:6), and, "Judge among yourself for a women to pray to God with her head uncovered" (1 Cor. 13).

To comply with their interpretation of Verse 15 ("But if a woman has long hair, it is a glory to her: for her hair is given to her for a covering"), Amish women do not cut their hair, which they arrange in a plain bun at the back of the neck. Hair is typically parted in the middle. A traditional style involves making plaits on each side before gathering them into a bun at the back.

Hair is covered with a handmade cap, and the style varies from one community to another. Some styles sit behind the ears; others come forward. The edges may be square or rounded, and the back section may be pleated or made into a heart shape. Unmarried women wear a black prayer covering and married women wear white ones, all made from a stiffened natural fabric, such as cotton organdy or muslin. On their wedding day, Amish brides wear a black prayer covering rather than a veil. For church services and other gatherings, women wear "covering caps" that fit over the prayer covering. These bonnets cover the entire head, with a piece of cloth that also covers the neck. Girls begin wearing this type of bonnet starting in infancy.

Amish men do not wear mustaches but do grow a beard after they are married. They keep their beards neatly trimmed. The accepted hairstyle for men covers the ears and is either parted in the center or cut into a short bang. Men and boys wear stiff, flat-brimmed black hats; in hot weather, they switch to straw hats.

See also: Beards, Men's; Religion and Hair

Further Reading: Hostetler, John, ed., *Amish Roots: A Treasury of History, Wisdom, and Lore* (1989); Seitz, Ruth Hoover, and Blair Seitz, *Amish Ways* (1991).

ANIMAL TESTING

Throughout the twentieth century, animals have been used in experiments to test cosmetics and personal care products, including hair care products. Rabbits, rats, monkeys, and other animals have been the subjects of laboratory tests conducted to determine the impact and safety of various products.

During testing, workers may rub substances onto an animal's shaved skin or force the animal to ingest or inhale the test compound. Some tests are done to evaluate the effects of irritation. Substances are placed on the eyes of the animal, usually a rabbit, to see the reaction, which may include redness, swelling, ulcers, bleeding, and even blindness.

Heated Debates

Animal testing is controversial, and some advocacy groups want to ban such testing. These groups, including People for the Ethical Treatment of Animals (PETA) and the National Anti-Vivisection Society (NAVS), have urged companies that make cosmetics and personal care products not to test on animals. People who oppose animal testing have lobbied legislators and held demonstrations and boycotts to express their views.

Opponents of animal testing also urge consumers to buy what they call "cruelty-free" products. The NAVS publishes a booklet called "Personal Care with

Principles," which contains a list of the companies that do not test products on animals.

As a result of these efforts, the use of animals to test cosmetics and personal care products has declined since the late 1900s. In 1989, Avon Inc. became the first U.S. company to announce that it would no longer test its products, which include shampoos and hair conditioners, on animals. More companies have followed suit, while others now conduct fewer tests with animals and/or treat the test animals in a more humane manner. In 1997 PETA compiled a list of 500 companies that do not test on animals. Companies that do not conduct animal tests sometimes use the phrase "cruelty free" in their advertising. PETA continues to publish lists of companies that do and do not test on animals. Its list for 2004 claimed that the following makers of hair care products were still conducting animal tests: Clairol, Helene Curtis, Procter & Gamble, and Unilever.

Many consumers refuse to use hair care products from companies that still conduct animal testing. A poll taken by the American Medical Association (AMA) showed that about 75 percent of Americans opposed animal testing for cosmetic products. In a 1996 survey of people between ages eighteen and forty-four by the Opinion Research Associates of Princeton, New Jersey, more than 52 percent of the respondents said that it was important for them to know which companies test their products on animals.

Alternative Testing Methods

For decades, people in various countries have been urging alternative testing methods that do not involve animals. In 1959, animal protection activists in England published "The Principles of Humane Experimental Technique," which set forth "Three Rs" for the future: refinement, reduction, and replacement.

Another organization, The Center for Alternatives to Animal Testing, is located at Johns Hopkins University in Baltimore, Maryland. It seeks sound alternatives that will still ensure that products are safe for humans. The European Centre for the Validation of Alternative Methods (ECVAM) also promotes alternative testing. ECVAM's main goal, as stated in 1993 by its Scientific Advisory Committee, is to promote the scientific and regulatory acceptance of alternative methods which reduce, refine, or replace the use of laboratory animals for testing products.

During the 1980s, the **Cosmetic, Toiletry, and Fragrance Association** launched a $5 million research effort to find alternatives for the Draize test, in which substances are injected into rabbits' eyes. Critics of the Draize test claim that it is painful and can cause blindness or death. They note that similar tests can be done on animal corneas from eye banks and from corneal tissue cultures, cell cultures, and frozen corneas that companies can obtain from hospitals and laboratories.

As of 2000, products, including those used for hair care, could be tested with computer software and by checking databases of previous test records, *in vitro* tests, cell or tissue cultures, and careful trials with human subjects. Some innovative methods for gauging skin reactions use pumpkin rind, or human skin tissue that was grown in sterile plastic bags.

Scientists note that, as of 2004, nearly every ingredient currently used in cosmetics or grooming products was once tested on animals. Therefore, companies cannot claim their products have never been tested on animals, only that they will not conduct such tests in the future, or that, aside from its ingredients, a product has not undergone animal testing in its "finished" state.

See also: Allergic Reactions; Shampoo

Further Reading: Canning, Christine, "Animal Testing Alternatives: The Quest Continues," *Happi*, February 1997, http://www.happi.com/special/febmain2.html; Center for the Study of Responsive Law, *Being Beautiful: Deciding for Yourself* (1986); People for the Ethical Treatment of Animals (PETA), http://www.peta-onlin.org; Rowan, A. N., *Of Mice, Models, and Men: A Critical Evaluation of Animal Research* (1984).

ANISTON, JENNIFER (1969–)

Emmy Award-winning actress Jennifer Aniston (born Jennifer Anastassakis) influences fashion and beauty trends, and *People* magazine has included her on its list of "Most Beautiful People in the World" four times: 1999, 2002, 2003, and 2004. Aniston popularized a hairstyle known as "the Rachel," named for her character on the hit television series *Friends*.

Jennifer Aniston, as Rachel Green from the sitcom *Friends*, with her famous "Rachel" haircut. *Photofest*

Born in California of Greek ancestry, Aniston spent a year in Greece as a child and then grew up in New York City and New Jersey, where her divorced mother and father lived, respectively. After graduating from New York's High School for the Performing Arts in New York City, she worked as a waitress and appeared in some off-Broadway productions. Aniston then moved to California to expand her acting career. She appeared in the television series *Molloy* (1990) and won small parts in other television shows, as well as in a 1990 film, *The Leprechaun*.

Aniston's breakthrough came in 1994 with the role of Rachel Green in a new television series called *Friends Like Us*, later shortened to *Friends*. The show was a hit and Aniston became both a star and trendsetter. Her formerly light brown hair became more blond, with golden highlights.

During the second season of *Friends*, Aniston had her shoulder-length locks cut into a distinctive layered "shag" style that framed her face. Los Angeles hair stylist Chris McMillan created the "Rachel cut" for Aniston. Throughout America, hairstylists were deluged with requests for the "Rachel." It was the most popular hairstyle to sweep the United States since **Farrah Fawcett**'s feathered look in the late 1970s. Stylists noted that the style allowed for some length and fullness at the crown, but also framed the face in a flattering way. In 1997, Aniston appeared in ads for L'Oreal shampoo.

Since the mid-1990s, she has starred in major motion pictures including *Rock Star* (2001), *Office Space* (1999), *Picture Perfect* (1997), *The Good Girl* (2002), *Bruce Almighty* (2003), and *Along Came Polly* (2004). In 2002 she won an Emmy award for her performance as Rachel on *Friends;* she has also won a Golden Globe for that role (2003) and two People's Choice awards as Favorite Female Television Performer (2001, 2002).

Aniston, who remained on *Friends* for all of its ten seasons, continued to change her hairstyle. She grew her hair longer, sometimes wearing it all one length or with bangs. Versions of the original straight and angled "Rachel cut" are still popular with many women.

See also: Bangs; Hairstyles, Twentieth-Century

Further Reading: "From Hair to Eternity: Jennifer Aniston, Friends," *TV Guide*, http://www.tvguide.com/features/hair/jennifer.asp; "Jennifer Aniston," http://www.tvtome.com/tvtome/servlet/PersonDetail/personid-896.

ARABIA, ANCIENT THROUGH MIDDLE AGES

People living in the land once called Arabia, in the Middle East, have a long history of careful personal grooming. Both women and men cared for their hair and skin, using preparations made from the materials around them. **Kohl**, a mineral substance, was used to darken eyelashes and eyebrows. **Henna**, a plant substance, has long been applied to the hair to add both shine and color. Another type of hair conditioner was made by brewing the peel from a quince.

Since Arabia was a center of the perfume trade, centered in Baghdad from 762 to 1258 CE, people in this region used various scents on their hair, beards, and bodies. Favorite scents included essences from roses, sandalwood, cloves, musk, civet, and red cyprus. To set their hair and give it a shine, some women used camel's urine, which has an acidic pH that can remove residues and parasites from the hair shaft. Ghee (clarified butter) was used as a conditioning agent.

Bathing was customary for both men and women in this Islamic country, and women removed all their body hair, except from the head, eyelashes, and brows. Europeans who returned home from the Middle East after the Crusades, which began in 1096 CE, brought back an appreciation for regular bathing and **hair removal**.

Muslim religious traditions require people of both genders to cover their heads in public. For women, this usually means a veil that also hides the face, while men have worn a fez, headcloth, or turban. Men's headgear was made without brims or other pieces that could obstruct them from prostrating themselves during worship. Traditionally, the color of a man's headgear helped to identify his status. Men who had made a pilgrimage to the Holy City of Mecca were entitled to wear a green turban. Jews and Christians living in the region wore their own distinctive clothing and headgear to communicate their status and religious affiliation so that people could identify one another easily.

See also: Fragrance; Religion and Hair

Further Reading: Alexander, Paul J., ed., *The Ancient World: To 300 AD* (1963); Bowen, Donna Lee, ed., *Everyday Life in the Muslim Middle East* (2002); Hall, Alice J., "Dazzling Legacy of an Ancient Quest," *National Geographic*, March 1997, 293–311; Wells, Rhona, "The Most Precious Incense," *The Middle East*, September 1993.

ARDEN, ELIZABETH *See* Salons, Hair and Beauty

ARTIFICIAL HAIR *See* Afro; Egypt, Ancient; Elizabeth I; Elizabethan Era; Eyebrows; Eyelashes; False Beard; Fontange; Gibson Girl; Greece, Ancient; Hair Loss; Hair Transplant; Hair Weave; Middle Ages; Roman Empire; Toupee; Wigs and Hairpieces

ASIA *See* Adornment, Ornamental; Baldness, Voluntary; China; Comb; Comb, Decorative; Coming of Age; Dredlocks; Eyebrows; Hair Weave; India; Japan; Monastic Styles; Mustache; Noda, Alice Sae Teshima; Religion and Hair; Salons, Hair and Beauty; Wigs and Hairpieces

ASSYRIA, ANCIENT *See* Mesopotamia

ATEF *See* False Beard

B

BABYLONIA *See* Mesopotamia

BAKER, JOSEPHINE (1906–1975)

African American entertainer Josephine Baker set beauty and fashion trends, especially during the Jazz Age—years following World War I into the 1920s. Baker overcame racism and childhood poverty to become one of the highest paid and most popular performers in Europe.

Born in St. Louis, Missouri, to an unwed mother, Freda Josephine McDonald had to leave school at age eight to work as a housemaid in order to help support her family, which grew to include an unemployed stepfather, a half brother, and two half sisters. At age thirteen, she began working as a waitress. Within a few years, she met and married Willie Wells; they were later divorced.

By 1920 and in her early teenage years, Josephine was touring as a comic performer with The Jones Family Band and the Dixie Steppers. While working as a dresser for the Dixie Steppers, she learned the chorus routines for the production *Shuffle Along* and was chosen to replace a dancer who left the show. She added comic touches that delighted audiences and drew larger crowds to the show. After performing in New York City, where *Shuffle Along* became a hit, she moved to Paris in 1925 as part of "La Revue Negre." By then, she had married and divorced Willie Baker, and she chose to be known thereafter as "Josephine Baker." In later years, she married twice more and divorced both men.

With her partner Joe Alex, Baker performed an exotic routine called *Danse Sauvage*. Her black hair was cut in a trendy **bob** featuring sleek Marcel waves sculpted around the head, with a spit curl on each cheek. Clad only in a skirt made of feathers, Baker captivated audiences with her dazzling personality and movements. When the revue ended, she performed at the world-renowned Folies Bergère, where she wore one of her most famous costumes—a skirt made from fake bananas. At the Casino de Paris, Baker introduced audiences to two popular American dances: the charleston and the black bottom. Her uninhibited dancing, soulful singing, and comic touch made her a star. She also became an international symbol of glamour. Among Baker's many fans was the novelist Ernest Hemingway, who called Baker "the most beautiful woman there is, there ever was, or ever will be" (Whitaker 1991).

In 1937, Baker, who had spoken out about the racism she experienced in America, became a French citizen. She proved her patriotism and courage during World War II (1939–1945), when she smuggled messages for the French resistance. She also worked as a Red Cross volunteer and entertained Allied troops

Josephine Baker. *Library of Congress*

stationed in North Africa. For her wartime work, Baker later received the Legion of Honor and Rosette of the Resistance.

In 1945, Baker resumed her stage career, using her earnings to support twelve children she adopted. Baker gathered orphans of different races and religions to demonstrate her belief that diverse people can live in harmony.

During a 1975 interview, Baker said of herself, "I have never really been a great artist. I have been a human being that has loved art, which is not the same thing. But I have loved and believed in art and the idea of universal brotherhood so much, that I have put everything I have into them, and I have been blessed" (Whitaker 1991, 30). Josephine Baker was still performing before live audiences a few weeks before she died.

See also: African Americans; Flappers; Hairdressing; Hairstyles, Twentieth-Century; Kohl; Marcel Wave; Styling Products

Further Reading: Haney, Lynn, *Naked at the Feast: A Biography of Josephine Baker* (1981); Phyllis, Rose, *Jazz Cleopatra: Josephine Baker in Her Time* (1989); Whitaker, Charles, "The Real Josephine Baker: What the Movie Didn't Tell You," *Ebony*, June 1991.

BALD-HEADED MEN OF AMERICA

Founded in 1973, this organization, which is open to both women and men, encourages people to feel comfortable and proud of their baldness. The organization promotes the idea that a positive attitude is the "best cure" for baldness. Besides publishing its "Chrome Dome" newsletter, which has a circulation of 20,000, the organization promotes "National Rub-a-Bald-Head Week," maintains a speakers roster, and raises money for charities.

Founder John T. Capps III began to lose his hair in his teens. Since baldness was typical for men in his family, Capps regarded his lack of hair as normal, though his teenage peers did not.

Each September, Bald-Headed Men of America holds its Bald Is Beautiful Convention in Morehead, North Carolina, a town located on the southern Outer Banks. A group of female judges selects a winner in the category of best "overall appearance" of a bald-headed person.

See also: Baldness, Voluntary; Hair Loss

Further Reading: Bald-Headed Men of America, John T. Capps III, http://members.aol.com/BaldUSA/info.htm.

BALDNESS *See* Aging and Hair; Allergic Reactions; Alopecia Areata; Bald-Headed Men of America; Baldness, Voluntary; Egypt, Ancient; Hair Loss; Toupee; Trichotillomania; Wigs and Hairpieces

BALDNESS, VOLUNTARY

Although baldness usually is associated with aging or an unwanted health problem, some people choose to shave or otherwise remove the hair from their head. They become bald for aesthetic reasons, for health reasons, to promote cleanliness, or to conform with religious or social customs.

Baldness has been fashionable from time to time, usually after rulers or celebrities started the trend. Some men shave their heads completely because their hair is thinning and they do not like the look of sparse hair, nor do they want to bother with hairpieces or hair restoratives.

> "It is foolish to tear one's hair in grief as though sorrow would be made less with baldness."
>
> CICERO (103–43 BCE), Roman orator and statesman

In **ancient Egypt**, members of the higher classes, both male and female, shaved their heads as a health measure in order to prevent parasitic infestations. However, the Egyptians wore wigs of various kinds since a bald head was not meant to be on public view. During the seventeenth and eighteenth centuries, men in some European countries shaved their heads in order to wear elaborate wigs.

Certain groups of men in northern Afghanistan have been shaving their heads for generations. They include the Aimaq, Hazara, Kirghiz, Tajik, Turkoman, and Uzbak. It has been customary for men to gather and shave one another's heads in turn, using the personal razor each brings with him, or they go to a local barber.

When they are in mourning, female members of certain Afghan communities shave their heads. Women in **Africa** and **India** also may shave their heads for this reason. Indian tradition advises that a widow shave her head, stop wearing jewelry, and dress in plain white or dark clothing. Some women in India offer their hair in shrines as a religious sacrifice.

Some women shave their heads for aesthetic or professional reasons or to make a political statement. In 1988 Irish singer Sinéad O'Connor made a bald head part of her personal style. Actors may become bald temporarily. For her role in the film *G.I. Jane* (1997), Demi Moore shaved her head and appeared in public without a wig or other head covering. Sigourney Weaver also shaved her head for the film *Alien 3* (1992).

Still other people have become bald to show solidarity with a friend or family member who lost their hair while undergoing medical treatments for cancer.

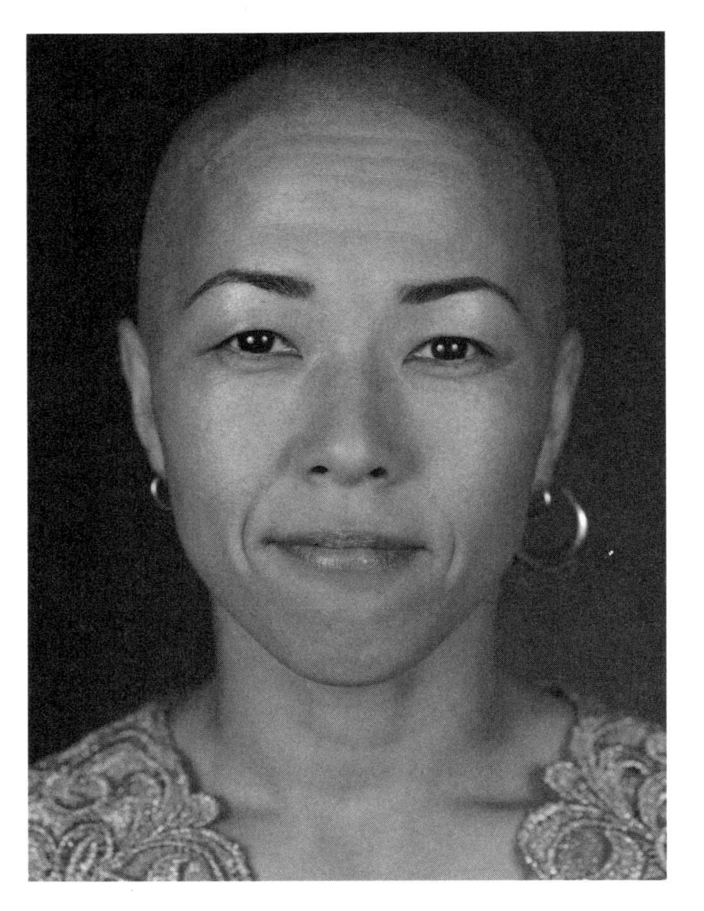

People have made news headlines for shaving their heads because a spouse or child had lost their hair. This type of event was dramatized on an episode of the popular television series *Sex and the City* when Samantha, portrayed by Kim Cattrall, decided to shave her head when her hair began falling out during chemotherapy for breast cancer. Her boyfriend then shaved off his own long blond hair. Groups of people have organized head-shaving events for charity. One such event took place on March 12, 2004, when hundreds of people around Glendale, Illinois, including police officers and firefighters, united to raise funds for the CureSearch National Childhood Cancer Foundation.

Famous people from the past who were openly bald and chose not to wear a hairpiece include Spanish artist Pablo Picasso, Indian political leader Mahatma Gandhi, and British film director Alfred Hitchcock. Well-known bald actors include Yul Brynner, Telly Savalas, Sean Connery, Danny DeVito, Louis Gossett Jr., Bruce Willis, Vin Diesel, Damon Wayans, Howie Mandel, Ving Rhames, Samuel L. Jackson, and Patrick Stewart of *Star Trek.*

More recently, famous athletes have opted for a hair-free head before baldness set in, explaining that a shaved head was easier to maintain, feels cooler in hot weather, and looks good. These athletes include basketball players Michael Jordan, Charles Barkley, and Shaquille O'Neal; tennis players Andre Agassi and James Blake; wrestler and former Minnesota governor Jesse Ventura; and soccer champion David Beckham. Jordan, who shaved his head in 1988, is credited with making baldness more popular. During the 1980s, the look became more fashionable, especially for young people. African American youths adopted it earlier than others.

Some companies offer special products, including gels, moisturizers, and sunscreens, for grooming bald heads. Certain shaving tools and blades, usually featuring a curved blade, may be used to remove hair from the head. Some of these razors do not have handles so that the hand can control the razor more easily as it moves along the contours of the scalp. Most men who shave their heads say they must shave every one to two days to maintain a clean look.

See also: Barbers; Egypt, Ancient; Hair Loss; Hair Transplants; Shaving; Toupee; Wigs and Hairpieces

Further Reading: Holmstrom, David, "For the Fashion-Conscious Man, Bald Is Beautiful," *The Christian Science Monitor*, October 1997, http://csmonitor.com/cgi-bin/durableRedirect.pl?/durable/1997/10/21/feat/feat.2.html; Kuntzman, Gersh, *Hair! Mankind's Historic Quest to End Baldness* (2001); Segrave, Kerry, *Baldness: A Social History* (1996); Theil, Art, "Like No Other," *Hoop Magazine*, April 1998, http://www.nba.com/jordan/hoop_oneforages.html.

BALL, LUCILLE (1911–1989)

A natural brunette, Lucille Ball became famous as a redhead on her popular 1950s television comedy, *I Love Lucy*. The show is still seen in dozens of countries around the world and continues to gain new generations of fans. From the 1930s to the 1970s, Ball also appeared in more than seventy feature films.

Born Lucille Desiree Ball in Jamestown, New York, she and her younger brother grew up with her grandparents and their mother Desiree (DeDe), who was widowed when Lucille was just four years old. As a teenager Lucille was tall, with striking blue eyes and a distinct personality. For example, she bobbed her hair before other local girls. When she was fifteen, her mother enrolled Lucille in a prestigious New York City drama school, in a class that included future screen legend Bette Davis. But her teacher said that the shy small-town girl had no special talent for the stage.

Ball found work modeling for New York designer Hattie Carnegie while she continued to pursue an acting career. Carnegie thought she resembled an actress named Joan Bennett who patronized her salon, and she had Ball bleach her hair platinum blond, like Bennett's. Health problems interrupted her modeling career, but she recovered and returned to Carnegie's.

Ball's first movie appearance was in *Roman Scandals*, released in 1933. In one part of the film, she played a slave girl and wore a long, blond wig over her brown hair. She also was asked to shave off her eyebrows. They did not grow back, so she used pencil to create brows for the rest of her life.

Ball took on more small roles during the 1930s, usually in "glamour" roles. She began her film career with her natural brown hair color, then switched to blond again. In 1935, she began dying her hair red, primarily to distinguish herself from other young actresses with blond hair. Author Stefan Kanfer writes that hairdresser Sydney Guilaroff suggested the change with this comment: "The hair is brown but the soul is on fire." Guilaroff chose a vivid shade called "Tango Red," which was, says Kanfer, "a cross between carrot and strawberry" (Kanfer 2003, 86).

While filming *Too Many Girls* in 1940, Ball met Cuban-born singer/actor Desi Arnaz, whom she married later that year. Ball also signed a contract with MGM in order to boost her film career; she later switched to RKO Studios.

In addition to serious roles and musicals, Ball began to show her flair for comedy in various roles, including on a 1949 radio program called *My Favorite*

Lucille Ball, 1948. *Library of Congress*

Husband. When CBS asked her to recreate that role for a new television series, Ball asked them to develop a program in which she could star with her husband. Although the studio initially did not like the idea, they ultimately agreed and the hit show *I Love Lucy* was born. It debuted before a live audience in 1951.

On the show, Ball played Lucy Ricardo, a lively redhead with a talent for getting in and out of zany situations. The program was filmed in black and white, but the live audience could see the star's bright red hair. One of the running jokes was that Lucy Ricardo dyed her brown hair red at the beauty salon, using henna rinse. In an episode where Ricky insists that the family must economize, Lucy laments the fact that her dark roots will soon show since she cannot afford to have her hair dyed. In real life, Ball used a written formula that was given to her by hair stylist Irma Kusely. It required an application of chemicals, followed by a henna rinse.

Ball and Arnaz formed Desilu Studios, which produced their top-rated show along with feature films and other popular television programs. (Ball would later run Desilu herself from 1962 to 1967, becoming the first woman to own a studio. She later sold the studio to Paramount Pictures in 1968.) After the couple decided to stop filming *I Love Lucy* in 1957, they starred in *Lucy-Desi Comedy Hour* specials during 1957 and 1958. According to author Coyne S. Sanders, in 1958 Ball started wearing wigs on television. That year, she wore a red wig in the popular "bubble-cut" hairstyle.

Ball and Arnaz separated in 1960 and were divorced the next year. Ball, who had two children with Arnaz, married comedian Gary Morton in 1961.

Lucille Ball continued to perform on stage, in films, and in new television situation comedies: *The Lucy Show, Here's Lucy!* and *Life With Lucy*. Filmed in color, these series showcased the actress' famous red hair and her gift for mimicry and physical comedy. From 1967 to 1989, Ball also headed Lucille Ball Productions. During her television career, Ball earned four Emmy awards as the best actress on television. She died in 1989 when her aorta ruptured during open-heart surgery.

See also: Hair Color; Hair Colorants; Henna

Further Reading: Brady, Kathleen, *Lucille: The Life of Lucille Ball* (2001); Higham, Charles, *Lucy: The Life of Lucille Ball* (1986); Kanfer, Stefan, *Ball of Fire: The Tumultuous Life and Comic Art of Lucille Ball* (2003); Sanders, Coyne S., and Tom Gilbert, *Desilu: The Story of Desi Arnaz and Lucille Ball* (1994).

BANGS

Bangs—hair cut shorter across the forehead—have been part of hair arrangements since ancient times. Styles in bangs, called "fringe" in Europe, vary in terms of length, thickness, and arrangement.

Ancient Egyptian hairstyles featured thick bangs cut straight across the forehead, both for wigs and natural hair. Both men and women in the **Roman Empire** sometimes wore bangs, as did people in ancient **Greece**. During the **Middle Ages**, bangs can be seen on paintings and drawings of both men and women in different European countries. They were out of favor during the **Elizabethan era** and Renaissance, a time when most women wore their hair off the forehead or parted smoothly in the center and drawn down and back.

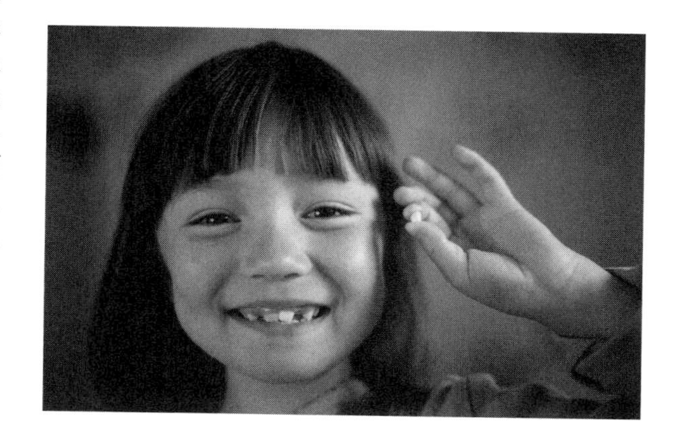

Though European women avoided bangs during the 1500s, they were found in men's styles both in western and eastern Europe. Some men and boys had bangs cut straight across the forehead but at least an inch above the eyebrows. A number of other men wore their hair swept back from the forehead without bangs.

At times, bangs were controversial. During the 1600s, conservative clergy said that women who cut and curled their hair into bangs represented "a slide into mortal sin." These bangs were regarded as a sign of vanity.

Bangs, or "fringe," were worn by women during the **Victorian era**. They tended to be short and wavy or curled and usually covered only part of the forehead. Short, frizzy bangs were popular for women during the early to mid-1880s. The style caught on after Alexandra, Princess of Wales (later queen of England as the wife of King Edward VII), wore her hair this way. Somerset Maugham referred to this style in his 1915 novel *Of Human Bondage*: "She seemed to have a great deal of hair: it was arranged with peculiar elaboration and done over the forehead in what she called an Alexandra fringe" (Bantam Classics, 1991 edition, 272).

Since 1900, bangs have been more or less in fashion, and women base this choice on the shape of their face and forehead, as well as on current trends. As First Lady of the United States from 1953 to 1961, Mamie Eisenhower was known for her signature short, tight, waved bangs. Stylish short haircuts from Italy also featured bangs, but these were more unstructured. Actress Audrey Hepburn popularized a short haircut called the "Pixie." Her hair was cut in an irregular fringe across the forehead and along both ears. Bangs became popular with men in the 1960s when members of the Beatles and other pop musicians were seen with bangs.

Bangs sometimes are viewed as a "youthful" look and many haircuts for young girls featured some kind of bangs during the mid-1900s. The "Dutchboy bob" featured a thick line of bangs cut bluntly across the forehead. Straight, thick bangs are also associated with certain classic haircuts worn by girls and women in Asia.

During the late twentieth century, bangs were in and out of fashion, but styles were more diverse and individualized than in the past. Bangs could be long, short, and every length in between as well as crimped, smooth, curled, waved, or spiky. Some bangs were cut to eyebrow length or longer.

In 2004, bangs seemed to be experiencing another surge of popularity in the United States. **Jennifer Aniston** helped to spark the trend after she appeared on the television series *Friends* with long bangs that were swept to the side. Actress Catherine Zeta-Jones also wore long bangs for some of her film roles and public appearances. Like many contemporary women, Zeta-Jones had versatile long bangs cut in such a way that they could be swept up or to the side to create different looks.

See also: Bara, Theda; Bob, The; Byzantine Empire; China; Egypt, Ancient; Flapper; Gibson Girl; Hairstyles, Twentieth-Century; Hepburn, Audrey; Pompadour; Regency; Renaissance Europe; Superstitions; Victorian Era

Further Reading: Doyle, Marian I., *An Illustrated History of Hairstyles, 1830–1930* (Atglen, PA: Schiffer, 2003); Nunn, Joan, *Fashion in Costume, 1200–2000*, 2nd ed. (2000); Turudich, Daniela, *1950s Hair: Hairstyles from the Atomic Age of Cool* (n.p.: Streamline Press, 2004).

BARA, THEDA (1890–1955)

Nicknamed "The Vamp," Theda Bara (born Theodosia Burr Goodman) was one of cinema's first *femme fatales*, and millions of women copied her hairstyle and makeup.

Born in Cincinnati, Ohio, to a middle-class Jewish family, Theodosia, nicknamed "Theda," grew up wanting to act. After high school graduation, she dyed her blond hair black for a more dramatic look and went to New York City in

1908 to pursue her dream. She appeared in a stage play and then began touring with a theatrical company in 1911.

Four years later, back in New York, she won a small role as an extra in a film called *The Stain*, produced by Fox Studios. The director thought Bara showed promise, and she was cast in the lead role as a vampire in *A Fool There Was*, released that same year. This led to her nickname, "The Vamp," and inspired a new, exotic look for women, which included bobbed hair, thick bangs, pale facial makeup, dark red lips, and eyes accented with **kohl** liner and thick mascara. Bara also wore her fingernails longer than other actresses of her day, often with sharply pointed ends. Vampish women were viewed as mysterious, aggressive, and seductive, and Bara became the movies' first "sex symbol."

Theda Bara. *Library of Congress*

Theda Bara made six more films in 1915 and eight in 1916. To generate more interest in their new star, Fox Studios invented stories about her background, claiming, for instance, that Bara's parents were an Italian artist and Arabian princess. They said she had lived in Europe, where she studied acting and starred onstage in Paris. To make herself more mysterious and provocative, Bara posed as the "Serpent of the Nile" with live snakes, crystal balls, skulls, and other startling props.

The following year, Fox Studios relocated to California and Bara moved west. In 1918, she ranked among the top three film stars of her day, along with **Mary Pickford** and Charlie Chaplin, and she earned about $4,000 a week. Bara continued to star in films and made seven new films in 1919, but Fox Studios dropped her contract that year as interest in "The Vamp" seemed to wane. After her marriage in 1921, Theda Bara retired, though she did attempt some unsuccessful comebacks in the years that followed.

See also: Bob, The; Flappers; Hair Color

Further Reading: Golden, Eve, *Vamp: The Rise of Theda Bara* (1996); Parrish, James Robert, *The Fox Girls* (1971); Pearson, David B., "Theda Bara," Silent Ladies and Gents, http://www.silentladies.com/Bbara.html.

BARBERS

Barbers—from the Latin word "*barba*" (beard)—provide hair care and personal grooming services, including cutting and styling the hair, **shaving**, and caring for beards and **mustaches**. Some barbershops also offer manicures, shoe shining, and other services. Centuries ago, barbers gave first-aid treatment and dental and surgical care.

"Long hair minimizes the need for barbers."

ALBERT EINSTEIN (1879–1955), German-American scientist

Ancient Roots

The barbering profession dates back over 6,000 years. Ancient barbers often were spiritual leaders, such as priests or medicine men. Some cultures believed that both good and evil spirits entered the body through the hair, so haircutting assumed a spiritual significance. In certain parts of **Africa**, Asia, and other regions, haircutting played a key role in rituals, including marriage. During some ceremonies, people wore their hair hanging loose so that evil spirits could leave the head and good spirits could enter. When the ceremony ended, barbers cut and styled the hair against the head to keep the good spirits inside and ward off evil ones.

In ancient **Mesopotamia**, religious leaders wore their beards in specific styles, and their barbers followed prescribed ways of shaving priests and other religious figures. Barbers were also employed to shave slaves so that their skin could be branded or marked in ways that showed their status.

Egyptian barbers who served upper-class men were well paid and prominent in the communities. Some personal barbers visited the homes of wealthy clients, while poorer citizens patronized barbers who moved about the community working outdoors. Their tools, made from sharpened flint and oyster shells, included razors with curved handles that resembled small hatchets. Among other things, barbers shaved off all body hair, a grooming practice that some Egyptians requested as often as every three days. Removing body hair helped people in this hot climate to stay clean because perspiration and dirt were less likely to cling to hairless skin.

People who followed Jewish laws, or the Laws of Moses, did not cut their hair or trim their beards like most other groups living in the Middle East. Barbers who worked among Jews were banned from shaving their heads or trimming their beards. References to these prohibitions can be found in the Old Testament, for example, in Leviticus 19:27: "You shall not round off the hair on your temples or mar the edges of your beard."

By about 500 BCE, barbers were important members of Greek society, where men prized their well-trimmed beards. Beards were often curled and then scented, so barbers became skilled in these areas and stocked fragrant essences. In these, the first real "barbershops," men gathered to socialize and exchange ideas as well as to have their hair and beards groomed. Personal barbers also made house calls to serve male members of wealthy households and their guests.

Barbers were found in other places, including the British Isles, Saxony, and Gaul. Barbers in ancient Ireland groomed the hair, beards, and mustaches of royalty and tribal leaders.

Roman men had scoffed at shaving and called it effeminate, but eventually they began to shave, too. In 296 BCE, a Sicilian, Ticinius Mena, brought Greek barbers to Rome. These *tonsors*, as they were called, worked in shops and in the elaborate Roman public baths. As was true in Greece, barbers were respected, and Roman barbershops became gathering places where men gossiped and exchanged news. Some meticulously groomed men spent hours in barbershops having their hair styled and receiving shaves, massages, and manicures. To set them apart from other Roman men, who shaved their facial hair, slaves were forced to wear beards.

Middle Ages

During the **Middle Ages**, barbers worked in European monasteries. Monks were expected to be clean-shaven at all times, as specified in a decree that Pope Urban II had issued in 1092.

Monks were performing minor surgery and a medical procedure called bloodletting, based on the notion that impure blood caused disease and should be removed from the body in order to relieve sickness. In 1163, barbers took over the job of bloodletting after Pope Alexander III issued a new decree that forbade clergymen from engaging in activities that involved blood. Barbers also dispensed herbal treatments and cared for cuts and wounds. For more than six hundred years, barber-surgeons, as they were called, provided medical care as well as some dental care, including extractions and treatment of abscessed teeth. This put barbers into conflict with physicians and dentists. From 1163 until 1745 barbers were called Doctors of the Short Robe.

Like other tradesmen and craftsmen, medieval barbers throughout Europe formed guilds. Barbers in France formed a trade group in 1096. Their business had increased after the Archbishop of Rouen banned men from wearing beards. New French barbers were trained through the apprenticeship system.

In the mid-1200s, the two major companies of Parisian barbers—the Brotherhoods of St. Cosmos and St. Domain—formed the first known school to train barbers (known in France as *chirurgists*) in surgical procedures. In 1383, the King of France authorized his personal barber and valet to oversee barbers and surgeons throughout the country. A guild for French barbers and surgeons was formed in 1391.

Likewise, English barbers organized trade guilds. The Worshipful Company of Barbers, which is still in existence, was formed in London in 1308. To promote quality and customer satisfaction, the king empowered a Master of Barbers to inspect barbershops and discipline barbers who did not meet the guild's standards of practice. As Master of Barbers in London, Richard le Barbour supervised all of the barbers in that city. Le Barbour conducted monthly inspections to make sure barbers were following the rules. Throughout England, each master of barbers supervised practicing barbers in his town and made sure no unauthorized man practiced barbering. Also during the 1300s, English barbers formed two separate groups: one group practiced surgical procedures, the other did not. In 1462 King Edward IV granted the barbers' guild a charter. By then, barbers in some countries were extracting teeth and carrying out other dental functions in addition to providing tonsorial (barbering and shaving) and/or surgical services.

The barber's pole developed during the medieval era. Barbers displayed a blue and white striped pole, while surgeons' poles were red and white. The pole symbolized the staff that patients held in their hands during bloodletting treatments. At the top of the pole was a brass bowl, like the one used to hold leeches that sucked the patient's blood. The basin also held blood. After the treatments, bandages were washed and hung on poles to dry, giving the effect of red and white spirals.

Changing Functions

During the 1400s, English physician-surgeons surpassed barbers in medical knowledge and skills. Parliament passed an act in 1450 that limited barbers to certain medical procedures: bloodletting, extracting teeth, simple care of wounds, and dissecting corpses. In order to perform these services, a barber-surgeon must have his diploma signed by two practicing barbers and two surgeons.

The Parliamentary restrictions remained in force even after barber-surgeons and surgeons once again joined the same guild. Barbers regained the prestige they had once enjoyed, and English monarchs gave them gifts and privileges. This continued until 1745, at which time the two professions became separate. In small communities that lacked dentists and physicians, barbers still provided dental and medical services, however. Women barbers also could be found in European barbershops during these years. English historians have identified certain women barbers working in London from the 1600s into the 1900s.

Since new medical discoveries were occurring rapidly, most barbers could not keep pace, and some patients complained about poor treatment. Physicians and dentists pushed for new laws to further restrict barbers' activities.

In colonial America, many barbers continued to combine traditional barbering with the work of surgeon and dentist. Signs reading "Barber and Chirurgeon" stood outside their shops, along with the red-and-white striped pole representing blood and bandages which had once stood inside the shops. Some barbers displayed red, white, and blue striped poles, possibly because these were the colors of the national flag or because blue represented veins.

During the 1700s in America, barbering was considered a working-class occupation, one that might be performed by household servants. In southern states, **African American** slaves often took on haircutting and shaving duties, and some freed African American men opened barbershops.

In 1745, English lawmakers passed new laws that made barbering and surgery separate fields and banned barbers from practicing medicine. Similar laws were passed in France and other countries. Barbers then focused on their haircutting and shaving (tonsorial) functions. Wigs were especially popular during the seventeenth, eighteenth, and part of the nineteenth century, so many barbers added wig making to their repertoire.

Improving Standards

After the 1750s, American barbers experienced a decline in both status and income. During the nineteenth century, many barbershops were unsanitary, and people regarded them as dingy places where men gossiped and read cheap magazines. Other barbers kept their shops clean and comfortable.

After the Civil War ended in 1865, new immigrants from Italy, Scandinavia, and other countries worked as barbers. African Americans continued to develop successful barbering businesses. For example, in Philadelphia, William Warrick gained a reputation for excellence during the 1880s when he established that city's first chain of barbershops. Warrick went on to found another barbershop in Atlantic City, New Jersey.

Barbershops were a common sight on the main streets of American towns and cities. A typical barbershop of the late 1800s was a small room with one or more straight-backed chairs with headpieces. To start their business, barbers needed a razor, scissors, soap, brushes, a water basin, and towels. Customers paid five or ten cents for a haircut and about three cents for a shave. Barbers no longer practiced bloodletting, which went out of favor after the 1850s.

To gain professional status, barbers worked for higher standards and organized themselves into groups called "boss barbers" and "master barbers." In 1886, the Barbers' Protective Union was founded in Columbus, Ohio, and the following year, the Journeyman Barbers International Union was formed in Buffalo, New York, where the group held its first annual convention. The union later changed its name to Journeymen Barbers', Hairdressers', Cosmetologists', and Proprietors' International Union of America, with headquarters in Indianapolis, Indiana. Today it is known as the Barbers, Beauticians, and Allied Industries International Association.

Barbers continued to upgrade their educational and licensing requirements. In 1893, A. B. Moler set up the world's first barber school, in Chicago, and he wrote the first American textbooks on professional barbering. Branches of Moler's school were established in cities around the country. The apprenticeship system was phased out, and men who wanted to become barbers attended classes on haircutting and shaving techniques, face and scalp treatments, sanitation, and proper care of their tools.

The first barber license law was passed in 1897, in Minnesota. This law set educational and licensing requirements for barbers and defined sanitary practices.

Twentieth-Century Barbers

During the 1900s, more laws were passed in the United States to regulate training and licensing and to ensure safe, sanitary conditions in the nation's barbershops. In 1920, Ohio became the second state to pass such laws; other states followed. These laws, coupled with regular inspections, improved services and helped to prevent infections and the transmission of scalp parasites and skin diseases, such as impetigo and ringworm.

The Associated Masters Barbers of America (AMBA) was formed in Chicago in 1924. Later, the organization changed its name to Associated Master Barbers and Beauticians of America. Now called Hair International, this association continues to promote the interests of barbers and beauticians.

Teachers were trained in Barber Science, and the AMBA set up an educational council. A standard textbook for barbering was published in 1931. Courses for barbers expanded to include chemistry, bacteriology, and anatomy, along with traditional technical classes.

During the early 1900s, men who insisted on being clean-shaven and well groomed visited barbers regularly, often for just a shave. Barbers were provided on ocean liners so that travelers could maintain their appearance during the voyage. For example, in 1912, the ill-fated RMS *Titanic* provided separate barbershops for first-class and second-class passengers so they could have professional shaves and haircuts during the trip, which was expected to last two weeks.

During the late 1910s and the 1920s, barbers served more female clients. Women came to have their long hair cut into a **bob**, which began as a trend for younger women but became a fashion for all ages. Some women had barbers cut their hair instead of visiting a beauty salon that catered to women.

From the 1940s into the early 1960s, barbers were busy giving male clients the haircuts and styles that were popular during those years, including the flattop, crew cut, ducktail, Princeton cut, and pompadour. Some of these styles required **tonics**, oils, and waxes. More men also sought professional shaving services in the days before effective safety razors, electric razors, and shaving foams became available.

When long hair for men became popular during the mid-1960s, the profession experienced a slump that continued into the 1970s. Thousands of barbers went out of business.

More changes took place during the 1980s. The Journeymen Barber International Union became part of the United Food and Commercial Workers International Union in 1981. That same decade saw a rise in the number of female barbers. By the mid-1980s, about half of all barber students were women, and by the 1990s, about half of all students were African Americans.

Modern barbers, both male and female, continue to provide haircutting and grooming services. Although some men now visit stylists in salons that serve both genders, others prefer the traditional "men only" barbershop. Barbers have expanded their repertoire and men who wish to keep their heads clean-shaven, a style that grew more popular after 1990, frequently rely on a barber. Barbershops have changed with the times and updated their facilities and equipment to attract more business, although many still display the traditional striped pole.

See also: Beards, Men's; Egypt, Ancient; Greece, Ancient; Hair Removal; Hairdressing; Hairstyles, Twentieth-Century; Religion and Hair; Roffler, Edmond O.; Roman Empire; Wigs and Hairpieces

Further Reading: Barlow, Ronald S., *The Vanishing American Barber Shop: An Illustrated History of Tonsorial Art: 1860–1960* (1996); Bibby, Geoffrey, *Four Thousand Years Ago: A World Panorama of Life in the Second Millennium* (1963); Cooper, Wendy, *Hair: Sex, Society, Symbolism* (1971); Dobson, Jessie, *Barbers and Barber-surgeons of London: A History of the Barbers' and Barber-surgeons Companies* (1979); Jenkins, Ian, *Greek and Roman Life* (1986); Jones, Christian R., *Barbershop: History and Antiques* (1999); Langdon, William Chauncey, *Everyday Things in American Life, 1607–1776* (1937); Lindsay, Jack, *The Ancient World: Manners and Morals* (1968); Plumb, Richard A., and Milton V. Lee, *Ancient and Honorable Barber Profession* (1974); Staten, Vince, *Do Bald Men Get Half-Price Haircuts? In Search of America's Great Barbershops* (2002).

BATTELLE, KENNETH (1927–)

Hairstylist Kenneth Battelle is known for his influence on western styles, particularly during the 1960s.

Battelle's hairdressing career began almost by accident. After serving in the navy during World War II, he was job hunting in 1945 and responded to a newspaper ad that was seeking people who could cut hair. Battelle discovered a talent for hairdressing and made a name for himself at the New York salon of Lilly Daché, a world-famous milliner who also designed clothing and beauty products.

In 1961, Battelle won a Coty Award for his work, and two years later he opened his own salon on East 54th Street. The multi-floored facility, known simply as "Kenneth," boasted a luxurious interior by celebrity decorator Billy Baldwin. Battelle's artistry attracted celebrities and socially prominent women.

During the early 1960s, Battelle became known to the general public as First Lady Jacqueline Kennedy's hairdresser. He created bouffant styles for the brunette Mrs. Kennedy, who set trends around the world with her hair and clothing styles. Battelle had begun working with her in 1954 and later did her hair for momentous occasions, including President Kennedy's inauguration ceremony and inaugural balls. According to Battelle, he suggested that Mrs. Kennedy wear a fuller hairstyle because she was tall, with a wide face and broad shoulders. He set her hair with specially designed large Lucite rollers before combing it out. For another client, film legend **Marilyn Monroe**, Battelle advised a softer, less curly look that he thought would flatter her facial features.

Battelle became vice president of Glemby Products (offering cosmetics and hair products) and opened a Glemby salon in London in 1976. Stylists at this salon promoted natural looking styles that did not require teasing and hairspray. Instead, said Battelle, "Hair must bounce and move" (Carter 1977, 169).

In 2002, still working as a hairdresser, he appointed his top stylist, Kevin Lee, as manager of his legendary salon in the Waldorf Astoria Hotel. Resisting the trend to charge hundreds of dollars for a haircut, Battelle was charging a relatively modest $155.

See also: Bouffant; Hairdressing; Kennedy, Jacqueline Bouvier; Salons, Hair and Beauty

Further Reading: Bradford, Sarah, *America's Queen: Jacqueline Kennedy Onassis* (2001); Carter, Ernestine, *The Changing World of Fashion* (1977); Dominus, Susan, "He's Still Hair," *New York Magazine*, May 13, 2002; Gordon, Michael, *Hair Heroes* (2002); Larocca, Amy, "Big Hair," *New York Magazine*, March 1, 2003.

BEARDS, MEN'S

Throughout history, men's facial hair has been a focus of appearance and changing grooming practices. Beards—hair growing on the chin, cheeks, and upper lip—have been common in certain cultures and eras. Since the potential to grow thick facial hair is a distinctly male trait, a beard has sometimes been a symbol of masculinity or male sexual potency. Beards also have designated rank, group affiliation, or social status. The decision whether or not to wear a beard can be influenced by custom, law, religion, or fashion trends.

The average man has about 25,000 hairs on the chin, and beard hair grows about five to six inches (125–150 mm) per year. Men of European or Middle Eastern ancestry tend to have the largest number of hair follicles on their faces. Asian men have the least, and men from Africa fall somewhere in between.

Fashions in beards and/or mustaches have undergone many changes. Men have grown, trimmed, and arranged their beards according to local customs and the styles of their times—or they have removed their facial hair for the same reasons. When beards are in style, they may be regarded as a sign of manliness, health, and honor. In places where shaving is the norm, however, a beard might be a sign that something is amiss. Perhaps the man is in mourning, lacks time to spend on his appearance, or does not care about social conventions? He might even be signaling his disregard for convention and conformity.

Laws or customs may require men either to wear a beard or shave their faces partially or completely. In some cultures, only certain men have been permitted to either wear a beard or to shave. Some religions also expect followers to remain unshaven. Sikhs, for example, do not remove beards or other body hairs.

In some cultures, men have devised elaborate beard styles and added decorative elements. Ancient Assyrian men curled their beards and added gold dust for special occasions. The Assyrians were renowned in the ancient world for their skill in styling both beards and other hair. Kings of ancient Persia laced their beards with gold threads or sprinkled on gold dust, as did the long-haired, long-bearded Merovingians, who lived in present-day France during the sixth to mid-eighth centuries CE.

Some conquerors or rulers forced men to shave against their will as a **punishment** or form of oppression. Losing a beard could be humiliating or go against a man's religion or culture. During the third century, Christian rulers demanded that the conquered Celts and Teutons shave off their beards. Centuries later, in the 1400s, Japanese conquerers ordered the indigenous Ainu men in present-day northern Japan to shave. Modern Ainu men do not shave their faces, which usually feature a thick beard.

Ancient Times

Cave drawings that date back to 10,000 BCE show some clean-shaven men and others with short beards. Since then, styles in facial hair have likewise varied, depending on the place and the times.

Sculptures from ancient Assyria (900–612 BCE) show men with full beards growing from ear to ear. The Assyrians wore this hair in three to five rows of small, tight curls. Assyrian men also dyed their beards, as well as their eyebrows and hair, with black pigments, whereas Persian men tinted their beards shades of red, using **henna**.

In **ancient Egypt**, men shaved their faces as well as their entire bodies, primarily for hygienic reasons. **Barbers** performed shaving services, and this gave them a prominent place in society as early as 500 BCE. During the period known as the Old Kingdom (3110–2000 BCE), men did grow some chin hairs, which they might dye or frizz. Some men also added gold threads. Egyptian rulers of both genders and priests attached **false beard** for ceremonies and other special occasions, but private citizens were banned from wearing them. The custom of wearing a false beard, which were made of metal, may have begun because an early pharaoh wore a real beard.

Jewish men were expected to wear beards, which were regarded as a sign of manliness. They usually trimmed their beards but let them grow longer during times of mourning. Modern Jews of the Chasidic group and certain other Orthodox Jews still follow this custom. Under certain circumstances, Jews could shave their beards. For instance, Moses, a Jewish leader, said that any man who recovered from leprosy should shave as a health precaution.

Other cultures eschewed beards. For example, in Sumeria, an African culture in western Asia (5000–1950 BCE), men carefully removed their facial hair. Ancient Indian men typically shaved their faces once or twice a week. Ancient tribes living in present-day Wales and Brittany shaved the chin area but did grow mustaches. In ancient Peru, now part of South America, the Incans had laws banning beards; likewise the Aztecs, who lived in present-day Mexico, went beardless. From ancient to modern times, Native Americans in North, Central, and South America removed facial hair, including beards.

Ancient Greeks wore beards, and the first sign of chin growth on young men was dedicated to Greek gods in a temple, according to religious customs. Beards lost favor after Alexander the Great (Alexander III of Macedonia, 356–323 BCE) rose to power. He sent Macedonian troops into Asia, where they lost several battles to Persian troops. The Persians managed to capture many Greeks by grabbing them by the beard and pulling them off their horses during a battle. To prevent this, Alexander banned beards in the military and other Greek men followed suit. Assyrian soldiers wore short beards, perhaps for the same reason and also for practical reasons. For soldiers in most countries, beards were kept short or removed for reasons of safety.

In Imperial Rome, before 296 BCE, men grew long beards, often adorned with curls and waves. They regarded shaving as effeminate. Adolescent men followed the custom of dedicating their first beards to the gods. From 78 to 117 BCE, the ruler Julius Caesar set the style of a clean-shaven face. Roman men began to shave their beards and Greek barbers were imported for that purpose.

Beards returned during the reign of Hadrian (from 117 to 138 CE), who wore a beard to conceal the scars and blemishes on his face. Hadrian was the first Roman emperor to wear a beard, which he kept trimmed. For decades, his successors also wore beards, which varied in length and style. During the second and third centuries CE, some emperors wore sideburns but no beards, while others shaved off their facial hair.

Religious customs determined the state of facial hair in some societies. In the **Middle East**, followers of the Prophet Muhammed were told to trim their mustaches and beards in a certain way to show that they were Muslim. Millions of men vowed to grow their beards in that way, which would also help to set members of their group apart from Christian men. Bedouin Arabs also had beards, which they wore pointed.

Changing Western Styles

Western styles have reflected changing ideas about fashion, often sparked by rulers or other prominent men. During the reign of Henry III (1216–1272), English men imitated his long, full beard. Edward II (1307–1327) wore an unusual beard formed with three ringlets, while Edward III (1327–1377) sported what is called a "forked beard." Richard II (1377–1399) wore twin tufts on both sides of his chin. Beards remained popular in England under King Henry VIII (1491–1547), whose beard was naturally red in color.

Some monarchs went beyond influencing fashion trends and made laws regarding beards. After he became czar of Russia in 1547, Ivan the Terrible demanded that all male subjects wear beards. He said, "To shave the beard is a sin that the blood of all the martyrs cannot cleanse."

Other rulers also decreed that their subjects must wear a mustache or beard, while in other countries men followed trends in their local communities. For example, during the 1600s many fashionable European men wore short pointed "Van Dyke" beards.

By around 1700, beards had gone out of style throughout Europe, in part because popular French actors were appearing onstage clean-shaven. Yet Russian men continued to wear beards. Then, in 1705, Czar Peter the Great imposed a tax of thirty to one hundred rubles per year or hard labor, on any Russian man who wore a beard or mustache. Peasants were exempted from this law. Some Russian men emigrated because they did not want to shave.

Colonial America

European explorers who crossed the Atlantic were usually bearded, often for practical reasons. These were men from Spain, France, England, and other countries, including Hernando Cortés, Ponce de León, Jacques Cartier, Samuel de Champlain, Sir Francis Drake, Sir Walter Raleigh, Captain John Smith, and Hernando de Soto. Male settlers who arrived during the 1500s and 1600s also had facial hair. The Pilgrims and Puritans who settled in New England wore beards.

Europeans noticed that most natives of the Americas removed their facial hair, with some exceptions. British soldier and trader Alexander Walker described men of the Chugach group living in Prince William Sound on the coast of present-day Alaska this way: "Their hair is black, and is generally worn short. Some of them shave or cut their beard, and others allow them to grow long."

In keeping with European styles, beards gradually became smaller until they went out of style in the American colonies around 1720. During the Revolutionary War, soldiers fighting both on the American and British side wore neither beards nor mustaches. The men who signed the Declaration of Independence and the first fifteen presidents were likewise beard free.

Clean-shaven faces remained the norm in North America during the 1700s. Prominent politicians and even men of the frontier, such as Davy Crockett and Daniel Boone, did not wear beards.

Nineteenth Century

When Abraham Lincoln took office in 1861, he became the first U.S. president to wear a beard. Many mid-nineteenth-century American men wore a full beard. After the Civil War ended, a more heavy-set and mature appearance for men was in vogue. Whiskers were thought to denote wisdom and respectability.

In 1869, cartoonist Thomas Nast put a beard on his drawings of "Uncle Sam," the tall, thin, white-haired man who became a symbol of the United States in 1812. Uncle Sam continued to wear red, white, and blue, but previous drawings of this national icon had shown him clean-shaven before Nast added the white goatee that remains to this day.

As beards became popular again, numerous products, including potions that promised to "grow beards," came into the marketplace. Manufacturers of various other products, including medicines, added bearded people to their ads and labels, since a beard symbolized trustworthiness and intelligence.

Although men living in settled parts of the eastern United States were likely to grow sideburns and beards to stay in fashion, men out west let their facial hair grow, since shaving was inconvenient and impractical. Army scout William "Buffalo Bill" Cody exemplified this rugged look with his long hair and beard.

In England, Edward VII influenced styles in clothing and personal grooming during the late 1800s when he was Prince of Wales and after he became king. At the turn of the twentieth century, gentlemen in various western cultures wore a beard that was neatly trimmed like King Edward's.

Changing fashions in beards could be seen in the portraits of U.S. presidents. Every man who followed Lincoln into the White House had a beard, or at least a mustache, until a clean-shaven William McKinley was elected in 1896. By the time Woodrow Wilson was elected in 1912, the vast majority of men were starting to shave daily, and facial hair never reappeared in the White House during the twentieth century.

Twentieth Century

After the early 1900s, beards became far less common in western cultures as men began to shave daily for a "well-groomed look." New shaving equipment made hair removal easier and more convenient. The **Gillette Company** began encouraging daily shaving with its 1910 ads that claimed women preferred men with clean-shaven faces. Gillette promoted the idea that shaving was more civilized and women appreciate "clean, healthy skin." Gillette ads showed beard-free men with a healthy look that signified an "outdoor man rather than the indoor man" (Atwan, McQuade, and Wright 1971).

Despite the trend toward a clean-shaven look, some men chose to wear beards anyway. Beards were sometimes associated with professors, scientists, artists, or other intellectuals. During the 1950s, members of the "Beat Generation," called "beatniks," often wore beards. They favored a narrow beard called a goatee.

Some men who grew beards during the 1960s and 1970s were members of, or wished to identify with, the counterculture. The so-called **hippies** often wore long hair, a beard, or both.

Since the 1980s, some men have opted for a light overall growth of beard—what once was called a "five o'clock shadow," meaning the appearance of hair late in the day after a morning shave. Actors Don Johnson and George Clooney were among those who wore this relaxed look, which results when a man doesn't shave for one or more days.

As the twenty-first century began, men in western cultures were wearing beards out of choice, either to express their personal style or conform to their religion. Those who wear beards do so because they like the look, it suits their occupation and lifestyle, or they have sensitive skin that makes daily shaving uncomfortable. Men who continue to wear beards for religious reasons include Orthodox Jews, particularly Chasidim, and the Todas, a group of people living in the

Tamilnadu State, located in southern India. The Todas are thought to have descended from Dravidians, Macedonians, or Romans.

See also: Beards, Women's; Byzantine Empire; Elizabethan Era; False Beard; Greece, Ancient; Laws and Regulations; Mesopotamia; Palmer, Joe; Politics and Hair; Regency; Religion and Hair; Shaving; Sideburns; Soul Patch; World Beard and Moustache Championship

Further Reading: Atwan, Robert, Donald McQuade, and John W. Wright, *Edsels, Luckies, & Frigidaires: Advertising the American Way* (1971); Grant, Michael, *A Social History of Greece and Rome* (1992); Hammond, N. G. L., *The Genius of Alexander the Great* (1998); Laver, James, *Taste and Fashion: From the French Revolution to Today* (1937); Lindsay, Jack, *The Ancient World: Manners and Morals* (1968); Moers, Ellen, *The Dandy: Brummel to Beerbohn* (1960); Oswalt, Wendell, *Alaskan Eskimos* (1967); Parker, Dan, *Corpus Christi (TC) Caller Times*, July 15, 2001, http://www.coastalbendfootball.com/2001/july/15/today/fea-livi/5277.html; Payne, Robert, *Ivan the Terrible* (2002); Peterkin, Alan, *One Thousand Beards: A Cultural History of Facial Hair* (2002); Reynolds, Reginald, *Beards* (1949); Sayce, A. H., *Babylonians and Assyrians: Life and Customs* (1899).

BEARDS, WOMEN'S

Women with beards have been described since ancient times. In those days, people did understand the scientific reasons for thick facial hair on a woman, so they speculated about the causes. It is now known that a genetic hormonal disorder can lead to this trait.

Since facial hair on women is unusual, bearded women often were regarded as curiosities to be ostracized, stared at, and exhibited in circuses, sideshows, and dime museums.

The medical literature has documented cases of bearded women. In **ancient Greece**, the physician Hippocrates (ca. 460–377) described a woman whose facial hair grew into a beard after the onset of menopause, the time when menstrual cycles end as a result of declining female hormones.

Since then, doctors also have written about younger women, including women in their thirties, with beards and/or mustaches. During the sixteenth century, Barbara Urster was known for her waist-length beard. In one case, a twenty-three-year-old woman told her doctor she had had facial hair since age three. This woman was a married mother of two children and her other physical and personality traits were regarded as "feminine."

Rosine-Marguerite Muller of Germany was one of the most famous bearded women in history. When she died in a Dresden hospital in 1732, Muller had a thick beard and heavy mustache. During the 1880s, American Annie Jones worked for P. T. Barnum as a museum attraction. Jones' beard began to grow in childhood but her other physical attributes were distinctly feminine. A Hungarian woman, Baroness Sidonia de Barcsy, had a natural full beard that began growing after her son was born. A postcard dated 1900 shows the baroness posing in a glamorous evening gown. A Frenchwoman named Madame Delait became famous for her beard during the early 1900s. Other bearded women "on exhibit" included Lady Olga, Madame Devere, and Princess Gracie.

According to the *Guinness Book of World Records*, as of 2001 American Vivian Wheeler (b. 1949) held the world record for the longest beard on a woman. Born in Illinois, Wheeler inherited a hormonal disorder from her mother, whose own mother also had facial hair. Wheeler's beard began to grow when she was ten years old. As an adult, using the stage name "Melinda Maxie," she traveled with carnivals and sideshow acts and dyed her naturally red hair black to make her beard even more dramatic.

Most cultures display negative attitudes toward facial hair on women, probably because it appears masculine rather than feminine. Social scientists believe that facial hair on a woman is considered unattractive because it looks rough and less "child-like," suggesting an older (and therefore infertile) woman, and therefore a "less desirable" mate. Most women who have hair growth on their upper lip or other parts of the face choose to bleach it or remove it with depilatories formulated for that purpose.

In 2004, newspapers told the story of Anica Birladeanu, a Romanian woman with a thick beard and mustache. Despite being ostracized by people in her village of Pechea, the thirty-four-year-old shepherd refused to shave, saying that the facial hair keeps her warm. Fellow villagers claimed that Birladeanu's beard was a sign of evil, and they accused her of being the offspring of the devil.

See also: Beards, Men's; Body Hair; Hair Removal; Hirsutism; World Beard and Moustache Championship

Further Reading: Gould, George M., and Walter L. Pyle, *Anomalies and Curiosities of Medicine* (1896); Reilly, Steve, "Bearded Woman Finds Shelter in Punta Gorda," *Sun Herald* (FL), May 21, 2003, http://www.sun-herald.com/NewsArchive2/05.../tp3ch17.htm.

BEEHIVE

See Bouffant; *Hairspray*; Hairstyles, Twentieth-Century; Styling Products; Styling Tools

BEGOUN, PAULA (1953–)

Consumer advocate Paula Begoun studies and writes about the cosmetics and hair care products industry, and she founded a company that produces her brand-name cosmetics, skin care products, and hair care products. Begoun, who was born in Skokie, Illinois, majored in science at Northwestern University. After working as a freelance makeup artist, skin care consultant, and department store cosmetics salesperson, Begoun decided to study cosmetics production. She believes that consumers need specific information about the ingredients and effects of various products so they can select the most appropriate items and receive value for their money.

During the 1980s and early 1990s, Begoun completed two detailed books with her findings and recommendations: *Don't Go to the Cosmetics Counter Without Me* (1991) and *Don't Go Shopping for Hair Care Products Without Me* (1995). These books, which have since been updated, contain articles and lists of products, along with information about their ingredients, performance, and cost. In her hair care book, Begoun discusses the anatomy and physiology of hair and describes how different chemicals, products, treatments, and styling tools and techniques can affect it. The 2004 edition of *Don't Go Shopping for Hair Care Products Without Me* contains information on more than 4,000 shampoos, conditioners, gels, mousses, styling creams, hairsprays, hair coloring products, and other hair care products.

To obtain information about products, Begoun and her staff purchase various products and try them. In addition, they study advertisements, commercials, and research abstracts, and they consult with chemists, dermatologists, and other experts.

Begoun also publishes a monthly newsletter, *Cosmetics Counter Update*, which describes new products and gives updates on existing products. Her Web site contains information about new products and cosmetics research, along with a question-answer column.

See also: Advertising; Shampoo

Further Reading: Begoun, Paula, *Don't Go Shopping for Hair Care Products Without Me* (1997); "Paula Begoun," http://www.cosmeticscop.com.

BIBLE *See* Amish; Beards, Men's; Dredlocks; Religion and Hair

BLEACH *See* Elizabethan Era; Hair Colorants; Harlow, Jean; Renaissance Europe; Roman Empire

"BLOND BOMBSHELL" *See* Hair Color; Hairstyles, Twentieth-Century; Harlow, Jean; Lake, Veronica; Monroe, Marilyn

BLOW DRYER *See* Hair Dryers

BOB, THE

The bob was a revolutionary short hairstyle that came to symbolize the so-called "new woman" in the United States, Europe, and other places during the 1910s and especially after 1920. The bob was a radical change from the long, contrived styles that predominated in earlier eras.

The rise of this style coincided with rapid social and political changes during and after World War I (1914–1918). Some historians think the hairdo spread after military nurses who had served on the war front returned home with short haircuts they had adopted for hygienic reasons. Meanwhile, on the home front, many young women had taken jobs to help the war effort or to gain economic independence.

New hairstyles reflected women's changing roles. Busy, active women found short hair easier to manage. Short hair also stayed in place better when women played sports, danced new fast-paced dances, or rode in convertible automobiles.

Some women went beyond driving their own cars to pilot airplanes. Pioneer aviator Amelia Earhart wore her blond hair in a short, no-fuss bob.

Greta Garbo with a bob hairstyle. *Photofest*

Bobbed hairstyles came in different lengths and arrangements and sported lighthearted names, such as "the Coconut." The early softer bobs that covered the ears gave way to "shingled" hair that was slightly longer around the face and tapered to become ever shorter as it moved toward the nape of the neck. The Eton crop, a very short bob, appeared in 1926 and 1927 and was modeled on a hairstyle that was popular with young British men. The Moana and Chesterfield were other popular cuts. Some women added spit curls, called "croche coeurs" (French for "heartbreakers"). Spit curls were arranged in front of the ears, usually one on each side, and sometimes a single curl adorned the forehead. To set a spit curl, women applied dried soap or homemade gel or they used a commercial product.

Critics complained that bobbed hair meant women were trying to "act like men." Short haircuts were associated with other controversial behaviors, such as wearing shorter skirts, "painting" the face, smoking, drinking, dancing, going out at night without a male escort, working at nontraditional jobs, and engaging in sexual activity without marriage. In 1920, women in the United States finally got the right to vote when the Nineteenth Amendment was passed—another change in the status quo.

People who wanted women to maintain their traditional roles and appearance urged them to keep their long hair. Preachers sermonized against the bob. Some schools banned girls from wearing it and/or offered bonus payments to female teachers who did not cut their hair. Pamphlets published during the 1920s warned young girls that bobbing their hair might cause them to grow a mustache, among other unpleasant effects. Charles Nessler (later Nestle), who had invented a **permanent wave** machine, claimed that cutting the hair could weaken a woman's scalp muscles, which, in turn, could cause baldness. Others said that bobbed hair might diminish a woman's chances of getting married, since men preferred women to look more "feminine."

Despite these admonitions, more and more women decided to bob their hair. Some women liked the convenience, or they found short hair more flattering for their features. Others liked being on the cutting-edge of fashion, or at least not out of style.

Trendsetters

During the 1920s, the woman who was known as the "Queen of Fashion"—French fashion legend and beauty products entrepreneur Coco (Gabrielle) Chanel (1883–1971)—helped to popularize the bob. Short hair harmonized with her simple, streamlined designs, often made from jersey fabrics. Chanel's sleek black dresses, trousers, and other garments offered more ease and comfort than older clothing styles. To go with short hair and slim silhouettes, she designed smaller hats with simple trimmings.

Actresses in the increasingly popular motion picture business also prompted many women to cut their hair. One of the most influential was Louise Brooks (1906–1985), a star of silent films from 1925 to 1938. A native of Kansas, Brooks began dancing professionally as a child and later appeared in the Ziegfield Follies in New York City. While working in English nightclubs in 1924, she became the first American to dance the charleston in London. Brooks favored a short "Buster Brown," or Dutch boy, bob with thick straight bangs and sleek sides framing her face—a hairstyle that was called her "black helmet."

Another prominent bobbed head belonged to Irene Castle, half of the world-famous ballroom dance team of Vernon and Irene Castle. The husband and wife team was known for stylish and elegant interpretations of dance crazes of the Ragtime and Jazz eras. When Irene Castle cut her hair in 1914, millions of women rushed to get a "Castle Bob." Another trend emerged when Castle wore a flat seed-pearl necklace around her forehead, which was dubbed the "Castle Band" but also called a "headache band." Castle explained that her husband had cut her hair for reasons of convenience just before she entered the hospital for an appendectomy. Castle wanted to avoid the problems of grooming long, styled hair afterwards.

Actress Mary Garden, another bobbed trendsetter, said that short hair,

> typified a progressive step, in keeping with the inner spirit that animates my whole existence. . . . Bobbed hair is a state of mind and not merely a new manner of dressing my head. It typifies growth, alertness, up-to-dateness, and is part of the expression of the élan vital! [spirit]. . . . To my way of thinking, long hair belongs to the age of general feminine helplessness. Bobbed hair belongs to the age of freedom, frankness, and progressiveness. (Garden 1927, 8)

Magazines published articles about the bob and tried to help readers decide: To cut or not to cut? In an article for the October 1921 issue of *Ladies' Home Journal*, Irene Castle wrote that she had not meant to fuel any trends when she cut her hair, and that a bob might or might not suit other women:

> To start with, one *must* have the right sort of hair; and rather small features also help to bring about satisfactory results. There is, however, no hard and fast rule to be followed, for I have often been fooled myself and delightfully surprised.

> The girl with coarse and straight hair, however, is likely to ruin a perfectly good disposition by cutting it. (124)

Some famous women kept their hair long but achieved a variation on the new look by sweeping their hair along the sides of each cheek, then gathering it into a bun or chignon at the nape of the neck. One actress who kept her long locks was actress **Mary Pickford**, a box-office phenomenon in the 1920s. Known for her long golden curls and girlish roles, "America's Sweetheart" finally did bob her hair at the end of the 1920s.

Economic Impact

The widespread fashion for short hair had economic repercussions as well as social ramifications. When hairnet sales fell dramatically, the Venida company, a leading maker of hairnets, hired public relations expert Edward Bernays (1891–1995) to help boost their business. Bernays talked with labor safety experts so they would publicize the dangers of loose hair getting caught in machinery at work. He also publicized the idea of germs from the hair spreading if food workers were allowed to leave their hair uncovered. States began passing new laws that required workers in certain jobs to wear hairnets.

While new bobbed hairstyles reduced hairnet sales, beauty salons gained business as more customers came for haircuts and trims. Between 1922 and 1924, the number of salons in the United States rose from about 5,000 to 23,000. During some weeks in 1924 and 1925, salons in large cities in the United States gave more than 1,000 bob haircuts. Reporters who described these thriving businesses noted that some barbers and beauticians kept containers of smelling salts nearby to revive women who fainted when they saw their long hair falling to the floor. Another new business began in 1922, when the "bobby pin" (also called a "**hairpin**") was designed to help women tend their short hair.

See also: Baker, Josephine; Bara, Theda; Bow, Clara; Flappers; Hairstyles, Twentieth-Century; Salons, Hair and Beauty

Further Reading: Basinger, Jeanine, *Silent Stars* (2000); Ewen, Stewart, *PR! A Social History of Spin* (1996); Gabler, Henry, "The Lives They Lived: Edward L. Bernays and Henry C. Rogers; The Fathers of PR," *New York Times*, December 31, 1995; Garden, Mary, "Why I Bobbed My Hair," *Pictorial Review*, April 1927, 8; Paris, Barry, *Louise Brooks, A Biography* (2000); Treman, Irene Castle, "I Bobbed My Hair and Then—," *Ladies Home Journal*, October 1921, 124; Turudich, Daniela, *Art Deco Hair: Hairstyles of the 1920s and 1930s* (2003).

BODY HAIR

Body hair refers to hair on the face, arms, chest, back, legs, pubic region, and other places aside from the head.

Evolutionary Changes

Scientists believe that the human body once had a thicker layer of hair but that humans evolved so that most of this hair became sparse, except for certain areas, including the pubic region. This change occurred as long as 1.7 million years ago. At one time, scientists theorized that body hair had diminished to help ancient humans stay cooler in hot climates. Newer theories suggest that body hair was lost through the process of natural selection as a way to prevent external parasites, such as fleas and **lice**, which infest fur-bearing animals. Not only are these parasites unpleasant, they also may carry deadly diseases, such as typhus. Scientists further suggest that humans began to perceive a nearly hairless body as more sexually attractive, since bare skin would signify that a potential mate had healthy (parasite-free) skin.

Patterns of Growth

Patterns of hair growth depend upon heredity and gender. People may inherit a tendency to have thick hair growth on various parts of the body, such as the chest or back. Abnormally dense hair on the arms, back, face, chest, or other areas is called **hirsutism**.

Males typically have thicker and more noticeable hair growth on their chins and upper lips than women do. This facial hair is a secondary sexual trait that differentiates males from females. Men may grow beards, sideburns, and/or **mustaches**, or they may shave their faces to conform with the trends in their culture.

Abnormal hair growth on a woman's face may be caused by genetics, hormonal disturbances, or the effects of aging. When women do have facial hair, the individual hairs tend to be thinner in diameter than a man's.

Male hormones also cause men to have more body hair than women. Their pubic hair is longer and covers a larger area, though it is finer in texture. Male pubic hair begins to develop around ages twelve to fourteen; facial and underarm hair appear a bit later.

Body hair grows somewhat differently than hair found on the head. While head hair tends to grow continually, body hair has cycles of growth followed by dormant periods. During the growth period, the hair follicles are long and bulbous, and hair grows at a rate of about one-third of a millimeter per day. After a few weeks, the follicle shrinks and the hair root becomes rigid, which causes the dormancy part of the cycle. Later, another growth cycle starts so that new hairs push out the old ones. This difference in growth patterns explains why head hairs grow much longer than body hairs, which reach a certain length and then stop.

Cultural Attitudes and Practices

Throughout history, attitudes about body hair have differed from one culture and era to another. While some people and cultures consider hair on the face, legs, underarms, or other parts of the body to be unsightly, others might find them attractive, or at least not offensive.

In some ancient cultures, including Egypt, Greece, and the **Roman Empire**, women removed all their body hair. Men in ancient **India** and Egypt also removed their body hair. Certain groups of Africans, Turks, and Tobriand islanders also have preferred a hair-free body. For example, in Uganda the Dodingo removed all body hair by applying a special resinous substance that was stripped off when dry, pulling off the hairs. At times, among certain cultures, it has been fashionable to remove the eyebrows and/or eyelashes.

Attitudes toward leg hair on women have undergone changes. Today, most cultures regard it as unattractive, leading to practices that remove it through **shaving**, waxing, cream depilatories, or sugaring. The practice of removing leg hair dates back to ancient times. One legend says that when Israel's King Solomon first saw Makeda, Queen of Sheba, the legendary African beauty, he commented on her leg hair, saying, "Thy beauty is the beauty of a woman, but thy hair is masculine; hair is an ornament to a man, but it disfigures a woman."

Ancient Caucasian peoples usually did not remove their body hair. During some historic periods, dense body hair was regarded as an asset. This attitude changed in the tenth century after European Crusaders returned from the Middle East to Christian Europe. They promoted the idea of regular bathing, which was the custom in the Middle East. Some European women started removing their body hair, as women did in the Middle East. The practice ended during the mid-1500s when Catherine de Medici, the Italian-born queen of France, objected.

See also: Aging and Hair; Barbers; Beards, Men's; Beards, Women's; Egypt, Ancient; Elizabethan Era; Eyebrows; Eyelashes; Gillette Company; Greece, Ancient; Hair Removal; Lice, Head; Lice, Pubic; Middle Ages; Pubic Hair; Religion and Hair; Shaving; Sideburns; Soul Patch; Unibrow

Further Reading: Caine, Kenneth W., and Perry Garfinkel, *The Male Body: An Owner's Manual* (1996); Camacho, Francisco M., *Hair and Its Disorders: Biology, Pathology, and Management* (2000); Imwold, Denise, et al., *Anatomica's Body Atlas* (2003); Olsen, Elise A., *Disorders of Hair Growth: Diagnosis and Treatment* (2003); Wade, Nicholas, "Why Humans and Their Fur Parted Ways," *New York Times*, August 19, 2003, F1, F4.

BOUFFANT

The bouffant, which became popular during the 1950s, was a full hairstyle that was turned over or under at the ends. To achieve the high top and wide sides, women often set their hair on rollers and then used teasing, later called backcombing, to add extra volume.

English hairdresser Raymond Bessone is credited with launching this look, which was nicknamed the "Teasy-Weasy." Sales of hairspray and hair rollers soared as more women adopted the bouffant look.

"I'd like to kiss you but I just washed my hair."

BETTE DAVIS (1908–1989), 1932 film *Cabin in the Cotton*

In 1956, a writer for *Life* magazine discussed this popular style: "The bouffant is basically a thick page-boy hairdo, 8 to 10 inches long, which has been puffed out at the sides and lacquered in place" (Corson, 628). Some women, said the article, had bouffants that measured fourteen inches wide.

Perhaps the most famous American woman to wear a bouffant hairstyle was First Lady **Jacqueline Kennedy**. Her hairstylist was **Kenneth Battelle**, who operated a prestigious salon in New York City. Mrs. Kennedy's everyday bouffant style was relaxed and youthful but also neat.

Upswept bouffants also were popular. These hairstyles could be seen in feature films and on television series of the 1960s, for example on actress Barbara Eden (*I Dream of Jeannie*) and comedian Jo Anne Worley (*Laugh In*). Members of the popular music group The Supremes wore both upswept and longer bouffant hairstyles.

To achieve a bouffant, girls and women used the newly developed mesh hair rollers in large sizes or they used clean juice cans. After rolling their hair, women used electric **hair dryers** or let their hair air-dry, sometimes in public. Newspapers and magazines noted that, suddenly, women in hair rollers could be seen in grocery stores, movie theaters, shopping malls, and other public places.

Bette Davis with a bouffant hairstyle. *Photofest*

Some women who wanted "big hair" could not achieve the look on their own. To add volume, they used hairpieces to or wore bouffant wigs made from either real or synthetic hair.

The beehive, a larger variation of the bouffant, emerged around 1958 and remained popular in the early 1960s. The beehive required a great deal of teasing (backcombing) and hairspray. In the United States, the beehive was also called the B-52, after the large bomber flown during World War II. From the United States, the style moved to Great Britain. In 1988, filmmaker John Waters featured exaggerated beehives in his film ***Hairspray***, which also became a Broadway musical.

Large bouffants and beehives aroused controversy, particularly in schools and workplaces. Teachers complained that these towering hairstyles kept students from seeing the teacher and blackboard. Some schools banned hairdos of a certain size.

Beehives that were not shampooed or combed for long time periods also could cause health problems. In 1962, a high school student in Canton, Ohio, developed a nest of cockroaches in her stiff hairdo, which had been teased, sprayed, and then left in place for several weeks.

See also: Hairspray; Hairstyles, Twentieth-Century; Styling Products; Styling Tools; Wigs and Hairpieces

Further Reading: Mulvey, Kate, and Melissa Richards, *Decades of Beauty* (1998); Scott, Susan Craig, *The Hair Bible: The Ultimate Guide to Healthy Beautiful Hair Forever* (2003); Simon, Diane, *Hair: Public, Political, Extremely Personal* (2000); Turudich, Daniela, *1960s Hair: Hairstyles for Bouffant Babes and Swingin' Chicks* (2003).

BOW, CLARA (1905–1965)

American film star Clara Bow, nicknamed the "It Girl," is regarded as the original screen goddess. The petite, auburn-haired Bow set trends with her hairstyle and makeup, which personified the popular "flapper" look of the 1920s.

Clara Bow, 1929. *Library of Congress*

Growing up poor in Brooklyn, New York, Clara Gordon Bow became a tomboy when neighborhood girls made fun of her shabby clothing. Bow's mother had a serious mental illness and her father was physically abusive. Plagued by problems at home, Bow escaped at the movies, which were then silent films, and she was determined to become an actress. Bow admired **Mary Pickford**, and she carefully studied Pickford's techniques and mannerisms, along with those of other successful actresses.

At age sixteen, Bow entered and won a contest called "Fame and Fortune," which was sponsored by a movie magazine. One of her prizes was a screen test. Despite her shabby clothing, the judges were impressed with Bow's acting. She won the national version of the contest, which earned her a small movie role, a trophy, and an evening gown.

In Hollywood, her film debut led to bigger and better roles, usually as a feisty yet vulnerable working-class heroine. Bow's most famous film was *It Girl*, made in 1927. Critics said she had "sex appeal" and could perform both comic and serious roles in a natural manner. Audiences loved the brown-eyed actress, and at the height of her fame, Bow received 45,000 fan letters a month. Women imitated her **bob** hairstyle, wide-eyed look, and full red lips. Many also imitated her characters' behavior, feeling more free to smoke, drink alcohol, and dance like "jazz baby" Clara Bow in some of her roles.

Between 1922 and 1933, Bow made thirty-six films. She retired soon after "talking films" debuted. Bow felt less comfortable speaking on film and she had been suffering from episodes of the mental illness that had afflicted her mother. At age twenty-eight, she married cowboy film star Rex Bell and retired from films to raise her two sons in Nevada. Bow died of a heart attack in Los Angeles at age sixty.

See also: Bob, The; Flappers; Hairstyles, Twentieth-Century

Further Reading: Morella, Joe, and Edward Z. Epstein, *The "It" Girl: The Incredible Story of Clara Bow* (New York: Delacorte Press, 1976); Stenn, David, *Clara Bow: Runnin' Wild* (1988).

BRAIDS *See* Africa; African Americans; Coming of Age; Cornrows; Middle Ages; Native Americans; Renaissance Europe; Roman Empire

BRECK GIRL

For more than thirty years, the "Breck Girl"—a female model featured in ads for Breck shampoo—was a cultural icon and one of the most recognized advertising symbols in North America. Using delicate pastel colors, artists painted lifelike portraits of Breck models. The portraits appeared in print advertisements that urged women to use Breck for shiny, healthy hair.

Edward J. Breck, son of founder Dr. John H. Breck, commissioned these ads in 1936 after he became head of the company. Dr. John H. Breck had launched his shampoo in 1930. At that time, many people were still using bar soap to cleanse their hair, and he stressed the idea that Breck's liquid formula was "gentler" than bar soap. It was produced in Springfield, Massachusetts, and sold throughout New England.

To further promote the shampoo, Edward J. Breck commissioned artist Charles Sheldon to draw women's portraits for some new ads. The first models were not professionals. They were "everyday" young women with wholesome good looks and, of course, lovely hair. Most of them were blond and they usually had long hair. Sheldon's photo-realistic pictures, done with pastels, featured soft colors and romantic, halo-like effects around the women's heads.

Early "Breck Girl" ads appeared in publications for hair care professionals and salon owners, but the campaign went national in 1946. These national ads featured Roma Whitney, who became known as the first "Breck Girl." Seven years earlier, in 1937, Sheldon had painted the teenaged blond in profile.

During the late 1950s, artist Ralph William Williams began painting the "Breck Girls." A third American artist, Rob Anders, produced portraits for ads from 1958 to 1973. After the 1960s, most of the Breck Girls were professional models.

Breck placed ads in *Glamour, Vogue, Ladies' Home Journal, Seventeen*, and other widely circulated magazines. Often, the ad appeared on the highly visible back cover. This campaign became one of the longest-running and most successful in advertising history, making Breck one of the most recognized brands in North America. Breck became America's bestselling shampoo, with a 20 percent share of the shampoo market during the 1960s.

Between 1936 and 1976, about 200 "Breck Girls" appeared in ads promoting the company's "Gold Formula" shampoo. Some of them were well-known models and actresses, including Erin Gray, Cheryl Tiegs, Jaclyn Smith, Cybill Shepherd, Christie Brinkley, and Kim Basinger. Model, and later actress, Brooke Shields appeared in the ads as a child. She was featured holding a baby doll in a 1974 ad released during the Christmas season. Some ads featured a mother and daughter together.

In the 1970s, as the feminist movement expanded, Breck stopped featuring young teens in its ads to avoid criticism that it was exploiting the looks of children to sell products. Breck models also became more diverse, and the first African Americans appeared in ads.

Dial Corporation bought the Breck brand name in 1990. The Breck Girls Hall of Fame was assembled in 1992, and 150 portraits were displayed in the lobby of the Dial Corporation building in Phoenix, Arizona. In 1994 and 1995, three new "Breck Women" appeared in ads, but this new campaign was short-lived. Breck sales continued to decline after the 1970s.

In 1995, entrepreneur Jeffrey Himmel bought the licensing rights to Breck shampoo. By then, Breck was being sold only in Mexico. The Himmel Group began developing shampoo from the original formula and made plans to market this still well-known brand in various countries. No new "Breck Girl" ads were created for this purpose.

A series of Breck Girl ads that ran from the 1930s into the 1970s can be seen in Washington, DC, at the Smithsonian Institution's National Museum of American History.

See also: Advertising; Hair Color; Shampoo

Further Reading: Daniels, Cora, "Return of the Breck Girl?" *Fortune Small Business*, http://www.fortune.com/fortune/smallbusiness/articles/0,15114,360967,00.html; Goodrum, Charles, and Helen Dalrymple, *Advertising in America: The First Two Hundred Years* (1990); Minnick, Mimi, "Breck Girls," *Smithsonian Magazine*, January 2000, http://www.smithsonianmag.si.edu/smithsonian/issues00/jan00/breck.html; Minnick, Mimi, "Breck Girls Collection" at Archives Center of the National Museum of American History, http://americanhistory. si.edu/archives/d7651.htm.

BROOKS, LOUISE *See* Bob, The

BRUMMELL, BEAU (1778–1840)

Englishman George Bryan Brummell, called "Beau Brummell," influenced styles in men's fashions and grooming. He is often called the prototype "dandy," referring to certain men who paid close attention to their appearance. Due largely to their influence, menswear became simpler and less effeminate, with fewer bows, laces, ruffles, and other adornments.

Born into a respected middle-class family, Brummell attended two of England's finest schools, Eton and Oxford, where he was known for his wit, charm, and personal style. Brummell was popular among his schoolmates and, despite his lack of wealth, he became part of the inner circle of King George IV when he was Prince of Wales. From 1794 to 1798, Brummell served in the military as part of the prince's own regiment.

After moving to London, Brummell could not afford to dress like his wealthy and aristocratic friends. He devised a wardrobe that cost less than the typical clothing of a London gentleman but looked more elegant than the styles worn in rural areas. Brummell's well-tailored starched shirts, understated dark-colored suits, neat cravats, and highly polished, simply designed boots earned him a reputation for refinement.

His peers regarded him as an expert in matters of dress, grooming, and etiquette. Following Brummell's lead, men began choosing long pantaloons over knee breeches. Brummell was also clean-shaven and he rejected powdered wigs in favor of his own hair, which was cropped fairly short. He wore no perfume, saying that regular bathing and clean hair made it unnecessary. It was rumored that Brummell spent five to six hours each morning to groom and dress himself and would not remove his hat to greet people on the street lest he dislodge his carefully arranged hair.

In 1816, after he quarreled with the future king and accrued large gambling debts, Brummell left England for France. There, he served time in debtor's prison until some friends paid for his release. They tried in vain to get Brummell a diplomatic post. Ironically, the man known for his elegant appearance died in shabby attire in a French asylum for the poor insane.

See also: Regency; Wigs and Hairpieces

Further Reading: Cole, Hubert, *Beau Brummell* (1977); Cosgrave, Bronwyn, *The Complete History of Costume & Fashion From Ancient Egypt to the Present Day* (2000); Moers, Ellen, *The Dandy: Brummell to Beerbohm* (1960).

BURMA SHAVE

Developed in 1926, Burma Shave was one of the world's first brushless shaving cream products. The company launched a now legendary ad campaign that bolstered its sales for four decades.

Burma Shave was founded in Minnesota where Clinton Odell owned a company that made Burma Vita Liniment. Sales were low, so Odell decided to try something new. During the early 1900s, beards and mustaches had gone out of fashion and, by 1920, most men were shaving daily using a razor, brush, soap, water, and shaving cup. Odell worked with a chemist to develop a more convenient and portable men's shaving product that he called "Burma Shave." In England, men were using such a product, called Lloyd's Euxesis.

Odell and his sons hoped their shaving cream would become a bathroom staple. Allan Odell traveled around the state marketing Burma Shave to druggists. He suggested that they try something new: paint advertising slogans on thirty-six-inch boards and place them along the highways—in effect, an early type of billboard. More and more Americans were buying cars, and highways were being built to accommodate them. The Odells placed a series of four three-foot long signs on Route 65 in Minnesota so that motorists could read the signs in sequence:

Shave the modern way

Fine for the skin

Druggists have it

BURMA-SHAVE.

As sales for Burma Shave increased, the Odells placed more signs in Minnesota and neighboring states. They gave landowners a small fee or a case of their product in exchange for the right to post signs on their land. Business continued to grow and revenues reached $3 million a year by the late 1940s.

The company continued to produce roadside ads, which ranged from four to six signs in a row. Allan Odell wrote many jingles himself, but the company generated even more interest by inviting the public to contribute jingles. If their ideas were chosen, people won cash prizes. Jingles poured in, sometimes at the rate of 50,000 per year.

Burma Shave ads praised the benefits of using the product, as in these examples:

A SILKY CHEEK / SHAVED SMOOTH AND CLEAN / IS NOT OBTAINED / WITH A MOWING MACHINE / BURMA-SHAVE.

HENRY THE EIGHTH / SURE HAD TROUBLE / SHORT-TERM WIVES / LONG-TERM STUBBLE / BURMA-SHAVE.

BEN MET ANNA / MADE A HIT / NEGLECTED BEARD / BEN-ANNA SPLIT / BURMA-SHAVE.

Some ads, like the following, contained a moral or safety message:

PAST / SCHOOLHOUSES / TAKE IT SLOW / LET THE LITTLE / SHAVERS GROW / BURMA-SHAVE.

THE ONE WHO DRIVES / WHEN HE'S BEEN / DRINKING / DEPENDS ON YOU / TO DO HIS THINKING / BURMA-SHAVE.

Over a period of nearly forty years, 7,000 sets of Burma Shave boards were erected in forty-five states. As a result, most Americans recognized the name "Burma Shave." The company hired crews to maintain the ads and replace broken signs.

Sales of Burma Shave continued to rise until 1947 and then remained stable for seven years. Sales declined during the late 1950s as more men began using electric razors and other shaving products. By then, highways were broader and cars moved faster, so the old style signs were less effective.

The last Burma Shave signs came down in 1963. Sales sank to the point that the line was discontinued in 1966. In 1997, however, the American Safety Razor Company brought Burma Shave back into the marketplace.

See also: Advertising; Beards, Men's; Body Hair; Hair Removal; Mustache; Shaving

Further Reading: "Burma-Shave in the Fifties," http://www.fiftiesweb.com/burma.htm; Rowsome, Frank, Jr., *The Verse by the Side of the Road* (1965); Vossler, Bill, *Burma-Shave: The Rhymes, The Signs, The Times* (1998).

BUTCH *See* Crew Cut

BUZZ CUT

The buzz cut, sometimes called a flattop, is an extremely short haircut, usually executed with electric clippers that do not have a guard comb in place. During the cutting process, which may take only minutes to complete, the barber or stylist closely cuts or shaves the hair along the sides. The top may be cut in the same way or clipped into a geometric shape and arranged so that it stands up from the head. Sometimes the clipper is moved in different directions until the hair is cropped evenly short all over the scalp.

The buzz cut also was traditionally given to men when they were inducted into the U.S. armed forces—hence its other name, "induction cut." Since this haircut is easy to maintain, inductees need not spend much time on their hair during their training at boot camp. Some people in the military choose to continue wearing a buzz cut after the induction period is over.

The buzz cut became fashionable as a unisex style during the 1980s and early 1990s. One of the best-known women to wear this hairstyle was the American diet and fitness crusader/author Susan Powter. Close-cropped, bleached blond hair became one of Powter's trademarks.

Television character Bart Simpson wore a version of a modern buzz cut in the popular animated series called *The Simpsons*. Another actor, Jason Sehorn, has worn a buzz cut on the television series *Third Watch*.

See also: Hairstyles, Twentieth-Century; Military; Styling Tools

Further Reading: Jones, Jim, *Men's Hairstyles and Beard Designs: Clipper Cutting, Razor Cutting, Blender Shears, Motivation* (1997); Rudoy, Marion, *The Complete Book of Men's Hairstyles and Hair Care* (1974).

BYZANTINE EMPIRE

The Byzantine Empire (395–1453 CE), was centered in Constantinople, now part of Turkey. Byzantium was the eastern part of the **Roman Empire** until Rome fell in the fifth century, so hairstyles were strongly influenced by Roman practices, particularly during the early days of the empire. Influences from Greek and Asian culture lent further complexity and decorative elements to Byzantine hairstyles. And, like their neighbors in Muslim Arab countries, the Byzantines bathed and washed their hair frequently.

Men cut and styled their hair like their Roman counterparts, with short bangs and sideburns extending about halfway down each cheek. Most of them removed their facial hair. Upper-class men often wore gold bands around the head, and many bands featured a central medallion.

By the time Justinian became emperor in 527 CE, Roman influence had waned. Men began growing longer hair, especially in the back, along with beards and mustaches. Long beards were favored during the reign of Constantine IV (668–685 CE), and some men grew waist-long beards, to which they added curls and plaits. Under Constantine V (741–775 CE), a new law banned facial hair. Beards and long hair returned to favor after the tenth century.

Theophilus (829–842 CE) issued an edict that required male subjects to wear their hair short. Some citizens concluded that Theophilus envied men with full heads of hair, since he himself was bald.

Hairstyles for women usually featured a center part on the forehead, with coils arranged on both sides of the face. Combs or bands made of gold, silver, pearl, ivory, or tortoiseshell were used to keep hair in place. Throughout much of the Byzantine era, women wore a round headdress that circled the head, and some wore turban-wrappings on their hair.

See also: Beards, Men's; Eyebrows; Roman Empire

Further Reading: Rice, Tamara Talbot, *Everyday Life in Byzantium* (1967); Severy, Merle, "The Byzantine Empire, Rome of the East," *National Geographic*, December 1983, 709ff; Treadgold, Warren, *A History of the Byzantine State and Society* (1997).

C

CELTS, ANCIENT

Hair cleansing and styling were important among the ancient Celts who lived in various parts of western Europe extending into present-day Ireland and Scotland and including a region known as Gaul. Images from the artwork of those times shows that long hair was popular, except among soldiers, who wore their hair cut in short, rounded styles that were longer over the forehead and shorter in the back.

In his history of the ancient world, the Greek writer and traveler Diodorus Siculus (90–21 BCE) described Celtic hairstyles this way:

> [T]heir hair is blond, and not only naturally so, but they also make it their practice by artificial means to increase the distinguishing color which nature has given it. For they are always washing their hair with lime-water [lime dissolved in water] and they pull it back from the forehead to the top of the head and back to the nape of the neck, with the result that their appearance is like that of Satyrs and Pans, since the treatment of their hair makes it so heavy and coarse that it differs in no respect from the mane of horses.

During the second century BCE, people applied chalk to their hair so they could make it form stiff tufts. For the majority who already had pale hair, chalk made it look even more striking.

Toward the end of the Iron Age (1000 BC to 50 BCE), Celts washed their hair with lime-water—a white, chalky substance. This process produced striking, white spikes of hair and soldiers believed that this would give them a more intimidating appearance on the battlefield, especially when it was combined with fierce-looking designs on the body made from blue paint (woad).

Long hair, which was typical for both men and women, was usually worn in a series of curls or braids. Women wore various knotted and braided hairstyles. Decorative pins sometimes were used to hold styles in place. Wealthier people adorned their hair with hollow gold balls, tied at the ends of curls or braids. Celts also wore ribbons or forehead bands made from gold, silver, or bronze. Women wore fillets—bands around the crown of the head—made from cloth or metal and adorned with beads, gemstones, and semiprecious stones. A thin band of gold hair called a *linn* also was worn around the head.

Upper-class men usually wore both a beard and a mustache. Often, beards were given a forked style or squared around the bottom. Men of the lower classes typically wore a long mustache with no beard, and curled mustaches were popular. These styles persisted into the Middle Ages.

Diodorus Siculus wrote about facial hair among men:

> Some of them shave the beard, but others let it grow a little; and the nobles shave their cheeks, but they let the moustache grow until it covers the mouth. Consequently, when they are eating, their moustaches become entangled in the food. (Siculus 1992, vol. 3)

Combs for grooming the hair were made from animal bone or horn. Wealthier people and royalty had personal barbers to perform shaving and hairstyling services.

See also: Beards, Men's; Comb; Hair Colorants; Middle Ages; Roman Empire

Further Reading: Corson, Richard, *Fashions in Hair: The First Five Thousand Years* (1965); Frey, Otto Hermann, et al., *The Celts* (1991); Siculus, Diodorus, C. H. Oldfather, trans., *Library of History,* vol. 3, book 5 (1992).

CHARM SCHOOLS

Traditional charm schools, which proliferated in the United States after 1920, offered courses on etiquette, fashion, and personal grooming, including hairstyling and cosmetics. Such courses usually began with an evaluation, followed by general information classes and personal consultations with each client.

One of the best-known and prestigious of these schools was the John Robert Powers School, founded in 1923 by actor-turned-model John Robert Powers. Often called the "founder of the modern modeling business," Powers started both his school and modeling agency in New York City and then added branches in other cities. First Ladies **Jacqueline Kennedy** and Betty Ford were among the most famous graduates of Powers' programs, as were many well-known actresses and models, including **Lucille Ball**, Ava Gardner, Grace Kelly, Lauren Bacall, and Diana Ross. The business, now called the John Robert Powers System, continues to operate today in the United States and Asia.

Starting in 1940, cosmetics and hair care giant Richard Hudnut offered his DuBarry Success Courses. Thousands of women enrolled in the classes held at Hudnut's Fifth Avenue salon in New York City, or they studied at home using the correspondence version of the "Success Course." Ads for this course appeared in national magazines. For example, in the June 1946 issue of *Woman's Day*, an ad entitled "Makes Herself Over During Summer Vacation" featured a photograph of a teenager who supposedly took the correspondence course during the school break. According to the ad, when school resumed, she surprised and impressed her classmates with her thinner shape, stylish clothing, and new hairstyle.

Charm school courses were popular with teenage girls, as well as adults who wanted to improve their appearance and social skills. Some of these women were immigrants or people who sought higher socioeconomic status. Other clients were sent by their employers, who included modeling and talent agencies. During the 1940s and 1950s, airline stewardesses (female forerunners of today's flight attendants) often attended charm school classes during their training. Members of the All-American Girls Professional Baseball League (AAGPBL), which ran from 1943 to 1954, also took a course designed to enhance their appearance and social skills. The charm school booklet urged players to care for their "crowning glory" and described a "daily program for the hair . . . to keep it in healthful and attractive condition" (http://www.aagpbl.org/history/hist_cs.html#foreword).

More charm schools were established during the 1940s and 1950s and some continued to operate through the 1960s and beyond. Charm school programs were conducted by various institutions, including secretarial schools, department stores, girls' clubs, and the Young Women's Christian Association (YWCA). Colleges offered classes to female students.

During the last half of the twentieth century, the name "charm school" was replaced with other terms, such as "modeling school" or "personal development course." Both men and women now enroll in programs that offer classes in hairstyling, personal grooming, makeup, posture, clothing selection, and etiquette, as well as personality development, public speaking, and executive skills. Some students are pursuing careers in modeling or acting or they plan to enter beauty contests. Other students work in politics, business, and other jobs where appearance and social skills are especially important.

See also: Occupations

Further Reading: All-American Girls Professional Baseball League available online at http://www.aagpbl.org/history/hist_cs.html#foreword; "Dubarry: The Secret of Everlasting Beauty," available online at http://www.dubarryusa.com/main.htm; John Robert Powers and Mary Sue Miller, *Secrets of Charm* (1954).

CHINA

Since ancient times, people in China have paid attention to personal grooming, including hair care. Hairstyles have reflected a person's social class, age, gender, religion, occupation, and the customs in their communities.

Among the Chinese, hair was an important aspect of appearance, so neglecting it was a sign of illness or grief. For example, a widow who did not want to remarry might cut off her hair to deter potential suitors. For a woman to cut off her hair or shave her head was regarded as disfigurement. A quote from the Chinese philosopher Confucius (551 to 479 BCE) reveals traditional attitudes:

> Since body, hair, and skin have all been received from one's parents, one dare not do them any injury—this is the basis of filial piety. To establish oneself by acting morally, and to make a name that resounds to later generations, thus bringing credit to one's parents—this is the final aim, of filial piety.

It was traditional to shave off a baby's hair, however. This was done when the child was a few months old for the purpose of allowing fresh, thicker, sturdier hair to grow. This custom, along with another shaving performed later in childhood, continued into the early 1900s and is still done among some Chinese today.

A version of the hair removal method called threading originated in China. Hair removal on the face aimed to create a clean hairline for women and to shape the brows, while Chinese men who did not wear full beards used threading to remove stray hairs on their chins.

Traditional treatments for hair loss included meditation and standing on one's head. Herbs, including vitex and ho-shou-wu, also have been used.

Mustaches for men were in fashion throughout Chinese history, although full beards were sometimes regarded as a sign of a barbarian. Different styles of mustaches can be seen on pictures of historical figures, ranging from the philosopher Confucius, who lived in the sixth and fifth centuries BCE, all the way to the twentieth-century political leader Sun Yat-Sen. A number of prominent philosophers and scholars wore long mustaches. Historians have found evidence that men living in the region of the Sarnath were wearing long, drooping mustaches during the third century BCE.

Ancient Times

Ancient Chinese hairstyles usually featured long hair for both genders that was arranged rather than left hanging loose. Women's styles ranged from simple buns, worn by women of the lower classes, to elaborate coiffures featuring various ornaments. Upper-class women and royals often wore styles that were both elaborate and symbolic. Both men and women wore hair ornaments, including **decorative combs** and **hairpins**. Men usually shaved their heads, leaving a long piece growing from the top. This was twisted into a topknot that was kept in place with gold pins, if people could afford them. Upper-class women adorned their buns with gold crowns trimmed with bells and/or gold hairpins. Poorer people wore ornaments made from cloth or paper. They used wooden dowels to secure their heavy buns.

Wealthier people had time for more elaborate hairdressing routines and could pay servants to perform these services, while poorer people cared for their own hair. People in the lower classes were banned from wearing certain kinds of clothing and ornaments even if they could afford them, because sumptuary laws forced people to dress according to their rank and socioeconomic class. Some of these laws, which also existed in Europe, persisted into the twentieth century.

The Chinese made various preparations to cleanse, condition, and color the hair, as well as to promote growth. Heavy pomade was used to wax the hair. Women believed that cedrela, a type of fragrant cedar, would promote hair growth, so they used it to rinse their hair after cleansing. Combs for grooming, holding, and decorating the hair were made in China, and comb-making became an important industry, as well as an art form.

Cleansing took place in baths, and many Chinese considered cold baths to be most healthy. During the T'ang Empire, wealthy people had baths build inside their homes. Baths were often scented with oils and aromatics and servants washed their master's or mistress's hair.

Eyebrows were an important aspect of personal appearance and sometimes took on dramatic shapes and colors in ancient and medieval China. During some periods, it was customary to pluck the eyebrows and then create new brow lines with pigments containing animal oil. The colors included blue, black, and green, and eyebrow styles often were given colorful names.

Styles changed over the years. In the second century BCE, sharply pointed arches were most popular. The next style favored a shape with curved arches.

Then, in the late Han period (202 BCE–220 CE), a shape called the "sorrow brow" predominated. In the T'ang period (618–907 CE), women preferred a design called "distant mountains."

Middle Ages to 1900

By the Middle Ages, the arrival of European explorers and increasing trade between countries was bringing new ideas about hair and fashion into China. During the eighth century, for example, Chinese women at court enjoyed wearing hairstyles that were popular in the Middle East, including the Uighur chignon.

More ornate hairstyles featuring false hair and adornments became popular among Chinese royals and their courts. During the T'ang Dynasty, the Empress liked to wear golden *buyaos*—a type of hair ornament—surrounded by flowers and birds, then attached to her ceremonial wig. Other upper-class women also wore *buyaos*. T'ang hairstyles for women covered their temples and formed a frame around the face. Hair was coiled high in a bun and the types of buns had special names, including "gazing-gods bun," "cloud bun," "double handing-down bun," and "flower bun." Elaborate hairstyles remained popular during the next era, known as the Sung dynasty (960–1276). Some women wore long braids cascading down the shoulders.

During medieval times, women began using long, sharp hair ornaments that looked like large pins or darts. They not only supported their hair but also could be used for the purpose of self-defense. During the 1920s, these hairpins were banned by law.

Simpler styles prevailed in some regions. During the twelfth century in the Western Xia empire, ruler Li Yuanhao became known for his conservative views. Encouraging the Tangut people to go back to their roots, he made laws that required them to wear traditional hairstyles, which meant short hair or bald heads on men instead of a long, knotted hairstyle.

The trade of barbering flourished during these centuries. As in many other cultures, Chinese barbers provided services beyond cutting men's hair. They frequently provided treatments for health problems, including skin problems, relying on their knowledge of herbal medicine and other skills. Barbers served a long apprenticeship before they were permitted to serve customers. While some worked in shops, others worked as itinerant barbers. They traveled about to ply their trade, carrying a pole on their backs with their barber stool tied to one end and their towel, basin, and other equipment on the other. The barber profession retained its high status in China into the twentieth century.

During the Ming dynasty (1369–1643), the most common hairstyle for Chinese men was long hair, plaited, and then wound around the top of the head. This image can be seen in many works of art from that period. Men's styles changed abruptly in 1644.

One familiar image of Chinese men shows them wearing a single pigtail down the back. This became customary when the Qing dynasty (1644–1912) was established. The new Manchu government decreed that Chinese men must shave the front top of their heads and grow the Manchu-style queue (*bianzi*) as a sign of submission to their new government. Any man who did not wear a long pigtail or queue could be arrested for treason against the emperor, a crime that was punishable by death.

The Manchu queue itself dated back about 2,000 years and had worked for practical reasons, since the Manchus traditionally were hunters who rode horses in mountainous terrain. Shaving the front of the head enabled them to see more clearly. The tail at the back could be rolled up as a sort of "cushion" for the head. The Manchus believed that the soul itself resided in this pigtail and when a soldier or military officer died, the pigtail was sent back to his hometown to be buried.

Traditional Manchu women's hairstyles required young girls to wear a long pigtail down the back before they reached adulthood. Bangs were cut in the front, and the pigtail was tied with red cord and sometimes ornamented with a gold or silver bead. Married women wore a specially shaped bun pierced with a silver ornamental stick. Some hairstyles involved tying bunches of hair and then plaiting them into special shapes, such as one that resembled a swallowtail.

During the Qing era, some families discarded other old traditions, such as capping males and binding up the hair of females to show that they were now adults. Other families carried out these customs only at the time of marriage, which took place between ages eighteen to twenty-one for men and ages sixteen to eighteen for women.

By the late 1890s, Manchus in the city of Peking were wearing hairstyles designed to stand high above a flat band on the head. This band projected to the left and to the right, and the finished hairstyle was decorated with flowers.

Dark, lustrous hair was still highly valued, and the Chinese made various hair-darkening preparations from plants and herbs to dye gray hair. During the late 1800s, wealthy people including the Empress Dowager of China, Tz'u-hsi, began using synthetic dyes imported from Paris. The Empress devoted more than an hour each day to her toilette and a eunich served as her personal hairdresser.

Twentieth Century

The twentieth century saw many changes in Chinese life, and those political and social changes affected hairstyles and other aspects of personal appearance. Author Yee Chiang, who grew up during in the early 1900s in rural China, said that fashions in hairdressing and clothing arrived there from Peking, Nanking, Shanghai, and other large cities.

During those years, it was still customary for children in Yee's region to have their hair shaved both a few weeks after birth and again as children. The second shaving left bunches of hair on the head, usually one or two bunches for boys and more for girls. The bunches might be left on the top above the forehead or at the nape of the neck. Yee, who had a bunch of hair above each ear and at the back, described the dreaded morning routine of having his hair tightly plaited as a young boy:

> Every morning I had to stand very still and endure a horrible strained feeling as my mother plaited my hair into three tight little plaits. They may have looked pretty, for they were tied with different-coloured ribbons, but what was that to me. Sometimes I tried to elude my mother. (Yee 1952, 48)

As children reached age seven, the hair was allowed to grow longer and boys could then wear a single plait of hair at the back, instead of multiple plaits.

When the Qing dynasty was overthrown and the Republic of China founded in 1912, China's new revolutionary government struck down that country's last imperial regime and decreed that the Manchu pigtails be cut off. Those who did not cut off their own pigtails could be forced to do so. Republican officials stood at the gates of Chinese cities, holding scissors to cut the hair from any man who arrived with his pigtail intact.

Although many younger people were glad to have short, plait-free hair, some older Chinese men felt differently. After the cutting, they might save their hair and express sorrow over the loss, quoting the sayings of Confucius regarding the hair. Still other Chinese said that the pigtail style had been a sign of political oppression and everyone should rejoice to see it go.

As was true in the past, women and girls spent time cleansing, conditioning, and styling their hair and the beauty standard remained the same: long, dark, shining hair. Numerous ways of dressing hair were popular. They included a single bun at the back of the head placed high or low, a center part with a coil of hair on either side of the ears, various types of chignons, long plaits, and looped or coiled hairstyles. For young girls, reaching the age of womanhood, at about age fifteen, meant changing the hairstyle to form a roll above each ear.

Women made a jelly-like liquid to add shine to their hair by soaking certain types of wood chips in water. Brushing this liquid through the hair added deeper color as well as shine. Chinese women liked their hair as dark as possible and used oil of tea seeds and various herbal infusions to make it blacker.

They often wore ornamental hairpins and/or flowers in their hair, choosing those with the most pleasing scents, and substituted artificial flowers when fresh were not available. For the special occasion of her wedding day, a young woman's hair was dressed by a close relative.

Braids, in some cases multiple braids, were common in hairstyles of young girls, as were bangs, often cut straight across. Some progressive young women began cutting their hair, as women were doing in western countries in the late 1910s and 1920s. Some faced harsh criticism from tradition-bound parents after they arrived home with their new haircut.

During the 1930s, more women in China, particularly in urban areas, followed the Western fashion of cutting their hair for political and aesthetic reasons. Some bobbed their hair and then had a **permanent wave**. Critics complained that some of the curled bobs worn by Chinese factory girls was not becoming and did not suit the natural texture of their hair. In the provinces, some women retained traditional ways of dressing their hair and did not wave or curl it.

Styles changed again after the Chinese Revolution ended with the formation of the communist People's Republic of China in 1949. Revolutionary leaders rejected Western values and culture and emphasized simple, practical styles of dress and grooming for both men and women. Individualism and a focus on appearance and material goods were frowned upon in this group-oriented society. People wore simple, uniform hairstyles and clothing.

Near the end of the twentieth century, the Chinese government became more tolerant of individual hairstyles and the use of cosmetics and relaxed former restrictions. The beauty industry, producing cosmetics and hair care products, contributes to the Chinese economy, and as of 2004, China was the leading source of hair for making wigs and hairpieces.

People in China now wear various hairstyles typical in other societies, although the government does set some standards for young people, certain professions, and members of national sports teams.

Despite modernization, some people continue to wear traditional styles—for example, people in Qiang province wear hairstyles and head coverings like those of their ancestors. Many women plait their hair, weaving in colored threads, then coil the plaits on top of a cloth arranged on the crown of their head. Their scarves may be plain or made from colorful embroidered pieces, sometimes festooned with gold or silver ornaments. Older women usually cover their heads with black or white turbans.

See also: Adornment, Ornamental; Body Hair; Comb; Hair Art; Hair Removal; Laws and Regulations; Monastic Styles; Mustache; Wigs and Hairpieces

Further Reading: "A Chinese Barber in New York" Harper's Weekly, March 10, 1888, reprint available online at http://immigrants.harpweek.com/ChineseAmericans/Items/Item124L.htm; Ayscough, Florence, *Chinese Women Yesterday & Today* (1937); Ko, Dorothy, *Teachers of the Inner Chambers: Women and Culture in Seventeenth-Century China* (1994); Muller, Max F., ed., and Rhys T. W. Davids, trans., *The Buddhist Suttas: The Sacred Books of the East* (2004); Smith, Richard J., *China's Cultural Heritage, the Qing Dynasty 1644–1912* (1994); Warner, Marina, *The Dragon Empress: Life and Times of Tz'u-hsi 1835–1908, Empress Dowager of China* (1972); Yee, Chiang, *Chinese Childhood* (1952).

CLAIROL

Clairol is a well-known brand that offers a wide range of hair coloring products, shampoos, and other hair care products for consumers and the beauty industry. As of 2004, Clairol was a major producer of hair products with annual sales totaling about $1.6 billion.

The company had its start in 1931 when, during a trip to Europe, Americans Lawrence and Joan Gelb discovered some new hair coloring products made by Mury of France. Gelb, a chemist, obtained the rights to this product, which could penetrate the hair shaft. After returning home to his chemical manufacturing plant, he worked with other chemists to improve Muray's formula, and within a few years was ready to launch this commercial oil-based hair tint.

Cofounder Joan Gelb took charge of the new company, called Clairol, and she used the professional name "Joan Clair." (She would serve as president until she and Lawrence Gelb were divorced in 1941.) Joan Gelb promoted "Instant Clairol Oil Shampoo Tint" in beauty salons around the country. At that time, Roux was the leading hair color brand in the United States. Although the nation was struggling through the Great Depression and money was tight, women still spent money on hair care and patronized beauty salons. Based at 1600 Broadway in New York, Clairol managed to carve out a share of the market, and annual sales reached $1 million in 1938. Many women, however, still shunned hair color because of its long association with "loose women." Those who did have their hair colored tended to keep it secret.

In 1940 Clairol moved its research, manufacturing, and distribution operations to Stamford, Connecticut. Sales of hair coloring products were relatively low during the 1940s, since many people continued to associate artificial hair color with "loose women" or chorus girls. In addition, some hair dyes or bleaches produced brassy, artificial-looking results. Clairol and other companies worked on new formulations that would produce more believable colors.

After graduating from the Harvard Business School, Lawrence and Joan's son, Richard Gelb, joined the company in time to launch "Miss Clairol Hair Color Bath" in 1950. (Another son, Bruce Gelb, would also join the company and serve as president of Clairol.) "Miss Clairol Hair Color Bath" was the first commercial formula that could lighten and color hair in one step. It looked more natural and lasted longer than previous formulations and was easier to use. The next year, the company introduced its revolutionary bleaching product, "Miss Clairol Whipped Crème" hair lightener.

In 1956, Clairol brought out "Miss Clairol," a home hair coloring kit that enabled people to color their hair in one step, by mixing the solution in the kit with peroxide. Consumers could see the results in about twenty minutes, and the cost was reasonable, so the sales opportunities seemed promising. In addition, beauticians were impressed by Clairol's demonstrations at the 1956 International Beauty Show in New York City.

Clairol hired the advertising firm of Foote, Cone, and Belding to launch a campaign for "Miss Clairol." They aimed to make the idea of hair coloring more socially acceptable to more women and to emphasize the natural-looking results. Shirley Polykoff created ads that contained these now-famous lines: "Does she or doesn't she? Only her hairdresser knows for sure." Ads appeared in major magazines, such as *Life*, as well as on television, and the product became quite successful. When Clairol introduced its "Nice 'n Easy" shampoo-in hair color, Polykoff came up with another memorable tag line: "The closer he gets, the better you look."

By 1959, Clairol was the undisputed leader in the U.S. hair color industry. Bristol-Myers, a large corporation, bought the company.

Fashion became more light-hearted during the 1960s and Clairol hair color names like "Just Peachy," "Tickled Pink," and "Frivolous Fawn" reflected that youthful, upbeat attitude. New tones of silver and gold became available, which increased hair coloring options. Clairol continued to develop new formulations, as well as shampoos, conditioners, hairspray, and styling products. To accommodate its growing business, the company had moved into a larger facility in Stamford in 1950. It moved into yet another larger new complex in 1968.

In 2001, Procter & Gamble Inc. bought Clairol from Bristol-Myers Squibb for $4.95 billion. The next year, Procter & Gamble announced that it would sell some Clairol brands, including the Condition 3-in-1 hairstyling products and the Vitapointe hair grooming lines. Procter & Gamble said that it regarded Clairol's hair color line as a good addition to its own hair products, which include Head & Shoulders, Pert, and Vidal Sassoon. The hair color line, which includes professional and mass-market products, included several brands: Nice 'n Easy, Hydrience, Herbal Essences, and Natural Instincts. In 2001, Clairol introduced a new line called Intensive Blends—shampoos, conditioners, hair balm and leave-in conditioner. Clairol Herbal Essences shampoos and conditioners remain popular.

Recent Clairol hair color ads have emphasized individuality and a modern, more relaxed attitude toward personal appearance. The tag line in 2001 was, "A beauty all your own." The 2002 ad campaign was called "Colorwonderful."

The quest for better hair color techniques continues. In 2003, Procter & Gamble announced that Clairol was developing a new hair color technology called "copper blocking" that would provide deeper, richer color than other similar products in the marketplace.

See also: Advertising; Hair Color; Hair Colorants; Procter & Gamble; Shampoo

Further Reading: Gladwell, Malcolm, "True Colors: Hair Dye and the Hidden History of Postwar America," *The New Yorker*, March 22, 1999; Healy, Peter, "A Market to Dye For," *The Wall Street Journal*, May 27, 2001; Kraft, Joy, "Hair Care Pros: Clairol Reliable, Not Cutting Edge," *The Cincinnati (Ohio) Enquirer*, May 22, 2001, available online at http://www.enquirer.com/editions/2001/05/22/fin_hair_care_pros.html; "Obituaries: Joan Bove, 99, Co-Founder of Clairol," *Newsday*, July 25, 2001; Peale, Cliff, "Clairol's Potential About to Be Tapped," *The Cincinnati Enquirer*, January 12, 2003; Pease, Theresa, "Finding That 'Something Special,'" 2000 Andover Academy, available online at http://www.andover.edu/publications/2000winter_bulletin/special/special.htm; Polykoff, Shirley, *Does She or Doesn't She? And How She Did It* (1975).

COLGATE-PALMOLIVE *See* Shampoo

COMB

The comb—a toothed implement made of solid material—has been a basic hair care tool since prehistoric times. The word "comb" comes from ancient Indo-European words that mean "tooth" or "to bite." Combs are used to clean the hair through mechanical action, as well as to smooth and separate strands and style the hair. They come in various sizes, styles, and materials but are almost always flat in shape. Special combs have been designed for particular hair types and hairstyles—for example, combs with wider teeth work better on thick, curly hair or tangled hair.

Early combs

Ancient combs resemble modern versions, though the materials and production methods have changed. They have been found underground and in tombs, since combs were among the burial gifts in some cultures.

Archaeologists have found boxwood combs from the Stone Age, which began about 2 million years ago and ended between 40,000 to 10,000 years ago, depending on location. A comb made from bone dating back to 2,500 BCE was found on the island of Gotland, off the east coast of Sweden. In **ancient Egypt**, combs were made from dried fish bones and other natural materials. They contain one or two rows of teeth and various decorations, ranging from simple to ornate. Ivory combs with carvings of peacocks or other animals have been found in the tombs of wealthy Egyptians.

Africans made combs from elephant ivory, wood, or bone. Since many people on that continent have curly or kinky hair that tends to tangle easily, these combs have long teeth set far enough apart to remove knots without pulling out hairs. The teeth usually have rounded tips.

People around the world also used animal horn and tusks to make combs. Native American peoples carved combs from the antlers of deer and other animals they killed for food, and from shells. The Inuit people of present-day Alaska made ivory combs from walrus tusks. Members of the Thule culture (at 1000 CE), ancestors of the Inuit, made carved graceful designs on their comb handles. During modern times, the Inuit peoples continued to make combs from ivory and bone.

Throughout the second, third, and fourth centuries, Romans made combs from polished bone. Most of these combs are flat, rectangular shaped, and double-sided, with a row of fine teeth on one side and thicker teeth on the other. Decorative carvings adorn the ends.

Ancient Greeks used ivory combs, while Anglo-Saxon peoples and Vikings made similar combs from ivory and bone. Some important comb-making centers were located in present-day Scandinavia.

In the city of Changzhou, China, a large comb-making business (now operating as the Palace Comb Factory or Changzhou Combs Factory) began operating in the fifth century. Workers crafted combs from different kinds of wood, including boxwood, sandalwood, cherry, photinia, and Chinese locust, which were chosen for their resilience and fine grains. The finished combs featured carved and/or burnt-on designs. Bamboo also was used to make combs, both for cleaning the hair and for smoothing strands. Pieces of bamboo were glued together with lacquer. This factory continues to produce handmade wooden combs.

Medieval Times

During the **Middle Ages** (in 500–1400 CE), combs still were made from bone, ivory, and wood, including birchwood and boxwood. Many combs had two sides—one row of fine teeth for cleaning and removing lice and their nits; the other row with wider-spaced teeth for grooming. Some combs had a central design between the rows, and well-to-do people could afford ivory or wood combs with fancy carvings. Combs were made to last and some people kept theirs for twenty to thirty years, even for a lifetime. Some combs made in Europe during and after the late Middle Ages featured a built-in mirror, and better quality combs had cases, often made from pieces of bone held together with iron rivets.

By the 1100s, comb-making was a guild industry, and comb-makers, like certain other craftspeople and traders, joined together to form guilds or to join existing guilds. In some countries, guild membership was based on the type of material people used in their work. For example, French comb-makers who worked with horn belonged to a guild with others who used horn as a raw material. At that time, horn for comb-making came from Europe, Brazil, South Africa, and Madagascar. Other guilds were based on the workers' location, and comb-makers might join printers, carpenters, druggists, blacksmiths, and others who worked in the same part of town. Greek comb-makers devised a special language to protect their secrets when they communicated with other guild members.

As a reflection of their religious faith, European guilds, including those for comb-makers, had a patron saint. This was true in other regions as well. In present-day Vietnam, comb-making guilds have a patron and certain temples in Hanoi are dedicated to these saints.

By the 1400s, Limoges, France, had become a center for crafting fine combs from boxwood, horn, and ivory. Some Protestant French comb-makers moved to Switzerland during the 1600s to escape religious persecution. As they set up successful comb-making businesses, Switzerland also became known for this product.

Comb-making also was an important craft in Turkey, where camel-leg bone and wood from the pear and annep trees were among the materials used to make combs. People believed that using these combs could improve the health of their hair and scalp and even reduce hair loss. Small combs made from camel bone were used to apply cosmetic materials to the eyelashes. Traditional comb-makers thrived in Turkey until the growth of the plastic comb industry forced most of them out of business during the 1900s.

Influence of New Hairstyles

During the seventeenth century, Europeans wore long wigs and beards, so the comb became even more important for grooming. In fact, people began to routinely use large combs in public. In Restoration England (1660–1688), especially during the reign of King Charles II, men kept a comb in their pocket and could be seen combing their hair at the theater or in people's homes. These combs were made from wood, animal horn, ivory, bone, and tortoise, and they came in different styles designed for natural hair, wigs, or beards. Some men with light-colored beards used combs made from lead since these were thought to impart a more fashionable darker shade. Centuries earlier, the Romans had found that they could create a liquid dye for gray hair by dipping a lead comb in vinegar.

Combing one's hair in public went out of fashion and was later considered to be a breach of etiquette. Hair historian Richard Corson quotes author Robert

Tomes, who criticized people for grooming their hair in public. In 1877 Tomes wrote, "The use of a comb, or even its habitual carriage in the pocket, is irreconcilable with all nicety of manners" (Corson 1965, 421).

Modern Combs

During the 1800s, new materials and machines for making combs became available. One of these materials was gutta-percha, a natural latex—plant sap that coagulates when exposed to the air. It comes from a resin found in the Isonandra Gutta tree, which grows in Malaya and other Pacific Rim countries. Beginning in the 1840s, gutta-percha was used for combs (both grooming and decorative), jewelry, golf balls, and cable insulation. This material was less brittle than rubber produced before the 1850s.

Hard rubber combs became available after the mid-1850s. Rubber trees grow in India and other parts of Asia, as well as in South America. Since ancient times, people living near rubber trees had used the sap from these trees to make solid yet flexible objects, such as balls for sports. During the mid-1800s, American inventor Charles Goodyear found a way to make hard rubber, through a process called vulcanization, which he patented in 1851. In 1854, the India Hard Rubber Comb Company began operating in Queens, New York, where it became a leading producer of combs. This company was licensed by Charles Goodyear to make various hard rubber goods for homes and businesses. The Goodyear Company and other comb companies around the world produced rubber combs for millions of customers. Although rubber combs could break if they were bent too sharply, they usually lasted longer than wooden combs.

Comb Manufacturing

The development of machines for comb-making led to the industrialization of this trade during the 1860s. Large comb-making companies employed hundreds, even thousands, of people. For example, in 1870 a horn comb factory in Licorne, France, employed 500 workers and produced 3 million combs. By 1930, at the peak of that factory's productivity, 1,500 workers made 30 million combs.

In some American towns, comb-making was the main industry or it made up a significant segment of the local economy. One example is West Newbury, Massachusetts, where farmer Enoch Noyes started making cattle horn combs in 1759. William Cleland, a former soldier, soon joined him to contribute his skills and tools to the enterprise. Noyes and Cleland built a successful business that, by 1793, employed seventy people in their area.

Another town in Massachusetts, Leominster, became known as the "comb capital of America." The first comb factory in Leominster was founded by Obadiah Hills in 1770. Hills, who had learned to make combs in West Newbury, made horn combs. The town boasted twenty-four comb shops in 1845. As the comb-making industry continued to grow in that region between 1845 and 1852, the number of employees rose from 146 to 400. Through the years, celluloid and other new materials replaced horn. Job opportunities brought new residents to the region, and the town retained its leading position in the industry into the 1900s. During the early 1920s, Leominster's Viscoloid Company Inc. was one of the nation's four largest makers of celluloid combs. Leominster then became a force in the plastics industry, and the Cardinal Comb & Brush Manufacturing Company, founded in Leominster in 1969, is still a major producer of plastic hair care items.

The demand for combs continued to rise during the 1800s. Most people still were not washing their hair frequently, so they used fine-toothed combs to remove oil and dirt and even to remove parasites. During the American Civil War, soldiers carried combs in their kits to help them to remove lice from their hair and beards. Hard rubber combs with teeth placed further apart were used for styling purposes.

Twentieth to Twenty-First Century

Regular shampooing became the norm during the twentieth century. As a result, people used combs more for styling than for cleansing their hair. Combs were still being made from horn and wood, as well as from newer materials, including metal, galalith, ebonite, and celluloid.

Developed in 1868, celluloid is a type of plastic made by mixing cellulose nitrate with camphor. American inventors Isaiah and John Hyatt developed celluloid while trying to win a contest offering a $10,000 prize to anyone who made a practical substitute for ivory billiard balls. It is cheaper than ivory and easier to work with. By the 1920s, celluloid had become the main material used to make combs and it launched a thriving plastics industry.

By the 1940s, new types of thermoplastic materials had virtually replaced ivory, tortoise, and animal bones for making combs. During World War II (1939–1945), natural rubber was in short supply, so plastics filled the gap. Besides, animal activists were protesting against the use of tortoise and ivory, which threatened some animals with extinction. Today, laws protect endangered species and ban the hunting of certain animals for their ivory or shells. One of these protected species is the hawksbill turtle, a major source of tortoise shell, which lives around tropical reef areas of the Atlantic, Pacific, and Indian Oceans.

By the late 1900s, hard plastic was used to make most combs. Today, most combs are machine-made from synthetic materials, but some companies still offer handmade combs, including combs made from wood or horn. Combs come in an array of different styles and sizes for barbers, hairstylists, and consumers. These include the styling comb, dressing comb, wide-toothed comb, flattop comb, Afro comb, rake comb, tail comb, and teasing comb. Special combs are available for use on beards, mustaches, eyebrows and eyelashes, as well as the head.

See also: Afro; Bouffant; China; Comb, Decorative; Comb, Liturgical; Hair Straightening; Hairstyles, Twentieth-Century; India; Japan; Religion and Hair; Roman Empire; Walker, Madam C. J.; Vikings; Wigs and Hairpieces

Further Reading: Corson, Richard, *Fashions in Hair* (1965); Doyle, Bernard W., *Comb Making in America* (1993); Haertig, Evelyn, *Antique Combs and Purses* (1983); Hague, Norma, *Combs & Hair Accessories Antique Pocket Guides* (1999); "History of Leominster Massachusetts," available online at http://members.aol.com/Leominster476/History.html; Macgregor, A., *Bone, Ivory, and Horn* (1985); Musser, Mary, "Massachusetts Horn Smiths: A

Century of Comb-making 1775–1875," *Old-Time New England* 58: 59–68; Williamson, Colin, *Plastics Collecting and Conserving* (1999); Woshner, Mike, *India Rubber and Gutta-Percha in the Civil War Era: An Illustrated History of Rubber & Pre-Plastic Antiques and Militaria* (1999).

COMB, DECORATIVE

Combs to anchor the hair and/or add decorative touches date back to ancient times. These combs come in various materials and designs and include "teeth" that position hair by gripping the strands. Some ornamental combs have numerous teeth while others resemble large hairpins, with two teeth and one opening.

Decorative hair combs fall into three general types: combs that hold up the sides; larger combs to hold up the back; and high combs worn at the back of the head to adorn a hairstyle or hold up a mantilla. In Spain and Latin American countries, a type of comb called a *peineta* is worn with a lace mantilla on festive occasions.

A Long History

Ancient combs were made from wood, often studded with gemstones or hand-painted designs, or from bones, feathers, or other natural materials. Historians can identify the source of many antique combs because certain types of wood were found only in certain regions. Likewise, some trimmings used in combs, such as the vivid blue feathers of the Chinese kingfisher, are unique to a country or region.

Ivory combs were popular among the Badarians and Amrateans, two groups of people who lived in pre-dynastic Egypt. Ancient Egyptians and some Asian peoples made hair accessories from ivory and copper, which they often adorned with beads.

Antlers from elk, moose, and deer also were used to make combs. Seventh-century graves of wealthy people who lived in present-day Scandinavia contain combs carved from animal antlers. The designs on these combs, including dots, spirals, circles, and geometric patterns, were adorned with gold leaf, amber, and garnet or other gemstones.

Native Americans made combs from bone, antler, and metal. By the seventeenth century, the Narragansetts and Wampanoags also made combs from brass. Popular designs included animals, such as bears and beavers, as well as a shape that resembled a whale's tail. Native Americans also designed combs with various patterns of dots.

Combs have been popular in Asia. From the 1600s into the 1800s, during the Edo historical period, women in **Japan** wore combs to secure and adorn their hairstyles. These combs were made from aromatic woods, including sandalwood, as well as cherry and plum woods, tortoise, ivory, horn, and various metals. An increasing number of styles evolved as people crafted intricate designs and decorations with colorful lacquers and inlays of gold, silver, and mother-of-pearl.

Women in the Philippines also often added a decorative comb to their hair. Traditionally, these combs, including the *peineta* and *suklay*, were made from horn, shell, and wood. Decorations for these combs included flowers made from copper wire or other metallic wires.

Animals provided much of the raw material for many decorative hair combs. Because ivory lent itself to fine carving, it was used in Asian and African countries where elephants lived and in places where people hunted walruses or other tusked animals. Animal bones and tortoise shell also were popular. Tortoise shell is durable and possesses naturally vivid colors and attractive patterns, making it desirable for decorative items. Ivory and tortoise were exported to countries where they were scarce or unavailable. Comb-makers heated or boiled horn and tortoise shell to make them more pliable. After the combs cooled, they hardened into their new shapes.

In Turkey and Armenia, where comb-making was a major trade, combs were made of wood, ivory, and camel bone. Egypt alone imported as many as 1,500,000 combs from these countries annually.

A Key Accessory

Combs have played an important role in Western hairstyles, especially during the 1800s and early 1900s. Millions of women around the world wore hair combs to adorn the long, upswept hair that was fashionable at that time. By 1900, the list of materials used to make combs included ivory, precious metals, pewter, aluminum, brass, tortoise, amber, coral, jet, bone, horn, and wood.

During the Victorian and Edwardian eras, some of the most coveted combs were made from sterling silver, tortoise shell, or gutta-percha, which came into use during the 1840s. Gutta-percha came from the sap of a tree found in Malaysia and was used to make furnishings and jewelry as well as hair accessories. Tortoise shell and ivory combs remained popular throughout the 1800s, but these raw materials were becoming scarce. Less expensive combs made from animal horn were also common.The development of celluloid, a synthetic that was a forerunner of modern plastics, enabled companies to keep up with the demand for hair combs. Sheets of celluloid were cut into combs and then hand-finished and decorated.

An article in an 1862 issue of *Godey's Lady's Book* shows the importance of decorative hair combs during those years. The author points out that the "small side combs" used in prevailing hairstyles "are made in endless variety." The article goes on to say the following:

> When worn in the daytime, these small combs are made of light tortoiseshell, either with a row of small pearls, also in shell, very closely ranged together, or cut in clubs, points, or hearts for the evening. They are made in dead gold, either quite plain or studded with pearl, coral, steel, gilt, or even precious stones . . . Ivory combs are still worn, also shell with ivory ball tops. Among the prettiest shell are some with ball tops studded with tiny gilt stars. (193)

The production of decorative combs boosted the economy of many towns. In Northborough, Massachusetts, for instance, comb making was the largest industry during the mid-1800s. In 1850, about 2.6 million combs were made in Northborough's factories. Companies often made both grooming combs and ornamental combs.

After 1870, the use of decorative combs began to diminish, and some businesses either were terminated or the owners began to produce other goods in their factories. As women's fashions and hairstyles changed, decorative hair combs were more or less in vogue.

Bakelite, a synthetic resin, was popular during the Art Deco period of the 1920s and 1930s. Combs were decorated with real or fake gems, beads, feathers, paint, enamel work, embossing, filigree, and/or pique—a method of placing inlaid gold or silver designs on tortoise shell. Some combs featured painted designs, such as clusters of flowers or leaves.

Decorative hair combs could be works of art. For example, glassmaker René Lalique (1860–1945), known for his artwork and jewelry, made combs with Art Nouveau designs, including his famous dragonfly. Lalique employed unexpected materials, including opals and Baroque pearls, in new ways and he combined them with enamel, glass, and semiprecious stones. These kinds of combs are highly prized by collectors.

Some people enjoy wearing or collecting vintage hair combs. The Antique Comb Collectors' Club International, which has members in the United States, the United Kingdom, France, and other countries, publishes a bimonthly newsletter that contains current and historical information for collectors.

Although most of today's hairstyles do not require the use of a decorative comb, women and girls may choose to wear them to create a certain hairstyle or accentuate their clothing. Natural, machine-made materials, and combinations of the materials, are used to make combs. Combs are decorated with crystals, rhinestones, feathers, pearls, wood, enamel, plastic and glass beads, among other things.

See also: Adornment, Ornamental; Comb; Hairstyles, Twentieth-Century; Roman Empire; Victorian Era

Further Reading: Bachman, Mary, *Collectors Guide to Hair Combs* (1998); Griffith, Susan R., "Salute to Leominster," *Massachusetts Review*, August 13, 1975, available online at http://members.aol.com/Leominster476/History.html; Haertig, Evelyn, *Antique Combs & Purses Gallery* (2000); Hague, Norma, *Combs & Hair Accessories Antique Pocket Guides* (1999).

COMB, LITURGICAL

During medieval times, Catholic priests used liturgical combs to arrange their hair before they celebrated the mass. Special liturgical combs were used to anoint new bishops, and the comb became the bishop's property after his consecration ceremony.

Most liturgical combs were made of ivory, and they featured ornate designs in the form of religious symbols or religious scenes, such as the "Adoration of the Magi." They also portray important people or events in church history, such as the life and martyrdom of Thomas Becket (on December 29, 1170 at Canterbury Cathedral), found on an English liturgical comb that dates from 1200 to 1210 CE. Some liturgical combs are regarded as artistic masterpieces. One example is the liturgical comb of St. Heribert (970–1021 CE). An example of Carolingian art, this comb is on exhibit at the Schnütgen Museum in Cologne, Germany.

See also: Comb; Middle Ages; Religion and Hair

Further Reading: Beckwith, J., *Ivory Carving in Early Medieval England* (1972); Herzog, Johann Jakob, *The New Schaff-Herzog Encyclopedia of Religious Knowledge*, Vol. 12 (1908).

COMING OF AGE

In many cultures, hairstyles have served as a visible sign that a young man or young woman has "come of age"; that is, moved from childhood to adult status. Some changes in hairstyle take place during special coming-of-age rituals or ceremonies.

In traditional African cultures, the hair may be cut or shaved during this life transition. For example, among the **Yoruba**, the head is shaved to signify the passage into a new stage of life, just as it is shaved in infancy and again after death. During the Temne male initiation ceremony, called the "Rabai de Temne," a male's head is shaved and then washed.

Young women of the Akan in western Liberia and the Sierra Leone region adopt specific new hairstyles at puberty. In the Sierra Leone, young women spend time at a special camp where their hair is cut. During the rest of their stay at the camp, they learn other rites of passage as their hair begins to grow out. Then the hair is combed and plaited in public. Braiding is a sign of their new status. Before marriage, Ibo girls in today's Nigeria used clay, ground coal, and palm oil to style their hair into a horn, tilting the hair forward over their brows. In India, the traditional hairstyle for younger girls was two braids, which was changed to a single braid once she reached puberty.

For **Native Americans**, traditions involving the hair also showed that young people reached maturity. Some tribes located in the southeastern region of the present-day United States allowed young women to grow longer hair once they reached a certain age. Among members of the Hopi tribe living in the American southwest, a special hairstyle that resembles butterfly wings shows that a young girl is ready for marriage, usually around age seventeen. This style is called the "squash blossom" hairstyle or "butterfly."

Males may also adopt a different hairstyle to show the coming of age. Young Turkana men of Kenya, Africa, sat for hours while their elaborate hairstyles were prepared to mark the end of their initiation rites. Among Polynesians living in the Cook Islands of the Pacific, a boy's hair was cut for the first time to mark his "coming of age." This haircut was also a way to show his masculine identity, since women wore their hair long. Because this culture believed the hair had a spiritual power, called *mana*, haircutting must be done carefully. The room was draped with quilts called *tivaevae* that contained special symbols to denote the significance of this occasion.

Samurai in Japan had a coming-of-age ceremony called *genpuku*. Sometime between the ages of twelve and eighteen, a young man changed his name and hairstyle to show his new adult status. This marked the time when he was given new responsibilities and also was the first age at which he could marry.

In western cultures, children have changed their hairstyles when they reached a certain age, such as sixteen. In Europe and the United States, until the early

1900s, young girls typically wore their hair down during childhood and then pinned it up in various ways after they reached maturity. For example, Victorian girls wore their hair down as children, then began to pin it up to show their new maturity as young women. Authors Kate Mulvey and Melissa Richards write, "Reaching the age when the hair could be put up was a rite of passage in her life, and often there were several interim stages, where a plait would be loosely put up with a ribbon, to signify the coming event" (Mulvey and Richards 1998, 18).

See also: Africa; Amish; Egypt, Ancient; Religion and Hair; Roman Empire

Further Reading: Arnoldi, Mary Jo, and Christine M. Kreamer, *Crowning Achievements: Africans Art of Dressing the Head* (1995); Mulvey, Kate, and Melissa Richards, *Decades of Beauty* (1998); Page, Jake, "Inside the Sacred Hopi Homeland," *National Geographic*, November 1982, pp. 607–629; Sieber, Roy, and Frank Herreman, eds., *Hair in African Art and Culture Munich* (2000).

COMPETITIONS

Competitions or contests relating to hair, beards, or mustaches are held around the world. Records are also kept in regard to the length of head and body hairs.

During the early decades of the twentieth century, women in various countries could compete in contests to determine who had "the longest hair." Many of these contests began during the late 1910s and 1920s after women began cutting their hair into shorter bobs and shingled styles, thus making long hair more rare. Contest winners in the United States and Europe often had hair that extended six feet or more from their heads, trailing onto the floor. Millie Owens, dubbed "Queen of Long Hair," had tresses that measured eight feet, two inches.

Women with unusually long hair also were featured in traveling exhibits and circuses. During the 1940s, Polish-born model Henrietta "Hanka" Kelter toured with the Ringling Bros. & Barnum and Bailey Circus.

Today, state fairs continue to sponsor hair contests of various kinds. For example, the Michigan State Fair has traditionally held a Longest Ponytail Contest. Girls and women compete in different divisions, according to their age.

Periodicals sponsor long hair contests. In 1981, with hair measuring 2.20 meters long, Californian Mary Tucker won a contest held by the *National Enquirer*. The 1986 winner, native Californian Judy Todd, had hair measuring a little over 2.20 meters long.

Hair magazine has sponsored a "Long & Lovely" hair contest. The 1989 winner, Balbir Kaur, is a native of India and a member of the Sikh religious group, who traditionally do not cut their hair. Her shining dark hair measured 1.5 meters at the time of the contest.

In China, women compete for the title of "Miss Dyq" to see whose hair is the longest. The 2000 winner, Dai YueQuin, had hair measuring more than three meters long. She became a popular winner and organized a Web site for her fans and for people who appreciate long hair. On her own Web site, Petra Schlesinger, whose thick 1.34-meter-long braid won her the German national "Rapunzel" title in 1998, calls herself the "hair goddess." As of 2000, Schlesinger's reddish hair reached her calves. In 1998, Ecih Sukaesih of West Java was named as the woman with the longest hair in Indonesia. At that time, her hair measured 240 centimeters, and by 2004, it had reached a length of 290 centimeters.

In 2003 Matrix, a hair care products company, sponsored the "Search for Rapunzel Contest." The contest was open to women who could donate at least 10 inches of healthy hair to "**Locks of Love**," an organization that provides human hairpieces to children who suffer from long-term medical hair loss. Six finalists in the contest appeared on the "Oprah Winfrey Show" in April 2004, and each woman donated more than 10 inches of hair to "Locks of Love."

When Gloria Tuason of Makati City in the Philippines won the Shopwise Book of Records long hair contest in April 2003, she described her hair care regimen. Tuason said she spent two hours each day washing and conditioning her hair, which measured over six feet long (208 centimeters), but she claimed that she could twist it into a bun in just five minutes. She said that she went to a salon for regular hot oil treatments.

The *Guinness Book of World Records* compiles lists of men and women with the longest hair in the world and also reports the results in individual countries. From 1983 to 1989, the record was held by Greek-born Georgia Sebrantke, who lived in Germany at that time. Sebrantke's hair was 3 meters long.

Men may also make the record books for longest head hair. At 5.97 meters (19.6 feet), a Hmong tribesman from Thailand named Hu Sengla was listed by Guinness as the longest-haired man in the world. He held the title until he died in 2001 at age seventy-seven. In 2004, the Associated Press reported that a Vietnamese man, Tran Van Hay, had hair that extended to 6.2 meters (20 feet) long. He told reporters that he had not cut it for thirty-one years. Yet his hair may not have been as long as that of a monk living in India in 1949: Swami Pandarasannadhi's hair reportedly measured 26 feet (7.93 meters). This was, however, not officially documented.

Diane Witt of Massachusetts is sometimes called the "living Rapunzel." She has held both the American and Guinness World records for the longest hair in the world. From 1989 to about 1996, Witt topped the list with over 3 meters (10 feet) of reddish-brown hair.

Guinness and other record-keeping organizations also collect statistics for the longest man's beard in the world, the longest ear hair, and the longest eyelash. In 2004, Mel Grubbe, a senior at the University of Chicago, claimed that she had an eyelash that measured 3 inches long, which might set a new record. A man in India set a record for ear hairs after his reached a length of 5 inches. In 2001, Ripley's "Believe It Or Not" reported that Paul Miller had grown a mustache that measured ten inches long.

See also: Bald-Headed Men of America; Beards, Men's; Bob, The; Flappers; Hairdressing; Harper, Martha Matilda; India; Locks of Love (LOL); Mustache; Salons, Hair and Beauty; World Beard and Moustache Championship

Further Reading: Guinness World Records, available online at www.guinnessworldrecords.com; "Vietnamese Man May Have Longest Hair," *Washington Post*, July 2, 2004, available online at http://www.washtimes.com/upi-breaking/20040702-071327-8216r.htm; "Woman Claims to Have World's Longest Eyelash," October 20, 2004, available online at http://www.nbc5.com/news/3837808/detail.html; "Woman With 6 ft.-Long Hair Wins Shopwise's Longest Hair Contest," *The Philippine Star*, April 15, 2003, available online at http://www.shopwise.com.ph/newsarch/15april03.html.

CORNROWS

Cornrows, which evolved in Africa and the Caribbean, are made by tightly braiding three strands of hair in a specific line, either straight or curved, along the scalp. To native peoples, the resulting rows resembled lines of corn planted in the ground and the hairstyle represented agriculture, order, and a civilized way of life.

Also known as "track braids," this styling technique became more widely known during the 1960s and 1970s. Cornrows experienced another surge of popularity during the 1990s, and they were worn by runway models at Paris couture shows in 2000.

From Africa to America

Africans have traditionally worn cornrows for certain festivals and celebrations or as a regular daily hairstyle. Members of the Temne and Yoruba groups in Africa might spend hours or even days creating a cornrow style, and cornrowing is regarded as an art as well as a hairstyling technique.

Beginning in colonial days, African American slaves wore cornrows in order to keep their traditions alive, as well as for practical reasons. Tightly braided hair looked neat, was easier to manage, and it stayed off the face as people labored for long hours. After the Civil War ended, most African Americans adopted the same kinds of hairstyles that white Americans were wearing. The larger society promoted standards of appearance that favored light skin, straight or smoothly waving hair, and other features associated with white Europeans. Many African Americans adopted mainstream hairstyles in order to "fit in" and gain access to social and economic opportunities. In so doing, they abandoned cornrows and other traditional African styles.

As the Black Pride movement expanded during the 1960s, more African Americans embraced their cultural roots and wore clothing and hairstyles that reflected that heritage. Famous African Americans known for their cornrow hairstyles during those years included singer/songwriter Stevie Wonder, actress Cicely Tyson, singer/songwriter Roberta Flack, and singer/songwriter Valerie Simpson. More recently, model Iman, singer Alicia Keys, rapper Snoop Dogg, and actresses Lisa Bonet and Angela Bassett have worn cornrows. Some athletes also wear them, including Philadelphia 76ers' Allen Iverson, Rasheed Wallace of the Portland Trail Blazers, and Latrell Sprewell of the New York Knicks. British soccer legend David Beckham wore his hair dyed gold and styled into cornrows during 2003. Bronson Arroyo, a member of the Boston Red Sox major league baseball team, wore cornrows during part of the 2004 season.

In 1979, cornrows became a major fad among whites after actress Bo Derek appeared in the feature film "*10*" wearing her long blond hair in beaded cornrows. As the fad spread, hairdressers who could create cornrow styles were in demand. In New York, Los Angeles, and other cities, hair salons that previously had never offered this style trained or hired stylists who could create cornrows. Customers were willing to spend hours having cornrows put in, at a cost of between $100 to $300. In addition to beads, some women had gemstones put into their hair. When cornrows became popularly known as "Bo Braids," people of color hastened to point out that this hairstyle has African roots and black women have worn it for millennia.

Some people experienced problems in the workplace when they wore cornrows or other unusual or "ethnic" hairstyles. During the 1960s and 1970s, some workplaces banned women from wearing cornrows, and lawsuits were fought over this matter.

Today, some hairdressers specialize in making cornrow styles for local residents and tourists. In the Harlem section of New York City, women may have their hair braided this way in numerous small salons where hairdressers, many of them born in Africa or the Caribbean, specialize in creating intricate cornrows. People of all ages, both male and female, may return from trips to the Caribbean with a cornrow hairstyle, which they can opt to keep for a few weeks or longer. Some people regard braiding is an art form, and they may spend hours, or even days, completing their creations. Stylists offer versions of the style that include hair extensions made from either human hair or synthetics, as well as beads and other ornaments.

See also: Africa; African Americans; Coming of Age; Dredlocks; Laws and Regulations; Yoruba

Further Reading: Byrd, Ayana D., and Lori L. Tharps, *Hair Story* (2002); Ferrell, Pamela, *Where Beauty Touches Me: Natural Hair Care & Beauty* (1995); Kovaleski, Serge F., "Cornrows a Bahamas Vacation Thing," *Washington Post*, May 17, 1998, available online at http://www.augustachronicle.com/stories/051798/fea_cornrows.shtml; Muhammad, Larry, "Top Rows: Braids are Trendy Coiffure of the Urban Black Male," *The Courier Journal* (Louisville, KY), August 27, 2001, available online at http://www.courierjournal.com/features/2001/08/fe20010827.html; Peters, Jacquelin C., "Braids, Cornrows, Dreadlocks, and Hair Wraps: An African Continuum," Paper presented at the 1992 Festival of Michigan Folk Life, Michigan State University, East Lansing, Michigan, available online at http://accad.osu.edu/~dkrug/367/online/ethnicarts4/r_resources/reading/Peters.asp; Sagay, Esi, *African Hairstyles: Styles of Yesterday and Today* (1983).

COSMETIC, TOILETRY, AND FRAGRANCE ASSOCIATION, THE (CTFA)

The Cosmetic, Toiletry, and Fragrance Association (CTFA) was organized in 1894 as a trade association for members of the personal care products industry, including products for cleansing, conditioning, styling, and coloring the hair.

The CTFA operates at the local, state, national, and international levels and it aims to provide its members with "a complete range of services that support the personal care products industry's needs and interests in the scientific, legal, regulatory, legislative, and international fields" (The Cosmetic, Toiletry, and Fragrance Association). As of 2004, the CTFA had 600 member companies, including active members (manufacturers and distributors of finished personal care products) and associate members (companies that supply ingredients, raw materials, and packaging materials and services that are used to produce retail goods).

As a service to members, CTFA informs companies about pending legislation that could affect their businesses—for example, laws that aim to ban or regulate products or ingredients, or that require new labeling procedures. It publishes information about the effects of various cosmetic ingredients in its Cosmetic Ingredient Review (CIR), which also is available online. Along with updates on products, the CIR lists safety alerts.

In 1998, the CTFA published its first International Legal and Regulatory Database, an electronic compilation that lists hundreds of cosmetic laws and regulations in sixty countries. Prior to 1998, CTFA had developed a similar database with information about laws and regulations in the United States. CTFA updates its roster of publications regularly. The organization also sends representatives to national and international conferences that deal with regulations and other matters that concern its members.

See also: Laws and Regulations

Further Reading: CTFA: The Cosmetic, Toiletry, and Fragrance Association, "About CTFA," "CTFA Annual Report," The Cosmetic, Toiletry, and Fragrance Association, 2004, http://www.ctfa.org and http://www.cir-safety.org.

COSMETIC EXECUTIVE WOMEN (CEW)

Founded in 1954, Cosmetic Executive Women Inc. (CEW) is a nonprofit organization for women working in the cosmetic, fragrance, and related fields, including the hair care industry. From its headquarters in New York City, CEW aims to keep CEW members informed about their profession and to promote the achievements of women in these industries. As of 2004, CEW had 3,000 members in the United States, France, and the United Kingdom.

The CEW honors people and products through its annual Beauty Awards and Achiever Awards, which debuted in 1975. Beauty awards are given each year to Hair Care and Coloring products in two categories: under $15 and over $15. The winners in 2004 were, respectively, Revlon High Dimension Color Accents Highlighting Kit and L'Oréal's Couleur Experte. Awards for eye makeup products are also given, and cosmetics for the eyelashes and eyebrows have won this prize. In 2004, both prizes went to a brand of mascara: Estee Lauder MagnaScopic Maximum Volume Mascara (over $15) and MAC Fibre Rich Lash mascara (under $15). These awards help consumers to identify products that "beauty insiders" have determined to be among the best in their categories.

CEW also performs charitable and philanthropic projects, such as providing funds for homeless women and children and helping women from low-income communities to start their own businesses.

Further Reading: CEW: Cosmetic Executive Women, "About CEW," "Achiever Awards," "Beauty Awards," Cosmetic Executive Women, http://www.cew.org.

COSMETICS, EYE

See Allergic Reactions; Eyebrows; Eyelashes; Factor, Max; Flappers; Kohl

COUNTERCULTURE

See Afro; Baldness, Voluntary; Beards, Men's; Bob, The; Dredlocks; Flappers; French Revolution; *Hair*; Hairstyles, Twentieth-Century; Hippies; Middle Ages; Politics and Hair; Punk; Puritans; Religion and Hair

CRABS

See Lice, Pubic

CRADLE CAP

See Dandruff

CREW CUT

The crew cut, a closely cropped hairstyle for men, became popular during the twentieth century, especially during the 1950s. This hairstyle got its name when it was adopted by American men who were members of Ivy League college rowing teams (called crews). It sometimes also is called a short taper haircut.

The typical American crew cut is short over most of the head, but the hair growing across the forehead is left up to one-inch long and can be combed or brushed to the side. Versions called a "Harvard Clip" and a "Princeton" feature slightly longer hair on top that is combed to the side. The back and sides also may be slightly longer so they can be tapered and shaped. Outside the United States, crew cuts are generally the same length all over the head—about one-quarter of an inch.

During World War II, men in the **military** wore crew cuts because they were easier to maintain and keep clean than longer styles. By 1950, the crew cut had become the mainstream fashion for civilians, as well as military men. It was regarded as a hairstyle that showed its wearer was clean cut, athletic, and patriotic.

During the late 1950s and early 1960s, the crew cut spread to Great Britain where it became popular among young men. Since then, it has been revived with slight variations during the late 1970s and early 1980s. A version called a flattop was worn in the 1980s.

Another hairstyle called the "butch" or burr cut is slightly different than the crew cut. The hair all over the head is cut very short, no more than one-eighth of an inch long.

See also: Hairstyles, Twentieth-Century; Shaving

Further Reading: Corson, Richard, *Fashions in Hair: The First Five Thousand Years* (2001); Severn, Bill, *The Long and Short of It: Five Thousand Years of Fun and Fury Over Hair* (1971); Trusty, L. Sherman, *The Art and Science of Barbering* (1956).

CRIME *See* Hair Analysis

D

DANDRUFF

Dandruff (*pityriasis capitis*) is a common scalp condition that results from shedding large numbers of dead cells from the scalp. On a normal scalp, dead skin cells are shed from the skin about once a month, a process that helps to remove dead cells from the scalp. However, when cells are shed more rapidly—for example, weekly or even more often—they tend to accumulate and become more noticeable. Dry white flakes fall from small, round patches of gray-white patches on the scalp. Scaling patches are most commonly found on top of the scalp but can occur in any hair-bearing area. This scaling may be accompanied by itching.

A severe form of dandruff is called seborrheic dermatitis, or seborrhea. Redness and itching accompany the shedding of dead cells, which appear as greasy yellow flakes. Seborrhea may occur around the eyebrow areas and the folds of the nose, as well as on the scalp. Cold, dry air and indoor heating in the fall and winter months seem to aggravate the condition. Other problems, such as infection, can occur if a person scratches the scalp so much that the skin breaks, allowing infectious organisms to enter.

When seborrhea occurs on the head of an infant, it is called "cradle cap." This condition, which is fairly common, may result from overactive sebaceous glands, which cause dead cells to accumulate as a greasy yellow substance on the scalp. Cradle cap usually appears within six weeks after birth. It is treated with a combination of mild shampooing and soft brushing of the scalp. For a severe condition, doctors also may prescribe a medicated cream.

Cradle cap usually disappears by itself, but in some babies, it persists for six to nine months after birth.

Scientists have studied possible causes of dandruff. Dandruff may commence after puberty begins, so sex hormones seem to play a role. Other theories blame a flaky scalp on shampooing too frequently or too infrequently, inadequate rinsing, or the use of harsh products, hair coloring products, or treatments that overheat the scalp. Some theories hold that excessive stress and anxiety and food allergies can cause or aggravate dandruff. If flaking is seasonal, or if it stops as a result of effective cleansing with products that don't irritate the scalp or leave a residue, then it may not be true dandruff. Instead, it may be a dandruff-like condition.

Recent research says that true dandruff is caused by a fungus called *Pityrosporum ovale*, which has been renamed *Malassezia furfur*. These fungi are present in everyone's body but normally occur in low numbers. They thrive on sebum, an oily secretion produced by the sebaceous glands on the scalp. Sebum may increase when a person eats a diet high in saturated fats and trans-fatty oils, which can, in turn, lead to an overgrowth of the fungus. Some people also inherit overactive sebaceous glands.

To control mild dandruff, people use special shampoos, conditioners, or scalp treatments. Some people control dandruff by shampooing their hair more often or by using shampoo or treatment that removes excess oil without drying the scalp.

Shampoos especially formulated to fight dandruff may contain one or more of these ingredients: sulfur, selenium sulfide, zinc pyrithione, alpha hydroxy acids, resorcinol, salicylic acid, and coal tar. Coal tar and other agents with a cytostatic action aim to slow the rate at which the cells on the top layer of the scalp grow and multiply. Alpha hydroxy acids and salicyclic acid help to exfoliate—remove dead cells. Selenium sulfide, zinc pyrithione, ketoconazole, sulfur, and resorcinol have anti-fungal properties, which will address the source of the problem. Some physicians prescribe anti-fungal ointments that are applied directly to the scalp. People also have used tea tree oil, a plant substance that has anti-fungal properties, or cider vinegar, either alone or mixed with water to deal with dandruff. Nutritional supplements, including kelp, B vitamins, Vitamin A, lecithin, salmon oil, and primrose oil, have also been recommended as nutritional methods to fight dandruff.

See also: Dermatology; Seborrheic Dermatitis; Shampoo; Tonics, Hair

Further Reading: American Academy of Pediatrics, *Caring for Your Baby and Young Child, Birth to Age 5* (1998); Baran, Robert, and Howard I. Maibach, eds., *Textbook of Cosmetic Dermatology* (1998); Baumann, Leslie, *Cosmetic Dermatology: Principles and Practice* (2002); Begoun, Paula, *Don't Go Shopping for Hair Care Products Without Me* (1997); Shai, Avi, Robert Baran, and Howard I. Maibach, *Handbook of Cosmetic Skin Care* (2002).

DERMATOLOGY

Dermatology is the branch of medicine that deals with conditions affecting the hair and skin. Medical doctors who specialize in dermatology may meet special qualifications in order to be certified by the American Academy of Dermatology, which was founded in 1938.

Dermatologists treat diseases of the scalp and offer help to people suffering from hair loss. These interventions may involve information about lifestyle changes to enhance hair health, medications, and/or surgical treatments. People with skin infections, including those that result from infected hair follicles, may consult a dermatologist. Some dermatologists perform cosmetic procedures relating to hair on the scalp and body. These include laser hair removal and hair transplants.

See also: Allergic Reactions; Alopecia Areata; Folliculitis; Hair Loss; Hair Removal; Hair Transplant; Trichology

Further Reading: American Academy of Dermatology, available online at http://www.aad.org; Baran, Robert, and Howard I. Maibach, eds., *Textbook of Cosmetic Dermatology* (1998); Baumann, Leslie, *Cosmetic Dermatology: Principles and Practice* (2002); Fitzpatrick, Thomas B., *Color Atlas & Synopsis of Clinical Dermatology* (2000).

DESSANGE, JACQUES (1928–)

Jacques Dessange is an internationally known hairstylist and founder of a company that sells his high-end hair care products. Born in Sologne, France, Jacques Dessange learned the art of hairdressing working with his barber father.

At age sixteen, he moved to Paris where he worked first in a barbershop and then moved on to prestigious salons, including the famous Louis Gervais salon, to develop his skills in women's hairdressing. Dessange began to attract celebrity clients who wanted the "tousled hair" styles that became his trademark. Dessange disliked the stiff, sprayed styles that were popular in the 1950s.

He opened his own salon on the posh Champs-Elysees in 1956. His fame spread as actresses Brigitte Bardot and Jane Fonda appeared with hairstyles that the press described as sexy and loosely styled and Dessange characterized as feminine and natural. For Bardot, he created a soft chignon with strands hanging free that became known as the *choucroute*, while Fonda wore a style with tumbling curls. Dessange also made several blond **wigs and hairpieces** for Bardot.

At age forty, Dessange ended his hairdressing career to focus on managing his salon business and developing his Phytodess hair care line. In 1977, the salon business was franchised and Dessange salons were developed around the world. As of 2003, the franchise had grown from 53 salons in 1980 to a total of 222 salons in France and 293 salons in over 39 countries, as well as 108 Dessange beauty institutes for educating new operators. A lower-priced chain of salons in western Europe, Camille Albane, was also part of the business. With sales exceeding $400 million, Dessange was one of the largest salon franchises in the world as of 2005 when the number of salons had surpassed 880. Dessange also marked his fifteenth year as the official hairstylist at the Cannes Film Festival in France.

Dessange salons advertise their focus on the "whole person" and offer clients a full range of hair care services, along with manicures, pedicures, makeup, waxing, permanent makeup, and skin treatments for face and body. Some famous Dessange clients include actors Brad Pitt, Kevin Costner, Julia Ormond, and Catherine Zeta-Jones.

See also: Hairdressing; Salons, Hair and Beauty

Further Reading: Dessange, Jacques, "Hair Care Products" and "History," available online at www.jacquesdessange.com; McGinnis, Laura, "Direct From Paris," *The Prague Post*, April 7, 2005, http://www.praguepost.com/P03/2005/spsect/0407/sp4.php.

DIAL CORPORATION

Based in Scottsdale, Arizona, Dial Corporation, which specializes in soap products for laundry and personal hygiene, is one of the largest multinational companies selling hair care products to consumers. In 1990, for the first time, Dial's revenues from consumer products exceeded $1 billion.

One branch of the company originated as Armour and Company in the 1860s after Philip Danforth Armour began producing and selling canned meats to people traveling to California during the Gold Rush. During the 1880s, Dial began marketing its soap products. By the 1950s, Dial was selling an array of cleaning products for the home, as well as its signature bar soap, which became the nation's bestselling antibacterial brand. In 1964, the company opened the world's largest and most modern soap-making facility in Montgomery, Illinois.

Dial became a larger and more diversified company after it bought Armour and Company in 1973, and again after purchasing the Breck shampoo brand and other hair care lines from American Cyanamid in 1990. Personal care products became a major source of Dial's revenues.

In 1996, the company was divided into two independent units, and the consumer products division was named The Dial Corporation. Two years later, Dial bought the Sarah Michaels and Freeman Cosmetics brands (later sold to the Hathi Group in Chicago in 2001). Known for natural products, Freeman was founded in 1976. It was the first company to use amino acids and proteins in its products, followed by botanical ingredients, including avocado, cucumber, orange, papaya, and oatmeal, in a line that now includes shampoos, conditioners, hairspray, gel, straightening balm, curl enhancer, and styling cream.

In 2000, Dial acquired the Plusbelle Company, Argentina's leading volume seller of hair care products.

In 2001, the company joined with The Himmel Group of New York to reintroduce Breck shampoo. Between 1936 and the 1980s, Breck was one of the top-selling shampoos in the United States. Since 1995, the shampoo had been sold primarily in Mexico. Dial Corporation also markets a body wash that can also be used for the hair.

In 2004, Dial became a wholly owned subsidiary of the **Henkel Group**, a multinational corporation based in Germany. Henkel's product lines include cosmetics and toiletries, adhesives, household detergents and cleansers, oleochemicals, and industrial and institutional hygienics.

See also: Breck Girl; Henkel Group; Natural Products; Shampoo

Further Reading: Dial Corporation History, available online at www.dialcorp.com; "Henkel to Acquire Dial," Press Release, available online at http://www.henkel.de/int_henkel/channelpress/channel/index.cfm?channel=281%2CPR_2003&picture=157&nav=281&base=2&pageid=281.

DIANA, PRINCESS OF WALES (1961–1997)

As Britain's Princess of Wales, the former Lady Diana Spencer influenced fashions in hairstyles and clothing. Known for her beauty and sense of style, the princess was widely loved for her warm personality and humanitarian efforts, including work on behalf of AIDS victims and the campaign against landmines.

Nineteen-year-old Lady Diana Spencer first gained international attention in 1981 when she became engaged to marry Prince Charles, heir to the British throne. During the engagement period and subsequent wedding that July, Diana was photographed numerous times and people noted every detail of her appearance. Her hairstylist was Kevin Shanley of the salon Head Lines, located in the Chelsea section of London. Before her engagement, Diana had been wearing a short, rather flat hairstyle that framed her face and showed part of her ears, with thick bangs across the right side of her forehead. Working with Shanley, she developed a fuller hairstyle, and he gave her light brown hair blond "multi-highlights" so that she was much blonder by the time of her wedding.

As Princess of Wales, Diana maintained a similar style but did grow her hair several inches longer, which gave it more volume and enabled her to vary the style to create waves and curls that complemented her clothing and headgear. Princess Diana experimented with variations on her "look," including sleeker hairstyles without bangs, but she consistently returned to her signature style. It was widely copied by women the world over.

Her hair often was a focal point of her appearance, because Princess Diana often wore hats or jeweled tiaras during her public appearances. She wore a variety of hats, including pillboxes, berets, boaters, and hats with veils and brims. Her signature hairstyle also worked well with Diana's earring collection, including valuable pieces made with pearls, diamonds, sapphires, rubies, or emeralds, often in the form of drop earrings.

Fashion and beauty writers chronicled the princess's trendsetting styles, noting any change in hairdos, and she was probably the most photographed woman of the twentieth century. Commentators said that Diana proved short hair can be elegant and regal while also looking modern and youthful.

During her marriage, Princess Diana gave birth to two sons, William and Harry, and was widely admired for her devotion to motherhood and her public duties and charitable projects. After her divorce from Prince Charles in 1996, she continued with her public appearances and work on behalf of various charities and organizations. She was known as a staunch advocate for people suffering from AIDS, homelessness, and landmine injuries. Diana Princess of Wales died in August 1997 after a car crash in Paris, France.

See also: Hairstyles, Twentieth-Century

Further Reading: James, Sue, *The Diana Look* (1984); Janaway, Alison, *Diana, Her Latest Fashions* (1984); Time, Inc., "Princess Diana," *Unforgettable Women of the Twentieth Century* (New York: Time, Inc., 1998).

DISEASES OF THE SCALP *See* Dandruff; Dermatology; Folliculitis; Lice, Head; Pityriasis amiantacea; Seborrheic dermatitis; Tinea Capitus; Trichology

DNA ANALYSIS *See* Hair Analysis

DREDLOCKS (also Dreadlocks; Dredlocs; Locs)

The word dredlocks refers to hair with a "nappy" texture that is allowed to grow naturally and is left uncombed so that it forms tight rope-like locks. The name may have emerged in the days of slavery. Authors Ayana D. Byrd and Lori L. Tharps write that when whites saw Africans who had spent months trapped in slave ships, they said that their matty, uncombed hair looked "dreadful." In recent decades, some people have come to prefer spelling dredlock without the "A" to avoid the negative connotation.

Today, some people adopt this hairstyle on purpose, but "informal" dredlocks also have occurred since ancient times. In places where people lacked the tools or methods to groom their hair, it could become matted or tangled in clumps. More recently, dredlocks have been associated with political and/or spiritual beliefs.

Some Biblical scholars believe that John the Baptist and Samson wore their hair this way. People in ancient Asia wore dredlocks. They include Hindu holy men called *sadhus*, who are mentioned in the Veda, writings from India that date back to 1800 BCE. Dredlocks also were found among the ancient Egyptians. A picture of the Egyptian King Tut shows a hairstyle that looks like dredlocks. Other people who wore similar styles include ancient Germanic peoples, Pacific islanders, and the Naga Indians.

Men and women in various African tribes, including the Masai of Kenya, created various forms of dredlocks. Before the fifth century BCE, priests of the Ethiopian Coptic religion adopted dredlock hairstyles. Many Kenyan warriors adopted the style, which they embellished by dying their locks red with root extracts. During the 1950 rebellion against the British in Kenya, Kikuya soldiers wore dredlocks and their valiant fight later inspired Rastafarians to adopt the style.

Jamaica and Rastafarians

Dredlocks are often associated with the Caribbean island of Jamaica, during the 1940s and 1950s when Jamaica was fighting for full independence from British rule. Former slaves wore their hair this way to show their rejection of the European ways they were forced to endure under Spanish and British colonial rulers.

Dredlocks also are associated with the Afro-Caribbean religion Rastafari, which spread in Jamaica during the 1950s. The religion takes its name from Ras Tafari, the name by which Haile Selassie ruled Ethiopia as regent and crown prince between 1916 and 1928. Selassie became king in 1928 and emperor in 1930. Dredlocks also resemble the mane on the Lion of Judah, which is a Rastafarian symbol and also one of the titles given to Ethiopian kings.

Rastafarians wear dredlocks to comply with the Nazarite Vow, which is drawn from Leviticus 21:5 in the Old Testament: "They shall not make baldness upon their head, neither shall they shave off the corner of their beard nor make any cuttings in their flesh." The Rastafarians also looked to the words of Numbers 6:5: "All the days of the vow of separation, no razor shall pass over his head. Until the day be fulfilled of his consecration to the Lord, he shall be holy, and shall let the hair of his head grow." Many Rastafarians wear beards and most are vegetarian, in keeping with their beliefs that life should be lived as naturally as possible. In adopting dredlocks, they let this hairstyle develop naturally over a period of time. Since the hair was not combed, it became twisted and matted.

Because the Bible also refers to the seven "locks" of Samson, many Rastafarians believe that their hair symbolizes strength. It reflects courage in the face of oppression during the times when Jamaican officials arrested Rastafarians and cut off their hair as a form of punishment. The colonial government regarded dredlocks as a sign of rebellion against their authority. People who wore dredlocks risked being expelled from school or fired from their jobs, among other penalties. To escape this fate, many early Rastafarians moved to the remote bush areas of Jamaica.

Into the Mainstream

The person who did the most to popularize dredlocks worldwide was Jamaican Rastafarian musician Bob Marley (b. Robert Nesta Marley), along with his group The Wailers. Their *Natty Dread* album became a hit during the mid-1970s, and people throughout the world saw the hairstyle on album covers and in reggae concerts. Marley was known throughout the world as the "king of reggae."

Other groups have adopted dredlocks for nonreligious reasons, as part of a "back-to-nature" philosophy, or to support African traditions.

By the mid-1970s, young white Londoners of both genders were wearing them. During the 1980s, some American and British fans of funk, soul, and hip-hop music adopted forms of dredlocks. People varied their look by dying all or part of their hair red with henna.

Whites who wanted this hairstyle usually had to work to get dredlocks. A London hairdresser named Simon Forbes devised dredlocks and extensions for Caucasian hair. Forbes said that dredlocks looked powerful and soft at the same time and were more flattering than braids. He styled the hair of some pop musicians, including Pete Burns and his group, Dead Or Alive.

In 1986, a salon in south London called Back to Eden became the first salon in Britain to specialize in dredlocks and other "natural" hairdos. During the 1980s, the musical group Soul II Soul, also called the Funki Dreds, wore "neat" dredlocks and opened a shop to sell clothing and accessories with their Funki Dred logo. People of different races wore variations, including more stylized dredlocks, which they then maintained with salon visits. The hairstyle was seen on people wearing business suits or various professional uniforms, as well as performers, writers, and artists. Actress Whoopi Goldberg and singer Tracy Chapman are among the celebrities who have worn dredlocks. Other performers known for their dredlocks include singers Erykah Badu and Lauryn Hill.

Writers also discussed their "locks." Novelist and poet Alice Walker wrote an essay about the liberated feeling she had during the years she allowed her hair to fall naturally without combing it out. British poet Dorothea Smart, who wore dredlocks for eighteen years, said that she felt proud and powerful from connecting with her African heritage through this hairstyle.

Today, dredlocks are worn in various parts of the world for different reasons (e.g., religious beliefs, tradition, personal preference). People who wear dredlocks include people in India (holy men called Sadhus); various people in Africa (Bahatowie priests in Ethiopia, the Himba peoples of Namibia and Angola, the Somali, the Galla, the Ibo of Nigeria, the Maasai, the Mau Mau, the Kau, the Ashanti, the Fulani); the Maori of Australia; the Rasto-Buddhists of Japan; and indigenous people in New Guinea. Whites who wear them, usually younger people, may do so as a form of rebellion. They often refer to their hairstyle as "dreds," whereas black people are more likely to call theirs "locs." Rastafarians are not obligated to wear this hairstyle but many choose to do so.

During the 1990s, members of prominent rock groups wore dredlocks, and more people asked hairstylists to create this look for them. New versions of dredlocks emerged, along with the "dred perm." Some people added bright colors to their hair.

At the Spring/Summer 2000 fashion collections in New York and Paris, some runway models wore dredlocks. Models for the Dior collection appeared in elaborate hairdos that included pins, ties, scarves, and dredlock hairpieces in different colors. Companies offered special waxes, shampoos, and jewelry to care for and adorn dredlocks.

For some people, however, wearing dredlocks brought unwelcome attention. Certain private schools banned the hairstyle and people in certain jobs may feel pressure to wear more mainstream or conservative styles in order to avoid conflicts in their workplace.

See also: Africa; African Americans; Laws and Regulations; Politics and Hair; Religion and Hair

Further Reading: Byrd, Ayana D., and Lori L. Tharps, *Hair Story: Untangling the Roots of Black Hair in America* (2002); Chevannes, Barry, *Rastafari: Roots and Ideology* (1994); Evans, Neckhana, *Hairlocking: Everything You Need to Know: Africa, Dread, and Nubian Locks* (1999); Johnson, Wanda, and Barbara Lawson, illus., *The Art of Locks* (1991); Mastalia, Francesco, and Alfonse Pagano, *Dreads* (1999).

DUCKTAIL *See* Hairstyles, Twentieth-Century

E

EBER, JOSE (ca. 1945–)

Called the "Stylist to the Stars," Jose (Joe-say) Eber gained celebrity status in the 1970s for his trendsetting designs. Eber became one of the world's best-known stylists and founded a chain of salons that bear his name.

Eber was born in Nice, France, and during his youth, he enjoyed styling his mother's and sister's hair. By age fifteen, he was working as an apprentice at a prestigious salon in Paris. As Eber developed his expertise and distinctive styling techniques, more and more clients at the salon began to request his services.

At age twenty-six, Eber visited the United States and decided to move to Los Angeles, where he worked at a salon in Beverly Hills before opening his own salon. Jose Eber created individualized styles for his clients, who soon included the rich and famous. Celebrities came to the Maurice/Jose salon for a new look that rejected the stiff, sprayed, structured hairdos that were typical in that era. Instead, Eber created loose, free styles that people called "sexy" and "touchable." He also encouraged women to find hairstyles that suited their lifestyles and were not difficult to maintain.

Eber gained increasing recognition during the late 1970s when he styled the hair of **Farrah Fawcett**. Fawcett's long, feathered mane of blond-streaked hair sparked an international trend after she became an international celebrity starring in the hit television series, *Charlie's Angels*. Eber's other celebrity clients included actress Elizabeth Taylor, singer/actress Cher, and television journalist Barbara Walters. Eber became a popular guest on television talk shows, where he did hair "makeovers." He continued to style the hair of celebrities for their appearances on television or at the Academy Awards, Emmy Awards, and other important ceremonies.

In 1982, Eber's first book *Shake Your Head, Darling!* was published. Eber described his approach to hairstyling, depending on a woman's hair traits, facial features, and lifestyle. He shared his techniques, using photographs of celebrity clients. Eber also made a popular home video that demonstrated his styling secrets. The year 1990 saw the publication of a second book, *Jose Eber: Beyond Hair, The Ultimate Makeover Book*.

During the 1980s, Eber introduced his "Secret Hair" human hair extensions, which can be added to a woman's own hair to add volume and styling options. Eber made a television infomercial to promote the "Secret Hair" line, which was also sold at his salons.

In addition, Eber is known for his charitable activities and philanthropy. He gives time and money to AmFar, an AIDS foundation, and to organizations that assist female victims of domestic violence. Eber also performs free makeovers for battered women to enhance their self-esteem and help them begin new lives.

Along with his original salon on Rodeo Drive, Eber opened nine others. Three are located in California (Palm Desert, Costa Mesa, and Carlsbad Canyon), while four are in Texas (Houston, Dallas, Austin, and Plano). The others are in White Plains, New York, and Bel Harbour, Florida.

See also: Advertising; Fawcett, Farrah; Wigs and Hairpieces

Further Reading: Eber, Jose, *Beyond Hair, The Ultimate Makeover Book* (1990); Eber, Jose, *Shake Your Head, Darling!* (1982); Shelton, Karen M., "Jose Eber: The Messenger of Love & Beauty," Interview, HairBoutique.com, April 3, 2003, available online at http://www.hairboutique.com/tips/tip3530.htm.

EGYPT, ANCIENT

Archaeological discoveries and tombs show that ancient Egyptians devoted special attention to their appearance, especially their hair. Favorable images of hairdressers are depicted on pottery and ancient works on art, and poems include romantic references to hair, which was considered sacred.

After the death of a loved one, ancient Egyptians expressed feelings of grief by tearing out their hair. Old images of funerals show mourners wailing as they pull out hair. During times of **mourning**, it also was customary to grow the hair and beard and to abandon regular grooming routines. At other times, these hairs were shaved or cut short. By ignoring their appearance, mourners showed members of the community that they were too distraught to care about such matters.

Texts dating back to 2000 BCE provide information about ancient grooming practices. They contain "recipes" that show the Egyptians used wet chemistry techniques to produce hair preparations, including a supposed "cure" for baldness. Gravesites provide still more information, since wealthy Egyptians buried cosmetics and grooming implements with the mummified bodies of their dead, believing that they would need these items in the afterlife.

People in ancient Egypt used combs, pins, ointments, and other tools and preparations to groom and style their hair. They wore wigs, ornaments, and **false beards**, often curled or braided. Some grooming practices were meant to beautify and scent the hair, while others helped to protect the hair and scalp from the intense sunlight in that region. Hair was also a means to "communicate." The cut and style correlated with a person's age, gender, occupation, and social status.

Cleansing and fragrance

Historians are not sure exactly how the Egyptians washed their hair, though it seems clear that they did cleanse both their natural hair and their wigs. Oils from plants, such as almond, olive, sesame, and palm, were used to make hair care products. One form of hair cleanser was made from water and citrus juice, and conditioners were made with plant oils and animal fats. To set their hairstyles, Egyptians applied beeswax, then let the wax set under sunlight until the style hardened.

Statue of Nefertiti, queen of Egypt, fourteenth century BC. *Library of Congress*

Hair and wigs were scented with special oils made from flowers, resins, and spices mixed with fats. Chips from the cinnamon twig also were used. For special occasions, women wore an aromatic cone of scented fat on their heads. As the evening proceeded, heat from their heads disseminated the fragrance.

Hair Care Services

Caring for hair and beards was a specialized occupation. Images of hairdressers can be found on ancient Egyptian urns, coffins, and fresco paintings. The Egyptians also had a "barber god" among their deities.

Wealthy people had **barbers** among their household staff or they relied on a personal barber who visited their home each day. Egyptian rulers had servants to care for their hair, just as they had servants to help with other aspects of their personal grooming. During the Old Kingdom era, royal servants included a personal barber and a team of wig makers, including a superintendent of wig makers and an upper and lower "wig maker of the king." The wig makers also were known as the "keepers of the diadem." Later, the person at court who filled the top position was called the "superintendent of the royal fillet."

Poorer people used the services of traveling barbers. These men moved from place to place, setting out their equipment and a stool for the customer outdoors under shady trees.

Facial and Body Hair

With the exception of the Old Kingdom period (2705–2213 BCE), Egyptian men removed all their facial hair. Statues from that era show that men wore very thin mustaches. Upper-class Egyptians often removed all their body hair, which also helped to prevent lice and other parasites. Priests were required to shave their heads and their entire bodies to remove all hairs, including eyebrows and eyelashes, as a form of religious purification. No hair of any kind was permitted in religious temples, not even any objects made from animal hairs.

Methods of **hair removal** included pumice stone, preparations made with sugar or beeswax, razors, and tweezers. The Egyptians made a kind of depilatory by mixing lime, starch, and arsenic. Their metal tweezers resembled those used today. The earliest shaving blades were made from stone; then copper was used until a form of hardened bronze became available during the Middle Kingdom era. Ancient Egyptian razors resembled surgical knives.

Hairstyles and Wigs

During the Early Kingdom period, Egyptians wore their hair fairly close to the head in simple styles. Blunt-cut hair, reaching from about the chin to below the shoulder, with straight-cut bangs, was the most common style. The Egyptians preferred thick hair, and the upper classes wore more elaborate styles than the lower classes. Workmen wore their hair cut short, with bangs, in a rounded shape around the head. Some men wore their hair longer and tucked it behind their ears. Women wore longer hair than men, sometimes falling a foot or more below their shoulders down the back. Most women wore bangs, and many preferred a center part.

Nearly every adult Egyptian, both men and women, wore some kind of false hair, including extensions and wigs. Wigs were worn as an adornment and to provide sun protection. Older people wore wigs to disguise baldness or gray hair.

Wigs usually were made in three sections, with one on either side of the chest and the third falling down the back. Women's wigs tended to be larger and longer than men's. Barbers and women who had learned the craft served as wig makers. The most costly wigs were made from human hair or the wool of black sheep, or some combination of both. Less expensive wigs were made from horse hair or plant fibers.

For many centuries, black and red were the preferred colors for hair, whether real or false, and for beards.

Henna, which comes from the dried leaves of the *Lawsonia inermis* plant, was used to dye hair various shades of orange-red. Cow's blood and crushed tadpoles, sometimes mixed with henna, were used to make different shades. Indigo was used to make black dye. After about 1150 BCE, however, people began wearing wigs in brighter hues, including vivid reds, greens, and blues.

After about 3000 BCE, Egyptian men favored a clean-shaven head or closely cropped hair, covered with a wig, but they did not pretend the wig was real hair. It was customary to allow part of their natural hairline to show at the sides or top of the wig. Ivory or metal hairpins or linen bands were sometimes used to hold the hair in place. People who could not afford a wig used hair extensions to add volume to their own short hair.

Children had their own distinctive hairstyles. During some periods, young girls wore their hair in a ponytail. The hair of male children was shaved off except for a small area on the top that was allowed to grow. Girls had hair cut to about mid-neck length, but also with one long lock left hanging. This strand—called the "Lock of Youth"—was often braided into a few sections that were then bunched together. During the New Kingdom, royal princes no longer wore this lock; instead, they wore a fringed band on their heads as a sign of their status. Ornaments for children's hair sometimes featured the image of fish, which may have been a good luck charm to protect them from dangers of the Nile River. At puberty, Egyptian boys and girls began to wear adult hairstyles.

More elaborate hairstyles prevailed during the New Kingdom period (1539–30 BCE). Hair was grown longer and arranged in styles with curls and plaits (form of braid). Some men wore their hair angled from the nape of the neck so that it hung longer in the front, just below the shoulders. Only queens and noble women were allowed to wear a style called the goddress, in which the hair was divided into three distinctive segments.

Grooming Tools and Hair Accessories

Wealthy Egyptians owned ornate cases in which to store or carry hair care lotions and implements. These tools included combs made from wood or ivory, hairpins, scissors, and hair removal devices.

For special occasions, people adorned their wigs with beads and other ornaments. Wealthier people could afford ornaments made from precious metals and gemstones, including garnets, turquoise, and malachite. People who could not afford such finery used berries, flowers, and inexpensive beads.

Headgear included ribbons, fillets, and diadems. Ribbons woven from linen cloth were tied around the head into a bow. Circular bands called fillets, made of leather or gold, were worn during the end of the Early Kingdom. Flowers, such as lotus buds, might be worn at banquets.

By the Middle Kingdom era, ornate diadems were created from precious metals, studded with gemstones, including carnelian, lapis lazuli, and turquoise. Craftsmen made floral designs or snakes and other symbolic objects. Both women and men wore diadems, and a gold diadem was found in the tomb of King Tutankhamen. Diadems could be large and elaborate, with trimmings that fell below the shoulders. Some headdresses featured rows of gold rosettes.

Modern Revival

Hairstyles, eye makeup, and grooming practices from ancient Egypt have been revived in modern times. In 1962, the release of a major feature film, *Cleopatra*, starring Elizabeth Taylor in the title role, brought renewed interest in these styles. Cleopatra, who reigned as Egypt's queen from 51 to 30 BCE, was renowned for her beauty, political skills, and intelligence. One of her most famous lovers, Roman emperor Julius Caesar, had a golden statue of Cleopatra erected in her honor and placed inside the Temple of Venus in Rome.

See also: Beards, Men's; Body Hair; False Beard; Hair Colorants; Religion and Hair; Shaving; Wigs and Hairpieces

Further Reading: Alexander, Paul J., *The Ancient World: To 300 A.D.* (1963); Breasted, James Henry, *Ancient Times: A History of the Ancient World* (1944); Brier, Bob, and Hoyt Hobbs, *Daily Life of the Ancient Egyptians* (1999); Granger-Taylor, Hero, *The British Museum Book of Ancient Egypt* (1992); Strouhal, Eugen, *Life of the Ancient Egyptians* (1992).

ELECTROLYSIS *See* Hair Removal

ELIZABETHAN ERA

The reign of **Elizabeth I** (1558–1603) was characterized by lavish attention to hair care and personal appearance. English men and women, particularly courtiers and members of the upper classes, followed trends in hairstyles and personal grooming that were strongly influenced by the queen.

One major trend for women was to show more hair. During the 1500s, the hoods that women wore to conceal most of their hair grew smaller in size. Short bangs became more popular, usually worn in a frizzed style high on the forehead.

Since Elizabeth had a distinctive reddish-gold hair color, these shades became especially popular. Some women dyed their hair or wore hairpieces or full wigs in red shades. One type of hair dye and conditioner was made from a mixture that contained rhubarb juice and oil of vitriol (sulfuric acid). Since vitriol was a corrosive agent, the use of this product could cause hair loss. Other dyes also contained corrosive ingredients that damaged both the scalp and hair. Hair lightening liquids made with sulfuric acid often caused the hair to fall out.

In Elizabethan England, modern shampoo was not available and most people did not bathe regularly. They cleansed their hair dry by combing it with a fine-textured clay powder that absorbed excess oil and dirt. Decorative hair powders were popular and women chose their powders according to their hair color. Those with light or gray hair used white powder or flour, while dark-haired women applied violet powder.

A high forehead was in style, partly because women's hairlines receded when they used caustic chemicals on their hair and faces. To whiten their complexion, women used a cosmetic paste called ceruse, which contained lead. This toxic metal caused hair loss, as well as long-term skin damage and other health problems. To dramatize their fashionably high foreheads, women preferred light or nonexistent eyebrows.

Hair accessories included feathers, jewels, and various kinds of nets and bags. Women used hairpins or gums to hold their hairstyle in place, or they secured their hair with metal hoops. If they could afford them, women bundled the hair at the back of their neck into a net made from silk threads, sometimes trimmed with jewels or gold. Women of lesser means wore a less expensive crepe net or simple cloth bag. Hair was either plaited or left loose and then put into the bag.

People who did not like the look of a bald head or sparse hair used wigs and/or hairpieces. Bald men usually wore light-colored wigs.

Elizabethan **barbers** created styles in which hair was perfumed, waxed, powdered, and/or starched to make it stiffer. Some men wore their shoulder length hair in "lovelocks"—curls created with hot irons. The lovelock, or "love-locke," originated in France in the 1590s. They also wore beards, which they would comb themselves or have trimmed by a barber.

See also: Elizabeth I; Eyebrows; Hair Color; Hair Colorants; Renaissance Europe; Wigs and Hairpieces

Further Reading: Corson, Richard, *Fashions in Hair* (1965); Turudich, Daniela, and Laurie G. Welch, *Plucked, Shaved, and Braided* (2004); Weir, Alison, *The Life of Elizabeth I* (1998).

ELIZABETH I (1533–1603)

During her long reign as Queen of England, Elizabeth I influenced hairstyles, as well as fashions in clothing and beauty. The queen had a strong interest in her appearance and was eager to try new beauty products and techniques, including those from other countries. After Elizabeth ascended the throne, it became much more common for British women to use hair dyes, cosmetics, and perfumes.

The daughter of Henry VIII and his second wife Anne Boleyn, Elizabeth was crowned queen in 1558 at age twenty-five. In her coronation portraits, she is shown with her hair hanging loose down around her shoulders, a style associated with youth.

From her Tudor ancestry, the queen inherited reddish-gold hair, and many of her subjects imitated this color. Ladies at court used dyes made from French recipes that included lixivium, a type of chalk, or Italian dyes made from plants and herbs. Some red hair dyes contained lead, sulfur, and quicklime. To show their esteem for the queen, some male subjects used red-gold dye on their beards. Queen Elizabeth even had the tails of her horses dyed in orange tones that matched her wigs.

Queen Elizabeth I. *Library of Congress*

Like other sixteenth-century European women, young Elizabeth had long hair, which she wore in various upswept styles held in place with pins, then covered with a "coif" or other cloth cap. Besides wearing crowns and tiaras, the queen frequently adorned her head with jeweled ornaments from her vast collection. One famous portrait shows her with a circle of pearls around the forehead. She also decorated her hair with garlands. As she aged, Elizabeth continued to wear sections of hair loose on various occasions, though she was no longer a young girl. She also began wearing blond wigs in her later years.

Legends sprang up about the queen's vanity. It was said that the queen had her hair cut short after being disappointed in love and then decided she would never marry. Other stories claimed that Elizabeth often wondered how she compared to other women, especially her cousin and arch-rival for the British throne, Mary Stuart, Queen of Scots. She asked people who knew Mary whether her cousin's hair (also reddish in color) was finer than her own, or whether Mary's skin was more fair.

Called the "Virgin Queen" because she remained unwed, an aging Elizabeth concealed her balding head with a curly red wig. She usually wore wigs with tight curls, but some of them featured large curls hanging down each side of the face to her shoulder. Historians estimate that Elizabeth I owned approximately eighty wigs, all made from expensive imported hair. As a result, wigs became much more popular in England during her reign.

See also: Beards, Men's; Elizabethan Era; Eyebrows; Hair Color; Hair Colorants; Mustache; Renaissance Europe; Wigs and Hairpieces

Further Reading: Jenkins, Elizabeth, *Elizabeth the Great* (1958); Smith, Lacy Baldwin, *Elizabeth Tudor: Portrait of a Queen* (1975); Weir, Alison, *The Life of Elizabeth I* (1998).

ETON CROP *See* Bob, the

EYEBROWS

Eyebrows are the short hairs that grow across the bony ridge at the top of the eye socket. Eyebrow hairs grow more slowly than scalp hair, and, compared to other hairs on the body, their growth is less influenced by hormonal changes. Eyebrow follicles are vulnerable to injury and may shrink or stop producing hairs if they are repeatedly traumatized or severely damaged.

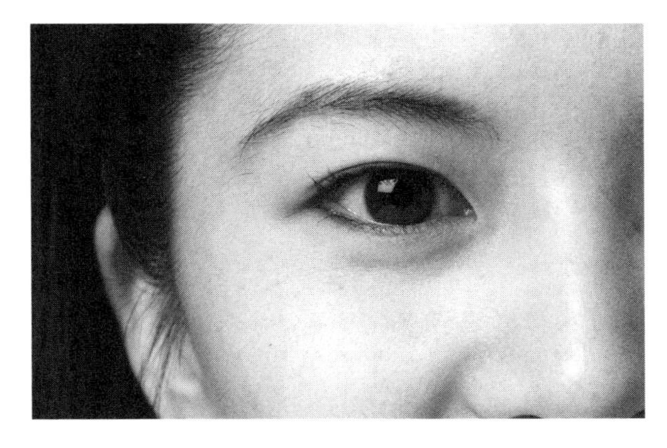

Changing styles and beauty standards have determined the preferred thickness, colors, and shapes for eyebrows, which frame the eye and play a key role in facial expression. For thousands of years, people around the world have altered the appearance of their eyebrows by removing them completely, thinning them, and/or reshaping them. They have used different cosmetics, either temporary or permanent, to make the brows look thicker, change their color, or alter their shape. False eyebrows have also been worn.

Cultures also have different attitudes about the space between the brows. In some cultures, a continuous line of hair across the bridge of the nose has been considered attractive. This once was the preferred style in some Asian countries. In other places, including most western societies, people have favored a hairless space between the brows.

Ancient styles

Color cosmetics and tools to change the appearance of the eyebrows date back thousands of years. People in **Egypt** used kohl to darken and define the eyebrows and they emphasized the area beneath the brows and the eyelids with colored eye shadows. In ancient **Greece**, women used soot—*asbokos*—or powdered antimony to darken their eyebrows. Some Greeks wore false eyebrows made from dyed goat's hair and attached them to the forehead with tree resin or natural gums. Babylonian men and women used bluish-black antimony to line and color their eyebrows and eyelashes while the ancient Celts dyed their brow hairs black with berry juice.

Women of the **Roman Empire** plucked hairs to change the shape of their eyebrows. At one time, it was stylish for **Byzantine** women to pluck the eyebrows in a straight line and then draw a black line beneath them.

When a high, bare forehead was in style, women shaved or plucked hair along their hairline and completely removed their eyebrows by plucking or shaving. Plucking all or most of the eyebrows became fashionable in Europe during the **Middle Ages**. Women in England also de-emphasized their brows during the **Elizabethan era** by plucking them into thin lines or removing them completely. One reason for the popularity of the bare forehead was that women were using corrosive hair dyes, as well as a lead-based powder called ceruse that was intended to whiten their complexions and cover blemishes. Long-term use of toxic substances damaged the skin and caused hair loss.

During the reign of Charles I (1625–1649), women were still using ceruse and the look of a high "empty" forehead with invisible eyebrows remained in style. To discourage hair growth, people rubbed walnut oil on their children's eyebrows. When this look lost favor, people began using false eyebrows made from mouse hide if their own eyebrows would not grow back.

Certain Asian cultures have emphasized the eyebrow and designed brow shapes that strongly affected facial expressions. In **Japan**, women once plucked their brows into specific designs with special names. For example, during the Heian era (794–1185 CE), men and women of noble birth plucked their eyebrows and drew new lines about one inch above the natural brow line.

In the Middle East, **China**, **India**, and other parts of Asia, eyebrows and other unwanted facial hairs were removed by "threading," a technique in which cotton thread is twisted around the hairs and turned in such a way that the hairs are secured. Then they are pulled out from the follicle. This technique still is used today for removing unwanted hairs.

Twentieth Century

Styles in brow-lines varied in western cultures during the twentieth century. Celebrities and famous beauties, as well as historical events, have influenced these changing styles.

During the 1920s, thin brows were fashionable, and more women plucked their brows into a thin line. Some historians believe that actors in silent films played a key role in influencing this look. Makeup artists strongly emphasized the eyes, since silent films relied on facial expressions to convey emotions that were not expressed through sound. Thin eyebrows could be seen more clearly on film as they moved up and down.

Brows became even thinner in western cultures during the 1930s. Prominent film stars popularized thin brows, which were sometimes drawn on after the natural brows were removed. Actress Greta Garbo plucked her brows to make a distinct arch that followed the shape of her eye socket. Marlene Dietrich eliminated her natural brows and drew a new and rather unnatural looking line above her normal brow line. Some women left a thin line of hairs while others removed all the hairs and then penciled in very thin "brows."

Some actresses preferred a thicker, more natural look. One of them was British actress Vivien Leigh. In the 1938 film classic *Gone With the Wind*, Leigh actively used her eyebrows in her role as Scarlett O'Hara. One of Scarlett's trademark behaviors was to raise just the right eyebrow.

Performers have used the appearance of their eyebrows to make a strong individual statement. For example, actor and comedian Groucho Marx used a black grease pencil to create his famous thick and expressive brows and reportedly began shaving his own brows to create entirely new ones. Actor and director Charlie Chaplin also used his mobile and prominent dark brows to convey emotions in his award-winning silent films.

Styles changed again during the 1940s, a time when many women entered the military and the workplace in order to help the war effort. Women working in factories and other jobs had less time to spend on their appearance, so brows were thicker and more natural. To many people, this "no-nonsense" look connoted the idea that women were strong and capable. Film stars of the 1940s era tended to emphasize their eyebrows and give them a distinctive shape.

The 1950s brought a wider and shallower eyebrow for women, still well-defined and often with a high arch at the center above the iris. Grooming and coloring the eyebrows took more time that it did in the 1940s. This more stylish brow was part of a "doe-eyed" look that included dark eyeliner and thick lashes, and it was regarded as highly "feminine." Actress Elizabeth Taylor's well-defined dark eyebrows were one style that other women tried to emulate. Actresses Lauren Bacall, Joan Crawford, **Audrey Hepburn**, and Sophia Loren also were known for their well-defined brows. During the 1950s, women emphasized both their lips and eyes with color and distinct lines.

During the so-called "Swinging Sixties," the eyes were a strong focus of female appearance, and women experimented with new brow-lines and creative eye makeup. A small percentage of women completely tweezed or shaved off their brows and used individual pencil strokes to draw in new ones. Some younger women painted their eyebrows with bright colors. Accessories for eyebrows included glitter, feathers, and small gems.

Women continued to try new brow designs during the 1970s. In general, brows were thinner and shorter, but thicker, darker brows also came in and out of fashion during that decade, when a healthy, natural look was in vogue.

More natural brows predominated during the 1980s, which was also a decade of "big hair." Women in the workplace were making a statement with business attire that included suit jackets with large shoulder pads. Women with thicker and more natural brows included model/actress Brooke Shields and Helena Bonham-Carter.

During the 1990s, eyebrows were not particularly thin or thick and the trend was to groom brows to suit a person's individual features. Julianna Margulies and Catherine Zeta-Jones were among the actresses admired for their brow-lines. Besides plucking, many people used waxing procedures to shape brows. People could also buy kits with eyebrow stencils in order to shape their brows at home.

Brow Specialists

By the 1980s, more makeup artists were specializing in grooming eyebrows, both for men and women. Well-known makeup artists who specialize in eyebrows include the Brazilian-born makeup artist Paulo Siqueira who has been called the "Eyebrow Guru." Actress Liv Tyler and model Naomi Campbell have worked with Siqueira.

Ramy Gafni, a New York makeup artist, is called "the king of brows." Gafni says, "There are many trends in makeup, but I think the eyebrows should be classic. I think of the eyebrow as a feature, like your nose. It shouldn't be trendy. It should be classic and flattering to your face" (Morago 2002).

Another brow expert, Victoria Gheorghias of the Frederic Fekkai salon in New York, says, "If eyes are the windows to the soul, then eyebrows are the window dressing: They can be gorgeous or they can ruin everything" (Morago 2002). She adds that most customers requested a thicker, more natural brow with a soft arch rather than thin or high penciled brows.

Two of the top eyebrow stylists in Beverly Hills, California, are Anastasia Soare, who works with actresses Renee Zellweger, Jennifer Lopez, and Julianna Margulies; and Valerie Sarnelle, who works with actresses Halle Berry, Nicole Kidman, Heather Locklear, and Goldie Hawn.

Los Angeles makeup artist Robyn Cosio's clients include actress Gina Gershon, Jamie Lee Curtis, and Joan Chen. Cosio wrote a book called *The Eyebrow* (2000) that is regarded as an authoritative guide to the history of eyebrow styles and the makeup techniques used to enhance them.

As of 2000, Americans were spending millions of dollars each year for professional eyebrow services, including eyebrow shaping and permanent makeup. They could also purchase eyebrow shaping kits in drugstores and department stores.

Current Trends

In most cultures today, people favor two distinctive eyebrows, and both men and women remove unwanted hairs between their brows. A rhyme that emerged in the twentieth century explained the need to rid the eyebrows of stray hairs between the brows: "If your eyebrows meet above your nose, you will never wear your wedding clothes." The most common methods for removing eyebrow hairs are plucking, chemical depilatories, and waxing. Electrolysis offers a permanent solution. In Asia, experts at threading continue to shape brows with this traditional method.

To define the eyebrows or alter their shape cosmetically, people can use colored eye pencils or brush-on eyebrow powders. As of 2003, 28 percent of all women were using an eyebrow pencil as part of their routine makeup.

People may also opt for permanent makeup—called dermapigmentation, or micropigmentation—as a replacement for temporary eyebrow makeup. During this process, which resembles tattooing, the operator injects colored pigments made from plant dyes to fill in the eyebrows. This gives the eyebrows a lasting and waterproof color. These kinds of procedures can be risky, leading to infections, scarring, and even blindness if they are no performed correctly. A person who lacks skill in applying permanent makeup also may produce an unnatural and/or unattractive brow line.

Brow-piercing became more popular during and after the 1980s. People wear eyebrow jewelry made from metals, gemstones, and synthetic materials. Popular designs for pierced brows include studs, barbells, rings, and one or more pieces may appear on the same brow. Usually the piercing is done on the outer edge, though some people choose to pierce the inner part of the brow.

See also: Body Hair; Elizabeth I; Flappers; Hair Removal; Kohl; Renaissance Europe; Unibrow

Further Reading: Corson, Richard, *Fashions in Makeup* (1972); Cosio, Robyn, with Cynthia Robins, *The Eyebrow* (2000); Damjanov, Milena, "Golden Arches," *TimeOutNY*, November 2, 2000, available online at http://www.timeoutny.com/checkout/267/267.checkout.html; DeCastelbajac, Kate, *The Face of the Century: 100 Years of Makeup and Style* (1995); Harris, Joyce Saenz, "Browmania: Celebrity Pluckers, New Products Can Shape Up Your Brows," *Dallas Morning News*, June 4, 2001, available online at http://amarillo.com/cgi-bin/printme.pl; McNeil, Daniel, *The Face: A Natural History* (2000); Morago, Greg, "Hairy Problem," *The Journal Gazette* (Fort Wayne, IN), November 27, 2002, available online at http://www.fortwayne.com/mld/journalgazette/4601209.htm; Mulvey, Kate, and Melissa Richards, *Decades of Beauty: The Changing Image of Women, 1890–1990s* (1998); Turudich, Daniela, and Laurie G. Welch, *Plucked, Shaved, and Braided* (2004).

EYELASHES

Eyelashes are specialized hairs on the upper and lower eyelids that help to protect the eyes from dust and other foreign matter. Aesthetically, they help to frame the eyes, which play a key role in human appearance and facial expression.

Cosmetic preparations, techniques, and tools for embellishing the eyelashes date back to ancient times. The twentieth century brought increasingly sophisticated versions of mascara and artificial eyelashes. Some people choose to dye their eyelashes with permanent makeup. People also use various substances that claim to condition the lashes and encourage their growth. Still other products are used to remove mascara from the eyelashes, and tiny combs are used to separate lashes and prevent mascara from clumping.

Early Cosmetics

In ancient times, people living in the Middle East used antimony (the mineral stibnite) ground into powder, then sometimes blended with oil, to darken both eyebrows and eyelashes. **Kohl** also was used to darken and thicken the eyelashes. The Egyptians also made lash-darkening preparations that blended kohl with ointment.

The *Kama Sutra*, a book about attracting the opposite sex written between the first and fourth centuries CE, provides a "recipe" for a product that will darken eyelashes:

> An ointment made of the tabernamontana corornaria, the costus speciosus or arabicus, and the flacourtia cataphracta, can be used as an unguent of adornment. If a fine powder is made of the above plants, and applied to the wick of a lamp, which is made to burn with the oil of blue vitriol, the black pigment or lamp black produced therefrom, when applied to the eye-lashes, has the effect of making a person look lovely. (Anand, 179)

The women of the **Roman Empire** used burnt cork to color and thicken their lashes. People who did not want to use a pigmented dye on their eyelashes might oil them to create a darker, thicker appearance.

During the **Middle Ages**, **Elizabethan Era**, and Renaissance, eyes were de-emphasized to bring more attention to the forehead and bosom areas. Some women even removed all their lashes and eyebrows to achieve the "blank-eyed" appearance that was popular in those days.

Twentieth Century

During the 1900s, modern mascara, worn to darken, thicken, and lengthen lashes, became the most widely used of all cosmetics. Some early versions appeared during the late 1800s, but these did not gain widespread acceptability until the 1920s. Women did find ways to darken their lashes, however. Some put lampblack, made by holding a small saucer over a flame, on their brows and lashes, using a small brush. Others used the juice of elderberries, burnt cork, or a mixture of frankincense, resin, and mastic.

The Maybelline Company, which originated in 1915, specialized in mascara. Founder T. L. Williams named the company after his sister Mabel, who gave him the idea of producing a commercial product to darken eyelashes. Williams, a chemist, had watched Mabel blend Vaseline petroleum jelly with coal dust to create a lash darkener. In 1917, he introduced a formula for cake mascara that was applied with a wet brush and was convenient enough to use everyday. At first, Maybelline cake mascara was advertised in magazines as a mail-order product, but as demand increased, drugstores and variety stores began stocking it. In 1932, Maybelline launched a hugely successful cake mascara package that cost ten cents.

Artificial (false) eyelashes also gained more acceptance during the twentieth century. They became popular during the early 1930s and again during the 1960s, when large, made-up eyes and a pale mouth were in style.

The 1940s brought new products to enhance the eyelashes. More women began to routinely use eyebrow pencil and mascara. False lashes, which were a staple in the film industry, became available to the public. Waterproof cream mascara and the first eyelash curlers appeared. The general design of the eyelash curler has remained much the same since the 1940s, though the materials have changed and some new curlers can be heated to give a more lasting curl.

During the 1950s, the "doe eye" became fashionable for women. This fashion originated in Paris, where the well-known makeup artist Etienne Aubrey created round, well-defined eyes with liner, shadow, and mascara. The look appeared in *Vogue* and other American fashion magazines and onscreen—for example, on actress Audrey Hepburn whose famous green eyes were naturally large. To achieve the look, millions of women drew a thick black line above the eyelashes, adding a "wing" at the outer corner.

New products for the eyelashes continued to arrive in the marketplace. In 1950, cosmetic giant **Revlon** introduced a cake mascara that competed with those offered by Maybelline and other companies. Eight years later, Revlon launched its "Roll-On Mascara," mascara in a tube. The wand featured a spiral tip, which is still a popular design for mascara wands. Then, in 1960, Maybelline introduced a waterproof product called "Ultra Lash Mascara," which was applied directly to the brush inside the tube.

These products made it easier for women to create the large, dark-rimmed eyes that were popular during the 1960s. That look often was exaggerated, especially since lip makeup was pale though often glossy. Women applied several coats of mascara, frequently with the new lash-lengthening formulations. More colored mascara, including indigo, dark green, and violet, became available. Revlon created its first colored mascara, Brush-On Mascara, in 1961. Some women used colored mascaras with contrasting colors of eyeshadow and eyeliner (e.g., violet mascara with frosted silver eyeshadow and navy blue eyeliner, or green mascara with gold shadow and dark copper eyeliner). Most women preferred liquid mascara in a tube with a built-in brush rather than the cake and cream varieties.

Consumers could buy false lashes made from human hair or synthetic materials in a variety of styles, lengths, thicknesses, and colors. Some women even applied two sets of strip lashes. More teens and women wore false eyelashes during the 1960s, and many did not hesitate to wear thick, black lashes that were obviously fake. Early in the 1960s, some women went to cosmetologists who applied individual lashes or clusters of lashes. Often, these would last up to a week. False lashes became available in strips that were trimmed to fit, then glued to the lash line on the eyelid. These lashes were made from human hair, sable, and mink, as well as synthetic materials. Some were produced in gold and other metallic colors or in combinations of colors and textures.

In 1971, Maybelline launched "Great Lash" mascara, which was destined to be one of the bestselling cosmetics of all time. Now America's number 1 selling cosmetic product, "Great Lash" is a water-based formulation that comes in a distinctive bright pink and green tube. As of 2002, it was selling at the rate of one tube every 1.5 seconds. By the year 2000, Maybelline was offering thirteen different types of mascara.

The 1980s brought more improved versions of mascara, including longer lasting formulations. In 1988 Max Factor created "No Color Mascara," a clear lash product that makes the lashes look thicker but will not smear.

In February 1996, Maybelline was purchased by L'Oréal USA Inc., and the company headquarters were subsequently moved to New York City. As of 2004, L'Oreal is a world leader in mascara sales.

Trends and Products

A global survey taken in 1998 showed that mascara was the top-selling eye makeup in six of seven surveyed countries—the United States, the United Kingdom, France, Italy, Spain, and Germany.

As of 2002, sales of mascara had reached $1.9 billion and mascara sales made up about 50 percent of all cosmetic sales. Around the world, 61 percent of women use mascara, and Maybelline remains the bestselling brand.

Manufacturers aim to produce mascara formulations that go on smoothly without smudging or irritating delicate eye tissues. Mascara formulae typically are either water based or solvent based. Water-based mascaras contain three major categories of ingredients that form an oil-in-water emulsion: waxes, such as beeswax, carnauba wax, and synthetic waxes; pigments, including iron oxides, chrome oxides, ultramarine blue, carmine, burnt umber, and titanium dioxide; and resins dissolved in water. Preservatives are added to prevent microbial contamination that can cause infection. Upon application, water-based mascara dries fairly quickly as it thickens and darkens eyelashes. Water-soluble mascara is easy to remove, but it also is more likely to smudge or run on the face. Adding more wax to the product can make it more resistant to the effects of water, perspiration, or tears.

Solvent-based mascaras contain a mixture of petroleum distillates, pigments, and waxes (e.g., candelilla wax, carnauba wax, ozokerite, and hydrogenated castor oil). This combination creates waterproof mascara that is unlikely to smudge or smear but also is more difficult to remove.

As with water-based formulae, preservatives are added to prevent the growth of bacteria, but the petroleum-based solvent also inhibits their growth. Some formulations contain talc or kaolin to thicken lashes and/or nylon or rayon fibers that add length. Consumers are more likely to report eye irritation from the use of solvent-based mascara.

Sometimes, manufacturers combine solvent-based and water-based formulae to produce a water-in-oil or oil-in-water mixture. The goal is to create mascara that will dry quickly and still thicken eyelashes but also be waterproof.

Since the Food and Drug Administration (FDA) banned coal tar color as an ingredient in mascara, manufacturers must use vegetable colors or inorganic pigments to add color. Iron oxide produces black, ultramarine blue creates navy, and umber or burnt sienna or synthetic brown oxide are used to make brown mascara.

In recent decades, new formulations for mascara have included more plant extracts and other natural ingredients. These include moss, beeswax, and algae extract, as well as dyes made from plants. This reflects the trend toward so-called "natural ingredients" that intensified during the 1970s.

False eyelashes are available for daytime wear and special occasions. Women who opt to wear them can choose either individual or cluster lashes or strips of lashes that cover the entire lash line. Strip lashes, both "one-time use" and reusable, come in various lengths and thicknesses. Some are pre-glued while others require a separate application of glue, and new formulations of eyelash glue adhere longer than those made decades ago. Lashes can make a fashion statement. In 2001, singer/actress Jennifer Lopez wore artificial eyelashes made from red fox fur to the Academy Awards ceremony.

New types of mascara continue to arrive in the marketplace. In 2003, Revlon introduced "High-Dimension Mascara," which aims to highlight the lashes by creating glints of reflective color. In addition to black and brown shades, this mascara comes in red and blue.

See also: Egypt, Ancient; Eyebrows; Factor, Max; Greece, Ancient; Renaissance Europe; Trichotillomania; Twiggy

Further Reading: Anand, Margot, *The Kama Sutra of Vatsayana* (2002); Corson, Richard, *Fashions In Makeup* (1972); Maybelline, "About Us: History," available online at http://www.maybelline.co.uk/about_us/l282l283.htm; Minor, Christina, "Still Lashing Out," *Herald-Tribune* (Waco, TX), December 6, 2003; Riordan, Teresa, *Inventing Beauty* (2004); Schervish, Susan, "Euromonitor: Global Report Market Direction for Makeup and Color Cosmetics," ECRM (Efficient Collaborative Retail Marketing), available online at http://www.ecrm-epps.com/Expose/V3_3/V3_3_A26.asp.

F

FACIAL HAIR *See* Barbers; Beards, Men's; Beards, Women's; Body Hair; Egypt, Ancient; Elizabethan Era; Eyebrows; Eyelashes; Gillette Company; Hair Removal; India; Mustache; Religion and Hair; Shaving; Soul Patch; Unibrow

FACTOR, MAX (Max Faktor) (1877–1938)

Born to a poor family in Lodz, Poland, Max Faktor became a world-famous makeup artist and wig maker. Factor founded the international cosmetics company that bears his name. He is thought to have coined the term "makeup" and is called the "Father of Modern Makeup."

As a young man, Max Faktor worked for a wigmaker and for a dentist, a job that taught him to mix chemicals. He moved to Moscow where he opened a store to sell his handmade cosmetics, face creams, fragrances, and wigs. After a theatrical troupe began using his products, Faktor became the official cosmetics and wig provider for the royal family and the Imperial Russian Grand Opera.

When he arrived in the United States in 1902, the spelling of his name was changed to "Factor" on his immigration documents. Factor headed west and settled in Missouri where he sold his products to visitors at the St. Louis World's Fair. He continued to work with people in the theater. Soon, other actors and filmmakers sought his services. In 1909, Max Factor moved to Los Angeles, California, where he opened a perfume store. The Pantages Theater hired him as makeup artist, and he saw ways to use his expertise for the developing film industry.

In 1914, Factor produced a form of makeup with a lighter texture than traditional theatrical "greasepaint." Factor's formulation was less likely to crack or cake on the skin. Actors and actresses who wanted to look more natural and attractive on film came to Factor's makeup studio. Filmmakers rented human hair wigs and **toupees** and other hairpieces from Factor's valuable collection.

Actresses **Jean Harlow**, Bette Davis, and Claudette Colbert were among the celebrities who frequented Factor's beauty salon for hair care services as well as cosmetic application. Factor designed the rooms in his salon to flatter the hair colors of his clients: Rooms labeled "For Blonds Only" were painted in shades of blue, while redheads were surrounded by mint green. For brunettes, the decor was dusty pink, and for "Brownettes," the rooms were pale peach.

Max Factor also made false **eyelashes**, lip gloss, and **eyebrow** pencil. He provided silent film star Phyllis Haver with false lashes, marking the first time these were worn onscreen.

As celebrities were seen wearing cosmetics in public, other women wanted these products. Negative attitudes toward the use of color cosmetics, once called "paint," were diminishing. In 1927, Factor began marketing to the general public. He continued to work with actors and came up with innovative ideas, such as sprinkling gold dust on Marlene Dietrich's hair to make it sparkle onscreen. The 20K gold dust cost sixty dollars an ounce and Dietrich used about half an ounce each day on the set.

After Factor died in 1938, his son Francis, who became "Max Factor Jr.," expanded their commercial cosmetics business. Born in 1904, Max Factor Jr. became involved in the business around 1916 and collaborated with his father to develop products and services. In 1935, they devised a foundation makeup product that prevented actors' faces from looking green when they were filmed in technicolor. Factor later sold the company to personal care and home care products giant Procter & Gamble in 1991. He died in 1996.

Max Factor is still a major international cosmetics brand known for its eye makeup, foundations, lipstick, fragrances, and other cosmetics.

See also: Salons, Hair and Beauty; Wigs and Hairpieces

Further Reading: Basten, Fred E., et al., *Max Factor's Hollywood: Glamour-Movies-Makeup* (1995); "Max Factor—the makeup of makeup artists," available online at http://www.maxfactor.com/about/about.jsp;jsessionid=pg-prodweb-b03-1d0:4130a378:269d2464fcb793; "P & G history," available online at http://www.petragroup.com.jo/history.htm; "The Max Factor Beauty Museum," available online at http://www.seeing-stars.com/Museums/MaxFactor.shtml.

FALSE BEARD

People have worn false beards for various reasons—as a form of disguise, to portray a character on stage or screen, or to show their professional or social status. False beards can be made of human hair, animal hair, or various synthetic materials.

In ancient Egypt, both men and women sometimes wore a false beard, called an *atef*, made from metal. There were two general types of false beards, both with tips that bent forward. One type was worn in a horizontal pattern while the other was made from two sets of plaited strands coarsely woven together. These long beards were tied around the neck with cords or straps or pasted onto the chin. Egyptian artwork shows lines from these straps running from the beard up to the face.

Long false beards were a sign of high rank for both men and women, and royal Egyptians wore beards made of bronze or gold. Gold false beards were associated with Egyptian queens. Papyrus images of Hatshepsut, the pharaoh of the Eighteenth Dynasty who ruled Egypt for more than twenty years, show her wearing a false beard. A royal false beard was passed on from one ruler to the next and was supposed to link rulers with a god named Osiris, the king of the Underworld who supposedly ruled forever. Besides kings and queens, priests also wore these false beards.

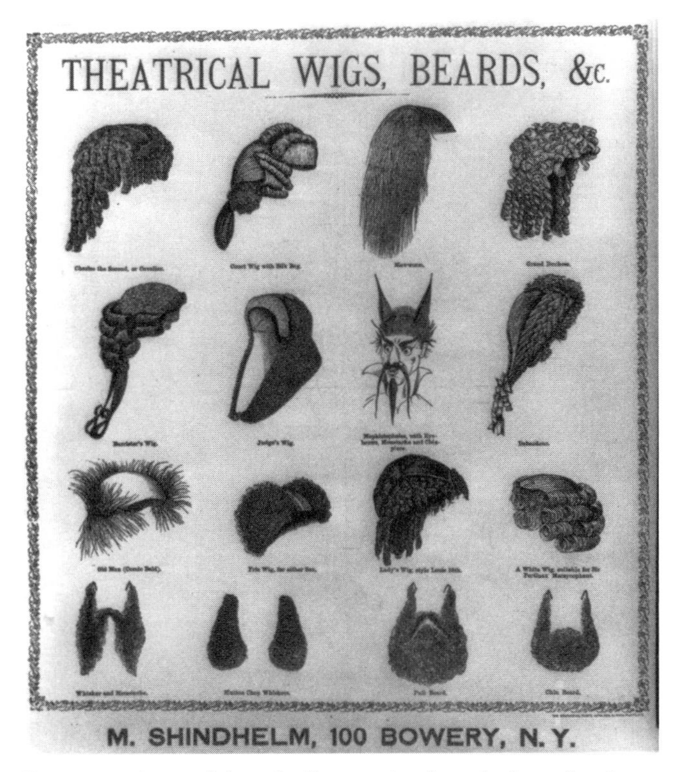

Costume wigs and beards for use in theatrical productions. *Library of Congress*

Rulers in other countries sometimes wore a false beard. During the **Roman Empire**, the emperor Caligula, who began his rule in 37 CE, occasionally wore a false beard made from gold.

In modern times, false beards most often are seen onstage, during Halloween, or at costume parties, and they are made to resemble human hair. People may don false beards to disguise their appearance, sometimes because they want to elude law enforcement officials or other people. Actors don false beards in order to portray certain characters, including historical figures and elderly men. False beards also are seen every December during the Christmas season, as men in the United States and some other countries don a long, full white beard to play "Santa Claus" or "Saint Nicholas."

See also: Beards, Men's; Beards, Women's; Egypt, Ancient

Further Reading: Clayton, Peter A., *Chronicle of the Pharaohs: The Reign-By-Reign Record of the Rulers and Dynasties of Ancient Egypt* (1994); Shaw, Ian, ed., *The Oxford History of Ancient Egypt* (2002).

FAWCETT, FARRAH (1947–)

During the late 1970s and early 1980s, millions of women and girls copied actress Farrah Fawcett's distinctive tousled hairstyle and bought the hair care products that she endorsed. Fawcett was known for her abundant blond hair, suntanned "all-American" looks, and wide smile. *Time* magazine once called her the "epitome of '70s glamour," and her hairdo may be the most widely copied style in history.

Born Mary Farrah Leni Fawcett in Corpus Christi, Texas, she later attended the University of Texas in Austin, majoring in art. In 1965, as a freshman, Fawcett was voted one of the ten most beautiful women on campus. A Hollywood publicist who saw her picture urged her to pursue an acting career.

Fawcett became a professional model and moved to California in 1967 to try acting. Soon she was hired to film ads for major grooming products, including Ultra-Brite toothpaste and Noxzema men's shaving cream. She also garnered small parts in episodes of popular television series. In 1973, she married actor Lee Majors, best known for his roles on two popular television series: *The Big Valley* and *The Six-Million Dollar Man.*

In 1976, a poster featuring Fawcett wearing a red one-piece knit swimsuit sold a record-breaking 6+ million copies. That year, she was cast as one of three glamorous female detectives in the television series *Charlie's Angels.* The series was a hit, and Fawcett became the most photographed of the three "angels."

Farrah Fawcett with a feathered hairstyle, which was made popular in the 1970s in America. *Photofest*

Her dark blond hair with sunny blond streaks styled in a distinctive layered "feathered" look (also called a "wing-back") received a great deal of attention. Millions of women around the world asked for a "Farrah" cut. Hairdressers Hugh York and Allen Edwards have both been credited with developing Fawcett's trademark hairstyle. Jose Eber also styled her hair during these years and developed his versions of the "feathered" look. As an icon of beautiful hair, Fawcett went on to sign a lucrative contract to endorse Wella Balsam hair products in television and print ads.

Fawcett embodied the natural, athletic look that was popular in America during the 1970s when people paid more attention to fitness and a healthy appearance. Fans wanted to know about her hair care routines, makeup, diet, and fitness regime. Hundreds of magazine articles discussed her beauty regimen, as well as her professional activities and personal life.

After one season, Fawcett left *Charlie's Angels* to act in feature films. She made guest appearances during the second and third seasons of the show. After her divorce from Lee Majors in 1982, Fawcett had a long-term relationship with actor Ryan O'Neil, and the couple had a son in 1985.

"Beware of her fair hair, for she excels / All women in the magic of her locks; / And when she winds them round a young man's neck, / She will not ever set him free again."

JOHANN WOLFGANG VON GOETHE (1749–1832), German author, *Scenes from the Faust of Goethe*, trans. Percy Bysshe Shelley, scene 2.

During the 1980s, Fawcett cut her famous hair and began tackling new roles onstage, in television movies and miniseries, and in feature films. She earned critical acclaim, including five Golden Globe nominations and two Emmy nominations. Fawcett appeared in *Playboy* magazine pictorials in 1995 and 1997. She continues to act in television and films, and in 2004, fans voted to give her the TV Land award as their "Favorite Fan-tastic Phenomenon."

See also: Advertising; Eber, Jose; Feathered Hairstyle; Hairstyles, Twentieth-Century

Further Reading: Burstein, Patricia, *Farrah* (1977); Friedman, Steve, "The Importance of Being Farrah," *Mirabella*, March/April 1998, p. 122ff; *Time*, "Time, 100 Most Influential Women of the Century," November 1999.

FEATHERED HAIRSTYLE

During the 1970s, the so-called "feathered hairstyle," sometimes called a "shag," wingback, or layered cut, became popular with men and women. Variations of the style have continued to appear since that time.

Some people credit the first feathered style to hairdresser Allen Edwards who styled the hair of actors on various television shows, including *Charlie's Angels* and *Ally McBeal*. Through her television appearances, commercials, and posters, actress **Farrah Fawcett** of *Charlie's Angels* helped to popularize the feathered hairstyle around the world. Since the 1970s, Edwards has styled the hair of other top actresses, including Jenna Elfman and Renee Zellweger, and other prominent women, including California attorney and prosecutor Marcia Clark.

Valerie Bertinelli, who costarred in the television series "One Day at a Time," was also known for her longer layered hairstyle. Her version of the feathered hairstyle, which featured bangs and a neat center part, is called "the Bertinelli" and was widely copied.

Short versions of feathered cuts also have been popular. In the 1971 feature film *Klute*, Jane Fonda wore a distinctive face-framing short layered cut that many women and girls copied. Goldie Hawn also has worn her blond hair in various feathered or "shag" styles.

Men also have worn layered and feathered hairstyles. One of the best-known was singer/actor David Cassidy, who appeared on the popular *Partridge Family* television series during the 1970s. Cassidy's "feathered shag" was cut to hang smoothly around the top and sides with longer strands falling around the shoulders. His brother, actor Shaun Cassidy, and Parker Stevenson wore feathered hairstyles on the *Hardy Boys Mysteries*, a television series that debuted during the late 1970s. Scott Baio of the television series *Happy Days* is another well-known actor who wore his dark hair in a feathered shag hairstyle. Actor John Travolta and singer Andy Gibb wore their own versions of the feathered cut.

See also: Aniston, Jennifer; Fawcett, Farrah; Hairdressing; Hairstyles, Twentieth-Century

Further Reading: Mulvey, Kate, and Melissa Richards, *Decades of Beauty* (1998); "The Feathered-Back Hair Site," available online at http://www.featheredback.com; Scott, Susan Craig, *The Hair Bible* (2003).

FEKKAI, FRÉDÉRIC (1958–)

During the 1990s, Frédéric Fekkai became one of the world's most famous hairstylists. He operates out of two luxurious salons and markets his own line of upscale hair care and beauty products, fragrances, and accessories.

Fekkai was born in Aix-en-Provence in southern France, of Egyptian, French, and Vietnamese ancestry. His parents encouraged him to enter law school and Fekkai considered becoming a sculptor. At age twenty, however, he decided to move to Paris, where he pursued a career in **hairdressing**. For three years, Fekkai worked with the well-known stylist **Jacques Dessange** before relocating to New York City in 1982. There he helped to launch the Bruno Dessange Salon on Madison Avenue.

After Fekkai moved into his own salon at Bergdorf Goodman in 1989, he became one of America's most celebrated hairstylists, attracting an exclusive clientele that included actresses, models, socialites, and executives. Fekkai was known for creating flattering, "clean," sexy cuts.

In 1996, Fekkai opened his new 12,500 square foot salon, Beauté de Provence, which occupies five floors of the Chanel building at 15 East 57th Street. Clients, who come from around the world, include actresses Salma Hayek, Julia Ormond, Liv Tyler, and Kristen Scott Thomas, and other prominent women, including Senator and former First Lady Hillary Clinton. In 1997, he opened another Fekkai salon in Beverly Hills, California. Both salons offer full hair care services, along with skin care and body treatments for women and men. People have paid $300 for a haircut by Fekkai.

In his book *A Year of Style*, Fekkai describes his philosophy of "effortless elegance" and tells women how to adapt their looks to the changing seasons and to the changes in their lives. Fekkai is a contributor to *In Style* magazine, and in 2002 he began writing a monthly column called "From Beauty to Business" for *American Salon* magazine, a publication for professional hairdressers and salon owners. In his work, Fekkai aims to help each client develop personal style and find an uncomplicated approach to beauty and fashion that suits her lifestyle and personality.

See also: Salons, Hair and Beauty

Further Reading: Fekkai, Frédéric, *A Year of Style* (2000); "About Frederic Fekkai," Frédéric Fekkai, http://www.fredericfekkai.com.

FLAPPERS

The flapper look for women became popular during the 1920s—the so-called "Roaring Twenties" or "Jazz Age" that followed World War I (1914–1918). During the post-war years, young people questioned traditional views of life and the wisdom of their elders, whose political decisions had sent many young men off to war, where they were injured or killed. While soldiers served in Europe, young women had taken jobs to help the war effort. After the war, more people adopted the attitude that they should enjoy life because it could end at any time. And since so many young men had died, more women faced the prospect of remaining unmarried. They decided to make the most of their lives, whether single or married.

The word "flapper" emerged in post-war Britain, where it referred to girls who had reached an awkward age between childhood and maturity. It may have come from the idea of a fledgling bird trying to leave the nest and "flapping" its wings to learn how to fly. In the United States, "flappers" came to mean youthful, fun-loving women who dressed and groomed themselves in certain identifiable ways.

A short, bobbed hairstyle was a key part of the look. Flappers, most of them younger women, cut their hair to around chin length or shorter. Some cut their hair in stages, growing progressively shorter with the changing styles. While some bobs were straight and sleek, others featured curls and waves. To set these styles, women wet the hair or applied gel from homemade recipes to sections of hair, then wound these "pincurls" around their finger and pinned them into place. Women adorned their hair with barrettes, headbands, bows, and combs. Evening styles were often ornamented with bands, beads, and feathers.

Flouting other traditional ideas about appropriate looks for women, "flappers" used obvious lipstick, face powder, cheek color, and eye makeup. Sleeveless dresses bared their arms and short skirts exposed their legs. Flappers also rejected the tight corsets that had confined generations of women. American actresses Louise Brooks and **Clara Bow** exemplified the flapper look. Brooks inspired John H. Streibel's popular *Dixie Dugan* cartoon strip.

In addition to wearing unconventional hairstyles and clothing, some flappers behaved in ways that were considered "daring" for women. They smoked, drank alcohol, and danced lively steps to the jazz music that became so popular during the 1920s. Many girls shocked their elders by kissing men they did not plan to marry.

The hairstyles and clothing of the 1920s showed that women were rejecting traditional roles and becoming more independent. American women, who finally gained the right to vote in 1920, continued to break new ground in education, the workplace, and other areas of life.

Louise Brooks with a classic flapper hairstyle. *Photofest*

See also: Bob, The; Water Wave

Further Reading: Blackman, Cally, *The 20s and 30s: Flappers and Vamps* (2000); Dumenil, Lynn, *The Modern Temper: American Culture and Society in the 1920s* (1995); Laubner, Ellie, *Fashions of the Roaring '20s* (2000).

FLATTOP *See* Hairstyles, Twentieth-Century

FLIP, THE *See* Hairstyles, Twentieth-Century

FOLLICULITIS

Folliculitis refers to an infection of hair follicles. The infection may involve a single follicle, a few follicles, or a large number. Infection can result from the overgrowth of organisms that normally occur on the body or from exposure to outside infectious agents.

The type called pityrosporum folliculitis occurs when a fungus called *pityrosporum ovale* or *Malassezia furfur* invades the hair follicles and multiplies, causing an itchy rash. This fungus, or yeast, is normally present on the scalp but usually does not grow so much that it causes a problem. This type of folliculitis may affect both males and females and is most common in people ranging from young to middle aged. People who contract this condition also tend to have severe dandruff and seborrhoeic dermatitis.

Certain conditions favor the growth of yeast. They include heat and humidity, tight clothing, a tendency toward oily skin, decreased immunity, stress, fatigue, being overweight, diabetes, the use of oral contraceptives, or the use of oral antibiotics, since these also kill organisms found on the body that prevent yeast overgrowth.

Treatment aims to reduce yeast overgrowth and the underlying causes. Local treatments include special shampoos containing selenium disulphide; topical preparations containing propylene glycol; solutions containing econazole; and ketoconazole cream. Oral treatments include pills that contain ketoconazole or itraconazole.

Other cases of inflamed hair follicles are classified as bacterial folliculitis, caused by the bacteria *staphylococcus aureus* or *pseudomonas auruginosa*, which lives in water. The latter condition, also called "hot tub folliculitis," may infect people who use pools or spa pools that lack enough chlorine to kill bacteria. "Hot tub folliculitis" tends to appear within one to three days after exposure to the infectious organism. Since the infection goes deep into the follicle, it can cause painful boils, as well as itchy bumps on the skin.

To determine whether infection is present, the pustules in the rash are swabbed, and then samples are sent to a laboratory for culture and analysis. Treatments include antibiotic creams or ointments, antiseptic cleansers, and/or oral antibiotics.

Irritant folliculitis may occur as a result of hair removal procedures that irritate hair follicles and cause ingrown hairs. Itching, redness, and swelling occur around the follicles as the hair regrows after plucking, tweezing, shaving, or waxing.

Chemicals found in cosmetic creams and lotions or in hair removal preparations may also irritate hair follicles.

To make a diagnosis, swabs are taken from the affected area are analyzed in a lab. If an irritant was responsible for the folliculitis, then these tests will show no evidence of bacterial infection.

To relieve this irritant folliculitis, people are advised to leave the irritated area alone while it heals and to avoid using hair removal methods that caused the problem. After irritation subsides, using an electric razor for hair removal may prevent a recurrence.

See also: Allergic Reactions; Hair Removal; Shaving

Further Reading: Baran, Robert, and Howard I. Maibach, eds., *Textbook of Cosmetic Dermatology* (1998); Fitzpatrick, Thomas B., *Color Atlas & Synopsis of Clinical Dermatology* (2000); Kerdel, Francisco A., *Dermatology: Just the Facts* (2003); Martin, Jeanne Marie, *Complete Candida Yeast Guidebook* (2000); Powell, J., et al., *An Atlas of Hair and Scalp Diseases* (2001).

FONTANGE

During the late 1600s and early 1700s, variations of the fontange hairstyle for women were popular in France and other European countries. The fontange, sometimes called a "top knot," arose by accident in 1680. Marie Angélique de Scoraille de Roussille, the teenage mistress of King Louis XIV of France, fell off her horse during a royal hunting jaunt. When her hat and hairpins fell out, her hairdo came apart, so she used a garter from her stocking to pile her hair in a loose knot on top of her head.

The style got its name from her title "Duchesse de Fontanges." As for its namesake, the young duchess became pregnant with Louis' child, which she miscarried. She was then sent to a convent where she died in 1681 at age twenty.

During the 1700s, the fontange changed in style and shape and became much higher, even eight inches or more above the head. Women added a linen or lace cap at the back, along with a wire structure, sometimes covered with lace. Two long streamers hung down from the cap, which was also called a "fontange" or "fontage."

In his Memoirs, Louis de Rouvroy, the Duke of Saint-Simon, called this hairdo "a structure of brass-wire, ribbons, hair and baubles of all sorts, about two feet high, which made a woman's face look as if it was in the middle of her body. At the slightest movement the edifice trembled and seemed ready to come down" (Saint-Simon 2004, vol. 4 [unpaginated electronic work]).

See also: Headgear; Wigs and Hairpieces

Further Reading: Arkwright, F., ed., *The Memoirs of the Duke de Saint-Simon* (1918); Corson, Richard, *Fashions in Hair* (1965); "Les Maitresses Royales," available online at http://maitressesroyales.free.fr/fontanges.htm; Pevitt, Christine, *Philippe, Duc D'Orleans, Regent of France* (1997); Saint-Simon, Duc de, "The Memoirs of Louis XIV, His Court and The Regency, Complete," 2004, available online at http://www.gutenberg.org/files/3875/3875.txt; Waugh, Norah, *The Cut of Women's Clothes, 1600–1930* (1984).

FRAGRANCE

Most products used for shaving and for cleansing, conditioning, and styling the hair contain fragrance. Some products are designed expressly to scent the hair.

The use of fragrances for the hair, head, and body dates back to ancient times. People applied fragrant oils to their heads or added flowers to add a pleasing scent to their hair. These fragrances derived from flowers, plants, or animals often were named according to their source (e.g., rose water, almond essence, or musk, which came from a sac found in the abdomen of the male musk deer before it was made synthetically).

People in **ancient Egypt** used scents from plant resins, roots, and saps. They found that adding fat to these materials or to scented powders would make the scent last longer. Egyptian wall paintings show dancers and musicians wearing solid ointments made from aromatic materials, including spikenard, an aromatic herb, on their heads. These "bitcones," as they were called, gradually melted during the performance. Persian kings scented their crowns with myrrh, and some Persian men scented their crowns with civet. After Roman men began shaving, they rubbed scented unguents on their chins.

In the Americas, native peoples added fragrant materials to the animal fats they used to condition their hair and relieve dryness. These ingredients included mint leaves, wild roses, sap from the balsam and juniper trees, vanilla, sassafras, and an herb called bergamot.

An Arabian doctor, Ali-lbn Sina, also known as Avicenna (980–1037 CE), developed a steam distillation process for obtaining oil—called attar—from flowers. He also studied the properties of hundreds of plants and wrote books about them. This knowledge and methodology propelled the fragrance industry in the Middle East.

In **ancient Greece**, merchants in the seventh century BCE sold scented unguents in decorative ceramic pots. Athenian markets featured various scents made from flowers and herbs, including lily, iris, rose, anise, marjoram, sage, and thyme, mixed into a base of almond, linseed, or olive oil. These thick pastes were used on the hair or body.

Women in Asia rubbed scented oils onto their hair and wrapped their hair into arrangements that contained jasmine and other flowers. People living in tropical climates also had a ready supply of fragrant flowers for their hair. Pacific islanders found orchids, plumeria, ginger blossoms, and other fragrant flowers growing wild.

During the **Middle Ages**, Europeans rarely bathed or washed their hair, so they relied on sachets and scented handkerchiefs to mask unpleasant odors. To scent their hair, people applied infusions of tea or herbal vinegars mixed with water. Rosemary was a popular herb for use on the scalp, since it has long been thought to improve hair growth. During the 1500s, people scented the powders they used on their hair and wigs.

By the 1800s, soap was being made in most parts of the world, and people added fragrances to soap formulas to enhance their appeal. Soap was used both for cleansing hair and the rest of the body. People who could not afford to buy it either made their own soap or went without. American settlers sometimes added bayberry to their homemade soap for a more pleasant scent.

Wealthy people ordered soap that was custom made with their favorite fragrances. Napoleon I of France preferred "Brown Winsor" soap, which contained bergamot, caraway, cassia, cedarwood, clove, lavender, rosemary, and thyme. He also liked a fragrance called "Jean Marie Farina." The Parisian firm of Roger & Gallet made Napoleon a soap in this fragrance after he became emperor in 1801.

The fragrance industry flourished after the 1800s when manufacturers also began using synthetic sources for scents. Modern perfume-making techniques led to the development of an array of fragrances and scented products.

The early twentieth century ushered in an era of simpler hairstyles and clothing for men, as well as a clean-shaven look. In promoting men's fragrances, companies focused on shaving products, since many men viewed cologne as a women's product and therefore "effeminate."

Ad campaigns for men's scented aftershave products stressed the alluring effects these scents would have on women. The ads showed images of virile, masculine-looking men. The ads focused on ingredients regarded as "masculine" (e.g., spices, lime, bay leaves, bayberry, and woodsy notes), and aftershave lotions were labeled as "manly," "sporty," or "invigorating." Product names reflected this same approach. For example, the 1961 ad for "King's Men After Shave Lotion" emphasized its "subtle, manly fragrance." The photo in the print ad showed an attractive woman sitting on a man's lap while he reads the morning paper at the breakfast table above this caption: "Why don't you take the 8:45 [train] instead?"

Since the mid-1900s, the number of scented products has continued to increase. Most personal products used for shaving and hair care include fragrances, whether they are single floral fragrances, mixed florals, herbs, spices, fruits, grasses, or other scents. Some fragrance makers include hair care products in their product lines so that people can use hair products that smell like their favorite perfume or cologne.

Since some consumers have allergic reactions to fragrances, consumers may also buy products labeled "fragrance-free." Permanent waves, hair coloring kits, hairsprays, and other products that once had strong chemical odors decades ago now come in milder-smelling formulations.

See also: Allergic Reactions; Arabia, Ancient through Middle Ages; Roman Empire; Shampoo; Shaving

Further Reading: Ackerman, Diane, *A Natural History of the Senses* (1991); Branna, Tom, "Fragrance and African-American Women," *Happi*, July 1997; Canning, Christine, "Fine Fragrances," *Happi*, November 1996, available online at http://www.happi.com/special/novmain.htm; Genders, Roy, *Perfume Through the Ages* (1972); Verrill, A. Hyatt, *Perfumes and Spices* (1940); Watkins, Julian Lewis, *The 100 Greatest Advertisements: Who Wrote Them and What They Did* (1959).

FRENCH REVOLUTION

During the French Revolution (1789–1799), fashions and hairstyles were visible symbols of political and social change. People who opposed the Old Regime wore simpler, more egalitarian styles to show their disdain for the aristocracy and their belief in "liberty, equality, and brotherhood."

Before the Revolution, elaborate hairstyles and towering powdered **wigs** were in style. The Muscadins, professional men who were members of the wealthier classes, were known for their fancy ringlets. Women's hairstyles were tall, wide, and ornate.

During the Revolution, hairstyles became more like those in classical **Greece**. The hair was arranged closer to the head, usually a simple chignon at the back of the neck. Women wore fillets, plain ribbons, pins, and tortoise shell combs instead of elaborate and expensive ornaments.

French men had been wearing wigs that differed in style, depending on their profession. By 1787, judges, lawyers, bankers, doctors, and merchants had stopped wearing wigs and were powdering their hair instead. Rejecting a wig was regarded as a patriotic gesture, much like wearing the Liberty Cap, a soft, shallow, cone-shaped hat that symbolized freedom from slavery or oppression. Revolutionary men called *sans-culottes* wore long hair combed straight under a red cap.

Some people of both genders wore a red ribbon around the hair at the back of their neck. This was a grisly symbol of the deaths of royalty and aristocrats who were beheaded by guillotine during the Reign of Terror. The family members of people who were beheaded during this time began holding balls solely for victims' families and they, too, wore the red ribbons around their necks.

To avoid antagonizing the Revolutionaries, the few aristocrats who remained in Paris during the Reign of Terror changed their hairstyles, clothing, and behavior. They remained in their homes most of the time, and when they did leave, they wore simple hairstyles and plain drab colored clothing.

One dramatic story about the Revolution involves the hair of Queen Marie Antoinette. When she and her husband King Louis XV tried to escape from France with their children, they were stopped near the border and brought back to Paris. As they arrived, the men who saw them leaving their carriage did not remove their hats as a sign of respect to the king. When they reached their quarters and the queen removed her hat and veil, the servants noticed that her blond hair had turned white, presumably from fright and from the strain of the ill-fated escape attempt.

After the Revolution ended, shorter and simpler hairstyles for men remained in fashion, and French women no longer wore large, elaborate hairdos.

See also: Hair Analysis; Politics and Hair; Regency

Further Reading: Doyle, William, *The Oxford History of the French Revolution* (2003); Fraser, Antonia, *Marie Antoinette: The Journey* (2002); Hibbert, Christopher, *The Days of the French Revolution* (1999); Willms, Johannes, Eveline L. Kanes, trans., *Revolution to the Belle Epoque* (1997).

FRIEDA, JOHN

See John Frieda Professional Hair Care Inc.; Styling Products

FRIZZEASE

See John Frieda Professional Hair Care Inc.; Styling Products

G

GEL, HAIR *See* Styling Products

GIBSON GIRL

During the 1890s into the early 1900s, many women in North America and parts of Europe wore their hair like the popular "Gibson Girl" featured in illustrations by American artist Charles Dana Gibson (1867–1944). Gibson based many of these images on his wife Irene Langhorne, a native of Richmond, Virginia. The ladylike and refined Gibson Girl look came to epitomize feminine attractiveness during the early 1900s.

The women in Gibson's pictures represent middle-class and prosperous women who also seem relatively independent. Often, they are portrayed outdoors—at picnics, rowing a boat, playing tennis or golf, riding a bicycle. Most were wearing natural-looking, wholesome garments that would allow freedom of movement—usually high-necked blouses and skirts without bustles, but with a small waistline. Men in Gibson's drawings also had a certain look, including neat hairstyles parted in the center.

Photofest

Women of all classes adopted this look. To achieve the Gibson Girl hairstyle, sometimes called a **pompadour**, women piled their locks high in the front. In variations of the style, one side of the hair was left hanging down over the shoulder, or a "stray" curl was left loose on purpose. Women with straight hair used a curling iron to create waves and curls; others used hairpieces to create the full, curving lines of the Gibson hairstyle. They piled their hair over a "rat" or postiche, made from horsehair or human hair. Some women made their own hairpieces by saving all the hair from their hairbrushes in a container kept on their dressing table. The puffs of softly waved or curled hair often created a hairdo wider than the woman's waist.

A Danish-born singer and actress, Camille Clifford (1885–1971) was regarded as Britain's "Gibson Girl." In 1906, Clifford appeared on the London stage in the play *The Belle of Mayfair.* Wearing a form-fitting black velvet gown, with her brunette hair arranged in a towering brunette pompadour, she sang "Why Do They Call Me a Gibson Girl?"

See also: Marcel Wave; Victorian Era; Wigs and Hairpieces

Further Reading: Gillon, Edmund V., Jr., *The Gibson Girl and Her America* (1969); Kitch, Carolyn, *The Girl on the Magazine Cover: The Origins of Visual Stereotypes in American Mass Media* (2001).

GILLETTE COMPANY

Gillette is one of the world's leading shaving products companies. The company had its roots in 1895, when its founder, King Camp Gillette, was a traveling salesman who sold bottle caps for the Baltimore Seal Company. King Gillette later said that the idea for a new type of razor emerged one morning while he was at home in Brookline, Massachusetts, trying to shave with a dull shaving blade. In those days, when a man wanted to sharpen the blade of his wedge razor, he had to take it to a barber or cutler. If it was not too dull, he could sharpen it himself on the strop men kept with their shaving equipment.

Gillette realized that a razor made with a separate and permanent handle holding a disposable blade would solve that problem. In an interview years later, Gillette said:

> I could see the way the blade could be held in a holder; then came the idea of sharpening the two opposite edges on the thin piece of steel that was uniform in thickness throughout, thus doubling its services; and following in sequence came the clamping plates for the blade and a handle equally disposed between the two edges of the blade. (McKibben 1997, 5)

Gillette convinced some friends to invest in this endeavor. He spent several years working with technicians who aimed to create a very thin but strong blade that would keep its sharp edge through numerous shaves. The disposable blade also would need to snap firmly into the permanent razor handle.

In 1901, Gillette formed his American Safety Razor Company and applied for a patent for his razor. It was granted in 1904 as Patent #775134. William Nickerson, an engineer and machinist from the Massachusetts Institute of Technology (MIT), worked with Gillette to make sure his safety razor, with its double-edged blade, could be removed when it grew dull and replaced with a fresh one. The final version used blades that were not forged but rather cut from a template.

Critics predicted that men would not buy disposable razors, and sales in 1903 were low—only 51 razors and 168 blades. Gillette remained optimistic, however, and he used the marketing skills he had practiced as a salesman to promote his razor. Consumers realized that the Gillette razor was easy to use and could minimize the chance of cuts, since most of the blade was covered. It also was reasonably priced. In 1904, sales rose to 90,000 razors and 123,000 blades.

In 1905, Gillette established an office in England to start selling his razors abroad. When the United States entered World War I in 1917, he negotiated with the U.S. armed forces to supply troops with individual "Khaki Sets," containing a safety razor and blades, which the men could take to Europe. During the war, Europeans saw Gillette razors in action, and the demand for disposable razors increased around the world. Soldiers received a total of 3.2 million razors and most then became Gillette customers who continued to replace their old blades with new ones.

Sales remained high during the 1920s. During the 1930s, electric shavers became available, but these were not as popular with men as disposable blades. Women were using Gillette razors, too. In 1916, Gillette had introduced the first razor designed expressly for women. More women were shaving their legs, especially during World War II (1939–1945) when stockings were scarce and women groomed their legs by shaving and then applying tints.

As other companies began to sell competing products in the shaving industry, Gillette developed new versions of its products. In 1960, the company introduced stainless steel blades in U.S. markets. Later, Gillette offered disposable razors with injector-style cartridges that were easier to use than previous models. Gillette promoted new versions of the twin-blade, wet-shave razor in the early 1970s, and in 1998 it launched the Gillette Mach3Turbo, which has three razor heads. The company developed a new razor with five blades called the Fusion.

Today, Gillette produces razors, blades, and shaving gel for men and women, as well as deodorant and other products. Its other corporate divisions include Duracell, Braun, and Gillette Oral Care.

See also: Beards, Men's; Hair Removal; Mustache; Shaving

Further Reading: McKibben, Gordon, *Cutting Edge: Gillette's Journey to Global Leadership* (1997); Pinfold, Wallace G., *A Closer Shave* (1999); The Men's Shaving Products Research Group, *The 2000–2005 Outlook for Men's Shaving Products* (2000); Zaoui, Myriam, and Eric Malka, *The Art of Shaving* (2002).

GRATEAU, MARCEL *See* Marcel Wave

GREECE, ANCIENT

Ancient Greece is divided into time periods known as the Archaic, Ionian, Classical, and Hellenistic periods, which ended in 30 BCE with the Roman conquest. Historical writings, including works by Homer and Aristophanes, mention hairdressing practices. The arts from those periods reveal changing fashions in hairstyles and facial hair. Mirrors, combs, and hair ornaments made from precious metals and jewels have been found in ancient Greek ruins.

A strong interest in physical fitness and personal appearance extended to hair on the head and body. Hair was regarded as a vehicle for personal expression and a form of social communication. A person's hairstyle could indicate age, social position, occupation, religion, and marital status. Hair also played a role in certain religious ceremonies. It could determine a person's success in their chosen profession.

Most Greeks had dark hair that remained thick during youth and young adulthood. Female children wore their hair short or arranged it in pigtails. Hairstyles for both genders usually were structured into definite patterns, with natural or artificial curls.

Grooming Products

The Greeks washed their hair in water and used olive oil to condition it. To soften and style their hair, they used mechanical means (brushing and massage), along with the oil. For a pleasing scent, they applied preparations made with spices and fragrant oils. Various lotions, pomades, and waxes were used to add shine.

The Greeks also colored their hair. During periods when blond hair was popular, they used dyes made from potash water and yellow flowers. Women also wore wigs that were dyed or were made from blond hair.

Women's Styles

Greek women took pride in their appearance and devoted time each day to styling their hair. Wealthier women may have spent most of the morning bathing and carrying out their grooming rituals, often with the help of slaves and servants. Slave women wore their short hair in simple styles.

Hairstyles revealed a woman's marital status, among other things. Young unmarried women wore their hair down and loose. In Sparta, one tradition decreed that a woman who was about to marry cut her hair short and dress like a man. During the Classical period, widows who were in mourning cut their hair short. During some other periods, women in mourning colored their hair with powders or pomades rather than cutting it short.

Minoan women wore their hair long and created elaborate styles, which can be seen on the sculptures and pottery of that era. Until the fifth century CE, women wore their hair hanging loose around their backs and shoulders, sometimes adding a headband or diadem. After the fifth century CE, they usually bound up their hair, often parting it in the center and pulling it back into a chignon or knot. The first ponytails may have originated in Greece.

During the Hellenistic period, women favored curls and waves, which were created by experienced hairdressers and held in place with combs made from wood or ivory. Greek women also used ribbons, metal hoops, and metal and cloth bandeaus in their hair during this era. Different kinds of oils, pomades, and lotions were applied to the hair for styling purposes and for their fragrance.

Women in Athens and certain other parts of Greece emphasized their eyelashes and eyebrows with cosmetic preparations. They used pulverized antimony or soot to darken the **eyelashes** and **eyebrows**. Unwanted hairs were removed with tweezers, razors, or plasters.

Men's Styles

Personal appearance was important to Greek men, and barbershops originated in Greece before spreading to other places. While Greek men were having a haircut, shave, massage, manicure, and/or pedicure, they socialized and exchanged news about politics, sports, philosophy, literature, and local events.

During the years before the Persian Wars (490–480 BCE), men in the Greek capital city of Athens favored long hair and elaborate hairstyles, often with an arrangement of curls, similar to fashions that were popular to the east in neighboring Asia Minor. The fifth-century historian Thucydides described one popular style, in which hair was tied behind the head into a kind of knot, or chignon, and then fastened with golden ornaments. Even in Sparta, where grooming rituals were simpler, men took the time to comb and plait their hair, though their hairstyles were shorter and less elaborate.

After the Persian Wars ended, men throughout Greece wore simpler hairstyles. The Greeks had managed to stop a Persian invasion, and long hair came to be seen as a symbol of eastern influence, and, therefore, unpatriotic. Most men cropped their hair short and stopped wearing chignons, curls, and ornate styles in order to avoid being regarded as effeminate or self-indulgent. They embraced a new standard for looking and feeling "Greek," in contrast to the long-haired "barbarians." Athenian men offered their cut-off hair as a sacrifice to the god Hercules.

Men's styles changed again under the influence of Alexander the Great (356–323 BCE), who had long, flowing hair. And although Greek men had been wearing beards for 500 years, the king's beardless face set a new fashion. Alexander reasoned that beards were dangerous in combat, where the enemy might grab hold of them. Other Greek men followed suit and preferred the clean-shaven look.

Ornaments and Fragrance

Both women and men wore hair ornaments. Women wore various types of "crowns," in the form of a diadem, meniskos, or wreath. They also wore hair ribbons, strings, and scarves—kerkryphylona, sakkos, sphendonei, stephanei, and taenia. Headbands called fillets, made from metal or cloth, were popular. Other hair accessories included hairpieces, decorative combs, and pins.

After conquering Persia, King Alexander the Great brought fragrances to Greece. Beginning in the eighth century BCE, myrrh and frankincense were imported from the Middle East. The Greeks boiled flowers, herbs, and other fragrant materials down to a concentrated essence, which they then mixed with olive oil.

The Greeks believed that scents were sent to earth by the gods. They applied fragrances to their hair and bodies and used them in their homes. They also anointed the bodies of their dead with scented oils.

See also: Adornment, Symbolic; Barbers; Beards, Men's; Comb; Comb, Decorative; Fragrance; Hair Colorants; Ponytail; Shampoo; Wigs and Hairpieces

Further Reading: Blumner, H., *The Home Life of the Ancient Greeks* (1966); Debrohun, Jeri, "Power Dressing in Ancient Greece and Rome," *History Today* 51(February 2001); Fantham, Elaine, et al., *Women in the Classical World* (1994); Grant, Michael, *A Social History of Greece and Rome* (1992); Jenkins, Ian, *Greek and Roman Life* (1986); Johnson, Marie, Maria Evans, and Ethel Abrahams, *Ancient Greek Dress* (1964); Lefkowitz, Mary R., and Maureen B. Fant, *Women's Life in Greece and Rome* (1982); Quennell, Marjorie, *Everyday Things in Ancient Greece* (1954); Robinson, C. E., *Everyday Life in Ancient Greece* (1933).

H

HAIR (the musical)

On October 17, 1967, an innovative musical by James Rado and Gerome Ragni (lyrics) and Galt MacDermot (music) premiered in an off-Broadway theater. *Hair*—subtitled *The American Tribal Love-Rock Musical*—featured characters known as "**hippies**," that is, members of the 1960s counterculture movement who, among other attributes, adopted certain distinctive hairstyles, including long hair for men. Hippies were also known for their political views, which included protesting U.S. involvement in the Vietnam War in Southeast Asia, and their rebellion against certain middle-class Western values and lifestyles, which were held by people they referred to as "the establishment."

The cast from the New York stage production of *Hair*, the musical. *Photofest*

The musical sparked heated debates, especially over one controversial scene in which male and female characters appeared onstage nude. Some observers considered the language obscene, and they objected to scenes in which characters were portrayed smoking hashish, voicing opposition to the Vietnam War, and burning their draft cards and an American flag.

Hair was a commercial success, and after moving to Broadway, it ran there from 1968 to 1972 for a total of 1,742 performances. It was nominated for two Tony Awards (Best Musical and Best Director of a Musical). *Hair* was also performed in theaters across the United States and around the world and is still being performed today. It was released as a feature film in 1979.

As the first rock musical on the American stage, *Hair* influenced theatrical history. Its success inspired new productions that were less structured and more daring than traditional musicals and that contained more modern types of music and controversial themes.

See also: Politics and Hair

Further Reading: Brantley, Ben, *The New York Times Book of Broadway* (2001); Gottfried, Martin, *Broadway Musicals* (1979); Horn, Barbara Lee, *The Age of Hair* (1991).

HAIR ANALYSIS

Hairs may be analyzed for health care purposes and to detect the presence of drugs, acquire evidence of a crime, or help determine someone's identity. Such tests can be useful because hair contains accumulations of minerals, including calcium and iron, and various chemicals that have been absorbed or ingested into the body. Hair is one of the places in which the body excretes waste products.

Health care professionals can analyze hair to determine the levels of certain nutrients in the body. They can also perform tests to find out if someone has been exposed to certain toxins and/or heavy metals, including aluminum, lead, mercury, arsenic, and cadmium. For this purpose, they use hairs that have not been treated with colorants or other chemicals.

Hair may also be tested to determine whether an individual has used drugs of abuse such as amphetamines, cocaine, marijuana, and opiates. This procedure is conducted by law enforcement agencies in criminal investigations and may also be used to test employees in the military and other workplaces. The use of these test results in court cases is controversial.

Hair is a common form of physical evidence, since it is easily transferred from person to person or from person to place. Hairs are typically gathered as evidence when they can be found at a crime scene or on the body of a victim examined during an autopsy. Some hairs are visible, while others, too small to be seen with the human eye, are collected with special equipment, such as a trace evidence filter. Hairs may show that a victim or perpetrator was at a certain place—the crime scene or another location—or that they handled objects found at the scene.

Investigators study evidentiary hairs to narrow down a list of suspects. They measure the length of the hair and observe its other characteristics. Using a light microscope, they examine the layers of the hair shaft—the outer cuticle, cortex, and inner medulla. The color and texture of the hairs may help them to identify the ethnic group of the perpetrator. They can also identify whether his or her **hair color** is natural or dyed. Law enforcement officials have developed a method called the "level system of hair color" to label the hair of suspected criminals. This 1–10 scale measures the darkness of hair. Lower numbers signify darker hair. Level 1 is black, moving into lighter shades as the numbers increase, with level 10 being light blond.

Further, lab tests can determine whether it is human hair, animal hair, or from a wig made of synthetic fibers. The shape of the cross section of the hair is typically different for Caucasians or African Americans, so this may indicate the hair's owner ethnic group. Although this type of hair analysis can aid investigators, such tests cannot prove a person's identity, since the hairs on any given individual's head can vary.

DNA testing of the sequence of genetic material found in the hair, on the other hand, can help to establish a person's identity. In one famous case, historians had long wondered whether young Prince Louis Charles, heir to the French throne, died during the **French Revolution**. After his parents, King Louis XVI and Queen Marie Antoinette, were executed in 1793, the ten-year-old prince was kept in a well-guarded prison, where he reportedly died of tuberculosis in 1795. During the 1800s, at least forty-three men claimed to be the prince, and some of them were so convincing that people continued to wonder whether or not the boy prince truly had died.

In 1999, scientists extracted DNA from the body of the boy who had died in the prison in 1795. They compared it with DNA samples taken from living and dead members of the French royal family. These samples came from a lock of Marie Antoinette's hair and hairs from two of her sisters, which had been saved in lockets. More DNA was obtained from tissue samples donated by contemporary descendants of the Hapsburgs, the noble family of Austrian-born Marie Antoinette. These tests confirmed that the deceased child was indeed related to Marie Antoinette.

Hair analysis also has been used in attempts to determine the exact cause of death for Emperor Napoleon I of France (1769–1821). His attending physician had noted that Napoleon had a stomach ulcer that became cancerous. His valet had kept a diary, wherein he described Napoleon's declining health during the months before his death. Based on this account and other findings, a Swedish dentist and amateur toxicologist named Sten Forshufvud published a paper in 1961 suggesting that Napoleon died from arsenic poisoning. An enemy could have given Napoleon small doses of arsenic over a period of time, creating a toxic accumulation. To back up his hypothesis, Forshufvud asked scientists at the Glasgow University Forensic Laboratory to test hair that reportedly belonged to Napoleon. During the early 1960s, a method called neutron activated analysis devised by Dr. Hamilton Smith was the most advanced test available for detecting trace elements in hair. The neutron activated analysis showed that the hair sample from Napoleon contained abnormally high levels of arsenic.

Yet, the controversy continued. Some skeptics said that the hair might not actually have belonged to Napoleon. Even if it was his hair, it could not be proven exactly when the hair had been removed from his head. During Napoleon's lifetime, members of his household staff had saved locks of his hair, and their descendants sold the hair to collectors. Scientists eventually obtained more hair samples and used newer technology to first confirm that it belonged to Napoleon and then to measure the arsenic levels. Studies done in 2001 showed that the hair contained levels of arsenic seven to thirty-eight times greater than normal.

Still, was Napoleon deliberately poisoned? When scientists conducted further studies on hair samples taken from Napoleon in 1805, 1814, and 1821, they found similar levels of arsenic through the years. These studies suggested that Napoleon was not assassinated by deliberate arsenic poisoning. He may have been exposed to arsenic in his hair tonics or in medications that once were commonly used to treat syphilis. Another possibility was that the arsenic came from wallpaper in the house where Napoleon lived from 1815 to 1821 while he was exiled on the island of St. Helena. Arsenic was a common ingredient in green pigment, and the wallpaper included prominent green designs. Since humans can absorb arsenic through the air, the arsenic in the wallpaper might have affected people living in the house, especially if the wallpaper became moldy. A few other people living with Napoleon had died of unknown causes, and the residents of the house complained of "bad air." In addition to hair tonic, wallpaper, or medical treatments, the arsenic in Napoleon's body may also have come from glue or rat poison used in the household. Scholars and historians continue to debate the actual cause of Napoleon's death.

See also: Hair Colorants; Memento

Further Reading: Cadbury, Deborah, *The Lost King of France* (2002); Dahlberg, John-Thor, "France Solves Mystery of What Happened to Marie Antoinette's Son," *San Francisco Chronicle*, April 20, 2000; Kintz, Pascal, *Drug Testing in Hair* (1996); Owen, David, *Hidden Evidence* (2000); Robertson, James, *Forensic Examination of Human Hair* (1999); Rousseau, Ingrid, "Who, or What, Killed Napoleon?" CBS News, October 30, 2002, http://www.cbsnews.com/stories/2002/10/30/tech/main527531.shtml.

HAIR ART

Hair art includes various decorative objects made from human hair, such as jewelry, wreaths, flower-shaped objects, and hair paintings, among other items. People have crafted baskets and even made sets of teapots and cups from hair, both for personal use and to sell. Historians trace commercial hair art to rural Sweden during the early 1800s.

Hair art and **mementos** made from hair were especially popular during the **Victorian era**. Popular forms of hair art included wreaths and arrangements made from hair "flowers." Hair-flower arrangements also included beads, lace, charms, and other items, which usually belonged to the hair's owner. Some people created these pieces as memorials to loved ones who had died. For example, they might have used the hair of the deceased to create a framed picture of a willow tree, a common symbol of **mourning**.

Hair flowers can be made by forming loops of hair that are attached to very fine wire stitched over a rod. Some people twist the wire over a knitting needle. The resulting flowers can be shaped into wreaths, including memorial wreaths, or fashioned into ornamental pictures.

Hair painting is another form of hair art. In the technique known as sepia hair painting, an artist uses finely ground hair to color paint. That paint is then used to create the objects in the painting, although pastel shades may be added to make paint for the sky or other features in the painting's background.

In palette work, or collage work, an artist arranges hairs against each other on a flat surface and glues them to a base material. After the glue is dry, the artist cuts out various shapes that can be used to form a pattern, such as a floral arrangement. This is then glued in place. All of these techniques can be used to make small works of art to tuck inside a pendant or brooch.

Hair art reached such prominence during the Victorian era that such pieces were displayed at important expositions in major European cities. At the Paris Exposition of 1855, visitors flocked to see a life-size portrait of Queen Victoria crafted entirely from human hair.

Hair work is classified as a folk art, and people continue to practice it today. Collectors can find antique hair art, as well as newly crafted pieces, for sale at auctions and on the Internet.

The Victorian Hairwork Society was formed to promote hair art. Its national headquarters is located at Leila's Hair Museum, in Independence, Missouri. The museum's founder, Leila Cohoon, also founded the Independence College of Cosmetology. As of 2005, Leila's Hair Museum contained more than 2,000 antique pieces of **hair jewelry** and 159 wreaths in glass frames. These pieces all were either made from or contained human hair.

See also: Hair Analysis

Further Reading: Bell, Jeanenne, *Collector's Encyclopedia of Hairwork Jewelry* (1998); Bernstein, Michael J., "Hair Jewelry, Locks of Love," *Smithsonian* 6 (12) (1976): 997–1000; Blersch, Stuart, "Victorian Jewelry Made of Hair," *Nineteenth Century* 6 (1) (1980): 42–43; Harran, Susan, and Jim Harran, "Remembering a Loved One with Mourning Jewelry," *Antique Week*, December 1997, http://www.hairwork.com/remember.htm; Jones, C. S., and Henry T. Williams, *Hair Work and Other Ladies' Fancy Work* (2003); Kliot, Jules, *The Art of Hairwork* (1989).

HAIRBRUSH *See* Styling Tools

HAIR COLOR

Hair color often is one of the first traits people notice about someone else's appearance. People usually identify each other by hair color, saying, for instance, "He has dark hair," or "She's a redhead."

Natural hair color is genetically determined, though people have altered their hair color for various reasons since ancient times. Like other aspects of appearance, certain hair colors have been more or less fashionable during various historical periods. Hair colors also have been associated with certain personality traits and behaviors and even with certain professions or political attitudes.

> "When red headed people are above a certain social grade their hair is auburn."
>
> MARK TWAIN (1835–1910), American author, *A Connecticut Yankee in King Arthur's Court*

Some cultures approach the concept of hair color in ways that may seem unusual to outsiders. For example, in the Dominican Republic, women with white skin are referred to as "blond" even if their hair is dark in color and regardless of hair texture. According to author Casandra Badillo, the hair of a light-skinned woman is labeled as "good," whereas the hair of other women may be labeled as "bad" (Badillo 2001).

Biological Origins

Hair gets its natural color from cells called melanocytes, which are located in the follicles at the cortical level of the hair. Melanocytes make pigments called melanins, and differences in the quantity and type of melanins result in various hair colors. In general, the darker the hair, the more melanin granules it contains. In darker shades of hair, the melanin cells also tend to be more densely packed. The two major types of melanin are eumelanin and pheomelanin. Hair that is lighter in color (e.g., blond, red) contains more pheomelanin, a pigment that is rich in iron, and less of the pigment eumelanin. Hair that ranges in color from brown to black contains higher levels of eumelanin.

As people age, melanocytes slow down their production of melanin or stop working altogether, which results in a lack of pigment. Hair that lacks melanin looks white, while a mixture of pigmented and unpigmented hair results in a gray appearance. At the turn of the twentieth century, gray hair generally was regarded as pleasing, since it was a normal part of aging and is a soft color that can flatter an older person's skin tones.

Hair of different colors also varies in thickness and in the number of hairs found on the head. Natural blonds tend to have the highest number of hairs on their heads, and individual hairs are thinner in diameter than those of dark hair, which falls between blond and red hair in terms of thickness. Red hairs tend to be thicker than other hues, and people with this hair color have fewer hairs overall on their heads.

Cultural Attitudes: Blonds, Brunettes, Redheads

Hair color has social ramifications because various cultures attach significance to different hues and even make assumptions about people's attitudes, behaviors, and intellect based on hair color. Different colors also go in and out of favor. During the early days of the **Roman Empire**, for example, blond hair was associated with prostitutes, who either dyed their hair or wore wigs. Later, golden hair became respectable for other women, including those who belonged to the upper classes.

Through the years, blond hair developed a certain mystique. Until the late 1300s, many Europeans regarded blond hair as provocative and a symbol of female seductiveness. Eve, who tempts Adam in the biblical story of the Garden of Eden, has usually been portrayed as blond haired, while artists have typically depicted the Virgin Mary, the mother of Jesus in the New Testament, with dark hair.

Golden hair fascinated many writers and artists. It was the most common hair color for the heroines of European folk and fairy tales, including those compiled by the Brothers Grimm and others. One notable exception was Snow White, whose hair was "black as ebony."

Throughout most of human history, blond hair has been considered attractive and alluring, possibly because this color is associated with gold and light, two things that people consider valuable and desirable. Lighter hair colors also are more rare, since the genes for darker hair are more dominant than genes for light colors. Sociologists also say that blond hair may connote youth, since children are far more likely than adults to have blond hair. Fewer than 25 percent of the women who are born blond keep that same hair color past their teen years. Traits associated with youth often appeal to men, since youth connotes health and fertility, and the urge to procreate is part of human nature. Writer Anita Loos dramatized this idea when she wrote her popular 1925 novel, *Gentlemen Prefer Blondes*, which later became a Broadway musical and 1953 feature film. To advertise its **hair colorant** products, **Clairol** used the catchy phrases "Is it true blondes have more fun?" and "If I have only one life, let me live it as a blonde." Blonds often are expected to have a certain type of personality as well, to go along with their sunny hair tones. Some women who have lightened their hair say that becoming blond made them feel more fun-loving and light-hearted and that other people expected them to be that way.

Blond hair also may be associated with certain sexy or seductive traits. In one of her many physical transformations, singer and actress Madonna bleached her hair and wore lingerie-like fashions, including a cone bra designed by Jean-Paul Gaultier, during her Blond Ambition Tour in 1990. During these concerts, she changed her hairstyles using various hairpieces. In this case, blondness was used to communicate blatant sexuality and aggressiveness.

Studies show that people may presume blonds are not only less serious-minded but also less intelligent than brunettes. This is reflected in the "dumb blond" jokes that became part of American culture during the 1900s. The concept arose in Europe. The original "dumb blond" may have been a French courtesan named Rosalie Duthe, who developed a reputation for being beautiful but empty-headed and incapable of carrying on a conversation (Pitman 2003). She was satirized in a one-act play, *Les Curiosites de la Foire*, which debuted in Paris in 1775. The "dumb blond" character resurfaced in 1925 in the form of Lorelei Lee, a fair-haired young woman searching for a rich husband in *Gentlemen Prefer Blondes.* **Marilyn Monroe** played Lee in the 1953 film version of the novel, while brunette Jane Russell portrayed her loyal and smart friend Dorothy.

Blond actresses have played parts that reinforced the "dumb blond" stereotype. They include Monroe, Judy Holliday, Jayne Mansfield, and Goldie Hawn during her years on the comedy variety show *Laugh-In.* Later, Hawn became a successful producer as well as actress and went against this stereotype by portraying independent, successful career women. Likewise, actress Loni Anderson portrayed an articulate, self-sufficient blond on the TV series *WKRP in Cincinnati* while still not hiding her voluptuous figure and stylish, long blond hair. In the 2001 hit movie *Legally Blonde*, Reese Witherspoon's petite, fashion-conscious character, Elle Woods, combines beauty with brains to succeed at Harvard Law School despite the biased opinions of people who cannot see beyond her Barbie-doll looks.

The "dumb blond" persona has been the topic of scholarly articles, university symposia, and research projects. A survey conducted in Great Britain in 1999 confirmed that many people still label women with platinum hair as less intelligent than dark-haired women. Other studies have reported similar results.

Blond hair is most characteristic of people with northern European ancestry and frequently is accompanied by fair skin tones and light eye colors, mostly blue or green. Naturally blond hair can be found throughout the world, however, even among people with dark skin, such as certain Africans and aboriginal peoples in Australia.

In his book, *Big Hair: A Journey into the Transformation of Self*, Canadian anthropologist Grant McCracken divided blond women into six categories, which he calls the "blondness periodic table." It includes the "bombshell blonde" (Mae West, Marilyn Monroe), the "sunny blonde" (Doris Day, Goldie Hawn), the "brassy blonde" (Candice Bergen), the "dangerous blonde" (Sharon Stone), the "society blonde" (C. Z. Guest), and the "cool blonde" (Marlene Dietrich, Grace Kelly) (McCracken 1995).

Dark hair colors have been less controversial than blond hair and usually received less attention. Around the world, brown or black is the predominant hair color, and in some regions and cultures, nearly everyone has dark hair. Although dark hair usually was not as exalted as blond hair, it was especially admired in certain times and places. Chinese women have sought even deeper shades of black hair, and long, black, gleaming tresses were a beauty ideal in **Japan** as well. Dark hair was elevated in seventeenth-century Europe and the Restoration period in England, when it replaced blond as the most desirable hair color for women. This trend developed during the early 1600s, when prominent French artists were painting in classical styles that coincided with a rationalistic movement in philosophy. One leading proponent of the classic, realistic style was Nicolas Poussin (1594–1665), an intellectual whose finely crafted paintings feature mostly dark- or auburn-haired people as well as angels and biblical figures. As dark hair became more fashionable for both genders, more people, including King Louis XIV, wore dark wigs.

Other European countries embraced this new beauty ideal, since France was an influential center of fashion and culture. By the late seventeenth century, most people in England also preferred dark hair to blond. People used various dyes to achieve this look, which was said to contrast especially well with pale skin. Women who bleached their hair or used blond wigs were regarded as unfashionable or low class. This trend can be seen in the British art of the Restoration period and in portraits that show elegant dark-haired men and women. One famous example is the portrait of Barbara Villiers, the countess of Castlemaine, which was painted by Peter Lely.

Throughout history, women with dark hair have been viewed in various ways—as competent, intelligent, and reliable, or as sultry, dramatic, exotic, and even "vampish." At times, brunettes have been associated with traits that were regarded as wifely or motherly. (The sequel to the 1953 film *Gentlemen Prefer Blondes* was *Gentlemen Marry Brunettes*.) Dark hair has been associated with higher intelligence or more common sense, in contrast to the "dumb blond" label. These stereotypes were dramatized in the popular television series *Three's Company* (1977–1984), in which brunette actress Joyce DeWitt played sensible, witty Janet Wood and blond actress Suzanne Somers played the part of sweet, childlike Chrissy Snow.

Although blond actresses achieved special fame during and after the 1930s, many top stars were brunettes. These brunettes included **Theda Bara**, known as "the Vamp." Bara dyed her light hair dark to achieve her dramatic look. During the early 1900s, film audiences had become accustomed to innocent-looking blonds, like the ones portrayed by "America's Sweetheart," **Mary Pickford**, so the Vamp characterization was a major change. Brunettes have starred in some of the screen's most famous romantic roles. Examples include Merle Oberon in *Wuthering Heights* (1939), Vivien Leigh in *Gone with the Wind* (1939), **Audrey Hepburn** in *Sabrina* (1954) and *Breakfast at Tiffany's* (1961), Ava Gardner in *Mogambo* (1953), Leslie Caron in *Gigi* (1956), Olivia Hussey in *Romeo and Juliet* (1968), Ali MacGraw in *Love Story* (1970), Jane Seymour in *Somewhere in Time* (1980), Debra Winger in *An Officer and a Gentleman* (1982), and Demi Moore in *Ghost* (1990). Screen legend Elizabeth Taylor often portrayed seductive or openly sensuous women during her long, successful career, including her lead role in the 1966 film *Cleopatra*. At the turn of the twenty-first century, actresses Halle Berry, Salma Hayek, Penelope Cruz, Lucy Liu, Jennifer Garner, Jennifer Lopez, and Catherine Zeta-Jones were regarded as some of the world's most glamorous celebrity brunettes.

Certain male actors have been regarded as prototypes for the label "tall, dark, and handsome." Silent-screen star **Rudolph Valentino** became a matinee idol during the 1920s in roles that earned him the nicknames "the Sheik" and "the Great Lover." The Italian-born Valentino became the screen's first international male sex symbol. Other dashing dark-haired stars include Clark Gable, Cary Grant, Gregory Peck, Rock Hudson, James Garner, Sean Connery, Christopher Reeve, Chris Noth, George Clooney, Jimmy Smits, Antonio Banderas, Ben Affleck, and Orlando Bloom, to name a few.

Although most high-fashion female models still are light haired, since the 1960s, more brunettes and women of color have become top models. Along with the popular "California blond"-type models, such as Cheryl Tiegs and Christie Brinkley, brunettes Janice Dickinson and Cindy Crawford became dark-haired supermodels, while Beverly Johnson was the first African American supermodel. Recent advertising campaigns by hair colorant and cosmetic companies have featured an array of spokeswomen with different hair colors. For example, to promote its Colorstay cosmetics, **Revlon** featured Halle Berry, Julianne Moore, Eva Mendes, and Jaime King in print and television ads.

Naturally red hair, in shades ranging from strawberry blond to auburn, is the most rare of all hair colors. It is most often found among people of Irish, Scottish, or English ancestry as well as in some small groups of people in Asia. About 2–5 percent of the population in the United States has naturally red hair. Of all the countries in the world, Scotland has the highest percentage (13 percent) of natural redheads. Frequently, light-colored eyes and fair skin, often with freckles, accompany naturally red hair.

Red hair has been popular in Greece and Italy for centuries but less popular in other places, especially during certain historical periods. Many cultures have associated red hair with a hot temper or a tempestuous nature. It even has inspired awe or fear. Some scholars trace negative attitudes about redheads to the belief that Judas Iscariot, the disciple who betrayed Jesus in the New Testament, was thought to have this hair color. Strong feelings about red hair also may stem from the fact that this color is relatively rare throughout the world and that red hair may be quite striking in appearance.

At times, red-haired people have been the targets of superstitions, prejudices, and persecution. In ancient Greek myths, they became vampires after death. During the sixteenth and seventeenth centuries, a high percentage of the women whom Puritan religious leaders branded as "witches" had red hair; most of them also were young and good looking. In seventeenth-century France, some scholars advised people with red hair to hide it under a wig. In India, male members of the Brahmin caste were traditionally banned from marrying red-haired women.

Red hair became especially popular in England during the reign of **Elizabeth I** and in Italy during the Renaissance, when Titian and other artists used brilliant red-gold tones to paint hair. People used caustic dyes and bleaches to obtain these hair colors.

Red hair became more popular in the twentieth century both in Europe and the United States. Some historians say that color films and television played a key role, since blond and red shades show up well in those media. Other analysts point out that red hair often was associated with a passionate personality type and that women's sexuality has become more open and acceptable since the 1960s. Studies have shown that, in general, female actors with red hair tend to be more popular with audiences than male actors with this hair color.

Salon owners reported that shades of red were the most popular with women when the use of **henna** was revived in the 1970s and again in the late 1990s and early years of the twenty-first century. As hair products became gentler, more African American women were trying hair colorants, including blond and red shades. In recent decades, Hispanic women frequently have used red shades when they changed their hair color.

Famous red-haired people include Cleopatra, Elizabeth I, Nell Gwynne (an actress and the mistress of King Charles II of England), American President Thomas Jefferson, Dutch artist Vincent Van Gogh, actress and London socialite Lillie Langtry, American author Mark Twain, British Prime Minister Winston Churchill, musicians David Bowie and Tori Amos, German tennis champion Boris Becker, Sarah Ferguson (the duchess of York), actresses Molly Ringwald, Nicole Kidman, Julianne Moore, Marcia Cross, and Lindsay Lohan, actors David Caruso and Eric Stoltz, actor/director Ron Howard, and comedian Conan O'Brien. Two of the most famous "redheads" of the twentieth century—actresses Rita Hayworth and **Lucille Ball**—dyed their hair.

See also: Aging and Hair; Albinism; Bow, Clara; Egypt, Ancient; Elizabethan Era; Factor, Max; Greece, Ancient; Harlow, Jean; Kennedy, Jacqueline Bouvier; Literature; Politics and Hair; Renaissance Europe; Temple, Shirley; Wigs and Hairpieces

Further Reading: Badillo, Casandra, *Only My Hairdresser Knows for Sure* (2001); Cooper, Wendy, *Hair* (1971); Douglas, Stephen, *The Redhead Encyclopedia* (1996); McCracken, Grant, *Big Hair* (1995); Phillips, Kathy, *The Vogue Book of Blondes* (2000); Pitman, Joanna, *On Blondes* (2003); Roach, Marion, *The Roots of Desire* (2005); Sacharov, Allen P., *The Redhead Book* (1985); Thomas, Karen, "She's Having a Blonde Moment," *USA Today*, October 27, 2003.

HAIR COLORANTS

The use of various substances to restore or alter the color of the hair dates back thousands of years. People have colored their hair to look more youthful, as a disguise, for theatrical purposes, or to acquire a new shade that they prefer or consider more fashionable.

> "My real hair color is kind of a dark blonde. Now I just have mood hair."
>
> JULIA ROBERTS (1967–), American actress

Hair colorants include temporary rinses, paints, sprays, and lotions that can be brushed or washed out of the hair; semipermanent color preparations that deposit color on the outer layer of hair (cuticle) and will last through several washings; and permanent tints that add color intended to last until the hair grows out.

Hair colorants are most often used to cover gray hairs associated with aging. The first gray hairs on the head usually appear around age thirty and increase to include about 50 percent of the hairs by age fifty. In many cultures, white or gray hair has been regarded as an undesirable sign of aging. In others, gray hair does not have negative connotations and is considered not only acceptable but also attractive. In **India**, for instance, gray hair is regarded as a sign of grace and charm. Certain African societies and the Maori of New Zealand do not hold negative attitudes toward gray hair or other signs of aging.

Ancient Times

Early hair dyes were made from materials found in nature (e.g., mineral and/or plant products such as chamomile, indigo, logwood, **henna**, berries, and walnut hull extract). Products derived from insects or animals also were used to make hair dyes.

Toward the end of the Iron Age (1000–50 BCE), the **Celts** and the Gauls used limewater, a type of lye, to wash and bleach their hair. This produced striking white hair. Soldiers with spikes of white hair and pale faces also painted their hair with woad, a bright blue dye, which resulted in a dramatic appearance that the Gauls used to intimidate their enemies on the battlefield. In some cases, woad also was used to accent the hair.

People living in the ancient societies of **Mesopotamia** and Persia dyed their hair, which they usually wore long. In **ancient Greece**, golden and red-gold shades of hair were admired, and Aphrodite, the goddess of love, was portrayed with golden hair. Light hair also was associated with health and youthfulness, which the Greeks admired. High-class prostitutes, called *hetairai*, colored their hair blond. One recipe for hair bleach mixed potash water with yellow flowers. Harsh bleaching agents and soaps were also formulated for the purpose of coloring the hair. During the fourth century BCE, most Greek women dyed their hair or dusted it with color.

Ancient Egyptian and Middle Eastern women sometimes colored their hair with henna, which is derived from the dried leaves and stems of the henna shrub that grows in the Near East and northern Africa. When combined with hot water and applied to the hair, henna imparts a variety of red tones and highlights. Tea sometimes was added to intensify henna's effects. To cover gray hairs, Egyptians mixed oil with the blood of a black cat.

Hair dyes were popular in ancient Rome, and historians have found more than 100 different recipes that the Romans used for bleaching or dying hair. Early Romans preferred dark hair, and at one time, blond hair was the mark of a prostitute. Light hair became fashionable after Greek culture reached Italy and the Roman legionnaires began bringing back fair-haired slaves from Gaul. Women, and some men, applied bleaching agents to their hair and then exposed it to the sun to achieve a golden or red color. Wealthier people could afford to sprinkle actual gold dust on their hair to create a blond look, as did the ancient Phoenicians. Another way to achieve a lighter shade was to cover their hair with flower pollen and the crushed petals of yellow-colored flowers. When harsh bleaching agents caused hair loss, Roman women resorted to wigs made from the hair of blond slaves.

To color gray hair, the Romans used a mixture made from ashes, boiled walnut shells, and earthworms. Another recipe for dark hair dye combined boiled walnut shells, charred eggs, leeks, leeches, and other ingredients. They also discovered that lead-coated combs dipped in vinegar would leave a dark residue on the hair. The color deepened over time as repeated use of a comb left more lead salts on the hair.

Some men in ancient cultures dyed their beards. Babylonian and Abyssinian men dyed their facial hair black, especially after it turned gray, while men in ancient Persia used henna to impart a red stain. Celts and Vikings used bleach to create pale blond beards. The Assyrians used black dye on their eyebrows, hair, and beards. On special occasions, wealthy Assyrians applied gold dust, gold thread, and scented yellow starch to add color to their hair and beards.

During times of celebration, people have used special hair colorant preparations. For example, Tunisian brides made mardouma by blending galls (a natural source of tannin found in trees), cloves, and copper sulfate. They used this substance to darken their hair as they prepared for their weddings.

Middle Ages to 1800s

During the early **Middle Ages** in Europe, Roman Catholic leaders condemned women who bleached their hair blond. The clergymen also expressed concerns that natural blonds with long, flowing hair were dangerously seductive to men. Yet women still dyed their hair, using various substances, and some women wore blond wigs. Bleaches made during the Middle Ages contained henna, gorse flowers, saffron, eggs, and calf kidneys as well as other ingredients.

Red hair was popular during the reign of **Elizabeth I** of England. High-ranking men in Elizabethan England dyed their hair auburn, and some male courtiers dyed their beards that color, too, as a sign of loyalty to their red-haired queen. Englishwomen who wanted to duplicate this color applied mixtures containing saffron and sulfur powder. This dye could have caused numerous side effects, including nausea, headaches, and nosebleeds.

Late in the sixteenth century, the Italian artist Titian helped popularize the red-gold **hair color** that appears in his oil paintings. Venetian women who wanted coppery hair colors applied bleaching mixtures, such as one that contained alum, sulfur, soda, and rhubarb. Then they sat in the sun, where heat produced a chemical reaction that developed the color. During those years, saffron was a prized and costly ingredient that people added to hair-lightening preparations. Some bleaching recipes included wine or even horse urine.

During the Renaissance, France became a leader in developing formulas for hair dyes. Marguerite de Valois (1553–1615), the first wife of Henry IV, is believed to have introduced more advanced hair-bleaching techniques to France. However, some women preferred to pulverize yellow flowers and then use a sticky substance to affix this powder to their hair instead of using a chemical dye.

During the 1600s, people used lead combs on their hair to darken it, especially after their hair turned gray, as the Romans had done. At that time, people did not realize that lead was poisonous and could cause kidney failure and death. People also continued to use plant products, such as lemon juice or chamomile, to lighten or highlight the hair. Perfumed powders in white and pastel tints also were becoming more popular for use on both hair and wigs.

Powdered hair peaked in popularity during the 1700s, and wheat flour often was used for this purpose. It is estimated that the amount of flour used by members of the British army alone for whitening their hair each year would have provided enough flour to make bread for 50,000 people.

1800s to 1900

After the 1700s, people continued to experiment with various ingredients to make hair dyes and bleaches, including animal by-products, lemon juice, wine, plant extracts, and roots. In the 1800s, however, many women avoided using products that visibly altered their hair color, just as they avoided using noticeable cosmetics. Most women faced social disapproval if they used obvious hair dyes or cosmetics. From colonial days through the 1800s in the United States, bleached hair was associated with vanity or immorality. Women were expected to fulfill their roles as wives and mothers and to exhibit modesty and virtuous conduct.

Some people did use cosmetics and hair colorants. In 1839, Jules Hauel began selling a vegetable-based hair dye in his Philadelphia shop, along with soaps, perfumes, and bear grease, which was used as a hair conditioner. Hauel's business prospered. Other merchants, including traveling salesmen, offered hair colorant products, and people also continued to make hair colorants and other personal care preparations at home.

A natural look was regarded as most suitable for women during the **Victorian era**. Even so, some women used subtle colors on their hair and sometimes powdered it for special evening occasions. Recipes for homemade dyes usually were composed of plant ingredients, such as herbs, roots, and leaves. Other recipes contained more unusual ingredients, including rust. A number of fashion-conscious women used henna on their hair, reflecting the rising interest in Asian and Middle Eastern cultures that developed as more upper-class Americans and Europeans began traveling to those regions. The world's most famous opera singer, Madame Adelina Patti, spurred the use of henna to add red tints to the hair. Women who wanted that look purchased boxes of henna imported from Turkey and other places where the plant was cultivated. Consumers could choose products labeled as "black," "red," "blond," "neutral," or "white." They contained henna, indigo, or cassia along with other ingredients. Women who used hair dye were said to "henna their hair," even if they used a different product.

During the late 1800s, people realized that the chemical hydrogen peroxide would remove pigment from the hair shaft, leaving it a yellow or orange-yellow color. Some historians believe that people might have used peroxide as hair bleach centuries earlier, even in ancient times. A colorless liquid, peroxide works by breaking down the natural melanin in the hair shaft, thus removing the color and lightening hair. One major drawback is that peroxide straight from the bottle tends to dry the hair.

Some men used a comb imbedded with dye to color their mustaches and/or beards. Hair dye also became available in the forms of crayon sticks and creams.

Modern Colorants

The late 1800s brought major developments in the field of synthetic organic chemistry. The 1863 discovery of paraphenylenediamine (PPD or PPDA), a chemical that was used to dye textiles, and research in coal tar dyes and anilines led to the development of modern hair colorant formulations.

The first modern chemical hair colorant was developed in France from a formula that contained paraphenylenediamine. During the early 1900s, Eugène Schueller, a young French chemist, developed a synthetic hair dye made with that chemical. Schueller sold batches of his hair color, which he called Aureole, to local hairdressers. People were still wary of using manufactured hair dye, and some reported adverse side effects. In 1909, Schueller tried to alleviate fears by naming his new business the French Harmless Hair Dye Company, a name that was changed in 1910 to **L'Oreal**. L'Oreal would grow into a multinational hair and beauty products business.

People continued to seek better hair coloring formulas. Many early synthetic hair dyes were harsh and drying to hair as well as irritating to the skin. Bleaching often was done with peroxide, ammonia, and soap flakes, and these chemicals could cause burns and blisters on the scalp. The chemical fumes sometimes caused headaches. In addition, the colors often looked unnatural, and results were inconsistent.

In 1917, a new double-process technique to create blond hair color was developed. The natural color was first stripped from the hair and then new color was applied during the second phase. During the 1920s, a small French company called Mury devised a formula that enabled colorant to penetrate the hair shaft rather than just coating the outside. Since this hair colorant formula lasted longer and looked more natural than previous formulas, it was more effective in coloring gray hair as well as enhancing a woman's natural color.

People still questioned the safety of hair dyes and bleaches, but attitudes began to change. The motion picture industry began to strongly influence attitudes about appearance as actors appeared onscreen wearing cosmetics and stylish hair. **Jean Harlow**, a popular film star during the 1930s, bleached her hair to a pale, platinum blond, and many women copied her "blond bombshell" look. Bleaching eventually damaged Harlow's own hair so severely that she began wearing wigs. When she died in 1937 at age twenty-six of uremic poisoning, people speculated that it had resulted from the toxic effects of hair bleach. Doctors pointed out, however, that Harlow suffered from kidney disease caused by previous injuries.

While some women used peroxide or laundry bleach in attempts to resemble Harlow or Mae West, other women used henna to enhance or alter their hair color in more subtle ways. As Technicolor movies reached theaters, the actors' hair colors became even more visible to audiences, but coloring the hair still was not easy or widely acceptable. Most people regarded it as immodest, daring, and somewhat "low class." Members of the clergy also criticized the use of hair colorants and cosmetics as a vain and sinful alteration of a person's God-given physical traits.

During the 1950s, several events combined to change attitudes even further. New and improved products made it possible to cover gray hair more effectively and to lighten hair without bleaching it first. Home hair coloring kits allowed people to color their hair privately at more affordable prices. These new products offered a wider selection of colors and yielded more natural-looking results.

The **Clairol** company played a key role in developing new products and helping to change attitudes. American chemist Lawrence Gelb had discovered Mury's products while visiting France in 1931. After obtaining the rights to the products, Gelb worked with chemists in the United States to develop an oil-based hair coloring product that women could use at home. With his wife, Joan Gelb, he founded Clairol. By 1938, Clairol's annual sales had reached $1 million. Still, most women hid the fact that they colored their hair, and salons tried to guard their privacy. Some salons even installed special entrances and exits where women could come for hair coloring services without being seen by other clients.

During the 1950s, Clairol launched new products with ad campaigns designed to make hair coloring more appealing and socially acceptable. In one 1956 ad, Clairol asked the provocative question, "Is it true blondes have more fun?" Another ad said, "If I have only one life, let me live it as a blonde." Women in the ads were portrayed as respectable wives, mothers, and proverbial "girls next door." Gradually, the social stigma attached to coloring hair dissipated. A 1950 survey of American women showed that 7 percent of them colored their hair. That number has steadily increased so that today more than half of all American women use hair colorants.

During the mid- to late 1950s, Clairol introduced other new products that were more convenient and delivered subtler and natural-looking results. The company launched another successful ad campaign in the late 1960s for their Loving Care hair color, a peroxide-free formula designed to cover gray hair. Since the idea of dying gray hair still carried some social stigma, the **advertising** firm labeled Loving Care as a "rinse" and came up with the slogan, "Hate that gray? Wash it away!" After the 1950s, the number of people coloring their gray hair steadily rose.

Clairol remained the top-selling hair color brand in the United States throughout the 1950s and 1960s, but L'Oreal eventually reached the top spot. Revlon is another well-known brand, while Redken and Allegretti are especially well known in the salon hair coloring market. Other brands excel in regional or national markets. For example, as of 2004, Framesi, a brand sold in seventy countries, was the best-selling hair color in Italy. Hair color made by Wella, a company founded in Germany, has sold well throughout Europe.

By the 1970s, other hair coloring options were available, and women were more open about using hair color. The technique of adding highlights to the hair appeared during this decade. These highlights tended to be more obvious and monochromatic than those resulting from techniques that have developed since then. Red tints also were popular in the 1970s, and more women in Western countries used henna. Revlon introduced Colorsilk, the first hair colorant made without ammonia. More companies introduced products with vegetable dyes, which were labeled as "natural" because they did not contain coal tar dyes or the chemicals ammonia, peroxide, or paraphenylenediamine.

The **punk** look, which originated among young people in New York City and in London and other cities in England during the 1970s, included vivid hair colors and/or colorful highlights. Punks who could not afford commercial hair coloring products used Kool-Aid powdered drink mix to dye their hair, although this caused obvious problems when their hair got wet. Likewise, people who wanted a macabre "Goth" look dyed their hair a deep black or used vivid colors and/or streaks. During the 1990s, Japanese teenaged "Goths" could be seen wearing vivid grass-green hair colors, for example.

Products and Trends

Today, consumers can choose from an array of hair products that offer permanent, semipermanent, or temporary color. Companies also offer kits that produce special effects such as highlights or streaks in natural-looking or obviously fake colors. New technology continues to drive the hair coloring industry as companies seek formulations that deliver appealing colors without undue damage to the hair.

Increasing numbers of women and men regularly enrich, change, or restore their hair color, choosing from among hundreds of shades of blond, brown, red, black, and silver/gray, or they add unusual effects. Blond shades have long been the best sellers for women, and an estimated 80 percent of all the women who color their hair use a blond shade. As of 2000, Clairol alone was producing more than seventy different shades of blond colorants in its various hair color lines. A new trend emerged in 2002, when sales of brown shades rose. Salons reported that an increasing number of clients were asking for darker hair colors and choosing highlights in shades of caramel, honey, and toffee rather than blond.

About 51 percent of the people who use hair colorants do so to conceal gray hairs associated with aging. Covering gray hair has become far more common, and members of the "baby boom" generation, who were born between 1946 and 1961, are more likely to dye their gray hair than any previous generation in the United States. Men and women who color their gray hair say that they do so to look younger and boost their self-esteem as well as to attract and maintain the interest of romantic partners. People working in the fields of entertainment, fashion, and fitness are most likely to color gray hairs for professional reasons. However, other people also say that gray hair can hurt their chances of getting a job or advancing in their careers since employers may perceive older people as less energetic or less motivated.

Since the mid-twentieth century, sales of hair colorants have risen each decade as more people of both genders began coloring their hair. In the early 1950s, 4–7 percent of all American women colored their hair. By the 1970s, that number had risen to more than 40 percent, and by 2004, different surveys stated that between 51 and 75 percent of American women had colored their hair at least once. By the 1990s, hair colorants were the strongest growth area in personal care products. An estimated 55 million Americans were using hair colorants as of 2000, and hair coloring products were a $1 billion a year consumer industry. In fact, so many people change their hair color that the designation "hair color" was deleted from U.S. passports as of 1969.

Hair coloring also has become more commonplace in countries where it was once quite rare. For example, until the late twentieth century, people in **Japan** tended to leave their hair in its natural color, which is usually black. Then more people began adding lighter streaks as well as dying their hair red, brown, or other colors.

Around the world, the use of hair coloring kits is more common than having hair colored at a salon. Most home coloring kits cost between $4 and $10, while a salon treatment may cost upwards of $50. However, in the United States at the turn of the twenty-first century, about 64 percent of the women who colored their hair did so in a salon. Salon receipts for hair coloring services reached $1.4 billion in 1999. L'Oreal was the top-selling brand in the United States with a market share of about 50 percent, while Clairol controlled 39 percent of the U.S. market.

An increasing number of men began coloring their hair after the 1970s. The old Roman practice of dipping a lead-coated comb in vinegar to darken the hair over time was the forerunner of modern hair coloring products such as Grecian Formula that gradually darken hair as metallic salt dyes deposit color on the shaft without penetrating it. The Grecian Formula name brand emerged during the twentieth century and appealed to men who wished to color their gray hair gradually, so that the change would not be so sudden or noticeable. Other popular men's hair coloring products include Just for Men and Men's Choice as well as male-oriented hair coloring kits made by the same companies that make hair colorants for women. These formulations produce permanent and semipermanent color using the same ingredients that are found in women's products but with names designed to appeal to men.

In 2002, sales of men's home hair coloring products reached $113.5 million, and about one in every twelve American men was coloring his hair. Most of these men were between ages thirty and fifty, and most were single or divorced. Surveys showed that Hispanic males were more likely than members of other ethnic groups to color their hair.

Young men in their teens or early twenties who like to wear distinctive clothing, hairstyles, and jewelry in pierced body parts also have used hair colorants to make personal statements. They have added highlights or bright color accents, sometimes combined with partially shaved heads. Basketball superstar Dennis Rodman inspired many young people with his unconventional use of hair colorants, including frequent color changes, the use of primary colors, and unique, multicolored styles.

More teens of both genders were using hair colorants by the turn of the twenty-first century—an estimated 30 percent in the United States. Marketing analysts said that teens regard hair color as a fun accessory that they can use to express their personal styles or make fashion statements, often through the use of bright, unusual colors and special effects such as stripes, highlighted tips, or bleached white hair. Surveys showed that boys preferred yellow and green colors while girls gravitated to reds and purples. To appeal to teens, companies have created products with whimsical names and youthful packaging designs. One example, launched in 1986, is L'Oreal's Hair Mascara. Some coloring kits geared for young people enable them to add striking temporary colors to their hair that last just for one evening or wash out over several shampoos.

Safety Concerns

Through the years, critics have questioned the safety of chemical hair dyes. Some consumers worry about the effects of certain ingredients used in these products. People also have developed **allergic reactions** after using certain products. Aniline dyes, which are found in semipermanent colorants, are liquid chemicals derived from coal tar. They can irritate the eyes, skin, and mucous membranes and cause allergic reactions. Blindness also can result if certain chemicals come into direct contact with the eyes.

Modern hair color formulations that deliver permanent or semipermanent color use ammonia and peroxide to open the hair cuticles, lighten hair, and then deposit color. Peroxide works by releasing oxygen, which combines with the dye molecules and helps them to develop and deposit color, which is a necessary step for covering gray. Allergic reactions may occur if a user is sensitive to the ammonia, peroxide, p-Phenylenediamine (paraphenylenediamine [PPD]) or diaminobenzene in hair colorants. Some consumers avoid using products that contain PPD, yet alternative products may contain mercury, lead, or other metals as well as ammoniated mercury, all of which may also be dangerous.

During the 1960s, consumer advocates suggested that certain materials used in hair dyes were associated with increased rates of cancer, especially cancer of the bladder. In 1975, tests conducted on common, commercial hair coloring products showed that certain permanent dyes contained mutagenic substances—that is, substances that can cause mutations in the genes of laboratory animals. Further testing showed that up to 89 percent of the chemical hair dyes on the market at that time might contain ingredients that are capable of causing genetic mutations. However, other scientists claim that the chance of being seriously harmed as a result of using hair colorants is quite slim, and hair colorant manufacturers contend that the products are safe to use.

Scientists have encouraged people to exercise caution when making decisions about coloring hair, and some have urged pregnant women to avoid using hair colorants to prevent any possible damage to their developing babies.

See also: Aging and Hair; Ball, Lucille; Beards, Men's; Egypt, Ancient; Elizabethan Era; Laws and Regulations; Monroe, Marilyn; Native Americans; Natural Products; Renaissance Europe; Revlon; Roman Empire; Wigs and Hairpieces

Further Reading: Balsdon, J. P. V. D., *Roman Women* (1962); Begoun, Paula, *Don't Go Shopping for Hair Care Products without Me* (2004); Center for the Study of Responsive Law, *Being Beautiful* (1986); Cooper, Wendy, *Hair* (1971); Fatham, Elaine, *Sex, Status, and Survival in Hellenistic Athens* (1973); Gladwell, Malcolm, "True Colors," *The New Yorker*, March 22, 1999; Hecht, Annabel, *Hair Dyes* (1978); Henkel, John, "A Colorful History," *FDA Consumer*, December 1993; Jorgensen, Anne D'Arcy, *Is There Cancer in Your Hair Dye?* (1982); Pitman, Joanna, *On Blondes* (2003); Pollak, Margie, "Hair Dye Dilemmas," *FDA Consumer*, April 1993; Ribeiro, Aileen, *Dress and Morality* (2004); Weiss, Michael J., "Guys Who Dye," *American Demographics*, June 1999.

HAIRDRESSERS, FAMOUS *See* Hairdressing

HAIRDRESSING

Hairdressing refers to the processes involved in cutting, cleansing, coloring, augmenting, and arranging hair. Hair care has been an important part of grooming practices for both men and women since ancient times, and certain people fulfilled the role of hairdresser. Hairdressing eventually became a profession, which some people also regard as an art form. Today's hairdressers use various tools and products to carry out their work.

> "Too bad that all the people who know how to run the country are busy driving taxi cabs and cutting hair."
>
> GEORGE BURNS (1896–1996), American actor and comedian

Ancient to Modern Times

Hairdressing as a specialized function or occupation dates back thousands of years. Ancient artwork includes drawings and paintings of people working on other people's hair. Greek writers, including Homer and Aristophanes, refer to hairdressing in their literary works.

Since hair had spiritual connotations in many ancient cultures, people who worked with hair were trusted and important members of their communities. In **Africa**, where a person's spirit was believed to reside in his or her hair, hairdressers were held in high esteem. People with a talent for hairdressing were encouraged to develop their skills so that they could serve others this way. Hairdressers developed close relationships with people as they spent hours washing, combing, oiling, styling, and ornamenting their hair. Male hairdressers served men, while women worked only with women. Before a master hairdresser died, he or she would give his or her combs and other tools to a chosen successor during a special ceremony.

Hairdressers in **ancient Egypt** had special decorated cases to hold their tools, which included scissors, lotions, and styling materials. **Barbers** also served as hairdressers, and personal barbers served wealthy men in their homes. Since Egyptians wore wigs, the wig makers were known for their hairdressing skills, too. In **ancient Greece** and Rome, household servants or slaves performed hairdressing functions, including dying hair and shaving. Men who lacked access to private hairdressing and shaving services or those who preferred a more social atmosphere went to a barbershop or street barber. Street barbers could be found in ancient Egypt and Greece, where they carried their equipment from place to place. Women had their hair groomed at home.

From the fifth century until the early 1300s, historians have not found many documents that discuss hairdressers in Europe. Barbers, including a very few female barbers, continued to perform hair care services, and they were in more demand after a papal decree in 1092 required all Roman Catholic clergymen to remove their facial hair. After the mid-1100s, hairdressers began to use an increasing number of tools and materials to carry out their work, especially when they colored the hair.

During the 1500s, men's barbershops again became the social gathering places they had been in ancient times. Barbers used curling irons as well as other tools to create the fancy hairstyles men favored during that time. A barber might have spent several hours washing and arranging a man's hair.

Development of the Profession

During the 1600s, the word "hairdresser" came into use in Europe, and hairdressing came to be regarded as a profession. As wealthier women began to favor large, complex, heavily adorned hairstyles, their personal maids and other people who spent hours arranging these styles were said to "dress the hair." A gentleman's valet cared for his master's hair.

In France, men began to style women's hair for the first time, and many leading hairdressers were men. The first famous male hairdresser was a man known as Champagne, who was born in southern France. After moving to Paris, he turned his gift for styling hair into a business and opened his own salon. Champagne continued to arrange the hair of wealthy Parisian women until he died in 1658.

During the first half of the seventeenth century, women's hairstyles were wide; over the next century they became progressively taller. A well-known hairdresser known as Madam Martin helped popularize tall hairstyles. Wealthy English and American women also relied on hairdressers to create the style called the tower—a tall pile of curls that people pomaded, powdered, and decorated with ribbons, feathers, flowers, lace, and various kinds of jewelry. This style was popular during the 1700s and spread throughout Europe.

Legros de Rumigny developed hairdressing into a genuine profession after he became the official hairdresser for the French court. In 1765, he published his *Art de la Coiffure des Dames*, a book about hairdressing that included pictures of dozens of hairstyles that he had designed. The book was regarded as essential for every fashionable Frenchwoman. Four years later, de Rumigny opened a school for hairdressers called Academie de Coiffure, where he taught men and women how to cut hair and create his special designs.

By 1777, approximately 1,200 hairdressers were working in Paris. Barbers had formed unions, and they insisted that hairdressers join their organizations. Conflicts also arose between hairdressers and wig makers, since wig makers claimed that hairdressers were not qualified to take away some of their trade. The hairdressers argued that their roles were not the same—hairdressing was a service in which people worked on the hair itself while wig makers made and sold a product.

By the time de Rumigny died in 1770, other hairdressers had risen to prominence. They included three French men known by the names Frederic, Larseueur, and Leonard. Both Larseueur and Leonard styled the hair of Queen Marie Antoinette. Leonard, who became the queen's favorite, designed some of the most fashionable styles worn by aristocratic Parisians. One of his trademark designs, the *loge d'opera,* towered about five feet above the wearer's head. During the **French Revolution**, Leonard managed to escape the country a few hours before he would have been arrested and put to death along with the king, queen, and his other aristocratic clients. Leonard emigrated to Russia, where he established himself as the premier hairdresser for the nobility.

Nineteenth Century

During the early 1800s, Parisian hairdressers continued to influence styles at home and abroad. Wealthy bourgeois French women hired their favorite hairdressers to arrange their hair in their homes, and hairdressers in other countries also visited the homes of wealthy clients. In France and most other nations, hairdressing services were available only to people wealthy enough to hire a professional or to pay servants who cared for their hair.

One of the most famous and notorious hairdressers in nineteenth-century America was Marie Laveau of New Orleans. During the early 1820s, she began working as a professional hairdresser for wealthy women. According to legends, Laveau used her social connections and the information these women shared with her during their hairdressing sessions to conduct a profitable practice of voodoo. People who believed in Laveau's "magic" asked her for help. When they received a favorable outcome, they paid her with money, gifts, or other favors. During the 1830s, Laveau was called the "Voodoo Queen of New Orleans."

At the end of the century, French hairdresser Marcel Grateau (1852–1936) introduced his influential **Marcel wave**. The style required a special hot iron and was best done by an experienced hairdresser. More and more women sought hairdressing services to have their hair "marceled."

Hairdressing became more organized as hairdressers opened salons in cities and small towns. Led by entrepreneur **Martha Matilda Harper**, hair care franchises, in the form of chains of salons, developed in the United States.

Twentieth Century

Hairdressing salons, often called beauty salons, continued to proliferate during the early 1900s. As with men's barbershops, these salons became places where women socialized as well as had their hair done and received other personal care services, such as facials. Hairdressers established luxurious salons in Rome, Vienna, London, Hamburg, New York, and other cities. Although wealthy women could still hire hairdressers to visit their homes, as the century continued, most women patronized salons, and certain elite salons, such as Elizabeth Arden's, attracted a wealthy clientele.

Advances in science and technology gave hairdressers more sophisticated tools for hair care and styling. With the advent of electricity and the development of **permanent wave** machines and **hair dryers**, hairdressers could offer professional services that their clients could not perform at home. A professional permanent wave required special training and took hours to complete. Hairdressers also learned to perform complicated hairstyling techniques and to apply new hair coloring formulations, starting with chemical hair colorants developed by Eugene Schueller in Paris.

After World War I, more women sought professional haircutting services in order to obtain **the bob**, the shingle, and other new, short styles. This remained true during the 1930s, when other complicated styles came into vogue. Some women continued to ask their hairdressers for Marcel waves. For women in the United States, hairdressing was one of a limited number of occupations, including teaching, nursing, and clerical work, that were considered suitable for women during these years.

Some Famous Hairdressers

The 1920s brought the first celebrity hairdresser—Polish-born Antek Cierplikowski (1885–1976), who founded the famous Antoine de Paris salon. Known as "Monsieur Antoine," he is credited with starting the fashion for short hair in 1910. During the 1920s, he created the shingle, which was cropped even shorter than most bobs and softly waved. The shingle became more popular than the conventional bob. Antoine himself was known as an eccentric who dyed his own hair and the hair of his poodle matching shades of lilac. In 1924, he gave his borzoi dog blue hair. One of his prominent clients, interior designer Lady Elsie Mendl, adopted the same tint, sparking a new fad. By the 1930s, Antoine was the world's best-known hairdresser. During that decade, he initiated a trend in upswept hairstyles. Antoine also introduced the idea of using a light blond streak to accent the hair. The Antoine salon at the Saks Fifth Avenue department store in New York City, which he opened in 1925, became America's most fashionable salon and spawned new generations of famous hairdressers. One of Antoine's protégés, Sydney Guilaroff (b. 1907), left New York for Los Angeles, where he became the first hairdresser to receive a film credit for styling hair. Guilaroff continued to work with actors in the movies, including Claudette Colbert, Joan Crawford, Clark Gable, Tyrone Power, Margaret Sullavan, Norma Shearer, Katharine Hepburn, Elizabeth Taylor, Ava Gardner, **Lucille Ball**, Jane Fonda, and many others.

Alexandre of Paris became another international hairdressing star. After founding his famous Paris salon, Alexandre established salons in other cities and at fashionable resorts where wealthy women spent their vacations. He often traveled at the request of his famous clients, who included the duchess of Windsor (the former Wallis Warfield Simpson), socialite Daisy Fellowes, and famous actresses. He also styled the hair of models who appeared in the couture collections for the world's top designers, including Christian Dior, Yves Saint Laurent, and Karl Lagerfeld.

During the 1940s, Maria and Rosy Carita opened their famous salon on Paris's renowned Boulevard St. Honoré. The Carita sisters worked with many famous women, including Farah Diba Pahlavi, the wife of the shah of Iran. They created a distinctive hairstyle for her wedding in 1959. During the 1960s, they were credited with sparking the trend in **wigs and hairpieces**, in the form of long falls and other pieces that augmented or changed a woman's hairstyle. The Carita sisters brought out their own hair care line, which became available in the United States as well as Europe.

As **bouffants** became fashionable, British hairdresser Raymond Bessone was nicknamed "Mr. Teasy Weasy" for his proficiency in creating these back-combed styles. Bessone, a hairdresser for many celebrities during the 1950s and 1960s, also was a television personality and racehorse owner who wore permed hair. One of his clients, actress Diana Dors, reportedly paid him $2,500 to fly to the United States and wash and style her hair for a special occasion.

The British hairdressers known as Toni & Guy—Anthony and Guy Mascolo—were born Guiseppe and Gaetano Mascolo in Italy. After the family moved to England, the two brothers learned hairdressing from their father and built a successful salon business, starting in 1963. The Mascolos won numerous awards for their hairdressing skills and developed a successful line of hair care products.

Londoner **Vidal Sassoon** became perhaps the world's most famous hairdresser during the 1960s, when he created his revolutionary bobs and geometric haircuts. Sassoon was paid $5,000 to fly to the set of the film *Rosemary's Baby* to cut the hair of actress Mia Farrow, one of his many celebrity clients. His Vidal Sassoon hair care products have been selling for more than thirty years.

Joshua Galvin, who has been called "The Godfather of Hairdressers," is descended from a family of wig makers, master barbers, and hairdressers. He became famous while working at Sassoon's London salon, where his clients included singer-actress Madonna and the late Princess Diana. Galvin remained with Sassoon from 1961 to 1975 and then opened his own salon business. He has remained in the field for over fifty years, and in 2004, he received the Lifetime Achievement Award from the Fellowship for British Hairdressing. His line of hair care products is known as Serum Solutions.

Nicky Clarke became familiar to the British public after he began doing weekly hair makeovers on the television program *This Morning.* Clarke, who was named British Hairdresser of the Year three times as of 2004, charges £350 for a haircut and endorses an aromatherapy hair care line. **Charles Worthington**, another hairdresser who is familiar to British television audiences, has won the British Hairdresser of the Year award several times. Worthington developed a popular line of pocket-sized hair care products.

Known for his creative styling, both for celebrities and regular clients, Trevor Sorbie won the British Hairdresser of the Year award four times as of 2004. Sorbie is the author of *Visions in Hair* (1998) and *The Bridal Hair Book* (2005). His hair care line includes shampoos, conditioners, and styling products.

Odile Gilbert began learning her craft in the famous Bruno Pittini salon in Paris. She then worked in New York City for seven years, creating studio hairstyles for prominent fashion magazines. By the 1990s, she had opened her own Paris salon. She continued to work part-time in New York, styling hair for top magazine photo shoots as well as creating unusual and show-stopping hairstyles for the spring and fall couture collections in Europe. Her work was featured in a 2003 book called *Her Style: Hair by Odile Gilbert.*

Charlie, a society hairdresser whose clients include prominent French actresses, first worked as an apprentice for the Carita sisters. After they began sending her to magazine studios to help with fashion shoots, photographer Sarah Moon asked her to style models' hair for her Cacharel ad campaign. After leaving the Caritas, Charlie spent the next twenty years doing only studio work. Another major career break came in 1992, when *Elle* magazine asked her to cut actress Catherine Deneuve's hair for a cover. Observers praised the resulting short haircut for its individuality and modern, feminine look. Within a week, numerous readers were requesting Deneuve's hairstyle. Charlie operated a private salon at Alexandre de Paris before opening her own salon, called Charlie en Particulier. In addition to cutting hair at a cost of 2,000 francs ($340) per cut, she works with clients to develop their personal styles.

Some hairdressers became famous for creating certain hairstyles that sparked trends. For example, British hairdresser Adee Phelan, who won the 2000 British Hairdressing Award in the "Men's" category, gave trendsetting soccer star David Beckham his Mohawk. After Beckham appeared in the World Cup matches, people asked about the haircut. Afterwards, Phelan reported that men from Japan and other countries made appointments to have him style their hair. Phelan and his business partner, Paul Merritt, founded the popular BLOWW hair salon in

London. Phelan and Merritt also starred on a popular British television reality show called *The Salon.*

Certain hairdressers, including **Frédéric Fekkai**, are known for their special expertise with **hair color**. During the 1980s, Louis Licari became one of the best-known hair color experts in the United States. A former art student and painter, Licari founded his flagship salon in New York City in 1987 and added his Louis Licari Color Group salon in Beverly Hills in 1992. He endorses a line of hair care products that aim to protect dyed hair from damage and fading.

By his mid-twenties, hairdresser Christophe Robin had established himself as a master colorist. A number of models and actresses rely on him for dramatic or subtle color changes in their hair. At his Paris salon, he is so busy that he can charge 1,000 francs for a coloring session. Once a month, Robin also sees clients in New York City.

Brad Johns became known for his approach to blond hair, in which he individualizes shades and highlights for each client. Johns, who worked at the Oribe salon in New York City before opening his own salon, also became known for adding "buttery chunks" of golden color and creating multicolored hair rather than a monotone look. He has devised coloring techniques to reflect the changing light conditions of various seasons. In one article, Johns said that successful coloring requires "the right vision, the right tools, and innovative techniques" (Johns 2004). His famous clients include actresses Natasha Richardson and Brooke Shields as well as male actors and models. As the artistic director of Avon Salon & Spa, Johns also developed hair care products and makeup that coordinate with certain hair colors.

At the beginning of the twenty-first century, the world's most talented hairdressers included Marcos Leonardo (Spain), Horst Chudy (Germany), Yasuko Inomaru (Japan), Johan Hellstrom (Sweden), Caterina di Biasi (Australia), Vivienne Mackinder and Antoinette Beenders (England), and Orlando Pita, **Sally Hershberger**, and Frankie Payne (USA).

Legal Requirements

Since 1900, hairdressers have been subject to more regulation from national and regional agencies than they had been before. Today, hairdressers in various countries are required to complete certain educational and training requirements before they can be licensed in their field.

Laws in the United States require candidates to complete an accredited cosmetology program that includes a certain number of training hours. States vary in terms of the precise number of hours and courses that must be completed, though schools usually offer courses in sanitation, hygiene, anatomy, chemistry, and laws governing beauty salons along with courses and practical experience in shampooing, haircutting, hair coloring, permanent waves, hair relaxing, and the use of wigs and hairpieces.

After completing an accredited course of study, a candidate may take an examination before receiving a license to practice. European countries may allow a candidate to apply for a license after he or she has served as an apprentice for a specific number of years. Salons also are subject to laws and regulations and may be periodically inspected by state officials.

During the 1990s, some disputes arose when women who perform hair-braiding services, including making cornrows, were told that they could not offer these services unless they attended a cosmetology program and received a license. To deal with this special branch of hairdressing, some states passed special laws. For example, New York and Michigan, among others, offered a license in natural hair care that did not require as many hours of cosmetology training as a general cosmetology license. Other states, including Maryland, exempted hair braiders from needing a license to practice their occupation. These states and others supplied them with brochures and other information about sanitary procedures they need to follow. The American Hairbraiders & Natural Haircare Association was founded by Taalib Din Uqdah as a trade organization to help members practice their trade and deal with the legal issues that affect them.

Organizations and Events

Hairdressers belong to various local, regional, national, and international organizations that advocate for people in their profession and promote educational activities and opportunities to meet other professionals. Among these organizations are groups that specialize in certain aspects of hairdressing, such as hair coloring or natural hair care.

Hairdressers receive recognition for their work and special achievements, both individually and in groups. Every two years, teams of hairdressers from different countries compete in the World Championships of Hairdressing, which are now held in conjunction with the beauty exposition called HairWorld. Teams vie for medals in three categories: ladies, gentlemen, and students. More than 100,000 beauty professionals attended the 2000 event, which was held in Berlin. Representatives from forty countries competed in events at the 2002 HairWorld, which was hosted by the National Cosmetology Association and held in Las Vegas. In 2004, Milan, Italy, hosted HairWorld.

Hair Color USA holds competitive international events in the area of hair coloring. More than 50,000 beauty professionals, including salon owners, managers, stylists, and cosmetologists, attend its annual events, which are combined with the International Beauty Show. This conference is held in Miami or New York City.

See also: Aniston, Jennifer; Battelle, Kenneth; Coming of Age; Dessange, Jacques; Eber, Jose; Fawcett, Farrah; Feathered Hairstyle; Hair Straightening; Hair Weave; Hamill, Dorothy; John Frieda Professional Hair Care, Inc.; Laws and Regulations; Masters, George; Michaeljohn; Noda, Alice Sae Teshima; Roman Empire; Salons, Hair and Beauty; Walker, Madam C. J.; Wigs and Hairpieces

Further Reading: Allan, Vicky, "A Career to Dye For," *Sunday Herald* (London), May 25, 2003, http://www.sundayherald.com/print34061; Bryer, Robin, *The History of Hair* (2003); Carter, Ernestine, *The Changing World of Fashion* (1977); Cooper, Wendy, *Hair* (1971); Corson, Richard, *Fashions in Hair* (2001); Gilbert, Odile, *Her Style* (2003); Guilaroff, Sydney, *Crowning Glory* (1997); Johns, Brad, "Dyeing to Know," *American Salon*, November 1, 2004, http://www.americansalonmag.com/americansalon/article/articleDetail.jsp?id=

129445; Kessler-Harris, Alice, *Out to Work* (2003); Loyer, Michele, "The Hands That Mold the Hair," *International Herald Tribune*, October 18, 1997, 13; Malagoli, Marisa, *Hairdressing throughout History* (1984); Potter, Eliza, *A Hairdresser's Experience in High Life* (2001); Rogozinski, Jan, *A Brief History of the Caribbean* (2000); Scott, Susan Craig, *The Hair Bible* (2003); Stuart, Julia, "Young Blades," *The Independent* (London), January 2003; Walton, Buddy, *High Styles* (2004); Zdatny, Steven, *Hairstyles and Fashion* (1999).

HAIR DRYERS

Hair drying machines came into use in 1920. Before that time, people had to dry their hair naturally or with machines designed for other purposes. After the electric vacuum cleaner was invented, women found that they could dry their hair by attaching the hose to the back end of the vacuum cleaner where the air blew out instead of being sucked in.

The first modern hair dryers were developed in Germany and were made from metal with wooden handles. By combining the technology used to make motors for vacuum cleaners with those found in electric heaters, inventors were able to create machines that emitted hot air. Because these hair dryers were large, bulky, and heavy, nearly all of them were purchased for salon use.

By the mid-1920s, hair dryers were being sold to both salons and individual consumers. They were still heavy as well as noisy, with a "bonnet" that fit around the head of a woman wearing curlers. The drying process could take an hour or more, depending on the length and thickness of the hair and the size of the curlers. From the 1920s into the 1960s, women could be seen in beauty salons sitting under dryers, reading or chatting while waiting for their hair to dry.

Some salon operators began using gas hair dryers during the 1930s. Although these machines were less expensive than previous versions, gas dryers produced fumes and tended to overdry the hair, so most people went back to using various electric models. Entrepreneur Robert Hoffman developed a successful professional hair drying system known as the Hoffman system. His electric machines became standard equipment in many American salons.

During the 1950s, a practical hair dryer for home use became available. These dryers were made of plastic in pastel colors chosen to coordinate with consumers' bathrooms. These dryers came with rigid hoods that were attached to the machine or more portable hoods that attached to a remote unit. Both types still required a user to sit under a dryer.

Over the next two decades, hair dryers became lighter and more portable. They also became safer when new versions included thermostats to regulate the temperature of the air so that it did not exceed 153 degrees Fahrenheit (85 degrees centigrade).

During the late 1960s, more women began wearing their hair long and straight or in short styles that did not require curlers. To achieve this look, many women let their hair dry into a loose, natural style or ironed it straight. In 1971, companies began to offer handheld hair dryers that became known as blow dryers. Some women used these dryers to achieve a straight look. Women who wanted curls or waves used heated hair rollers or new types of curling irons instead of sitting under a hair dryer wearing curlers, or they combined curlers with a blow dryer.

Today's hair dryers came in various sizes and designs for salon and personal use. Consumers can adjust the temperature and flow of air, and some dryers include attachments for styling purposes, such as diffusers, combs, and brushes. Cordless versions are also available. Hair dryers have become standard equipment in many hotel bathrooms, so travelers can blow-dry their hair without packing their own dryers.

Professional hairdressers and consumers alike use blow dryers to create hairstyles that look less "done" than the hairstyles of the 1950s and early 1960s. These hairstyles also can be finished more quickly, often within minutes after a shampoo.

See also: Hairdressing; Hairstyles, Twentieth-Century; Salons, Hair and Beauty; Styling Tools

Further Reading: The Research Group/The Hair Dryers Research Group, *The 2000–2005 World Outlook for Hair Dryers* (2000); Riordan, Teresa, *Inventing Beauty* (2004); Scott, Susan Craig, and Karen W. Bressler, *The Hair Bible* (2003).

HAIR GROWTH DISORDERS *See* Alopecia Areata; Beards, Women's; Hair Loss; Hirsutism; Hypertrichosis

HAIR JEWELRY

Hair jewelry refers to pieces that are either crafted from hair itself or that contain human hair—for example, a brooch or locket with a lock of hair tucked inside. Such sentimental objects, particularly **mourning** jewelry, were especially popular during the **Victorian era**.

The custom of wearing specific pieces of jewelry during periods of mourning may have begun during the reign of England's King Charles II in the late seventeenth century. During the 1800s, Queen Victoria played a major role in popularizing mourning jewelry. After her husband, Prince Albert, died in 1861, the queen wore clothing and jewelry in a mourning style for the next forty years. New types of mourning jewelry emerged, and its popularity spread throughout the British Empire and to the United States. During the Civil War (1861–1865), thousands of Americans wore black jewelry to commemorate loved ones. As well, soldiers leaving for war often carried gold or silver lockets containing locks of hair from their girlfriends and wives as love tokens.

Mourning brooches that could be pinned on the owner's clothing were common during the 1800s. A lock of the deceased person's hair was kept inside the brooch, which often had a clear window in front. Such pins might have held the likeness of the deceased person on one side with their hair attached to the other side.

Some mourning brooches were studded with gems, such as jet, a black or very dark brown stone that can be carved. Brooches also featured ornate designs in the metal. The hair inside often was sculpted to form the shape of a willow tree, a plume of feathers, or some other object.

More than 100 mourning rings were made in honor of the English author and diarist Samuel Pepys (1633–1703). These rings were distributed to Pepys' family members, servants, godchildren, and friends. U.S. President George Washington also requested that rings made from his hair be given to his mourners along with a memorial card.

Hair has been crafted into many different types of jewelry. Often, the hair is braided before it is arranged in various designs to make pins, bracelets, pendants, earrings, and rings. During the 1800s, people made their own hair jewelry or paid a professional hair worker to complete a commissioned piece. Some people preferred to create their own hair jewelry so they would know it was authentic and not made from hair that a hair worker obtained elsewhere.

People could find instructions for making hair jewelry or **hair art** in booklets and magazines, and they could order the items they needed for this craft. Many of these pieces were complex, requiring careful handling and numerous steps to complete. One major source for hair jewelry patterns and accessories was *Godey's Lady's Book*, a popular magazine published in the United States from 1830 to 1898. The magazine offered items that people could order to make hair jewelry in the form of breast pins, belt buckles, earrings, bracelets, cuff links, rings, necklaces, fob chains (for pocket watches), and charms. Readers also could send in their hair and pay someone else to make their hair jewelry.

See also: Hair Analysis

Further Reading: Bell, Jeanenne, *Collector's Encyclopedia of Hairwork Jewelry* (1998); Campbell, Mark, Jules Kliot, and Kaethe Kliot, *The Art of Hair Work* (1989); Harran, Susan, and Jim Harran, "Remembering a Loved One with Mourning Jewelry," *Antique Week*, December 1997, http://www.hairwork.com/remember.htm; Luthi, Ann L., *Sentimental Jewellery* (2002).

HAIR LOSS

Hair loss, or thinning of the hair, occurs when hair follicles die and stop producing hairs or when hairs are produced at a slower than normal rate. A normal scalp usually contains about 100,000 to 150,000 hairs. For hair loss to be noticeable, about 25 percent (25,000 or more hairs) must be lost.

Hair loss as a result of hormonal changes is a normal part of the physical aging process for both men and women. It also may occur as a result of disease, including inflammatory skin diseases that cause scarring and permanent death of hair follicles, or by chemical or physical damage to the scalp, hair, or hair follicles. Diseases that can cause hair loss include lichen planopilaris (a form of lichen planus that affects the scalp), discoid lupus erythematosus, and folliculitis decalvans. Systemic diseases, including diabetes, also can cause hair loss. In traction hair loss, hair falls out because of long-term pulling caused by certain hairstyles, such as wearing the hair in a tight ponytail or braids.

One type of excess shedding of hairs called telogen effluvium may result from illness, prolonged emotional or physical stress, malnutrition, a poorly functioning pituitary or thyroid gland, fungal infections including ringworm, intense fever, pregnancy, chemotherapy or radiation treatments for cancer, and certain medications, such as anticoagulants. When temporary conditions cause hair loss, normal growth tends to resume within six months to one year. Although telogen effluvium may affect hairs all over the body, hair loss on the scalp usually is most evident.

Hair loss can cause emotional distress, diminish self-esteem, and make people feel less attractive. Such feelings are most common in cultures that value youth, since thick, healthy-looking hair is considered attractive, and hair loss usually is regarded as a sign of aging.

For thousands of years, people have sought ways to reverse or stop hair loss. In addition to magic or spiritual rituals, they have tried special shampoos, tonics, hairbrushes, massages, and other treatments. The first truly effective medical remedies were developed during the late twentieth century.

Male Hair Loss

Men experience normal hair loss as a result of aging and/or hormonal influences, resulting in the condition called male pattern baldness (MPB), known to scientists as androgenetic alopecia. The hair loss usually starts at the crown and/or temples and follows a pattern that includes a receding hairline and bald spot on top of the head. As hair loss continues, a horseshoe-shaped area of hair remains on the head or the entire head gradually becomes bald.

Heredity affects the timing, speed, pattern, and extent of the hair loss. Scientists believe that at least four genes are involved in transmitting the tendency to male pattern baldness.

Male pattern baldness affects about two-thirds of all men—approximately 40 million American men in 2004. This process typically begins between the ages of twenty and forty-five, although it may start as early as the teen years. It affects about 12 percent of men by age twenty-five, and by age thirty, about 25 percent of men have begun to lose some hair. Some 45 percent of men have lost hair by age forty-five, and by age seventy, only about 15 percent of all men have little or no bald areas on the scalp. Understandably, hair loss with MPB tends to be more extensive the earlier in life it begins.

The incidence and severity of male pattern baldness differs among members of different nationalities. For example, Asian men are less likely to lose their hair than their European counterparts.

Through the years, researchers have proposed theories about the cause of male pattern baldness. At one time, people thought that it resulted from tightening of the scalp, or more specifically, tightening of the galea, a membrane of tendons covering the crown of the head. A Swedish physician named Lars Engstrand suggested that this process begins in puberty and causes the blood vessels on the head to constrict, thus reducing blood flow to the hair follicles. Engstrand devised a surgical procedure designed to alleviate this problem.

Today, most scientists believe that MPB results from an interaction between genetics and hormonal influences. On areas of the scalp prone to baldness, an enzyme called 5-alpha reductase changes testosterone circulating in the blood to the hormone called dihydrotestosterone (DHT). Scientists theorize that high amounts of free testosterone and 5-alpha reductase lead to more hair loss. DHT affects hair follicles in several key ways. It shortens the anagen (growing) stage of hair follicles and seems to prolong the telogen (resting) phase. DHT also seems to shrink, or "choke," hair follicles, resulting in hair that is thinner in diameter, and it may constrict capillaries, which then reduces blood flow that brings oxygen and nutrients to the follicles.

Female Hair Loss

In women, hair loss or noticeable thinning of the hair often occurs when levels of the female hormone estrogen decline after menopause. Prior to that time, estrogen helps to counteract testosterone, which can be converted into the hormone DHT, which can cause hair follicles to shrink or enter the resting stage of the hair growth cycle earlier than normal. About 15 percent of all women are affected by noticeable thinning of the number of hairs.

Whereas older males may have certain bald areas or total baldness, age-related hair loss in women tends to be more diffuse. An overall thinning of hair occurs and the hair at the top of the forehead continues to grow rather than having the hair line recede, as it does in males. Women's hair loss as a result of aging tends to occur at a later age than it does for men and is less extensive.

Treatments for Hair Loss

People deal with hair loss in various ways, including accepting the condition and not trying to disguise it. Some people change their hairstyles or replace missing hair with removable hairpieces, wigs, or hair extensions. Others opt to attach nonremovable hair replacements to their remaining hair, or they undergo surgical transplants to place growing hair into the scalp itself. Still others use topical treatments, massage, dietary changes, nutritional supplements, or prescription drugs that claim to grow hair.

Since ancient times, people have tried to reduce or conceal hair loss, primarily in attempts to look more youthful. Author Wendy Cooper described one remedy that was recorded about 4000 BCE by the mother of King Chata of Egypt: "She recommended rubbing the head vigorously with a preparation made of dog's paws, dates, and asses' hooves ground and cooked in oil" (Cooper 1971, 151). Other ancient Egyptian remedies called for animal fats to be applied to balding areas on the scalp. Animals used for this purpose included cats, lions, goats, ibexes, geese, hippopotamuses, and various snakes. Yet another recipe combined bear grease, deer marrow, horse teeth, and burned domestic mice. This was the remedy that Egypt's famous queen, Cleopatra, suggested for Roman Emperor Julius Caesar. The use of snake oil, particularly from reptiles that were captured during a full moon, was common to many cultures. In parts of the Middle East and Mongolia, men used yogurt on their balding scalps. Around 400 BCE in Greece, the physician Hippocrates, known as "the Father of Medicine," recommended a blend of opium, essence of roses, wine, and the oil of green olives or a mixture combining cumin, pigeon droppings, crushed horseradish, and nettles. Sometimes he used pigeon droppings alone. When the philosopher Aristotle began losing hair, he rubbed goat's urine on his head.

The Romans used pastes made from ashes, earthworms, and boiled walnut shells to prevent hair loss or graying of the hair. Another Roman formula combined tar and sulfur with urine taken from various animals that lived in the Mediterranean area.

Various plant remedies also were popular. Ancient Egyptians made a paste from chopped lettuce that was applied directly to the scalp. Other plant remedies for hair loss included the use of castor oil, almond oil, and extracts from evergreen trees. Fenugreek seeds and rosemary were among the herbs that people thought would improve hair growth in bald men.

The use of rosemary was especially popular in ancient **China**. The Chinese also massaged their scalps with safflower oil or with a mixture made from herbs and animal testes, which were first dried and then ground up. In China and India, headstands also have been among the traditional remedies for baldness. This stems from the belief that improved circulation helps hair growth. An herb called bhringaraj also was recommended for hair loss in India. Another common Indian remedy was made by boiling sage leaves in coconut oil and then applying that to the scalp.

Native Americans favored the juice from the aloe plant. They also applied bear oil or bear grease to their head and hair. Some early European settlers in America adopted this practice and began using bear grease or oil on their own hair.

Old and new remedies for baldness were used during the **Middle Ages**. Some men swallowed drinks brewed from mandrake root to restore hair growth. Medieval monks and alchemists concocted new recipes for restoring hair, and sometimes these substances were applied with prayers or special incantations. During the 1500s, the book *Natural Magick*, written by Giovanni Battista della Porta, offered various formulas for helping hair to "grow again." Some recipes were complicated and contained unusual ingredients, such as "ashes of a Land Hedge hog" (Cooper 1971, 152). Faster treatments could be carried out with "burned barley bread, horse fat, and boiled river eel" (Cooper 1971, 152). A seventeenth-century Italian chemist offered his "vine dew" to French royalty at high prices. After the product was shown to contain mostly water, the chemist was banished and left for Italy, where he sold another "cure" for hair loss called "calf water."

Nineteenth Century

The quest to delay hair loss or restore hair continued as people made and used various lotions, oils, hair tonics, and mechanical devices. Bear oil grew even more popular during the early 1800s. Various merchants placed ads for "genuine bear's oil," claiming that such products could restore the hair of bald people and prevent others' hair from falling out. Sales reached a peak during the 1830s.

During the nineteenth century, treatments for baldness were concocted of snake oil, beef marrow, butter, onion juice, flower water, and other substances. Although many products claimed to increase hair growth, none of them was proven effective. Some treatments for hair loss included toxic substances, such as sulfur or mercury.

One famous hair tonic from the middle of the nineteenth century was Barry's Tricopherous, made by Alexander C. Barry, who used the title of "professor." A former wig maker, Barry came up with a formula that contained 97 percent alcohol, 1.5 percent castor oil, and 1 percent tincture of cantharides, commonly known as Spanish fly. Cantharides is an irritant, and during those years, irritating the scalp was thought to stimulate hair growth by increasing circulation. It was commonly used in tonics for hair loss during the 1800s, as was capsicum, another irritant. People also used massage treatments to improve blood flow to the scalp, and mechanical devices were made for this purpose.

Another well-known commercial hair tonic sold in the United States during the 1880s purported to contain cantharides. In 1882, Fletcher Sutherland patented his famous Seven Sutherland Sisters Hair Grower, which was sold through ads featuring his seven daughters, who had long, thick hair. After entrepreneur J. Henry Bailey married Naomi, one of the sisters, he promoted the hair tonic around the country by having the sisters tour with a circus, showing off their tresses. Bailey claimed that the tonic was made with borax, salt, quinine, cantharides, bay rum, glycerin, rose water, alcohol, and soap. When a pharmaceutical journal conducted a chemical analysis of the compound in 1896, however, it found that the tonic contained 56 percent water of witch hazel, 44 percent bay rum, hydrochloric acid, and trace amounts of magnesia and other salts.

According to the American Medical Association, twentieth-century consumers wasted millions of dollars each year buying shampoos, lotions, tonics, massagers, and other products that did not fulfill their claims. Still, new products appeared in the marketplace seeking a share in the very profitable hair products industry, which earned $1 billion a year after the mid-1900s.

Hoping to find an effective remedy for baldness, researchers and physicians experimented with ointments containing testosterone, the major male hormone, during the 1960s. The results were disappointing, however.

Medications for Hair Loss

The late twentieth century brought new medications for treating hair loss, which were shown to be effective for some people. These drugs aim to reduce the amount and effects of DHT or to stimulate hair follicles.

Minoxodil, a drug used to treat hypertension (high blood pressure), was found to promote hair growth in the people who took it. Doctors Charles A. Chidsey and Guinter Kahn worked to develop a topical formulation for direct use on the scalp, and the Upjohn company launched this drug under the brand name Rogaine. Clinical tests showed that consistent use of Rogaine did encourage hair growth in some people, but the results continued only as long as they used the product. However, for those with temporary hair loss caused by radiation therapy or trauma and using Rogaine, hair growth will resume as normal after the treatment or the trauma is over, even when the drug is discontinued.

Scientists were not sure exactly how minoxidil worked. They thought that since it dilates blood vessels, it might increase circulation, which would bring more nourishment to hair follicles. However, other drugs that dilate the blood vessels did not have the same impact on hair growth. Another theory was that minoxidil increases the size of hair follicles so that they produce hairs of normal diameter instead of thin hairs. Scientists thought the drug also might extend the anagen phase of hair growth. A widely held theory is that minoxidil affects the hair cycle by causing the follicles to extend the growing stage and perhaps shorten the resting stage. A longer growing stage would enable hair to become longer and thicker.

In 1988, the FDA approved Rogaine for use in men as a medically prescribed treatment for hair loss; in 1991, the drug was approved for use in nonpregnant women. In the late 1990s, Rogaine became available to consumers without a prescription. It is now available in different strengths (2 percent and 5 percent) as well as in versions for male and female consumers. It is sold as a topical solution that can be sprayed on or massaged into areas of the scalp where hair is thinning.

Finasteride, commonly known by its brand name, Propecia, works by hindering the action of DHT. Merck & Company offers Propecia in the form of a pill taken orally once a day. Originally used to treat urinary problems and benign prostate enlargement, this drug was approved by the FDA for the treatment of male pattern baldness in men only. Scientists explained that the drug slows the conversion of testosterone into DHT by partially neutralizing the enzyme 5-alpha reductase. In some studies, men who took 1 mg of finasteride daily showed a decrease of almost 60 percent in the level of DHT in their scalp tissue. As with minoxidil, men must continue to take finasteride or their baldness will proceed on course. The drug is available only by prescription.

Some studies have shown that minoxidil and finasteride are about 35 to 45 percent effective in promoting hair growth on the crown area of the head within a one-year period. They appear to have less impact on the front of the scalp.

Other Remedies

People also address hair loss by nonmedical means, including improved nutrition and the use of nutritional supplements. This may help reduce hair loss if malnutrition is a factor. Iron-deficiency may contribute to hair loss. Eating iron-rich foods or taking iron supplements helps bring up the level of ferritin, an iron-containing protein, in the blood in people who are iron deficient.

Some scientists also recommend a diet that is low in fat, especially animal fat, because fat reduces the amount of a protein called sex hormone binding globulin (SHBG) in the blood. SHGB binds to testosterone in the blood, which means that less testosterone is then available to be converted into DHT.

Supplements that improve circulation also have been recommended in order to bring more oxygen and nutrients to the scalp. Saw palmetto has been promoted as an herb that stimulates hair growth. Other herbs and treatments come from traditional Chinese and Indian (Asian) medicine.

As of 2004, American men were spending more than $1.3 billion per year on treatments for baldness, including drugs and **hair transplants**. Others made use of nonmedical treatments, including changing their hairstyles or wearing hairpieces or hair extensions. Women also sought help from hairdressers, hair replacement specialists, and dermatologists. Founded in 1976, the Hair Club for Men & Women is a commercial enterprise that offers people information about various treatments and products for dealing with hair loss.

Some men choose to accept their hair loss or simply shave off their remaining hair. Baldness became more fashionable after well-known celebrities, notably basketball superstar Michael Jordan, deliberately shaved their heads. Actors, models, and athletes are among those who have made baldness more fashionable. Some of the best known are actors Ving Rhames and Vin Diesel and wrestler Steve Austin.

See also: Aging and Hair; Alopecia Areata; Baldness, Voluntary; Folliculitis; Hair Weave; Shaving; Toupee; Trichotillomania; Wigs and Hairpieces

Further Reading: American Hair Loss Council, "Causes of Hair Loss," http://www.ahlc.org/causes-m.htm; Baudet, A. L., et al., eds., *The Metabolic Basis of Inherited Disease* (1989); Cooper, Wendy, *Hair* (1971); Dunn, Carolyn A., "The Ethnic Hair Care Market," *Happi*, April 1997; Ellingwood, Finley, MD, *The American Materia Medica* (1919); Greenwood-Robinson, Margaret, *Hair Savers for Women* (2000); Hitzig, Gary S., MD, *Help & Hope for Hair Loss* (1997); Hudson, Patrick, MD, "Causes of Male Pattern Baldness," http://www.phudson.com; Kuntzman, Gersh, *Hair: Mankind's Historic Quest to End Baldness* (2001); Muller, Richard W., *Baldness: Its Causes, Its Treatment and Its Prevention* (1918); Olsen, E. A., et al., "Five Year Follow-Up of Men with Androgenetic Alopecia Treated with Topical Minoxidil," *Journal of the American Academy of Dermatology* (April 1990): 643–646; Pine, Devera, "Hair! From Personal Statement to Personal Problem," *FDA Consumer*, December 1991; Scott, Susan Craig, *The Hair Bible* (2003); Van Deusen, Edmund, *What You Can Do about Baldness* (1978).

HAIR NET

Containers for the hair made from knotted material date back at least to the eleventh century. Hair nets hold the hair while still revealing it and allowing the air to circulate. They were widely worn during the **Middle Ages** and the Renaissance, and different versions have been used into the twenty-first century. Hair nets have been worn for aesthetic reasons, to maintain a hairstyle, to keep a setting in place, or to contain the hair for sanitary purposes.

Early hair nets were made by knotting loops of single-ply silk threads in various shades of brown. Some nets were decorated with golden threads or gemstones. Poorer women wore nets made from less-expensive material, such as crepe. During the Middle Ages and the Renaissance, women wore hair nets along with other **headgear**, such as hats, chin straps, or veils.

During the fourteenth century, hair nets changed in designs and materials. Thicker cords replaced fine threads, and the nets were decorated with ribbons, beading, and other accessories. Later, woven or crocheted nets were made to hold chignons or buns in place while still showing the hair. These nets, often called snoods, came in plain or decorative designs.

By the twentieth century, many women were wearing utilitarian hair nets at night to secure their hairstyles or keep hair rollers or pin curls in place. Some women also wore a hair net over their curlers or pin curls in the daytime. Manufacturers offered nets made in different shades, such as blond, brown, black, auburn, to match the hair color of the consumer. Nets also came in different sizes to fit various hairstyles and heads.

During the twentieth century, laws regarding hair nets have affected certain workers. These laws were passed, in most cases, for health and safety reasons. In some cases, manufacturers of hair nets and hairpins spearheaded these laws, such as when their sales declined dramatically in the 1920s after millions of women bobbed their hair. Laws have required people working in food-service jobs, including cooks, caterers, and servers, to wear hair nets so their hair does not make contact with food. Before and during the early 1900s, some hospitals required nurses to wear hair nets. Workers who handle certain kinds of machinery also are required to wear a hair net or other covering for safety reasons. Some high school and college music departments require members of their marching bands to wear a hair net to contain their hair if it might otherwise touch or fall below their collar while they are performing in uniform.

See also: Advertising; Bob, The; Laws and Regulations; Renaissance Europe; Victorian Era

Further Reading: Geist, William E., "Selling Soap to Children and Hairnets to Women," *The New York Times*, March 27, 1985, http://partners.nytimes.com/books/98/08/16/specials/bernays-selling.html; Horsting, Ruth, and Rosana Pistolese, *History of Fashions* (1970); ICON Group International, Inc., *The World Market for Hair Nets* (2003); Lester, Katherine Morris, and Bess Viola Oerke, *Accessories of Dress* (1940).

HAIRPIN

Hairpins are slender, straight or U-shaped hair accessories used to hold a hairstyle, hairpiece, hat, or headdress in place. Hairpins have been used to secure and/or adorn the hair since ancient times. Early hairpins were simple, with one prong that ended in either a rounded or sharp tip. Such pins have been found during archaeological digs in parts of **Africa**, Asia, Europe, and the **Middle East**. They were made from pieces of wood, bone, thorns, or stone. Wooden hairpins worn in ancient Rome were studded with gems and other trimmings.

Early hairpins also were crafted from metal. As early as 2000 BCE, the Greeks were making decorative gold hairpins studded with gold flowers. Some Roman hairpins from the third and fourth century CE were made from bronze. Gold and silver hairpins also have been found in fourth-century Scythian tombs that were excavated in present-day southern Russia.

Two-pronged hairpins may have emerged in Asia. Some Chinese hairpins dating back to 300 CE were made from bone, horn, wood, and metal and were designed with two prongs. Many of them are decorated with gemstones and carved into various designs, such as flowers. People also continued to wear one-pronged hairpins made from jade, ivory, and other materials. Some featured detailed carvings of dragons, for example. Japanese hairpins tended to be simpler in design. These hairpins, as well as those made in Korea during medieval times, were fairly thick. Some wooden pins were lacquered and inlaid with ivory, silver, and mother-of-pearl. Throughout Asia, hairpins also were made from tortoiseshell. In modern times, **China** and Korea became the top producers of the commercial hairpins that women use for styling their hair.

Modern, two-pronged hairpins have been used to set hairstyles or keep sections of hair in place. They have been especially useful as hair accessories in times and places in which women wore their hair in buns, chignons, French twists, or swept on top of their heads.

The name "bobby pins" came into use during the late 1910s. After women began cutting their hair into the style called **the bob**, which became very popular during the 1920s, people used hairpins to hold back sections of their hair. In England, the name "grip" was used.

During the 1950s, most women owned hairpins, which they used to anchor pin curls to create curly hairstyles or to hold back strands of hair when they wore ponytails. As mesh and plastic hair rollers came into use, hairpins were used to secure them to the hair.

Plain metal hairpins designed for utilitarian purposes are manufactured in shades of gold, brown, and black. Decorative hairpins come in numerous shapes, sizes, colors, and designs. The ends of these hairpins are trimmed with bows, flowers, rhinestones, pearls, crystals, and other decorations. Children's hairpins may feature beads, plastic animals, cartoon characters, or other childlike designs.

See also: Adornment, Ornamental; Comb; Styling Tools

Further Reading: Belinkskij, Andrej, and Heinrich Harke, "The 'Princess' of Ipatovo," *Archaeology*, March/April 1999, www.archaeology.org/9903/newsbriefs/ipatovo.html; Carter, Ernestine, *The Changing World of Fashion* (1977); Hashimoto, Sumiko, *Okazaki Collection* (1989); Turudich, Daniela, *1940s Hairstyles* (2001).

HAIR REMOVAL

Removal of **body hair** in humans—known as depilation—dates back to prehistoric times. People have used various devices and materials to remove unwanted body hair. These include cutting tools, tweezers, abrasive materials, sharp-edged objects, chemicals, electrolysis, and lasers. **Shaving** is the most common method of hair removal.

Except for certain medical situations, such as surgery, childbirth, or to prevent parasites, people remove body hair for reasons of aesthetics, cultural and religious traditions, social norms, and personal preference. For example, social norms prompt men in many countries to keep their faces clean-shaven. Buddhist priests have traditionally shaved their heads for religious reasons. In the Middle Eastern countries of Egypt, Turkey, Lebanon, and Palestine, it was customary for a bride's attendants to remove her body hair, except for the **eyebrows** and head hair, the night before the ceremony. Some tribes in central Africa followed a similar custom, removing hair from their arms and legs by shaving and by plucking **pubic hairs**. Some athletes remove the hair on their legs and/or arms. For example, body builders remove hair for a sleeker look that shows nuances of muscle development. Swimmers remove hair because it reduces friction, which can improve their performance. Cyclists also sometimes remove their leg hair to promote faster healing of any cuts or abrasions they might receive during falls or crashes.

Archaeologists believe that humans have removed their facial hair since prehistoric times, when they used the sharpened edges of rocks or shells or pushed two shells together in order to tweeze the hairs. Ancient Sumerians and Romans made devices resembling modern tweezers. People in ancient **China** and Arabia used pieces of string to tie and pull out unwanted hairs, a hair removal method that still is used today.

Shaving and abrasion were common methods of removing hair from larger areas. In ancient **India**, Hindus shaved the face and pubic area. In **ancient Egypt**, people shaved their heads, which was a practical way to keep cool and prevent lice infestation. Egyptian women shaved other parts of their bodies, and they used beeswax or cream depilatories made with an alkali, such as quicklime, to remove hair from their legs. Ancient Egyptians, Romans, and Greeks also used abrasive materials, including pumice stones, for hair removal.

On other continents, **Native Americans** and Pacific Islanders removed hair by scraping the skin with sharp-edged seashells. Samoan Islanders removed the hair from their armpits but left women's pubic hair intact. Ancient Mayans and Aztecs of Latin America sharpened obsidian to an extremely fine edge, which made this volcanic glass useful for shaving. Native tribes in Brazil used tweezers made from pieces of split bamboo to pluck body hair, including their eyebrows and lashes. In northern Rhodesia, warm ashes were massaged into areas slated for hair removal before those hairs were plucked.

The ancient Turks may have been the first to remove hair with chemical preparations, which dissolved hair at the skin's surface. A mixture called *rhusma* was made from arsenic trisulphide, quicklime (an alkali), and starch. *Rhusma* was made as early as 4000–3000 BCE. Likewise, modern chemical depilatories have been formulated with an alkali in a solution. During the 1700s, European settlers observed that Native Americans were using caustic lye on the skin to burn away hair.

Another method for removing hair was sugaring. In the Middle East, this depilatory was made by cooking sugar, lemon, and other ingredients to form a paste that was applied directly on the skin. Various sugaring techniques still are used today.

During the **Middle Ages**, women plucked their eyebrows and the hair on their foreheads and hairlines to achieve the pale look and high forehead that were considered beautiful at that time. They used tweezers or forceps to pull out these hairs. To inhibit hair growth, young girls applied walnut oil to their foreheads. Another method of hair removal was the application of vinegar and dried cat dung directly to the site. A recipe for hair remover from the early eighteenth century called for pulverized eggshells.

By the 1840s, powdered depilatories were available in the United States. Some powders were mixed with water, and the resulting paste was applied to the skin. A man named Dr. Gouraud advertised his hair removal powder in New York City newspapers, claiming that the preparation was one of the Queen of Sheba's cherished beauty secrets.

Modern Methods

As in ancient times, the most commonly used modern techniques for hair removal achieve temporary, not permanent, results. Abrasive methods to remove hair are still available, though they have been less popular since the 1940s. Such methods involve mitts or disks made from fine-textured sandpaper, which are rubbed on the legs or other area to get rid of hairs. Abrasive materials have been used primarily to remove fine hair from the legs, since they can irritate skin on the face, arms, or pubic area. Since the effects may not last longer than a few days, some women only used this technique to remove stray hairs between shaving or waxing sessions.

Shaving is the most common way to remove unwanted hair, particularly on the face, legs, and underarm area. In the United States and many other countries, leg hair is regarded as unattractive on females once they reach puberty. Girls who wish to remove this hair frequently begin by using a razor, cream, or lotion depilatory. During the late twentieth century, new shaving devices that pull out hairs from the root became available. The results last longer than shaving off hair at skin level.

Waxing, which also removes hair at the root, can be used on various parts of the body, including the eyebrows, face, bikini area, legs, arms, back, abdomen, and feet. Early forms of waxing used natural substances, mainly beeswax. In Brazil and Venezuela, people discovered that the waxy sap of the coco de mono tree could be used as a depilatory. Today, either cloth strips coated with a waxy preparation or manufactured wax strips are placed over the skin and then pulled off quickly once the wax has had a chance to set, taking hairs with the wax. New hairs usually do not grow back in a waxed area for three to eight weeks.

Companies offer various waxing kits and formulations for use at home or in salons. Since the late 1900s, an increasing number of customers have visited salons for waxing services. Women most often wish to remove hair on the legs and pubic area (which is called a bikini wax or Brazilian wax); both men and women have their eyebrows waxed.

Permanent Hair Removal

Starting in the late 1800s, new methods were developed to permanently remove hairs that people are sure they do not want anymore, including those on the upper back, between the eyebrows, and on a woman's breast or chin. In 1875, Charles E. Michel, an ophthalmologist practicing in St. Louis, Missouri, invented electrolysis as a means to remove ingrown eyelashes. Michel's device operated with galvanic current and a surgical needle.

Electrolysis works by destroying the hair follicle itself so the hair cannot grow back. An electrologist inserts a very slender probe into the follicle and then transmits a low electrical current into the follicle and the papilla, which nourishes the hair.

Hair also may be permanently removed through laser treatments. Laser—an acronym for "light amplification stimulated emission of radiation"—works by generating an intensely focused emission of light rays. People may undergo several laser treatments to remove hair from a fairly large area of the body.

Cultural Aspects

Choices about hair removal may reflect a desire to conform with prevailing customs or to flout convention. One example is removing hair from the legs. This cultural standard, which prevails for women in Western societies, developed during the twentieth century as women's clothing became more revealing and their legs were more visible to the public. During those decades, new forms of safety razors made shaving more convenient, and companies knew they could earn higher profits if women, as well as men, began using razors on a regular basis.

Some social historians also note that when women cut their hair shorter, wore trousers, gained the right to vote, and entered professions that were once strictly male, the differences between the sexes became less distinct. Fashions that dictated shorter hair for men and hairless legs for women emphasized their physical differences. Since the 1920s, the majority of American women have opted to remove the hair from their legs, either with a razor or a depilatory.

Some women, however, choose not to do so. They may prefer a "natural look" or consider this act of hair removal to be irrelevant, a waste of time, or a form of oppression in a male-dominated society. Some women who do not remove their leg hair reject social norms that tell women how they 'should' or 'should not' look.

See also: Arabia, Ancient through Middle Ages; Baldness, Voluntary; Barbers; Beards, Men's; Beards, Women's; Elizabethan Era; Gillette Company; Greece, Ancient; Hirsutism; Hypertrichosis; Latin America, Ancient Times to 1500s; Mustache; Pubic Hair; Roman Empire; Salons, Hair and Beauty

Further Reading: Bickmore, Helen, *Milady's Hair Removal Techniques* (2003); Cooper, Wendy, *Hair* (1971); Godfrey, Sheila, et al., *Principles and Practice of Electrical Epilation* (2001); Goldberg, David Joseph, *Laser Hair Removal* (2000); Simon, Diane, *Hair: Public, Political, Extremely Personal* (2000); Tyldesley, Joyce, *Daughters of Isis* (1995).

HAIRSPRAY

Hairspray is a product designed to hold a hairstyle in place and minimize the effects of wind and humidity. It also is used for styling purposes. Some hairsprays contain sunscreen or ingredients intended to help prevent hair color from fading.

The technology used in modern hairspray was developed during the late eighteenth century and was initially used for carbonated beverages that were self-pressurized in their containers. Inventors developed valves and propellants that led to the first aerosol products during the 1920s.

The hairspray industry began to thrive after the aerosol process was patented and practical aerosol cans were made during the 1940s. After the United States entered World War II in 1941, the U.S. government funded research to find ways for military personnel serving in the Pacific to transport insecticide sprays that would limit the spread of malaria. A Norwegian engineer, Erik Rotheim, had developed and patented a modern form of aerosol spray in the 1920s. In 1943, researchers Lyle David Goodhue and W. N. Sullivan, who worked for the U.S. Department of Agriculture, developed a practical small aerosol can that was pressurized by a liquefied gas (a fluorocarbon).

Another inventor, Robert H. Abplanal, introduced a crimp-on valve that could dispense gases under pressure. Abplanal later also invented the "aquasol," or "pump spray," which uses water-soluble hydrocarbons as propellants. With aerosol cans and a clog-free valve, hairspray formulas could be packaged more effectively for consumers.

Early hairsprays contained alcohol, lacquer, and other ingredients. The lacquer in these products often felt heavy and/or tacky on the hair and resulted in stiff hair. Once the spray was applied, women generally left their hairstyles alone until they were ready to brush them out or wash their hair. Hairdressers who worked during the 1950s and early 1960s have said that the floors of their salons became tacky with hairspray residue. The lacquer also clung to their clothing and skin. Some stylists preferred not to use commercial hairspray and made their own, using sugar and water.

After 1951, the new high and wide **bouffant** hairstyles boosted hairspray sales. During the early 1960s, hairstyles were created with teasing and using hairpieces, rollers, and liberal amounts of hairspray. Competition intensified as various companies brought out their versions of this product and advertised them via television, radio, and the print media. During that decade, new forms of hairspray became available in different strengths and for different hair types.

By 1964, hairspray had become the top-selling beauty product in the United States, outselling even lipstick. One of the most popular brands was Aqua Net, from Chesebrough Pond's, a brand that is still sold today. Sales of hairspray in Great Britain reached more than £200 million in 1974.

Hairspray sales declined after new haircuts and long, straight styles predominated during the late 1960s and the 1970s. Women wore their hair in looser styles that "moved." Hairspray manufacturers began developing new products that gave a lighter or "softer" hold and did not feel as stiff to the touch.

Today, hairsprays are made with components that offer holding power, including acrylates, crotonic acid, and methylacrylate copolymer. Adding certain plasticizing ingredients, such as acetyl triethyl citrate or lauramide DEA, makes the product more pliable so that the hair can be brushed after spray is applied.

Environmental Concerns

During the 1970s, more research was conducted on the effects of chlorofluorocarbons (CFCs) on the environment. Scientists concluded that the CFCs in air conditioning units, refrigerators, certain industrial processes, and some aerosol cans were causing damage to the ozone layer, as well as increasing indoor pollution and outdoor smog.

As a result, numerous manufacturers switched from CFCs to alternative propellants and mechanical pump sprays. In 1978, the U.S. Environmental Protection Agency began making regulations that phased out the use of fluorocarbon gases in most aerosol products, including hairsprays.

During the 1980s, Canada, Mexico, Australia, and some European nations banned CFCs in aerosol products. California passed laws, effective in 1993, banning the sale of any hairspray that contained more than 80 percent volatile organic compound (VOC) (CFCs are a type of VOC). Both New York and California passed laws stating that, as of 1998, no hairsprays containing more than 55 percent of these compounds could be sold in those states. The Montreal Protocol, an international agreement, called for a ban on the production of all CFC propellants by January 1, 1996, in industrialized nations, while these compounds were set to be phased out in developing nations by 2010.

See also: *Hairspray*; Hairstyles, Twentieth-Century

Further Reading: Begoun, Paula, *Don't Go Shopping for Hair Care Products without Me* (1995); Colwell, Shelley M., "Shape of the Future," *Soap/Cosmetics/Chemical Specialties*, October 1993, http://members.aol.com/lishelley/hair.htm; Consumer Aerosol Products Council, "Aerosols and the Environment," January 2004, http://www.nocfcs.org/ae.html; U.S. Environmental Protection Agency, "Government Ban on Fluorocarbon Gases in Aerosol Products Begins October 15 [1978]," October 15, 1978, http://www.epa.gov/history/topics/ozone/01.htm.

HAIRSPRAY

Hairspray is the name of a popular feature film and Broadway musical. It portrays the lives of several high school students living in Baltimore in 1962, at a time when huge **bouffant** hairstyles, anchored with **hairspray**, were at the height of their popularity. The main character is plus-sized Tracy Turnblad, whose dancing talent and enthusiasm win her a spot on a local TV dance show for teenagers. The script takes a humorous look at social cliques, 1960s fashions, and teenage romance as Turnblad speaks out for former outsiders like herself, models plus-size fashions, and supports the growing movement for racial integration.

Written and directed by John Waters, *Hairspray* debuted as a feature film in 1988. The film received praise from the critics and was successful at the box office. In 2002, it debuted as a Broadway musical, with ads describing its heroine as "a big girl with big dreams—and even bigger hair." Since the musical debuted, it has won nine Tony Awards, including awards for direction, book, costumes, and musical score (by Marc Shaiman). The musical was still on Broadway as of 2005, and plans were being made for a new film version.

See also: Hairstyles, Twentieth-Century

Further Reading: *Empire Online*, "*Hairspray* Remake," March 4, 2004, http://www.empireonline.co.uk/site/news/newsstory.asp?news_id=15653; *Hairspray* (the musical), http://www.hairsprayonbroadway.com; O'Donnell, Mark, et al., *Hairspray: The Roots* (2003).

HAIR STRAIGHTENING

Hair straightening is a process designed to remove the natural curl or wave, thus imparting a straighter look. People have used mechanical and chemical methods to straighten their hair. Commercial products designed to straighten or "relax" the hair are available for use at home or in salons, and most of the people who use them are female.

One product used for centuries to temporarily flatten the hair is pomade, a greasy and somewhat heavy substance that pushes curly hair down on the scalp. Men were most likely to use pomade as a way to tame curly hair when sleeker hairstyles were in fashion.

Efforts to straighten hair may reflect a desire to follow cultural norms or current fashions or to gain more styling options. Women whose hair is not naturally straight may want a smoother look or the option to wear their hair either straight or curly.

Racism also has influenced people's efforts to attain straighter hair. For centuries, **African Americans** faced discrimination based on their appearance. People with racist attitudes favored traditional northern European features, including lighter skin and hair that looked more "white" (i.e., straighter, silkier in texture, lighter in color). Long hair that was smooth or softly curling has frequently been a beauty ideal in many cultures.

During the days of slavery in the United States, some white slave owners forced sexual relations on black women, which resulted in children of mixed race with various hair types. In addition to facing sexual assaults from their masters, female slaves also had to worry about the masters' wives. Historical records show that some jealous wives punished female slaves who had long, smooth hair by having their heads shaved so they would be considered less attractive.

After the Civil War, many newly freed slaves, especially those who moved to cities, tried to fit in with the dominant society so they would have more access to jobs, education, and social acceptance. They rejected traditional African styles in favor of the hairstyles and clothing that white people wore. For decades, the notion that straight hair looked better than natural African hair continued to prevail among both whites and blacks. As a result, African American men and women straightened their hair, and some women wore wigs for a straight look.

Early Straightening Methods

During the 1800s, most people straightened their hair at home. One basic method was to tie the hair with pieces of cloth to pull it straight. Frequently, people used a combination of oil and heat. After applying oil to the hair, they pressed it with an iron or other object that was heated over a fire. Hot combing was another technique. Pressing oil was applied to clean hair and then a metal comb heated to 300–500 degrees Fahrenheit was quickly run through the hair. The effects were temporary, and dampness or humidity would bring back the curl. The heat sometimes damaged the hair or burned the scalp.

Commercial, chemical hair-straightening products also became available during the nineteenth century. They included Curl-I-Cure, which was made by a company in Virginia and offered through mail order. Ads for straightening products targeted African Americans and other people who came from regions where the hair usually was curly or kinky instead of straight. Attaining smooth hair was one way that immigrants could fit in as they became assimilated with mainstream Americans.

Madam C. J. Walker founded a successful, ethnic hair care products business that sold Madam Walker's Wonderful Hair Grower and her version of a hot comb and pressing oil. The comb was heated over a stove and used to distribute the pressing oil along hair shafts. Walker claimed that her product was intended to help hair grow longer and healthier rather than make it look more like white women's hair. She promoted the idea that all women have the potential for beauty through the self-confidence that comes from proper grooming and caring for the body, mind, and soul. For example, she urged women to wash their hair more often—weekly, instead of monthly, as was common practice before the mid-1900s—to promote cleanliness and a healthy scalp.

Larger numbers of African American women began straightening their hair after 1905, when Walker's products became available. Generations of women had lived with stereotypes that viewed black women as less physically attractive than white women. Hair care and other forms of personal grooming helped elevate black women's concepts of beauty and reverse negative attitudes based on racism. In her book *Ain't I A Beauty Queen?*, Maxine Craig wrote, "Straightened hair represented access to hair products, sanitation, leisure, and relative prosperity. A woman who put time and money into her appearance was dignified, and her dignity spoke well of the race" (Craig 2002, 35).

An Ongoing Debate

As more African Americans straightened their hair, the practice became increasingly controversial. It was discussed in newspaper articles and church sermons and by people in their homes. Groups of black women formed clubs that rejected the practice of hair wrapping—straightening hair by oiling it and then wrapping heated flannel on the head. Some African Americans criticized hair straightening as an attempt to emulate whites. Prominent African American leaders advocated racial pride and urged people not to adopt white standards of appearance.

They faced stiff competition from the growing hair care products industry. By the 1920s, newspapers and magazines featured numerous ads for cosmetics, toiletries, and hair care products, including hair-straightening products. Some women used them at home while others received their hair treatments at the beauty parlor. Maintaining straight hair was expensive and time-consuming, since most people needed a weekly treatment to maintain a straight look.

Educator and activist Booker T. Washington was among the prominent African Americans who continued to criticize the practice of hair straightening. He criticized the people who made and sold these products as well as salon owners who performed hair-straightening services. After Washington founded the National Negro Business League in Boston in 1900, he refused to admit people who engaged in these businesses as members. Yet, these hair care businesses helped tens of thousands of African Americans gain financial independence, and advertisements for hair-straightening products contributed significant revenues to African American–owned newspapers and magazines.

Observers noted that many white women also were straightening their hair during the 1920s. **The bob** and other popular hairstyles worked better on straight hair, and many Americans, including immigrant women from Southern Europe or Mediterranean countries, did not have naturally straight hair.

Twentieth Century

Individual inventors and companies continued to develop new straightening products. In 1920, at the onset of the **flapper** era, Philadelphia native Walter H. Sammons received U.S. Patent 1,362,823 for the design of a heated straightening comb he devised especially for African Americans. White women whose natural hair was curly or frizzy bought straightening devices, too.

African American men developed chemical processes to straighten hair, which were used both at home and in barbershops. One type of straightening product became popularly known as a conk. The name may have come from Kink No More, a straightening mixture that was developed by New York barber William Hart, or from another product called Kongolene Knocks Kinks. Many stylish young men, as well as their elders, used these preparations from the 1920s into the 1960s.

People have written about the discomfort they endured with chemical straightening preparations. Conks contained lye, which could burn the scalp if the mixture was applied incorrectly or left on too long. Another difficulty was keeping all the hair straight at one time, since new hair would grow out curly or kinky. The process had to be repeated regularly, which was irritating to the scalp.

In 1948, Jose Calva, working from a lab in Minneapolis, created a straightening formula called Lustrasilk Permanent. This foaming product was available in salons, where operators used it with a special electric comb and shampoo. It purported to "give curly, uncombable, felty hair a silken, straight quality for months" (Byrd and Tharps 2002, 84). Madam C. J. Walker's company launched a competitive product called Satin Tress shortly thereafter. Again, the product was used in salons, where beauticians applied Satin Tress after using a special shampoo. That step was followed with the application of Satin Tress conditioning cream and then the use of a hot comb.

The 1950s brought new straightening products that were more comfortable and convenient to use. In 1954, entrepreneur **George E. Johnson** began selling Ultra Wave, the first of several very successful "hair relaxers" offered by his company, **Johnson Products**. Johnson's Ultra Sheen line for women included a cream-press **permanent** that was used to straighten hair without the use of a hot comb. Ultra Sheen relaxers could be used at home, which saved the cost of salon visits. Fewer treatments often meant healthier-looking hair for consumers. Also, nearly all of Johnson's customers were African Americans, and many of them liked the idea of supporting an African American–owned business. Like other hair straighteners of that era, Johnson's formulas contained lye as one of the ingredients. These chemical straighteners produced more lasting results than heat used with pressing oil.

Ads for hair-straightening products sometimes featured African American celebrities. A 1955 ad for Perma-Strate claiming that the product was "proved by over 1,000,000 happy users" featured photographs of singer Sarah Vaughan, musician Count Basie, and a musical trio that included Sammy Davis Jr., who later achieved fame as a solo singer and actor.

During the late 1960s, the civil rights movement and a growing sense of ethnic pride inspired more African Americans to wear their hair in its natural state and embrace the natural texture. Actors, athletes, and other celebrated African Americans wore **Afros** or other natural styles. While some of these hairstyles carried political connotations during the 1960s, later they reflected a person's individual choice and sense of style and also offered ease of care. More hairstylists and salons offered hairdos that worked with the natural texture of African American hair and did not require straightening treatments. During these years, sales of hair-straightening chemicals and hot combs declined, although some women still preferred straightened hair.

More white women also straightened their hair during the **hippie** era in the late 1960s and earlier 1970s. Girls and women sometimes used a household iron on their hair to achieve the long, free-flowing styles that were popular during that time. They also rolled their hair on oversize juice cans to pull it straight. Some men, both black and white, also wanted straighter hair, and they used various products to achieve that look.

During the 1970s, author and chemist Willie Lee Morrow began marketing a formula designed to relax hair that was tight and kinky to create looser curls. Morrow, who wrote several books, including *Curly Hair and Black Skin* (1973), originally called his product Tomorrow Curl but changed the name to California Curl in 1977. This product offered people a middle ground between straight hair and tightly curling hair. Since the product worked with the hair's natural tendency to curl, the resulting style was easier to maintain than completely straight hair. Other companies, including those founded by Jheri Rhedding and Edward Gardner, brought out their versions of products that relaxed hair into softer curls. Beauticians offered these services at a cost of between $80 and $100.

In the 1980s, many women of color and others who wanted softer though not totally straight hair used new brands of "curly permanents." These products involved a two-step process in which the hair was first straightened and then styled into soft curls. Their popularity declined, however, after women found that the treatments had a drying effect, especially when they were repeated on a regular basis. Styles also changed so that straighter hair became more fashionable again.

African Americans still debate the ideas of straightening hair versus wearing natural styles. In 1998, a controversial children's book called *Nappy Hair*, written by African American author Carolivia Herron, sparked fresh debates. Some African Americans said that the word "nappy" is insulting, and they asked teachers not to read the book in their classrooms. In an interview, Herron said of her own hairstyle, "I love my hair in its Afro. . . . It's like a halo, like antennae, like some idea that started in the soul and couldn't stop so it had to keep on going until it found its conclusion back in the source of creation" (Byrd and Tharps 2002, 175).

As the twenty-first century began, hairstyles were more diverse than ever before. Men and women could opt to straighten their hair, wear it naturally curly, or choose hairstyles in between.

Current Products and Techniques

Since the late 1980s, new types of chemical straighteners and mechanical straightening devices have come into the marketplace. The chemical relaxers include permanents designed to straighten the hair rather than adding waves and curls. Some straighteners work by breaking down the hydrogen bonds in the keratin layer of the hair. These formulations are less harsh than the chemical straighteners that were made in previous decades.

As straightening methods have improved, more women have opted to use them. At the turn of the twenty-first century, about 66 percent of all African American women were using hair straighteners (or relaxers, as they are often called). Statistics showed that chemical hair straighteners were the top-selling category of hair care products for black women. Among African Americans, long, straight hair has been regarded as an attractive feature, and black women have admired the hair of singer and actress Beyonce Knowles, actress Queen Latifah, and supermodels Tyra Banks and Veronica Webb, all of whom have worn their (sometimes lightened) hair in long, smooth styles or in various other styles, including curls, weaves, and braids.

New types of combing irons deliver varying levels of heat and come in lightweight, portable versions. Theora Stephens patented a more efficient pressing and curling iron in 1980. More recently, companies began making flat irons that are designed with a ceramic layer over the metal plates. The ceramic material helps to diffuse the heat, which protects hair from damage caused by concentrated heat from the metal plates. This smooth ceramic finish also is gentler on the hair, which can break from the rough pull of a metal surface. Since hot irons reach temperatures as high as 200 degrees Fahrenheit, people must be extremely careful not to burn their scalp or skin while using these appliances. As a result, many people rely on salon professionals to carry out straightening treatments, whether with hot appliances or chemicals, to minimize the health and safety risks and avoid damaging their hair.

In addition to hot irons and chemical treatments, companies also offer shampoos, gels, lotions, mousses, creams, and hairsprays that aim to reduce or remove curl or frizziness from the hair. Some companies, including **John Frieda Professional Hair Care, Inc.**, specialize in products that aim to reduce frizziness. Frieda's line includes products designed for red, brunette, and blond hair. Many of the products that reduce frizziness contain silicone.

The U.S. Food and Drug Administration publishes articles warning consumers about the hazards of chemical hair straighteners and relaxers. Each year, the administration receives complaints from consumers who experienced hair loss, **allergic reactions**, or other problems while using these products, some of them purchased from companies that advertise on television or over the Internet.

In 1994, major problems were reported by women who used a product called Rio Hair Naturalizer System, which was sold by the World Rio Corporation, Inc., and marketed through television infomercials. The product was described as "all-natural" and made from plants found in the Amazon rainforest. The women in the ads claimed that they achieved their long, bouncy hair after using Rio. Thousands of women who used the product complained that it caused massive hair loss, scalp irritation, discoloration, and other problems. When the Food and Drug Administration conducted tests on Rio, they found that the product contained high levels of acid. In addition, because the product merely coated the outside of the hair, it did not result in any long-term straightening. People who used the product subsequently filed a class action suit against the company that sold Rio. In 1997, a federal district court ruled in their favor and awarded the plaintiffs $4.5 million, which was divided among approximately 53,000 women who suffered damages after using the product.

See also: Advertising; Barbers; Ouidad; Styling Products; Styling Tools; Wigs and Hairpieces

Further Reading: Banner, Lois, *American Beauty* (1983); Craig, Maxine, *Ain't I A Beauty Queen?* (2002); Dunn, Carolyn A., "The Ethnic Hair Care Market," *Happi*, April 1997; Herron, Carolivia, *Nappy Hair* (1998); Meadows, Michele, "Hair Dyes and Chemical Relaxers," *FDA Consumer*, February 26, 2001; Ogunnaike, Lola, "Some Hair Is Happy to Be Nappy," *The New York Times*, December 27, 1998, section 9; Parker, Emanuel, "Efforts Made to Stop Sale of Rio Products," *Los Angeles Times*, February 2, 1995; Rooks, Noliwe M., *Hair Raising: Beauty, Culture, and the African American Woman* (1996); Simon, Diane, *Hair* (2000).

HAIRSTYLES, EIGHTEENTH-CENTURY *See* Adornment, Ornamental; China; Fontange; French Revolution; Hair Color; Hair Colorants; Hairdressing; Headgear; Japan; Puritans; Wigs and Hairpieces

HAIRSTYLES, NINETEENTH-CENTURY

See Adornment, Ornamental; African Americans; Brummell, Beau; Comb; Comb, Decorative; Gibson Girl; Hair Color; Hair Colorants; Hairdressing; Harper, Martha Matilda; Malone, Annie Minerva Turnbo Pope; Marcel Wave; Native Americans; Pompadour; Regency; Salons, Hair and Beauty; Sideburns; Victorian Era; Wigs and Hairpieces

HAIRSTYLES, TWENTIETH-CENTURY

The twentieth century was a time of major technological advances and social, economic, and political change, and these were reflected in hairstyles for men and women of all ages. These developments also gave people of different economic classes more access to hairstyling tools, products, and services.

> "Why don't you get a haircut? You look like a chrysanthemum."
>
> P. G. WODEHOUSE (1881–1975), British author

At the millennium, people had many options for selecting and maintaining colors and styles that expressed their personal tastes. Yet while some women have followed new fashions, others have chosen to wear conservative styles or a classic look (e.g., a chignon, bun, ponytail, neat bob, pageboy, French twist, shoulder-length wave). Likewise, some men have continued to wear short, simple hairstyles despite changing trends. This overview describes some of the major styles in Western cultures during the century.

Women's Styles

At the beginning of the century, women still wore long hair, styled in braids or hanging loose, until they reached young adulthood, at which time they began pinning it up. The **Gibson Girl** look that emerged late in the 1800s featured a soft, full **pompadour**, often with one or more curls hanging loose. The **Marcel wave**, with its crimped, undulating waves, remained popular in the early 1900s, and some women used a curling iron to apply a similar waving look after they cut their hair into **the bob** style.

New, short hairstyles for women began to emerge in the United States after World War I ended in 1918, a time when women's roles and opportunities in education and the workplace began expanding. At first, only the most daring young women cut off their long hair. Some of these women pursued a more liberated lifestyle, and they were nicknamed **flappers**. The style caught on, however, and by the end of the 1920s, millions of women of all ages were wearing shorter hair.

By the 1920s, more women were visiting beauty parlors and hair salons. Many women in Asia, Europe, North and South America, and Africa who could afford it had their hair washed and set weekly.

Styles in the 1930s featured more constructed curls and waves, including the Marcel wave and the **water wave**. The development of the **permanent wave** during the 1930s meant that hairstyles would last longer. An increasing number of women went to salons to have a permanent wave or to have access to the newly developed **hair dryers**. **Jean Harlow** was among the film stars who influenced hairstyles during this decade.

World War II meant that metal for permanent wave machines was less available because that material was being used in the war effort. The development of cold-wave permanents during the 1940s meant that women could still achieve long-lasting waved or curled styles. Longer, wavy hair was popular during the 1940s and could be seen on various actresses, including **Veronica Lake**, who popularized "peekaboo" **bangs**. At the request of the war department, Lake changed to a neatly secured hairstyle that did not droop over her eye. This style was considered safer for women working in factories and other wartime jobs. For evening wear, many women wore decorative **headgear** called snoods.

Celebrities and the mass media influenced trends more strongly as the century continued. Women emulated the styles and hair colors that they saw on their favorite film actresses and other people in the media. Fashion magazines became increasingly influential, and top models influenced hairstyles, as did other famous people. During the 1930s, many mothers created **Shirley Temple**–style sausage curls on their daughters' hair. Later, women copied first lady Mamie Eisenhower's short **bangs** during the 1950s.

The 1950s saw hairstyles covering diverse lengths, although women older than twenty tended to wear short or medium-length hair. Many women got short, "elfin" haircuts that were sometimes called Italian cuts or poodle cuts. Actress **Audrey Hepburn** appeared on film in these popular haircuts, and future first lady **Jacqueline Bouvier Kennedy** wore a short style at her 1953 wedding. Later in that decade, Kennedy wore a **bouffant**, which, along with the even larger beehive and shorter bubble cut, became a top women's style during the early 1960s. For teenagers, a signature look of the 1950s was a high **ponytail**, often tied with a scarf. This popular hairstyle can be seen on the earliest versions of the Barbie doll, which the Mattel Toy Company launched in 1959. A few years later, the doll also came in a version with a "bubble cut" hairstyle.

Pageboys (ends of the hair turned under) and flips (ends turned up) were popular during the 1960s. This hairstyle had originated during the 1930s and evolved into straighter, longer versions. One famous television flip belonged to actress Mary Tyler Moore when she appeared on the series *The Dick Van Dyke Show* during the 1960s. Marlo Thomas, star of the series *That Girl*, also wore a trendsetting version of the flip. False hair was used during that decade to add fullness, and some women wore bouffant wigs. During the late 1960s, **Twiggy**, a model, sparked a new trend for a very short cut that people called boyish, waiflike, or genderless. Two other women known as trendsetters for their very short haircuts during the 1960s were American actress Mia Farrow and Brazilian singer Ellis Regina.

Women again used hairpieces, called falls, to get the long, straight hair popular from the late 1960s into the 1970s. The look of 1970s was exemplified by actress Ali MacGraw's long, shining, dark hair in the hit film *Love Story* and by blond actress Peggy Lipton on the television show *Mod Squad*. Men and women alike chose longer hairstyles during the late 1960s and 1970s, varying from neatly groomed to natural looking and even unkempt. More people had their hair cut at unisex salons that served both genders. Female members of the counterculture group called the **hippies** wore long, straight hair, usually with a center part. As part of the black pride movement, many **African American** women wore some version of the **Afro** or had their hair styled in **cornrows**. More white women also wore cornrows after actress Bo Derek had her blond hair styled this way in the movie "*10*." A popular short style during the 1970s was the wedge, popularized by figure-skating star **Dorothy Hamill**. Actress **Farrah Fawcett** and a number of other women wore **feathered hairstyles** and shags.

The "big hair" look resurfaced in slightly different forms during the 1980s, with various layered hairstyles and long, full waves or crimped hair, either short or long. Some people of both genders, usually young people, adopted the **punk** look, which featured bright colors, spikes, and versions of the Mohawk style. More lesbian women felt freer to openly express their lifestyle and wear distinctive hairstyles, sometimes adopting very short hair, including buzz cuts, but despite stereotypes, there was no one typical lesbian haircut for women in every region or community.

The 1990s brought the unusual looks known as grunge and heroin chic. Emaciated-looking models who adopted the heroin chic look wore stringy hair and messy hairstyles, sometimes punctuated with seaweed or other unexpected materials. The extremes of this look, which appeared mostly on high-fashion runways, were short-lived. Versions of the grunge look became chic, however, and many women preferred the unstructured, spiky, or tousled layers of hair that were part of that style. Bleaching or dying hair while leaving the roots dark for an inch or more also became more fashionable. Ponytails changed to become less structured, with an undone look that left ends hanging. This look was also achieved with plastic claws that gripped hair to leave loose strands around the face, for example. Many African American women visited salons for **hair straightening** or a **hair weave**.

At the millennium, some of the most popular women's hair care products included antifrizz products and those that produced unusual colors. More women than ever before were coloring their hair. Ads for hair care products tended to emphasize individuality and a woman's own uniqueness rather than a limited beauty ideal.

Men's Styles

At the beginning of the 1900s, men wore neat hairstyles, and those with beards or **mustaches** groomed them carefully. By the 1920s, most American men were shaving daily. Men used a variety of grooming creams, pomades, and oils to slick their hair in place. Silent-screen idol **Rudolph Valentino**'s hair exemplified a popular look for men during the early decades. Hairstyles remained generally short until the 1960s.

During the 1930s, a distinct style emerged among Latinos living in coastal cities in California. They slicked their hair back to form a "tail" at the base of the neck, a style that was known as the Argentine ducktail because it was thought to have originated in that country. These men, who often wore a style of clothing called the zoot suit, identified themselves with the name "pachucos."

During the 1930s and 1940s, versions of the crew cut were popular. Men who went into **military** service during World War II had closely cropped hairstyles, which many of them kept after the war ended. Actor Steve McQueen was one of the most famous men to wear a crew cut on film. Some people improvised to personalize this cut. Jazz musician Gerry Mulligan wore his short hair combed forward, often combined with his signature sunglasses and turtleneck. This look was called hip and cool.

One style that spread during the 1940s and 1950s was the DA, which stood for "duck's ass" but was usually called a ducktail. These hairstyles evolved from looks that became popular among the pachucos during the 1930s. Joe Cirello, a well-known men's hairstylist working in Philadelphia, said that he developed this hairstyle in the United States. Cirello later said, "I invented the D.A. in 1940 at 6th and Washington Avenue, on a blind kid." When that boy's classmates at Southern High School saw the haircut, more teenagers came to Cirello's barbershop asking for the same cut. Cirello's celebrity clients included actors Humphrey Bogart, Wallace Beery, and James Dean as well as musician **Elvis Aaron Presley**. Presley's darkened hair, arranged in a high wave in the front, influenced many teenagers and older men to wear a style that communicated an energetic, youthful image. The legendary singer and actor Frank Sinatra wore a version of the DA.

With the arrival of the mid-1960s, the slicked down "wet look" in men's hair lost favor. Revolutionary new looks were coming from England, where the Beatles had risen to the top of the pop charts and Carnaby Street designers were setting fashion trends. The Beatles and other pop bands had long, swinging hair. During the early 1960s, the Beatles wore a haircut called a "moptop," which resembled the shape of a bowl with bangs above the eyebrows. Pop musicians, including the Beatles, began to wear their hair longer in the early 1970s. Many men followed suit, and some who identified themselves as hippies wore facial hair as well as long hair.

For African Americans and some whites, the Afro was a popular new version of former natural hairstyles and was seen on musician Jimi Hendrix, among many others. Rock musicians appeared with different versions of Afros and long hair, and reggae artist Bob Marley was known for his **dredlocks**. Many men adopted the new long or natural hairstyles to make a political and/or social statement, whereas other men kept their hair in short styles to show that they were more traditional and conservative.

The 1980s and 1990s saw more individualized hairstyles for men, including versions of the buzz and flattop, sometimes coupled with a Mohawk and vivid dyes. The top often was cut and styled to stand straight up from the head.

Men's styles went on to become more daring and creative than they had been since the eighteenth century, a time when men wore elaborate wigs. The punk look featured hair in bright colors, sometimes in several different colors. Spikes and partially shaved heads could be seen, along with asymmetrical designs. Mohawks were worn by both men and women. Country singer Billy Ray Cyrus wore a version of the mullet, which was short on top and long in back and was popular during the 1990s.

Pop musicians and other celebrities continued to spark trends after the 1960s, especially after music videos began appearing regularly on television. Along with actors and musicians, athletes also have strongly influenced men's hairstyles. Basketball star Michael Jordan influenced men around the world by shaving his head. Fellow basketball player Dennis Rodman became known for his daring styles and hair colors. Rodman has worn curls and bleached his dark hair blond, among other changes. One of the international sports stars known for his trendsetting hairstyles is British soccer player David Beckham. Beckham has worn an array of styles, including a mullet, a ponytail, and cornrows. Other celebrities maintained the same style for decades. One example is singer Willie Nelson, who has kept his long hair, tied back in a ponytail or braid, through the years.

During the last decades of the century, more men were using hairstyling services as well as using more mousse, gel, and other **styling products**. A higher percentage of men were coloring their hair than ever before. There was no longer a uniform or universal look in men's hair, and many men had individualized, stylized hairdos that required blow-drying and the use of diverse products. Men's hair care was one of the fastest-growing sectors in the hair products industry.

At the millennium, men had numerous hairstyle options, ranging from long hair that resembled looks from the hippy era to a completely shaved head. They could choose smooth, straight looks or waves, curls, cornrows, or dredlocks. Some of the most popular men's styles included spikes. Many fashionable men chose a medium-length cut with a longer top fashioned into spikes, often bleached. One male celebrity who wore this style was Ty Pennington, a former male model and the host of the popular television show *Extreme Makeover: Home*.

See also: Advertising; Aniston, Jennifer; Baldness, Voluntary; Beards, Men's; "Blond Bombshell"; Buzz Cut; Crew Cut; Diana, Princess of Wales; Hairdressing; Hairspray; Presley, Elvis Aron; Salons, Hair and Beauty; Shampoo; Styling Tools; Wigs and Hairpieces

Further Reading: Charles, Ann, *The History of Hair* (1970); Cooper, Wendy, *Hair* (1971); Corson, Richard, *Fashions in Hair* (2001); Innes-Smith, James, *Big Hair* (2003); LaForte, James, *Men's Hair* (1979); Larson, Mark, and Barhey Hoskins, *The Mullet* (2000); Mulvey, Kate, and Melissa Richards, *Decades of Beauty* (1998); Rudoy, Marilyn, *The Complete Book of Men's Hairstyles and Hair Care* (1974); Severn, Bill, *The Long and Short of It* (1971); Turudich, Daniela, *Art Deco Hair* (2004); Turudich, Daniela, *1940s Hairstyles* (2001).

HAIR TRANSPLANT

Hair transplants involve removing live ("donor") hair follicles from one area of the body and then implanting them on some other area of the body. Most hair transplants are done on the scalp in order to cover bald areas or places where the hair is thin. Techniques have become increasingly sophisticated, and today physicians can perform single hair grafts or grafts with just a few hair follicles.

> "They see hair down to there, / Say, "Beware" and go off on a tear! / I say, "No fair!" / A head that's bare is really nowhere."
>
> GEORGE CARLIN (1937–), American comedian and author, "Hair Poem"

The idea of scalp hair transplants dates back to at least the **Middle Ages**, when the writer Francois Rabelais predicted that grafting of hair would one day be a remedy for baldness. In 1822, a prominent German surgeon named Johann Friedrich Dieffenbach tried transplanting some hair follicles from his scalp into his arm. After poking holes in his skin with a needle, he inserted six hairs. While four did not take hold, two of the hair follicles did survive and grow. The idea of hair transplantation did not catch on at that time, however, and surgical instruments were not yet sophisticated enough to allow doctors to carry out such procedures.

Practical methods of cosmetic surgery to replace lost hair developed during the 1900s. In the 1930s and 1940s, some Japanese scientists tried inserting hair shafts on the scalp to treat **hair loss**. During the 1950s, this work resumed and was tried on patients who had lost their eyebrows because of leprosy. Pieces of skin that contained hair follicles were used.

Some early hair transplants were done with artificial hairs made from polyester, modacrylic, and polyacrylic. A number of men who underwent these procedures developed infections and their transplants fell out of the infected sites. Others were permanently scarred when the fibers, which were attached to knots placed under the scalp, could not be removed. The U.S. Food and Drug Administration banned artificial hair transplants in 1984.

Transplants using live human hair became available after the 1930s. Physicians developed methods for moving hair from one part of the scalp to another, usually to replace hair lost on top as a result of male pattern baldness. In 1939 and 1943, dermatologists in Japan pioneered methods of transplanting grafts of skin that contained live hair follicles. Their work was described in Japanese medical journals, but people around the world did not learn about it until after World War II ended in 1945. In New York City during the 1950s, dermatologist Dr. Norman Orentreich conducted research showing that grafts of hair-bearing skin would grow on bald areas of the scalp. Orentreich developed a procedure in which "plugs" of live hair follicles from the back of the head were removed and then implanted into prepared holes of the same size on the bald areas. Each plug contained from ten to fifty hairs. Men from around the world traveled to Orentreich's office for this procedure. One of his most famous clients was singer Frank Sinatra. By 1970, other physicians who studied with Orentreich to master his techniques were performing hair transplants in various countries.

Since the 1970s, doctors have found ways to transplant even smaller plugs of hair, which are called minigrafts or micrografts. New punch-graft tools are sharper, and doctors also have learned how to cut grafts in ways that cause less damage to the tissues. Some grafts are round in shape and contain from ten to fifteen hairs per punch. A minigraft consists of two to four hairs, while a micrograft has only one or two hairs. Slit grafts contain from four to ten hairs each and are placed in slits cut into the recipient area of the scalp. Strip grafts, which are long and thin, contain more hairs—about thirty to forty. The grafts are carefully positioned and spaced to promote healing and enable hair to grow in a natural direction on the scalp.

A hair transplant usually is done on an outpatient basis using local anesthesia. After a procedure, most patients leave with sterile dressings in place over the surgical area. People must take care not to disturb the transplant area while it heals. New hairs begin growing from the transplanted plugs in about two to six months. The risks of hair transplantation include infection, scarring, and/or excess bleeding as well as other problems that may occur with surgical procedures.

By the 1990s, more sophisticated tools and techniques allowed hundreds, and even thousands, of small grafts to be transplanted during one session. Usually, two or more sessions are needed to completely fill in the bald spot that typically results from male pattern baldness. Some clients receive these treatments over a period of months or even years as the physician fills in areas in a series of grafts. Most transplant patients are men, but women also use hair transplants to deal with hair loss.

Another type of surgical treatment involves anchoring a hairpiece to attachments implanted in the scalp. In other cases, knotted synthetic hair (which uses the trade name Biofibre) is sewn into the scalp. Artificial hair transplants, including Biofibre, are still banned in the United States and in Canada. In 1995, the Biofibre process was approved for use in Italy; it also is available in Japan and Australia.

See also: Aging and Hair; Dermatology; Hair Loss; Wigs and Hairpieces

Further Reading: American Medical Association, *The AMA Book of Skin and Hair Care* (1976); Buchwach, Kenneth A., *Contemporary Hair Transplant Surgery* (1997); Hitzig, Gary S., MD, *Help & Hope for Hair Loss* (1997); Norwood, O'Tar T., and Richard C. Shiell, *Hair Transplant Surgery* (1984); Pine, Devera, "Hair! From Personal Statement to Personal Problem," *FDA Consumer*, December 1991; Van Deusen, Edmund, *What You Can Do about Baldness* (1978).

HAIR WEAVE

A hair weave is a type of hair addition carried out with real or synthetic hair, usually by a trained hairdresser. Bunches of hair are sewn into the person's own hair or onto netting that has been sewn into the hair.

Hair historians Ayana D. Byrd and Lori L. Tharps say that hair weaves might have existed in some form for thousands of years, but modern hair weaving originated in 1950 when an Ohio housewife, Christina Jenkins, invented and patented her technique. Early weaves usually were made by putting the hair into cornrows and then sewing strips of hair that had first been sewn onto netting onto the cornrows. Many early weaves did not look natural, however. According to an article in the August 1990 issue of *Essence* magazine, "Most weaves [in the 1960s] looked too fake, too voluminous and too much alike" (*Essence* 1990).

Since then, methods for creating more natural-looking hair weaves developed. One method, called bonding, involves gluing strips of hair to the roots. Another method, called singeing, uses heat to machine-press synthetic hair onto the natural hair. Contemporary techniques can produce more natural-looking weaves, often for shorter hairstyles that include bangs or layers. The hair used in the weaves comes in more colors and textures, including wavy, straight, curly, and kinky.

During the 1980s, American hairdressers noted that more African American women liked the look of long, straight hair. Some commentators believe this occurred because people were watching more music videos on television and most videos for black music featured black women with longer hair that "moved."

Women make up the vast majority of people who have hair weaves, and most of them are **African Americans**. As of 2000, about 25 percent of all African American women were wearing some type of hair addition, often incorporated into a braided hairstyle. The natural hair sometimes is straightened before it is blended or braided with extensions.

Hair weaves can be both expensive (costing from $200 to more than $1,500) and time consuming, requiring several hours or more to complete. However, women appreciate the convenience of having weaves and the ways that weaves can enhance their own hair. Weaves add thickness and enable women with tightly curling or short hair to have the look of longer, straighter hair. The weaves can last up to several weeks and make hair care easier, since they require only shampooing and oiling. That eliminates the need for frequent styling, blow-drying, setting, heated combs, or chemical hair straighteners, which can lead to hair damage. As a result, using a hair weave may promote healthier natural hair. Some hair experts, however, note that heavy hair weaves or extensions and/or tight braiding can tug on hair, causing pressure on hair follicles that can lead to hair loss.

A number of celebrities have worn hair weaves. They include musician Janet Jackson, actresses Lisa Bonet and Garcelle Beauvais-Nilon, and supermodels Iman, Naomi Campbell, and Tyra Banks.

The popularity of hair weaves since the 1990s produced a boom in the importation of human hair. Each year, more than a million pounds of hair purchased from women in **China**, **India**, Indonesia, and Korea is imported into the United States. It is then processed for use in beauty supply shops, salons, and hair retailing enterprises.

See also: Hair Straightening; Salons, Hair and Beauty; Wigs and Hairpieces

Further Reading: Begoun, Paula, *Don't Go Shopping for Hair Care Products without Me* (2004); Bonner, Lonnice Brittenum, *Good Hair* (1994); *Essence*, "Sisters Love the Weave," August 1990, http://www.findarticles.com/p/articles/mi_m1264/is_n4_v21/ai_9252025; Love, Toni, *The World of Wigs, Weaves, and Extensions* (2001); Weitz, Rose, *Rapunzel's Daughters* (2004).

HAMILL, DOROTHY (1956–)

During the mid-1970s, Olympic figure-skating champion Dorothy Hamill popularized a short haircut called the wedge. Before the competition, she asked her New York City hairstylist, Suga, to cut her shining, dark-brown hair in a way that would not get in her eyes and also would blend in well with her movements on the ice to enhance her performance. The resulting hairstyle was a version of the wedge cut that Trevor Sorbie had developed in 1974 at the world-famous **Vidal Sassoon** salon in London. Hamill's wedge sparked a trend among the general public and also influenced female athletes. In the past, most figure-skating champions had worn more controlled hairstyles. Frequently, they secured their hair in ponytails, buns, chignons, or French twists.

Hamill was born in Chicago, but her family moved to Riverside, Connecticut, shortly thereafter. When she began taking formal skating lessons at age eight, Hamill showed talent and a desire to excel. She worked with top coaches, including Gus Lussi and Carlo Fassi, to become a world-class skater.

In 1969, Hamill won the national novice title for women at the U.S. Figure Skating Association Championships and then won the silver medal at the Junior Women's Championship in 1970. She was U.S. National women's figure-skating champion in 1974, 1975, and 1976. Hamill received attention for her athletic spins and leaps and versatility on the ice as well as her appealing personality and natural good looks. One of her trademark moves was the Hamill camel—a camel spin that flowed into a sit spin. International figure-skating judge Charles Foster commented, "Dorothy skates with finesse. She performs a difficult program, works at high speed, plus she interprets the music with feeling. She's a beautiful skater" (Hilton).

After she won the women's world championship and an Olympic gold medal in 1976, Hamill turned professional and became a commercial spokesperson for Clairol Short & Sassy hair conditioner and shampoo. *Life* magazine said that her trademark hairstyle was "one of the most important fashion statements of the last 50 years" (quoted in *The New York Times*, "This Day in Sports," February 13, 1995).

The Clairol product line became successful. In 1977, the Ideal Toy Company produced a Dorothy Hamill doll, which featured her famous hairstyle and came with a plastic ice rink.

From 1977 to 1984, Hamill starred in the Ice Capades and was the first female skater to receive a $1 million contract. In addition to these and other performances, she won the World Professional Figure Skating Championship five years in a row. In 1991, Hamill was inducted into the U.S. Figure Skating Hall of Fame. She bought the Ice Capades organization in 1993 and sold it in 1994.

Hamill has actively worked for charitable organizations, including the American Cancer Society, the Ronald McDonald House, the International Special Olympics, and the March of Dimes, where she has been involved in a program that helps blind children learn to skate. In 2004, she served as a spokesperson for Merck, a pharmaceutical company that makes a medication for osteoarthritis, a chronic and inflammatory disease of the joints. Hamill began to notice symptoms of osteoarthritis at age forty. She takes medication for this condition and has continued to skate. She competed at the 2000 Goodwill Games and performed with a professional show, Tom Collins Champions on Ice. Hamill, who has been married and divorced twice, is the mother of a daughter.

See also: Hairdressing; Hairstyles, Twentieth-Century

Further Reading: Hamill, Dorothy, with Elva Fairmont, *Dorothy Hamill, On and Off Ice* (1983); Hilton, Lisette, "Skating Was Passion, Therapy for Hamill," *ESPN Classic*, http://espn.go.com/classic/biography/s/Hamill_Dorothy.html; Sorbie, Trevor, *Visions in Hair* (1998); Tarshis, Joan, "Dorothy Hamill's Amazing Grace," *Reader's Digest*, January 2001, http://www.rd.com/common/nav/index.jhtml?articleId=9520003; *The New York Times*, "This Day in Sports," February 13, 1995, http://www.nytimes.com/packages/html/sports/year_in_sports/02.13.html.

HARLOW, JEAN (1911–1937)

Known for her softly waved platinum-blond hair, actress Jean Harlow (born Harlean Harlow Carpenter) was nicknamed the original "Blond Bombshell." During her short film career, Harlow came to symbolize blond glamour.

Harlow was born into a wealthy household in Kansas City, Missouri, and she attended private schools. At age sixteen, she left home to marry twenty-three-year-old Charles McGrew; they divorced two years later.

> "Only God, my dear, / Could love you for yourself alone / And not your yellow hair."
>
> WILLIAM BUTLER YEATS (1865–1939), poet, "For Anne Gregory"

By 1927, Harlow was living in Hollywood, California, and she accepted a small role in the film *Why Is a Plumber?* She had not set out to pursue an acting career but continued to receive film offers. In the 1930 movie *Hell's Angels*, Harlow appeared in scanty costumes and spoke suggestive lines. She had her straight eyebrows shaved off and created her trademark highly arched brows with a pencil.

The press began referring to Jean Harlow as a sex symbol and a "blond bombshell." In 1931, after her next hit film, *Platinum Blonde*, she made several films with screen legend Clark Gable. Harlow received strong reviews for her comedic role in 1933's *Dinner at Eight*.

Harlow's platinum-colored hair was a key part of her image. During those years of black-and-white photography, movie executives realized that pale blond hair filmed well, so they promoted certain female stars with pale hair, including Harlow and Mae West. To achieve that shade of platinum, Harlow's naturally ash-blond hair was bleached each week with a mixture of peroxide, ammonia, Clorox, and Lux soap flakes. The harsh chemicals caused escalating damage to her hair, so Harlow had to wear wigs to hide it.

She sometimes appeared with other hair colors besides blond. Instead of dying her hair for her role in *Red-Headed Woman* in 1932, Harlow wore a wig. Her hair was tinted brown for her 1936 role in *Riffraff*.

In May 1937, Harlow was the first actress to be featured on the cover of *Life* magazine. Imitating her hair color and style, other women began bleaching their hair, and sales of peroxide soared. For evening wear, many women also chose the slinky, bias-cut satin gowns that were another of Harlow's signature looks.

During her ten years as an actress, Harlow made thirty-six movies. She married two more times, but both unions ended in less than a year.

When Jean Harlow died at age twenty-six, rumors began to circulate that she had died from the poisoning effects of hair dye. However, Harlow had long suffered from kidney problems that began after she contracted scarlet fever at age fourteen.

Harlow has become a screen legend, one of the first women to appear on a list of "bombshells" that grew to include Marilyn Monroe, Jayne Mansfield, and others. In her hit song, "Bette Davis Eyes," singer and songwriter Kim Carnes refers to a woman's hair as "Harlow gold."

See also: Hair Color; Hair Colorants; Monroe, Marilyn

Further Reading: Golden, Eve, *Platinum Girl* (1991); Stenn, David, *Bombshell* (1993).

HARPER, MARTHA MATILDA (1847–1950)

Entrepreneur Martha Matilda Harper founded a successful chain of hairstyling salons that used hair care and skin care products that Harper developed. She has been called the "Mother of Modern Franchising" as well as the "Inventor of the Beauty Salon."

A native of Ontario, Canada, Harper went to work as a servant for relatives when she was about seven years old. She continued in domestic work until age thirty-two. During those years, she learned how to make and apply herbal treatments to the hair and skin while serving as a personal maid who cared for her mistresses' hair and other grooming needs. She also was devoted to the Christian Science religion, which continued to inspire her throughout her life.

In 1882, Harper moved to Rochester, New York, where she planned to start her own business. Six years later, with her life savings of $360, she founded her first hair salon and began performing treatments with a hair tonic made from a recipe she had brought from Canada.

During the late 1800s, most American women regarded personal grooming as an activity that should be conducted in the privacy of the home. Wealthy women relied on their personal servants or hairdressers who made home visits; women who could not afford a maid or hairdresser styled their own hair. To attract a wealthy clientele, Harper was determined to present both herself and her business as ladylike and respectable. She rented space in the most prestigious building in Rochester and studied with tutors to improve her education, etiquette, and manner of speaking. To further boost her business, Harper provided excellent service in a spotless and relaxing setting.

In addition, Harper emphasized health rather than vanity as the rationale behind her hair care treatments. She promoted the idea that "health is beauty." Products made from natural, simple ingredients were used on the skin and scalp to enhance what Harper called "natural beauty." These measures succeeded in drawing Rochester's most prominent women to Harper's salon.

Harper skillfully promoted her business in other ways. Her remarkable floor-length, chestnut-colored hair was one of her greatest business assets, and she posed for advertisements that displayed it. The company's logo featured a horn of plenty, which was meant to show that women who were willing to work hard could become successful business owners like Harper.

Soon, out-of-town clients were asking for similar salons in their communities. Over the next three years, Harper developed a plan to franchise Harper Hair Dressing Salons along with beauty schools to train managers and operators to use "the Harper method." Harper salons opened in Buffalo, New York, and then in Chicago, New York City, Detroit, and San Francisco as well as in Berlin, Germany, and Edinburgh, Scotland. By 1928, 500 Harper salons were operating around the world.

To maintain quality in every location, Harper set high standards for hiring and training her managers and operators. She preferred to hire reliable working-class women, especially former servants, to work in her salons because they were used to working hard and providing good service. These women, called Harperites, attended her training schools, where they were taught to use standard tools and techniques. That way, customers could rely on consistent service and products in every Harper salon. Each owner also was expected to keep her salon neat, clean, and attractive.

Further, salon branch owners were required to purchase all their supplies from Harper, but they could keep the profits they earned from the business. As a result, thousands of women became upwardly mobile and financially independent by working in the hair care business. Harper encouraged these women, in turn, to devote time and money in their communities to improve the lives of women and children.

Both men and women visited Harper salons for hair and skin treatments as well as soothing head, neck, and shoulder massages. Playwright George Bernard Shaw, President Calvin Coolidge, first ladies Grace Coolidge and Eleanor Roosevelt, and Susan B. Anthony were among Harper's most famous clients. Anthony, a famous suffragist and women's rights advocate, praised Harper's business skills.

Through the years, Harper added new products to her line, including more hair care and coloring products, hair-waving products, skin creams, and makeup. All of these were organic, and they were produced in Harper's own factories. Besides developing products, Harper also created practical equipment for her salons, including the "tip-back chair," a chair for shampooing that could recline, and a sink made with a cutout area where the neck could rest.

At age sixty-three, Harper was married for the first and only time to thirty-nine-year-old Captain Robert McBain, an Iowa native. She retired from the business in her seventies. After Harper died in 1950, her chain of salons continued to operate until 1972. That year, a competitor purchased the business. As of 2000, two Harper salons were still operating, including the Harper Method Founder's Shop in Rochester.

See also: Hairdressing; Salons, Hair and Beauty

Further Reading: Larsen, Polly, "Bonny LeVine Award 2001 (Celebrating Franchising's Success, Martha Matilda Harper)," *Franchising World*, February 2, 2002, 2, 3; *The New York*

Times, "Martha M. Harper, Pioneer Beautician" (obituary), August 5, 1950, 15; Plitt, Jane R., *Martha Matilda Harper and the American Dream* (2000); Public Broadcasting System (PBS), "Martha Matilda Harper (They Made America)," http://www.pbs.org/wgbh/theymadeamerica/whomade/harper_hi.html.

HEADDRESS *See* Egypt, Ancient; Headgear; Middle Ages

HEADGEAR

Headgear refers to items of clothing that cover the hair or head or that enclose or anchor a hairstyle. They include different types of bands, bonnets, caps, hats, hoods, veils, helmets, and scarves.

Headgear may be worn for decorative, practical, or symbolic reasons or to conform to cultural or religious customs that require people to cover their hair. For example, people living in Islamic countries traditionally cover their heads, men with turbans and women with head cloths and veils. Headgear also may be part of a uniform for people who belong to the armed services or certain organizations. Headgear sometimes has an important symbolic significance, such as when monarchs wear special crowns or when members of the Catholic clergy wear miters. Hair accessories and replacements, such as wigs, also may be considered a form of headgear.

In **ancient Egypt**, members of the royal family wore special head coverings. The pharaoh wore a crown, a helmet, or a folded cloth kerchief. During the New Kingdom period, the pharaoh's sons wore kerchiefs with broad bands along with royal headbands called diadems. The queen wore a special headdress that featured an image of a vulture, a bird that was considered sacred and was believed to protect the king in battle. Ordinary Egyptians wore wreaths or colored ribbons in their hair.

Everyday headgear was especially important during the **Middle Ages** and the Renaissance in Europe. By the 1300s, European women were wearing various types of circlets around their foreheads. These were made of metal or of decorative ribbon wrapped around a metal wire. Veils were attached to the back of these pieces of headgear.

During and after the 1500s, people of both genders wore various accessories that covered part of the hair. Different hair coverings that are sometimes grouped together under the heading "snoods" include cauls, balzos, Italian coifs, and bun covers. Depending on the cost and the degree of formality, these items were made from netting, lace, ribbon, and various kinds of cloth, including cotton, muslin, velvet, or silk. Sometimes they were worn with hats or other head coverings. In such cases, after a snood was attached to the bottom section of hair, a hat was placed over it.

Snoods themselves were a type of large, loose bag that covered nearly all of the hair. Some were designed to lightly cover yet still show the hair, which allowed a woman to appear modest without completely hiding her hair. During the Middle Ages, most snoods were made of fillet-knotted lace, and after the

1600s, many were crocheted. Snoods could be ornate and artistic, with beads, jewels, and precious stones sewn onto the cloth or net. Other snoods that were made to hide or protect the hair were made from heavier materials that were not sheer or translucent, such as muslin or linen.

Whether they were worn for decorative or protective reasons, most snoods were worn on the middle of the head. Medieval women usually pinned their snoods in place or tied them with ribbons or pieces of cloth. Most of the snoods made in modern times are kept in place with elastic cording.

Cauls were made from cloth rather than open netting or crocheted material, although both cauls and snoods could be ornamented with jewels or pearls. Cauls were smaller than snoods, covering a specific area rather than most of the hair.

Similarly, bun covers were designed to cover and adorn just one portion of the hair. These hair coverings, which looked like small, tight cauls, sat around the top part of a bun. They were made from lace, silk, and other materials. Modern bun covers have been made from chain metal as well as cloth or crocheted fibers.

Sixteenth-century Italians developed a version of the snood called the balzo. It was worn higher on the head than a snood or caul and resembled a roll. An Italian coif was larger than a caul but smaller than a snood. During the late sixteenth century, this hair accessory was popular with Flemish men and women.

Women wore various kinds of caps on their hair during the late 1500s. One type, the Mary Stuart cap, formed a heart-shaped outline around the face. Some hairstyles required a woman to brush her hair up over pads before adding a cap. Other hairstyles featured curls placed close to the sides of the head, while the long hair in back was gathered into a bun and then covered with a net or small cap.

During the Middle Ages and Renaissance, headgear could indicate a woman's status or economic condition. Older or widowed European women usually covered most or all of their hair. Working-class women often wore simple kerchiefs or cloths on their heads. For practical reasons, these women often preferred to braid their hair, wind the braids into a circle at the nape of the neck, and then cover it with a cap.

In France, women favored small caps, often made of lace and worn low on the head, until the mid-1700s. Some of these caps had flaps on each side; these could be worn down or folded back. During the **French Revolution**, women's caps became simpler in design, as did their hairstyles.

During colonial days in America, women and girls wore caps on their heads both for decorative and practical reasons. Caps minimized the need to style the hair everyday and helped to keep dust and dirt from settling in the hair. These caps generally were made from white linen or cotton, sometimes trimmed with lace or ruffles.

Since the 1800s, headgear has not been part of everyday clothing for most Americans. Until the late 1960s, however, it was common for both men and women to wear hats for social occasions, and most women wore hats to church throughout the year.

Some kinds of headgear have been associated with political movements or professions. In France during the Revolution, a red cap called the *bonnet rouge* was a symbol of the fight for liberty. During the 1960s, members of the counterculture group known as the **hippies** popularized the wearing of bandannas and headbands worn across the top of the forehead. Certain kinds of headgear are associated with professions. For example, a French beret came to be identified with artists.

See also: Adornment, Ornamental; Adornment, Symbolic; Africa; Amish; Arabia, Ancient through Middle Ages; Comb, Decorative; Fontange; Greece, Ancient; Hair Net; India; Japan; Latin America, Ancient Times to 1500s; Monastic Styles; Native Americans; Religion and Hair; Renaissance Europe; Roman Empire

Further Reading: Amphlett, Hilda, *A History of Fashion on Headgear* (2003); Brooke, Iris, *English Costume From the Early Middle Ages through the Sixteenth Century* (2000); Houston, Mary G., *Medieval Costume in England and France* (1996); Norris, Herbert, *Medieval Costume and Fashion* (1999); Norris, Herbert, *Tudor Costume and Fashion* (1997).

HENKEL GROUP

The Henkel Group is a multinational company based in Düsseldorf, Germany. Henkel's products include the Schwarzkopf and DEP professional hair care lines.

In 1876, Fritz Henkel, a German merchant with a strong interest in science, founded the business under the name Henkel and Cie. Henkel's first products were detergent and glue; hair pomade was added in 1883. The products were made in Düsseldorf, and traveling salesmen brought them to customers in other parts of Germany.

By 1900, the company was selling other products, including wallpaper paste and tea, and it had expanded its business to Austria, Switzerland, the Netherlands, Italy, and England. The company continued to expand as Henkel's children and their descendants joined the business. Innovative new products were developed, particularly in the area of soaps, detergents, adhesives, and personal care products.

In 1960, the company entered the U.S. chemical-products market. That same decade, Henkel expanded its operations in France, and during the 1970s, it founded subsidiaries in Canada, Hong Kong, Nigeria, Thailand, Japan, Brazil, Ireland, and other countries. The company began operating in China in 1988.

In 1995, Henkel acquired the Schwarzkopf Company, which originated in 1898 when Hans Schwarzkopf combined a drugstore and perfumery business that were both located in Berlin. During the 1900s, Schwarzkopf became a major cosmetics firm. The company launched Germany's first powdered **shampoo**, Schaumpon, in 1903 and offered three versions of that product (tar, chamomile, and egg) by 1908. In the decades that followed, Schaumpon became Germany's most popular shampoo. Schwarzkopf hair colorants were introduced in 1949, and the company's first hairspray, Taft, was launched in 1955, followed in 1960 by Igora Royal hair colorants, which were made for salon use. Henkel went on to acquire the DEP Corporation, which was located in Los Angeles, California.

As of 2003, Henkel was the leading company in hair care for Austria and Germany and the second leading company in Russian hair care markets. It had a strong sales presence in numerous other countries.

In 2004, Henkel made three major acquisitions of companies that produce hair care products. One was Advanced Research Laboratories, a California company that makes Smooth 'n Shine and the Got2Be hairstyling line. Henkel also made its largest acquisition to date when it purchased **Dial Corporation**, which makes several well-known hair care products. From **Alberto-Culver**, Henkel acquired Indola, a worldwide consumer products group with professional brands sold to salons and wholesalers in Italy, the United Kingdom, France, Spain, Belgium, the Netherlands, and Luxembourg.

Further Reading: Associated Press, "Germany's Henkel to Buy U.S.-Based Dial," MSNBC.com, http://www.msnbc.msn.com/id/3717086; Euromonitor International, *Cosmetics and Toiletries Company Profile* (2003); Gabel, Medard, *Global Inc.* (2003).

HENNA

Henna, also known as Egyptian privet, has been used to color and condition the hair for more than 6,000 years. It is derived from *Lawsonia inermis*, a plant that grows in hot climates and is indigenous to North Africa, the Middle East, and possibly India. Henna is also cultivated in Australia and the Americas. The name "henna" comes from the Arabic words *al khanna.*

In ancient times, people thought that henna had magical properties to ward off evil spirits that cause disease and other misfortunes. Ancient Egyptians applied it to the hair and fingernails of the dead before they were mummified.

To prepare henna for use on the hair, the shoots and leaves of the shrub are first dried and then crushed and made into a paste. This paste, which is red in color, can be mixed with water. It works by coating the hair with color rather than causing a chemical effect, such as bleaching. The color and depth of henna hair dye depends on the strength of the henna and how long the preparation remains on the hair. Shades of red vary from orange to deep red-brown shades. Because it is a protein, the color tends to last a long time.

The first recorded use of henna as a hair dye has been traced to an ancient Egyptian queen named Ses, who also used henna preparations to cure hair loss. Cleopatra and Nefertiti are two other famous Egyptian beauties known to have colored their hair with henna. People in Africa, India, and the Middle East continued to use henna for cosmetic purposes into modern times.

During the late 1800s, Turkey was a major producer of henna for use on the hair. During those years, Turkish women used thousands of pounds of henna every year, and vendors sold henna in mixtures that they had developed to provide different tints along with pleasing fragrances.

Europeans learned about henna through travel and when famous people used it on their hair. Opera star Madame Adelina Patti (1843–1919) has been credited with popularizing henna hair dye during the late 1800s. Known for her long, thick auburn hair, Patti, the daughter of two Italian opera singers, used henna to attain her trademark hair color and to cover gray hairs as she continued to perform until 1906. As a result, more European and American women tried using henna on their hair, nails, and the soles of their feet during the Victorian Era, using henna imported from Turkey and the Middle East.

During the early 1900s, American silent-film stars **Theda Bara** and **Clara Bow** used henna on their bobbed hair. At that time, henna was still one of the most common materials used to color the hair.

More people in the United States became familiar with henna hair dye in the 1950s while watching the popular television comedy series *I Love Lucy*. Actress **Lucille Ball**'s character, Lucy Ricardo, occasionally commented that she used henna rinse to dye her brown hair red.

The use of henna became more widespread during the late 1960s when some people in the counterculture group known as the **hippies** used it on their hair. Henna and other plant products were used as part of a "back to the earth" movement that promoted natural ingredients.

Today, both women and men use henna products. Some men use it to dye their beards. Henna is used to condition the hair as well as to color it. Advocates of henna conditioners claim that it coats the hair shafts and helps to protect them from the effects of sun and environmental pollutants. Henna hair conditioners have long been popular in the Middle East.

In addition, henna is used to make dyes for body painting and temporary tattoos. The art of *mehndi*, a form of body painting that dates back to ancient times, spread throughout the Middle East and to Asia. Today, men and women in various countries have revived the practice, and celebrities, including actress Demi Moore, have been seen wearing temporary tattoos done this way.

See also: Arabia, Ancient through Middle Ages; Baker, Josephine; Egypt, Ancient; Eyebrows; Eyelashes; Hair Colorants; Natural Products

Further Reading: Abercrombie, Thomas J., "Arabia's Frankincense Trail," *National Geographic*, October 1985, 474–513; Miczak, Marie Anakee, *Henna's Secret History: The History, Mystery, and Folklore of Henna* (2001); Weinberg, Norma Pasekoff, *Henna From Head to Toe* (1990).

HEPBURN, AUDREY (1929–1993)

Actress Audrey Hepburn became a fashion icon, setting numerous trends in clothing and hairstyles during the mid-twentieth century. Her style combined elegant simplicity with a charming modesty and a waif-like manner.

The daughter of a British father and Dutch mother, Hepburn was living in England when World War II broke out in Europe. Her mother decided they would be safer in neutral Holland, but Germany invaded that country in 1940. Hepburn was then studying ballet at the Arnhem Conservatory of Music and planned to become a professional dancer. Her family endured many hardships during the war, including being forced from their home by the Nazis. Hepburn performed in dance programs to raise funds for the resistance movement, and she served as a courier, carrying messages, forged documents, and ration cards for the Dutch underground.

After the war, Hepburn and her mother moved back to London, where relatives helped them find housing. Hepburn resumed her ballet studies but was considered somewhat too tall for that career. However, her talent, unique beauty, and charm caught the attention of theatrical directors, who saw that the wide-eyed brunette would be quite photogenic. They offered her parts in plays both in England and the United States.

In 1948, Hepburn began her movie career and moved to Los Angeles. Her performance in her first major film, *Roman Holiday*, made her a star. During the course of the 1953 film, which is set in Rome, Hepburn's character has her long, dark hair cut into a gamine-style short hairdo that framed her face, with its large eyes and distinct dark brows, and set off her long neck. Hepburn won the Academy Award for Best Actress, and many women copied her hairstyle as well as the overall Hepburn look.

Fans saw a similar transformation in the movie *Sabrina*, in which Hepburn portrayed a chauffeur's daughter in love with the wealthy employer's son. Her shy, dowdy character leaves for Paris to attend culinary school with long, plain hair and then returns home with a chic, short, face-framing Paris hairstyle and a new wardrobe. Once again, women wanted the Audrey Hepburn haircut. More women also began wearing toreador pants with ballet flats and simple black turtlenecks.

Audrey Hepburn with her dog, 1963. *Library of Congress*

Hepburn continued to make fashion headlines as she went on to star in more than thirty films, which included historical stories, serious dramas, musicals, and contemporary romances. Critics praised her natural quality, melodic and aristocratic voice, and captivating personality, saying that Hepburn brought a new kind of sex appeal to films. At a time when the "blond bombshell" look was popular, she kept her dark brown **hair color** and refused to dye it, even for a film. When her role in the play *Ondine* called for light hair, she did not like bleached hair and hated wearing a wig, so she used gold dust onstage and washed it out at night. While playing Holly Golightly in *Breakfast at Tiffany's*, she popularized the "little black dress," in the form of a simple sleeveless sheath worn with pearls, and she wore a sleek but soft upswept beehive hairdo with honey-toned streaks.

Through the years, she was also photographed wearing a simple

ponytail, sometimes with bangs, different versions of the pageboy, and various short hairstyles with bangs. In her later years, the actress wore her hair pulled back from her face with a simple bun at the back, showcasing her wide green eyes and much-admired bone structure.

Beginning in the 1960s, Hepburn began making fewer films in order to spend more time with her two sons. During the 1970s, she took part in a documentary for UNICEF, the United Nations Children's Fund. In 1988, she became a goodwill ambassador for UNICEF, helping to publicize the work of the organization and raise funds. She made numerous trips to war-torn countries and places where children lived in poverty to raise public awareness of their plight. Hepburn was still working with UNICEF when she was diagnosed with cancer in 1992. She died in 1993 at her home in rural Switzerland.

Throughout her life, Hepburn was known for her charm, grace, and professionalism as well as her compassion. When people commented on her beauty, she expressed her belief that real beauty comes from a loving heart and acts of kindness. Hepburn often said that above all things in her life, she valued human relationships.

Further Reading: Vermilye, Jerry, *Audrey Hepburn: Her Life and Career* (1995); Woodward, Ian, *Audrey Hepburn* (1984).

HERSHBERGER, SALLY (1961–)

Sally Hershberger is a prominent hairstylist best known for her individualized, "choppy" hairstyles. She was the first New York hairdresser to officially charge $600 for a haircut.

Born to a wealthy family in Kansas, Hershberger later moved to California. Instead of enrolling in college after high school, she decided to attend beauty school. Her talent earned her an apprenticeship at the famous Arthur Johns salon, located in Hollywood, before she had even completed her training. There, she impressed both clients and photographers, which led to jobs styling celebrities' hair for fashion shoots.

Hershberger gained widespread attention when she created a distinctive, choppy-looking short hairstyle for actress Meg Ryan for the 1995 feature film *French Kiss*. The Meg Ryan shag became a major trend across America during the mid-1990s. In 2000, actress Jane Fonda appeared at the Academy Awards ceremony in another version of the choppy cut designed by Hershberger, and hairdressers across America reported that women were asking for similar styles.

Hershberger works on both coasts. Her Los Angeles base is the Melrose Avenue salon called Sally Hershberger-John Frieda, and her New York City salon is located in a loft in the meatpacking district. As executive style director at John Frieda Professional Hair Care, Inc., she has helped to develop new products, including the Sheer Blonde collection, which debuted in 1998, and then the Beach Blonde collection.

Besides Meg Ryan and Jane Fonda, Hershberger's celebrity clients include actresses Michelle Pfeiffer, Kate Capshaw, Sarah Jessica Parker, and the Olsen twins,

Mary Kate and Ashley, and U.S. Senator Hillary Clinton. Male clients have included Tom Cruise, Steven Spielberg, Jon Bon Jovi, Brad Pitt, and Jimmy Fallon. She has styled actors' hair for various films, including *Message in a Bottle, Bowfinger*, and *Magnolia*. Since the 1980s, Hershberger has styled the hair of models and actors for the covers of *Vogue* and other top magazines, as well as major ad campaigns.

See also: Hairdressing; Salons, Hair and Beauty

Further Reading: Harris, Judith Solomon, "More Women Turn Their Rug into a Shag," *The Detroit News*, November 3, 2000, http://www.detnews.com/2000/features/0011/03/e03-143237.htm; Kinetz, Erika, "Sally Inc.: Stylist Shapes Business in Her Own Image," *The New York Times*, September 25, 2005, Section 9: 1, 6; Landman, Beth, "Prime Cut," *New York*, October 27, 2003; Larocca, Amy, "Big Hair," *New York*, March 1, 2003; Reynoso, Patricia, "In the Cut: The Name behind the World's Most Wanted Hair—Sally Hershberger," *W*, July 2003.

HIPPIES

Members of a counterculture movement in the United States that developed during the early and mid-1960s and was associated with certain sociopolitical attitudes were called hippies. They opposed the Vietnam War, the proliferation of nuclear weapons, materialism, traditional roles for men and women, and attitudes that discriminated against minority racial and ethnic groups. This movement, made up mostly of young people, was associated with distinctive styles in hair and clothing and led to longer and less structured hairstyles for both men and women.

Photofest

Hippies were identified by their long, flowing hair, often including beards and sideburns for men. They also wore distinctive clothing featuring bright colors, African-inspired prints, and tie-dyed patterns. Blue jeans were a staple item along with bell-bottomed trousers, ruffled men's shirts, military fatigues, and clothing imported from India, including loose cotton gauze shirts, peasant blouses, and long skirts for women. Conversely, the miniskirt, a very short skirt, also became popular as a symbol of revolt against the modest fashions of earlier eras. Many hippies wore headbands around their foreheads, which were sometimes made by folding bandannas. Often, the headbands featured the peace symbol, which was also a popular motif for jewelry during that era. Some hippies chose to live in communes and/or engage in "free love" (sex outside of marriage not limited to one partner). Recreational drugs, particularly marijuana, LSD, hashish, and psilocybin, were also associated with the counterculture.

Some people who did not espouse the hippies' liberal political beliefs or lifestyle choices still adopted the hair and clothing styles associated with this movement. Long hair for men became far more common and gradually more acceptable. Men in various walks of life, including business, politics, education, medicine, and other fields, began wearing their hair either slightly longer or much longer than their previous styles. Some secured their long hair in **ponytails** when they were at work.

See also: *Hair* (the musical); Hairstyles, Twentieth-Century; Henna; Natural Products; Politics and Hair

Further Reading: Braunstein, Peter, and Michael William Doyle, eds. *Imagine Nation* (2001); Farber, David, and Beth Bailey, *Columbia Guide to America in the 1960s* (2003).

HIRSUTISM

Hirsutism is defined as excess hair growth in women in places where hair growth is normally absent or minimal. This may occur above the lip or on the chin, chest, nipples, upper and lower back, buttocks, and above the pubic region into the abdomen. Increased growth also may occur on the legs and other areas where men typically have more hair than women. The hair follicles become enlarged, and the resulting hairs are thicker and darker than usual.

According to dermatologist Herbert P. Goodheart, MD, hirsutism occurs in one out of every six women in the United States. Other experts estimate that hirsutism affects about 6 percent of all women of reproductive age in the United States. The condition is most common in women of southern European and southern Asian heritage, and it is least common among **Native Americans** and people from East Asia. Women in some ethnic groups normally have denser and darker hair than women in other groups.

Hirsutism is not life threatening, but it may cause emotional distress. It also may be a symptom of other problems, or it may be accompanied by other disorders, such as menstrual irregularities.

The most common causes of hirsutism include heredity, ovarian cysts, certain medications, and androgenic oral contraceptives. Abnormal hair growth can occur when the body produces higher than normal amounts of androgenic hormones (testosterone and androstenedione) or when the hair follicles themselves become more sensitive than usual to normal levels of androgen. About 60–80 percent of all women with hirsutism have higher than normal levels of circulating androgens.

Hirsutism also may be caused by inherited disorders of the adrenal glands, ovarian tumors, pituitary tumors, adrenal tumors, Cushing disease, and syndromes that cause severe insulin resistance in the body. The majority of people with hirsutism also are overweight, and some have acne or other skin problems.

Most women deal with the unwanted hair by bleaching it or removing it by means of waxing, shaving, plucking, or using a depilatory. Other treatments aim to stem the abnormal hair growth. A prescription cream may halt the growth of facial hair. Medications used for this purpose include antiandrogenic pills or non-androgenic contraceptive pills, which increase the estrogen levels in the body. If tumors are involved, these can be surgically removed so that the glands function normally.

See also: Beards, Women's; Hair Removal; Hypertrichosis

Further Reading: Elias, Alan N., *Hirsutism* (1983); Goodheart, Herbert E., MD, "Hirsutism," http://www.emedicine.com/derm/topic472.htm; Griffing, George T., MD, "Hirsutism," http://www.emedicine.com/med/topic1017.htm; Hunter, Melissa H., and Peter J. Karek, "Evaluation and Treatment of Women with Hirsutism," *American Family Physician,* June 15, 2003, http://www.aafp.org/afp/20030615/2565.html.

HYPERTRICHOSIS

Hypertrichosis refers to the abnormal and excessive growth of hair of the lanugo, vellus, and terminal types in either men or women. The condition is not androgen related—that is, not caused by high levels of male hormones or hypersensitivity of the hair follicles to male hormones. It may be congenital (present at birth) or acquired. Certain medications, including hydrocortisone, minoxidil, interferon, and streptomycin as well as heavy metals may lead to hypertrichosis. Some people develop hypertrichosis on the face during the late stages of cancer. It may result from injuries that require plaster casts, but that type usually is temporary rather than permanent.

Two major types of hypertrichosis are congenital. With congenital hypertrichosis lanuginosa, excess hair appears on the body at birth in the form of lanugo—long, fine-textured, silky hair without pigment. This hair remains on the body for life. Normally, lanugo is shed during the eighth month in utero and replaced by fine vellus hair and terminal hair on the scalp, which are then present at birth. Congenital hypertrichosis lanuginosa is extremely rare, and since the 1600s, fewer than sixty cases have been recorded around the world.

In some forms of congenital hypertrichosis, excess terminal hairs with full pigmentation grow all over the body. Nearly everyone with this condition also has dental defects. As a result of their appearance, some cultures have labeled people with this form of hypertrichosis as "dog-men," "werewolves," "ape-men," or "hairmen."

Hypertrichosis may date back to prehistoric times, since ancient drawings of people with excess hair on their faces appear on some cave walls. Between the seventh and tenth centuries, some physicians in the Middle East described men with the condition. During the late sixteenth century, physicians in France, Flanders, Switzerland, and Italy examined a man from the Canary Islands named Pedro Gonzales, also known as Petrus Gonsalvus, and his children to determine what caused the excessive hair on their faces and bodies.

During modern times, people with hypertrichosis have been featured as curiosities in circuses and sideshows, particularly during the nineteenth century. In some cases, siblings or families with hypertrichosis have appeared together. Mexican Julia Pastrani (1834–1860) toured with various circuses in Europe, where people called her the "Ape Woman." A well-educated and multilingual Polish man born as Stephan Bribowsky (1890–1932) had a six-inch growth of hair on his face. Known as "Lionel, the Lion-Faced Man," he traveled with America's Barnum and Bailey Circus. An acrobat, the Russian-born Fedor Jeftichew, was known to circus audiences as "Jo Jo the Dog-Faced Boy."

One of the most famous "wolf-people" was Manuel Diaz (1938–2003), who appeared with circuses in Mexico and the United States as Manuel Diaz or Manuel Diaz-Aceves. Diaz's facial hair covered about 98 percent of his face, including his eyelids and nose. While growing up, he was ostracized, and some people were afraid of him. Later, as an adult, he was featured in *Ripley's Believe It or Not, The Guinness Book of World Records*, and on numerous television shows as well as traveling with circuses. None of Diaz's fifteen children inherited his hypertrichosis, although his nieces and nephews were born with it. In an interview about his condition, Diaz said, "I want people to remember that no matter how different a person may appear, they are still human beings inside. I want people to see the heart of a person and not judge the outside appearance. I want parents to teach their children to respect others" (Diaz).

To deal with hypertrichosis, people may opt to remove the hair, using mechanical or chemical means. Some choose permanent methods of hair removal, including electrolysis and laser treatments. Others find that hair removal is too painful or that the chemicals burn their skin, so they leave the hair alone.

See also: Beards, Women's; Body Hair; Hirsutism

Further Reading: "Q & A With Manuel Diaz, the Wolf Man," http://www.circusfolks.com/circus/interview.html; Rook, Arthur, *Textbook of Dermatology* (1986); Ruiz-Maldonado, Ramon, et al., *Textbook of Pediatric Dermatology* (1989); Speroff, Leon, and Marc A. Fritz, eds., *Clinical Gynecologic Endocrinology and Infertility* (2004); Stockinger, Günther, "The Curse of the Hair," *Der Spiegel*, December 31, 2004, http://service.spiegel.de/cache/international/spiegel/0,1518,335660,00.html.

I

INDIA

Since ancient times, grooming practices in India have included cleansing and conditioning the hair and applying scented oils and other materials. Bathing and shampooing became especially important in the hot and often dusty environment. Hair care preparations have been made with natural substances, including coconut oil, almond oil, honey, and *ghee* (clarified butter). Hairdressing (*shringar*) and **comb** making can be traced back to 2000 BCE. Special techniques of head massage also date back more than 1,000 years. Massage is regarded as a way to reduce stress and improve hair growth. **Henna** has long been used to color the hair and add shine. Tweezers and shaving razors have been used for removing hair.

An Indian priest. *Library of Congress*

Most people of Indian ancestry have black hair, usually straight and smooth in texture, although some people have curly or frizzy hair. A small number of natural redheads also are found in India.

Hair ornaments are important, and handcrafted ornaments made in various parts of India are admired all over the world. They include combs made from gold, silver, ebony, bronze, shell, or ivory, some of them decorated with gemstones, filigree, or carvings. Certain groups in the states of West Bengal and Orissa are known for their handcrafted, ornamental hairpins. Craftspeople in Uttar Pradesh make ebony combs carved with floral designs. Another traditional ornament is a comb shaped like a cobra that can be worn over a woman's long braid.

Real flowers are a common hair ornament for women, and in southern India, floral garlands are especially popular. Certain flowers are used to signify special occasions, such as weddings.

Spiritual Significance

Hair plays a role in certain spiritual customs. The majority of people in India follow the Hindu religion, and most others are Muslim, Buddhist, Sikh, Christian, or Jain. Hindu families have followed the tradition of having a child's head shaved as a way to get rid of impurities and so that fresh hair can grow in its place. The first cutting of the hair, called the *chudakarana* or *chudakarma*, has been performed in the first to the third year from the date of the child's birth, although it may be done up to age seven. Dates for this ceremony are planned based on the northern solstice and certain phases of the moon.

When the hair is cut, one or more tufts of hair—called *sikha* or *kuduma*—are left on the head to protect the brain from excess heat and to serve as a symbol of religious beliefs. The number and placement of tufts differ, depending on a person's affiliation and family traditions. For Namboothiris, the tuft has traditionally been located on top of the head and twisted into a knot; Tamil Braamahnins have worn their tuft more toward the back.

The removal of the hair is believed to bring strength, energy, long life, and other virtues. The shorn hair is offered as a religious sacrifice. During the ceremony, the child's father may use a porcupine quill, darbha grass, and a fake razor in symbolic ways. Special words are spoken to promote the child's future health, prosperity, and usefulness to others.

The custom of offering hair as a sacrifice continues to the present day, and this hair has been a major resource for companies that make wigs and hairpieces. Pilgrims still travel to Hindu temples where they give up their hair as a faith offering in the hope of fulfilling a special request, such as a good rice crop for their family or to give thanks for a special blessing. At the temples, the hair of these pilgrims is shaved off at the scalp and then processed at factories in India, China, or the United States before it is made into wigs and hairpieces that are sold around the world. The hair is particularly valuable for wig making because people keep it in a natural, healthy condition and refrain from using chemicals, permanent solutions, or dyes.

One of the major temples for hair offerings is Sri Venkateswara, located in Tirupati. The shaving area is located at the base of the temple. As of 2003, some 600 barbers shaved the heads of about 25,000 male and female pilgrims, including children, each day, for a total of about 450 tons of hair annually. Sales of this hair made Sri Venkateswara the richest Hindu temple in the country and enabled the funding of various hospitals, schools, and charitable institutions.

Women's Styles

Indian art and literature have showcased women's hair. Hair care, styling, and ornamentation are regarded as ways to reveal a woman's beauty, character, and sensuality.

Hair historians have noted that versions of modern hairstyles can be seen on Indian art dating back centuries. For instance, some sculptures of Indian gods from the first century BCE have braided hair that looks like cornrows. Other sculptures show women wearing hairstyles that resemble the buns and chignons that were popular in Western countries during the nineteenth and early twentieth centuries.

For centuries, long braids have been associated with Indian women, whose hair may grow to forty inches or longer. Braiding works well on the hair texture that is most common in this country. For generations, young women showed that they had left their childhood years by switching from two braids to a single long braid down the back. Many women also choose to wear their hair coiled or rolled into a simple bun or tied back in a long ponytail.

Traditions also dictated special wedding hairstyles and specific cosmetics for the hair and brows. During a Hindu wedding ceremony, a red dot called a *bindi* may be placed on the forehead of the bride and groom. Colored powders are applied along the line of the bride's eyebrows. Another tradition, performed by the groom, is to apply the red powder used for the *bindi* along the part on his bride's hair. This symbolizes her new status as a married woman.

In recent decades, more Indian women have been cutting their hair, adopting Westernized styles, and using manufactured products, including colorants. This practice is most common in urban areas. Women in rural India still usually wear their hair long, in traditional styles.

Men's Styles

For thousands of years, wealthy Indian men performed complicated grooming rituals each day that included hair care. Hindus usually shaved their faces twice a week and shaved their body hair every five to ten days. Members of the Namboodiri and some other castes were banned from shaving during times of mourning.

One of the ancient hairstyles for Hindu men was called *kudumi*. Men shaved their heads except for a small oval area toward the front. This unshaved patch was allowed to grow long and was then twisted into a knot. The knotted hair hung loose over the forehead or was worn on the side, usually the left. People living in remote regions left their hair long until modern times.

The profession of barbering dates back to ancient times in India, and barbers were highly respected in Indian society, since they performed the work of helping people to stay clean and well groomed. Wealthy people had personal barbers. Rural barbers moved from place to place with their equipment or sometimes were attached to a specific community. Those barbers might accept crops or other material goods in lieu of money. Modern barbershops usually have a glass front, which is reserved for only a few businesses in India. Inside the shops, a senior barber supervises a group of employees and trainees. During the late twentieth century, barbers stopped using traditional blades and began using disposable razors to prevent the spread of AIDS, which has become a serious problem in India. Although barbering was once a male-only profession, a few women have been accepted as barbers, usually after taking over the businesses of their deceased fathers.

Ute Indian chief at Ute Mountain tribal park in Colorado. *Getty Images*

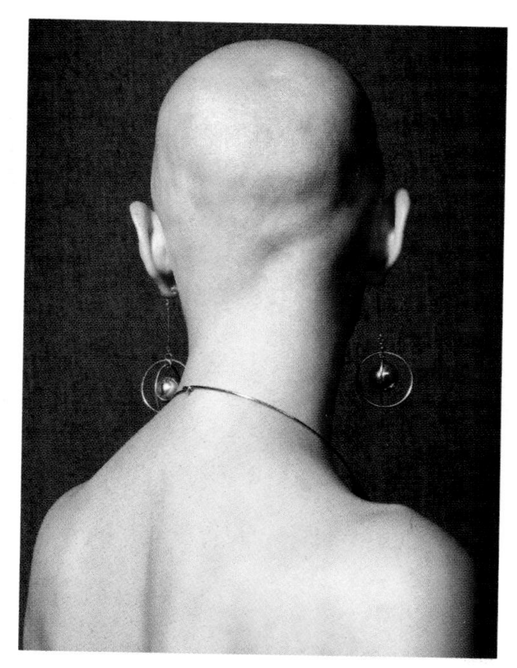

Getty Images

A Hindu holy man with streaming dredlocks at prayer in Bodhnath, Nepal. *Getty Images*

A girl from the Long Horn Miao minority with ancestral hair woven into a headpiece, China. *Getty Images*

Portrait of a Young Man, by Vincenzo di Biagio Catena, showing the pageboy hairstyle. *Corbis*

Ramesses II, Egyptian pharaoh. *Corbis*

Corbis

A patent medicine label for an unnamed woman's hair tonic that "restores gray hair . . . cures dandruff and prevents baldness." *Library of Congress*

Lady Lilith, by Dante Gabriel Rossetti, 1868 (oil on canvas). *Getty Images*

Getty Images

Head of Medusa, by Gian Lorenzo Bernini, showing snakes in her hair. *Corbis*

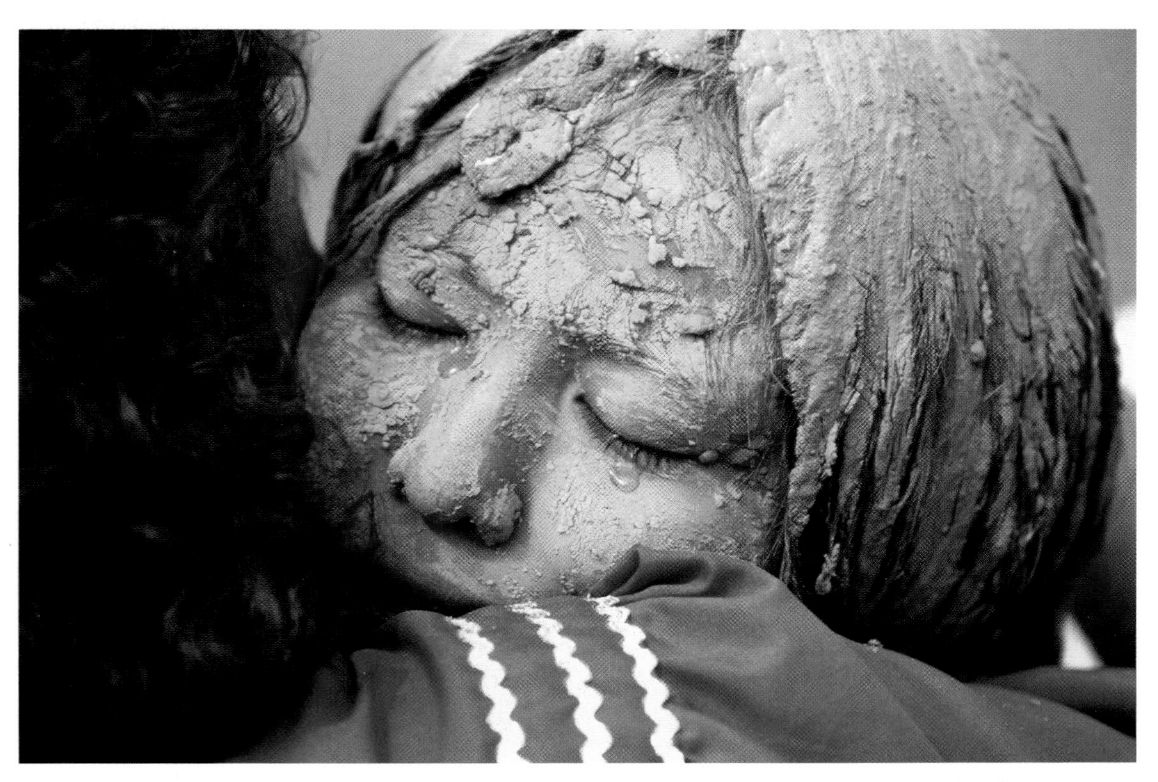

Arizona, Whiteriver, White Mountain Apache, Sunrise Ceremony where girls pass into womanhood. *Getty Images*

A South Yemen, Hadramaut, woman veiled in traditional dress. *Getty Images*

Getty Images

A Hibma woman sits with her two children. *Getty Images*

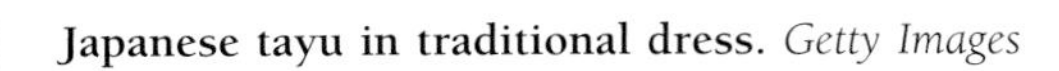

Japanese tayu in traditional dress. *Getty Images*

Portrait of a Woman, by Antonio del Pollaiolo. The subject is wearing a hair ornament from the Renaissance period. *Corbis*

Masai Moran men coat their heads with red ochre after getting their hair cut and shaved as part of the initiation ceremony that marks their passage into manhood. *Corbis*

Roman sculpture of a young boy showing typical ancient hairstyle of Roman men. *Corbis*

A man at a Bush/Cheney rally showing his political support by dyeing "Vote Bush" in red onto the back of his head. *Corbis*

Women's hairstyle from ancient Roman Iron Age. *Corbis*

A warrior from the Asaro clan at sing-sing in West Highlands, Papua New Guinea, Pacific. *Getty Images*

Turbans—long strips of cloth wound around the head or around a hat form—have been a traditional form of headgear for Indian men. Styles vary in different regions and may indicate a person's social class, religion, or other attributes. The Indian word for turban is *pagdi.*

Members of the Sikh religion leave their hair uncut and usually wind it around their heads under a turban. Male Sikhs are also advised not to shave or otherwise remove their body hair. Haircutting is considered to be an unnatural act, which makes it sacrilegious. A Sikh who does cut his hair is not forced out of the religion but does not enjoy the same status as those Sikhs who strictly follow their religious guidelines.

Modern Hair Care

Today, more people in India, especially those living in cities, use commercial shampoos and conditioners to care for their hair, as well as hair colorants. Young women living in cities may have their hair trimmed in shorter styles than were worn in the past. Some salon customers ask for hairstyles like those worn by their favorite actresses. In rural areas, girls still usually let their hair grow long, and knee-length hair is not unusual.

Traditional methods and materials are still popular, however. Coconut oil, and to some extent, safflower oil, are used to condition the hair. The oil may be applied before and/or after shampooing. It also is used to moisturize a dry scalp. Many Indians continue to believe that a healthy diet, cleansing, oiling, and avoiding the use of chemicals in shampoos or dyes are the best ways to maintain a healthy scalp and hair. Some make their own hair care preparations from oils, plants, and herbs.

In parts of India, comb making remains an important industry. Certain tribes living in Orissa are particularly skilled in this handicraft. Members of these comb-making tribes, which number about twelve, sell combs and also trade them in exchange for crops or other things they need. The combs are made in a variety of sizes, designs, colors, and materials for different uses. Different tribes are known for their particular designs, and a comb is regarded as a valued personal item. Some combs contain special scented oils that are released onto the hair when the combs are used.

Hairdressing

Hairdressing is a profession in India, and people attend training schools to receive licenses as beauticians. Hairdressing once was governed by stricter social rules. Before the 1950s, for example, it was considered improper for women from the upper classes to touch other people's hair. Those who chose a career in hairdressing were regarded as daring or as members of the avant-garde.

Veena Shroff (b. 1924) is perhaps India's most famous female hairdresser. She is well known for styling the hair of actresses and other celebrities and for her extensive knowledge of the history of Indian hairstyles and ornaments. As a child, Shroff was fascinated by classical dance and the hairstyles of the performers. She began writing columns about traditional hairstyling when she was still in her teens. To perfect her art, Shroff studied thousands of hairstyles in Indian paintings, sculptures, and works of literature. She has served as the stylist for more than 200 films, working with actresses Suraiya, Meena Kumari, Usha Kiran, Sandhya, Nirupa Roy, and Kamina Kaushal in the Indian film industry, which is called Bollywood. In the course of her career, Shroff has collected fine hair ornaments from different regions of India and from different eras that she uses to accentuate traditional and modern hairstyles. Shroff has lent these works of art for exhibitions throughout India. She has given hairstyling demonstrations in Paris, London, and other cities. In addition to using valuable ornaments in her hairstyles, she shows people how to create amazing hair designs using flowers, leaves, and beads strung on twigs. Her book *Indian Hairstyles* was published in 1962.

One of today's leading hairstylists, Nadeem Ahmed, grew up in a family that included an uncle who operated a salon. Nadeem later decided to pursue that career himself, and, in 1998, he began working at Rex Salon and Academy in Chandighar. He is known both for his skill in designing hairstyles and his ability to teach others. In his seminars and workshops, he emphasizes the need for effective communication with the client, along with an understanding of fashion, art, and technical skills. He has earned hair-coloring certificates from both **L'Oreal** and Schwarzkopf.

Uma Jayakumar, who grew up in a village near Bangalore, has achieved recognition as a hairdresser, beautician, and teacher. Jayakumar is known for her efforts to help women in rural India and women with special needs support themselves as hairdressers and beauticians. She began her career working out of her home and built a thriving salon business and training school that graduates about 100 students each year. As of 2005, she had trained almost 5,000 people, most of them women with physical challenges. Jayakumar also conducts free workshops during which she teaches people how to create various hairstyles and make hair care preparations, including a conditioning paste made from yogurt and hibiscus leaves and a tamarind paste that adds body to the hair. She has visited women's prisons to improve morale by giving the inmates haircuts and showing them how to style their hair. Jayakumar is known for her ability to style different hair types and work with children as well as adults. In 2004, she achieved a new distinction when she set the record in India for doing the fastest hairstyle, makeup, ear piercing, and sari tying. She broke her own record in 2005. That same year, she was listed in the *Guinness Book of World Records* when she created sixty-two hairstyles (French twists) in one minute, using a chopstick. The previous record holder was Spain's Marco Aldeni (twenty-five French twists in one minute).

As of 2005, other important stylists include Javed Habib, Adhuna Bhabani, and Hakim Aalim. Habib, who trained in London, returned to join his father's hair salon business where he became well known as a stylist and teacher. The business has expanded throughout India and into some other countries. Bhabani has done work for music videos and feature films as well as launching her own salon business. Aalim is known for his fresh, creative styles and his work with India's top film stars.

Hairstylists from India take part in the Middle East Golden Hands Awards, which are considered to be the "Oscars of hairdressing" in that part of the world. The awards are sponsored by the Wella Corporation's Middle East division.

Hair Industry

India has a thriving hair trade. More than twenty large companies and about 100 smaller businesses operate factories that process tons of hair. This hair comes from Sri Venkateswara and other temples where pilgrims sacrifice their hair for religious reasons. When sacks of hair arrive at these factories, workers sort out the bundles to identify the hairs that go together, making sure they do not mix the hairs from different people's heads. Then they smooth the strands to remove tangles and visible debris and put them in piles, according to length. Other workers wash the hair and lay it out to dry. Metal combs called hacklers are used to detangle the dry hair. Workers then measure and pack the hair so that it can be shipped to factories where it is made into wigs and hairpieces.

Hair regarded as "lower grade" is collected from combs and hairbrushes and from salons and barbershops. Some of this hair is used to make doll's hair and wigs for beauty school mannequins. The short hair taken from men who have their heads shaved is used as raw material for coat linings and other products.

See also: Competitions; Dredlocks; Hair Removal; Laws and Regulations; Monastic Styles; Religion and Hair

Further Reading: Auboyer, Jeannine, *Daily Life in Ancient India* (1965); De, Aditi, "Trappings for Tresses," *The Hindu* (India), March 17, 2003; De, Aditi, "Trappings for Tresses," *The Hindu*, March 17, 2003, http://www.hindu.com/thehindu/mp/2003/03/17/stories/2003031701680300.htm; Kalsi, Jyoti, "Makeover in a Minute," *Gulf News* (Florida), May 8, 2005, http://www.gulf-news.com/Articles/people-places.asp?ArticleID=87461; Mehta, Narenda, *Indian Head Massage* (2003); Padmini, Sengupta, *Everyday Life in Ancient India* (1955); Shroff, Veena, *Indian Hairstyles* (1962); Sivananda, Sri Swami, *All about Hinduism* (1977); Wadhwani, Anita, "From India to Nashville: The Human Hair Trade Links People a World Apart," *Middle Tennessee News and Information*, March 9, 2003, http://www.tennessean.com/special/hair/archives/03/03/29911318.shtml.

J

JAPAN

Special bathing and grooming practices, including hair care, have been part of Japanese life since ancient times. Keeping the body clean was considered vital for hygienic and spiritual reasons.

For centuries, hairstyles could indicate a person's marital status, social class, age, occupation, and/or religious affiliation. For example, during the Meiji period (1868–1912), unmarried women wore a butterfly hairstyle that they would change after marriage to a different type of bun. Historically, members of the lower classes (*hinin*) had short haircuts rather than the long, carefully tended hair worn by upper-class Japanese. Also, like members of certain other religious traditions, Buddhist priests and nuns in Japan shaved their heads to show they were entering a spiritual existence apart from the physical world. Otherwise, short hair on a woman was a sign of illness or disgrace. A traditional punishment for women who committed crimes was to have their hair shaved off.

Special hairstyles also were reserved for certain occasions. A traditional Japanese wedding hairstyle was an elaborate upsweep adorned with peach blossoms and silk ribbons. The famed geishas wore special styles and hair ornaments for different events and holidays.

Hairstyles with topknots are often associated with Japanese men. The wearing of topknots emerged during the Asuka age (550–710 CE), when Prince Shotoku adopted a hairstyle he had seen on members of the Chinese royal family. When young Japanese men came of age, they received an adult name and their foreheads were shaved, leaving a ponytail in the back. Facial hair was common for Japanese men until the seventeenth century. Mustaches were popular, and many men, especially members of the **military**, wore a narrow beard.

Perhaps the most famous and distinctive men's hairstyle was that worn by members of the *samurai* (the warrior class). A neat hairstyle and clean shave were part of a samurai's mandatory morning routine, as set forth in the code of knighthood. Samurai shaved the tops of their heads and then gathered hair from the sides and back together into a queue. They applied oil to the queue before doubling it forward over the crown, then tying it at the point where it was doubled over. The ends of their bunched hair were kept neatly trimmed. As part of their gear, samurai carried *kogai* (long, matching hairpins) that were used to anchor the hairdo. It was considered disgraceful if an opponent managed to cut off a samurai's queue.

For Japanese women, hair was a chief aspect of personal appearance, as shown by an old proverb: "Hair is women's life." Poems and other literary works celebrated women's long, shining hair. Some historians say that certain rulers

Japanese geisha girls. *Library of Congress*

enforced laws that banned women from cutting their hair in order to maintain the status quo in their male-dominated societies. In the past, people in Japan believed that long hair piled upon the head put pressure on a woman's brain so that she would not think too much.

The ideal hair for women was long, thick, black, and shiny, and women who possessed such hair were considered attractive, regardless of their other features. Hair shorter than waist length was regarded as a misfortune. To add sheen, women applied oil with a cloth. They, or their servants, carefully combed and dressed their long tresses.

Eyebrows were regarded as a particularly expressive feature, and distinctive fashions in eyebrows marked various historical periods in Japan. During the Heian era (792–1192 CE), for example, women and men at court plucked their eyebrows and drew in new, thick, black brows high on their forehead. Some chose instead to dip their thumbs into black makeup pigment and then press them against their foreheads to create two symmetrical prints. Styles in eyebrows were also used to communicate. Women who plucked their brows during the early part of the Edo era (1601–1867 CE) indicated to others that they were married and had at least one child.

Medieval Styles

Throughout the Middle Ages, people in Japan followed certain rituals and superstitions related to hair as well as other activities of daily life. Haircutting was supposed to be done only at certain times, depending on the calendar.

During the late seventh century, women and men both wore a hairstyle that some people described as shaped like a mallet. Men wore very long beards, some of them extending four feet or more. People used simple hairpins called *kogai* to part and style their hair and also to scratch the scalp.

During the Nara Period (710–794 CE), Chinese culture arrived in Japan and exerted its influence. One change involved hair accessories. From the Chinese came **combs** designed with a horizontal shape rather than the stick-shaped hair prongs the Japanese had been using. Relations with China ceased around 800 CE and were not resumed until centuries later.

The Heian era, which lasted from about 792 to 1192 CE, brought distinctive styles based on Japanese, not Chinese, culture. Men continued to wear topknots in different shapes, and they used a variety of hats.

For women, a high forehead with a distinct widow's peak was considered attractive. Women emphasized that feature or created a widow's peak by drawing a line around the forehead with makeup. Such lines were also used to soften the line between the face and a wig.

During this period, long hair was still the norm, and a woman's hair might have reached the ground or been grown even longer. Washing and combing this long hair was a time-consuming process, and some servants devoted as many as six hours a day to their mistresses' coiffures. The most common style for women during this period was center-parted hair that fell straight down a woman's back. According to G. Sansom, author of *History of Japan to 1334*, women at court "prided themselves on their hair, which must be glossy black, straight, and very long. . . . It was usually worn uncut, without any arrangement other than a parting, and it was thought right that the hair of a beautiful woman should reach the ground" (Sansom 1958, 408). Some women gathered their long locks into a low ponytail. Oil from the camellia tree was used to condition the hair.

Edo Period (1603–1867)

During the 1600s, the preference for long, loose hair on women gave way to elaborate, upswept styles or buns at the back of the neck. The trend seems to have started with courtesans and fashionable merchants' wives.

To create these coiffures, women usually began by dividing their hair into six sections—on the two sides, the front, the back, the nape of the neck, and the center (which was secured with string). The hairdresser then created the desired style, which might require pads, frames, and combs, eventually bringing all six sections together at the center. A thick, greasy substance was applied to keep these styles intact.

Each style had a name, and some were reserved for particular groups of women. They included the *shimada*, the *hyogo*, and the *katsuyama* (for married women). Courtesans adopted a coiffure that featured a forelock, side locks, back hair, and a chignon. Brides and the daughters of samurai were among the others who had special coiffures.

Many wealthy women had their hair styled twice a week. Some women often wore the same style for a week to ten days in a row without washing it. Women slept on their backs, using special pillows and neck rolls that propped up their heads so the hairstyles would remain in place.

A variety of ribbons, pins, combs, picks, and fancy ornaments were worn on the hair. Since wealthy Japanese did not wear necklaces or other pieces of jewelry typical in Western countries, hair ornaments were their primary adornments. These *kanzashi*, as they were called, came into wide use during the Edo period and were thought to give women a flower-like beauty. They were crafted from aromatic woods, plum and cherry wood, ivory, crystals, horns, tortoise shells, gold, and silver and then decorated with colorful lacquer, silver, gold, coral or jade beads, and/or mother-of-pearl inlays. Some women wore these ornaments with pairs of long *kogai* hairpins. Japanese artisans competed to design the most beautiful ornaments. *Kanzashi* have been handed down as family heirlooms and are now collectibles.

Men also wore somewhat fancy hairstyles during the Edo period. One popular style was the *chommage*, a style formerly worn by warriors. The top of the head was shaved, and the rest of the hair was grown long. That hair was formed into a topknot and then folded or tied to make a stiff ponytail in back of the head. Barbershops thrived during this era, as priests, soldiers, merchants, and men frequented the shops, which were off-limits to women. While having a haircut, a shave, or receiving other grooming services, barbershop patrons would socialize and discuss politics and current events.

In rural areas, people wore simpler hairstyles that did not require much maintenance. Historians note that, lacking fine ribbons or cords, Japanese peasants used straw to tie their hair. During the late 1700s, however, the economy improved, and peasants could be seen devoting more time and money to their appearance. Local rulers protested that the peasants were anointing their hair with oil and using cords to style their hair. They objected to these practices and said that it was improper for villages to have hairdressers.

Working-class women and farm laborers did not spend as much time styling their hair as the wealthier classes. According to Gail Lee Bernstein, author of *Recreating Japanese Women, 1600–1945*, male and female field workers were hard to tell apart because the women "dressed like men and left their hair unkempt" (Bernstein 1991, 57).

Changing Times

The Meiji period (1868–1912) brought changes as Japan modernized its government and connected more with other nations. After the military adopted new uniforms with Western-style caps, the traditional topknot hairstyle no longer worked, and men's hairstyles changed accordingly. The government urged men to "crop" their hair.

As hairstyles changed, class and occupational distinctions diminished. Most women started wearing more natural eyebrows instead of plucking them off. A number of younger women and some older ones preferred to wear short hair instead of fancy hairstyles that required time and money to maintain. Some women went even further and wore men's clothing styles. In 1872, the government passed laws banning short hairstyles for women. Other laws passed during the Meiji period required women to obtain permission from their husbands or fathers before cutting their hair. Short hair was said to be too radical and unsupportive of Japanese traditions.

In 1885, an organization called the *Sujin Sokuhatsukai* (Women's Upswept Hair Society) was formed by men and women who wanted to promote a version of an upswept style that was simpler than prevailing hairdos. The new style reflected both Western styles and Japanese traditions. The society spread its ideas through mass print media. Several versions of the style became popular and were worn by prominent Japanese women, including the empress. Certain schools required girls to wear the upswept style. After the 1880s, the upsweep became a standard hairdo for middle-class women.

Twentieth Century and Beyond

During the Showa period (1926–1989), both men and women increasingly adopted Westernized clothing and hairstyles. By the late 1920s, some Japanese women were bobbing their hair. The press referred to women who wore short hairstyles and short skirts as the "modern girl." The first beauty parlor in Japan opened in Tokyo in 1923.

Hairstyles continue to be influenced by trends from the West, especially by film stars and other celebrities. For example, during the 1950s, numerous women opted for a short, "pixie"-style cut with bangs like the one actress **Audrey Hepburn** wore in the 1953 film *Roman Holiday*. The ponytail gained popularity when it was seen on Hepburn and French actress Brigitte Bardot, among others. Many Japanese women wore the French twist and modernized versions of the chignon.

Women continued to wear various kinds of braids (called *mitsuami*), including multiple braids wound around the head in different configurations, such as ones that looked like coronets. They also continued to use traditional conditioning oils and eat certain foods, including kelp and seafood, for healthy hair.

Before the late twentieth century, dress codes banned girls from curling or dying their hair or using colored barrettes or other hair accessories while at school. Boys were expected to keep their hair very short, and girls were advised to wear either a bobbed hairstyle or braids. Still, the mass media and celebrities continue to exert a strong influence. Pop singer Seiko Matsuda (b. 1962) strongly influenced hairstyles when she appeared with feathered layers and bangs. The hairstyle required careful blow-drying and hairspray to keep it in place, but young women were willing to make the effort to attain the "Seiko-chan" look. More girls were washing their hair every morning before school, which caused extra strain on family bathrooms. Some schools tried to ban this hairstyle, but it remained extremely popular through the mid-1980s.

In recent years, Japanese hairstyles have covered a wide range, including long, traditional-looking effects, curls, feather cuts, "buzz cuts," and other fashionable styles from the West. Today, more people are experimenting with color and diverse hairstyles. Young women have been choosing shorter, trendy cuts, while women in their twenties and thirties have been growing their hair longer. As women grow older, they usually wear their hair shorter. Some Japanese, usually young people, wear styles influenced by African American culture. They visit salons that offer hair extensions, dredlocks, cornrows, and permanents to create curls, waves, or frizzy hair textures. Some young men and women opt for Afro styles reminiscent of the late 1960s.

Recent trends also include more hair coloring. Until about 1979, few Japanese people colored their hair, except women who wanted to keep the natural black color from going gray. Stylists contend that since most people in Japan are born with the same kind of hair, they look for a color and shade that will set them apart from other people. Young people are more likely than their elders to experiment with unusual hair colors or streaked hair. At the millennium, shades with a red or pink base were popular, and women were looking for a natural appearance whether they used streaking, highlighting, or an all-over dye. Japanese soccer players also have become known for their individualized, dyed hairstyles.

Hair salon businesses flourish in Japan today, and hairdressing is one of the top-ten favorite professions among young people. According to Kaori Shoji, writing in *The Japan Times*, "People will pay 10,000 yen for a hair job and only 500 yen for lunch" (Shoji 2005). Both women and men have their hair straightened during especially humid times of year.

Some hairstylists and salons specialize in traditional hairstyles, called *nihongami*, which means "Japanese coiffure." They include stylists for kabuki theatrical companies and hairdressers for Japan's traditional puppet theater. Hideo Tanikawa, who styles hair for the Zenshinza, a theatrical company, has amassed a collection of historical prints and accessories so that she can reproduce old styles accurately. Tanikawa admires the classical hairstyles of the Edo period and says, "*Nihongami* looks most beautiful when viewed from the back. . . . *Nihongami* and kimono made a perfect combination" (Takashima 1999, 7).

Elaborate traditional Japanese hairstyles can still be seen during festivals and special occasions, such as New Year celebrations. A festival called Shimada-mage is held in Japan on the third Sunday in September. Female beauticians wearing traditional hairstyles parade along streets in the downtown district of Shimada and near the Uda-ji Temple. Some Japanese brides choose to wear a classic *nihongami* wig for their wedding.

Geisha Styles

Certain women called *geisha*—"beautiful person" or "one who lives by art"—represent a specialized feminine look in Japan. The earliest *geisha* were male professional actors, dancers, musicians, and storytellers, but by the 1700s, women dominated the profession. These women are traditionally entertainers, trained to provide a sense of luxury and relaxation. As *maiko* (geishas in training), they learn to speak, move, sing, write, dance, recite poetry, and serve food and drinks in ways that are considered graceful and attractive. They learn to play a three-stringed instrument called the *samisen* and master special rules of etiquette.

The geisha's use of makeup, clothing, hairstyles, and ornaments corresponds to different seasons and months of the year. For instance, the hair is adorned with cherry blossoms in April and with chrysanthemums in November. Other adornments include combs carved into different shapes and then adorned with flowers or lacquered designs. Hairstyles also have special names, such as "peach blossom."

The geisha's large hairstyles use extensions and hairpieces, some of them made from the hair of yaks or other animals. They are heavy, weighing as much as six pounds. The strain from hairstyling and the weight of the hair can cause hair loss, including bald spots.

Such hairstyles are meant to last several days or even a week. Wax holds the hair in place. At night, a geisha also sleeps with her head on a wooden neck rest called a *takamakura* to keep her hairstyle intact. If it becomes flat or disheveled, she will need to visit the hairdresser again the next day.

Hairdressers who create geisha styles are called *keppatsu-shi*. They use special tools for their trade, including combs designed to cut through the heavy, waxed hairstyles that can cost hundreds of dollars. Traditionally, *keppatsu-shi* were women until the mid-1970s, when a male hairdresser, Tetsuo Ishihara, began styling hair for geishas in the famous Gion district of Tokyo.

Traditional Comb Making

Comb making is one of Japan's traditional crafts, and fine combs have been regarded as practical works of art that respect the hair while providing a lifetime of service. Combs were made with care, starting with the selection of the wood, which might have been sandalwood or another fragrant wood with a fine, suitable grain. A comb was carved by hand and oiled, sometimes more than 100 times and then put them aside to "rest" for a few years before being put into use.

Before the early 1900s, young apprentices, often no older than ten, would learn this trade by living with a master comb maker and his family. While carrying out odd jobs, the apprentices would learn about woods, tools, cosmetics, hair-dressing, and other things. A master comb maker might have had to study for twenty years before he could have produced a comb that could be sold in the shop.

See also: Adornment, Ornamental; Comb, Decorative; Laws and Regulations; Wigs and Hairpieces

Further Reading: Bernstein, Gail Lee, ed., *Recreating Japanese Women, 1600–1945* (1991); Daidoji, Yuzan, et al., *Code of the Samurai* (1999); Faiola, Anthony, "The Geisha Stylist Who Let Her Hair Down," *Washington Post*, August 17, 2004, C01; Hempel, Rose, *The Golden Age of Japan, 794–1192* (1983); Henshall, Kenneth G., *A History of Japan* (2001); Morris, Ivan, *The World of the Shining Prince* (1964); Sansom, G., *History of Japan to 1334* (1958); Shoji, Kaori, "The Mane Attraction," *The Japan Times*, May 25, 2004, http://202.221.217.59/print/features/life2004/fl20040525zg.htm; Takashima, Miki, "Black and Beautiful," *Daily Yomiuri* (Japan), November 18, 1999, 7; Yamamura, Kozo, *The Cambridge History of Japan* (1993).

JAZZ DAB *See* Soul Patch

JOHN FRIEDA PROFESSIONAL HAIR CARE, INC.

John Frieda Professional Hair Care, Inc., is a leading manufacturer of hair care products for retail markets. Based in Wilton, Connecticut, the company distributes its products in fourteen countries and also operates salons in the New York City, Los Angeles, London, and Paris. It was founded by British hairdresser John Frieda, who became a well-known celebrity stylist during the 1980s and later was named British Hairdresser of the Year.

The John Frieda company is known for its Frizz-Ease line. Launched in 1990, Frizz-Ease Hair Serum, which contains silicone, was designed to help control frizzy hair and "fly-aways," thus creating a smoother, silkier look. The company also offers shampoos, conditioners, serums, hair spray, **styling products**, and finishing products for various hair textures and hair colors.

Founded in England, John Frieda expanded into the United States in 1990 and by 2000, it had become one of the top-ten manufacturers of hair care products in the nation. Sales of the Frizz-Ease line steadily rose during the 1990s, and Frizz-Ease Hair Serum, the company's first product, became the number-one styling product in hair care. As of 2001, annual sales were about $160 million. The company went on to develop several new lines, including products specially geared for blond, brunette, and red hair.

In 2001, Kao Corporation, a Japanese soap and cosmetic firm, acquired John Frieda for $450 million, through its American subsidiary, the Andrew Jergens Company. The John Frieda salons were not included in this transaction, which Kao hoped would enable it to expand its beauty products operations in North America. At the millennium, John Frieda himself stopped working as a stylist to manage the growing business.

See also: Hershberger, Sally

Further Reading: Geracimos, Ann, "Hair Peace," *The Washington Times*, March 8, 2004, http://washingtontimes.com/metro/20040317-091612-2002r.htm; Naughton, Julie, "Frizz Pays Dividends for Frieda," *WWD*, November 5, 1999.

JOHN PAUL MITCHELL SYSTEMS

In 1980, with an initial investment of $700, Paul Mitchell and John Paul DeJoria established the partnership that became known as John Paul Mitchell Systems. As a hairdresser himself, Mitchell aimed to design a hair care line for hairdressers, by a hairdresser, while DeJoria brought his expertise as a consultant to companies in the professional hair care business.

Although Mitchell and DeJoria had great confidence in their products, they faced numerous challenges in building up the business, including limited resources. To promote the products, the two founders visited numerous cities to carry out demonstrations for salon operators. They also pledged that customers would receive full refunds if they were not able to sell the products they ordered.

Sales steadily grew, and John Paul Mitchell Systems became one of the fastest-growing privately held companies in the United States. As of 2005, John Paul Mitchell Systems has annual retail sales of approximately $800 million. The company offers more than ninety products, including color treatments, shampoo and conditioning systems, smoothing and texturizing systems, and styling products, including serums, gels, and hairspray. Other products include styling tools and body products, for a total of about 100 trademarks. In the United States, the company sells products to approximately 90,000 hair salons. Internationally, John Paul Mitchell Systems works with distributors in forty-five countries, and about 15,000 hair salons carry their products.

Paul Mitchell The School was also created to carry on the legacy of John Paul Mitchell Systems. Numerous schools located throughout the United States offer training and education in beauty care.

DeJoria and Mitchell are active in philanthropic efforts, including those that help the homeless and preserve the environment. They donate time and money to various charities, including the Rainforest Foundation and the Creative Coalition.

See also: Hairdressing; Styling Products

Further Reading: "John Paul DeJoria," Horatio Alger Association of Distinguished Americans, http://www.horatioalger.com/members/member_info.cfm?memberid=DEJ04; Mitchell, Paul, "About Us: The Story," http://www.paulmitchell.com/intro.asp; http://www.islandconnections.com/edit/mitchell.htm.

JOHNSON, GEORGE ELLIS (1927–)

A native of Richton, Mississippi, George Ellis Johnson founded **Johnson Products**, a successful multinational hair care products business.

When Johnson was two years old, his mother relocated from Mississippi to Chicago, where he grew up and attended school through the eleventh grade. While his mother worked in a hospital cafeteria, young George helped by shining shoes and then by working as a busboy. In 1944, he began working as a door-to-door salesman for the Fuller Products Company, a black cosmetics firm. He was promoted to production chemist and then to production manager.

In 1954, shortly after he married Joan Henderson, Johnson decided to start his own company. Dr. Herbert A. Martini, a German-born chemist who ran the laboratory at Fuller, urged Johnson to produce and sell hair care products for people of color, and he helped to develop those products. With a $250 loan from a finance company, Johnson made plans to manufacture and sell Ultra Wave, a **hair straightening** product for men. He began working with Orville Nelson, a prominent Chicago barber who served well-known clients such as musician Duke Ellington. While Johnson handled the production aspects of the business, Nelson took charge of marketing and sales, targeting barbers.

In less than a year, Nelson left the business and Johnson took full control. Sales for that first year reached $18,000. Joan Johnson and her brother joined the business in 1955, a year that saw sales expand to $75,000. As Johnson branched out beyond Chicago to sell products to barbers in Indianapolis, Detroit, and other cities, sales of Ultra Wave products continued to grow. By 1957, the company also was producing its Ultra Sheen line. This product line brought increasing profits, and Johnson moved the business to a three-story building in Chicago to keep up with the demand. Gross sales for 1958 totaled $250,000.

During the 1960s, the company began selling products to the general public through drugstores and other retail outlets. By then, Johnson had become a millionaire known for his ability to develop and promote popular new products and to maintain strong brand-name recognition in a competitive marketplace.

In 1971, Johnson Products became the first company owned by an African American to be listed on a national stock exchange when its stock was offered on the American Exchange. That same year, Johnson was the first African American to be elected to the board of directors of the Commonwealth Edison Company, a large utility corporation. He also was known for his cultural and civic contributions. Through the George E. Johnson Foundation and George E. Johnson Educational Fund, he has supported the arts, Junior Achievement of Chicago, the Chicago Urban League, Northwestern Memorial Hospital, and Operation PUSH. In 1978, *Ebony* magazine gave Johnson its prestigious American Black Achievement Award.

In 1989, Johnson's son Eric, one of his four children with wife Joan, took over as president of the company, while Johnson continued to serve as a consultant. He retired from active involvement with the company in 1992, when it was sold to IVAX, a large pharmaceutical firm.

See also: African Americans; Afro

Further Reading: "Johnson, George," Business & Industry Hall of Fame biography, http://www.businessandindustryhalloffame.com/Johnson_George.html; Phelps, Shirelle, ed., *Who's Who among African Americans* (1996); Silverman, Robert Mark, "The Effects of Racism and Racial Discrimination on Minority Business Development," *Journal of Social History* 31 (1998).

JOHNSON PRODUCTS

Johnson Products is a multinational company that is known for its innovative hair care products designed specifically for people of color. It was the first African American–owned company to be listed on a national stock exchange.

In 1954, entrepreneur **George Ellis Johnson** started his business with a $250 loan from a finance company. Johnson Products began manufacturing Ultra Wave, a product that straightened men's hair.

Within three years, Johnson Products also was offering its Ultra Sheen line of products for professional beauty operators who worked with female clients. Ultra Sheen included a cream-press permanent that was used to straighten hair. This was regarded as a major advancement over previous straightening methods, which involved oiling the hair and then using a hot comb, which could cause damage. Ultra Sheen hair relaxing cream could be used between visits to the beauty salon.

Profits from these successful products brought the company's earnings to $250,000 in 1958. Johnson moved to a three-story building to accommodate the growing business.

During the 1960s, the company began selling to retail markets as well as professionals. In 1969, the company became the first African American advertiser to sponsor its own television show, *Soul Train*, which was syndicated across the United States. Johnson Products went public in 1971, with a listing on the American Stock Exchange. Ultra Sheen cream hair relaxer continued to be one of Johnson's most popular products.

During the late 1960s, the black pride movement inspired many African Americans to stop straightening their hair artificially and wear more natural styles, including the **Afro**. In response, Johnson Products launched its new Afro Sheen line for natural hair. The line grew to include more than ten different products, but sales of these products declined as the Afro became less popular.

During the 1970s, Johnson Products became the largest black-owned manufacturing company in America. Sales quadrupled between 1968 and 1973. The company grossed $14 million in 1971 and $24 million in 1973; by 1976, that figure reached $39.4 million.

However, during the next ten years, sales leveled off and then declined. Johnson Products entered the fragrance market with a new men's cologne called Black Tie, but it was not a success. As more competitors began producing ethnic hair products, Johnson Products' market share declined from 60 percent in 1971 to 40 percent in 1980. The company reported a net loss of $4.1 million in 1984.

In 1985, the company brought out a new line of men's personal grooming products called Team Jordan, endorsed by superstar basketball player Michael Jordan of the Chicago Bulls. The new line faced intense competition from larger companies that had a stronger pull in mainstream markets, and Johnson Products was forced to downsize.

Eric Johnson, George Johnson's son, became president in 1989. During the next two years, he worked to help the company recover its profitability. Then, in 1992, he left to manage another business.

By the 1990s, Johnson Products offered more than 200 items, including Soft Touch, Classy Curl, Sta-Sof-Fro, GT for Men, and Ultra Sheen's Bantu. Johnson Products Research Center was one of the largest development laboratories in the world specializing in hair care products for African Americans. In addition to its hair care products, the company featured several successful lines of cosmetics, including beauty products from Flori Roberts, Posner, and the model and actress Iman.

In 1993, Ivax Corporation, a pharmaceutical company based in Miami, bought Johnson Products. The company experienced further changes and consolidations. In 2001, Wella Corporation, a multinational hair care products business, bought the Ultra Sheen and Gentle Treatment product lines. In 2002, a semipermanent hair color and a line of children's products, U.S. Kids by Ultra Sheen, were added to the Gentle Treatment line. A line called JP Professional RefleXions was introduced only for the salon market.

Johnson Products are sold in both beauty supply and retail stores in the United States, Europe, Africa, the Caribbean, and Latin America.

See also: Hair Straightening

Further Reading: Byrd, Ayana D., and Lori L. Tharps, *Hair Story* (2002); "Johnson, George," Business & Industry Hall of Fame biography, http://www.businessandindustry-halloffame.com/Johnson_George.html; Silverman, Robert Mark, "The Effects of Racism and Racial Discrimination on Minority Business Development," *Journal of Social History* 31 (1998).

JOYNER, MARJORIE STEWART (1896–1994)

Marjorie Stewart Joyner was a prominent cosmetologist, educator, inventor, and activist. For her invention of the **permanent wave** machine, she became the first **African American** woman to be granted a U.S. patent.

Born in Monterey, Virginia, in the Blue Ridge Mountains, Joyner was one of thirteen children. She moved to Chicago at age sixteen and decided to study cosmetology. In 1916, she was the first African American woman to graduate from the A. B. Moler Beauty School. That same year, she opened a beauty salon in Chicago and married podiatrist Robert Joyner, with whom she would have two daughters.

Joyner soon began working with the hair care products company founded by **Madam C. J. Walker**. She helped Walker organize the nationwide chain of beauty schools that trained thousands of operators called "Walker agents," who sold the company's hair care products and tools door-to-door. Joyner soon rose to higher positions in the organization and was named vice president of the company after Walker died in 1919. As an expert in her field, Joyner was asked to help write Illinois's first beauty culture law in 1924.

While working at the Walker company, Joyner invented her version of the permanent wave machine, made with a combination of curling irons and clamping devices to "set" a hairstyle. Joyner wanted to provide women with a device that would keep their hairstyles in place for several days after they left the salon. Since she was a Walker employee when she developed her invention, she did not directly profit from sales of the machine, which she patented in 1928.

Joyner became more involved in political and charitable activities during the Great Depression of the 1930s. While she continued teaching and working in the field of cosmetology, she also helped people find housing and jobs. Joyner opened her beauty salons to people for various community functions. During World War II, her salons provided gathering places for African Americans serving in the military who were excluded from racially segregated social events for white servicemen.

A staunch supporter of education and self-help, Joyner worked with nationally known educator Mary McCleod Bethune to cofound the United Beauty School Owners and Teachers Association. She also worked with organizations that raised funds for African American colleges. Joyner worked with people of all races to promote civic programs that she believed in.

For several decades, Joyner served as head of the Chicago Defender Charities, Inc., an organization that began operating during the 1920s. During her seventies, she went to college and earned a bachelor of science degree. Still actively working for social causes in her nineties, Joyner was known as the "Grand Dame of Black Beauty Culture."

Further Reading: Macdonald, Anne L., *Feminine Ingenuity: How Women Inventors Changed America* (1992); Salem, Dorothy C., *African American Women: A Biographical Dictionary* (1993); Worley, Kelly, "Joyner Marks a Century of Black Progress," *The Chicago Reporter*, December 1993, http://www.chicagoreporter.com/1993/12-93/1293JoynerMarksaCentury ofBlackProgress.htm.

KAZAN, MICHEL (1920–2000)

Hairdresser Michel Kazan has been credited with creating several influential hairstyles, including the **bouffant**, which became popular with women around the world during the 1950s. Kazan's devoted clientele included celebrities and socialites.

Born in France, Kazan originally studied art and began his career working on theatrical productions at the Comedie Francaise in Paris. When he decided to focus on hairstyling, Kazan opened a Paris salon in 1938. After World War II broke out in Europe in 1939, Kazan emigrated to the United States, where he became the chief stylist for Helena Rubinstein, Inc., an international beauty products company with salons in New York, London, Paris, and other cities.

During the next twenty years, Kazan was known as one of the world's most talented and influential hairstylists. Clients praised his ability to individualize hairstyles, foresee trends, and create styles that would become popular around the world. Kazan was credited with designing the modern French twist, the bouffant, and the pageboy as well as some lesser-known styles—the cockatoo, the bubble, the Cleopatra, and the frizz. The bouffant, which was most popular during the 1960s, was a full hairstyle cut above the shoulders. Stylists used a combination of large rollers and hairspray to create height and fullness that would last for hours. Kazan also added false hairpieces called "falls," which became more popular in the 1960s.

In the early 1960s, Kazan left Rubinstein's organization to develop his own salons, which were affiliated with Bonwit Teller's chain of high-end department stores. Three dozen Kazan salons were opened in the United States and Europe. His regular clients included actresses, socialites, and top models who appeared in the pages of *Mademoiselle, Vogue, Cosmopolitan*, and other prestigious magazines. Some of the best known were first lady **Jacqueline Bouvier Kennedy**, actresses Natalie Wood, Raquel Welch, and Greta Garbo, and socialite Doris Duke. One of his assignments involved styling the hair of nearly 2,000 female flight attendants employed by Eastern Airlines.

Kazan also lent his name to a line of hair care products, cosmetics, perfumes, and women's wigs and hairpieces. During the 1980s, he stopped working directly with clients but continued to supervise his salon business.

After the Bonwit Teller department stores closed in 1990, Kazan's salon business declined along with it. By then, Kazan, who was in his seventies, suffered from health problems. His original Manhattan salon, the Townhouse of Beauty, continued to operate into the 1990s with a reduced staff that served some loyal customers.

After a long illness, Michel Kazan died in 2000.

See also: Hairstyles, Twentieth-Century

Further Reading: *Business Week*, "Reinventing the House That Dad Built," September 16, 1996, http://yahoo.businessweek.com/1996/38/b349325.htm; Englert, Jonathan, "Michel Kazan, Hair Designer to Celebrities and Inventor of the Bouffant," http://www.michelkazan.com.

KEEPSAKE *See* Hair Art; Hair Jewelry; Memento; Mourning

KENNEDY, JACQUELINE BOUVIER (1929–1994)

As first lady of the United States from 1961 to 1963, Jacqueline Kennedy (Onassis) helped popularize the **bouffant** hairstyle and strongly influenced other trends in hairstyles, beauty, and fashion. Her thick, brunette hair, which had some natural curl, was cut to an above-the-shoulder length and worn in various bouffant styles, including a version called the bubble cut. Millions of women admired the first lady's casual elegance and copied her various bouffant and upswept styles, which she usually wore with bangs. As one of the world's most famous women, she popularized an elegant simplicity that became known as "the Jackie Look."

During the 1960s, one of Mrs. Kennedy's favorite stylists was **Kenneth Battelle**, also known as "Mr. Kenneth." When Battelle began working with Kennedy in 1954, her hair was cut short and worn in a curled cap around her head. He encouraged her to grow it longer so that he could use large rollers to add volume, creating a bouffant look. The bouffant hairstyle was developed by French-born stylist **Michel Kazan** at Kazan's Manhattan salon, where Battelle had worked before launching his own world-famous salon on East Fifty-fourth Street.

The first official White House photograph of First Lady Jacqueline Bouvier Kennedy. *Library of Congress*

As first lady during an era when women typically wore hats for various social functions, Kennedy preferred pillbox hats and hats of other designs that were set back on her head so they would not crush her hair. As a result, sales of pillbox hats increased dramatically during the early 1960s. Sales of wigs also increased, since many women were not able to achieve a bouffant hairdo with their natural hair.

The first lady helped promote a modern new look that combined American ease with classic elegance. Fine fabrics, simple lines, and expert tailoring were part of her individualized stylen and her hairstyle was part of this overall look. The first lady was photographed in a variety of fashions, including formal ball gowns, suits, sundresses, and simple sportswear for riding horses or playing with her children, Caroline and John F. Kennedy Jr. Outdoors, her hair sometimes became windblown but managed not to look "messy."

After President John F. Kennedy was assassinated in 1963, Jacqueline Kennedy moved to New York City, where photographers continued to follow the former first lady and magazines chronicled her hairstyles and clothing. In 1968, she married Greek billionaire and shipping magnate Aristotle Onassis, from whom she was later divorced. As Jacqueline Onassis, the former first lady worked as a book editor in New York City from 1978 until her death in 1994. Throughout her life, she remained one of the most photographed women in the world and an icon for understated elegance.

See also: Alexandre of Paris; Hairstyles, Twentieth-Century

Further Reading: Cassini, Oleg, *A Thousand Days of Magic* (1995); Keogh, Pamela Clarke, *Jackie Style* (2001); Mulvaney, Jay, *The Clothes of Camelot* (2001); Tapert, Annette, and Diana Edkins, *The Power of Style* (1994).

KOHL

Kohl (from an Arabic word that means "brighten the eyes") has been valued as a cosmetic item since ancient times in parts of **Africa**, Asia, and the Middle East. Used mostly to enhance the eyes, kohl is made by mixing powdered antimony, carbon, and copper oxide with gum resins. In ancient times, kohl was made from galena, a dark compound of sulfur and lead that came from a mine near the Red Sea, and cerussite, a white lead that also came from that area. Kohl also has been made from various mixtures of crushed antimony, burnt almonds, copper oxide, ash, malachite, and/or lead. Chemical analyses of kohl found in tombs dating back to 2000 BCE show the presence of compounds that do not occur in nature, which indicates that the ancient Egyptians used chemical processing to develop some formulations of kohl. Scientists also think that this substance was used for medicinal purposes, because it has disinfectant properties.

After mixing kohl powder with fat or oil, people typically applied this material with a small stick, which some people in the Middle East called "the needle." This applicator is made of wood, ivory, bone, silver, or another material, sometimes in a decorative shape.

In ancient times, people stored their kohl in seashells; later, they made special pots from limestone, ivory, silver, alabaster, wood, or other materials. Kohl pots, which often were painted and/or glazed, had disc-shaped lids.

Many ancient kohl pots have survived in Egyptian tombs, in which owners were buried with certain personal possessions. Archaeologists have found containers made into decorative shapes, such as the form of a palm tree or a monkey holding the pot in its hands. Others featured carved designs, and monkeys were a popular choice, since the ancient Egyptians kept monkeys as pets.

Men, women, and children in **ancient Egypt** used kohl (called *mesdemet*) to darken their **eyebrows** and **eyelashes** and to line their eyes. This practice not only dramatized the eyes, it also helped protect their eyelids from the intense sunlight. As well, kohl helped repel tiny flies that carried diseases that could cause infection and inflammation of the skin and eyes.

Kohl was valued so highly that it was used as a form of currency in Middle Eastern trade. It remained popular in Africa, the Middle East, and some other regions into the eighteenth and nineteenth centuries and still is used today. Berber women living in the Atlas Mountains of North Africa traditionally line their eyelids with kohl, placing a large black dot in each corner.

Some Western women, including popular entertainers, began using kohl during the late 1800s and early 1900s. They included French actress Sarah Bernhardt (1844–1923), American actress **Theda Bara** (1885–1955), and American-born singer and dancer **Josephine Baker** (1906–1975). During the 1920s, women who wanted to emulate the dramatically lined eyes they saw on film stars began using kohl as an eyeliner. During the 1960s, a renewed interest in **natural products** prompted some manufacturers to produce new eye pencils and other cosmetics made with kohl.

Modern kohl is made in Morocco, Pakistan, and **India**, among other places. People living in rural Egypt sometimes still make their own kohl, and one popular recipe includes charred almond shells and soot from sunflowers. Yet another method involves holding a pot over a stick of burning incense, then mixing the burnt residue left in the pot with *ghee* (clarified butter) to create kohl.

For some people, wearing kohl has religious connotations, since Muslims believe that the daughters of the prophet Muhammad wore kohl around their eyes. In some Middle Eastern cultures, both men and women line their eyes with kohl.

See also: Arabia, Ancient to Middle Ages

Further Reading: Alexander, Paul J., ed. *The Ancient World: To 300 AD* (1963); Hall, Alice J., "Dazzling Legacy of an Ancient Quest," *National Geographic*, March 1997, 293–311; Scarce, Jennifer, *Women's Costume of the Near and Middle East* (2003); Wells, Rhona, "The Most Precious Incense," *The Middle East*, September 1993.

L

LADY GODIVA (ca. 1004–1067)

The subject of historical debate, legend, and works of art, Lady Godiva (Godgyfu of Mercia) was an English noblewoman and patroness of the arts who lived during the Middle Ages. Her husband, Leofric, who was made an earl in 1017, became wealthy in the mutton trade and through his real estate holdings.

The famous legend about Lady Godiva riding naked on horseback covered only by her long hair may have arisen around 1167, about a century after her death. Supposedly, while the couple was living in Coventry, Warwickshire, Leofric imposed higher taxes on the people and used large sums of that money to erect ornate public buildings. His wife, known for her compassion, tried to convince him to use this money to benefit the poor. According to legend, Leofric told her that if she would ride her horse naked along a public street in Coventry, he would revoke the tax. She accepted the dare and rode her horse unclothed on July 10, 1040. Some accounts of this famous ride state that her long thick hair covered her entire body except for her lower legs, while others state that she wore her hair in two long braids. It also was said that the townspeople showed their respect and gratitude by covering their eyes and not looking at Lady Godiva as she rode down the public street.

Lady Godiva riding through town nude on a horse, with her long hair wrapped around her. *Library of Congress*

By the year 1678, the people of Coventry had begun a custom of reenacting Lady Godiva's ride at the annual Coventry Whitsun Fair. Women who played the part of Lady Godiva wore flesh-colored body coverings and long, flowing wigs. The Godiva pageant attracted many visitors—at its peak,

200,000 people in 1936—and proceeds from the ticket sales were donated to charity.

See also: Literature

Further Reading: Donoghue, Daniel, *Lady Godiva* (2002); Lancaster, Joan C., *Godiva of Coventry* (1967).

LAKE, VERONICA (1919–1973)

Born Constance Frances Marie Ockleman in Brooklyn, New York, film star Veronica Lake popularized a hairstyle in which one side of her long, ash-blond hair hung over her eye. Women around the world copied this wavy, side-parted, shoulder-length look, which became a representative hairstyle of the early 1940s.

At age twelve, Lake lost her father, a ship's master for an oil company who died in a ship explosion. Her mother remarried artist Anthony Keane, and the family moved several times. They were living in Beverly Hills, California, in 1938, when nineteen-year-old Lake enrolled in acting classes. A casting agent noticed the petite, fledgling actress and helped launch her film career, using the name Constance Keane. The next year, she made her screen debut in the RKO picture *Sorority House*.

> "And yonder sits a maiden, / the fairest of the fair, / With gold in her garment glittering, / And she combs her golden hair."
>
> HEINRICH HEINE (1797–1856), German poet, "The Lorelei"

During a publicity shoot for the 1940 film *Little Mothers*, a strand of hair kept falling across her right eye. The signature hairstyle was born, and it inspired the nickname "Peek-a-boo Girl." Women began asking for hairstyles with a "peek-a-boo bang."

In 1941, the actress signed a long-term contract with executives at Paramount Studios. That year, she appeared as a torch singer in Paramount's *I Wanted Wings*, using her new screen name, Veronica Lake. Soon, Lake joined a list of actresses who were known as "blond bombshells." People were eager to learn more about Lake's hair, and a feature article in one issue of *Life* magazine gave facts about her hair, including its length. The article said, in part: "Miss Lake has some 150,000 hairs on her head, each measuring about .0024 inches in cross-section. The hair varies in length from 17 inches in the front to 24 inches in the back and falls about 8 inches below her shoulders" (Corson 1965, 587).

Known for her roles as an aloof seductress with a sultry voice, Lake made three successful films with screen legend Alan Ladd: *This Gun for Hire, The Glass Key*, and *The Blue Dahlia*. Her other well-known films included *Hold Back the Dawn, Sullivan's Travels*, and *Isn't It Romantic?* During her career, she made twenty-eight films.

After World War II began, Lake changed her "peek-a-boo" hairstyle for patriotic reasons. Many women had copied Lake's famous hairstyle, and the U.S. War Department feared that it could endanger women working in factories and war-industry jobs. The War Womanpower Commission asked Lake to adopt a neat, upswept hairdo for the duration of the war. In 1943, Paramount released a newsreel that showcased that new look, with no locks hanging over her eyes. Lake wore a version of that upswept style while portraying an army nurse in the 1943 film *So Proudly We Hail.*

Lake was married four times and divorced three times. She had four children, including one who died in infancy. Recurring problems with mental illness and alcoholism and a reputation for being difficult on the job led to a decline in her career. After leaving California for New York in 1952, she occasionally appeared onstage and on television. After 1960, Lake made only two more films before she died of hepatitis at age fifty-three.

See also: Hairstyles, Twentieth-Century

Further Reading: Lake, Veronica, with Donald Bain, *Veronica* (1971); Lenburg, Jeff, *Peekaboo* (2001); Parish, James Robert, *The Paramount Pretties* (1972).

LASER *See* Hair Removal

LATIN AMERICA, ANCIENT TIMES TO 1500s

Ancient peoples of present-day Latin America developed distinctive ways of grooming and caring for their hair. Mummies of some pre-Incan people dating back to at least 500 BCE show that women styled their hair in bobs and plucked their **eyebrows**. Archeologists have also found tools that these people used to pluck their brows and pigments that they used to tint their remaining brows.

Aztecs

The Aztecs, who established an empire at about 1100 CE in what is now Mexico, used local materials to cleanse, condition, and style their hair. The style of their hair indicated their age and social status.

Boys were expected to wear their hair long, in a ponytail on top of their heads, until they had captured or killed an enemy. After they reached that milestone, males could wear a topknot. Adult males usually grew their hair as long as the napes of their necks, with a fringe of bangs over the forehead. Aztec warriors wore pigtails, with a type of scalp lock, and warriors who had captured many prisoners were entitled to wear a high ridge of hair on their heads.

Priests, however, were expected to leave their hair alone as a way to honor the Aztec gods, so they did not cut it or wash it. They wore black cloaks with hoods that covered their hair.

The Spanish conqueror Bernal Diaz described the Aztec chief Montezuma at age forty, stating, "He did not wear his hair long, but so as just to cover his ears, his scanty black beard was well-arranged and thin" (Diaz 1963, 219).

Aztec women wore their hair long, and unwed women kept it loose. Many young women grew their hair down to the waist. On festive occasions, women braided their hair with material dyed in different colors or they made two plaits and wound these around their heads with the ends sticking out on either side of the forehead above the eyebrows. Married Aztec women wore their hair in two horn-like tufts, one on each side of the head.

Cleanliness was important to the Aztecs, who bathed often and made hair-cleansing preparations with juice from the yucca plant. To moisturize the hair and scalp, they used jojoba oil and mashed avocado. Another type of conditioner was made from the berries of the yiamolli plant. They boiled sunflowers to extract oil used to condition the hair. Avocado was regarded as a stimulant for hair growth. Women wore flowers in their hair for decorative purposes and for their pleasing scent.

A present-day Latino man.

Along with flowers, head ornaments were made from shells, precious metals, gemstones, and feathers. Montezuma owned an elaborate headdress trimmed with vivid blue continga feathers and green quetzal feathers. The quetzal bird was considered to be sacred, so quetzal feathers were reserved for people of noble birth.

Facial hair, which grew only sparsely on these people, was regarded as undesirable. Among both the Aztec and the Maya, pieces of a volcanic glass called obsidian were sharpened into very fine points to use in shaving unwanted hair. Plucking was another method of removing facial hair. Aztec mothers began applying hot cloths to their sons' faces during childhood in the belief that this would discourage hair growth.

Mayans

The Mayans, who lived in present-day Mexico and Central America from 2600 BCE to around 1200 CE, paid a great deal of attention to the appearance of the hair and head. Their hair was nearly always black in color. They valued elongated heads, which they achieved artificially by pressing wooden boards against the skulls of growing babies.

Both men and women wore their hair long and arranged it into plaits, usually two or four in number. Sometimes they wrapped these plaits around the nape of their necks or let them hang loose down the back. The hair was cut in a fringe across the forehead.

Women wore various individualized hair ornaments and headdresses. They adorned their braided hair with flowers or strips of leather as well as feathers and jewels. Both the *pañuelo*, a traditional woven headdress, and *cintas*, which are woven ribbons, four to five feet long, that are incorporated into braids, are still worn today. Vivid shades of red and orange were popular colors for these cloth hair trimmings.

Mayan nobles of both genders had elaborate hairstyles and often wore tall, fancy headdresses. A nobleman's headdress, adorned with big, colorful feathers, might be as large as his whole body. Other Mayans wore headdresses only for special ceremonies. One headdress that might have been worn only by rulers was made from wood, fibers, feathers, and precious stones.

Like other **Native Americans** who lived in Central and South America, the Mayans used fruit and vegetable oils and herbs to make hair care preparations. Avocado was a popular hair conditioner agent. Mayans used combs to groom and style their hair.

Incas

The Incas, who lived in present-day Peru in South America, built an empire that lasted from around 1438 to 1532 CE. They did not leave behind any writings, so scientists have relied on archaeological finds, including mummies, to learn about their way of life. Other information comes from the written accounts of Spaniards who arrived in South America during those years.

One custom involving hair took place when a baby was about one or two years old. At that time, the child received its name during a special ceremony called a *rutuchicoy*. During the ceremony, relatives, beginning with the baby's oldest uncle, cut off locks of the child's hair. The cut hairs were kept in a safe place, because the Incas believed that hair contained a person's essence. The eldest uncle also cut his own hair and offered it to Incan gods as a sacrifice for the welfare of the child. Another custom was carried out when an Incan emperor died. For example, during his lifetime, the emperor Pachakuti saved hairs that were either cut or fell out. After he died, these hairs were used to form a statue that served as a public symbol of the dead ruler. Hair was also used to make medicinal preparations. For example, when a person was poisoned, a lock of their hair was burned, and these ashes were mixed with *chicha* (a beverage made from fermented corn) to serve as an antidote.

Some groups who lived among the Andes Mountains used mechanical devices to shape their heads in peaks. Other groups of Incas, usually those living on flatter areas, flattened the tops of their heads.

Incan men kept their hair, which was almost always black, relatively short. A man revealed his rank and status by the length of his hair and the way he wore his headband. Shorter hair was a sign of higher rank. Men wore colorful cloth headbands wrapped around their heads in specific ways, depending on their class. Leaders wrapped their headbands five times. Nobles had shorter hair and fewer turns of their headbands, while chiefs could be identified because they had even shorter hair and still fewer turns of their headbands. Commoners had the longest hair in Incan society and the fewest turns of their headbands. The Incan ruler had a special headdress adorned with gold tubes and red tassels that was worn during coronation ceremonies. Men sometimes braided their hair with colored strings.

Women in Incan society also wore headdresses. Examples of fine woolen headgear, made from the wool of llamas, have been found in ancient tombs. They wore their hair long, hanging down their backs or plaited with pieces of cloth. Women who were in mourning often cut their hair.

Further Reading: Bray, Warwick, *Everyday Life of the Incas* (1968); Coba, Bernard, *Inca Religion and Custom* (1990); Coe, Michael D., *The Maya*, 4th ed., rev. (1987); Diaz, Bernal, *The True History of the Conquest of New Spain* (1963); Fagan, Brian M., *The Aztecs* (1984); Hewett, Edgar L., *Ancient Life in Mexico and Central America* (1968); Malpass, Michael A., *Daily Life in the Inca Empire* (1996); Schrieberg, David, and Sharon Begley, "Children of the Ice," *Newsweek*, November 6, 1995; Trout, Lawana Hooper, *The Maya* (1991).

LAWS AND REGULATIONS

Since ancient times, religious and political leaders and governing bodies have made laws regarding hair on the head and body. Some laws were formal, and people who disobeyed them faced specific penalties, including fines and/or imprisonment. In other cases, cultures or religious groups have promoted strong norms about people's hair, and people who did not conform to these standards faced ostracism or other punishment from members of their community or religious group.

Since the early 1900s, governmental agencies in the United States have been empowered to make and enforce laws regarding hair care products and businesses that provide hair care services. Also, legal cases have resulted from conflicts over regulations that affect hairstyles in educational settings and the workplace.

Ancient to Medieval Times

Laws regarding hair date back to ancient times. In some cases, a haircut was the punishment for certain crimes or behaviors. For example, Babylonian laws made it a punishable offense to disobey one's parents. The law stated that if a son "denies his father, his hair shall be cut, he shall be put into chains and sold for silver. If he denies his mother, his hair also shall be cut, city and land shall collect together and put him in prison" (Sayce 1899, 196). In that society, shorn hair was the mark of a slave, so a lack of hair was a visible sign that a person had committed some offense.

Long hair was customary in many cultures during and immediately after the Christian era began. Laws protected a man's hair because long hair typically was worn both by aristocrats and warriors. During some eras, the cutting of too much hair, either on the head or face, was illegal among the Anglo-Saxons, Lombards, Frisians, and Alamans. Anyone who unlawfully cut the beard of another man faced heavy fines and/or other penalties.

In Burgundy during the fourth and fifth centuries, only slaves wore their hair cut short and slaves were not allowed to disguise themselves. Anyone who gave a slave a wig to hide the slave's true status had to pay a fine or face imprisonment. Grabbing another person by the hair also was illegal and could result in a fine.

Laws in the Frankish kingdoms banned cutting the hair under certain conditions. Under the Pactus Legis Salicae (Salian law), which was set forth in the sixth century, a heavy monetary fine was levied on anyone who cut a boy's hair without the consent of his parents. The Burgundians imposed fines on people who cut the hair of a woman against her will unless she was a slave.

King Alfred, who ruled West Saxony from 871 to 899 CE, set a fine of twenty shillings as the penalty for cutting off a man's beard. In some parts of Europe, it was illegal to seize another man by his beard or to pull hairs from his beard or his head.

As time went on, however, shorter hair became more fashionable, primarily because church officials decided that long hair should be reserved for women. Various Catholic clergymen said that long hair on men was barbaric, effeminate, and a sign of low moral character. Some clergymen also criticized pointed beards, saying that they made men look like goats. On the holy day of Ash Wednesday in 1094, the archbishop of Canterbury, England, refused to bless men who had long hair, which he likened to the hair of girls. Similarly, in Rouen, France, in 1096, church officials said that long hair on men was un-Christian. An archbishop in Normandy, France, clashed with King Henry I (1006–1060) and the men of his court when they continued to wear long hair. The archbishop convinced them to let him cut their hair after one particularly strong sermon. The clergymen themselves were expected to obey church laws, which were passed during the sixth century and forbade long hair and beards.

As for women, starting in the fourth century, Catholic clergymen had begun enacting decrees that forbade them to cut their hair. Women who broke this rule faced excommunication from the church.

1500s to Present

After the **Middle Ages**, rulers were less likely to make laws about hair, although customs and social pressure still strongly influenced hairstyles for both men and women. The power of the Roman Catholic clergy diminished as a result of the Protestant Reformation and new political attitudes that aimed to separate religious institutions from government.

As Western societies became more secular, religious leaders did not dictate government policies as much as they once had. Yet, even in countries founded on principles of freedom of expression, some local governments have passed laws regarding hair. In certain countries located in Asia and the Middle East, religion and government have remained intertwined, and religious beliefs regarding hair are the law. In other countries, such as modern China, leaders passed laws about hair and other aspects of appearance that were based on politics rather than religion.

Laws Regarding Facial Hair

As late as the 1700s, certain European rulers still were enforcing laws about hair, and some of those laws involved facial hair. In 1705, Peter the Great of Russia expanded a law that banned beards in the **military**, and he insisted that all Russian men shave their beards, regardless of class. Men throughout Europe had stopped wearing beards, yet Russian men still maintained their facial hair, as they had done since ancient times. Men who disobeyed this law had to pay a tax of 100 rubles. An exception was made for serfs and Orthodox priests, who were charged just one copeck for wearing beards. They had to pay this fee whenever they passed through gates that allowed people to move from one part of a town to another. Although members of various ethnic groups in Russia felt quite strongly about their beards, they knew that they might face harsher penalties than fines if they organized to defy their powerful ruler.

Men who did pay fines in order to keep their beards received a special copper coin called a *borodovaia* (the bearded) that was minted for this purpose. One side featured the image of a face with a long, full beard and the official stamp mark of a black eagle, and the other side bore the date. In order to pass through various city gates, men with beards had to present this coin. People who did not pay were imprisoned.

In 1838, the king of Bavaria, Germany, signed a law that banned **mustaches** on civilian men. Men who defied this law faced arrest and could be forcibly shaven. Observers noted that Bavarian men were quick to obey the new law.

State and Local Laws

During the eighteenth and nineteenth centuries, some states and municipalities in the United States also passed laws regarding facial hair as well as other hair-related matters. A Massachusetts law said that men must pay for a license in order to wear a goatee in public, while a law in Brainerd, Minnesota, required men to wear beards. Officials in Eureka, Nevada, once passed a law banning men with mustaches from kissing women. Some states, such as Michigan, passed laws stating that a woman could not get her hair cut unless she had her husband's permission. This law was based on the notion that a man "owned" his wife's hair. An old Florida law levied a fine on a woman for falling asleep under a hair dryer; the salon owner also was fined. In Alabama, it once was against the law for a man to wear a mustache that caused people to laugh in church. A state law in Nebraska made it illegal for mothers to give their children a home **permanent**. In the capital city of Omaha, Nebraska, **barbers** were banned from shaving a customer's chest.

Some of these laws remain on the books today, though they are not enforced. Many of them reflect attitudes that prevailed when women were regarded as second-class citizens under the control of men, while other laws are based on religious practices in certain communities. Still others, such as bans on the use of home permanents, were enacted because salon operators lobbied for laws that would prevent them from losing business.

Regulating Products and Services

The twentieth century brought a new kind of lawmaking that regulated certain aspects of the personal care and cosmetics industry. During the late twentieth century, for example, various nations passed laws that require companies to list the ingredients on hair care products, cosmetics, and other items. Such laws were enacted in the United States (in 1978), Australia (in 1993), and the European Union (in 1997).

In the United States, companies that make personal care products and cosmetics must comply with certain laws. The Food and Drug Administration (FDA) is the agency set up by the federal government to enforce regulations dealing with the safety and purity of these and other products. The FDA is part of the U.S. Department of Health and Human Services. It was organized when the U.S. Congress passed the Pure Food and Drug Act of 1906 to protect consumers from unsafe drugs. At that time, the FDA regulated only the pharmaceutical industry.

Reformers wanted laws that would protect consumers from other unsafe products, false **advertising**, and/or misrepresentation. Consumer advocates asked the federal government to give the FDA authority over cosmetics and personal care products.

In the meantime, some states, including New York, passed laws that required cosmetologists to pass a test before they could be licensed. More and more states began requiring barbers to pass tests in order to receive their licenses, and state inspectors checked barbershops and beauty salons to ensure that certain standards were met.

The American Medical Association (AMA) set up its own board of standards to address issues relating to cosmetics and personal care products. The board urged companies not to make claims that their products would not cause **allergic reactions**. It banned these kinds of ads from its magazine, *Hygeia*, along with ads from companies that claimed their products would stop hair loss or restore lost hair. The AMA also banned ads from companies that refused to reveal the ingredients in their products, either on the package or at the consumer's request.

In 1938, the U.S. Congress passed the Wheeler-Lea Amendment to the Food and Drug Act, which became known as the Food, Drug, and Cosmetic Act of 1938. It gave the FDA authority over cosmetics as well as pharmaceuticals.

The FDA now maintains a list of banned ingredients and specifies how products must be labeled. Other regulations deal with FDA inspection procedures and the penalties for violations. In addition, the FDA conducts research to evaluate the safety of various products and ingredients.

Federal and state governments continue to regulate the licensing of people who work in the hair care industry. These laws affect people who own and work in the salon and barber industry as well as those who perform electrolysis and other professional hair removal services or permanent makeup services. Schools that train hair care professionals must meet certain standards, including adequate facilities and staffing, to be accredited. State officials also evaluate such schools' equipment, textbooks, courses, and testing procedures to determine if students are being taught to operate in a way that is safe for consumers.

Dress Codes

Legal conflicts have ensued when people disagree over what kinds of hairstyles are appropriate in a given setting. Many controversies involve public school dress codes. Students have objected to rules that limit the style and color of their hair. Many American schools have banned students from wearing headgear except when it is worn for medical or religious purposes. During the era when the **bouffant** was a popular hairstyle for females, schools also banned hair rollers, as exemplified by this line from a 1971–1972 dress code in Perryville, Arkansas: "Girls will not come to school with hair in rollers."

Numerous lawsuits over hair length for male students arose in the United States during the late 1960s and early 1970s. More males had begun growing their hair below the ears, even to shoulder length or longer. Some males chose this look because they thought it suited them, while others wanted to identify with members of the counterculture (who were sometimes called "**hippies**"). The case of *Karr v. Schmidt* began in 1970 when sixteen-year-old Chesley Karr was banned from enrolling at his high school in El Paso, Texas, because his hair was longer than the school board regulations allowed. Karr filed a lawsuit claiming that, by denying him a free public education because of his hair length, the school board had violated his rights to due process of law and equal protection under the Fourteenth Amendment to the Constitution. After the district court ruled in Karr's favor and said that he should be reinstated, the school board appealed this decision to a higher court. In 1972, the Court of Appeals for the Fifth Circuit reversed the decision by a narrow margin of eight to seven. The majority opinion stated that public school students do not have a constitutionally protected right to wear a particular hairstyle and that these matters are best determined by local and state officials, rather than the federal government. Justice Hugo Black wrote:

> There can, of course, be honest differences of opinion as to whether any government, state or federal, should as a matter of public policy regulate the length of haircuts, but it would be difficult to prove by reason, logic, or common sense that the federal judiciary is more competent to deal with hair length than are the local school authorities and state legislatures of all our 50 States. Perhaps if the courts will leave the States free to perform their own constitutional duties they will at least be able successfully to regulate the length of hair their public school students can wear. (*Karr v. Schmidt*)

These kinds of cases continue to reach the courts. The case of *Toungate v. Bastrop Independent School District* also arose in Texas after the school board in Bastrop, a small, rural community outside Austin, made a regulation for the 1990–1991 school year banning male students from wearing their hair longer in the rear than the bottom of a standard shirt collar. The regulation stated that the sides of the hair must be short enough so that the bottoms of the ear lobes were visible and the front must not fall below the top of the eyebrows. Zachariah Toungate, a third grader at Bastrop Elementary School, refused to cut his hair to comply with the regulations, and his parents supported that decision. Toungate's "rat tail" fell five to six inches below his shirt collar, and he wore a seven-inch **ponytail**. As per the board's regulations, Toungate was given an in-school suspension. He was removed from his regular classroom and confined to a small alternative classroom, where he worked with a substitute teacher. He was not permitted to join his classmates for recess or lunch or to attend school functions. (In 1991, as the case was unfolding, his parents removed him from public school; he attended private school and then was home schooled.)

The District Court and Third Court of Appeals both found in Toungate's favor, but the Texas Supreme Court overruled that decision. The State Supreme Court said that local school districts have great discretion to determine the standards for dress and hair among their students and that these regulations do not necessarily violate the Equal Rights Amendment or the Civil Rights Act of 1964.

In 1993, a group of male high school students in Texas succeeded in their suit against the local school district, which had banned long hair and earrings for males. In the case of *Barber v. Colorado Independent School District*, the Court of Appeals did not uphold the dress code because it found that the bans discriminated on the basis of gender.

That same year, Native American high school students challenged a law in another part of Texas. In the case of *Alabama and Coushatta Tribes of Texas v. Big Sandy Independent School District*, Native American students claimed that school hair codes violated their rights under the First Amendment to free expression and symbolic religious expression. The students pointed out that for people in their tribes, long hair symbolizes moral and spiritual strength and is part of their religious tradition. A federal court ruled in their favor, saying that the school could not force Native American students to cut their hair in order to attend school because it violated their sincerely held religious beliefs under the free exercise clause of the First Amendment as well as their right to symbolic expression.

Courts have ruled that college officials do not have the same authority as high school officials to regulate students' hairstyles. In the 1972 case of *Lansdale v. Tyler Junior College* (Tyler, Texas), the Fifth Circuit Court of Appeals ruled in favor of students who sued a public college that refused to admit them because they would not cut their hair according to the college's dress code. The court said that that while high school officials have the right to make rational rules about hairstyles in those settings, these rules are not appropriate for college students. In the majority opinion, the court said, "The place where the line of permissible hair style regulation is drawn is between the high school door and the college gate" (*Lansdale v. Tyler Junior College*).

Courts have also upheld the right of college employees to wear beards or the hairstyles of their choice so long as the colleges cannot prove that these choices prevent them from performing their jobs. Judges have made distinctions in cases where a beard or long hair could be hazardous to the employee or to others.

Prisons also make regulations about hair on the head and face. In many cases, they do not permit inmates to wear beards or to grow their hair beyond a certain length. Some inmates have brought court cases claiming that these rules violate their civil rights. One such case was brought by Billy Soza Warsoldier, a member of the Cahuilla American Indian tribe. While serving nineteen months at Adelanto Correctional Facility in California, Warsoldier refused to cut his hair to comply with rules that set a limit of three inches for the length of male inmates' hair. A local judge extended Warsoldier's prison term when he refused to cut his hair. Warsoldier took his case to the Ninth Circuit Court of Appeals, where he won a favorable ruling. The court said that forcing him to cut his hair was a violation of Warsoldier's religious rights, because male members of his tribe do not cut their hair except as a sign of mourning when a family member dies.

Around the world, officials continue to grapple with laws and regulations that apply to hair. In 2004, Chinese officials in Beijing banned ponytails on youths playing on soccer teams. The China Football Association stated that members of its national boys' soccer team could not copy the ponytail worn by British soccer legend David Beckham, shave their heads, or wear certain other hairstyles. Beckham had become a major celebrity in **China**. When his Madrid team played against the all-star Chinese team in August 2003, fans mobbed him and his teammates. In 2004, Beckham changed his hairstyle and wore plaits adorned with ribbons. As reported by the Chinese official government news agency, the order read, "Dyed hair, long hair and weird hairstyles are all strictly prohibited in the training camp and all players must cut hair short" (Associated Press, February 26, 2004). The officials seemed to base their rulings on the idea that young athletes should wear simple, unobtrusive styles that do not require a great deal of care and look more traditionally male.

French officials came into conflict with members of the Sikh community in 2004 when they decided to ban all religious apparel in France's public schools. The law was enacted in March of that year after a vigorous debate in the nation's parliament. It forbids students from wearing obvious symbols of religion, including headgear such as Jewish skullcaps and Muslin headscarves or turbans. The law did permit students to substitute a hair net for a turban if they wished to do so, because the net was less conspicuous. Muslim girls also were allowed to wear a bandanna if the local school considered it appropriate. These regulations were part of a broader law that banned students from refusing to attend certain classes on religious grounds or from objecting to a teacher based on the teacher's gender. It was intended to emphasize the fact that French public schools are secular institutions. After this law was passed, members of the Sikh community in France, who numbered around 7,000 in 2004, continued to protest. They said that wearing turbans posed no threat or problems in the schools.

As of 2004, the dictatorial government of North Korea made an edict setting a two-inch limit for the length of men's hair in that country. An exception was made for older men who are balding: their hair is allowed to reach two and eight-tenths inches. The North Korean government said that long hair on men was both unhygienic and a sign that the man was incompetent. To urge conformity, the state-run television began running pictures of men who violated the edict.

See also: Beards, Men's; Occupations; Palmer, Joe; Politics and Hair; Pubic Hair; Religion and Hair; Salons, Hair and Beauty; Wigs and Hairpieces

Further Reading: Associated Press, "China Bans Ponytails for Youth Soccer," February 26, 2004, http://www.dailypress.com/broadband/sns-othernews-0226soccerhair,0,219935. story; Associated Press, "French Law Bans Sikh Turbans in School," May 16, 2004, http://web.mid-day.com/news/world/2004/may/83552.htm; Associated Press, "North Korea

Tells Men: Be Patriotic and Cut Hair," *MSNBC News*, February 1, 2004, http://www.msnbc.msn.com/id/6894691; *Colorado Independent School District v. Barber* 864 S.W.2d 806 (Tex. App. Eastland 1993); Driver, Godfrey Rolles, and John Charles Miles, eds., *The Babylonian Laws*, 2 vols. (1952–1955); Edwards, Chilperic, *The World's Earliest Laws* (1934); Freeman, Jo, ed., *Women: A Feminist Perspective* (1995); *Karr v. Schmidt* 460 F.2d 609 (5th Cir. 1972); *Lansdale v. Tyler Junior College* 470 F.2d 659 (5th Cir. 1972); *Texas News (Abilene Reporter News)* "Court Agrees to Hear Ponytail Case," March 28, 1995, http://texnews.com/texas97/hair032897.html; U.S. Food and Drug Administration, http:www.fda.gov; U.S. Food and Drug Administration, "Cosmetic Labeling," *FDA Consumer*, http://vm.cfsan.fda.gov/~dms/cos-labl.html; U.S. Food and Drug Administration, "Decoding the Cosmetic Label," *FDA Consumer*, May 1993, http://vm.cfsan.fda.gov/~dms/cos-labl.html.

LEGENDS *See* Lady Godiva; Literature

LICE, HEAD

Human head lice (*Pediculus humanus capitis*) are a type of parasitic insect that live among the hairs on the human scalp and neck, feeding on the blood of their human host. Body lice (*Pediculus humanus*) are another form of this insect, and they are closely related to head lice. They feed on the body and only occasionally appear on the scalp or in facial hair. Infestation by head or body lice is called pediculiasis, while pediculosis is the medical term for the disease.

Head lice have specialized features that enable them to live on human hosts. Since these lice are wingless and cannot fly, they move about by crawling. With their six legs, each ending in a claw, they can grasp hair shafts.

A female louse lives for about seventeen to twenty-two days, during which time she lays approximately six to ten eggs per day until she has deposited as many as 200 eggs. About eight days after being hatched from its egg, a louse begins to develop, and it reaches the adult state in about nine to twelve days. When a person becomes infested, the scalp will show both active lice and eggs that have yet to hatch.

Scientists believe that head lice date back to prehistoric times, since they have identified nits (lice eggs) on Egyptian mummies and ancient **combs** found in the Middle East. As well, head lice date back thousands of years in the Western Hemisphere, since their remains have been found in pre-Columbian Peru. Fine-toothed combs designed to remove lice also date back to ancient times.

The Centers for Disease Control and Prevention estimate that about 6–12 million people around the world are affected by head lice infestation each year. Head lice spread by head-to-head contact and by the shared use of infested combs, brushes, hats, sports helmets, or other headgear. Although lice may remain on bedding, furniture, and other objects for brief periods of time, they require a host for their survival. They cannot live for more than a day or so without feeding.

Lice prey upon people of all socio-economic classes, regardless of their personal practice of hygiene or sanitation. In the West, lice are most common among children age six to eleven. Children in this age group are more often in contact with other children's heads when they play together, take nap breaks at school, and go to sleepovers or camps. Young people also may share their hats, helmets, or headphones.

In the United States, lice have evolved to grasp hair that is round-shaped in cross section. This means that they rarely infest the heads of African Americans, since their hair shafts have an oval shape, not the round shape that is found on people of Caucasian, Asian, or **Native American** descent. Lice that live in the United States are also tan in color, enabling them to blend in with lighter skin tones. African lice are darker in color and have a different type of leg that enables them to grasp oval-shaped hair shafts.

Lice may be difficult to spot on hairs because they are tiny—about the same size as a sesame seed. Also, head lice can sense when hair is moving, so they quickly crawl to another patch of hair when someone moves a section of hair in order to locate them. As a result, inspecting the head of an infested person usually will reveal only a few live parasites. The nits remain in place, however, so they are easier to spot, using a magnifying glass or special combs.

In ancient times, people relied mostly on the mechanical action of combs to remove both lice and their nits from the hair. In some cultures, such as **ancient Egypt**, people tried to prevent lice by shaving off their hair.

Today, various shampoos and topical products are used to treat lice infestations. Before recommending these treatments, health care providers examine heads carefully to make sure that lice infestation is the problem rather than residues from hair products or other conditions that leave foreign matter on the hair or cause itchy scalps.

Ordinary combs and washing usually do not get rid of lice nits, which become stuck to the hair with a glue-like substance. Special fine-toothed combs are used to remove nits from the hair shaft.

Further Reading: Bakalar, Nick, et al., *Wiping Out Head Lice* (1997); Pollack, Richard, MD, "Head Lice: Information and Frequently Asked Questions," Harvard School of Public Health, http://www.hsph.harvard.edu/headlice.html; Sawyer, Joan, and Roberta Macphee, *Head Lice to Dead Lice* (1999).

LICE, PUBIC

Pubic lice (*Pthirus pubis*) are most often found in the pubic region of their human hosts, but they may also infest facial hair, armpits, and eyelashes. Pubic lice are transmitted by sleeping in infested bedding, wearing infested clothing, or, most frequently, through sexual contact. In the latter case, they are classified as a sexually transmitted disease. Pubic lice are found throughout the world.

In contrast to head and body lice, public lice have short, flat bodies that resemble a crab shape, which gave them their colloquial name, "crabs." Their six legs are spaced further apart than the legs of **head lice**, and the two front legs are larger than the other four. These front legs resemble the pincers on a crab. The body of a louse is only about as large as the head of a pin.

A female louse lays her eggs (nits) on hair shafts along with a glue-like substance that keeps them firmly in place while they develop and hatch, which takes about one week. Once it has hatched, a louse cannot survive more than one or two days without feeding on blood. They feed from tiny blood vessels located near the skin's surface.

For most people, these bites cause itching, and the itching is more severe for people who are allergic to the bites. Red sores and/or a rash also may develop. Sometimes a person who is infested will notice visible nits on pubic hairs or crawling adult lice in that area, although these light-brown insects may be difficult to spot.

Treatments for pubic lice and their nits include mechanical means (combs), prescription medications, and over-the-counter preparations. Special fine-toothed combs are designed to latch onto adult lice, nits, and nymphs (newly hatched lice). Doctors may prescribe a medication called Lindane. Shampoos containing permithrin or pyrethrin may be used before combing to kill adult lice. Bedding and clothing also need to be treated by washing them in very hot water to prevent reinfestation.

Further Reading: Centers for Disease Control and Prevention, Division of Parasitic Diseases, "Pubic Lice," http://www.cdc.gov/ncidod/dpd/parasites/lice/factsht_pubic_lice.htm; Icon Health Publications, *The Official Patient's Sourcebook on Pubic Lice* (2002); Schulz, David, *Human Sexuality* (1984).

LICENSING *See* Barbers; Salons, Hair and Beauty; Laws and Regulations

LITERATURE

The subject of hair has appeared in many written works, dating back to ancient myths, stories in the Old and New Testaments, and folk and fairy tales. Modern authors also have written stories and novels in which hair plays a central role in the plot or takes on a symbolic role.

These literary works reflect cultural attitudes about the role of hair in personal appearance, society, and spirituality as well as the author's perspective. Through folk and fairy tales, cultures transmit standards of beauty from one generation to the next. Many old European tales, for example, featured a heroine described as "fair" and with silken hair, showing that those traits have been part of a persistent standard of beauty in western European cultures. Often, great power and rewards, as well as approval and admiration, have been accorded to those blessed with "beautiful hair."

In certain other morality tales, people are admired and rewarded when they value virtue over beauty, for example by sacrificing their hair to attain some spiritual goal. Some tales also show people suffering dire consequences when they break social norms regarding hair.

The subject of hair occurs in creation myths. For example, the creation story passed down by a group of pre-Incan Indians, who lived in present-day Bolivia, states that their creator painted people on stones before bringing them to life and that he painted some people with short hair and some people with long hair. In the

Norse creation story, after the dead body of a giant named Ymir falls down to earth, his hair became the trees while his bones became mountains.

Historians have pointed to myths featuring the Greek god Pan as being influential in ancient thinking. Pan was described as half goat and half human, thus possessing both a human nature and an animal nature. The hairiness was said to represent the animalistic side.

Other stories show hair as a fearsome thing or a tool of destruction. A Greek myth features Medusa, whose beautiful hair was turned into serpents by the goddess Athena. Similar stories about women whose hair turns into snakes can be found in African and Indian tales. In the German myth about the Lorelei, sirens living in the water entice sailors to their death, in part by using their long, blond hair in a seductive manner.

Early Christians believed that unruly hair was "sinful" and made onlookers prone to temptations of the flesh. As a result, well-groomed and controlled hairstyles were regarded as more righteous and less sexual in nature. During the **Middle Ages**, based on these ideas, the Catholic Church passed clerical laws that dictated hairstyles.

Conversely, the writings and oral traditions of some ancient cultures regarded hair as a gift from God, and hair is shown as a symbol of positive human attributes as well as a connection to the spirit world. This was true among certain African and Native American cultures. In the Old Testament story of Samson and Delilah, Samson's hair is the seat of his strength and vitality. When Delilah finds a way to trick Samson and cut off his hair, he loses that strength. Variations of this same plot, with its strong symbolism, exist in tales told in numerous cultures.

In other ancient tales, people express feelings of grief through their hair. For example, Achilles tears out his hair when he is mourning the death of his dear friend Patroclus, who was killed by a Trojan during the Trojan War.

Hair figured strongly in certain medieval folk and fairy tales. In "Rapunzel," a maiden who is trapped at the top of a tower manages to gain her freedom by letting down her very long hair so that her suitor can climb up to rescue her.

A number of tales of sacrifice involve hair. In O. Henry's short story, "The Gift of the Magi," a young couple living in poverty in New York City faces Christmas without money for gifts. The ironic ending shows the husband arriving with combs for his wife's beautiful, long hair as she awaits him with her gift of a new chain for his watch. They discover that she sold her hair to buy the chain and he sold his watch to buy the combs.

In Louisa May Alcott's classic Civil War–era novel, *Little Women*, protagonist Josephine March sells her long, chestnut hair, which the family has always called her "one beauty." She returns home, her hair shorn off, and gives her mother the money so that she can travel to Washington, DC, where Mr. March, a chaplain in the Union Army, lies ill in a military hospital.

Hair sometimes plays a role in modern tales of treachery or revenge. In F. Scott Fitzgerald's story "Bernice Bobs Her Hair," which is set in the 1920s, a young girl visiting her cousin agrees that she will cut her hair if the other will do likewise. Bernice accepts the dare but the other girl then backs out. During the night, Bernice sneaks into her room and cuts off her rival's beautiful, long hair while she is asleep.

See also: *Hair* (the musical); *Hairspray*; Lady Godiva; Religion and Hair

Further Reading: Brothers Grimm, *Grimm's Fairy Tales* (1993); Fitzgerald, F. Scott, "Bernice Bobs Her Hair" (2004); Leeming, David Adams, ed., *The Dictionary of Folklore* (2002); Leeming, David Adams, and Margaret Adams Leeming, *Encyclopedia of Creation Myths* (1994); Weitz, Rose, *Rapunzel's Daughters* (2004).

LOCKS OF LOVE (LOL)

Locks of Love (LOL) is a nonprofit organization that provides human-hair wigs for children younger than eighteen who are financially disadvantaged and suffer from short-term or long-term hair loss. The organization was formed in 1997 by Madonna Coffman, a retired nurse who saw the impact of hair loss on girls suffering from cancer and other diseases that directly cause hair loss. Since its inception, LOL has received attention from various television networks, newspapers, and magazines. For example, in 2004, talk-show host Oprah Winfrey featured a show on which women with very long hair received a complimentary makeover that included a haircut, and their hair was donated to Locks of Love.

Among the organization's sponsors are corporations, privately owned companies, and individuals. The companies and foundations included Fantastic Sams, Computer Associates, *Child* magazine, the Cherese Mari Laulhere Foundation, the Teammates for Kids Foundation, and the Martha G. Moore Foundation. The organization also accepts financial contributions to help it carry out its work.

Individual donors include men, women, and children of all races and ethnicities. Typically, donors provide ten or more inches of hair, which is then used to produce custom-fitted hairpieces. Each hairpiece requires hair taken from about six donors. They are carefully manufactured to ensure a high-quality product that would retail for about $3,000–$6,500.

Many salons in the United States and Canada aid Locks of Love by promoting its work and offering free haircuts and other services in order to collect hair. Matrix and The Hair Cuttery are two chains of salons that take part in this effort.

To receive a wig, potential recipients apply to Locks of Love and may reapply every eighteen months for a total of five hairpieces each. All children, regardless of creed, race, or ethnicity, can receive a hairpiece if they meet the eligibility requirements, including financial need. When a child is fitted, she has a chance to express her preference about the kind of hairstyle she will receive.

Some of the people who donate hair to Locks of Love are children themselves who want to help other children. Communities also have organized special events to encourage people to donate hair.

Further Reading: Locks of Love, "About Us," http://www.locksoflove.org; Stapley, Karen, "Locks of Love," *Desert Dispatch* (Barstow, CA), May 25, 2005, http://www.desertdispatch.com/2005/111702689685478.html.

L'OREAL

L'Oreal is a leading international beauty products business. Along with hair care products, L'Oreal offers consumers a variety of cosmetics and fragrances.

Based in Clichy, France, the company began in 1907 in the Paris apartment of Eugène Schueller, a young French chemist. Working from his home laboratory, Schueller developed a hair dye made from synthetic ingredients, including the chemical paraphenylenediamine (abbreviated to PPD or PPDA). Schueller called his formulation Aureole, which signifies a halo-like effect in French. He then made batches of the **hair colorant** and sold them to local hairdressers.

In 1909, Schueller registered his new company under the name Société Française de Teintures Inoffensives pour Cheveux (French Harmless Hair Dye Company). It later was renamed L'Oreal. During these years, Schueller continued to research new products and expand the company's offerings, adding more people beyond himself. As of 1920, three chemists were working for the company.

By 1950, the company's research team totaled 100 people, and L'Oreal was poised to become a leading hair care and beauty products business. After Schueller died in 1954, ownership of the company passed to his daughter Liliane Bettencourt, who was born in 1922. Under the leadership of Francois Dalle, who had worked closely with Schueller, L'Oreal expanded its operations into the United States and other profitable markets. In 1953, L'Oreal signed an agreement with Cosmair, Inc., to be the exclusive licensee for L'Oreal products in the United States. Located in Clark, New Jersey, Cosmair (short for "cosmetics for hair") then had twenty employees at its headquarters.

By 1963, sales for L'Oreal products to customers in the U.S. beauty industry had reached $6 million. Two years later, the company moved its American headquarters to a larger facility in New York City. By 1966, sales had reached $14 million, largely the result of increased sales of the new hair colorant brands that L'Oreal was bringing into retail markets.

During those years, L'Oreal set out to gain an increased share of the market from Clairol, which was the leading hair colorant brand in the United States during the 1950s and 1960s. L'Oreal ads claimed that their products embodied European elegance, with formulations that left hair soft, natural looking, and lustrous. In 1973, L'Oreal worked with a top New York City **advertising** agency, McCann Erickson, to develop a strong, new ad campaign. Written by Ilon Specht, the new campaign noted that L'Oreal's Preference was "the most expensive hair color in the world" and featured the famous tag line, "I'm worth it." Starting with Meredith Baxter Birney, a series of popular, blond, American actresses were spokespeople for Preference, which became the top-selling hair colorant in the United States during the 1980s. Polls showed that more than 90 percent of Americans could connect the Preference brand name with the phrase "I'm worth it," which was featured in print and television ads.

L'Oreal continued to look for ways to improve products and develop new ones. By the 1980s, the research branch of the company had expanded to include 1,000 people. L'Oreal also expanded through acquisitions. In 1993, it acquired Redken Laboratories, which marketed a high-end line of hair colorants, shampoos, conditioners, and styling products designed for salon professionals. Three years later, it bought cosmetics giant Maybelline, maker of the world's top-selling brand of mascara as well as other beauty products. L'Oreal reported sales of $2 billion in 1997.

The company also added ethnic hair care products when it acquired Soft Sheen Products, based in Chicago, in 1998. It added another ethnic hair care company, Carson Products, in 2000, and also acquired Matrix, Dermablend, Kerastase, and Kiehl. Sales for L'Oreal topped $3 billion in 2000, and they reached $12 billion in 2002.

Part of this growth came from the expanding men's hair colorant market and sales of Garnier Nutrisse. Noting that more men were coloring their hair, L'Oreal added a new colorant line for men in 2001. The next year, it began marketing its Garnier Nutrisse hair colorant and Garnier Fructis hair care products for women in the United States. Sales steadily grew, especially after actress Sarah Jessica Parker, known for her thick hair, which is often styled in casual curls as well as straight smooth styles, appeared in Garnier ads. As of 2003, L'Oreal had more than a 50 percent share of the U.S. home hair color market.

As the twenty-first century began, L'Oreal continued to look for ways to improve techniques and products. Researchers in L'Oreal's laboratories are using computer-assisted design software called Catia V5 to analyze the growth and development of hair follicles. This new technology has enabled scientists to create clear, detailed, three-dimensional images of the hair follicle system. With this new information, they can examine a hair follicle from new angles and have thus learned more about the growth cycle.

By 2004 L'Oreal had added new pharmaceutical and dermatological product lines. The company was offering more than 2,000 hair care and beauty products to retail and beauty industry markets. Hair products included various hair colorant lines (Preference, Excellence, Garnier) shampoos, conditioners, styling products, styling tools, permanents, and cosmetics for eyebrows and **eyelashes**. The company was operating five research and development centers (two in France and one each in the United States, Japan, and China) with a combined staff of 2,000.

L'Oreal continues to profit from the increasing number of people who color their hair. Since the 1950s, the number of men and women using some kind of hair colorant product has steadily risen. In the early 1950s, about 4–7 percent of all American women colored their hair. By the 1970s, that number had risen to more than 40 percent, and by 2004, the number was at 75 percent. Sales of men's home hair colorant products reached $113.5 million in 2002. At the turn of the twenty-first century, hair colorant products were a billion-dollar consumer industry.

L'Oreal also owns the four top-selling brands of mascara in the world. As of 2004 they were: Great Lash (by Maybelline, #1), Voluminous (by L'Oreal, #2), Double Extend (by L'Oreal, #3), and Volume Express (by Maybelline, #4).

Further Reading: *Happi*, "Happi Breaking News: L'Oreal Uses Catia V5 to Study Hair," October 24, 2002, http://www.happi.com/new/break6.htm; "L'Oreal Company History," http://www.lorealusa.com; "L'Oreal USA Products and Brands," http://www.lorealusa.com.prodbrand/home; Redding, Marie, "Packager of the Year," Cosmetic/Personal Care online, http://www.cpcpkg.com/03/12/PackagerOftheYear.html.

LOUSE *See* Comb; Lice, Head; Lice, Pubic

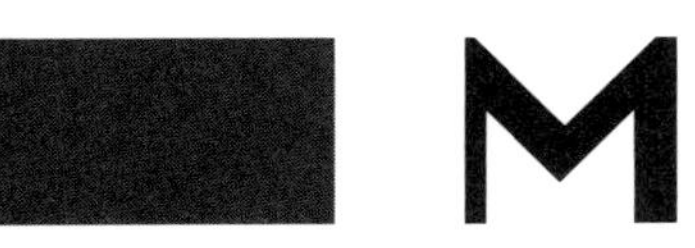

M

MALONE, ANNIE MINERVA TURNBO POPE (1869–1957)

Entrepreneur and philanthropist Annie Minerva Turnbo Pope Malone overcame childhood poverty and racism to found a successful hair care products company.

Born in Metropolis, Illinois, Malone was the eleventh of twelve children. After being orphaned at a young age, she lived with an older sister in Peoria, Illinois. Malone suffered from health problems as a child, and she developed an interest in herbs and the healing arts.

She then became interested in hair care. At the end of the 1800s, **African Americans** could not find many products that suited their hair texture and styling needs. They used kitchen oil and goose fat, among other substances, to condition and straighten their hair. These oils often were too heavy as well as harsh and ineffective. Malone began trying out formulas for products that would heal scalp problems and reduce hair loss and breakage.

Her first commercial product was a conditioner that contained egg and sage, among other ingredients. After she and her sister moved to Lovejoy, Illinois, they began making and selling Annie's "Wonderful Hair Grower" door-to-door in African American neighborhoods. While selling to these customers, they demonstrated how to use the products and discussed effective ways to cleanse and care for the hair and scalp. Soon, the sisters were selling enough of their products that they were able to hire three assistants. In 1900, Malone patented a design for a hot comb that was used along with oil to straighten hair. The steel comb had widely spaced teeth so that it would work with thick, curly, or frizzy hair.

The business continued to grow. In 1902, the sisters moved to St. Louis, Missouri, where they continued to sell the Hair Grower door-to-door and also through some retail drug stores. During the next few years, the business expanded into the Southern states and other regions of the country.

In 1906, Malone registered the name "Poro" as her trademark. "Poro" comes from West African words that mean "devotional society." This reflected Malone's belief that her business would relate to more areas of life than hair care and that she and her employees would be able to improve the quality of life in their communities. Working as Poro agents enabled thousands of African American women to earn higher salaries than they could have earned in most of the other careers that were open to them at that time. As a result, employees gained independence and pride along with higher incomes. The most famous agent was Sarah Breedlove, who worked for the Poro organization in St. Louis. As **Madam C. J. Walker**, she later founded her own multimillion dollar hair products business.

Malone married Aaron Malone in 1914, and he also worked in the company she had founded. By then, white business owners were stocking Poro products in their stores, and ads for the products appeared in magazines and newspapers. Malone decided to add skin care products and cosmetics to the Poro line. With the profits from her business, she funded various community organizations, including churches, schools, and recreational facilities.

In 1918, Poro College opened. This institution included offices, a factory, and educational and cultural facilities for employees and other people in the community. By the mid-1920s, about 75,000 people had graduated from the college. They went on to work as Poro agents throughout the United States and the Caribbean.

Malone may have been the first African American female millionaire. In the 1920s, it was estimated that her net worth reached $14 million. She continued to contribute large sums of money to favorite causes, including $25,000 to Howard University—the largest donation ever given to an African American college by a black American as of that time. She also paid the expenses of numerous individual African American college students so that they could earn their degrees.

Another favorite charity was the St. Louis Colored Orphan's Home (later renamed the Annie Malone Children and Family Service Center). Malone founded this institution and served as its first president.

When the Malones divorced in 1927, they fought an intense court battle over the Poro company. By the time Annie Turnbo Malone won control, the company's assets had been depleted, and Poro was not doing well in competition with newer hair care lines. The Great Depression, which had begun in 1929, made it even more difficult to recover. When Malone died of a stroke in Chicago in 1957, her personal fortune was about $100,000.

See also: African Americans; Walker, Madam C. J.

Further Reading: American Mothers Committee, comp. *Mothers of Achievement in American History, 1776–1976* (1976); Majors, Monroe A., *Noted Negro Women* (1971); Peiss, Kathy, *Hope in a Jar* (1998); Poinsett, Alex, "Unsung Black Business Giants; Pioneer Entrepreneurs Laid Foundations for Today's Enterprises," *Ebony* 45 (March 1990); Silverman, Robert Mark, "The Effects of Racism and Racial Discrimination on Minority Business Development: The Case of Black Manufacturers in Chicago's Ethnic Beauty Aids Industry," *Journal of Social History* 31 (1998); Smith, Jessie Carney, ed., "Annie Turnbo Malone" in *Notable Black American Women* (1992).

MARCEL WAVE

Named after French hairdresser Marcel Grateau (1852–1936), the Marcel wave was created by using a curling iron to make deep, regular waves in the hair all over the head.

As a teenager, Grateau worked as a horse groomer who sometimes helped a friend in his hair salon business. At age 20, he started his own hairdressing business in a low-income district of Paris. For a small fee, he used a curling iron to make frizzy waves in his clients' hair. One day in 1872, while trying to fix his mother's hair in a hurry, he found that he could create a more natural-looking wave by turning his curling iron upside down. He invited his clients to try this new look, which he called a "watered effect" or *ondulations*.

As more women came to Grateau's salon and praised his work, he discovered that the same waving technique would work on straight hair as well as hair with a natural curl. By 1880, he also was serving wealthier clients, including prominent actresses and singers, which enabled him to establish a new and more lavish salon in 1882. He continued to design styles that delighted clients, and his reputation grew. Grateau became so busy that women actually began to outbid each other for an appointment with him.

To further his work, Grateau devised a new type of hot curling tongs that enabled him to arrange smooth waves at intervals around the head. This curling device usually was heated over a gas burner. M. Marcel, as he was called, would take hold of the strands of hair and flip them upside down to produce a natural-looking effect that resembled real curls rather than the "crimped" look that had resulted from previous methods. Both the technique and the "Marcel curling iron" spread around the world.

Wavy hair often had been in fashion for women, and at the turn of the century, most women in westernized countries sought that look. Marcel waves remained in style for about fifty years and were especially popular during the 1920s and 1930s, when some women wore their bobbed hair curled around the head. Performer **Josephine Baker** is one of most famous people to wear this style. Hairpieces were also waved into a "Marcel."

Although the 1920s ushered in new short, boyish hairstyles, the Marcel wave became more popular again during the 1930s. New techniques in hairdressing made this style easier to achieve and longer lasting. Some methods involved steam, pin curls, or a permanent wave. Actresses Joan Crawford, Gloria Swanson, and Mae West were among the celebrities who wore this style. At salons, women who had their hair put into Marcel waves with a hot iron and some macassar hairdressing oil could expect this style to last for up to a week. A popular song of that era, "Keep Young and Beautiful," advised women to "wear a Marcel wave" as one key way to remain attractive to men.

Subsequent generations have also adopted the Marcel wave. For example, singer Gwen Stefani, of the group No Doubt, wore this hairstyle during the 1990s, along with a tank top, sneakers, red lipstick, and black eyebrow pencil.

See also: Baker, Josephine; Hairstyles, Twentieth-Century; Permanent; Styling Tools; Water Wave

Further Reading: Corson, Richard, *Fashions in Hair* (1965); Mulvey, Kate, and Melissa Richards, *Decades of Beauty* (1998).

MASTERS, GEORGE (1936–1998)

During the late twentieth century, George Masters was one of the world's most famous hairdressers and makeup artists. His clients included actresses, first ladies, socialites, and other prominent people.

Masters was born on April 1, 1936, in Los Angeles, and he grew up in the suburb of Highland Park after his family moved to Michigan. He dropped out of high school to pursue a career as a hairdresser. In his book *The Masters Way to Beauty*, Masters says that he began working as a "shampoo boy" at Anthony Collett's beauty salon in Grosse Pointe, Michigan. By observing Collett at work, Masters learned his trade and began to work with important clients, including Anne Ford, who was then the wife of Henry Ford II. She brought other members of her family to see the talented new stylist and then used her connections to help Masters get a job as an apprentice at the world-famous Elizabeth Arden salon in New York City. Within three years, he had become one of Arden's top stylists.

Masters moved again in 1959, when he began working at the Saks Fifth Avenue salon in Beverly Hills. In addition to his expertise as a hairdresser, Masters was known for his blond good looks and casual style. He usually worked in jeans and an open-necked shirt. Wealthy clients began requesting that he make home visits to style their hair for important events. One of his favorite celebrity clients was Marilyn Monroe. He designed a softer, curlier look for her, and at Masters' suggestion, she lightened her hair to a paler shade of blond. Other regular clients included actresses Jennifer Jones and Ann-Margret. In 1966, Lynda Byrd Johnson, daughter of President Lyndon B. Johnson, asked Masters to style her hair and apply her makeup before she attended the Academy Awards ceremony with actor George Hamilton.

That same year, Masters opened his own salon but soon closed that business in order to work as a freelance personal stylist and makeup artist for individual clients. He became a traveling stylist for Glemby International, a London-based company that operated hundreds of department store beauty salons. One of his specialties was a "makeover," which he performed on people of different ages during his visits to various Glemby salons. They paid $350 (a high fee during the 1970s) for a consultation with Masters that included hairstyling and makeup application. In 1977, he and Norma Lee Browning wrote *The Masters Way to Beauty*, a book about his techniques.

For more than twenty years, Masters also worked as a hairstylist and makeup artist for various television programs and feature films. His screen credits included hairstyling for actresses Marlene Dietrich, Doris Day, and Joanne Woodward. One of his most challenging assignments came when he helped transform actor Dustin Hoffman into a woman for his role in the acclaimed 1982 comedy *Tootsie*. As part of the team that executed the makeup for that film, Masters received the British Academy of Film and Television Arts award for Best Makeup Artist.

In March 1998, George Masters died in Los Angeles of heart failure.

See also: Monroe, Marilyn; Salons, Hair and Beauty

Further Reading: "George Masters," obituary, *The New York Times*, March 7, 1998; Masters, George, and Norma Lee Browning, *The Masters Way to Beauty* (1977).

MEMENTO

Throughout history, family members and/or friends have saved the hair of a loved one for sentimental reasons. A lock of hair can serve as a memento of an earlier stage in life, such as infancy or childhood. For generations, mothers have saved their children's hair and kept these strands inside a locket, scrapbook, or other place, along with other mementos.

Hair also may be saved as a keepsake of someone who has died. Since hair is already dead once it grows from the head, it remains much the same after it has been cut. Saving the hair of deceased loved ones dates back to ancient times and was common in various cultures.

During the 1700s, more people began to place locks of hair inside pieces of jewelry called lockets, some of which were made with glass windows. Hair was also woven into brooches, watch chains, and bracelets. As with lockets, these items of jewelry were worn by loved ones. Some women gave these mementos to their sweethearts. Lockets and other pieces of romantic jewelry sometimes were made with strands of the couple's hair, and both people wore these items to show their attachment to each other. During the 1800s and early 1900s, women also sometimes attached a lock of their hair to a postcard or Valentine's Day card. Some romantic postcards were specially designed to hold hair.

Mourning jewelry made with human hair became increasingly popular during the Victorian era. This jewelry often took the form of a glass-covered brooch, which was used to hold the hair of a deceased loved one. The owner sometimes added more strands of hair when other friends or relatives died. Mourning jewelry was meant to serve both as a memento of the loved one and as a reminder that death is inevitable. Today, some of these pieces, and other works of **hair art**, can be seen in museums and personal collections.

Hair has also become more popular as a collector's item. The hair of famous people can fetch high prices to collectors. Some of this hair comes from barbers or hairdressers who save the hair of their famous clients and then sell it, often via Internet auctions. Other strands from historical celebrities were cut from their heads at the time they died and then passed on. John Reznikoff, a well-known hair historian and collector in Connecticut, owns hair from Napoleon, Abraham Lincoln, Charles Dickens, Albert Einstein, and Marilyn Monroe. The *Guinness Book of World's Records* claims that Reznikoff's collection, which is insured for $1 million, is the largest collection of historical celebrity hair in the world. During 2001, collectors traded hair from George Washington, Robert E. Lee, Jefferson Davis, Henry Ford, John F. Kennedy, John Lennon, and others.

See also: Hair Analysis; Hair Jewelry; Mourning; Presley, Elvis Aaron

Further Reading: Bell, Jeanenne, *Collector's Encyclopedia of Hairwork Jewelry* (1998); Campbell, Mark, Jules Kliot, and Kaethe Kliot, *Art of Hair Work* (1989); Good, David L. "Collecting Hair," *Maine Antique Digest*, May 2001, http://www.maineantiquedigest.com/articles/hair0501.htm; Good, David L., "Hair Today, Sold Tomorrow," *The Detroit News*, March 29, 2001, http://www.detnews.com/2001/decorating/0103/29/c01-205246.htm; Harran, Susan, and Jim Harran, "Remembering a Loved One With Mourning Jewelry," *Antique Week*, December 1997, http://www.hairwork.com/remember.htm.

MESOPOTAMIA (9000–500 BCE)

The ancient Middle Eastern region known as Mesopotamia lay around the Tigris and Euphrates rivers and included present-day Iraq. The earliest people to inhabit the region were probably Semites, and major dynasties ruled the regions of Sumer, Akkad, and Babylonia. Around 1300 BCE, Babylonia was conquered by its longtime rival, Assyria.

Archeologists have unearthed artifacts from graves and other sites that provide information about ancient grooming practices in this region. Babylonian women were buried with their cosmetics, mirrors, and certain other possessions, which included tweezers for plucking hairs. Wealthy Babylonians kept these in gold cases.

The king of Mesopotamia with traditional headgear dating back centuries. *Library of Congress*

Some wealthy Babylonian men were buried with helmets made of beaten gold, shaped into "wigs" that had locks of hair and individual hairs etched in the metal. Evidence shows that people in these ancient civilizations curled, oiled, dyed, and decorated their hair.

For cleansing their hair and bodies, wealthier Babylonians had bathrooms built inside their homes, while less affluent people used streams or public sources of water. Soap was made from plant oils mixed with ashes and clay. They smoothed their skin with pumice stone.

Babylonians of every socioeconomic class used oils on their hair and skin to counteract the effects of living in a hot, dry climate that was prone to sandstorms. Certain oils were used to kill parasites that lived on the scalp. Oils for the hair and body were stored in small stone vases.

Most Babylonians styled their hair carefully. Upper-class Babylonians tended to wear more elaborate and highly decorated hairstyles. The men favored thick, long hair, and some added ringlets with heated curling irons. **Wigs and hairpieces** were also used to create a fuller look.

Likewise, women preferred thick hair and used wigs with braided hair extensions to achieve the desired styles. The wigs were pinned in place, using either gold hairpins or less expensive versions. Wealthier women powdered their hair with gold dust; women of lesser means used a yellow-colored starch. Scented powders were also used. People of both genders used scented oils on their hair.

During the earliest period, men were clean-shaven. Babylonians used the services of a barber—a *gallâbu,* which means "high hand" in Sumerian. These **barbers** were assigned to shave the priests according to religious customs. Barbers also shaved the heads of slaves so that they could be branded.

Later, around the time King Sargon II of Assyria (721–705 BCE) came to power, full **beards** were popular, sometimes cut into a square shape. Prominent men would have been identified by their long, square-trimmed beards. Commoners kept their beards short. The Assyrians tended to wear more facial hair than the Sumerians. Akkadian men also grew beards. In the bas-relief of Diarbekr, the ruler Naram-Sin wears a beard and **mustache** and his hair is curled. Sculptures of other rulers show them wearing long beards.

Babylonians sometimes colored their hair and beards. Black was fashionable, especially for men, and it also was the most common natural hair color in the region. Babylonians were called the "people of the black heads." Hair dyes were made from cow's blood, crushed tadpoles, and other materials. Red colors were made from **henna**, a dye obtained from plants. Henna was used to color hair and also to paint fingernails and skin on various parts of the body.

Metal or cloth bands were worn to keep hair in place. These bands ranged from quite simple to ornate, depending on a person's social class. One of the most popular decorations was a rosette or double rosette; these often appeared on the metal bands Babylonians wore around their foreheads. Another type of headband, made of woven material, resembled a turban but was less bulky. It was constructed from pieces that were shaped to fit around the head. Artisans wrapped long pieces of fabric around their heads and then knotted a narrow strip at the crown. During the later Babylonian period, people of the lower classes wore simply designed fillets, while upper-class people wore ornate caps or tiaras. Members of the royalty and upper-class Babylonians wore ornaments made from precious metals and gems. Queen Shubad's tomb contained elaborate gold and jeweled headdresses and a **comb** made of gold and lapis lazuli.

Babylonians applied fragrance to their hair and bodies. During the seventh century BCE, they built perfume centers, and over the next two centuries, Babylonia became a perfume-trading center. Babylonians traded for Arabian gums, Chinese camphor, spices from India, cedar of Lebanon, cypress, pine, myrtle, and juniper, among other ingredients they used to make scented products.

After the Assyrian conquest of Babylonia, hairstyles for men and women became even more elaborate and people of both genders added oil and perfumes to their hair. Braids were popular. Men regarded their facial hair as a sign of power and masculinity, and many men trimmed their beards into unusual and sculpted shapes. To cover graying hair, the Assyrians mixed oil with crushed daisies to create a dye.

See also: Beards, Men's; Facial Hair; Fragrance; Hair Color; Headgear; Laws and Regulations; Mourning; Mustache; Wigs and Hairpieces

Further Reading: Contenu, Georges, *Everyday Life in Babylon and Assyria* (1954); Corson, Richard, *Fashions in Hair* (1965); Frame, Grant, *Rulers of Babylonia* (1995); Frankfort, Henri, *The Birth of Civilization in the Near East* (1968); Sayce, A. H., *Babylonians and Assyrians* (1899).

MICHAELJOHN

The Michaeljohn salon, located in London, is one of the world's foremost salons. Michaeljohn hair products are sold in various countries.

Michaeljohn was founded in 1967 by British stylists Michael Rasser and John Isaacs, who envisioned a salon with expert services delivered in a comfortable, relaxing atmosphere. Rasser and Isaacs had met when both men were working as stylists at the famous Leonard salon in London. Rasser's celebrity clients included musician Mick Jagger of the Rolling Stones, singer-actress Madonna, and supermodel Iman, who later patronized his business.

In 1978, a second Michaeljohn salon was opened in Beverly Hills, California, to accommodate more American clients. Co-owner John Isaacs left the London salon to manage this new venture and work as a stylist there. Isaacs also became known for his work with film stars, including Julie Andrews. He styled Andrews' hair for the movies "*10*" (1979), *S.O.B.* (1981), and *Victor/Victoria* (1982), and also styled the hair of Candice Bergen, star of the television series *Murphy Brown*. Also in the late 1970s, Michaeljohn began offering its own line of shampoo, conditioner, and other hair care products, packaged in distinctive blue and white containers that echoed the blue-painted door of the original London salon.

During the early 1990s, Michaeljohn moved into a new facility in London that could accommodate its growing business. The new, spacious salon and beauty clinic on Albemarle Street was staffed by 100 people. At 5,000 square feet, Michaeljohn remains one of the largest beauty facilities in London.

Clients at Michaeljohn have included actors Minnie Driver, Liza Minelli, Julie Andrews, and Dustin Hoffman, members of the royal family, politicians, and diplomats. Some clients have remained loyal to the Michaeljohn salon for thirty years.

See also: Salons, Hair and Beauty

Further Reading: "Another British Invasion?" *Happi* magazine, August 1997; Howard, Jenni Baden, "The Hair Necessities," *Daily Telegraph* (London), March 15, 2001; "Michaeljohn, Salon and Agency," http://www.michaeljohn.co.uk.

MIDDLE AGES (Europe, ca. 476–1270)

During the Middle Ages—the medieval era—in Europe, hairstyle often signified a person's socioeconomic class, marital status, and religious status. The Middle Ages began after the fall of the Roman Empire, leaving the Roman Catholic Church as a major influence on European politics, culture, and society. Some historians divide the Middle Ages into three periods: Early, ca. 476–1000 CE; Middle, ca.1000–1300 CE; and Late, ca.1300–1500 CE.

Early in the Middle Ages, upper-class men and women wore their hair longer and often styled in waves or loose curls. Tying gold balls to the ends of the hair was a popular form of ornamentation. Members of the lower classes had shorter, plainer hairstyles. Usually, their hair was cut to fall between chin level and the shoulders. As the merchant class grew after 1000 CE, more people could afford finer clothing, headgear, and ornaments as well as the services of barbers and servants to dress their hair.

A child's first haircut could have special significance. During the eighth century, it was customary to have a respected friend or relative perform this haircut in a ceremonial manner. Afterwards, the person who cut the child's hair held a special role in his or her life. This custom may have dated back to ancient times. Emperor Constantine the Great, who ruled from 306 to 337 CE, sent the freshly cut hair of his son to the Roman Catholic pope as a sign that he hoped the pope would be a surrogate father to the child.

Women's Styles

Women, especially members of the upper classes, usually had long hair, which could extend to knee length or below. A center part was most common.

Young girls tended to wear their hair loose or in two long plaits on either side of the head, while married women secured theirs into a chignon or other contained style, using pins or a cloth covering. Many women plaited their hair then gathered these braids into coils above the ears or arranged them at the nape of the neck. One of the most popular styles during the middle to late Middle Ages was created by gathering plaits on either side of the head to make a "bundle" above each ear. These were held in place with woven nets made from gold thread and/or silk.

Long braids remained popular until the 1200s, and in some places women wore them hanging loose, although covered for the sake of modesty. Women who could afford false hair used it to enhance their braids if their hair was thin or fine-textured.

Throughout most of the Middle Ages, women's hair was styled to reveal the entire forehead, which was considered to be an important physical feature during this era. To give the appearance of a higher hairline, women often shaved the hair around their hairline or plucked these hairs. The forehead was further adorned with decorative headbands or circlets made from real or artificial flowers. Wealthier women wore headbands studded with pearls and/or other gemstones. During the Carolingian period (752–987 CE) in France, fine nets were woven from gemstones and beads.

Women generally covered their hair, based on religious decrees and community customs. Hair was regarded as an erotic feature. Married women were expected to cover their hair with a hat, hood, veil, or shawl to discourage unwanted attention from men. Many medieval hats were shaped like a cone with a veil attached to the front, and wealthier women sometimes wore turbans or tall hats with long ribbons trailing behind. Their hair coverings were made from fine linen, silk, and gold netting.

During the early Middle Ages, flat bonnets were in style, but as the Middle Ages continued, less and less hair was revealed, and head coverings grew larger. Hats, veils, and bonnets were worn to church and other public places. After women began wearing their hair in coils above each ear, headgear was designed to cover the coils. Elaborate headgear shaped like butterflies or hearts became popular. Some women wore them with fine silk ribbons. For special occasions, gold threads were added to the hair.

Men's Styles

During the Middle Ages, men began wearing hairstyles that were simpler and somewhat shorter than styles of the previous era, but still fairly long unless they were servants or members of the lower classes. A typical male hairstyle during the middle to late Middle Ages was a pageboy or bowl-cut style, which became shorter after the 700s. Some versions of the pageboy were curled under the chin. Wealthier men wore their hair about neck length with a roll of hair at ear level. They could afford to pay people to care for their hair and maintain more complicated styles.

Among the Franks, long hair was popular during the Merovingian period (481–752 CE). Red was the most popular hair color, and some men used dye to achieve it. Men plaited their long hair and wore it on top of their heads. The Merovingian rulers were renowned for their long, flowing hair, which they wore parted in the center. These men also wore long beards, and it was considered an honor to touch even one hair from the beard of the ruler. The hair was worn loose or was curled or knotted above the shoulders. It also was common to shave the back of the head. Merovingian men did not typically wear headgear unless they were rulers or warriors. Soldiers wore their hair in a roll and shaved their necks.

During most of the early Middle Ages, men wore beards as one clear way to separate mature males from youths. Historians noted that when the Norman ruler William the Conqueror ascended to the throne of England in 1086, he complained that he had defended Normandy from the French "whilst still unbearded." By this, King William meant that he was still just a boy when he assumed responsibility for that military effort.

During the eleventh century, men who parted their hair tended to wear a center part. Fashions in beards changed, too.

The Catholic Church strongly affected European politics during medieval times, and church officials made rules about facial hair, the length of men's hair, and women's head coverings, among other things. During the 1000s, the pope supported regional ecclesiastical bans on long hair. In 1073, Pope Gregory banned beards among the clergy. Clerics in France declared that men should not wear long hair or beards. Clergymen began issuing edicts that told Christian men to shave their beards. In 1096, the Archbishop of Rouen, France, announced that men who wore beards would be excommunicated from the church (Peterkin, 2001, 25). This official church decree boosted the barbering profession, since more men sought haircuts and shaving services. Likewise, church officials in Venice, Italy, issued a decree banning long beards in 1102. After the English clergy denounced long hair and beards, King Henry I (reign 1100–1135) and his noblemen continued to wear long curls. After a particularly forceful sermon, the king finally agreed to cut his hair and shave off his beard. Within less than a year, however, King Henry and his friends resumed wearing ringlets. Two centuries earlier, the French king Louis II (reign 846–879) had obeyed a clerical imperative against long hair and had his own hair cut nearly as short as a monk's.

Although men began to wear their hair somewhat longer during the twelfth and thirteenth centuries, it still reached just above the shoulder. Usually, men wore a center part and no bangs. Beards and mustaches were rare during these centuries. By the fourteenth century, men were curling the ends of their shoulder-length hair, and the curl became tighter as the century continued. Long mustaches were fashionable, and beards, often a goatee with two forked segments, became more common. Few men wore a full beard, however.

Church officials continued to exert their influence on personal grooming into the 1400s. People who broke these rules risked being excommunicated—banned from the sacraments of the church—and priests could refuse to pray for their souls after death.

As was true for women, medieval men wore hats and other headgear. Hoods were popular, and styles varied according to social class. Members of the lower classes wore simple hoods, which might be merely a folded piece of cloth with a seam up the back. One popular style featured a long piece of cloth called a linpipe, which extended from the point of the hood and hung down the back. Upper-class men wore more ornate and fitted hoods, often with ornamentation. Some winter hoods were made from fur.

Hair Treatments

Hair and scalp treatments were made from plants, minerals, and animal products. One recipe for hair conditioner was made by boiling a lizard in olive oil. The use of the lizard in hair care recipes probably came from the Moors, as Europeans learned about Moorish culture during the Crusades. Egg whites were applied to the hair to add body and firmness. Other conditioners were made with flax oil, flax seeds, hemp oil, and fat called lanolin that was made by boiling sheep's wool in water and then collecting the grease that floated to the top. Honey also was used in various hair treatments, including formulas people hoped would minimize hair loss.

Hair rinses often contained herbs, such as rosemary, and various types of vinegar. Vinegar mixed with nettles was used to treat dandruff. Recipes to fight parasites and other unwanted scalp conditions called for vinegar, rosemary, thyme, mint, or other herbs.

The Trotula, attributed to a woman healer named Trota who practiced in Salerno, Italy, was a book of recipes for cosmetics and other personal care products from the late eleventh century. It contained instructions for making various hair products. For example, one recipe for getting rid of "itch-mites" (lice) included vinegar, myrtleberry, clary, and broom. A formula designed to increase hair growth was made with burnt barley bread, salt, and bear fat. The author advised people to anoint their hair with a mixture of agrimony, elm bark, vervain, willow root, burnt linseed, and root of reed, which was first cooked with goat milk, to increase hair thickness.

Hair Color

During medieval times, people used dyes to change their hair color or cover gray hairs. Blond shades were much admired, and ingredients for hair bleaches included henna, gorse flowers, saffron, eggs, and calf kidneys, among other things. Another dye was made from white wine and honey. Some people used recipes from *The Trotula* to achieve "golden" hair. One of these recipes called for walnut shells and walnut tree bark, boiled together and then strained. After adding alum and oak to this water, people applied the resulting mixture to clean hair. They then covered their head with leaves and left the mixture in place for two days. Next, they applied a coloring agent made from henna, crocus, and other ingredients, leaving that in place for three days. This process was supposed to create lasting results. Another recipe for golden dye from *The Trotula* read as follows: "Let cabbage stalks and roots be pulverized and let pulverized shavings of boxwood or ivory be mixed with them, and it should be pure yellow. And from these powders let there be made a cleanser which makes the hair golden" (Green 2001, 116–117). For women who were willing to undertake a complicated process to obtain light hair, the book offered these instructions:

> After leaving the bath, let her adorn her hair, and first of all let her wash it with a cleanser such as this. Take ashes of burnt vine, the chaff of barley nodes, and licorice wood (so that it may the more brightly shine) and sowbread; boil the chaff and the sowbread in water. With the chaff and the ash and the sowbread, let a pot having at its base two or three small openings be filled. Let the water in which the sowbread and the chaff were previously cooked be poured into the pot, so that it is strained by the small openings. With this cleanser let the woman wash her head. After the washing, let her leave it to dry by itself, and her hair will be golden and shimmering. (Green 2001, 114)

For black hair dye, people boiled gall nuts, iron, and alum in vinegar, then applied that to the hair and left it in place for two days. They could also carry out a two-step process described in *The Trotula*: First, they applied a mixture made by cooking a green lizard in oil without its tail and head. The next steps involved burning oak apples with oil in a dish, pulverizing them, and then mixing them with vinegar along with a blacking ingredient that came from Gaul.

For styling the hair, people used simple tools, including crimpers. Papers and ribbons were used to produce curls and other desired styles. Hair was scented with powders made from dried roses, cloves, nutmeg, and other spices or dried flowers, often mixed with rosewater. These scents also were combed through the hair.

See also: Adornment, Ornamental; Barbers; Beards, Men's; Comb; Comb, Liturgical; Eyebrows; Hair Color; Hair Removal; Headgear; Lady Godiva; Laws and Regulations; Military; Monastic Styles; Politics and Hair; Religion and Hair

Further Reading: Boucher, Francois, *20,000 Years of Fashion* (1987); Collins, Roger, *Early Medieval Europe, 300–1000* (1999); Green, Monica H., ed and trans., *The Trotula* (2001);

Gregory of Tours, *The History of the Franks* (1983); Simon, James, *The World of the Celts* (1993); Turudich, Daniela, and Laurie G. Welch, *Plucked, Shaved, and Braided* (2004); Wallace-Hadrill, J. M., *Long-Haired Kings and Other Studies in Frankish History* (1982).

MIDDLE EAST *See* Arabia, Ancient through Middle Ages; Body Hair; Dredlocks; Headgear; Henna; Kohl; Laws and Regulations; Mesopotamia; Middle Ages; Religion and Hair

MILITARY

Members of the military are subject to rules regarding their hairstyles and facial hair. These rules have been made for reasons of hygiene and/or safety, to promote a uniform appearance, and to enhance a sense of group identity.

Military hair regulations date back to ancient times. For example, among the Masai of Africa, a chief and military leader was required to have chin hair to retain his leadership qualities.

During the fourth century BCE, tens of thousands of soldiers under the command of Alexander the Great (Alexander III, ruler of Macedonia from 356 to 323 BCE) were obliged to shave their beards. In those days, soldiers often engaged in hand-to-hand combat, and a beard made them more vulnerable because the enemy could grab it.

British military guards.

Ancient Celtic warriors were known for their long hair, which they often dyed white with lime. Using blue dye from the woad plant, they painted designs on their faces and bodies. Against their long, pale hair, this created a dramatic look intended to intimidate the enemy. Celtic warriors also shaved the hair on their bodies and faces, leaving a line of hair across the upper lip.

Viking warriors wore long hair, sometimes along with beards and mustaches, which usually were kept short. Hair was styled to prevent the enemy from being able to grasp it during a battle. Some ancient Viking art shows warriors with braided beards that were wrapped around their ears.

Soldiers of the **Roman Empire** wore short hairstyles like those of other men in their society. Until Hadrian came to power, these troops did not wear beards or mustaches. Germanic warriors, on the other hand, often wore long mustaches and long hair, which they pulled into a topknot on their heads. These soldiers regarded long hair as a sign of manliness.

By the 1600s, European troops were wearing long hair styled in various prescribed ways. One reason for these distinctive styles was to set them apart from slaves and manual laborers, who were required to keep their hair short. Soldiers secured the back of their hair in a ponytail, while the sides often were carefully curled. Military barbers attached to a specific unit used hot irons and other tools to create these side curls. Soldiers slept in positions that did not crush their curls. During the 1700s, the back of the hair often was formed into a queue, made by twisting the long strand tightly to resemble a rope.

French military general Napoleon Bonaparte (1769–1821), later emperor of France, prompted a major change in military hairstyles in Europe. His own hair was cut short in 1800, which gave him the nickname *petit tondu*, meaning "little shaved." Short styles were easier to maintain, and other armies began to adopt them. The side curls were eliminated, and eventually the long tails at the back of the head also disappeared.

Meanwhile, in **Japan**, the fabled samurai warriors, who were prominent from 1185 to 1867, had their own distinctive hairstyle. A samurai shaved the hair on top of his head, then gathered the remaining hair on the sides and back up into a queue, or topknot. This was a special mark of the samurai, who lived by a code of "death before dishonor." Samurai who had been defeated in battle cut off their topknot as a sign of shame. In the 1870s, the emperor of Japan decided to train a new, more Western-style military. Samurai were phased out, and it was illegal for a former samurai to wear the traditional topknot hairstyle.

Inductees into the French Foreign Legion, which was founded in 1831, were required to have their hair cut very short—about one-half millimeter in length. Officials said that this practice was intended to help prevent lice. After basic training was completed, however, the men were permitted to wear longer hair if they wished.

During the Civil War in the United States (1861–1865), male soldiers wore hairstyles much like their civilian counterparts. Most men parted their hair in the middle or on the side and swept up the rest, either backward or forward, to create a "crest" shape. Then, some kind of oil or pomade was applied. Hair was not short but the sides usually did not fall below the bottom of a man's ear or hit his uniform collar, as it had in previous eras. The back might be longer, falling to the collar or even the shoulder. Long sideburns were stylish, and beards became more popular among men who liked the look of President Abraham Lincoln's short beard.

Military Regulations (United States)

By the 1900s, most men were shaving their facial hair, and short hair was the dominant trend among men in westernized countries. Inductees visited a military barber as they prepared to enter basic training. As men's hair grew longer in the 1950s and still longer during the late 1960s, an induction cut produced a haircut much shorter than those worn by most civilian men.

Perhaps the most famous military haircut of the twentieth century took place on March 25, 1958, when pop singing idol Elvis Presley received his GI haircut at Fort Chaffee in Arkansas, when he entered the U.S. Army. Photographers recorded this moment for the news media, which reported that Presley commented, "Hair today, gone tomorrow." Some female fans cried over the haircut. In 1999, the Mattel Company issued a collectible doll called "Elvis Presley Goes to the Army," showing him in uniform with his new, shorter haircut.

When women began to officially serve in the U.S. armed forces, dress codes specified how they could wear their hair. These codes were usually more detailed than those written for men, and they covered more aspects of personal appearance, including hair accessories and the use of cosmetics. In all service branches—Army, Air Force, Marines, Navy, and Coast Guard—hair was not permitted to reach the shoulder. Many women chose to wear a bun or other upswept style rather than cut their hair.

Before the 1970s, women in branches of the military were required to attend classes on hairstyling and other aspects of personal grooming as well as posture and etiquette. During the 1960s, for example, U.S. Navy regulations stated that a woman's hair must be "arranged and shaped to present a conservative, feminine appearance." These dress codes reflected the attitudes of the prefeminist era.

After the 1970s, regulations regarding women's hair were worded more like the regulations written for men. Today, similar uniform and grooming regulations govern both men and women in the military, with few differences based on gender. Dress codes for all service branches emphasize neatness, cleanliness, and professionalism. They call for hairstyles that do not interfere with job performance or call undue attention to the wearer. For example, U.S. Marine regulations say that hairstyles for all marines must look neat and professional and that a woman's hair must not fall below the lower edge of the uniform collar. These regulations say, in part, "Marine Corps uniform standards of grooming do not allow eccentric or faddish styles of hair, jewelry, or eyeglasses. Eccentricities in individual appearance detract from uniformity and team identity." The corps further bans the use of barrettes, hair ribbons, or other hair accessories that can be seen while the marine is in uniform. Hair must be styled so as "not to interfere with the proper wear of uniform headgear." The code goes on to say that, if hair color is used, it must not look unnatural. Men are required to be clean-shaven except for a mustache, which must be neatly trimmed according to Marine specifications.

According to U.S. Navy regulations, "Grooming standards are based on several elements including neatness, cleanliness, safety, military image and appearance" ("United States Navy Uniform Regulations"). People of either gender may wear a wig if it looks natural and conforms with other regulations. As for facial hair, the code says:

> The face shall be clean shaven unless a shaving waiver is authorized by the Commanding Officer. . . . Mustaches are authorized but shall be kept neatly and closely

trimmed. No portion of the mustache shall extend below the lip line of the upper lip. It shall not go beyond a horizontal line extending across the corners of the mouth and no more than inch beyond a vertical line drawn from the corner of the mouth. ("United States Navy Uniform Regulations")

Since the 1970s, women have assumed more active and diverse roles in the military, including serving aboard Navy ships and in combat areas. The 1997 feature film *G.I. Jane* shows a woman having her head shaved as she becomes the first female member of the elite Navy SEALS. Demi Moore agreed to have a buzz cut for her role in the film to make her character more believable.

Legal Issues

People have legally challenged military rules regarding hairstyles. Some litigants were members of the Sikh religion, who believe that men should not cut their hair or shave their beards and that a turban should be worn in public. From 1958 to 1974, the U.S. Army permitted Sikhs to follow these religious teachings, and they were exempted from complying with rules regarding hair and headgear. In 1974, however, that practice was changed, and Sikhs challenged it in court. In the 1985 case of *Khalsa v. Weinberger*, a court of appeals confirmed a ruling by a lower court that the military has the right to enforce rules regarding hairstyles. The court acknowledged that people have the constitutional right to follow their religious practices but that the military has no obligation to admit people who will not comply with military regulations. The courts also ruled, however, that Congress can pass laws that make allowances for people in the military and that the various service branches would be required to follow these laws. Therefore, Sikhs and others who wish to join the military while retaining their distinctive hairstyles and headgear can ask Congress to pass laws that give them an exemption.

See also: Beards, Men's; Buzz Cut; Celts; Greece, Ancient; Japan; Laws and Regulations; Mustache; Presley, Elvis Aaron; Punishment; Roman Empire; Vikings

Further Reading: Bryer, Robin, *The History of Hair* (2003); Cooper, Wendy, *Hair* (1971); Holm, Jeanne, *Women in the Military* (1992); "Marine Corps Uniform Regulations," http://www.usmc.mil/directiv.nsf/Pdocuments?openview&count=5000&start=1; Peterkin, Allan, *One Thousand Beards* (2001); Shep, R. L., *Civil War Gentlemen* (1995); Turnbull, Stephen R., *The Samurai, A Military History* (1977); "United States Navy Uniform Regulations," http://buperscd.technology.navy.mil/bup_updt/508/unireg/toc/tableOfContents.htm.

MOHAWK *See* Hairstyles, Twentieth-Century; Native Americans; Punk

MONASTIC STYLES

Both men and women traditionally had their hair cut or removed in specific ways when they entered a monastery or convent. These haircuts symbolized religious devotion, group identity, and humility as well as the renunciation of worldly things and personal vanity. The practice may relate to ancient rites in which people in various cultures offered their hair as a religious sacrifice. Monks and nuns also take a vow of celibacy, and hair has historically been associated with eroticism and sexuality and as a means to attract the opposite sex.

Historians say that monastic hairstyles also may relate to the ancient custom of shaving the heads of male slaves. Some early monks who began shaving their heads voluntarily referred to themselves as "slaves of Christ." Such hairstyles thus would show that a person entering religious life intends to subordinate his own will to the will of God.

Groups of Christian men began to form organized religious communities during the second and third centuries. These men, who became known as monks, lived apart from other people and developed distinctive modes of dress and appearance. Some monks cut their hair short, while others shaved it off completely or shaved part of their head.

Partial shaving may have its origins in **ancient Egypt**, **Greece**, and other places where men shaved a circular bald spot on top of their heads to honor the sun god. Some orders of monks who left a narrow crown of hair around their heads said that this signified the crown of thorns placed on Christ's head during his crucifixion.

The distinctive style, which is called the tonsure (from the Latin word *tondere*—"to shear"), often is associated with Catholic monks. Historians are unsure about the earliest origins of the tonsure, but church officials came to accept it and then required that all Catholic monks adopt this hairstyle. The tonsure is "a sacred rite . . . by which a baptized and confirmed Christian is received into the clerical order by a shearing of his hair" (*The Catholic Encyclopedia*).

In Roman Catholic monasteries, novices who had just entered the community had their hair cut short with scissors. When the novice took his vows to become a monk, he received the tonsure. The hair was cut short and then the hair on top of the head was shaved off, leaving a round bald area on the crown. These haircuts were carried out as part of the initiation into the group and were maintained by monastic barbers.

Three main variations of the tonsure developed among various orders. The eastern style involved shaving the head completely, according to a style attributed to St. Paul, while others shaved just the crown, a style associated with St. Peter and known as the Roman tonsure. A third style, called the Celtic (or transverse tonsure or tonsure of St. John) evolved in the British Isles. Celtic monks shaved the front part of their head from ear to ear but left the hair in the back hanging longer. Some Celtic monks pulled that hair around to form a semi-circle from one ear to the other.

During the seventh century, a fierce debate raged between Celtic monastic orders and church officials in Rome over the tonsure. Officials wanted the Roman style to prevail. Some French monks in Bayeux also came into conflict with officials in their country when they adopted the Celtic style.

Nuns also have had their hair cut during the initiation rites into their monastic communities. Usually the abbess (the head of the monastic community) performed this haircut at the time a postulant became a novice. Nuns also wore headgear that covered their forehead, head, and neck. The haircut is meant to symbolize the voluntary renunciation of the vanities associated with worldly life outside the convent or monastery.

The custom of tonsures for Buddhist monks dates back to ancient times. As with Christian monastics, it showed that the wearer had given up worldly attachments and no longer cared about appearance or spending time on vain pursuits. Buddhist monks shave their entire heads, as well as their faces, and do not let their hair grow beyond a certain length before shaving it again. This is done on a biweekly, monthly, or more frequent basis. The razor a monk keeps for this purpose is one of his few personal possessions. Monks also are banned from dying or plucking out gray hairs, which are considered a natural part of the aging body and thus a reminder that life on earth is transient, whereas the spirit is eternal.

Buddhist nuns shave their heads as a way to communicate to the outside world their status as spiritual seekers and to avoid attachment to worldly pursuits. Simple robes and the lack of styled hair permit more time for spiritual growth. This practice also helps nuns maintain a group identity with other members of the spiritual community, and it removes a potential source of pride.

Among Buddhists, hair also is known as "ignorance grass." Removing it can be a sign that someone wishes to eliminate ignorance that is a barrier to looking inside oneself for the purpose of spiritual growth.

In **India**, monks in the Vedic tradition shave off their hair, leaving a small tuft called a *sikha* at the back of the head. Facial hair also is shaved off. Cutting the hair is done on days when there is a full moon. Korean nuns and monks both shave their heads to show that they reject materialism and focus on things of the spirit.

In 1972, the Roman Catholic Church declared that monks are no longer required to wear the tonsure. Today, some Christian monks still wear the traditional tonsure, but others opt not to do so.

In the Eastern Orthodox orders, the tonsure survives in three main forms. At baptism, the hair of the infant is offered during the rites. The three levels of monastic tonsures are called rassophore, stavrophore, and great schema; they are used to bring men into the monastic community. The clerical tonsure is cut before a man is ordained as a cleric by a process called the "laying on of hands." Four locks of hair are cut so as to form a cross going from front to back and side to side on the head.

See also: Baldness, Voluntary; India; Japan; Middle Ages; Punishment; Religion and Hair

Further Reading: Bede, *Ecclesiastical History of the English People*, rev. ed. (1991); Burton, Janet E., *Monastic and Religious Orders in Britain, 1000–1300* (1994); *Catholic Encyclopedia*, "Tonsure," http://www.newadvent.org/cathen/14779a.htm; Decarreaux, Jean, trans., and Charlotte Haldane, *Monks and Civilization* (1964); Eliade, Mircea, editor in chief, *The Encyclopedia of Religion* (1987); Hiltebeitel, Alf, and Barbara D. Miller, *Hair: Its Power and Meaning in Asian Cultures* (1998); Larkin, Geraldine A., *First You Shave Your Head* (2001).

MONOBROW *See* Unibrow

MONROE, MARILYN (1926–1962)

Although her natural hair color was reddish-brown, actress Marilyn Monroe became a legendary "blond bombshell" and one of the world's most famous actresses as well as a cultural icon of the twentieth century.

Born Norma Jeane Mortenson on June 1, 1926, in Los Angeles, California, the future star endured a traumatic childhood. Her father abandoned the family before she was born and her mother, Gladys, a film cutter who worked for RKO Studios, suffered from recurring mental illness. During Gladys' numerous hospitalizations, Monroe (whose mother changed the family last name to "Baker" after her husband left) spent much of her childhood in foster homes and orphanages. In 1937, she began living with Grace McKee, a friend of her mother's. McKee provided a warm and loving home and reassured Monroe that she was beautiful and could become a movie star someday.

At age sixteen, Monroe was married for the first time, to her twenty-one-year-old neighbor, James Dougherty, an aircraft plant worker. After Dougherty joined the merchant marine in 1944, she began working in a munitions plant in Burbank, California. There she caught the eye of photographer David Conover, who was taking pictures of women working in the war industry. Because she was so photogenic and curvaceous, Conover used several pictures of her in his article and recommended her for other modeling jobs. Over the next two years, she appeared on dozens of magazine covers and in swimsuit ads. She enrolled in acting classes to pursue a film career like her childhood idol, the famous platinum blond, **Jean Harlow**.

In 1946, Monroe and Dougherty were divorced, and she signed a film contract with Twentieth Century Fox. Adopting her grandmother's surname, she changed her name to Marilyn Monroe and bleached her hair blond. Movie executives saw some of her photographs and "pin-up" shots and invited Monroe to do a screen test. She made her onscreen debut in 1947 but did not gain much attention for her small roles in films between 1947 and 1949. That changed in 1950, when Monroe's appearance in a thriller called *The Asphalt Jungle* garnered some attention from film critics. That same year, she was praised for her role in the acclaimed screen hit *All About Eve*.

Monroe continued to build up her career in subsequent films and became a bona fide star with her role in the 1953 dramatic film *Niagara*. That same year, two other hit films—*Gentlemen Prefer Blondes* and *How to Marry a Millionaire*—displayed Monroe's comedic talents and physical glamour, which was coupled with a "little-girl" vulnerability. In *Gentlemen Prefer Blondes*, Monroe also sang and danced. *Photoplay* magazine named her "Best New Actress of 1953." Her screen image was that of a somewhat fragile woman who relied on her looks rather than intelligence—what some people referred to as a "dumb blond."

The next year, fans were excited when Monroe married baseball hero Joe DiMaggio, whom she had been dating for two years. The marriage ended nine months later, though the couple remained close through the years. Friends said that DiMaggio resented the attention Monroe received from male fans and that she refused to give up her career, as he requested.

Marilyn Monroe, 1953. *Library of Congress*

Meanwhile, Monroe was the world's most famous blond, and she endorsed shampoos, such as Lustre-Crème, and other beauty products. It was rumored that she would not allow other actresses with the same shade of blond hair to appear with her on film.

In 1955, Monroe left Hollywood to study acting in New York. She hoped to take on more serious roles and diminish her dumb blond reputation. A year later, she founded her own production company and proceeded to star in two films released by Marilyn Monroe Productions: *Bus Stop* and *The Prince and the Showgirl.* Together with her starring role in 1959's *Some Like It Hot*, these films proved she was a capable, versatile actress. Reviewing her role in *Bus Stop*, the *London Times* said, "Miss Monroe is a talented comedienne and her sense of timing never forsakes her. She gives a complete portrait, sensitively and sometimes even brilliantly conceived. There is about her a waif-like quality and an underlying note of pathos which can be strangely moving." For *Some Like It Hot*, Monroe earned a Golden Globe award as the best actress in a comedy.

In 1956, Monroe married Arthur Miller, a critically acclaimed playwright. During their marriage, Miller wrote a story called *The Misfits* with a female lead tailored for Monroe; it was made into a movie starring Monroe and screen idol Clark Gable. Released in 1961, the same year that the couple divorced, *The Misfits* turned out to be the last of Monroe's twenty-nine films.

On the morning of August 5, 1962, Monroe was found dead in the bedroom of her Brentwood, California, home. During the last years of her life, she had been using prescription sleeping pills and tranquilizers. Although some people speculated that Monroe's death was a suicide and some believed that it was the result of foul play, other observers have concluded that it was an accidental drug overdose. During the months before she died, Monroe had been seeing DiMaggio again, and friends reported that the couple planned to remarry. She had also agreed to complete a film called *Something's Gotta Give* for Fox.

Her tragic death at age thirty-six became part of the Monroe mystique. The story of Marilyn Monroe, the most famous blond bombshell in film history, continues to captivate and intrigue new generations of moviegoers. Her look, which is instantly recognizable nearly everywhere in the world, has inspired other performers, including singer-actress Madonna, who wore a platinum blond hairstyle with clothing similar to Monroe's during one phase of her career.

See also: Advertising; "Blond Bombshell;" Hair Color; Masters, George

Further Reading: Buskin, Richard, *Blonde Heat* (2001); Conrad, Barnaby, *The Blonde* (1991); Guiles, Fred L., *The Life and Death of Marilyn Monroe* (1991); Woog, Adam, *Marilyn Monroe* (1997).

MOURNING

Customs relating to the treatment of hair during periods of mourning date back to ancient times. While in mourning, people in certain cultures have styled their hair in a different manner, cut or shaved off their hair, or stopped grooming it for a specific period of time. These customs also may extend to facial hair. For example, in ancient Egypt men in mourning customarily let their beards grow, though they shaved them off at other times.

Customs involving hair at times of mourning may have evolved because hair often was offered as a sacrifice and had a spiritual significance in ancient cultures. Traditions involving hair and mourning are still followed in some form today. Some Hindu women in India still follow the ancient tradition of shaving their heads when they are widowed. It also is still customary to refrain from washing the hair during the initial mourning period. In Nigeria and certain other parts of Africa, the hair of a widow is shaved off to signify that her relationship with the deceased is now severed. The hair from her head and other parts of the body may be scraped or burned off to make the woman look unattractive to other men.

Women in some ancient cultures would tear out their hair as a visible sign of mourning. As they lamented their losses, some ancient Egypt women tore out their hair. This also was true in **Babylonia**, where women who had lost a family member would wail and tear out their hair as they watched the corpse go by. They also threw dust on their heads to symbolize the body returning to the earth for burial.

In ancient Persia, people bared their heads as an outward sign of mourning for a member of the royal family. Members of the Persian army cut their hair to show their grief, and some cut off the manes of their horses and mules.

The Torah and Talmud, two sacred Jewish texts, forbid the cutting of hair as a sign of mourning. Samaritans were forbidden to shave their heads for a year after a death in the family. Today, among adherents of this religion, that time period has changed so that the hair and beards must not be shaved for seven days, and it applies only to close relatives of the deceased.

In Athens during the classical period in **Greece**, women would beat their heads and/or tear out their hair during a funeral service. A loud display of grief was regarded as a sign of respect for the dead, and some families hired mourners to attend a funeral, where they cried and tore out their hair. This custom persisted into modern times.

The sight of women pulling out their hair at funerals also was common in ancient Rome. According to the historian Tacitus, women showed their grief either by pulling out their hair or letting it hang down in an unkempt manner.

Letting down the hair as a sign of lamentation also occurred during the **Middle Ages**. Agnellus, archbishop of Ravenna, wrote that during the ninth century, crowds of women appeared at funeral ceremonies, where they wailed and tore at their hair even though they had no personal connection with the deceased person. Reginald of Durham, a twelfth-century monk and author, described chaotic, noisy scenes during funerals in his native England. As a result of similar scenes, officials in Italy passed laws to keep funerals more private and prevent crowds from behaving this way.

Although Colonial Americans did not have elaborate mourning rituals, such rituals developed in the United States during the 1800s. People in mourning were expected to wear certain types and colors of clothing and headgear for specified periods of time, and they were expected to follow rules that restricted and prescribed their behavior. Since **hair jewelry** often was worn during those years, mourning hair jewelry was common. To set it apart from other types of jewelry, mourning jewelry featured tombs, lilies, weeping women, weeping willow trees, and other recognized symbols of mourning.

Another Hindu tradition says that male relatives, including sons, are to shave their heads when a father in the family dies. In 2001, to show their respect for their late king, thousands of young men in Nepal shaved their heads. Many of them were not Hindu, but they believed that it was important to show solidarity and support for the ruler, who was considered a "father" to all the people.

See also: Egypt, Ancient; Greece, Ancient; Hair Art; India; Japan; Memento; Religion and Hair; Roman Empire

Further Reading: Coulton, G. G., ed. *Social Life in Britain from the Conquest to the Reformation* (1918); Dhakal, Sanjaya, "People at Loss," *Spotlight*, The National News Magazine, June 8–June 14, 2001, http://www.nepalnews.com.np/contents/englishweekly/spotlight/2001/jun/jun08/national9.htm; Garland, Robert, *The Greek Way of Death* (1985); Morris, Ian, *Key Themes in Ancient History* (1992).

MUSTACHE

The term "mustache," or "moustache," refers to hair growth above a man's upper lip. In some cases, men wear both **beards** and mustaches; in other cases, mustaches are worn alone.

Since prehistoric times, men have worn mustaches for reasons related to religion, social custom, occupation, fashion, or personal taste. For example, different styles of mustaches once were associated with military men in various countries, and the size and style were determined by the man's rank. Facial hair may signify a man's social status or group membership or show that he admires certain celebrities or political leaders. A man may show that he does not wish to conform to the prevailing fashions by wearing or not wearing a mustache. This choice also might be determined by the rules of the military organization, monastic order, religious group, or occupation to which he belongs. Facial hair also may be worn for practical reasons—as a way to protect the skin in harsh weather or because circumstances make shaving inconvenient or impossible.

The long list of men who have worn mustaches includes the famous and infamous, heroes and villains, kings and commoners, and people from diverse occupations and professions. That list also includes famous siblings such as the Smith Brothers (founders of a cough drop company), the Ringling Brothers (circus entrepreneurs), the Herbert Brothers (acrobatic act), and the Moustache Brothers (three brothers from the Myanmar Republic known for their comedic talents, including political satire).

Care of a mustache may include one or more of these activities: trimming, shaping, coloring, waxing, combing, setting, and styling. Tools and materials used for grooming mustaches include dyes, bleaches, powders, waxes, ointments, combs, brushes, razors, and scissors.

Changing Fashions

Styles in facial hair have changed repeatedly throughout history. The mustache has been the subject of heated debates, and some societies have passed laws on the subject.

In ancient Egypt, most people shaved off virtually all their body hair, including the hair on their heads. Men apparently did not wear beards other than the **false beards** that Egyptian rulers wore on special occasions, possibly because one or more early pharaohs wore a real beard. During the early Old Kingdom (2650–2152 BCE), however, men with thin mustaches appear on pottery and other artifacts. Then, around 1800 BCE, Pharaoh Teqikencola banned men from wearing mustaches.

In ancient **Greece**, facial hair was in vogue until Alexander the Great shaved off his beard. He banned beards on his soldiers to prevent enemy troops from being able to grab them by their facial hair. In Roman society, men were clean-shaven, and only barbarians, slaves, or certain philosophers were likely to wear beards and mustaches. The Romans considered certain kinds of facial hair to be barbaric. As the **Roman Empire** expanded, Roman troops encountered warriors from Gaul and Anglo-Saxon lands wearing facial hair. The military general and future emperor, Julius Caesar, noted that Anglo-Saxon soldiers used powders in vivid shades of red, orange, green, and blue to color their long mustaches.

In Gaul from about 27 BCE to 290 CE, the aristocracy wore mustaches but not beards, since these were reserved for commoners. Early Gauls shaved off their chin hairs but let the hair above the upper lip grow, while also growing out the hair on the back of their heads. Charlemagne (742–814), who ruled the Franks and became emperor of the Roman Empire, wore a small mustache. He decreed that all his descendants must wear a mustache.

In the Middle East, Muhammad prescribed facial hair on all followers of Islam, in part so they would stand out from the Christians who lived in that region. Early Christians wore facial hair in the form of a beard, often accompanied by a mustache.

Asian men also wore mustaches and/or beards. These usually were thin, though some men wore thick and/or long mustaches. Paintings of famous Chinese philosophers and religious leaders, such as Confucius and Lao-tzu, show them with mustaches. Mongolian military leader and emperor Genghis Khan (1162–1227) wore a style of mustache now referred to as a "Fu Manchu." His grandson, Kublai Khan (1215–1294), wore a mustache with thin tapered ends. In some Asian cultures, a mustache was regarded as a sign of wisdom. A style often associated with Chinese emperors is a thin, vertical mustache growing from the middle or outer end of the upper lip as far down the side of the face as possible.

During the **Middle Ages**, European men wore beards and mustaches, and styles differed from one country to another. Celtic men tended to wear both a mustache and beard or to shave off all their facial hair. Aristocrats disliked the look of a mustache alone, without a beard. Some men asked their barbers to create an upward curl at each end of their mustache.

During the mid-1400s, men in England were banned from wearing mustaches. (In later centuries, however, British soldiers were expected to keep theirs.) As the **Renaissance** continued, men in England and France began wearing rather long mustaches with the ends curving upward, but facial hair became less popular after the late 1600s as both men and women began wearing wigs. That trend in mustaches continued into the 1800s, even though wigs went out of favor.

As the 1800s progressed, mustaches became popular again. During the 1820s, more men in France began to wear small mustaches. These also were common among soldiers in France, Prussia, and England, though rulers in Bavaria (now Germany) outlawed mustaches among their troops.

Soldiers fighting away from home made up most of the small number of European males who wore mustaches until the 1850s. Then in the Crimean War, members of the English military, including male volunteers, admired the Turks' large mustaches and grew their own. They kept their mustaches after returning home. The trend spread throughout the British Isles and across the Atlantic to the United States.

During the 1860s, more American men also grew beards and/or mustaches as a result of the influence of President Abraham Lincoln, the first bearded president. While Lincoln was campaigning for office in the fall of 1860, he received a letter from eleven-year-old Grace Bedell saying that he would look better with facial hair. Bedell urged Lincoln to "let your whiskers grow." She told him, "You would look a great deal better because your face is so thin," and besides, "All the ladies like whiskers."

The style even prompted some popular verse, including one that said, "I'll put my trust in Providence and let my whiskers grow." Musicians wrote songs about mustaches, including a humorous tune called "If You've Only Got a Moustache," written by George Cooper and Stephen Foster and published in 1864. The song said that even if a man lacked other attributes, he could attract a woman "if you'll only get a moustache" (Foster). A British playwright, Robert Barnabas Brough, created a dramatic farce called *The Moustache Movement*, which debuted on the London stage in 1854.

A mustache that was part of a style called "burnsides" (sometimes called "mutton chops") became popular during the U.S. Civil War (1861–1865). Union Brigadier General Ambrose Everett Burnside sported a distinctive, full-sized, well-groomed mustache with ends down each side of the mouth that blended into bushy side-whiskers.

During the 1870s and 1880s, the long, drooping "handlebar" mustache, worn without a beard, became popular. One of the prominent men who wore a handlebar mustache was John C. Breckinridge, who served as vice president under James Buchanan and as a Confederate general during the U.S. Civil War. Other styles were also worn. American author and humorist Mark Twain wore his distinctive walrus mustache from the late 1800s until his death in 1910. In Europe, Franz Ferdinand (1863–1914), archduke of Austria, wore a somewhat more manicured version of the walrus mustache.

Various tools and accessories for facial hair care were developed during the 1800s, and some of them are now considered collectibles. Inventors received patents for their mustache guards, protectors, trainers, curlers, holders, adjusters, shapers, and bands. Some items were worn at night to preserve the mustache's shape. For travel, men could buy a portable mustache curler with a heating device.

The mustache cup made it easier for men to keep their mustaches neat and dry. A raised lip guard on the rim or ledge prevented beverages from coming into contact with the mustache. These were available in both right- and left-handed versions.

One styling device, the *Schnurbartbinde*, or mustache binder, was designed in Germany. It was used to keep the ends of a mustache pointed and curled in the style worn by Kaiser Wilhelm II. The binder was made of silk with two small leather straps and two pieces of plastic webbing. After pressing the binder over his mustache, a man strapped it to his head and wore it while sleeping and sometimes also in the daytime.

During the 1900s, new products and shaving equipment made it easier to remove facial hair. In Western cultures, clean-shaven faces became the prevailing style after the 1920s. By then, most men were shaving themselves at home. The shaving products industry promoted the clean-shaven look through persuasive **advertising** techniques that said men without facial hair were more attractive and well groomed. Some men, including intellectuals, men in the arts, or people who belonged to a counterculture group, continued to wear a mustache.

During the 1960s, mustaches became more prevalent in Western societies. Some men wore longer hair and more facial hair to express their political views and protest against conformity in various areas of American life. More pop musicians, such as the members of the Beatles, began to wear mustaches. This trend continued into the 1970s as athletes and others wore mustaches for the first time.

In 1975, Charles E. Barbarow patented a styling device that helped men choose a flattering style and then groom and maintain their mustache. A template attached to a clamp was placed in the mouth. The user could cut this template to the desired shape, then place it above his upper lip. This left both hands free for trimming the mustache.

Since the early 1900s, most American political leaders have not worn a mustache, regardless of changing styles in facial hair. As of 2005, the last U.S. president to wear a mustache was William H. Taft, who left office in 1913. His predecessor, Theodore Roosevelt, also kept his mustache during his two terms as president (1901–1909).

Today, some men wear facial hair for religious or practical reasons, but in most cases, the decision to wear a mustache is based on personal taste.

Styles and Namesakes

Different kinds of mustaches that developed through the years were named for famous people who wore them or for the appearance of the mustache itself. For example, the bushy walrus mustache hangs over the upper lips and may even cover the mouth and fall below, like the tusks of a walrus. The bottom line of this mustache is horizontal. As its name would suggest, the horseshoe is designed to curve downward on both sides. To wear the bulletheads style, a man creates ball-shaped ends on his mustache. The major has a small space under the nose halfway between the two ends of the mustache, while the painter's brush is relatively thick and resembles a straight line across the upper lip. The box is a tight, trimmed-back style that can be worn either thick or thin. In contrast, the triangular style fills the upper lip area. It is shaped so that the top points from the upper lip to the nose while the sides grow toward each side of the lower lip.

A mustache named for Mexican revolutionary leader Emiliano Zapata (1879–1918) is thick, natural looking, and bushy. Zapata's mustache drooped over his upper lip but left the bottom lip uncovered, with thick ends growing across both cheeks.

Artist Salvador Dali (1904–1989) wore a distinctive, long, thin mustache with curling ends. Dali said that this style, which bears his name, was inspired by the mustache worn by seventeenth-century Spanish painter Diego Velasquez. A curled mustache with pointed ends also was popular with fashionable gentlemen and "dandies" during the nineteenth century.

Film stars and fictional characters have helped to publicize certain styles. The Fu Manchu mustache was named for a fictional Chinese villain by the same name. This character was featured in books and in several movies during the 1930s and again in the 1960s as well as on a television series. Fu Manchu's mustache usually fell below the chin, with slim, tapered ends that pointed downward. The "Charlie Chaplin" style, named for the legendary actor and director, is a thick, nearly square mustache that reaches the upper lip and does not extend to the ends of the mouth. Some observers said that it resembled a push broom. Chaplin's dark mustache made a strong statement in combination with his thick, dark brows and black-lined eyes. Musician George Harrison, a member of the Beatles during the 1960s, sometimes wore a Chaplin-style mustache later in his career.

Actor Errol Flynn (1909–1959), a screen idol during the 1930s and 1940s, was one of the most famous men to wear the "pencil" mustache, sometimes called the "Errol Flynn." This mustache, which was extremely popular during those two decades, is narrow and carefully clipped to follow the line of the upper lip. To achieve this look, a man must shave the area between the nose and mustache. Clark Gable was another leading man of this era whose mustache became an integral part of his look.

One of the best-known mustaches in show business belonged to comedian and actor Groucho Marx (1890–1977). Together with his bushy eyebrows, thick glasses, and fat cigars, the mustache was central to Marx's image. During the years he worked in vaudeville with his brothers, he glued on an exaggerated horsehair mustache before going onstage. According to legend, Marx began using greasepaint to paint on a fake mustache one night after he arrived at the theater too late to attach his horsehair mustache. Later in his life, he grew a real mustache.

A handlebar mustache fills the whole upper lip and resembles the handlebars of a bicycle. This style is worn in different lengths and styled by waxing and twirling the ends. The Handlebar Club, an international organization for men who wear a handlebar, is based in London, England. It was founded in 1947, after World War II, to support servicemen who did not want to shave their mustaches like most civilian men of that era. As of 2005, the Handlebar Club had members from nine different countries. Members must have a handlebar mustache, but no beards are allowed. Each year, the club awards prizes for the longest handlebar mustache, as measured from tip to tip. The 1957 champion was John Roy, with a mustache that measured nineteen inches.

Some people have tried to correlate certain personality traits with the type of mustache a man chooses to wear. A British psychiatrist, Major Geoffrey Peberdy, studied 400 men with mustaches who applied for officer training in the British military. He divided the mustaches into five classes: trimmed, bushy, toothbrush, hairline, and divided. Peberdy associated personality traits with the different types of mustaches and concluded, for example, that military boards regarded men with a toothbrush style as less imaginative and less open-minded than certain others.

Record Holders

Certain people have become famous for their unusually long or distinctly styled mustaches. Hans Steininger, burgomaster of Braunau, Austria, grew his whiskers to eight feet, nine inches. An account of his death in 1567 says that he tripped over them and fell down the stairs, breaking his neck. His whiskers were removed and put on display in Braunau Museum.

When General Gaishi Nagaoki, the father of Japanese aviation, died in 1933, his twenty-inch-long mustache was buried beside him in a separate mound. As of 2005, according to the *Guinness Book of World Records*, the longest known mustache belonged to a Turkish man, Mohammed Rashid. Rashid's mustache reached a length of five feet, three inches after he did not cut it for more than ten years.

Clayton Bailey won first prize at the 1993 Bull Valley Mustache Festival held in Hayward, California. Tip to tip, his mustache measured twenty-four inches. Bailey came up with a formula called Clayton Bailey's Mustache Grower, which he used for conditioning his mustache. He claimed that the product also acts as a fire retardant.

The *Guinness Book of World Records* lists Masuriya Din (1908–) of India as the owner of the longest mustache in the world. Din, who is brahmin of the Partabgarh district of Uttar Pradesh, grew his mustache to a length of 102 inches between 1949 and 1962. He told reporters that he spends $30 a year to maintain it.

See also: Advertising; Aging and Hair; Barbers; Beards, Men's; Body Hair; China; Competitions; Gillette Company; Greece, Ancient; Hair Removal; Japan; Laws and Regulations; Middle Ages; Military; "Mustache Gang"; Religion and Hair; Renaissance Europe; Roman Empire; Shaving; Victorian Era

Further Reading: "Abraham Lincoln in Buffalo: The Legend of the Whiskers," http://www.buffalohistoryworks.com/lincoln/whiskers.htm"; Atwan, Robert, Donald McQuade, and John W. Wright, *Edsels, Luckies, & Frigidaires* (1971); "Burnside, Ambrose Everett," Civil War Indiana, http://civilwarindiana.com/biographies/burnside_ambrose_everett.html; Foster, Stephen, "If You've Only Got a Moustache" (song lyrics), http://www.stephen-foster-songs.de/Foster12.htm; Grant, Michael, *A Social History of Greece and Rome* (1992); Laver, James, *Taste and Fashion* (1937); Lax, Roger, and Maria Carvainis, *Moustache* (1979); Lindsay, Jack, *The Ancient World* (1968); Moers, Ellen, *The Dandy* (1960); *The New York Times*, "The Saga of the Moustache," August 20, 1944; Peterkin, Allan D., *One Thousand Beards* (2001); Reynolds, Reginald, *Beards* (1949).

"MUSTACHE GANG"

In 1972, when members of the Oakland Athletics baseball team grew mustaches, they were nicknamed the "Mustache Gang." Although many athletes had worn mustaches during the nineteenth century and the early part of the twentieth century, by the 1920s, nearly every major league baseball player was clean-shaven. Styles in facial hair had changed during the mid-1910s, and American men were shaving off both their beards and mustaches. Ballplayers were no exception. Although the officials in charge of the major leagues had not instituted a specific regulation banning facial hair, some individual teams put this "unwritten rule" into words. For example, during the 1960s, at a time when men in the counterculture began growing long hair and beards and/or mustaches, the Cincinnati Reds banned facial hair on its players.

By 1970, a few players sported a mustache or other facial hair but removed it before opening day of the playing season. This pattern changed in 1972 when Reggie Jackson, one of the sport's top players, grew a sizable mustache and did not shave it off after spring training. Jackson, a right fielder with the American League's Oakland Athletics, made it known that he would continue to wear his mustache during the regular season. This had not been done since 1914.

As some former teammates recall the story, the owner and the manager of the Oakland team wanted Jackson to shave but hoped to avoid a big conflict over the matter. They thought that if other players also grew mustaches, Jackson would shave because he prided himself on being an individual with his own sense of style. Four of the "A's" pitchers—Jim "Catfish" Hunter, Rollie Fingers, Derold Knowles, and Bob Locker—grew their own mustaches. Fingers' "handlebar" mustache made him one of the most recognizable men in his sport. He later said, "Playing in the World Series, with all the media attention, the mustache became my signature. There were times where people would recognize the mustache rather than me" (Parry 2002).

The look began to appeal to the members of Oakland's management, and they decided that the whole team should wear mustaches. Some players also began wearing trendy, longer hairstyles and beards. This gave the team a different look than other ball clubs that year.

Capitalizing on publicity generated by the players' facial hair, team owner Charlie Finley decided that Father's Day that year would be called "Mustache Day," and any man who wore a mustache to the Oakland Coliseum would be admitted free to the game. Players who grew a mustache by that day were offered a $300 bonus.

All twenty-five players did grow a mustache in time for the Father's Day game, though some players later shaved them off. At the end of the season, most of the players again sported mustaches. The so-called "Mustache Gang" of baseball won that year's World Series—one of three world titles in a row for the team.

See also: Beards, Men's; Mustache; Occupations

Further Reading: Bergman, Ron, *The Mustache Gang* (1973); Markusen, Bruce, "Thirty Years Ago," Baseball Museum, http://www.baseballlibrary.com/baseballlibrary/submit/Markusen_Bruce5.stm; Parry, Jason, "Milwaukee Mustaches: Rollie Fingers," February 5, 2002, http://www.onmilwaukee.com/articles/print/rollie.html.

N

NATIVE AMERICANS (North American)

In the Americas, native peoples took pride in their hair and believed that hair had special spiritual significance. As a result, people were careful not to let their enemies have any contact with their hair. They believed that this would give the enemy power over them. Fallen hair and hair combings were burned or otherwise destroyed.

Hair also played a role at times of **mourning**. Members of some tribal groups traditionally cut or shaved off their hair when someone died, while others let it hang down, ungroomed.

Native Americans wore their hair in diverse styles, influenced by regional and tribal customs. Both men and women groomed their hair, and hairstyles differentiated men from women. Haircutting and styling sometimes were group activities. Historians have noted that Sioux women as well as women from some other Native American groups scheduled their haircuts for the same times.

The most common hair colors were dark tones of blue-black and brown-black, though intense sun could turn the hair of some Native Americans to a bronzy color. They had sparse body hair, which they removed, and seemingly did not lose enough hair to become bald during their lives.

Tools and Adornments

To comb their hair, people used their fingers or combs made from bone, wood, river cane, or deer antler. Hairstyles were ornamented with natural objects, including feathers, shells, beads, horn, bone, animal hair, porcupine quills, flowers, leaves, metals, and gemstones. Some of these items were made into headdresses that symbolized a person's status in the tribe or their specific achievements. Men of a certain rank could wear elaborate headdresses made up of many feathers and buffalo horns. Among plains Indians, shells obtained from coastal Indians in trade were made into tubular ornaments that hung from cords near the ears. After Europeans arrived on their lands, Native Americans also began wearing ornaments made from manufactured cloth and silk or cotton ribbons.

Styling Agents and Colorants

Native Americans used animal fats, such as bear grease or oil, and roots, herbs, and plant extracts for hair care. Bear oil was regarded as a lice killer as well as a conditioner. Sometimes, oil was mixed with fragrant plant substances. Different preparations were made to add shine to the hair, moisturize and condition the hair and scalp, treat itchiness, and get rid of parasites. The ingredients varied by region. For example, the Chippewa (Anishinabe), who lived in the upper Midwest, mixed balsam fur tree gum with bear grease. The pollen from cattails, which grew in several regions, was used in hair conditioning mixtures. In North Carolina, people mixed bear's oil with a red powder they made from a scarlet root they obtained near the foot of the mountains. The mixture was used to kill lice as well as condition the hair. According to a historian who visited them, "They have this *Scarlet Root* in great Esteem, and sell it at a great Price one to another, and the Reason of it's being so very valuable" (Brickell 1968, 256). The Omaha, who lived on the southern plains, used prairie rose petals and wild bergamot leaves in their hair conditioning oil. In the Southwest, people found that oil from the jojoba plant made an excellent hair balm. Another plains tribe, the Blackfoot, used needles from balsam trees, which grew abundantly in their region. The Cheyenne used a brew made from mint leaves as a hair rinse. Chaparral was used to treat flakiness or itching on the scalp.

In the Southwest, the Navajo used yucca to make soap and shampoo. Yucca comes from a plant that grows in the southwestern United States and Mexico. A member of the lily family, the yucca has roots that contain saponins, which have a cleansing action.

Other mixtures gave color to the hair, either for decorative reasons or as a dye. Walnut hulls were used to give hair a deep color. One account written by a former white hostage relates how the blond hair of a captive was colored with bear grease and charcoal. Mixtures of buffalo or bear grease, blood, red ochre, and/or charcoal were used to make paints to decorate both the body and hair.

Hair Removal

For shaving, Native Americans used sharpened pieces of stone or shell, and they used pairs of clamshells as tweezing instruments to remove hair. Many people carried a small leather belt pouch to hold bear grease, paint, and tweezers, which were made from copper after Europeans began arriving.

Certain groups of Native American men, including the Wampanoag, grew scalp locks by shaving their heads and leaving just one section of hair. Scalp locks were said to symbolize the person's manhood or spirit. The scalp locks varied in diameter and style, and the way they were adorned (with a feather, for example) could indicate the man's clan membership within the tribe. A scalp lock was supposed to remain untouched, and its loss could lead to social ostracism.

Regional Styles

Specific ways of styling the hair were common to groups living in certain geographic regions. Members of certain groups wore short hair, including styles in which men shaved off a portion, or most, of their hair. Some Native American hairstyles were dramatic. For example, in the style that became known as the "Mohawk," men shaved off all but a ridge of hair that ran from the front to the back of the head. Among the groups who wore false hair were the Mandan, who lived in present-day Missouri, and the Mohave and Yuma (today called Quechan), who have lived in the present-day southwestern United States.

Iroquois men and other men in the Northeast wore a distinctive hairstyle known as a "ridge" or "cockscomb," with feathers on top. A scalp lock hanging down the back was braided and ornamented with shells, stones, and other objects. Sometimes a patch or red-dyed deer bristles were arranged on the ridge. This style was achieved by shaving around a round or square ridge of hair on top of the head. Women in the Northeast wore their hair long, in a braid down the back.

Among the Assateague of Virginia, hair was fairly long, and grave sites show that children's hair was longer than adults. Some men shaved off part of their hair on the side where they held their arrow when they went hunting with a bow. It was customary for women in mourning to shave their heads.

Male members of the Cherokee, who lived in the Southeast, shaved or plucked their hair to leave a patch on top, while women grew long hair. After European colonists arrived, women began wearing silk ribbons as hair ornaments. Long ribbons in vivid colors were attached to hairstyles, and women sometimes wore dozens of these streamers. Other hair ornaments were made from bells, ostrich feathers, and combs of horn and ivory.

Before Europeans entered their land in present-day Mississippi, the Choctaw of both genders wore their black hair long and loose. Hair ornaments included combs made from antler, bone, or copper, and for special occasions, women wore beaded, decorative combs on the crown of their heads. Men wore feathers from eagles and other birds. Elaborate headdresses adorned with feathers that showed rank and accomplishments were worn for certain ceremonies. Specific hairstyles and ornaments were worn during spiritual ceremonies, such as the eagle dance.

Chickasaw men and women also wore their hair long. Warriors wore a different style that featured a scalp lock. The foreheads of Chickasaw infants were pressed on a board while the bones of the head were still growing to create a distinctive, flat, elongated head shape.

Among the Creek, women grew their hair long, sometimes leaving it uncut their entire lives. For special occasions, they looped their long, plaited hair on top of their heads forming a wreath-like shape, then added colorful ribbon streamers, some of which reached the ground. One naturalist and author who visited during the 1730s wrote that Creek women "[rolled up their hair] in a bunch to the crown of their head, others braid it, and bind it with wreaths of peak and roanoak" (Catesby 1996, 60). During times of mourning, however, women did not groom their hair and might cut it or singe it.

In the Carolinas, Native Americans also grew their hair long and decorated it with colored cloth in red, green, and yellow. Men did not wear beards or other facial hair, which was removed by plucking.

Osage men wore a style known as a "roach," achieved by shaving their entire face and head, leaving only a scalp lock about two inches high and three inches wide running from the neck up to the area just over the forehead. Women wore their long hair hanging simply down their backs.

Male members of the plains tribes known as the Sioux and the Dakota wore long hair that was parted in the middle and then left loose or braided. Sometimes the braids were wrapped with cloth or skins from otters or beavers. The style was created by parting the hair back to a circle that formed the scalp lock on the crown of the head and then pulling the hair down the back from the scalp lock to the base of the neck. The scalp lock and the hair on each side were all braided separately.

Another plains group, the Pawnee, got their name because of their hairstyle. Some people thought the crest on the Indians' otherwise shaven heads looked like a horn, and "Pawnee" derives from an Indian word for horn.

Like plains Indian males, those in the northwestern groups, including the Nez Perce, also wore long hair. They did not braid their hair, however, or only plaited sections of hair and left the rest hanging free.

In contrast, Seminole men, who lived in present-day Florida, wore short, blunt haircuts with bangs, which may have been more comfortable in a hot climate. Seminole women also wore bangs, although the rest of their hair was long and gathered together at the back. Similar styles could be found among the Inuit, often called Eskimos, who lived across the continent and much further north than the Seminole.

In the Southwest, Pueblo men also wore their hair cut shorter than plains Indians, with bangs. For special ceremonies, they wore wigs made from black wool.

The Hopi, who lived in desert villages in present-day New Mexico, developed wedding and coming-of-age customs relating to hair. In a traditional Hopi wedding, relatives of the bride and groom wash the hair of their new son-in-law or daughter-in-law before the ceremony. For centuries, the Hopi have known how to make a hair-cleansing liquid by pounding the roots of the yucca plant. This soapy liquid they got from the root was applied to the hair. By custom, the bride and groom stood beside each other with their soapy hair mixed together, a symbol of their coming union.

Hopi women braided their hair in a single plait after marriage. Before marriage but after reaching the age when they were ready for marriage, young women wore a distinctive, whorled, "squash blossom" hairstyle that resembled butterfly wings on either side of the head. This hairstyle was part of the coming-of-age ceremony for young Hopi girls and is still sometimes worn today. A special shampoo made from the yucca plant also was used for the ceremony.

Changing Customs

By the 1850s, most Native Americans had been forced to leave their ancestral lands. The U.S. government assigned them to reservations that were located either on small parts of their homelands or in Indian Territory in present-day Oklahoma. The government policy of assimilation reflected a belief that native peoples should adopt the customs and religion of white society, including the manner of dress and personal grooming. A law passed in 1865 required Native American children to attend government-run boarding schools, where they were taught English and the Christian religion. They were dressed like white children and forced to cut their hair and style it like whites. People who refused to obey this law faced penalties, such as the loss of food rations, and some children were taken from their families against their will.

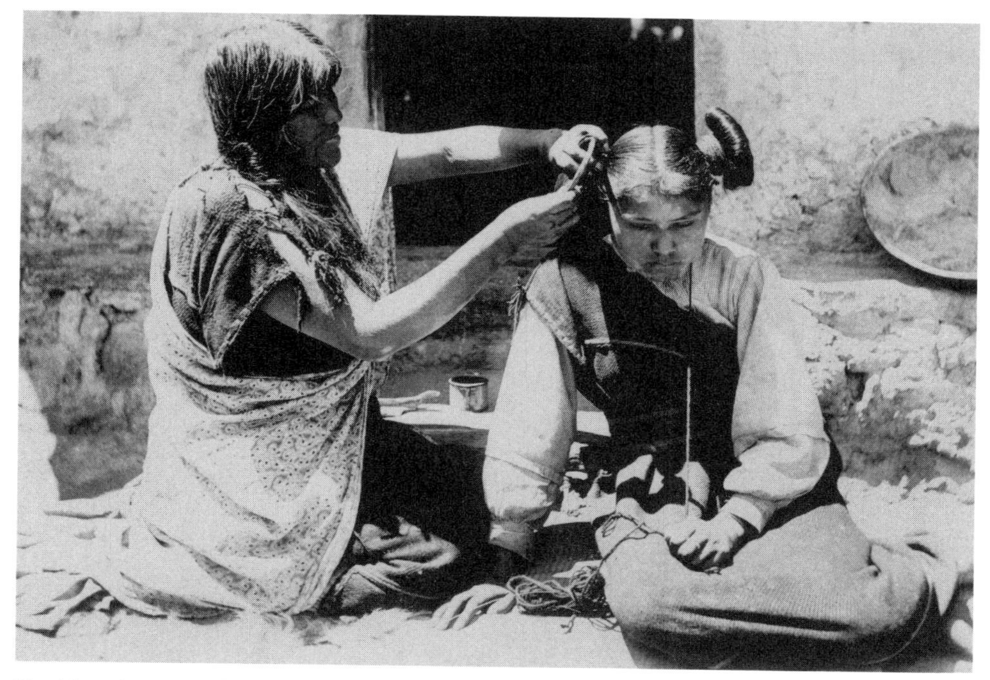

Hopi hairdresser. *Library of Congress*

During the 1900s, these policies were reevaluated and gradually were abandoned. Native Americans were free to decide matters of personal grooming for themselves. Since some Native Americans regarded long hair as essential to their spirituality, they returned to that custom. During the 1960s, when the black civil rights movement expanded, many Native Americans embraced the idea of "red power" and chose to wear traditional hairstyles and clothing.

See also: Adornment, Symbolic; Comb; Coming of Age; Headgear; Latin America, Ancient Times to 1500s; Laws and Regulations; Shampoo; Tonics, Hair

Further Reading: Andrews, Ralph W., *Curtis' American Indians* (1962); Axtell, James, *The European and the Indian* (1981); Braund, Kathryn E. Holland, *Deerskins and Duffles* (1993); Brickell, John, *The Natural History of North Carolina* (1968); Catesby, Mark, *The Natural History of Carolina, Florida, & the Bahama Islands* (1996); Dutton, Bertha P., *American Indians of the Southwest* (1983); Hoxie, Frederick E., ed., *Encyclopedia of North American Indians* (1996); Hutchens, Alma R., *Indian Herbology of North America* (1991).

NATURAL PRODUCTS

People have used hair products made from plants, animals, and minerals—materials found in nature—for thousands of years. Although synthetic ingredients from chemicals became available during the 1800s, some companies today specialize in so-called "natural products," and many popular brands feature botanical ingredients.

People living in ancient civilizations used oils, particularly oils derived from the olive, palm, corn, and coconut plants, as well as other plant and animal products to cleanse, condition, color, style, and/or scent their hair. They also used natural substances to treat parasites or other unhealthy scalp conditions. In **Africa** and other parts of the world, certain kinds of mud were used to style the hair. For thousands of years, native Australians found that oil from the leaves of the tea tree (*Melaleuca alternifola*) was useful in certain scalp cleansers and treatments.

The use of these products continued into the 1800s. Many popular hair tonics and other grooming aids were made by blending herbs and/or plant extracts with plant or mineral oil. Products were sold in stores, door-to-door, and by traveling salespeople. People also made their own products at home, and the housekeeping guides and cookbooks of this era contain recipes for hair preparations and other grooming aids.

Even after preservatives and synthetic ingredients became available, some people relied on homemade hair and beauty products or looked for natural ingredients in the products they bought. For example, during the 1940s, some of the most popular shampoos contained eggs, and women sometimes applied homemade hair masks made with eggs, or they used mayonnaise, which contains egg yolk. Some well-known shampoos emphasized the natural plant oils in their formulas.

Increasing Interest

Personal care products made from so-called natural ingredients became more popular in the United States during and after the late 1960s. More people began seeking products that were derived from plant and animal products rather than chemicals processed in a laboratory. This coincided with the health and fitness movement of the 1970s and a desire to go "back to nature" in other areas of life, such as eating whole, natural foods instead of processed foods and wearing clothing made from natural fibers. Increasing concern about the global environment also focused attention on the potential effects of chemicals in food, air, water, soil, and consumer goods. The year 1970 marked the first international Earth Day, organized to address global environmental issues.

By the 1970s, some companies already were producing lines of hair care products designed for people who wanted natural ingredients. A number of European companies, including several based in Germany and Switzerland, had been operating for decades. Aubrey Organics, founded by Aubrey Hampton, was one of the first U.S.-based companies to offer organic cosmetics and hair care products. The company began to voluntarily list product ingredients on its labels in 1967, which was a decade before the U.S. Food and Drug Administration began to require this information. The company offered shampoos made with coconut oil, primrose oil, lavender, chamomile, green tea, nettle, and aloe, among other ingredients, and without artificial colors or fragrances, sodium lauryl sulfate, or petrochemicals. During the 1980s, Aubrey Organics produced a styling formula made with herbal gums and vitamin B-5 rather than the more commonly used synthetic PVP/VA copolymer.

The Body Shop became the first large cosmetics company known around the world for emphasizing products made from natural ingredients. The company, which opened its first store in England in 1976, declared its commitment to environmental causes. Founder Anita Roddick (1944–) said that the company aimed to provide jobs for people in developing countries who cultivate plants the Body Shop would use for its products. Roddick's first store offered twenty-five products for the hair and face, sold in five sizes. The products reflected the beauty customs of women around the world, and some ingredients were cultivated by indigenous peoples. For example, Brazil Nut Hair Conditioner contains nuts grown by members of the Mebengokre Indians (also known as Kayapo) who live in the Brazilian rainforest. Customers were urged to recycle product containers by bringing them back to the store for refills. The Body Shop has grown into a multinational company with more than 1,400 stores in forty-five countries. By the late 1990s, annual retail sales reached $1 billion.

During the 1970s, large, well-established companies, including Alberto-Culver and Procter & Gamble, also introduced new, natural products along with their other lines, and they emphasized the plant ingredients in their shampoos and conditioners. Faberge offered a new line of shampoos and conditioners that contained wheat germ oil and honey.

Several companies have produced hair care products that include balsam, which comes from a type of evergreen tree. Two other popular plant ingredients are aloe vera, from a plant that grows in warm climates, and jojoba oil, from a shrub that is native to Mexico and the American Southwest. More commercial growers in California also began cultivating these shrubs when the demand for jojoba oil increased during the 1970s. Some organic and natural hair care product lines feature both aloe and jojoba. Yucca, a plant that belongs to the lily family, and soap bark extract also can be found in organic or botanical shampoos. Still others contain juniper, chamomile, lecithin, and/or rosemary.

Before the 1970s, organic and natural hair care products were sold primarily in health food stores. As consumer demand and product lines grew, more drugstores, variety stores, and department stores began stocking them. The ads for these products often emphasize the fact that they contain fruit and vegetable extracts and/or herbs. New product lines for hair cleansing, conditioning, and hair coloring may feature the words "botanical" or "nature" in their names.

All-natural hair color products are also available. The dyes used in these products are made from vegetables instead of coal tar or artificial coloring, and the products are formulated without ammonia and peroxide. Most consumers find these hair color products at health food stores or through the Internet.

Products made with botanicals experienced another surge of popularity during the 1990s. Companies introduced new hair care products that contain shea butter, palm oil, coconut oil, bamboo medulla, nut extracts, tea tree oil, emu oil, and/or other ingredients.

In 1998, sales of natural personal care products reached $1.62 billion in the United States. They accounted for about 6 percent of the total sales in cosmetics and toiletries. Between 1995 and 1999, sales of natural shaving products also rose. A steady annual rise in the sales of these products has occurred in European and Asian countries as well as the United States. Surveys conducted during the

1990s show that most of the people who buy natural products are high-income women between the ages of sixteen and forty-five.

An Ongoing Debate

People disagree about whether cosmetics and personal care products made primarily with plants are better and/or safer to use than products made from synthetic ingredients. Some critics point out that ingredients from plants may cause **allergic reactions** and that preservatives are useful in killing bacteria that can proliferate in personal care products. These critics claim that synthetic ingredients are not inherently more hazardous than plant, animal, and mineral ingredients and may even be less likely to cause allergic reactions than certain plant extracts.

Some research scientists claim that they have not found any scientific evidence that natural ingredients are safer and/or more effective than synthetics. The U.S. Food and Drug Administration has published articles saying that any claims to the contrary "have no basis in fact or scientific legitimacy" (Lewis 1998).

Laws do not prevent companies from labeling a product as natural even when it contains some synthetic ingredients, such as artificial colors and fragrances. Consumer advocates say, therefore, that people must read labels carefully to know the contents of a specific product.

See also: Advertising; Africa; African Americans; Allergic Reactions; Animal Testing; Clairol; Egypt, Ancient; Elizabethan Era; Fawcett, Farrah; Fragrance; Greece, Ancient; Hair Color; Mesopotamia; Middle Ages; Renaissance Europe; Roman Empire; Shampoo; Walker, Madam C. J.

Further Reading: "Aubrey the Company," www.aubreyorganics.com; Begoun, Paula, *The Beauty Bible*, 2nd ed. (2002); Begoun, Paula, *Don't Go Shopping for Hair Care Products without Me* (2004); The Body Shop Team, *The Body Shop Book* (1994); Lewis, Carol, "Clearing Up Cosmetic Confusion," *FDA Consumer*, May–June 1998, http://www.fda.gov/fdac/features/1998/398_cosm.html.

NESSLER, KARL *See* Permanent Wave

NESTLE, CHARLES *See* Permanent Wave

NODA, ALICE SAE TESHIMA (1894–1964)

Entrepreneur Alice Sae Teshima Noda developed a chain of beauty salons in Hawaii and brought the hairstyles and beauty culture of the "flapper era" to her homeland during the 1920s.

Noda's parents, who were Japanese immigrant laborers, arrived in Hawaii in 1909 and worked on a plantation until they could afford to buy land for their own pineapple business. After graduating from high school, Noda attended the Hawaii Japanese Language School, where she met her future husband, Steere Noda, with whom she would eventually have four children.

After pursuing a career as a dental hygienist, Noda became interested in health and hygiene. She began working part-time in beauty culture and earned her salon certification. In 1923, Noda opened a salon in Honolulu, which became so successful that she was able to expand her business into a chain of four popular salons.

Noda traveled to New York City in 1927 to study new techniques in hair care and cosmetics at the Nestle Institute of Hair Dyeing and the Emile Shoree School of Facial Beauty Culture. When she returned to Hawaii, her salon business continued to thrive as customers came for the new bobbed hairstyles and flapper look that had swept the mainland during the 1920s.

By then, Noda was regarded as Hawaii's foremost expert in her field, and she was appointed first examiner of the Territorial Board of Beauty Culture. In 1930, she was elected president of the Honolulu Hairdressers and Cosmetologists Association. Noda also was active in various civic organizations, such as the Girl Scouts and League of Women Voters.

Noda expanded her salon business to Tokyo, Japan, in 1936. As was true in Hawaii, her clientele included celebrities and women of different nationalities who were affiliated with foreign embassies in Japan. Noda was credited with bringing Western hairstyling techniques, including the use of permanent waves, to Japan. In turn, she learned more about traditional Japanese methods of caring for the skin and hair. She sold her Tokyo salon in 1941 as war between Japan and the United States became imminent.

Noda continued to be active in Hawaiian business and civic affairs until her death in 1964. Known for her energy and personal charisma, she also was regarded as a role model for young Hawaiian women who hoped to pursue careers.

See also: Bob, The; Flappers; Japan; Salons, Hair and Beauty

Further Reading: "Famed Asahi Ball Club Celebrates Centennial," *Honolulu Advertiser*, September 12, 2005, http://the.honoluluadvertiser.com/article/2005/Sep/12/ln/FP509120333.html; Peterson, Barbara Bennett, "Alice Sae Teshima Noda," American National Biography, http:www.anb.org/articles/20/20-01408-article.html.

NORMANT, SERGE (1966–)

Serge Normant, one of the world's leading hairstylists, is known for his creative work with individual clients and in fashion work. Clients praise his ability to find a style that flatters each individual woman rather than following a trend or satisfying his own ego. Says Normant, "My philosophy is not about putting my mark. It's not important for me that when someone sees a picture, they know it's a Serge Normant hairdo" (Wulff and Paley 2004, 115–116).

Born in Paris, Normant was the son of a military officer who encouraged his son to pursue a career in medicine or a similar profession. Serge, however, became interested in hairdressing at an early age, and he began cutting and styling the hair of his mother and other female relatives.

Normant began his formal career at the Bruno Pattini Salon in Paris, and by age eighteen, he was working at the prestigious Jacques Dessange salon. As he mastered his craft and revealed a distinctive talent, Normant attracted more prominent clients. He was asked to serve as a stylist for women who performed on French television.

When he was twenty-one, Normant moved to New York to work at the Jacques Dessange salon in Manhattan. Important clients began to request his services for special events and photo shoots. Normant was able to launch a new career as a freelance stylist. His celebrity clients have included Jennifer Aniston, Susan Sarandon, Sharon Stone, Kate Hudson, Beyonce Knowles, Julianne Moore, Julia Roberts, and Sarah Jessica Parker. In September 2004, he contracted to train stylists at the John Frieda salon in New York City and to see clients by appointment there.

Normant's first book, *Femme Fatale*, was published in 2001. It describes the history of hairstyles during the twentieth century and features contemporary celebrities posing as famous women of the past. In 2004, Normant's second book, *Metamorphosis*, was published. In it, Normant describes techniques that he uses to transform the hair of various clients to produce special looks.

See also: Hairdressing

Further Reading: Normant, Serge, *Metamorphosis* (2004); Normant, Serge, et al., *Femme Fatale* (2001); Wulff, Jennifer, and Rebecca Paley, "Mane Attraction," *People*, September 13, 2004, 115–116.

NUBA

The Nuba, who live in mountains located in the Sudan region of Africa, have a tradition of paying special attention to the hair, which they imbue with spiritual significance. The Nuba shave off their facial hair, believing that this is an important way to distinguish humans from other species.

Hair care and styles change as people age. When Nuba babies reach the age of about one month, or when they have enough hair on their heads, they receive their first haircut. The style depends on the child's clan membership.

At the time of puberty, Nuba boys get a haircut in the shape of a small skull-cap with a small knot of longer hair called a *rum*. This section is used to anchor different kinds of decorations on the head. A young man's hairstyle changes as he grows from age nine to seventeen, and the skullcap of hair grows longer.

From ages seventeen to twenty-three, a Nuba man is allowed to grow his hair over a larger section of the head. Two strips of the scalp are shaved from the *rum* to the face. These strips are gradually widened as the man ages, resulting in a triangular-shaped design on the hair. At age thirty, men stop wearing the *rum* strip, and at age forty-five, they shave their heads completely.

The Nuba groom their hair with beeswax, and they pay special attention to grooming and hair care during the time they are searching for a mate. They place beeswax on top of the hair rather than rubbing it in, then create textural designs with a stick. Dust made from red and yellow ochre is added for color, and they also may adorn their hair with ribbons, feathers, thorns, pods, and/or herbs. When these materials look worn, they are removed and replaced with new ones.

Since the Nuba perceive hair as a vulnerable spot on the body, they handle it carefully and bury loose hair. One Nuba superstition says that stepping on hair will cause bad luck. They also take care to prevent an enemy from touching their hair, since this, too, is thought to bring bad luck. During the months after someone dies, people perform special hair care rituals to ward off evil spirits.

See also: Africa; Coming of Age

Further Reading: Faris, James C., *Nuba Personal Art* (1972).

O

OCCUPATIONS

Hairstyles have been used to denote the wearer's role or occupation. Since ancient times, people engaged in certain occupations have been expected to follow rules that dictated their hairstyles while in uniform or on the job. In some societies, a hairstyle enabled people to immediately identify the status or occupation of the wearer. For example, in the **Roman Empire**, male slaves were expected to shave their heads to set them apart from other men. Slaves in other cultures also could be recognized by their shaved heads or very short hair. At times when beards were in style, male slaves in the Roman Empire were forced to shave; when beards were not in style, slaves were forced to wear them. At the top of the social order, the only Roman entitled to wear a laurel wreath around his head as a sign of his office was the emperor. Yet another Roman law said that prostitutes must reveal their trade by bleaching their hair blond or wearing a blond wig.

Members of the clergy often have worn their hair in specified ways to show that they belonged to a monastic community or religious order. These hairstyles identified them to other members of the community as well as symbolizing their vows. The style of the haircut also sometimes showed the type of religious order to which they belonged. For example, monks in the British Isles wore a different type of tonsure than those in Italy.

Some hairstyles have been regulated for practical reasons, such as when Alexander the Great had his troops shave off their **beards** so that enemy soldiers could not grab them during a battle. Males of the Manchus, a tribe that lived in northeastern China, found that a shaved forehead worked well with their lifestyle. It kept their hair out of their faces while they rode through mountainous terrain on horseback. The hairstyle also was meant to signify the unity of the group.

In more recent years, many occupation-related hairstyle rules or regulations have been more concerned with safety or with the image of the company or type of business. Hygiene prompted rules about the use of the **hair nets** for people in food-service occupations. People who entered the nursing profession or became airline stewardesses (forerunners of today's flight attendants) before the 1970s often were compelled to wear their hair above the collar and in a style that was approved to work with uniform caps.

After more men started wearing longer hair in the 1970s, some professions, such as firefighting and law enforcement, developed rules for maintaining safety while allowing people some freedom in their personal appearance.

Sports is an area in which certain hairstyles have prevailed, often because they were easier to manage or helped the wearer to be more comfortable and able to see and move freely during the sport. For that reason, women athletes with longish hair often tied it into a ponytail or put it in an upswept hairstyle. Since long hair became more fashionable for Western males during the late 1960s, male athletes have been wearing ponytails, too. Tennis player Andre Agassi wore this style during his early career.

Some sports, such as baseball, have had unwritten rules about hair and facial hair. Such rules were relaxed after members of the Oakland Athletics formed the **"Mustache Gang"** in the 1970s. During the 1940s, the people who organized the All-American Girls Professional Baseball League required the players to maintain a look they considered "feminine." The players' handbook contained instructions telling the women how to take care of their hair and maintain certain styles:

> One of the most noticeable attributes of a girl is her hair, woman's crowning glory. No matter the features, the clothes, the inner charm or personality, they can all suffer beneath a sloppy or stringy coiffure . . . . Neatness is the first and greatest requirement. Arrange your hair neatly in a manner that will best retain its natural style despite vigorous play. Off the diamond, you can readily arrange it in a softer and more feminine style, if you wish. (All American Girls Professional Baseball League)

Some employees have come into conflict with their employers regarding hairstyles. One recent case involved Janel Rankins, who worked at the historical tourist attraction Colonial Williamsburg in Virginia. Rankins, an African American, had bleached her hair blond, and employers said that violated their ban on "extreme dye jobs." Colonial Williamsburg asks employees to personify their "living history" concept and look like eighteenth-century Americans. Rankins contended that her hair color is not unnatural, since blond hair does occur in nature. She pointed out that other women at her job who are Caucasians also have dyed-blond hair.

See also: Beards, Men's; Charm Schools; Hair Net; Hairstyles, Twentieth-Century; Laws and Regulations; Monastic Styles; Mustache; Religion and Hair

Further Reading: All American Girls Professional Baseball League (AAGPBL), http://www.aagpbl.org/league/charm.cfm#beauty; Bergman, Ron, *Mustache Gang* (1973); Crossley, Pamela Kyle, *The Manchus* (2002); Spencer, Jim, "Argument over Dyed Hair Is a Tangled Mess," http://www.digitalcity.com/hamptonroads/hampton_issues/main.adp#story.

OUIDAD

Ouidad founded a salon and the successful line of hair care products that bear her name. These products are designed for people with curly or frizzy hair, and Ouidad has become known as the "Queen of Curl." Ouidad has said that women should learn to live with and enjoy their curly hair rather than fight it: "It's a gift, not a curse."

A native of Beirut, Lebanon, Ouidad grew up with an interest in hair care, and she experimented with ways to style her own thick, curly hair as well as the hair of various family members. While attending beauty school in Lebanon, she had a special interest in chemistry and the growth and characteristics of hair.

When civil war broke out in Lebanon in 1970, her family emigrated to the United States. There, Ouidad finished her undergraduate studies and worked in a hair salon. During the summers, she studied and practiced her craft as an apprentice stylist in salons located in Sicily, London, and Paris. After working at England's famous Chadwick Salon, she decided to relocate to New York City during the late 1970s. There, Ouidad began styling hair for the women who appeared in top fashion and beauty magazines. Her work for *Harper's Bazaar, Elle, Vogue*, and other publications gained Ouidad a reputation in her industry as an expert on curly and frizzy hair.

In 1983, shortly after her marriage, Ouidad opened her own New York City salon in partnership with her husband. Now a mother of two children, Ouidad has continued to expand her business to include new services and products. Ouidad products are formulated to address the special needs of curly hair, which is more fragile and more easily damaged than straight hair.

Women from all over the United States and around the world visit Ouidad's Manhattan salon, where stylists work exclusively on curly hair. Her clients have included **Sarah Jessica Parker**, Julia Roberts, and Nicole Kidman. Many customers come from Mediterranean countries, where naturally wavy or curly hair is quite common, and many African American women also use her products. Ouidad stylists are trained to use haircutting techniques that she developed to avoid clumped areas in the hair. This patented method is called the "carving and slicing method." By 2004, the business had grown so that Ouidad moved into a salon five times larger than her original salon.

See also: Salons, Hair and Beauty

Further Reading: Haddad, Ann, "New York Loves Lebanese Hair Stylist," *The Daily Star* (Lebanon), May 25, 2004, http://www.dailystar.com.lb/article.asp?edition_id=10&categ_id=4&article_id=4344; Ouidad, *Curl Talk* (2002); Schuck, Jill, "A Curl's Best Friend," *Platinum* magazine, July 2002, reprinted at http://www.ouidad.com/news_and_events/press_magazines_detail.asp?detail=320&start=92.

OVERTON, ANTHONY (1864–1946)

Entrepreneur Anthony Overton founded a successful personal grooming products business. The son of former slaves, Overton was born in 1865 in Monroe, Louisiana. His family moved to Kansas after the Civil War ended, and Overton attended public schools. As a teenager, he worked in a dry goods store, and within a few years he started his own small business as a green grocer. Overton used the money he saved from that business to attend Washburn College in Topeka, Kansas. After he received his bachelor of laws degree in 1888, he practiced law for a few years and then served as a judge.

Hoping to use his creativity and skills to develop his own business, Overton studied manufacturing, retailing, and marketing practices, and he observed how various businesses grew and became profitable. He used his savings of about

$2,000 to move to Kansas City, Missouri, where he founded the Overton Hygienic Manufacturing Company, which produced and sold a product called Hygienic Pet Baking Powder.

Overton developed hair products and cosmetics that were expressly designed for African American women. Agents were recruited and trained to sell his High Brown line of products and fragrances directly to consumers. Sales of High Brown products steadily grew in the United States, and Overton began selling to international markets, including Japan, Egypt, and Liberia. In 1911, he moved his company to Chicago, where he built factories and a larger headquarters. Within a year, Overton's company offered fifty-two products, and by 1915, that number increased to sixty-two. The company was earning more than $1 million annually in 1921.

With the profits from his business, Overton could develop more enterprises. In 1916, he founded a magazine, *The Half-Century*, devoted to African American issues and interests. Overton promoted his beliefs in racial pride, self-help, and full civil liberties for people of color.

In addition, he founded a bank, newspaper, and life insurance company. His four-story building in Chicago housed the offices for his Overton Hygienic Manufacturing Company, Victory Life Insurance Company, the *Chicago Bee* newspaper, and the Douglass National Bank, the first nationally chartered bank to be founded by African Americans (Overton and his partner, Pearl Chavers). He also leased office space to African American entrepreneurs so that they could found their own businesses.

The Great Depression of the 1930s adversely affected Overton's company, and his bank folded in 1932. Although he suffered financial losses, Overton still was able to support himself comfortably until he died in 1946.

See also: African Americans

Further Reading: *Issues & Views*, "Anthony Overton: Born Entrepreneur," 1997; Poinsett, Alex, "Unsung Black Business Giants," *Ebony*, March 1990, 96–99; Silverman, Robert Mark, "The Effects of Racism and Racial Discrimination on Minority Business Development," *Journal of Social History* 31 (1998): 571.

P

PAINT *See* Hair Color; Hairstyles, Twentieth-Century; Punk

PALMER, JOE (1788–1875)

During the nineteenth century, Joe Palmer was ostracized and attacked for wearing a beard at a time when clean-shaven faces were in fashion.

In 1830, forty-two-year-old Palmer, who was married and the father of a son, moved from his farm to the village of Fitchburg, Massachusetts. Palmer's father was a Revolutionary War veteran, and he himself had fought in the War of 1812. Soon after he arrived in Fitchburg, Palmer was criticized and ridiculed for not shaving his facial hair. Although men in America had worn **beards** in early colonial days and on the frontier, by about 1720, American men had stopped wearing beards. This trend continued into the 1800s.

Palmer's beard made him conspicuous among the other clean-shaven men in the community. Though his character and citizenship were not in dispute, other people verbally attacked him and avoided both him and his son Thomas. Children threw stones when he passed by, and crowds jeered at him in public. The local minister even criticized him, but Palmer continued to attend church. Some people said that Palmer should be arrested for wearing what they called "a monstrosity." At one point, a group of four men grabbed him and tried to shave off his beard. Palmer managed to get away by fighting back, but was later arrested and charged with "unprovoked assault." When he called the fine unjust and refused to pay it, Palmer was jailed for more than a year.

During his imprisonment, Palmer wrote letters that his son smuggled out of the jail and sent to newspapers around the state. These letters described the poor conditions in the prison and Palmer's plight. He began to gather public support, and the local sheriff let him leave the jail because officials feared Palmer would become a martyr. When Palmer refused, on grounds of principle, his jailers physically carried him out to the street.

By the time he left the jail, Palmer was known as the "Bearded Prisoner of Worcester." His beard had become famous outside New England, and people in the community left him alone. Palmer pursued his life as an intellectual and abolitionist and worked with people in the temperance movement to abolish alcohol. His friends and scholarly associates included Ralph Waldo Emerson, Henry Thoreau, and Bronson Alcott, whose daughter, the famous author Louisa May Alcott, later based one of her characters on Palmer: Moses White in her novel *Transcendental Wild Oats.*

During the last twenty years of his life, Palmer lived with his wife and family on a farm in central Massachusetts called Fruitlands. This was the site of a failed utopian commune that had been organized by Bronson Alcott. There, he entertained friends and others who wanted to meet him or see his famous beard.

During Palmer's later years, beards came back into fashion. The change began during the Civil War years (1861–1865). President Abraham Lincoln wore a beard at his inauguration in 1861 and continued to wear a beard until he was assassinated. The leaders of the opposing armies in the Civil War, generals Ulysses S. Grant and Robert E. Lee, wore beards. Other men in various socio-economic groups embraced beards and mustaches, too.

After Palmer died in 1875, he was buried in North Leominster, not far from Fitchburg. His monument, which measures nearly six feet tall, features a white marble medallion with a carving of Palmer's full-bearded head. The legend below reads: "Persecuted for Wearing the Beard."

See also: Beards, Men's; Facial Hair; Laws and Regulations

Further Reading: Holbrook, Stewart, "The Beard of Joseph Palmer," *The American Scholar*, Autumn 1944, 455–458; "The Palmer Grave," http://edutel.musenet.org:8042/gravenet/grave_palmer.html; Wright, Les, ed. *The Bear Book II* (2001).

PARKER, SARAH JESSICA (1965–)

Actress and producer Sarah Jessica Parker became a fashion and hairstyle icon during the 1990s. Her signature looks included both long and short casual, curly styles; straight and sleek looks; and the various upswept hairstyles she wears for "red carpet" appearances at the Emmy Awards and other award shows.

Parker was born in Nelsonville, Ohio, the fourth of eight children that included three full siblings and four half siblings. At an early age, she began studying ballet and singing, as did several of her siblings, and she soon became a child actress. Her parents divorced shortly after she was born, and her mother remarried.

After the family moved to New Jersey in 1976, Parker landed her first Broadway role in a play called *The Innocents*. She and four of her siblings performed in the national touring cast of *The Sound of Music*. Then, in 1979, she became the third actress to play the coveted title role in the Broadway hit *Annie*. After a year in that role, she performed in other plays until she moved to California in 1982 for a role in the TV series *Square Pegs*.

"Beauty draws us with a single hair."
ALEXANDER POPE (1688–1744), English poet

When the series ended, Parker began appearing in various feature films, moving from supporting roles to larger roles opposite well-known actors. Parker also continued her stage career and received a Drama Desk Award nomination for Best Actress for her role in the play *Sylvia*. She performed in the hit musical *How to Succeed in Business without Really Trying* with Matthew Broderick, whom she married in 1997. Their son, James, was born in 2003.

Parker achieved major celebrity status in her role as Carrie on the hit HBO television series *Sex and the City*. Since the series began in 1998, Parker has won two Golden Globes and an Emmy as Best Actress, and the series has also won several awards as best comedy series. Women copied Carrie's flowing, casual golden curls, a style that suited Parker's naturally curly hair. Another trend she popularized was intentional root lines—letting natural-colored hair show at the roots while the rest of the hair is lightened or highlighted. During the later seasons, she wore shorter curled or waved hairstyles as well as both long and short straight hairstyles. While she was pregnant, Parker avoided using hair dyes or straightening chemicals.

Sarah Jessica Parker with short hair. *Photofest*

In 2000, Parker became the spokesperson for L'Oreal's Garnier Nutrisse hair color. At that time, Garnier Nutrisse was the top-selling hair color brand in France, and Maybelline/Garnier hoped that Parker's popularity would increase sales in the United States. In the December 11, 2000, issue of *Chain Drug Review*, the senior vice president of marketing, Ketan Patel, said, "Sarah Jessica Parker's unique style, warm approachability and broad appeal make her the ideal spokesperson for Nutrisse. She will complement the brand's image while creating increased recognition for Nutrisse and Garnier." During the time she represented the product, Parker used several Nutrisse shades, including a golden blond and a warm light brown.

Stylist **Serge Normant** has created many of Parker's special-occasion hairstyles. In Normant's book *Metamorphosis*, Parker is presented as a Botticelli beauty and as the nineteenth-century French actress Sarah Bernhardt.

Further Reading: *Chain Drug Review*, "Parker to Promote Nutrisse Hair Color," December 11, 2000; Normant, Serge, *Metamorphosis* (2004); Shapiro, Marc, *Sarah Jessica Parker* (2001).

PAUL MITCHELL *See John Paul Mitchell Systems*

PERMANENT (Permanent Wave)

Since the early 1900s, people have been able to achieve longer-lasting hairstyles with a permanent, originally called a "permanent wave." The first versions of the permanent wave were carried out in beauty salons, where operators used bulky equipment to apply heat and chemicals that changed the structure of the hair shaft. Later, salon permanents became less complicated, and people could also buy kits to give themselves a "home permanent."

Early permanents were based on methods used in the textile industry to straighten wool fibers before they were spun into cloth. In 1906, German American Charles Nestle (born Karl Nessler) introduced his newly invented permanent wave machine. Nestle, who had created other hair products, developed an electrically powered machine, which was attached to hair pads that were used to protect a client's head from the heat used to curl the hair. From his home in New York City, Nestle began advertising his machines. Within a few years, these machines had become standard equipment in most American beauty salons.

The process of permanent waving took about ten hours from start to finish. After the operator finished applying substances that would break down the chemical bonds in the hair strands, he or she rolled up the hair on hot, cylindrical hair rollers to create the desired style. Then an oxidizing agent was used to maintain the new position of the hairs.

Permanents were somewhat risky because electric current was less predictable in the early 1900s, and the timing of each step was crucial. The harsh chemicals used in this procedure often caused hair breakage. Hairstylists would quickly hide the broken hairs in their pockets before the clients saw them—a practice that led to the nickname "pocket perm."

In 1928, Marjorie Stewart Joyner was granted U.S. Patent 1,693,515 for her version of a permanent wave machine. Described as a "hair wave machine," it featured sixteen pot roast cooking rods hooked up to a hooded hair dryer. The rods were connected with an electrical cord.

Despite improvements, permanent machines were cumbersome to operate, and many women disliked the idea of spending so many hours in a beauty salon hooked up to machines. For example, to receive a popular wave called a croquinole, women were connected to a bulky machine with heated wires. Clamps covered the curlers so that the machine could deliver the necessary levels of heat. Heat levels had to be carefully monitored, and timers were set to make sure each step was carried out on time.

In 1932, **Zotos International, Inc.**, a global beauty products company, brought out a chemical permanent wave process that did not require electrical heat or machines. This new process was easier and less time-consuming than earlier methods. As a result, more customers made salon appointments for the "machineless" permanent.

Permanent waves became more popular as techniques improved, and celebrities sported hairstyles with curls and waves. In 1936, beauty operators in the United States gave more than 35 million permanent waves. Permanents remained popular during the 1940s, when new cold-wave formulations appeared on the market. Researchers had found that using chemicals such as thioglycolates made it possible to produce lasting waves or curls without heat. Different companies introduced their versions of the cold-wave permanent for salon use.

By the late 1940s, home permanent kits were available for consumers. These kits contained strong-smelling solutions that were used with plastic curlers and end papers. They tended to produce tight curls or waves.

Companies continued to look for ways to improve products and cause minimal damage to the hair. In 1946, Nelson Harris, a home permanent manufacturer in Minnesota, introduced a formulation invented by Carl Koch that was relatively easy to use and less costly than salon permanents. Foote, Cone, & Belding Advertising, Inc. of Chicago developed a famous campaign to market the product, which became quite popular. The ads showed attractive twin girls with identical hairstyles and a slogan that read: "Which twin has the Toni?" The text of the ad then explained that one twin had spent from $15 to $24 on a salon permanent, while the other twin had achieved similar results using a Toni home permanent kit that cost $1.25 (later $2). Toni home permanents became so popular that the Gillette Safety Razor Company bought the company in 1948 for $20 million.

As more people used home permanents, beauty salons lost customers. Beauty operators became so concerned that they urged state legislatures and government agencies to pass bills banning home permanents or forcing the manufacturer to label them as unsafe unless they were in the hands of professional hairdressers. These bills did not pass, however.

In the meantime, in 1949 Gillette sponsored a "Toni Twin Caravan" tour to promote its home permanent. Six sets of twins from the ads traveled 20,000 miles to seventy-six cities in the United States. They rode in Lincoln Continental automobiles with a luggage trailer that was painted pink and white to resemble the Toni box. During the six-month tour, the young women visited drugstores, department stores, hotels, and nightclubs as well as special events. Feature articles in *Reader's Digest* and *Life* magazine described the tour.

That same year, the Ideal Novelty and Toy Company introduced its Toni dolls, which also helped to promote the brand name. Just as the dolls were intended to boost sales of the permanent, the success of the permanent helped to sell more dolls. For the next five years, these were the top-selling dolls in America. Made from hard plastic, the Toni dolls came in different heights ranging from fourteen inches to twenty-one inches, with an attached nylon fiber wig in either pale blond, medium blond, red, brown, and black. It came with a "home permanent kit" that contained end papers, plastic hair curlers, a comb, and permanent solution (made of sugar and water) so that girls could imitate their mothers by giving their dolls a "permanent." Later, the dolls' hair was rooted and made from saran, a thermoplastic resin. Doll owners were told that the hair was strong enough to be shampooed and styled over and over but that they should treat it with care. During the mid-1950s, the American Character company also produced a Toni doll that had a more adult look and also came with a "permanent wave" kit.

In 1950, the home permanent was promoted on a fifteen-minute television variety show called *Toni Twin Time*. During the show, twins in identical outfits and hairstyles would model for the audience members, who were asked to guess which twin had the Toni. Toni's Prom Home Permanent kit became popular with consumers, as did its White Rain shampoo and Toni Crème Shampoo.

The Toni ad campaign ran on radio and television throughout the late 1940s and early 1950s. Millions of women and girls in North America and western Europe bought a Toni to give themselves, or each other, a permanent wave at home. Other top-selling home permanents brands were Bobbi, Richard Hudnut, and Lilt. Some brands, including Lilt's Party Curl, Tonette by Toni, and Richard Hudnut's for Children, were expressly designed for young girls.

During the late 1960s, as hairstyles became looser, straighter, and less structured, fewer women used permanent waves, or "perms" as they had become known. That trend continued into the twenty-first century, although various curled, waved, and crimped styles were in and out of fashion. Formulations for permanents changed during those years, enabling people to achieve the desired hairstyle without a tight, unnatural effect.

Today's cold-wave permanents offer more styling options, including formulas that straighten hair or create various styles ranging from tight to loose. Permanents are made to suit different hair textures and lengths as well as different age groups. The chemical solutions are gentler, with milder scents. Ogilvie and Zotos are two leading brands of hair permanents.

Gillette sold its White Rain division, and, in 2001, the new White Rain Company, the current owner of the Toni brand name, decided to reintroduce Toni products. White Rain offered three improved versions of Toni permanents along with a new product called Toni Weeklong Waves, which was geared mostly to younger women. Other companies, such as Ogilvie, offered permanents formulated to last through seven or more shampoos.

A "perm" played a key role in the 2001 film *Legally Blonde*. During a dramatic courtroom scene, law student Elle Woods, played by Reese Witherspoon, resolved a murder case by figuring out that the real murderer lied on the witness stand when she claimed she had come home after a salon permanent and then taken a shower. Elle was able to break down that alibi by pointing out that people who have had a permanent know they must not get their hair wet for a certain number of hours.

See also: Advertising; Hairstyles, Twentieth-Century; Salons, Hair and Beauty

Further Reading: American National Business Hall of Fame (ANBHF), "Fairfax Cone Ad Samples: 'Toni,'" http://www.anbhf.org/cone_ads.html; Corson, Richard, *Fashions in Hair* (1969); Kurien, Miriam, and Alexis Petrosa, "Sugar and Spice and Everything Nice," http://www.trincoll.edu/~mkurien; Robison, Joleen, and Kay Sellers, *Advertising Dolls* (1980).

PERUKE (or Periwig) *See* Wigs and Hairpieces

PICKFORD, MARY (1893–1979)

Born in Toronto, Canada, on April 8, 1893, as Gladys Louise Smith, the actress known as Mary Pickford was perhaps the most popular star of the silent film era. Some historians regard her as the first Hollywood superstar. Pickford's distinctive blond sausage curls resulted in her nickname as the "Girl With the Golden Hair." As a result of her innocent appearance and the sweet-natured, childlike roles she performed, Pickford also became known as "America's Sweetheart." She later was called the "World's Sweetheart" as her fame spread to other continents.

"Little Gladys" began performing onstage at age five. Her father, an alcoholic, had deserted the family, which included three children, and then died in 1898, leaving them destitute. Her mother, Charlotte, took in boarders and worked as a seamstress, sometimes for theater productions. She became determined that her daughter would succeed as an actress after a stage manager at a local theater offered the attractive young girl a small part in a play. By age sixteen, when "Little Gladys" starred in her first film, *Mrs. Jones Entertains*, she had appeared in numerous stage plays. David Belasco, a New York theatrical producer, gave her a new name: Mary Pickford. On film, Pickford was known for two youthful-looking hairstyles. One featured two waist-length braids, and the other was her trademark long sausage curls. During the early 1900s, new curling irons made it possible to keep a curled style for longer periods of time. Women in Western cultures also began wearing their hair down instead of piling it on top of their head, as they had done during the Victorian and Edwardian periods.

Mary Pickford, 1915. *Library of Congress*

By age twenty, Pickford had appeared in 176 films. In just one year, 1909, she made fifty-one films. She had begun her film career earning $10 a day, and by age nineteen, she earned $150 a week. As her fame grew, that amount rose to $10,000 a week. During the early 1920s, Pickford was earning $500,000 a year, more than any other film star, and only one other film star, actor and director Charlie Chaplin, was as famous.

Fans were shocked and upset when Pickford finally cut and bobbed her famous hair in 1928. She commented, "You would have thought I murdered someone" ("Mary Pickford," *The American Experience*). She had decided to change her image so that she might take on more mature and challenging film roles, such as her critically acclaimed lead role in *Rosita*, which she had undertaken in 1923 to expand her repertoire. In 1929, she appeared in *Coquette*, which was less popular with fans than her "little girl" roles but which gave Pickford the only Academy Award of her career. She also received excellent reviews for other films that she made during the 1920s, including *The Taming of the Shrew* in 1929.

By then, Pickford also had become a film executive, known for her strong business skills and expert knowledge of filmmaking. In 1919, with fellow actors Douglas Fairbanks, D. W. Griffith, and Charlie Chaplin, Pickford formed the motion picture company United Artists. It was the first motion picture company formed by people who either directed or performed in films.

Married in 1920, Pickford and Fairbanks were idolized as Hollywood's golden couple, and many people considered them to be the most glamorous couple in the world. They were divorced in 1936, and Pickford married actor and bandleader Buddy Rogers the next year. She continued to act until age forty-one and also wrote a book and performed on the radio. In 1956, she sold her share of United Artist for $3 million dollars. She devoted time and money to charitable causes, including the Motion Picture & Television Country Home and Hospital, which Pickford had helped to found to aid actors who found themselves homeless, sick, or retired without health insurance or retirement benefits.

See also: Bob, The; Victorian Era

Further Reading: Eyman, Scott, *Mary Pickford* (1991); "Mary Pickford," *The American Experience*, Public Broadcasting System transcript online: http://www.pbs.org/wgbh/amex/pickford/filmmore/pt.html; Simpson, James B., comp., *Simpson's Contemporary Quotations*, rev. ed. (1997); Whitfield, Eileen, *Pickford* (1997); Windeler, Robert, *Sweetheart* (1973).

PIERCING *See* Eyebrows

PITYRIASIS AMIANTACEA

In the condition known as pityriasis amiantacea, deposits of thick, yellow-white scales form on the scalp and stick to hairs at the point where they leave the scalp. These scales form an overlapping pattern of flakes that resemble tiles on a roof. *Pityriasis* comes from a Greek word meaning "bran," and the flakes caused by the condition are said to resemble pieces of wheat bran. The scalp itself may turn red or remain normal in color.

The causes of this condition are not clear, but the condition may occur along with psoriasis, seborrheic dermatitis, lichen simplex (also known as neurodermatitis), and other health problems of the scalp. It may affect just part of the scalp or the entire scalp.

In areas affected by this condition, some hair loss may occur, especially if someone with pityriasis pulls on the comb or brush while trying to groom hair that is sticking to the scales on the base of the hair shafts. Normal hair growth typically resumes after successful treatment, unless scarring results from the infections that occur along with this condition.

Further Reading: Powell, J., et al., *An Atlas of Hair and Scalp Diseases* (2001); Sinclair, Rodney D., et al., *Handbook of Diseases of the Hair and Scalp* (1999).

POLITICS AND HAIR

The length and/or the arrangement of hair have been used as political symbols as well as signs of social status and religion, both of which have been bound with politics. People have worn their hair in certain identifiable ways to show that they belonged to a particular political group or agreed with certain political ideas. Ideas about hair also have been promoted to push political agendas.

In some cases, people have adopted styles that showed their opposition to the existing regime or government. One such example comes from ancient Greece during the fifth and fourth centuries BCE, when a group of young men from Athens, known as Laconisers, showed their distaste for the democratic government and their preference for the more conservative government in Sparta. These men wore long hair, long beards, and clothing styles that prevailed in Sparta, which made them stand out from their fellow Athenians. They were mostly well-educated members of the upper classes.

Another example comes from the **Middle Ages**. The Merovingian kings who ruled in Gaul from ancient times until 751 CE regarded their long, uncut hair as sacred and a sign of royal birth. Known as the "long-haired kings," they did not cut their hair from childhood until death. Other men in Gaul were expected to keep their hair cut as a sign of respect and of their lower status.

When the Carolingians planned to conquer Gaul and end the rule of these long-haired kings, they kidnapped King Childeric III and cut his hair by force. Afterwards, Childeric was sent to a monastery, where he remained a prisoner for the rest of his life. Charlemagne was then installed as the new ruler, authorized by the Roman Catholic pope. A haircut had played a role in bringing down a dynasty.

Hair played a role in the political conflicts between the Roundheads and the Cavaliers in sixteenth-century England. The **Puritans**, a reform religious group, associated the long, curled wigs of King Charles I and his courtiers with immorality, vanity, and corruption. The Royalists, in turn, scorned the short, rounded haircuts of their rivals. Short-haired men stood out sharply among the be-wigged Royalists in London.

In colonial America, as conflicts grew between the colonists and their rulers in England, some political leaders and patriots rejected certain hairstyles associated with Britain. Among them was Benjamin Franklin, who refused to wear a wig, as was the fashion during the late 1700s in both Britain and colonial America.

Changing styles in hair and fashion occurred during the **French Revolution**. Revolutionaries decried the luxurious hairstyles, wigs, and clothing of the aristocracy and wore shorter, simpler haircuts and plainer clothes. They also wore distinctive hats that showed themselves to be part of the revolutionary movement. To avoid bringing attention to themselves and risking arrest and execution, wealthy French people adopted simpler modes of dress themselves.

Some of the women who cut their hair during the 1910s and 1920s did so for political reasons as much as fashion. **The bob** became a symbol of women's changing roles and reached its popularity around the time that women in the United States won the right to vote.

During World War II, ideas about hair and other aspects of physical appearance became a key part of Adolf Hitler's Nazi ideology. The Nazis claimed that people of Nordic or northern European ancestry were a "superior" race and that their features—including smooth blond hair, blue or gray eyes, fair skin, delicate facial features, and a tall, athletic physique—were ideal. In publicizing their ideas, the Nazis sometimes included pictures showing the "right" kind of hair versus hair from other ethnic and racial groups that they considered inferior.

In America during the 1960s, people known as **hippies** were outspoken against the Vietnam War, and their long hair, often accompanied with facial hair, became associated with the antiwar movement. Similarly, African American men and women who wore an **Afro** hairstyle were presumed to support the antiwar movement and/or the civil rights movement, which had gathered momentum during the 1960s. Long hair and Afros, especially on men, became a significant way to make a political statement about the values and politics of government officials and previous generations who had different ideas.

Likewise, women who wore their hair unusually short could make a political statement defying traditional views about women's roles and appearance as well as the social restrictions women traditionally faced. Some leading members of the women's liberation movement, or feminist movement, of the 1960s and 1970s chose to wear very short or otherwise unconventional hairstyles, and some also objected to shaving off body hair, regarding it as a way of oppressing women.

See also: Bob, The; Dredlocks; French Revolution; Middle Ages; Mustache; Roman Empire

Further Reading: Fest, Joachim C., *The Face of the Third Reich* (1970); Gregory of Tours, *The History of the Franks* (1983); Hibbert, Christopher, *The Days of the French Revolution* (1999); Wallace-Hadrill, J. M., *Long-Haired Kings and Other Studies in Frankish History* (1982).

POMPADOUR

Pompadour refers to a type of hairstyle, worn in different versions by both men and women. It was named for Jeanne-Antoinette Poisson (1721–1764), the Marquise de Pompadour. As the mistress and longtime friend of King Louis XV, Madame de Pompadour influenced some political decisions and was a patroness of the arts.

The marquise set a trend among women by wearing tall hairstyles built around a wire frame. To create this look, eighteenth-century French women frizzed their hair to create more volume and swept it high off the face, usually rolled over a frame that was stuffed with straw or fabric. Pomade was used to set the style.

These hairstyles became larger and more elaborate. Women added ornamental objects of different kinds and began using the services of professionals called "hairdressers" to execute their fancy hairdos. A large, embellished pompadour was regarded as a sign of wealth and status.

Since the eighteenth century, the pompadour has survived in different, often simpler, forms. During the 1800s, women sometimes combed their upswept hair over a mound of false hair or other kind of padding, known as "rats." During the Edwardian era in England, the pompadour was the prevailing hairstyle for women, often worn with a frizzy set of bangs named the "Alexandra fringe" after the Princess of Wales, wife of the future King Edward VII.

The male pompadour is combed back off the face without a part, forming a mound of hair above the forehead. The well-known singer Elvis Presley wore a version of this hairdo during the 1950s, as did movie idols, including Marlon Brando and James Dean. Musician James Brown was known for his exaggerated pompadour during the 1950s and 1960s. Since then, a number of other musicians, including members of rockabilly groups, have worn pompadours. Musician David Bowie has been credited with popularizing an updated and more "edgy" version of the pompadour.

See also: Gibson Girl; Hairstyles, Twentieth-Century; Presley, Elvis Aaron

Further Reading: *Civilization*, "The Golden Age of Big Hair," September/October 1995, 29; Hyde, Melissa, "The 'Makeup' of the Marquise," *The Art Bulletin* 82 (2000), reprinted at http://www.findarticles.com/p/articles/mi_m0422/is_3_82/ai_66304031; Pevitt, Christine, *Madame de Pompadour, Mistress of France* (2002).

PONYTAIL

The hairstyle now known as the ponytail can be seen on frescoes painted thousands of years ago in Crete, so it may have emerged in Greece during ancient times. These images show women wearing their hair pulled up away from the face and secured high on the back of the head. Girls and young dancers in ancient Egypt and young girls in ancient Rome also wore their hair in the style that we now call a ponytail.

Since then, people in various cultures have worn different versions of this hairstyle, usually secured on the top of the head or at the neck, although it can also be worn on the side. A ponytail can be neat, simple, and practical, since it keeps the hair off the face during certain jobs, sports, or other activities, and it can be more comfortable in hot weather. It also enables people with long hair to achieve a "shorter" style if they wish.

Ponytails have been more common among women, since women are more likely to have long hair, but men wear ponytails, too. During the Edo period (1603–1868), for example, Japanese men wore short ponytails. Japan's sumo wrestlers wear a version of a ponytail that is oiled and then styled on the top of the head into a fan shape. Men in Europe and the American colonies wore short ponytails during the 1700s, or they wore wigs with a type of ponytail that was called a *queue*, from the French word that means "end." During the late eighteenth century, most men tied their queue with a simple black ribbon.

Ponytails were especially popular in Western cultures during the 1950s and 1960s, when millions of teenage girls wore high ponytails, often tied with colorful ribbons or scarves. This look was especially common among female cheerleaders. Sandra Dee, known for her performances in the film *Gidget* and other popular films for teenagers, and British actress Hayley Mills were among the young celebrities who wore ponytails. Older actresses, including **Audrey Hepburn**, also wore ponytails onscreen and off.

When the Mattel toy company launched its very successful Barbie dolls in 1959, the dolls wore long blond hair in ponytails. Soon, brunette Barbies wearing similar ponytails were available. Another popular doll, Ideal's Miss Revlon, wore a shorter, wavier ponytail than Barbie's, along with curved bangs.

Women athletes have worn ponytails for practical reasons as well as to show their personal styles. As a teenager, tennis champion Chris Evert was known for her sun-streaked, dark-blond ponytail, which was often adorned with colorful ribbons. Many other athletes, including world-class gymnasts and figure skaters, have chosen to wear ponytails. In 1999, new sports helmets designed with a hole in the back for ponytails became available.

Ponytails became more common among males during the late 1960s, as more men grew longer hair. Although longer hair and ponytails became less common among men after the 1970s, some men continued to wear a ponytail, and others began wearing them during the 1980s and 1990s. Famous men who have worn ponytails include comedian George Carlin, rapper Ice-T, tennis champion Andre Agassi (during the early 1990s), and soccer players David Beckham, David Seaman, and Roberto Baggio. Some men have adopted a hairstyle that combines a mullet, which is short on the top and sides, with a ponytail. Fashion historians have concluded that some members of the baby boom generation (those born between 1945 and 1961) enjoy their long hair as one way to maintain their youth and memories of the 1960s and 1970s, and a ponytail gives them a more conservative look for various jobs and other activities.

Some men have faced discrimination in the workplace when they insisted on wearing a ponytail. For example, in 2001, Mark Pell, a twenty-one-year-old British man, sued a pub owner who said he must cut his ponytail in order to work there as a part-time bartender. Pell brought the case to an industrial tribunal, claiming that he was the victim of sexual discrimination. The tribunal awarded him 566 pounds for emotional injury and loss of wages.

New versions of the ponytail arise from time to time that are tied in different ways and adorned with various ornaments. New types of ponytail holders, in the form of clasps, clips, bands, and fashionable elasticized "scrunchies" became available during the late twentieth century. Some ponytails are casual, while others are formal enough for special occasions. During the fall 1995 and spring 1996 fashion shows in Paris and New York, a number of models, including Kate Moss and Claudia Schiffer, wore their hair in ponytails. Singer and actress Jennifer Lopez also is known for a style that sweeps her hair completely off her face into a sleek ponytail.

See also: China; Egypt, Ancient; Greece, Ancient; Hairstyles, Twentieth-Century; Hepburn, Audrey; Laws and Regulations; Occupations; Roman Empire; Wigs and Hairpieces

Further Reading: de Witt, Barbara, "The Big Swing: Ponytails Again Turn Heads with Decidedly '90s Blend of Innocence and Seduction," *Daily News* (Los Angeles), May 16, 1996; Krenz, Carol, *Audrey Hepburn* (1997); Mulvey, Kate, and Melissa Richards, *Decades of Beauty* (1998); Stokes, Paul, "Pay Out for Man Denied Bar Job over His Ponytail," Telegraph.com (United Kingdom), January 13, 2000, http://www.choisser.com/longhair/telegraph.html; Strodder, Chris, *Swingin' Chicks of the 60s* (2000).

PRESLEY, ELVIS AARON (1935–1977)

Rock and roll legend Elvis Presley helped to popularize a slick **pompadour** hairstyle with **sideburns** and a "ducktail." During the 1950s, millions of males around the world copied "the King's" signature style.

Elvis Presley. *Library of Congress*

Presley was born on January 8, 1935, in Tupelo, Mississippi. As a child, he began singing country gospel music. He won his first talent show when he was six years old, and at age eleven, Presley began to play the guitar. In 1948, the family moved to Memphis, Tennessee, where Presley finished high school and continued to sing and play the guitar.

In 1954, using money he had earned driving a delivery truck, Presley recorded some songs for Sun Records in Memphis. Sam Phillips, the owner of the studio, thought he had the potential to sing the kind of rhythm and blues music that had been developed by **African American** musicians, including Johnnie Johnson and Little Richard, who had begun recording in 1951. Two years later, Presley recorded his first big hit, a rhythm and blues song called "Heartbreak Hotel." That same year, he became a film star in the movie *Love Me Tender*.

Presley's musical career boomed after tens of millions of viewers saw him perform on Ed Sullivan's popular Sunday evening TV variety show. Along with his vocalizing abilities, critics said that Presley expressed strong emotions through his music, whether he was performing a sorrowful ballad or upbeat dance piece.

His charisma onstage was enhanced by natural good looks that included a glistening modern pompadour. During his teens, Presley had begun dying his hair black for a more dramatic look. Conservative critics expressed shock over Presley's longish hair, seductive mannerisms, and rotating hip movements. They complained that teenage girls in the audience were swooning and screaming over the "crooner." After one TV appearance, the new star was nicknamed "Elvis the Pelvis."

By 1960, Presley had recorded eight of the ten songs that would later be listed as the top-selling rock and roll singles of all time. He had attained worldwide fame and millions of males copied his look, including the hairstyle. They used pomade, creams, tonics, and brilliantine to imitate the slicked-back, patent-leather appearance of Presley's hair. Teenage boys carried pocket combs that they used to groom their hair in public.

Fans became so attached to Presley's hair that they grieved in 1958 when he was inducted into the army and received the regulation short haircut. Newspapers around the world ran photos of Presley sitting in the military barber's chair. Two years later, this situation was dramatized in the hit Broadway musical *Bye-Bye Birdie*. In the play and subsequent feature film, the character Conrad Birdie, a rock and roll idol, receives a similar haircut when he is drafted into the army, upsetting his millions of fans.

After Presley was honorably discharged in March 1960, he continued to record and perform, and he expanded his film career. During his army assignment in Germany, he had met Priscilla Beaulieu, the daughter of an army officer. They were married in 1967, and Presley's only child, Lisa Marie, was born the next year. The press noted that Presley had insisted that his wife dye her own naturally light hair black to match his, and she wore it in the large bouffant style he preferred. The couple was divorced in 1973.

After the mid-1960s, Presley often headlined at Las Vegas nightclubs, where he was known for his dazzling costumes and dynamic performances. He continued to wear different versions of the pompadour he had adopted early in his career. His friends worried about his weight gain, however, as well as his frequent use of prescription painkillers.

In 1971, Presley was honored with a special Grammy Award for lifetime achievement. He continued to deal with personal problems and health issues during the 1970s. When Presley died in 1977 of heart failure brought on by abuse of prescription drugs, he had become the most famous popular musician and the most photographed person of his era. During his career, Presley had more songs on *Billboard* magazine's Hot 100 list than any other recording artist. In 1986, he was inducted into the Rock and Roll Hall of Fame.

Presley's likeness has appeared on numerous objects as well as in newspapers, magazines, and books. Also, tens of thousands of performers have worked as "Elvis impersonators," mimicking his signature hairstyle, clothing, and mannerisms. Since his death, people have sold and collected Presley memorabilia, including locks of his hair. Fans who wanted to own a half-pound collection of Presley's hair had the opportunity to bid for it in October 2002 on the Internet auction site Mastronet.com. Presley's former hairstylist, Homer "Gill" Gilleland, of Memphis, had saved clippings from Presley's haircuts over a period of twenty years. The mass of hair measured about three inches in diameter and was estimated to contain thousands of hairs. A famous hair-collecting authority verified that the hair did belong to Presley. Thirty-two people bid on the hair, and the anonymous winner paid $115,120.

See also: Hairstyles, Twentieth-Century; Memento; Pompadour

Further Reading: Gentry, Tony, *Elvis Presley* (1994); Love, Robert, *Elvis Presley* (1986); *Miami Herald*, "Elvis Hair Sells for Over $100,000," November 16, 2002, http://www.miami.com/mld/miamiherald/4536571.htm; Shirley, David, *The History of Rock & Roll* (1997).

PROCTER & GAMBLE

A large conglomerate based in Cincinnati, Ohio, Procter & Gamble manufactures and sells hair care products and other personal care products as well as household products, paper products, and foods.

The company originated in 1837 when James Gamble, a soap maker, joined forces with William Procter, a candle maker. The company grew steadily as the two men made good use of the nation's rivers and developing railway system to transport goods from place to place. By 1859, they were selling $1 million worth of products. Procter & Gamble was the leading supplier of soap and candles to Union troops during the U.S. Civil War (1861–1865).

During the 1800s, many people were using cake soap to wash their hair as well as their bodies. Procter & Gamble's Ivory Soap, introduced in 1879, became popular for that purpose. Promoted as "99 and 44/100 percent pure," the soap was white in color and would float on water.

During the 1900s, Procter & Gamble continued to expand its product lines. Its Head and Shoulders became one of the world's leading antidandruff shampoos. During the 1980s and 1990s, Procter & Gamble acquired Max Factor and Noxell, two beauty products companies that produce products for use on hair, eyebrows, and eyelashes. As of 2004, Procter & Gamble included these prominent hair care product brands: Clairol, Pantene, Daily Defense, Pert, Herbal Essences, Aussie, Infusium 23, and Physique. Clairol included several leading hair color brands, including Nice 'n Easy, Ultress, Herbal Essences, Balsam Color, Hydrience, Natural Instincts, Miss Clairol, Loving Care, Lasting Color, and A Touch of Sun.

See also: Advertising; Clairol; Dandruff; Hair Color; Shampoo

Further Reading: Dyer, Davis, et al., *Rising Tide* (2004); Editors of *Advertising Age, Procter and Gamble* (1988); Goodrum, Charles, and Helen Dalrymple, *Advertising in America* (1990); "Procter and Gamble," "General Information," "History," and "FAQs," http:/www.pg.com.

PSORIASIS

Psoriasis is a skin condition in which dry, red, raised patches are covered with white, flaky material. These patches, called lesions or plaques, may be painful as well as itchy. Scalp psoriasis may occur behind the ears and on any area extending from the hairline at the forehead to the nape of the neck. About 80 percent of the people who suffer from psoriasis also have the condition on their scalps.

Psoriasis is classified as an immune system disorder, one in which the skin cells receive faulty signals to grow at a faster rate than normal—about every three to four days instead of the normal rate of about every thirty days. Since the condition is genetic, it frequently is seen in members of the same family and can be passed from generation to generation. Both males and females are afflicted, and about 4.5 million people in the United States have this disorder, which is not contagious.

Psoriasis can be mild (involving a small area of the body), moderate, or severe. Severe cases, in which psoriasis covers more than 10 percent of the body surface, can be both physically uncomfortable and emotionally upsetting. Outbreaks tend to occur in cycles. They may be triggered by stress, infection, injuries, allergic reactions, drug reactions, and changes in climate.

As of 2005, there is no cure for psoriasis, though it can be controlled. Treatments include ultraviolet light, topical medications, and oral medications called "biologics." Since the scalp is covered with hair, applying topical creams, ointments, and lotions is more difficult than it would be on hairless parts of the body. Patients need to use the treatments over a period of weeks to see results. Some doctors prescribe medicated shampoos and shampoos that contain coal tar or ketoconazole. Severe cases require topical treatments that remain on the scalp longer than a shampoo. Preparations that contain steroids, salicylic acids, sulfur, or calcipotriol (or two or more of these ingredients) may be prescribed. People may need to repeat the treatments if the scales do not completely disappear or if they return.

See also: Dermatology

Further Reading: National Psoriasis Foundation, http://www.psoriasis.org; Papadopoulos, Linda, et al., *Understanding Skin Problems* (2003).

PUBIC HAIR

Pubic hair is located in the frontal genital area and crotch and sometimes also the upper inside of the legs, in the area that forms the pubic region. This hair begins to grow during puberty for both genders. For boys, hair growth in this region tends to occur before the growth of facial hair. The purpose of this hair is to protect the skin from injury resulting from the friction that occurs during sexual intercourse and to disseminate sex pheromones—chemicals that are produced to stimulate sexual attraction.

The growth patterns and texture of pubic hair vary from sparse to thick and from fine to coarse. The pattern also differs by gender. Females tend to have a triangular-shaped patch of hair, while men's hair tapers up toward the navel. The color of pubic hair is usually darker than hair on the scalp and usually is more like the color of the eyebrows.

Grooming practices have differed from one culture to another and at different times in history. The hair may be left in its natural state, trimmed, or completely removed through shaving, waxing, or other means. The reasons for modifying or removing pubic hair may be aesthetic, hygienic, sexual, religious, or cultural.

In **ancient Egypt**, people of both genders removed their body hair, and most women in **ancient Greece** removed their pubic hair, believing that it looked uncivilized. Ancient Greek artists did not show signs of pubic hair on statues that portrayed women. Historians believe that by at least 1500, European women, along with some men, were removing their pubic hairs. Some people replaced their natural hairs with a false hairpiece called a merkin. These hairpieces were sometimes made from goat hairs.

Women are more likely to modify their pubic hair. For centuries, women in India and some Arab countries have trimmed their pubic hair or removed it completely. More women in Western cultures, including North America, began to follow these practices during and after the 1960s. Some women remove just enough hair so that nothing is visible when they wear a bikini or other revealing swimsuit. Women younger than forty are more likely to completely remove their pubic hair. A procedure known as the "Brazilian" or "Brazil waxing" removes all or most of the hair in the pubic and anal region. Some salons specialize in this type of hair removal.

A survey taken in 2003 showed that, among women in the United States and Canada, about 30 percent completely removed their public hair, 60 percent trimmed it, and 10 percent left it in its natural state. In India, the figures were, respectively, 70 percent, 10 percent, and 20 percent, and in Europe, 10 percent, 15 percent, and 75 percent. Some women create designs as they shave this area—for example, a heart shape.

Men may also trim or remove their pubic hair. This practice has become more common in Western cultures since the 1990s and has been more common among homosexual men. One survey showed that about 10 percent of the men living in nudist colonies remove all their pubic hair, usually by shaving. Special tools have been designed and marketed for removing hair in this area.

The indigenous peoples of the Amazon basin, such as the Yanomami, tend to pluck out all body hair, including pubic hair. Anthropologists believe that this is done for hygienic reasons, to prevent lice infestation. Other reasons may be aesthetic, because the Yanomami, who often wear no clothing, consider body hair unattractive.

At the turn of the twenty-first century, fashions influenced more people to remove their pubic hairs so that they could wear revealing swimsuits, lingerie, and low-cut jeans without showing any hairs. Businesses developed products expressly designed for pubic hair removal, including special scissors, shaving gear, gels, depilatories, lotions, creams, and decorations for the pubic area. Salons and day spas reported that more people of both genders were making use of pubic hair–removal services, such as waxing.

In recent years, physicians have seen an increasing number of patients, particularly teenage girls, suffering from vulvar **folliculitis** that results from shaving or waxing pubic hair. Symptoms of this condition include swelling, redness, and irritation around the hair follicles.

See also: Body Hair; Hair Removal; Lice, Pubic; Shaving

Further Reading: Alexander, Brian, "Personal Grooming Down There," MSNBC News, April 22, 2004, http://www.msnbc.msn.com/id/4751816; Bickmore, Helen, *Milady's Hair Removal Techniques* (2003); Johnson, Kate, "Vulvar Folliculitis Often Caused by Waxing, Shaving," *OB-Gyn News*, July 1, 2003; Lizot, Jacques, *Tales of the Yanomami* (1991); Robinson, Julian, *The Quest for Human Beauty* (1998).

PUNISHMENT

Since hair has strong personal significance and can indicate a person's social status or religious beliefs, forcibly cutting it off was sometimes used as a form of punishment, oppression, or humiliation. Individuals or members of a community may also punish another individual by cutting that person's hair against his or her will.

In ancient Rome and Greece, slaves could be identified by their shaved heads. This practice showed that a slave was utterly submissive to a master, even in matters of personal appearance. When Julius Caesar conquered Gaul, a region where long hair was much admired, he ordered that the Gauls cut their hair as a sign of submission to Roman authority. Roman officials also shaved the heads of the early Christians as a form of ridicule and humiliation.

In Asia, Chinese Manchu rulers (1644–1912) designated a special hairstyle for Huan men under their control. Their heads were partially shaven and the remaining hair was tied into a braided queue.

In some societies, women who committed adultery might have had their hair cut off as a penalty. This was true in India, ancient Teutonic nations, and ancient **Babylon** under the Assyrians.

More recently, during World War II, Nazi Germany under dictator Adolf Hitler had a policy of cutting off people's hair and beards as a form of subjugation, humiliation, and religious persecution. Nazi SS troops operating in Germany and in Austria, Poland, the Netherlands, Czechoslovakia, and other occupied nations cut off the beards and/or side locks worn by Orthodox Jewish men as part of their religious observances. The Nazis allowed and encouraged other citizens to commit similar acts against Jews. Jewish prisoners and other people sent to concentration camps were forced to have their heads and bodies shaved upon arrival. To further demean their prisoners, the Nazis identified them with numbers, not names, and gave them identical, shabby garments. Those who were not instantly killed endured forced labor, often followed by death in gas chambers, or they died as a result of abuse or disease. Visitors to the sites of these former death camps often express shock when they see piles of belongings, such as eyeglasses, baby clothing, and shoes that belonged to the victims. At Auschwitz, the notorious death camp in Poland, a massive pile of different-colored hair, most of it from women inmates, is displayed at the museum. Hair shorn from prisoners at these camps was packed into bundles and shipped to Germany to be used in various ways. When Soviet troops arrived to liberate Auschwitz early in 1945, they found seven tons of hair wrapped and stored in a warehouse.

After World War II, some French citizens cut off the hair of women in their communities who had collaborated with or socialized with Nazi troops during the war. Their shorn heads were a visible sign of their association with the enemy, and they brought public condemnation and shame upon these women.

In other countries, such as Northern Ireland, women have been given forcible haircuts when they engaged in political activities that upset people in their community.

See also: African Americans; China; Greece, Ancient; Laws and Regulations; Monastic Styles; Roman Empire

Further Reading: Byrd, Ayana D., and Lori L. Tharps, *Hair Story: Untangling the Roots of Black Hair in America* (2002); Ferencz, Benjamin B., *Less Than Slaves* (1979); Hilberg, Raul, *The Destruction of European Jews* (1961); Simon, Diane, *Hair: Public, Political, Extremely Personal* (2000).

PUNK

The punk look originated during the 1970s among young people in New York city and London as an "antifashion," antiestablishment, urban look. It was popular with people who rebelled against conventional looks and had little money to spend on clothing. Punk outfits often were assembled from remodeling worn-out clothing or pieces that came from thrift shops. Chains, spiked leather jackets, safety pins, body piercing, tattoos, and bondage pants were part of the look. Punk was associated with a movement in pop music as performed by American musicians, including the Ramones, Blondie, and Talking Heads, and by British groups, including the Sex Pistols, the Clash, and others. The look spread across continental Europe and other parts of North America during the late 1970s and the 1980s.

> "Uncle Dave is concerned about a hairstyle . . . where the sides and back of the head are shaved completely naked, while the hair on top is grown really long and pulled straight back into a ponytail. Young people, this haircut looks even stupider than the one where you shave words into the side of your head."
>
> DAVE BARRY (1947–), humorist and author

Punks wore their hair in unusual colors and configurations. Many styles featured horns and spikes, set with hair gel or egg whites, as well as some version of the "Mohican," or "Mohawk," haircut. Some punks shaved sections of their hair in unusual ways, or they shaved their heads completely. To create the Mohawk, the scalp was shaved except for an upright strip of hair running across the crown of the head from the forehead to the nape of the neck. Some punk styles featured short hair in vertical arrangements or tall spikes.

Hair was dyed with vivid shades of green, pink, dark blue, orange, red, purple, and combinations of colors. Some people preferred a dramatic pitch-black color,

Two teenagers in punk fashion.

or they bleached their hair a stark white. "Punk" styles often involved strips that towered a foot or more above the top of the head.

Punk clothing and hairstyles were adapted into mainstream fashion. Celebrities and others could be seen wearing punk hairstyles, ripped jeans, body piercings, clothing fastened with safety pins, and other parts of the look. Some people wear punk-inspired hairstyles, vivid hair accents, and fashions today.

See also: Eyebrows; Hair Colorants; Hairstyles, Twentieth-Century

Further Reading: Boot, Adrian, and Chris Salewicz, *Punk* (1997); de la Haye, Amy, et al., *Surfers, Soulies, Skinheads, & Skaters* (1996); Hebdige, Dick, *Subculture: The Meaning of Style* (1981).

PURITANS

The Puritans (so-called because they wished to "purify" the Church of England) were members of a Protestant reform movement that arose during the 1600s. They believed that the English king and members of his court had become vain, frivolous, and immoral. The Puritans valued hard work, self-discipline, sobriety, and simple styles in dress.

Personal appearance became a matter of intense political debate during the seventeenth century. At that time, King Charles I and his supporters, called

Cavaliers, wore long, curly wigs and ornate hats with ostrich plumes and other trimmings. Both men and women wore bright-colored clothing trimmed with lace, ruffles, fringes, embroidery, and braiding. Puritans favored short hair for men and particularly objected to hair on the face. Many Puritan men wore a short hairstyle that led the Cavaliers to nickname them "Roundheads." Members of the Parliamentary Party, which politically opposed the monarchy, were then classified as Roundheads. Most Roundheads were clergy, middle-class merchants, or country gentry.

In contrast to the king and his supporters, the Puritans wore plainer clothing, often in shades of gray, brown, or black, and the men eschewed the single earring that was popular among the Cavaliers. They believed that long hair was meant exclusively for women and that men should not wear hairstyles or clothing that blurred gender differences, which they believed were necessary for a stable and "godly" society. To support their position, Puritan clergy quoted the words of St. Paul in Corinthians, in the New Testament of the Bible: "Does not nature itself teach you that for a man to wear long hair is degrading to him, but if a woman wears long hair it is her pride?" (11:14–15). Women were expected to cover their hair with a modest white cloth cap.

After the English Civil War (sometimes called the Puritan Revolution) broke out in 1642, Charles I was executed, and the monarchy and Church of England were abolished. Puritan leader Oliver Cromwell took over as head of the new republic in 1653 and ruled England for five years. The Puritan government shut down taverns and theaters and banned activities that they considered sacrilegious, such as gambling and dancing in public. They also enforced rules of conduct on Sunday such as banning all unnecessary forms of work, since Sunday was regarded as the Sabbath, a day of rest and religious observance.

When groups of Puritans left England to settle in colonial North America, they formed communities based on their religious principles, beginning in 1630 when the first Puritans settled in Salem, Massachusetts. Laws regarding personal appearance were passed in Massachusetts Bay Colony and enforced during the 1600s. It was illegal for women to cut their hair so that it resembled a man's. In 1648, the general court of the colony declared that long hair on men would not be tolerated and that "wearing of long haire after the manner of Ruffians and barbarous Indians hath begun to invade New England contrary to the rule of God's word" (Simon 2000, 20–21). Puritan clergy and political leaders also insisted that women avoid tall, frizzled, powdered, or otherwise fancy hairstyles. Women were also urged not to cut bangs across their foreheads. Students at Harvard College were forbidden to wear long hair, lovelocks, foretopps, curls, or powder.

See also: Politics and Hair; Wigs and Hairpieces

Further Reading: Allen, David Grayson, *In English Ways* (1981); Hibbert, Christopher, *Cavaliers & Roundheads* (1997); Prynne, William, *The Unloveliness of Lovelockes* (1976); Simon, Diane, *Hair: Public, Political, Extremely Personal* (2000).

Q

QUAKERS *See* Society of Friends (Quakers)

R

RAT *See* Bouffant; Victorian Era

REGENCY

The Regency period in England (ca.1790–1840) was a time of distinctive hairstyles for both men and women. Political events influenced hairstyles, as when some young men in England supported the **French Revolution** and emulated the shorter, simpler hairstyles worn by French patriots. In general, Europeans favored simpler styles in hair and dress during this period.

The word "dandy" was used to describe certain Englishmen who developed a distinctive new style of dress and personal grooming during the 1790s. Shorter hairstyles prevailed, including curled, short hair worn with sideburns. Reflecting changing tastes, men's styles became more understated as they eschewed ruffles, bows, and other adornments and traded short pants for longer ones. This new look aimed for refinement and elegance in the form of starched white shirts, well-cut, dark-colored suits, neat cravats, and polished, simple boots.

One well-known pioneer of this look was **Beau Brummell** (1778–1840) a charming London socialite who was part of the prince regent's (the future king's) inner circle. Brummell was known for his meticulous grooming that included expertly fitted clothing, shorter hair, and a clean-shaven face. One of Brummell's contemporaries, Captain William Jesse, had watched him perform his daily grooming ritual and wrote, "Brummell took a dentist's mirror in one hand and a pair of tweezers in the other and closely examined his forehead and well-shaved chin, and he did not lay the tweezers down till he had mercilessly plucked every stray hair that could be detected on the polished surface of his face" (Murray 2000, 26).

Dandies also stopped powdering their hair, as did many other members of society. In 1795, the government of Prime Minister William Pitt placed a tax on hair powder. Opposition to the tax grew, and within a year, more and more people declared that they would not buy hair powder. Even after the tax was reduced, few people resumed wearing wigs or using hair powder. Legal records for the year 1812 show that 46,000 people paid the hair powder tax. According to author Venetia Murray, these people would have included footmen, coachmen, and certain other servants in wealthy households who were expected to wear powdered hair or wigs.

From the 1820s to 1840, classical Roman styles influenced hairdos as men copied the coiffures of Roman emperors. These styles aimed to create height and required rather dense hair for the desired effect. Hair was clipped at the back, with ringlets and piles of hair on top. Some men wore locks that dangled down on their forehead. During the 1830s, some men brushed their hair forward or wore a soft side part. Other styles were curled up at the neck. Small mustaches and sideburns also were popular.

Early in the 1800s, women wore a simple topknot or a knot of hair at the base of the neck, with curls arranged around the forehead. Both women and men also wore earlocks—curled locks of hair in front of each ear. By the 1810s, many women were wearing a plain center part, with some curls or loops of hair at the sides. Curls were especially popular during the 1820s and 1830s, often forming a cloud of soft ringlets around the head. From the 1810s to 1840, women's topknots were styled higher on the head.

Like men, women added false hair to achieve certain styles. Hairpieces to enhance a hairstyle or cover thinning hair were common among women who could afford them. A hairpiece called an Apollo knot, worn during the late Regency period, was styled into coils, loops, or braids, then placed on a wire frame that made it stand high on the head.

As was true in the previous century, hair was rarely washed—sometimes not for months at a time. Nightcaps helped to prevent dirty hair from soiling bed pillows and kept heads warm during cold nights. Both genders applied oil to their hair. Popular scented hair pomades included Pomade de Nerole and Pomade de Graffa. Decorative doilies and other cloths were placed on the backs of chairs to minimize stains.

Observers noted that the influence of Beau Brummell and his fashion followers did not change the prince regent's taste for colorful, ornate clothing and a hairstyle that featured curls, frizzing, and fluffed-out sides. On one occasion during the 1780s, the future king could be seen wearing pink, high-heeled shoes. Later in life, after he had become king, he did stop powdering his hair. He did continue to wear a wig, which was shorter and more natural looking than eighteenth-century styles.

See also: Beards, Men's; Brummell, Beau; Wigs and Hairpieces

Further Reading: Cole, Hubert, *Beau Brummell* (1997); McCutcheon, Marc, *Everyday Life in the 1800s* (2001); Moers, Ellen, *The Dandy* (1960); Murray, Venetia, *An Elegant Madness* (2000); Severn, Bill, *The Long and Short of It* (1971); Walden, George, *Who's a Dandy?* (2002).

RELIGION AND HAIR

Since prehistoric times, cultures around the world have imbued hair with spiritual significance. Certain symbolic uses of hair—for sacrifices, in fertility rites, in major life passages—have been carried out among numerous cultures. The world's major religious groups also expressed specific attitudes and customs regarding hair for lay members, clergy, ascetics, or members of religious orders. Distinctive hairstyles and practices regarding hair on the head, face, and body have been part of various spiritual traditions.

Sacrifices

Hair offers a convenient form of sacrifice because it can be cut without producing pain or blood. It also will grow back. People in many cultures believed that by sacrificing their hair, they could obtain certain requests. Hair was used in ceremonies that asked the gods for favors, including fertility in humans and animals or good crops. This was true in ancient cultures of Greece, Rome, Egypt, Phoenicia, Arabia, and countries in the Near East.

Ancient Greeks offered their hair to the gods as sacrifice in exchange for fertility and strength. They scattered the cut pieces of their hair into streams, which were supposed to carry the hair to fertilize the land and crops. Greek women offered their hair as a sacrifice to a goddess in exchange for favors, such as the safe return of a husband fighting in the military. Youths offered some of their first beards to the god Apollo at the temples of Delphi or Delos. In some parts of Greece, young men had to offer some of their hair or beards to the god Hippolytus before they could marry. Mariners offered their hair to Poseidon or other sea gods, while military leaders gave theirs to Zeus or other gods who might aid their victory. Hair was also sacrificed at times of death. For example, Hercules left some of his own hair on his son's tomb. Offering large amounts of hair was regarded as more of a sacrifice. People in the **Roman Empire** carried out similar rituals. The emperor Nero offered hairs from the first time he shaved to the god Jupiter.

Ancient Jewish and Muslim rituals also include sacrifices involving hair, particularly at key points in the life cycle such as birth, the onset of puberty, marriage, and death. One ceremony occurs the first time an infant's or child's hair is cut, after it has been allowed to grow anywhere from several days to more than a year. This initial haircutting is regarded as a time when the child is spiritually "cleansed" and becomes eligible to join the religious group. A Buddhist ceremony for newborns in Thailand is called the fire hair shaving.

In **India**, many Hindu children have their hair shaved around the time of the first birthday. The hair is offered as a sacrifice as also to permit fresh hair to grow, since birth hair is regarded as more prone to tangling and disarray.

Cleansing and Cutting

Certain groups carry out special rituals involved with cleansing and cutting—or not cutting—the hair. For the **Yoruba** of Nigeria, head-cleansing rituals are performed to nourish and refresh the head, which is regarded as the seat of the soul. Muslims, both men and women, have shaved their pubic and underarm hair as an act of religious cleansing and purification.

In ancient Israel, some Jews took the vows of a Nazarite, which meant that they lived apart from society to pursue religious ideals. These practices could include leaving the hair uncut and ungroomed until they completed their experience. Modern Rastafarians have taken similar vows and resolved not to cut their hair, leading to the formation of matting known as **dredlocks**.

Among the Sikhs, hair is viewed as a source of strength and vitality and is supposed to be left in its uncut, natural state. Cutting the hair is also criticized as an arrogant act that asserts one's personal will against the will of God. Sikhs also cover their heads with turbans and follow rules about the care of their hair and beards. Some Sikhs feel so strongly about following their religious precepts that they have endured harsh punishments, even death, when governing authorities ordered them to cut their hair.

In India, people known as forest hermits or ascetics do not cut or otherwise groom their hair. They let it fall in natural clumps that show their physical separation from society and their disinterest in social conventions. These ascetics spend their time in prayer and meditation.

The Confucians of Korea also ban haircutting among adherents. Both men and women are expected to let their hair grow and also to control it by styling it with knots or braids that indicate a person's status.

A Vietnamese priest.

Eliminating a Source of Vanity

Removing all or part of the hair on the head is traditional among monks, nuns, and others who join certain religious groups. This practice reflects the fact that people who follow a **monastic** lifestyle aim to let go of materialism, worldly attachments, ego-based activities, and vanity. Lack of hair also gives people more time and energy to pursue the life of the spirit through prayer, meditation, and other activities, and it tends to decrease concern over one's appearance.

According to Bishop Isidore (560–636) of Seville, Spain, the physical removal of a monk's hair had a strong spiritual impact: "By this sign, the vices in religion are cut off, and we strip off the crimes of the body like hairs. This renewal fittingly takes place in the mind, but it is shown on the head where the mind is known to reside" (Isadore of Seville 1970, 271).

Today, some Christian priests still have a lock of their hair cut off as a symbolic gesture at the time they enter religious life.

For Hindus, Buddhists, and Jains, the removal of head and facial hair symbolizes separation from society and acceptance of celibacy. This ritual takes place when people are initiated into the ascetic life.

For related reasons, some religious groups believe that hair should be covered or otherwise concealed. Concealing the hair is regarded as a way to suppress vanity and feelings of sexual attraction that could lead to unsanctioned behavior. Orthodox Jewish women and Muslim women traditionally kept their hair covered. Christian nuns both cut off and then covered their heads with a *collareum* to symbolize their withdrawal from vain and worldly pursuits and their vows of chastity.

Traditions in Judaism, Christianity, and Islam

Many Orthodox Jews still follow traditional customs regarding the hair that arose from ancient traditions and beliefs. Among Hasidic Jews, men wear side locks (*pe'ot*) that are styled in curls. The style may have arisen from a passage in the Torah that bans rounding off the hair of the temples, which ancient Jews regarded as a pagan custom. Jews wished to set themselves apart from pagan neighbors who did not share their monotheistic beliefs. Beards also are worn, following the tradition that sees facial hair as a source of strength and virility. Jewish religious laws banned shaving "the four corners of the face." The first haircut for boys occurs at age three and is a ceremonial occasion.

Some Orthodox Jewish women cut off their hair at marriage and then conceal it with a wig of false hair, called a *sheitel*. Others do not wear wigs but place their hair inside some sort of covering.

In countries where Islam became the major religion, such as those in the Middle East, south Asia, and northern **Africa**, people have followed certain rules, some connected with rituals, for cleansing the body and hair. The laws of Islam require careful grooming of the hair and beard rather than a disheveled appearance, and they advocate modesty in hairstyles and clothing.

With the rise of Islam in the seventh century, millions of Muslim men wore beards to set themselves apart from Christians, who were clean-shaven. Men covered their hair in public with a turban, headcloth, or fez, while women wore veils that covered their heads and faces.

Scholars have found passages from the Koran that mention hair and led to certain customs. These passages include bans against wearing false hair, plucking gray hairs, and shaving the head. Hair should be combed starting on the right side, as was done by the Prophet, and when it is cut, preferably the cut hairs should be buried or destroyed. Women should maintain styles that are not like those of men and should not wear all of their hair on top of their heads.

For Christians, the influence of the Roman Catholic Church was particularly strong during the early Christian era and the Middle Ages. In medieval Europe, the church regarded long, loose hair as immoral for women, which led to styles in which hair was contained and kept under various kinds of coverings. The church hierarchy also emphasized the need for modesty and lack of extravagance.

Religious leaders also criticized practices that minimized differences between the genders, such as curled hair or long hair on men. They quoted from Biblical passages such as 1 Corinthians 11:14–15: "Does not even nature itself teach you that if a man has long hair, it is a dishonor to him, but if a woman has long hair, it is a glory to her? For her hair is given to her for a covering."

Church leaders criticized the use of hair dyes, wigs, elaborate hairstyles, and hair ornaments. The influential Christian writer Tertullian (ca. 160–230 CE), known as the Father of the Latin Church, complained bitterly about curled hair on men. He also criticized women who spent time arranging their hair with fancy curls or false hair, saying that these practices were immodest and disrespectful toward their Creator. Other clergymen agreed that wigs were sacrilegious, as well as vain and unnatural.

In some European communities, church leaders worked for laws that banned people from buying and wearing certain kinds of wigs, hair ornaments, jewelry, and clothing. During the **Renaissance**, clergymen in some communities in Italy organized mass burnings called "bonfires of the vanities" for people to bring wigs and other items of which the church disapproved.

After the 1500s, Christian religious leaders continued to comment on hair and advise their members about styles and ornamentation. In England during the 1630s, the **Puritans**, a conservative Protestant group, set themselves apart from the Royalists by cutting their hair and eschewing wigs such as those worn by King Charles I and other members of the royalty. The group's members, male and female, were expected to wear simple hairstyles. English clergymen advised men to stop wearing the popular lovelock, a long strand of hair that fell down the side of the face. They regarded this as another dangerous blurring of the differences between the genders. Since that time, conservative Christian sects have continued to emphasize the need for men and women to adhere to specific roles that include wearing different hairstyles according to gender.

Some modern religious groups became known for their distinct hairstyles and headgear. In America, they include monks of various faiths, nuns in orders that wear habits, Hasidic Jews, Mennonites, **Amish**, and conservative Muslims. Before the twentieth century, members of the **Society of Friends**, also known as Quakers, also wore distinct headgear and hairstyles that tended to be simpler than those in the larger population.

See also: Beards, Men's; Coming of Age; Latin America, Ancient Times to 1500s; Laws and Regulations; Middle Ages; Monastic Styles; Mourning; Politics and Hair; Renaissance Europe; Wigs and Hairpieces

Further Reading: Berg, Charles, *The Unconscious Significance of Hair* (1951); *Catholic Encyclopedia*, "Hair in Christian Antiquity," http://www.newadvent.org/cathen; *Catholic Encyclopedia*, "Tonsure," http://www.newadvent.org/cathen/14779a.htm; Cole, W. Owen, and Piara Singh Sambhi, *The Sikhs* (1978); Eliade, Mircea, editor in chief, *The Encyclopedia of Religion* (1987); Gregory of Tours, *The History of the Franks* (1983); Hiltebeitel, Alf, and Barbara D. Miller, eds., *Hair: Its Power and Meaning in Asian Cultures* (1998); Isadore of Seville, *Letters of St. Isadore of Seville* (1970); Leyser, Conrad, "Longhaired Kings and Short-haired Nuns," *Medieval World* (March–April 1992); Peterkin, Alan, *One Thousand Beards* (2002); Reynolds, Reginald, *Beards* (1949); Schaff, Philip, *History of the Christian Church* (1997); Segraves, Daniel L., *Women's Hair* (1979); Tertullian, *The Apparel of Women* (2004); Wallace-Hadrill, J. M., *Long-haired Kings and Other Studies in Frankish History* (1982).

RENAISSANCE EUROPE

The historical period known as the Renaissance stretched from about the mid-fourteenth century to the late seventeenth century in England, France, Italy, the Netherlands, Germany, Spain, and other European countries. Following the **Middle Ages**, the Renaissance (from a French word for "rebirth") marked a time of heightened interest in art and beauty, with slightly more freedom in dress and hairstyles.

Several factors influenced social and cultural changes during these years. Thousands of Europeans broke away from the Roman Catholic Church to form new denominations classified as "Protestant," because their founders, including Martin Luther from Germany, protested the policies of Roman Catholic leaders. As a result, the church had less control over matters of appearance as well as politics and religious doctrines. The middle class also was increasing in many European countries, and more people could buy goods and services that were previously considered luxuries for the wealthy. New technology also made it possible to produce glass mirrors at a cost more people could afford, increasing people's awareness of their own appearances.

Sumptuary laws still were in place during the Renaissance in various countries. The purpose of these laws was to maintain distinctions among members of different classes and to curb excess spending. They specified what types of cloth, garments, and trimmings, including **headgear** and head ornaments, could be worn by members of different segments of society. Often these laws were ignored, however, and they gradually disappeared.

During the Renaissance, people still rarely washed their hair or bathed. They might have wiped their hair with a damp sponge or a towel dipped in scented water before combing it each day. Cleansing waters, which were used on both the hair and body, often were scented with rosemary, rose petals, lavender, violet, orange flower, verbena, mint, chamomile, bergamot, myrrh, patchouli, or frankincense.

Rulers, especially popular ones, continued to influence styles in appearance. English styles reflected the preferences of Henry VIII and his daughter, **Elizabeth I**. Both Henry and Elizabeth cared about personal dress and grooming. Elizabeth devoted a great deal of time to maintaining an attractive, imposing, and youthful image, going so far as to destroy portraits and drawings of herself that she disliked. Images of Elizabeth had to be approved before they were displayed.

In Italy, the development of the merchant class and increasing trade with other lands led to the more widespread use of **fragrances** and cosmetics, including hair care products. Scholars translated more classical Latin texts that discussed ways to beautify the hair and body. New books joined these older ones, and recipes for cosmetics and hair products were exchanged and passed on. One popular text, *The Nobility and Excellence of Women* by Lucrezia Marinella (1571–1653) was published in 1600.

Wealthy Europeans could afford to visit hot springs, which were regarded as beneficial to a person's overall health. When frequent bathing was impossible, people in England and other countries sponged their bodies with scented waters. Bathing was more common in Italy than in certain other parts of Europe, so many wealthy Italian homes featured heated bathing facilities.

Small mirrors became the most popular beauty accessories of the Renaissance. People also used various kinds of combs, hairpins, and woven hair coverings. For setting elaborate hairstyles, they used pomades made from animal and plant products.

Women's Styles

Women's hair remained long during the Renaissance, but the styles became more ornate and revealing than they had been during the Middle Ages. Upswept hairstyles went well with the high, stiffened collars and starched neck ruffs that were in style. One popular style, often worn by Mary Queen of Scots, was created by arranging the hair over a heart-shaped wire frame. A high forehead also was much admired in several countries, so people shaved or plucked their hairlines, and even their brows, to achieve that look. A favorite style among French women involved frizzing the hair that surrounded the face. The hair at the back was then coiled and placed inside a net that rested above the collar.

In sixteenth-century Italy, the ideal look for women included long hair, preferably a golden brown color, although some artists and writers also admired very dark hair. White skin and black eyes, black **eyebrows**, and black **eyelashes** were admired on women. Those with light eyebrows used a lead pencil to darken them. Oil was applied to the eyelashes to make them look darker and thicker, while **kohl** was used to line the eyes and create a more distinct lash line.

Renaissance headgear did not cover as much of a woman's hair as the medieval versions. Women wore various types of hair nets, cauls, snoods, veils, bonnets, and hats. The author Agnola Firenzuola, who helped popularize certain looks for women, warned them not to wear too many flowers in their hair, lest it resemble a garden patch.

Italian women wore a special style that involved hair taping, which originated around 1350 and remained popular into the early seventeenth century. They bound their hair to their heads using a ribbon or length of silk or linen cloth called a *benda*. This cloth could serve several purposes—as a cover or wrap or for braiding the cloth strands with the hair.

The use of false hair was quite common during the Renaissance, even though laws were passed against it and clergymen denounced it as vain and extravagant. Strands of white or yellow silk were used to make many hairpieces.

Under the influence of the Dominican friar Girolama Savonarola, who became abbot of San Marco in Florence, first of his "bonfires of the vanities" was held on February 7, 1497. As citizens brought "vanities" to be burned, a large number of hairpieces were cast onto the pile, along with musical instruments, songbooks, playing cards, artwork, masks, magic charms, and other items religious leaders had condemned.

Men's Styles

During the early Renaissance, men's hairstyles became longer and more complex. In France, King Francis I (reign 1515–1547) started a new trend when he burned the ends of his hair with a torch. His subjects copied this shorter look, accompanied with shorter beards and mustaches. Some men preferred a style in which the ends of their hair were turned under. Later, men wore longer styles in both hair and beards.

Styles in England also were strongly influenced by rulers. Under King Henry VIII, men wore more facial hair, in the form of beards and mustaches, and hairstyles were more varied. Men had their beards trimmed in decorative shapes and used scented pomades or waxes to hold the style. At night, men wore special caps or wooden presses to preserve the style of their beard.

During the fifteenth century, French kings and other nobles often preferred a style with blunt-cut bangs and straight hair that was cut near the chin. French King Louis XIV of France ruled from 1643 to 1715. After he began wearing long, thick curls, other men adopted that look, which usually required a wig.

Hair Colorants

Hair color became more popular during this era, and various hair colorants were made from plants, minerals, and animal products. Although wigs and false hair were commonly used, hair dye was used to change the hair color. Elizabeth I was born with a vivid shade of red-gold hair that she dyed later in life, first in red shades, then blond. Loyal subjects imitated her hair color both on their heads and facial hair. In Renaissance France, people pulverized flowers into powder and then used gluey substances to apply the powders to their hair.

Renaissance hair coloring recipes have survived to the present time. These dyes, some of which contained harmful ingredients, were intended to turn the hair shades of gold, red, and black. Men as well as women dyed their hair, and elderly men often dyed their hair to appear younger.

One recipe designed to turn black hair to a warm chestnut color contained a warning: "This is done with oyle of Vitrioll: but, you must doe it verie carefully not touching the skin" (*Raffaela of Master Alexander Piccolomini*, 1968, 71).

Another recipe for bleaching hair blond required the user to mix the following ingredients with lye: pulverized beech-wood shavings, box-wood shavings, fresh licorice, dried lime peel, swallow wort, yellow poppy seeds, leaves and flowers from the glaucus plant, saffron, and wheat flour. Still other dyes were made with onion skins. Before using a dye, people were advised to wash their hair with lye so that it was very clean.

Hair dyes were especially popular in Italy, and numerous recipes were used to color the hair. One major influence in that region came from Italian artists. Among them was Titian, who produced paintings during the late 1500s featuring beautiful women with red-gold hair, which became known as "Titian red."

Venetians in particular were known for their love of hair dyes. Women in Venice attained red and golden shades with preparations made from saffron flowers mixed with lye. Other recipes contained alum, sulfur, soda, rhubarb, turmeric, and/or henna. Women first removed the color from their hair and then added a preparation to produce the desired tint. After applying a bleaching mixture with sponges tied to long sticks, they sat in the sun for hours wearing special straw hats called *solanas*. These hats were made with broad brims but with the crowns cut out so women could expose their hair to the sun by pulling it through the holes while the brims protected their faces. After this process was completed, they rinsed out their hair.

Author and artist Cesare Vecellio (1521–1601) wrote:

> It is customary, in Venice, to erect square, wooden, open loggias on to houses, called *altane*. There the greater part of the women of Venice devoted themselves intensely to the art of dyeing their hair blond, employing different kinds of washes and rises especially devised for this purpose. They choose the hottest moment of the day to sit there, enduring great discomfort in order to achieve the desired result. Dressed in a particular sort of gown of silk or very thin cloth that is called a *schiavonetto* [a Dalmatian-style dress fashionable in Venice in the fifteenth and sixteenth centuries]. The women wet their locks with small sponges attached to a slender stick, while admiring themselves in a mirror. (Vecellio, 1590 [quoted in Lawner, 1987, 67])

See also: Fragrance; Hair Colorants; Hairpin; Styling Products; Wigs and Hairpieces

Further Reading: Bryer, Robin, *The History of Hair* (2003); Burkhardt, Jacob, *The Civilization of the Renaissance in Italy* (2000); Chamberlin, Eric Russell, *Everyday Life in Renaissance Times* (1966); Emerson, Kathy Lynn, *The Writer's Guide to Everyday Life in Renaissance England from 1485–1649* (1996); Firenzuola, Agnola, *Tales of Firenzuola* (1987); Holmes, George, *The Oxford Illustrated History of Italy* (2001); Lawner, Lynne, *Lives of the Courtesans* (1987); Marinella, Lucrezia, *The Nobility and Excellence of Women* (2000); Nicholas, John, ed., *Illustrations of the Manners and Expenses of Ancient Times in England, in the Fifteenth, Sixteenth, and Seventeenth Century* (1997); Paassen, Pierre Van, *A Crown of Fire* (1961); Peterkin, Alan, *One Thousand Beards* (2002); Saslow, James M., *The Medici Wedding of 1589* (1996); Vecellio, Cesare, *Degli habiti antichi et moderni di viverse parti del mondo (The Clothing, Ancient and Modern, of Various Parts of the World)* (1590).

REVLON

In 1932, brothers Charles and Joseph Revson and their partner Charles Lachman, inventor of a formula for longer-lasting nail polish, founded the Revlon company with their combined savings of $300. The company began by selling nail polish before expanding to lipstick in 1940 and then to other cosmetics and hair care products. By the 1970s, Revlon was the largest retail cosmetics and fragrance in the United States, with billions of dollars in annual sales by the 1990s.

Primary founder Charles Haskell Revson (1906–1975) served as president from 1932 to 1962, then as chairman of the board from 1962 to 1975. Born outside Boston in a tenement, Revson was the son of a cigar maker. He had keen business and marketing instincts and the ability to anticipate the kinds of products consumers would buy. Under his direction, Revlon moved from salon markets to drugstores and department stores.

In 1956, Revlon was listed on the New York Stock Exchange, and it became a top international cosmetics company during the 1960s. The company launched its Braggi line of men's products in 1965. Revlon continued to expand its international operations and was selling products in more than eighty-five countries as of 1980.

In addition to its products, Revlon also operated a luxury beauty salon called the House of Revlon. The salon opened in 1959 on the second floor of New York City's fashionable Gotham Hotel. Clients went from a lavish reception area to elegant dressing rooms, where they changed into robes by French designer Pierre Balmain. In the salon's gold-and-white décor, they sat among fresh lilies and other flowers as various services were performed. The salon's hairstylists wore suits and neckties and used gold-plated (actually brass) hairdryers. Members of royalty, dress designer Pauline Trigere, and actresses Ingrid Bergman, Judy Garland, and Zsa Zsa Gabor were among the famous women who patronized the salon. The salon was not a financial success and was closed in 1972.

In 1985, a subsidiary of MacAndrews & Forbes Holdings purchased Revlon. During the 1990s, Revlon reached the position of top brand in the United States in color cosmetics; as of 2004, it ranked number three, after Maybelline and Cover Girl.

Revlon currently offers a wide array of hair-related products, including **hair colorants** (Colorsilk, High Dimension, Roux, and various highlighting kits), shampoos, conditioners, thermal protecting balms, hair dryers, tweezers, eyelash curlers, and wigs. Its cosmetic offerings include different kinds of mascaras and pencils and powder for eyebrows.

See also: Advertising; Eyebrows; Eyelashes

Further Reading: "Revlon History," http://www.revlon.com/corporate/corp; Tobias, Andrew, *Fire and Ice* (1976).

RINGWORM *See* Tinea capitis

ROFFLER, EDMOND O.

Edmond O. Roffler is credited with bringing new, European methods of haircutting and styling to the United States and adapting them to suit American preferences. In 1959, Roffler introduced his technique, which involved using a straight razor to cut and blend various lengths of hair. He taught others how to use this technique and promoted his line of razors and other products.

Roffler already had developed his own barber chair design, which was first advertised in 1950. Twenty barbers began using the Roffler Sculptur-Kut Razor Hair-Styling Technique as the 1960s began. Within a few years, thousands of barbers and beauticians were offering customers this type of service. New tools and methods enabled barbers to build their business because the technique worked on the longer hairstyles that were becoming more popular with men.

As of 1975, an estimated 6,000 barbers were using Roffler's technique. That year, Roffler was inducted into the Barbering Hall of Fame, which is now located in Canal Winchester, Ohio. Today, cosmetology and barbering schools still teach the Roffler Sculptur-Kut Razor Hair-Styling Technique. The styling technique includes analyzing a client's face and features carefully in order to design a flattering, individualized haircut. The Roffler hair care products line includes shampoo, conditioner, and styling gel. The company is based in Phoenix, Arizona.

See also: Barbers; Hairdressing; Salons, Hair and Beauty

Further Reading: "Roffler Then and Now," http://www.roffler.com; The Barbering Hall of Fame http://barbershop.com/barberfame.htm.

ROMAN EMPIRE (ca. 27 BCE–476 CE)

Based in ancient Rome, the civilization known as the Roman Empire placed a strong emphasis on "proper" dress and grooming practices as a sign of character as well as social status, age, and religion. Wealthier citizens spent part of every day caring for their hair, with the help of servants, while people of lesser means groomed themselves. Bathing also was common, and luxurious public baths provided rooms for massage, dining, exercising, and socializing as well as cleansing the hair and body. Roman hairstyles and fashions in facial and body hair strongly influenced styles in other countries that were a part of the empire.

Men's Hairstyles

Roman men began wearing shorter hair and shaving off their beards during the late republic (100–31 BCE) and early empire period (31 BCE–100 CE). To remove their facial hair, they used razors made from sharpened bronze. The cultural imperative to follow these styles was strong. Roman men who wore beards were not admitted to their places in the senate unless they shaved their beards. Slaves still wore beards, however, as a way to distinguish them from other men. Later, they were expected to shave their faces when beards came back in style for Roman citizens.

More frequent shaving and shorter haircuts meant more business for **barbers**, called *tonsors*. Wealthy Romans could afford to retain barbers as part of their household staffs, while other Romans received hair care and shaving services at the local *tonstrina* (barbershop). The barbers shaved their faces with iron razors. To soothe razor cuts, barbers applied an ointment that contained spider webs. Barbers used hot irons to curl their customer's hair. Some younger Roman men began wearing sculpted, short styles featuring curls.

Certain styles aroused criticism from conservative citizens or the political enemies of those who wore such styles. Cicero, the great Roman politician and orator, made many speeches in which he broached the subject of hair and personal appearance, relating these traits to what he considered political failings. In 58 BCE, Cicero described the very different appearance of two consuls he regarded as corrupt. He said that Gabinius was "heavy with wine . . . with hair well-oiled and neatly braided," probably with a curling iron (Everitt, 2003, 152). Calling Gabinius's appearance "foppish," Cicero said that it reflected his immoral lifestyle. In his speech in defense of Publius Sestius, Cicero described Gabinius's colleague Piso this way:

> How horrible was his approach, how savage, how terrible was he to look at! You would say that you were beholding one of those bearded men, an example of the old empire, an image of antiquity, a prop of the republic. His garments were rough, made of this purple worn by the common people you see around us, nearly brown; his hair so rough that at Capua, in which he, for the sake of becoming entitled to have an image of himself, was exercising the authority of a *decemvir*, it seemed as if he would require the whole Seplasia [a street occupied chiefly by perfumers and hairdressers] to make it decent. (Yonge, 1891, 348)

According to Cicero, Piso's appearance, with the old-fashioned full beard and long hair, was deceptive because it evoked traditional Roman values whereas Piso did not support those old values in his public life.

On another occasion, Cicero made a fiery speech about the behavior of young men and women he considered of low character, saying:

> There is the last class . . . the especial body-guard of Catiline . . . whom you see with carefully combed hair, glossy, beardless, or with well-trimmed beards; with tunics with sleeves, or reaching to the ankles; clothed with veils not with robes all the industry of whose life, all the labour of whose watchfulness is expended in suppers lasting till daybreak. In these bands are all the gamblers, all the adulterers, all the unclean and shameless citizens. (Yonge 1917 [an unpaginated electronic work])

Women's Styles

During the early Christian era, women's hairstyles were fairly simple, and most women wore their hair coiled into a bun or knot at the back. They let their hair grow long (unless they chose to cut it as a sign of mourning), but respectable women were expected to contain their hair and cover it when they were out in public. Prostitutes, on the other hand, wore their hair loose as a sign of their occupation and did not cover their heads. Young girls could wear their hair loose until a certain age. Female slaves were expected to grow their hair long until it could be cut off to make wigs for Roman women.

Between the early and late republics, hairstyles for women became shorter and more elaborate. The new styles featured curls and poufs. Some women wore a bun at the back and arranged waves or small curls around their faces. Later, Julia, sister of Emperor Augustus (reign 27 BCE–14 CE), wore a fancier style that required her hairdresser to use hot irons to create towering curls on her head. Elaborate forehead curls also were popular during this time. Around 70 to 200 CE, braids were in vogue, and some women coiled their braids into buns at the back of their necks. During the second century, women wore headpieces made from hair to resemble a tiara. These were woven either from a woman's own hair or hair from slaves.

By the third century, styles were so elaborate that certain servants called *ornatrices* were assigned to do nothing but groom the hair of their wealthy mistresses. They created long ropes of braids coiled on top of the head and used false hair to add height and volume. Wealthy women who had their portraits sculpted asked the artists to make separate sculpted "wigs" so that hairstyles could be changed at will. To ornament their hair, women added jewels, diadems, silk ribbons, and various woven nets, sometimes trimmed with gold ornaments.

Hairstyles and hair ornamentation changed so often during these years that, speaking of one woman, the poet Ovid (43 BCE–17 CE) wrote, "Have you ever winced as you arranged it in a hundred styles? . . . Just think of the horrible tortures those down-soft curls had to endure at your hands. How patiently they endured the rack of hot curling irons as you twisted them into ringlets" (Ovid, *Amores*, 114 [in Rayor and Batstone, 1995, 104–105]).

Younger women tended to wear simpler styles, however. One popular style for adolescents was to knot the hair simply at the back of the neck. For another style, a pile of rod-shaped curls was pinned on top.

Wealthy Roman women usually were the trendsetters. Hairdressers called *matrices* helped them to cleanse and care for their hair, using fragrant emollient oils along with massage and brushing. Other servants called *cosmetae* were in charge of mixing beauty preparations for the hair and body.

Most middle-class and upper-class Roman women owned numerous cosmetic items, including pigment to darken the eyebrows, razors, hairbrushes, tweezers, mirrors, and wigs. They could look at themselves in a mirror made from polished metal, not glass. Razors, pumice stone, and tweezers were used for **hair removal**. Women also made depilatory creams to remove hair from larger areas of the body. It was said that Poppaea, wife of the notorious emperor Nero, used depilatory creams every day. These creams were less risky than the razors of that era, which often produced nicks and cuts, but the ingredients in the cream could irritate or burn the skin. Some depilatories contained material taken from the root of the bryonia plant, while others mixtures were made from resin, pitch, wine, bat's blood, or powdered viper.

Hair Color

Romans used many different types of hair dyes to alter their natural color or cover gray hair. For example, the mineral quicklime was used to give hair a red-gold tint. Walnut oil, made by steeping walnut shells in olive oil, produced a brown substance that hid gray hair. In his book *The Art of Love*, Ovid suggested covering gray hair or turning dark hair amber or red with preparations made from German herbs. Historians think Ovid may have been referring to herbs found in the Rhine district (now Germany) that were used to make substances known as Batavian foam or Wiesbaden soap.

In ancient Rome, blond hair was initially considered to be a symbol of a prostitute, and these women were required to bleach their hair blond or wear blond wigs. After slave girls were acquired from Scandinavia and Germany, noblewomen began to wear more wigs made from their hair, and the stigma attached to blond hair diminished. Women also began dying their hair lighter shades using infusions made from saffron flowers. Unfortunately, some dyes and bleaches caused such severe damage to the hair that people resorted to wearing wigs. People also wore false hairpieces to augment their own hair or create special effects.

Men also colored their hair for various reasons. One ruler during the days of the Republic, the notorious emperor Lucius Aurelius Commodus (161–192 BCE) was known for his vain and cruel behavior. Commodus was rumored to spend hours bleaching his hair, which he wore in curls, to the desired shade of blond. The emperors Caligula, Caracalla, and Hadrian also wore blond wigs dusted with powder made from gold, as well as gold-dusted beards.

See also: Barbers; Beards, Men's; Comb, Decorative; Hair Color; Hair Colorants; Hair Removal; Hairdressing; Headgear; Politics and Hair; Religion and Hair; Shaving; Styling Tools; Wigs and Hairpieces

Further Reading: Balsdon, J. P. V. D., *Roman Women* (1962); Cicero, Marcus T., *Selected Works* (1960); Debrohun, Jeri, "Power Dressing in Ancient Greece and Rome," *History Today* 51 (February 2001); Everitt, Anthony, *Cicero* (2003); Gardner, Jane F., *Women in Roman Law and Society* (1986); Johnston, Mary, *Roman Life* (1957); McKeever, Susan, *Ancient Rome* (1995); Pitman, Joanna, *On Blondes* (2003); Rayor, Diane J., and William W. Batstone, eds., *Latin Lyric and Elegiac Poetry* (1995); Yonge, C. D., trans. *The Orations of Marcus Tullius Cicero*, vol. I (1891); Yonge, C. D., trans., *The Orations of Marcus Tullius Cicero* vol. II (1917).

S

SALONS, HAIR AND BEAUTY

The occupations of barbering and **hairdressing** date back to ancient times. **Barbers** worked both in private homes and in shops or outdoors, while certain servants, often slaves, served as hairdressers within the home. In **Africa**, master hairdressers sometimes served a whole village or community, visiting homes or designated areas outdoors.

In modern times, hairdressers operate in places of business called salons where they offer various hair care services, including cutting, coloring, cleansing, conditioning, straightening, styling, and permanents. Other beauty services include **hair removal**, manicures, pedicures, and facials, among other things. Commercial hair salons can be found around the world and usually are subject to certain licensing, business standards, and other **laws and regulations**.

Although men had visited barbershops for centuries, historians identify a salon in Paris, France, as the first bona fide hair salon for women. Called Champagne, it opened in 1635.

Other salons operated for women who could not afford a private hairdresser, although some began to attract wealthy women as well. The salon of Marcel Grateau, creator of the **Marcel wave**, was among the most successful nineteenth-century hair salons.

As more salons sprang up in France and other countries, hairdressers devised special techniques for cleansing, conditioning, and styling hair in order to attract customers. In England, for example, a scalp massage was often included as part of the shampooing service. Hairdressers also attracted clientele by offering effective products, often made from their own recipes, and by selling these products in the salon.

In the United States, hairdressing salons for women did not become a widespread phenomenon until after the Civil War. Most American women took care of their own hair, or they had servants or slaves as hairdressers. A small number of male hairdressers and an even smaller number of female hairdressers visited the homes of wealthy clients.

Growth of Modern Salons

In North America, the first commercial hairdressing services appeared near the end of the nineteenth century, at a time when more lower-class and middle-class women sought to enter the workforce in jobs that took them beyond factory work, farm labor, or domestic service. A social stigma had been attached to jobs where people had physical contact with others, but these attitudes began to change. For many women, hair salons offered a chance to own and run their own businesses, as women were doing with dressmaking and hatmaking.

While some establishments were called hairdressing salons, the names gradually changed to beauty salons or beauty parlors. Most of these salons were operated by women or owned and operated by families. One of the earliest salon operators was Anna D. Adams, a physician who left that profession because of gender discrimination. Instead, Adams pursued more studies in chemistry and founded a chain of salons.

Most of the women who opened salons at this time came from poor or working-class backgrounds. In 1872, Mary Williams, an African American, opened a successful salon in Columbus, Ohio, that served a multiracial clientele. Madame Gold S. M. Young built a successful salon business in Greenwood, Mississippi. A hair care products entrepreneur as well, Young started styling hair in 1900, using petroleum jelly as a styling product, and her first clients were her friends and neighbors. In 1911, she opened her first beauty shop, followed by the Gorine Beauty School. By 1913, she had obtained a patent for the hair oil she manufactured, called Gorine Hair Grower. Gorine products, along with Young's shop and school, grew into a $50,000 business, which was a substantial sum for that era. In 1920, Young and her friend, Madame Beautchet, organized the first chapter of the National Beauty Culturists League in the South.

One of the most successful salon operators at the turn of the century was **Martha Matilda Harper** (1847–1950). This Canadian-born former housemaid became known as the "Mother of Franchising" after she founded her successful chain of Harper Hair Dressing Salons and beauty schools. At the business's peak in 1928, there were 500 Harper salons around the world. (A competitor bought the business in 1972.)

Annie Minerva Turnbo Pope Malone and **Madam C. J. Walker** were two of the most successful African American beauty entrepreneurs. Starting with door-to-door sales of their hair care products, they built profitable businesses that included salons and training schools. One woman from Indianapolis later recalled, "Before the entrance of Mme Walker, there were no beauty parlors as such, [though] there were a few women who would come to your house to give you a shampoo" (Bundles 2002, 103). Further, she said that the few beauty parlors in her city served a white clientele or people working in the theater. Walker salons continued to operate into the late twentieth century. Walker encouraged the growth of salons in more places, including areas near women's colleges and factories.

In 1911, a Virginia native, Madam J. L. Crawford, opened a business that is regarded as New York City's first African American–owned hair salon. Located in Harlem, this thriving business combined sales of dry goods with Crawford's beauty parlor. Walker opened her own luxurious Harlem salon in 1915. The décor featured subtle gray tones and white marble, with furnishings in royal blue velvet and was said to surpass that of the fine salons operated by white owners on Manhattan's posh Fifth Avenue.

African American women who operated and patronized salons found important common ground as they worked to improve their own lives and life in their communities. According to author Kathy Peiss, "New visions of economic self-sufficiency, personal autonomy, and social participation . . . arose to combat the deepening privations and assaults of everyday life" (Peiss 1998, 94). Women encouraged each other, shared information, and looked for ways to deal with their individual and group concerns.

Meanwhile, other salons offering professional hair care services were opening in various countries, especially in European and Asian capitals. In Tokyo, Hatsuko Endo opened a salon in the main commercial section of that capital city. Endo's business, which began as a bridal salon offering clothing and wedding planning, expanded to include hairstyling services and makeup. Endo salons continue to operate today, including one at the Radisson Miyako Hotel in Tokyo.

Several other women opened successful salons during the early 1900s. Canadian-born Florence Nightingale Graham (1878–1966), who became famous as Elizabeth Arden, went into business in New York City. After opening a luxurious salon specializing in skin care in 1910, Arden asked two hairdressers to offer their services in that facility. She opened a second salon in 1914 in Washington, DC, followed by salons in Paris and other cities, all featuring her trademark red-painted door at the entrance. Along with hairdressing and skin care services, Arden salons offered massage and exercise rooms. The Elizabeth Arden Red Door salon is still operating today in New York City.

Other salons were linked to a well-known brand name in the hair care business. Breck International, maker of the shampoo, set up shop in the 1930s, and **Revlon** opened a New York salon during the 1950s. In Los Angeles, hairdressers who worked in the film industry, including the famous makeup artist **Max Factor**, founded successful beauty salons.

During the early 1900s, salons found creative ways to establish themselves as refined, comfortable places where women could enjoy themselves. Salons operators sponsored fashion shows and tea parties. Ads for salons encouraged groups of friends to treat themselves to a pleasant outing consisting of lunch and a trip to a hair salon.

New technology and other developments spurred the beauty salon business during the early to mid-1900s. Electricity became more widely available, which meant that salons could operate **permanent wave** machines, which had been invented in 1906. By the 1930s, these machines were standard equipment in American and European beauty and hair salons. Salons also featured electric **hair dryers** and electrical curling tools, and they offered new kinds of hair coloring processes. Women also were more apt to seek professional hair care, as they favored short **bobs** and other new styles during and after the 1920s.

In addition, cosmetology developed as a profession, and the use of cosmetics and hair care preparations became more widely accepted. More women continued to enter the workplace, and jobs in the beauty industry came to be regarded as suitable for women. Cosmetology schools opened around the country. Moreover, salon jobs often paid better than other jobs women typically held at that time. For example, a clerk or salesgirl might have earned about $17 a week during the 1920s, while a beginning salon operator could have earned $20 to $30, and more in tips. More-experienced operators could have earned hundreds of dollars per week if the business was successful.

During the 1920s, women in the United States and many other industrialized countries were visiting salons on a regular basis, sometimes weekly. By 1925, there were about 25,000 beauty parlors in the United States alone. The average American woman spent about $150 annually for beauty products and services; wealthier women often spent more than this sum each week. Women also continued to pay for hair care services during the Great Depression of the 1930s, even if they had to sacrifice other things. American women spent $6 million on hair care services in 1936. More schools to train cosmetologists opened around the country during the 1930s and 1940s.

As had been true during earlier historical periods, some critics complained that women should not spend so much money or time on their appearance. Some clergy members preached sermons urging women to avoid personal vanity and to maintain their natural looks without using cosmetics or hair colorants. Attitudes had changed, however, and fashion and beauty were increasingly regarded as worthwhile pursuits. Mass media, the film industry, and companies in the beauty business promoted these ideas. Popular songs even urged women to "stay young and beautiful."

Women enjoyed trips to the beauty shop for social and emotional reasons as well as the practical benefits of a professional hairstyle. During their visits, they felt pampered and cared for as they conversed with the staff members and other patrons. Many beauty shops became social gathering places in neighborhoods and communities. **Marjorie Stewart Joyner** was among those who opened their shops for other community meetings and activities.

By the 1950s, the beauty parlor was a significant part of American culture. Most customers were women, as men continued to see barbers for hair care and shaving services. More men were pursuing careers as hairdressers, too, and many of the world's top stylists were men, as is true today.

After the 1960s, beauty parlors were usually called hair salons, and men and women often patronized the same salons, which featured hairstylists who had been trained to create styles for both genders. Some salons advertised themselves as "unisex." More men also began seeking other salon services, including manicures, pedicures, facials, and hair-removal treatments.

In addition to freestanding businesses, salons often are located in facilities that sell other products and services. For example, salons can be found on cruise ships, in hotels, and in multipurpose stores like J. C. Penney's and Walmart. Some salons operate as day spas where people can spend hours, or even a full day, receiving various treatments and services for the hair and body.

Popular Services and Costs

As styles and trends have changed through the years, different hair care services became more popular than others. In 2003, a survey conducted by Sally Beauty Supply and Harris Interactive, a market research company, showed that highlighting was the number one salon service requested by clients. About 20 percent of adults age eighteen to thirty-four have had their hair highlighted, and 60 percent of them were visiting a salon at least four times per year. Most customers were asking for one change in their hairstyle per year (*Happi*, 2004, 14).

Different ethnic groups differ in how often they request certain services. When this survey was broken down by race, the responses showed that about 80 percent of the salon visits for white customers involved some type of hair coloring service, while 20 percent involved permanents. Before the mid-1980s, those figures were reversed. For African Americans, 90 percent of their hair services were straightening permanents, with various other services making up the remaining 10 percent.

Surveys taken in 2004 showed that, in the United States, the average women's haircut cost about $21 in a small salon (one with fewer than six chairs). In a salon with fewer more than thirteen chairs, the average cost of a haircut was about $44 (Kuczynski 2004).

One notable trend that emerged during the 1990s was the increasing cost of a prestige haircut at top salons. People had taken notice, sometimes critically, in the 1990s when New York's **Frédéric Fekkai** began charging $300 and again when John Sahag raised his fee to $400. A new high occurred when **Sally Hershberger**, who works in New York City and Los Angeles, began charging $600. By 2004, some hairdressers were charging $800. In New York City, Orlando Pita, who has worked with celebrities Jennifer Connolly, Kirsten Dunst, and Naomi Campbell, was charging $800 for an appointment that lasted about 80 minutes. Hairdressers who charged premium prices pointed out that such a hairstyle is instantly visible and that clients receive value every day from an expert haircut. They also said charging high fees is practical, since there is a high demand for their services and time is limited. Critics, including other hairdressers, claim that these fees are too high. Speaking bluntly to the press, legendary hairdresser **Kenneth Battelle** called an $800 fee "an ego trip." As of 2004, Battelle was charging $155 for his services; he also did not accept tips (Kuczynski 2004).

Salon operators belong to various professional organizations. The largest organization for people in this field is the National Cosmetology Association (NCA), founded in 1921. Along with licensed professionals, cosmetology students are eligible to join NCA. As of 2005, NCA had about 30,000 members and all fifty states were represented. NCA provides information, educational opportunities, insurance programs, and other benefits for members, including industry conferences. In an interview in 2000, NCA President Derl Green said, "Our primary goal is to help salons expand their service and retail business. Our second goal, though no less important, is to instill pride in their profession among all licensed cosmetologists" (Salon Channel). NCA has sponsored National Beauty Salon Month in the United States to recognize the work of salon professionals and to help consumers appreciate the value of professional beauty services.

Other professional organizations include the **American Beauty Association**, Intercoiffure Atelier, and The Salon Association. Key industry events include the International Beauty Show for licensed cosmetologists and people who operate a salon or spa business. Beauty professionals from at least eighty-two countries attended the 2005 International Beauty Show in New York City.

See also: Breck Girl; Eber, Jose; Japan; John Frieda Professional Hair Care, Inc.; Masters, George; Michaeljohn; Noda, Alice Sae Teshima; Normant, Serge; Sassoon, Vidal

Further Reading: Banner, Lois W., *American Beauty* (1983); Beer, Thomas, *Mauve Decade* (1926); Bundles, A'Lelia Perry, *On Her Own Ground* (2002); Gill, Tiffany M., "Civic Beauty," *Enterprise & Society*, December 2004, 583–593; *Happi*, "Survey," March 2004, 14; Kuczynski, Alex, "You Paid *How Much* For That Haircut?" *The New York Times*, November 21, 2004; Lewis, Alfred Allen, and Constance Woodworth, *Miss Elizabeth Arden* (1972); Mark, Vernice, *The National Beauty Culturists' League History* (1994); National Cosmetology Association, http://www.ncacares.org; Peiss, Kathy, *Hope in a Jar* (1998); Plitt, Jane R., *Martha Matilda Harper and the American Dream* (2000); Salon Channel, "NCA Plans Second National Beauty Salon Month," http://salonchannel.com/articles/beauty_salon_month.htm; Scranton, Philip, ed., *Beauty and Business* (2000); Smith, Adelaide, *Modern Beauty Culture* (1934); Walker, Juliet E. K., *The History of Black Business in America* (1998).

SASSOON, VIDAL (1928–)

During the second half of the twentieth century, Vidal Sassoon became an internationally known hairstylist and the founder of a highly successful line of hair care products. His revolutionary approach to haircutting and styling sparked a new trend toward "wash and go" hair that required less maintenance than previous styles. So profound was Sassoon's influence that one analyst said, "Sassoon is to hair care what Picasso is to painting" (Horovitz [an unpaginated electronic work]). Former model Grace Coddington put it this way: "Sassoon changed the thinking of hair" (Horovitz [an unpaginated electronic work]).

The man who became known as the "Living Legend of Hair" was born in London in 1928. His family endured poverty after his father left them. Vidal and his brother Ivor spent six years in a Jewish orphanage until their mother remarried and reunited the family. During his school years, Sassoon excelled in athletics and showed a strong interest in health and fitness.

At age fourteen, he left school to become an apprentice at Adolph Cohen's Beauty and Barber Shop so that he could contribute to the family income.

World War II had begun in Europe in 1939, and England had joined the Allied troops fighting Nazi Germany in 1939 after Germany invaded England's ally, Poland. By 1942, the Nazis had occupied several more European countries, and Sassoon had heard grim stories about the mass murder of Jews and other people. Now in his teens, Sassoon joined antifascist groups to fight the Nazis. After the war, in 1948, he went to Israel to help work for an independent Jewish nation.

When he returned home, Sassoon went back to **hairdressing** and studied with two top stylists, Silvio Camillo and Frank Blaschke. Demonstrating his talents, he won several hairstyling competitions during the next few years. He was able to open his own salon in 1954.

Although stiff and sprayed styles were popular during that time, Sassoon disliked the uncomfortable practice of wearing hair rollers to bed at night. He preferred more natural styles that required less maintenance. His innovative cuts, including the torro, bronte, and le swish, were designed to complement the hair's natural texture and move more freely. Each style was incorporated into the cut itself. Women were pleased to find that they could take part in sports and other activities without ruining their hairstyles.

Sassoon's ideas were in sync with the fashion and beauty trends of the 1960s. London was the center of revolutionary changes in pop music and fashion, as miniskirts and other fresh, youthful styles swept the nation and then the world. Fashion designer Mary Quant had Sassoon give her dark hair a geometric cut in 1961 and asked him to create styles for her runway models. He designed artful but simple-looking short haircuts in a style that became known as the Sassoon bob.

Sassoon generated even more excitement with his famous five-point cut in 1964, creating his signature asymmetric cuts. Other Sassoon classics were the angular Bob cut and Nancy Kwan. He explained that he was aiming for a neat, clean line that showcased natural, shining hair. Because he considered a woman's individual features, his haircuts could be adapted to suit individuals. They also worked for women of diverse nationalities and ethnic groups during an era when ideas about beauty were becoming more inclusive.

As London's most famous stylist, Sassoon's reputation spread to other countries. He was invited to design hairstyles for top models who were wearing the collections of couturiers, including Emmanuelle Khan, Paco Rabanne, Ungaro, Mila Schon, and Rudi Gernreich. He styled hair for models appearing in prestigious fashion magazines. Meanwhile, actress Mia Farrow, known for her long, straight blond hair, decided she would wear an extremely short hairdo for her role in the 1968 film *Rosemary's Baby*. Sassoon flew to Hollywood, where he cropped Farrow's hair in what became known as the "$5,000 haircut."

In 1968, Sassoon's hairstyles appeared in the first fashion video, *Basic Black*, which featured clothing by Rudi Gernreich. The next year, he became the first foreign hairstylist to be invited to Le Style de Paris, an elite annual French hairstyling event. About 600 stylists attended the 1968 event, at which Sassoon demonstrated eight of his famous cuts. In 1969, Sassoon visited several countries, including **Japan**, to demonstrate his styling techniques.

By 1968, Sassoon had written about his work in his first book, *Sorry I Kept You Waiting, Madam*. He went on to write two books about hairstyling techniques for professionals: *Super Cuts* (1972) and *Cutting Hair the Sassoon Way* (1972).

Sassoon moved to Los Angeles in 1974 and made that the location of his world headquarters. His salon was known for its chic atmosphere and friendly staff. Numerous celebrities, including singer Rod Stewart, actresses Liza Minelli and Catherine Deneuve, and actor Cary Grant, were Sassoon clients, but he also welcomed people from all walks of life. During the 1970s, Sassoon's chain of salons grew to more than twenty facilities in six different countries. He also set up Vidal Sassoon schools for training hairstylists.

Sassoon's interest in the science of hair led him to work with chemists on formulas for hair care products. He developed a line of products for men and women that included shampoos, conditioners, and styling products. The Sassoon ad campaign featured the catchy slogan, "If you don't look good, we don't look good."

In 1975, Sassoon married actress and model Beverly Adams, with whom he had four children, they later divorced. The couple collaborated on a book called *A Year of Beauty and Health*, which discusses their ideas about diet and exercise as well as hair care. Vidal and Beverly Sassoon also appeared together on television programs, including *Your New Day* (1980–1981), and Vidal Sassoon made numerous other TV appearances. He continued to develop haircuts that had his distinctive look but also changed with the times.

To fund various philanthropic causes, Sassoon set up the Vidal Sassoon Foundation. It has funded social programs and institutions, especially programs to help educate disadvantaged youth, as well as arts programs. The Vidal Sassoon International Center for the Study of Antisemitism was set up to bring together young people from different racial and national backgrounds to promote understanding and better international relations. Sassoon gave time and money to Hair Cares, a fund that helps hairstyling professionals who suffer from AIDS.

Sassoon's many honors include the 1982 Patron of Honour Citation from the Fellowship of Hair Artists of Great Britain. The award cites his "outstanding achievements, revolutionary ideas and creative techniques in hairdressing." In 1982 he was inducted into the United States Cosmetology Hall of Fame. Sassoon was the official hairstylist for the 1984 Olympics held in Los Angeles. Then in 1991, he was inducted into the British Hairdressing Hall of Fame. That same year, Sassoon became only the second person ever to receive the North American Hairstyling Award for Lifetime Achievement. The **American Beauty Association** gave him their award for Outstanding Achievement in 1993. A fifty-year retrospective of Sassoon's work was organized in London in 1992, after which it was exhibited in other countries.

Sassoon hair products continued to sell well into the 1990s and reportedly earned $300 million a year as of 1991. In 1983, Sassoon sold the line to Richardson Vicks, who sold the line to Procter & Gamble two years later. Sassoon also sold his chain of salons to Regis Corporation in 2002, as well as his academy business. He and his wife Ronnie have a primary residence in Beverly Hills.

See also: Twiggy

Further Reading: Fishman, Diane, and Marcia Powell, *Vidal Sassoon* (1993); Horovitz, Bruce, "Vidal Sassoon Takes on a Hairy Fight Against P & G," *USA Today*, July 7, 2003, http://www.usatoday.com/money/industries/retail/2003-07-07-vidal_x.htm; Sassoon, Beverly and Vidal, *A Year of Beauty and Health* (1976); Sassoon, Vidal, *Cutting Hair the Sassoon Way* (1972); Sassoon, Vidal, *Sorry I Kept You Waiting, Madam* (1968); Sassoon, Vidal, *Super Cuts* (1972).

SCALPING

Historians trace the practice of scalping—cutting off the scalp of a human enemy—back to pre-Columbian times in the Americas. It echoes the custom of headhunting, which was once practiced in Europe and Asia. In some cultures, hair was regarded as a center of strength and power, so removing the hair of the enemy was a way to prevent him from causing harm. Bringing back scalps after a battle also showed that a warrior had succeeded against the enemy.

Some **Native American** groups in North and South America engaged in scalping, and their languages included words for scalping, the scalp, and the victims of scalping. Archaeologists have found the remains of men, women, and children dating back to before 500 BCE that show evidence of scalping.

Some scalping involved cutting away a small, circular area of hair while other circular cuts removed nearly the entire hair-containing area from the head. Although some victims died, others survived. Doctors sought ways to treat their wounds, and in 1806, one physician published "Remarks on the Management of the Scalped-Head" in a Philadelphia medical journal.

Indian warrior with a scalp. *Library of Congress*

After taking scalps, a warrior gave a special war cry. Scalps were carried back home on a pole, tree branch, or bow. To prepare them for display, they were dried and stretched and sometimes painted. Scalps often were displayed like battle trophies and served to intimidate the group's enemies or impress other tribes. Some were hung on sticks in public places, while others were given to tribal chiefs or carried on horses into battle. When a warrior died, his collection of scalps might be buried with him or hung over the grave.

In early America, some colonists retaliated by scalping Native Americans during conflicts between the two groups. In some places, bounties were offered for scalps, which increased the practice even more.

Aside from Native Americans, a group of nomadic central Asian warriors called the Scythians also scalped people they conquered. Members of the Scythian culture, which lasted from the fourth to the eighth centuries, were known to decorate their horses, clothing, and homes with hair taken from scalpings.

See also: Superstitions

Further Reading: Axtell, James, *The European and the Indian* (1981); Starkey, Armstrong, *European-Native American Warfare, 1675–1815* (1998).

SCALP LOCK *See* Native Americans

SEBORRHEIC DERMATITIS

Seborrheic dermatitis is an inflamed version of the common scalp condition called dandruff. It appears as a scaling rash that can affect the scalp, face, and other areas of the body. It occurs most often in areas with a large number of sebaceous glands, which make the skin oily. On the face, it is most common within the eyebrows, on the edges of the eyelids (where it is called blepharitis), and in the creases around the nose. It may appear inside and behind the ears and in the skin folds of the armpits and groin. Scaly patches may also develop in the middle of the chest or on the back.

Like dandruff, seborrheic dermatitis has been attributed to the overgrowth of a normal skin fungus called *Pityrosporum ovale*, or *Malassezia*. This yeast tends to proliferate when a person's resistance is lowered by a weakened immune system, illness, stress, fatigue, seasonal changes, and other factors. It may appear anytime after the onset of puberty and is not contagious. People with seborrhoea may be more vulnerable to psoriasis. The plaques that develop in psoriasis tend to be thicker, deeper red in color, and more persistent. It may affect more areas of the body, including elbows and knees.

Cradle cap in babies may be a variation of this condition. It is probably caused by overactive sebaceous glands as dead cells build up to form a greasy yellow substance. Cradle cap is fairly common and usually appears within six weeks after birth. It is treated with a combination of mild shampooing and soft brushing of the scalp, but doctors may prescribe a medicated cream if the condition is severe. Cradle cap usually disappears within a few weeks or months, but in some babies, it persists for six to nine months after birth.

To control this condition, adults are given antifungal agents or topical steroid creams. For the scalp, they may use medicated shampoos with dandruff-fighting ingredients such as ketoconazole, selenium disulphide, zinc pyrithione, coal tar, and/or salicylic acid. They may also apply steroid creams or lotions to the scalp to reduce symptoms. For severe symptoms, people may take oral antifungal medications or be given ultraviolet radiation treatments.

See also: Pityriasis amiantacea

Further Reading: Powell, J., et al. *An Atlas of Hair and Scalp Diseases* (2001); Sinclair, Rodney D., et al. *Handbook of Diseases of the Hair and Scalp* (1999); Verbov, Julian L., *Superficial Fungal Infections* (1986).

SHAMPOO

The word "shampoo" is derived from *champoo,* the Hindu word for massage. In India and Persia, the *champoo* involved massaging the body with warm water and rubbing the skin with herbal extracts.

Today, "shampoo" is both a noun and verb that refer to a product used to cleanse the hair as well as the cleansing process itself. Modern shampoos include commercial liquids, creams, and powdered soap products used for cleansing hair. These forms of shampoo began to emerge in the nineteenth century as more people gained access to running water in their homes and new technology became available for formulating and manufacturing shampoos. Before that time, most of the people in the world did not wash their hair very often. When they did, they often used the same kinds of soap they used for bathing or for cleaning other items.

> "I'm a big woman. I need big hair."
>
> ARETHA FRANKLIN (1942–), American pop singer known as "the Queen of Soul"

Ancient Times to 1700s

To cleanse their hair, ancient people sometimes mixed plant juices with water. The first forms of soap may have developed in **ancient Egypt** as people discovered a natural cleanser called saponin. This substance comes from the root of the soapwort plant, a member of the carnation family, and produces a foam when wet. The Egyptians added animal fats for their conditioning properties and fragrant oils for a pleasing scent. Sumerians found that mixing water with alkali and cassia oil produced a substance that could be used for cleansing.

Native Americans also used the soapwort plant to cleanse the hair, and they used chapparal to make a rinse for treating dandruff. Natives in **Latin America** obtained saponin from the soapberry tree. It can also can be obtained from the yucca plant, which grows in Latin America and the American southwest.

The word "soap" comes from Sapo Hill, a place near ancient Rome where animals were sacrificed. Fats dripped through the wood ashes of the fires into the clay soil, then ran down to the Tiber River where women went to wash clothes. These women discovered areas where the blend of fats, ashes, and clay had formed a cleaning agent. This mixture of acids (from animal fat) and alkali (from ashes) became the basis of soap formulas used into modern times. The Romans worked out new formulas to create more-effective and refined soaps, adding olive oil and special types of ash. A soap factory was found in the ruins of Pompeii, but it is not clear whether that soap was used for people or the process of making cloth.

Other cultures found ways to make soaps. The Latin scholar Pliny the Elder (23–79 CE) wrote about a type of soap used in Gaul that cleaned and brightened the hair. North Africans found ways to combine clay with fragrant oils to make soaps. Other Africans mixed ash, papaya, and fat. People in **China** and Brazil added honey to their soap formulas.

Soap making became a trade. By the seventh century, guilds for soap makers had formed in medieval Europe. These guilds promoted the trade and regulated the training process for new soap makers and soap-making establishments.

Although bathing was not common among most Europeans during the **Middle Ages**, soap making continued to advance. During the 800s, Spain became known as the best source of fine soap, containing high-quality olive oil from the district of Castile. The resulting soap, which became extremely popular during the late Middle Ages, had a finer texture and whiter color than other soaps. Wealthy people prized their Castile soap, known as the "queen of soaps."

By the tenth century, France was making excellent soaps with pleasing fragrances, while Italian soaps were highly prized during the Renaissance. England built up a strong soap industry during the late Renaissance. Although these soaps could be used directly on the scalp or hair, some people, including hairdressers, created a more liquid mixture by adding more water.

As of the 1300s, commercial soap was sold in European stores, but it was a luxury item that few people could afford. Some countries, such as England, also levied a high tax on soap. Consequently, most people made soap at home, or they did without.

Early America

As people settled the American colonies, they rarely washed their hair and used a **comb** and/or brush to control dirt, remove parasites, and distribute oil from the scalp. A full bath was a rare event that took place about once a month or no more than once a week.

People continued to use homemade soap as a shampoo. The process of making soap took hours. First, people made lye with water and ashes from the fireplace or stove. They mixed the lye with fats saved from cooking and bits of leftover candles. Early Americans boiled their soap outdoors in a large kettle over an open fire. As it simmered for hours, a family member was assigned to stir the kettle from time to time so that the soap would not boil over. This smelly and complicated chore usually was done in the spring or fall, and the soap was stored in buckets or jars to last for the rest of the year.

During the slavery era, Africans brought their own hair care methods with them to North America and began using what they found in their new surroundings to wash and groom their hair. Kitchens provided cornmeal for a dry shampoo and fats, oils, and eggs that could be used as conditioners.

Dry shampooing was done with powder, starch, or cornmeal. This was often more convenient than using soap and water, since most people did not have running water in their homes.

Nineteenth Century

During the 1800s, people continued to use homemade soaps for hair washing, bathing, and household use.

Lye-based detergents from ashes and fats did clean the hair but often left a residue. People used acidic substances, such as vinegar or citrus juice, to remove the scum for a shinier appearance. Hairdressers often came up with special formulas for rinsing out soap scum. One popular formula combined lemon juice, potash, and fragrance.

Early manufactured cake soap became widely available during the 1800s, when manufacturing processes using sodium hydroxide helped to make a hard soap product. Cake soaps were used on the hair, or shavings from these soaps were softened in water for a liquid soap. Coal tar soap was regarded as effective for cleansing the scalp, but many people did not like the smell.

By the 1890s, German companies were selling commercial shampoos that did not leave a dulling film on the hair. These popular shampoos were marketed and sold throughout Europe.

Early Twentieth Century

During the 1900s, various manufacturers introduced shampoos containing water, detergent, and other ingredients such as fats, coloring, plant substances, and proteins. Fragrances were added to appeal to consumers, and some people became devoted to a brand because they liked its smell.

Most American homes now had bathrooms with running water. Instead of spending hours making their own soap, people could buy a variety of soaps and shampoos for different purposes and for a reasonable price at their local store. This meant that cleanliness, achieved by regular bathing and shampooing, was more feasible. This became the standard practice for wealthy and middle-class Americans and eventually for all segments of society.

Shampoo soon became one of the most heavily advertised products in the United States. Companies competed for business by **advertising** in newspapers and magazines, using catchy and compelling texts accompanied by pictures of models with lustrous, carefully styled hair. Later, radio and television provided fertile ground for shampoo ads.

The 1930s brought a variety of successful commercial shampoos. Dr. John Breck developed a brand of shampoo while seeking a cure for baldness. Although the product did not stop his hair loss, it led to the development of the successful Breck shampoo company with its familiar image of the **Breck Girl**.

In 1933, Hans Schwarzkopf, a German, introduced the world's first nonalkaline shampoo, called Onalkali. He had previously introduced a popular form of powder shampoo in 1903. The year 1934 brought **Procter & Gamble**'s detergent-based shampoo, Drene, which became one of the nation's best-selling brands. In the 1930's, Wella Corporation in Germany worked on formulas to control static in the hair.

For times when washing hair with water was inconvenient or impossible, people could buy various dry shampoos in the form of powders and foams. They contained a powder ingredient to absorb oil along with a mild alkali. Hospitals were one market for these shampoos.

During the 1940s, popular formulas for soaps included coconut oil. To achieve a clear liquid, manufacturers aged their products until the precipitate sank to the bottom of the vats and then filtered the liquid into bottles.

New Products

The technology involved in shampoo making continued to evolve, and synthetic surfactants were used as a base in various formulas. One formula used a substance called ammonium coconut monglyceride sulfonate. Synthetic shampoos often started with triethanolamine lauryl sulfate, which was made by sulfating lauryl alcohol, a fatty alcohol that comes from hydrogenating the fatty acids in coconut oil.

The first synthetic shampoo, Colgate-Palmolive's Halo, was marketed in 1950 and became the best-selling brand in the United States. Colgate-Palmolive had begun in 1806 as a soap and candle business in New York City, and the company produced several popular hair products after 1950. At its peak, Halo achieved a market share of 60 percent. Other popular brands at mid-century were Drene, Lustre-Crème, Breck, and Prell.

As American teenagers became a profitable consumer group in the 1950s, hair care companies designed products and ads just for them. Many teenagers had their own spending money and could buy the products they preferred—or could convince their parents to buy them. Shampoo ads stressed the importance of clean, shining hair for a teenager's personal appearance and social success and implied that using their products would result in compliments, more dates, and more friends. Teens shown in the ads appeared happy, attractive, and popular. Lovely, well-groomed hair became a core aspect of personal appearance.

Commercial hair conditioners also made their first appearance in the 1950s. They developed from the technology that was used in making fabric softeners. Ads emphasized the way that hair conditioner, also known as "cream rinse," would make hair shinier and easier to comb and style after shampooing. In 1986, Procter & Gamble introduced a shampoo and conditioner in one product—Pert Plus.

During the 1940s, the emergence of detergent-based cleansers made the adjustment of pH levels more critical. New formulas emphasized a balanced pH level so that the product was not too alkaline, which opened hair cuticles and exposed the hair to more potential damage. Excess alkalinity also tended to leave a film on the hair.

Dandruff shampoos became more prominent, and ads for these products emphasized that dandruff was an unattractive and embarrassing grooming problem. In the United Kingdom, 1963 brought ZP11, the first approved shampoo to treat dandruff. Other companies developed antidandruff shampoos to treat itchiness and flaking on the scalp. Head & Shoulders shampoo became the top-selling brand, and it remains so today. Shampoos designed to address dandruff now come in various formulations, including shampoos with conditioners.

New products continued to reach the marketplace, with special formulations or ingredients designed to improve the hair's appearance. One of these ingredients was protein. Researchers thought that applying hydrolyzed protein to hair could help to fill in damaged areas and improve hair strength. Shampoo manufacturers have added protein ingredients in the form of nucleic acids, nucleo proteins, and others. During the 1960s, **Revlon** launched Flex as the first protein-treatment shampoo for hair. Redken brought out pH-balanced products and shampoos that contained proteins. The proteins used in shampoos once were derived from animals, a practice that bothered some consumers. As a result, shampoo makers found new protein sources in wheat, silk amino acids, and human hair.

In the 1970s, a renewed interest in so-called "**natural products**" also affected the shampoo industry. The idea of natural shampoos was not new. Helene Curtis had introduced an egg shampoo during the late 1940s, and other formulations had emphasized plant ingredients. During the 1970s, more companies added jojoba oil, wheat germ oil, honey, herbs, flowers, and other similar ingredients. Labels often mentioned the words "botanical" and "natural." During the 1990s, this interest resurfaced, and companies again sought ways to add plant substances to their shampoos and other hair care products. One such line came from the Ales Group, a French firm. Their products contain a higher-than-usual level of botanical ingredients. In some, botanicals make up to 65 percent of the formulation.

Companies also added vitamins to shampoos and other hair care products. Procter & Gamble brought out its Pantene Pro-V line during the 1990s. The ingredients in these kinds of products evolved in Switzerland during the 1940s, when medical researchers sought ways to help burn victims during World War II. They found a derivative ingredient they named panthenol that seemed to increase the hair's elasticity.

Children's Shampoos

A number of companies have developed shampoos especially for babies and children. These products are recent innovations, since children used the same cleansing products as adults before the twentieth century. These products usually feature packaging in designs and colors that will appeal to children and may be advertised on television. Often, these shampoos are named for popular TV or film characters or children's toys, such as the Barbie doll, characters on *Sesame Street*, or Disney characters. The names may also come from popular fairy tales or children's books.

Shampoos for infants are formulated to meet special requirements. They may contain fewer sulfates, which can be drying. They also may be formulated to cleanse more gently than shampoos made for adults. One of the best-known and earliest baby shampoos is Johnson's Baby Shampoo, which comes as a gold-colored liquid. Johnson & Johnson advertised this shampoo as mild enough for young children, using the slogan, "No more tears." Teenagers and adults also use this product. More recently, companies have produced shampoos that contain particular botanicals or fragrances the companies say will be "soothing" for babies.

Shampoo Industry Today

Today, the shampoo industry is one of the largest consumer-goods industries in the world. New products to cleanse the hair, with added features meant to beautify, protect, and improve hair's condition, appear regularly. Research chemists continue to seek new ingredients and formulations that will improve products and increase sales.

Most existing formulations are designed to produce lather, although lather is not essential to removing dirt. Shampoos aim to remove dirt without stripping all the natural oil from the hair. The pH level is adjusted to be slightly acidic so that the hair shaft will contract rather than expand, giving hair strands a smoother, shinier appearance.

According to author **Paula Begoun**, shampoos contain:

> primarily water, surfactants (surface-active agents or detergent cleansers), lather builders, quaternary ammonium compounds (antistatic and detangling agents), humectants (ingredients that attract water to the hair), thickeners (ingredients that give the shampoo a pleasing consistency), and preservatives. Many shampoos also contain . . . conditioning agents, including panthenol, collagen, protein, elastin, dimethicone, stearic acid, amino acids, and a host of others. (Begoun 1995, 70)

Consumers can choose from among hundreds of different shampoos to suit their needs and tastes. Shampoos come in formulations designed for various hair textures, colors, lengths, levels of oiliness or dryness, permed hair, straightened hair, color-treated hair, and damaged hair. Some shampoos are geared to appeal to just men or women.

Among the diverse products in the marketplace are shampoos that contain sunscreens and other ingredients designed to appeal to athletes and other people who spend a great deal of time outdoors. Swimmers can buy shampoos and conditioners that claim to remove chlorine and other pool chemicals from their hair. Specialty shampoos also include formulations expressly for beards.

Data compiled by Information Resources, Inc. showed that the top-selling shampoos in the United States for fiscal year 2003 were: **Clairol** Herbal Essences (76.9 million units), Head & Shoulders Classic Clean (42.2 million units), Pantene Classically Clean (39 million units), Pantene Sheer Volume (37.9 million units), Dove Regular (34.9 million units), Thermasilk Regular (33.1 million units), **L'Oreal** Kids Regular (30.2 million units), Neutrogena T-Gel (27.7 million units), and Finesse (26 million units). Procter & Gamble owns the Clairol, Head & Shoulders, and Pantene brands, which sold a combined total of 196 million bottles of shampoo in 2003; **Unilever** owns the Dove brand name.

See also: African Americans; Alberto-Culver Company; Dial Corporation; Elizabeth I; Fekkai, Frédéric; Hair Color; Henkel Group; Michaeljohn; Renaissance Europe; Sassoon, Vidal; Seborrheic Dermatitis

Further Reading: Begoun, Paula, *Don't Shop for Hair Products Without Me* (1995); Contenu, Georges, *Everyday Life in Babylon and Assyria* (1954); Cooley, Arnold J., *The Toilet and Cosmetic Arts in Ancient and Modern Times* (1970); Frazier, Gregory, and Beverly Frazier. *The Bath Book* (1973); Henson, Melanie, "Baby Care Update," *Happi*, August 2004, http://www.happi.com/current/August041.htm; Hunting, Anthony, *Encyclopedia of Shampoo Ingredients* (1983); Macdonald, Veronica, "The Hair Care Market," *Happi*, December 2001, http://www.happi.com/special/Dec011.htm; Steinman, David, and Samuel S. Epstein, MD, *The Safe Shopper's Bible* (1995); Stuller, Jeff, "Cleanliness Has Only Recently Become a Virtue," *Smithsonian Magazine*, February 1991, 126–134.

SHAVING

The process of shaving off unwanted body hair dates back to prehistoric times. Shaving off hair—or choosing not to shave—has been done for various reasons related to hygiene, religion, personal style, sexuality, customs, and social mores.

Modern shaving tools have made the process safer, faster, and more convenient than the methods people used thousands, or even hundreds, of years ago.

> "Between the cradle and the grave, lies a haircut and a shave."
>
> SAMUEL HOFFENSTEIN (1890–1947), Russian-American author and composer

Ancient Times

Drawings in caves dating back tens of thousands of years show that some men had hairy faces while others were devoid of hair. Historians think the earliest shaving devices were made by sharpening shells, stone, and pieces of flint. While flint could be formed into a sharp edge, it became dull with use and had to be replaced rather often.

Studies of Egyptian art, tombs, and excavation sites dating back to 4000 BCE show that most people removed all of their body hair, including the hair on their heads. Copper and bronze razors have been found inside the tombs of Egyptian pharaohs, and copper razors dating back to 3000 BCE have been found in India. Wealthy Egyptians and members of the royalty had servants, including personal **barbers**, to help with shaving. For these men, shaving the hair was regarded as good hygiene.

While some cultures developed shaving tools, men in other cultures removed hairs by plucking. In **Latin America**, some native peoples shaved with razors made from obsidian, a volcanic glass.

The materials and techniques used to make razors changed through the centuries. By 3000 BCE, people had learned to work with metals and were making razors from copper alloys. Bronze razors developed sometime between 1567 and 1320 BCE. Embossed bronze razors dating back to 1300 BCE have been found inside grave sites located in present-day Denmark. The handles on some of these razors were carved into horse-head shapes, showing that people cared about the style of their personal razor. By 1000 BCE, men were using razors made from iron.

Ancient Greeks began shaving more often around 323 BCE, when Alexander the Great demanded that his soldiers remove their beards so they could not be grabbed by enemy troops. Among the Celts and Britons, it was common practice to shave the entire body except the head and a narrow strip of the upper lip.

Shaving also became common in present-day Italy around 296 BCE and during the time of the Roman Republic and the **Roman Empire**. The Etruscans who lived in that region used bronze razors. Roman barbers used iron razors with thin blades, which they sharpened on a stone. At about age twenty-one, young, Roman men had their first shave, which was celebrated with a ritual party that included the man's friends. This event signified his passage to male adult life, and the hairs from the initial shave were offered as a gift to the man's favorite god.

Among members of the **military**, the fashion for being clean-shaven was reinforced when Scipio Africanus Major defeated Hannibal in 202 BCE and became a hero in the Roman world. Roman legionnaires who did not want to shave daily rubbed their faces with volcanic rock.

Artwork shows a clean-shaven Emperor Julius Caesar (100–44 BCE), whose servant plucked out his stray hairs. However, starting with Hadrian (76–138 CE), Roman emperors wore beards again. After some early Christians started shaving their facial hair, Roman Emperor Julian (332–363 CE) grew a beard to set himself apart.

Middle Ages and Renaissance

Shaving became more common during the **Middle Ages** in Europe, as more men removed their facial hair on a weekly basis. Shaving more often than weekly was extremely difficult, since shaving at home required soap, which was scarce and costly. Most forms of lye-based, cheap soap also irritated the face during shaving. Moreover, the crude shaving tools of that era left stubble on the shaved area.

Monks shaved their faces and also most of their hair. In the style known as a tonsure, they shaved the center section of their heads, leaving the rest of the hair. Some medieval men wore a pageboy hairstyle on the sides of their head but shaved off the back.

Women shaved or plucked the hair on their foreheads and temples, and frequently also their eyebrows, to achieve the bare look that was popular during those years. That look remained popular during the **Renaissance** and throughout the reign of **Elizabeth I**.

The soldiers who returned from the Crusades (1096–1270) introduced some new ideas about grooming to Europe. Women in the Middle East removed their body hair, and some European women decided to follow this custom, so they began to shave theirs. By the end of the twelfth century, most men in France were shaving their chins, and that trend spread to other countries.

In Tudor England, King Henry VIII revived the beard around 1520, which meant that many men stopped shaving during these years. Henry later began to wear his trademark close-cropped beard and mustache. That fashion remained in England throughout the 1500s. In France, Louis XIII shaved what remained of his hair and wore wigs, sparking a fashion among French men that spread to other countries. A new type of straight razor made shaving easier. Developed in the 1680s, it featured a narrow, folding blade. Like other razors, it was made by sword smiths and had to be sharpened on a regular basis. A shaving brush to apply soap lather before shaving was developed in France during the 1750s.

New Shaving Tools and Markets

During the eighteenth and nineteenth centuries, shaving tools became more efficient. A French barber named Jean-Jacques Perret played a key role in this process. Perret wrote a guide to shaving products and techniques called *La Pogonotomie* (*The Art of Learning to Shave Oneself*). In 1762, he went on to develop what some historians consider to be the first version of a safety razor. Perret's razor featured an L-shaped guard along one edge of the metal blade, which meant that the blade was less likely to cut the user.

The Perret razor was manufactured and sold to barbers and individuals. This razor was a boon during the years when people of both genders were wearing elaborate powdered wigs, and many men would shave their heads before putting on these wigs.

Straight steel razors became available during the early 1800s in England. They were made in Sheffield, a city known for its fine quality steel. Like previous razors, these required regular honing to keep a sharp edge. Men used a strop to maintain the razor's edge at home. At the turn of the century, razor blades were made from forged steel.

In the mid-1800s, most men switched to the new hoe-type razor, invented by Englishman William Henson in 1847. Henson's razor featured a handle placed perpendicular to the blade for easier handing and better control. Otto and Frederick Kampfe patented their own version of a safety razor in 1880. A wire skin guard was placed along one side of the Kampfes' razor, and only the other side was used for shaving. As in the past, the razor had to be sharpened frequently.

A clean-shaven face was in fashion for men during the **Victorian era**. In addition to razors and strops, men used soaps especially made for shaving, along with brushes and shaving cups. Some lathering agent—soap or a special "shaving cream" or foam—was used before shaving to minimize skin irritation. After shaving, men applied special shaving lotions, often homemade from plant substances.

A major innovation in shaving equipment took place during the early 1900s, when a traveling salesman named King **Gillette** worked with a professor from the Massachusetts Institute of Technology to develop a disposable razor, which was patented in 1901. The Gillette safety razor had a disposable, double-edged blade that was cut from a template instead of being forged. It became available for consumers in 1903.

The Gillette razor, priced for the average consumer, became immensely popular. By 1904, sales had reached 90,000 razors and 123,000 blades. Shaving offered major opportunities in the business of men's personal care products. Ads for razors stressed the convenience and privacy of shaving at home rather than in a barbershop as well as the money-saving aspects. Gillette ads featured athletes, soldiers, and professional men with traditionally masculine good looks. Men with clean-shaven faces, said the ads, could be seen "in the store, the counting-room, the classroom, the office—in work and sport out of doors." A Gillette ad from 1910 equates the self-shaver with the "American spirit," while another ad claims that using a Gillette razor daily helps a man develop healthy routines and self-respect.

As new types of shaving equipment and supplies were developed and marketed, companies emphasized the importance of a man's face and appearance in the modern job market. More and more men in Western nations became convinced that shaving was important to their appearance, hygiene, professional advancement, and social status. During the early twentieth century, most men in Western societies began to shave daily.

Gillette's business continued to expand with sales in European countries. During World War I (1914–1918), U.S. soldiers stationed in Europe were equipped with Gillette razors, in part for strategic reasons: clean-shaven faces enabled gas masks to fit more snugly. For Gillette, this meant sales of about 3.5 million razors and 36 million blades as well as extensive publicity because more

Europeans saw the razor in action. By the 1920s, millions of men around the world were shaving their faces daily, and that has remained the norm in Western cultures since.

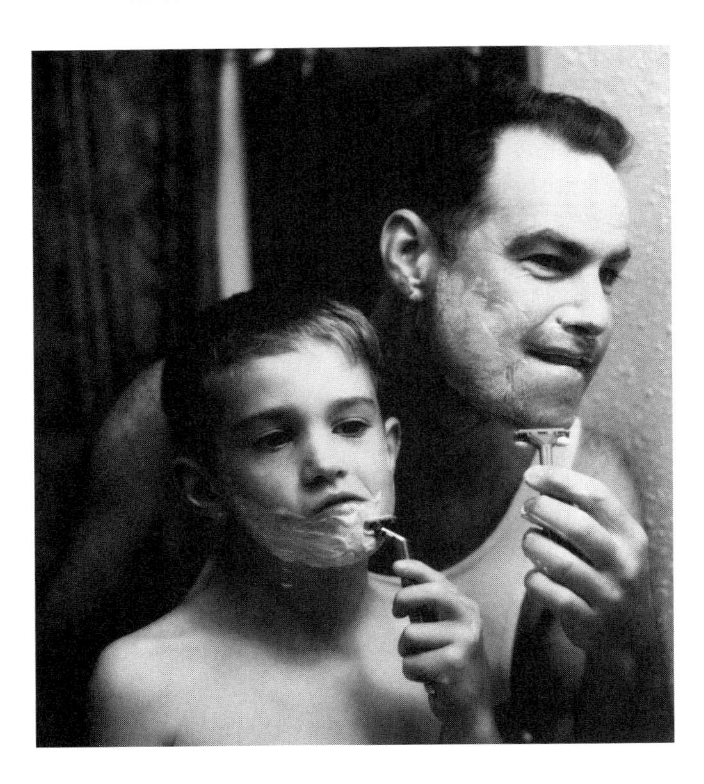

The forerunner of the electric shaver arrived in 1910. Willis G. Shockey patented his wind-up safety razor, which operated for a set amount of time after the user wound up a flywheel by hand.

During the early 1900s, more women began shaving their legs. Fashions became more revealing during the 1910s and 1920s. The makers of razors and blades realized that they would sell far more products if women shaved their armpits and legs regularly. One major force in this campaign was the Wilkinson Sword Company, a British company that produces razor blades. Fashion editors took up the cause of shaving by labeling underarm hair as unfeminine and a sign of poor hygiene. They pointed out that underarm odors tended to cling to these hairs. Sleeveless dresses featured models with neatly shaved armpits, and smooth, shaved legs appeared beneath the short skirts that emerged during the Roaring Twenties.

During those years, the word "shaving" was considered masculine. Ads for women's shaving products did not mention the word "shaving," and razor companies instructed their salesmen to use other language when selling the products, as Gillette used in ads saying that shaving could help a woman acquire a "smooth underarm" (Riordan 2004, 137). One example comes from the May 1915 issue of *Harper's Bazaar*, which featured an ad for Gillette's Milady women's razor. The model in the ad wore a sleeveless dress that revealed her smooth armpits, and the ad copy read: "Summer Dress and Modern Dancing combine to make necessary the removal of objectionable hair." In 1922, razors were offered for sale in the Sears, Roebuck catalogue alongside an illustration of a girl looking at her hairless underarms in the mirror. Sales of Gillette's Milady razor increased dramatically as more women began shaving.

During the 1920s and 1930s, women shaved more than their underarms and legs. Some also shaved their **eyebrows** and drew in new lines to emulate the look of film stars, such as **Jean Harlow**, who created new brows in this manner.

According to author Teresa Riordan, "Before World War I, virtually no American woman shaved her legs. But by 1964, ninety-eight percent of all American women under the age of forty-four did" (Riordan 2004, 117). Uncommon in most other parts of the world, the practice of leg shaving among women is common in North America, Australia, and much of Western Europe.

Through the years, special razors, somewhat different in shape from razors designed for men, have been marketed for women. They come in colors and shapes designed to appeal to women or teenage girls. Advertising campaigns promote the idea that using these tools will create "sexy" or "silky smooth," hair-free skin.

A Competitive Industry

The 1920s brought more competition in the shaving equipment industry. Jacob Schick (1878–1937), a lieutenant colonel in the U.S. Army, patented his "magazine repeating razor," which had replacement clips of blades inside the handle. The razor was designed so that users could insert new blades without touching any sharp edges. It became available to consumers in 1926. Schick's next innovation, the injector razor, was even more popular. In 1929, Schick unveiled the first electric dry shaver, which featured oscillating blades and a small motor. Early versions required two hands, but Schick went on to develop a one-handed version by 1931. Schick's razors were produced and marketed by his American Chain & Cable Company; in 1930, he renamed it the Schick Dry Shaver Company. The razor company was acquired by Warner, Lambert (now a division of Pfizer) in 1969. (In 1981, the Schick company manufacturing electric razors would become part of Europe's Philips DAP and its Norelco division in the United States, with domestic headquarters in Stamford, Connecticut.)

The electric shaver did not immediately appeal to the public, though Schick's injector razor still sold well. When using safety razors, men were now applying shaving creams designed expressly for that purpose. One popular brand, **Burma Shave**, began a unique ad campaign during the 1920s, as Americans were spending more time in automobiles. Catchy rhymes praising the product were written on billboards posted along American highways to catch the eye of passing motorists. The billboards were arranged in groups of four to six, with the first signs each containing one line of the short rhyme and the final sign containing the Burma Shave name.

In The Netherlands, Philips benefited from the creativity of engineer Alexandre Horowitz, who would eventually patent 136 ideas for products. During the 1930s and early 1940s, Horowitz developed the first double-headed shaver, which Philips marketed as the Philishave Electric Razor.

By the 1930s, more companies were making shaving creams and aftershave products, including powders, creams, and lotions. To avoid any hints that these products were in any way "feminine," companies gave them masculine names, and ads stressed that using these products was a manly thing to do. Old Spice, which became America's top-selling aftershave lotion, was first sold in 1938. When the Mennen company brought out its Skin Bracer aftershave lotion in the 1940s, the ad campaign stressed that the product was "100 percent male." In the United States, the Food and Drug Administration Office of Cosmetics and Colors was responsible for regulating shaving creams, foams, and gels, while the Consumer Product Safety Commission regulated razors.

During the 1930s, Schick's electric razor became more popular. Since the shaver did not require soap, water, or shaving cream, it was convenient and portable. The shaver initially cost $25. Despite the fact that it was launched during the hard economic years of the Great Depression, sales reached nearly 2 million by 1937. One year earlier, the Sunbeam company, known for its household appliances, also began selling an electric shaver.

During the 1960s, improved forms of the razor blade were introduced. Stainless steel blades from Wilkinson Sword first appeared in 1962 and became standard for use in razors, since they were more durable and longer lasting. Cartridge razors and new kinds of injector-style cartridges, similar to those used today, made their debut, followed by new and improved twin-blade razors in the early 1970s. Remington electric shavers became a well-known brand during that same decade.

Companies also began making disposable razors. Available for both men and women, these razors, made from plastic products and metal, were designed to be used two or three times, then discarded.

Despite many improvements and innovations, people still complained about the amount of time they spent shaving. A Texan named Herbie McNinch developed a new double-headed, wet-shave razor in the 1990s called the Quik Shave. McNinch said that his razor worked "like two razors in one." He went on to manufacture, market, and sell his product, via print media and television ads, as well as the Internet.

Today, people can choose from a variety of disposable razors and razors with replaceable blades, often with two or three cutting edges as well as electric razors. Companies continue to seek new products or improvements that will make shaving a more efficient and pleasant experience. In 2002, men and women spent around $8 billion on shaving razors and blades.

See also: Advertising; Africa; Beards, Men's; Body Hair; Gillette Company; Greece, Ancient; Hair Removal; Mustache; Native Americans; Politics and Hair; Religion and Hair; Salons, Hair and Beauty; Wigs and Hairpieces

Further Reading: Atwan, Robert, Donald McQuade, and John W. Wright, *Edsels, Luckies, & Frigidaires* (1971); Debrohun, Jeri, "Power Dressing in Ancient Greece and Rome," *History Today* 51 (February 2001); Grant, Michael, *A Social History of Greece and Rome* (1992); Laver, James, *Taste and Fashion* (1937); Riordan, Teresa, *Inventing Beauty* (2004); Zaoui, Miriam, and Eric Malka, *The Art of Shaving* (2003).

SIDEBURNS

The term "sideburns"—or "side-whiskers"—refers to hair extending from the head down the sides of the face. The first sideburns may have been worn during ancient times by male Hittites, a group of Indo-Europeans who lived in present-day Turkey and northern Syria around 1600 to 1200 BC and who shaved off all their facial hair, including their eyebrows. They left hair along the side of their face beside the ears and then braided these side-whiskers. Sculptures of ancient Celts also show men with long sideburns.

Side-whiskers were worn in eighteenth-century France, where they were called *favoris.* Men wore them in various forms, including sparse, full, short, long, or shaped to cross the cheek at various angles. Sideburns also were part of many styles in **Regency** England. During the 1800s, new styles continued to appear, and they were named for people or for the way the sideburns looked. For example, dundrearies were named for the character of Lord Dundreary in a play called *Our American Cousin*, while Piccadilly weepers fell about six inches below chin level.

Sideburns became especially fashionable in the United States during the Civil War. They were named for Vermont native General Ambrose Everett Burnside, who served as a Union commander in charge of the Army of the Potomac. Though many men had worn sideburns before, Burnside's were especially thick and pronounced. By 1900, the name had changed from "burnsides" to "sideburns." Through the years, several American presidents wore sizeable sideburns. They included Martin Van Buren, Andrew Jackson, and Zachary Taylor.

During the **Victorian era** (1837–1901), "mutton-chop" sideburns were also worn. These large sideburns got their name from their shape, which looked like two meat chops sitting on either side of the face. One famous set of sideburns belonged to Franz Josef, emperor of Austria from 1848 to 1916. Russian male monarchs also favored sideburns, as can be seen in portraits of Alexander I, Alexander II, Alexander III, Nicholas I, and Nicholas II. In the early 1900s, silent film star **Rudolph Valentino** wore his sideburns neatly trimmed and gave this look a new glamour.

Sideburns made a big comeback in the 1950s, when millions of men copied rock star **Elvis Presley**'s long, gleaming pompadour hairstyle that he wore with sideburns. Singers Engelbert Humperdinck and Elton John wore large sideburns during the 1970s, as did actors Clarence Williams III (in television's *Mod Squad*) and Richard Roundtree (in the film *Shaft*).

By the end of the 1900s, men's sideburns generally were smaller in size than those of the 1800s or the 1950s and 1960s. Some men continued to wear them, however. Well-known celebrities who wore distinct sideburns during the 1990s were actors Luke Perry and Jason Priestly, who costarred on the popular television series *Beverly Hills 90210.*

See also: Beards, Men's; Body Hair; Facial Hair; Mustache

Further Reading: Moritz, Robert, "A Brief History of Whiskers Starting with God," *GQ*, September 2000, 345–350; Peterkin, Alan, *One Thousand Beards* (2002).

SOCIETY OF FRIENDS (Quakers)

The Society of Friends, often called the Quakers, is a Christian religious group founded during the 1650s by Englishman George Fox.

During the late 1700s, many members of this sect had developed a distinctive and conservative style of dress and grooming based on principles of simplicity and avoidance of luxury, ostentation, or vanity in personal appearance. Clothing and hairstyles were similar to those of the mainstream but simplified and without ornamentation. For instance, they avoided unnecessary cuffs, collars, lapels, and buttons. They also did not add showy ribbons, bows, excess lace, braiding, embroidery, and other decorative elements to their clothing, headgear, or hair. Many members of the group avoided bright colors and prints, choosing instead to wear shades of brown, gray, and other dark colors. They avoided wearing elaborate hairstyles and jewelry.

During the 1600s, when most Englishmen and American colonists wore wigs, Quaker men either wore a simpler, smaller wig or did not cover their own hair, which was grown to about shoulder length. Powdering the hair was regarded as vain and unnecessary. The minutes of the Annual New England contained these directions: "That all men Friends, both young and old be careful not to Imatate [*sic*] the vain Fashions of the World in wearing their hatts [*sic*] set up in three sides with Ribins [*sic*] (broad or Bunched) nor powder the hair to be seen . . ." (Case 1683–1789).

As for hats, cocked hats (sometimes called bicorn or tricorn hats) were popular among Englishmen from about 1680 to 1800. These hats were designed with the brim turned up in two or three places and were worn at an angle—"cocked"—to show off men's wigs. Quaker men wore simpler versions of the hat with a smaller "cock" section, or they wore hats with a natural wide brim. They also did not remove their hats as often as a sign of respect to royalty or nobles because the Friends believed that all people are equal in God's sight. Women wore simple caps at home. For summer, they had plain straw bonnets, and in cooler weather they wore simple gray bonnets with sides that laid flat against the side of the face.

Today, members of the Society of Friends are not compelled to follow any official restrictions or rules regarding their hairstyles or manner of dress. Those who choose to dress and style their hair more simply than people in mainstream society do so because they prefer to focus on their inner selves and spiritual goals instead of their outward appearance. As expressed in the *Book of Discipline of the Ohio Valley Yearly Meeting Religious Society of Friends, 1978*, "It is urged that Friends be watchful to keep themselves free from self-indulgent habits, luxurious ways of living, and the bondage of fashion. . . . Undue luxury often creates a false sense of superiority, causes unnecessary burdens upon both ourselves and others, and leads to the neglect of the spiritual life."

See also: Religion and Hair

Further Reading: *Book of Discipline of the Ohio Valley Yearly Meeting Religious Society of Friends, 1978,* http://www.quaker.org/ovym/friends.htm; Case, Clarence M., Minutes of New England Yearly Meeting, 1683–1789, vol. 1; Davies, Adrian, and T. A. Davies, *The Quakers in English Society, 1655–1725* (2000); De Saussure, Cesar, *A Foreign View of England in 1725–1729* (1995); Fiske, John, *The Dutch and Quaker Colonies in America* (1902).

SOUL PATCH

The soul patch, or soul spot, is a deliberate growth of hair running from a man's lower lip to his chin. This small area of hair has been called a "dab" of beard and an imperial, coming from the French word *imperiale*. Members of the Organization for the Advancement of Facial Hair call it an attilio. Founded in 1996, this group is based in California.

The soul patch can be worn long or short and shaped in various ways, although the modern version is usually short and narrow. Soul patches became quite fashionable during and after the 1990s but were also worn in earlier times. One of the best-known people to wear a small area of beard beneath the chin was English author William Shakespeare. Napoleon III of France also wore a triangular tuft of hair beneath his lower lip.

During the 1950s, when jazz trumpet player Dizzy Gillespie wore this style, it was known as a jazz dab. It was especially popular with musicians who played jazz or rhythm and blues. Other men who regarded themselves as members of the beat generation (nicknamed "beatniks") also could be seen wearing this form of beard.

Performers continued to wear this small beard, which most people now call a soul patch. During the 1970s, they were seen on pop musicians Frank Zappa and Tom Waits. The Blues Brothers characters—Jake and Elwood Blues, as performed by John Belushi and Dan Aykroyd from the comedy show *Saturday Night Live*—also sported the style. A. J. McLean of the Backstreet Boys band was among the celebrities who adopted the style. Several bands have taken the name Soul Patch. They include a band from Berlin, Germany, a band from Colorado, and a band in New York City. In recent years, actors, including Keanu Reeves and Ethan Hawke, have worn a soul patch.

Irregular and untidy soul patches were part of the "grunge" look of the 1990s. The look also became more common among athletes. American Olympic speed-skater Apolo Anton Ohno wore a soul patch at the 2002 Winter Olympics. Baseball players Mike Piazza and Randy Johnson have worn a soul patch, as has English soccer legend David Beckham, who set numerous trends in hairstyles. Beckham sparked another fashion among men when he wore a soul patch combined with a mustache and "chin curtains." Chin curtains refer to facial hair grown along the jaw line on the lower part of the face at the chin.

See also: Beards, Men's

Further Reading: Organization for the Advancement of Facial Hair, "About Us" and "History," http://www.ragadio.com/oafh/page2.html; Peterkin, Alan, *One Thousand Beards* (2002); Peterseim, Locke, "Minds, Bodies and Soul Patches," http://espn.go.com/page2/s/closer/020221.html; Rickard, Ken, "Facial-Fuzz-Challenged Reflections on the Hip Hirsute Look," *Honolulu Advertiser*, February 17, 2003.

SPORTS *See* Baldness, Voluntary; Beards, Men's; Hamill, Dorothy; Mustache; "Mustache Gang"; Occupations; Ponytail; Soul Patch

STYLING PRODUCTS

Styling products for the hair include pomades, creams, lotions, oils, gels, waxes, hairspray, mousse, straighteners, and other materials designed to help people groom and style their hair.

The use of such materials dates back to ancient times, when people found ways to use natural substances and mixtures of those substances for styling purposes. Recipes for hairstyling products were passed on to new generations of individuals and hairdressers.

Modern technology makes it possible to mass-produce a vast array of items for use on the hair, and sales of these products yield billions of dollars in revenues annually. Women have been the major consumers of such products, and most products are geared for their use. However, the number of male consumers grew steadily during the twentieth century, and that trend continues. Many hairstyling products are used by both men and women.

> "People bring up my hair quite a bit. It's strategically tousled. The flatiron is the key."
>
> RYAN SEACREST (1974–), TV host of *American Idol*

Early materials for styling hair came from plants, animals, and minerals. In **Africa**, women mixed ochre and animal fats together and applied it to their hair to keep styles in place and to provide color. *Tavo*—a blend of animal fat and honey—stiffened the hair and kept braids and rolls in place. Some groups of people continue to use these natural substances on traditional hairstyles.

In Asia, Chinese women used a heavy pomade-like substance that contained wax. This substance helped to fix their buns in place. They also made a finishing rinse for their hair from the seeds of the Chinese cedrela tree. Later, Japanese people found that a variation of the lacquer product they used in their arts served as a hair fixative. In the Philippines, women soaked aloe in water to produce a hair conditioner.

Egyptians styled and set their wigs with damp mud. Later, they found that soaking quince seeds in water would produce a thick, jelly-like material that worked well for styling hair. This mixture was used in other parts of the Middle East.

Oils were popular for hair grooming, and people used what they found in their surroundings—for example, olive oil, palm oil, coconut oil, almond oil, and shea butter. Bear oil was used widely in the Americas and other places where bears were hunted. As conquest and exploration brought more cultures in contact with each other, the use of various substances spread and new products were imported.

During the **Middle Ages**, a time when many colorants and hair treatments called for exotic animal ingredients, a conditioner was made with boiled lizards and olive oil. One popular medieval recipe for hair gel blended lizard tallow and swallow droppings. A more attainable gel was made by boiling flax seeds and then adding oil of rosemary to the strained flax water. Flax contained oil, and the herb rosemary has long been regarded as a hair tonic in many parts of the world. Rosemary was said to enhance curls. **Henna** also arrived in Europe at that time, having been used for millennia to color and condition hair in the Middle East.

By the sixteenth century, numerous herbs were used to make hairstyling products. Other hair lotions were made with lemon, flaxseed, gelatin, and/or Irish moss.

In seventeenth- and eighteenth-century Europe, powder for coating hair and wigs was an essential hair product for fashionable people. These powders came in shades of pink, blue, yellow, violet, and white, often scented with lavender, orange flower, orrisroot, or other floral essences. They were applied over pomade so that the powder would stick. Historians say that these hair powders were made from potato or rice flour or wheat starch; some mention plaster of Paris. Hairdressers used glue and paste to hold up the styles of the towering wigs, which had numerous curls, loops, poufs, and other features.

During the 1800s, women could find recipes for hair care products in magazines and books. *Godey's Lady's Book* was a popular source for American women who wanted to find out about the latest fashions in hairstyles and clothing. Along with dress patterns and household hints, the magazine contained instructions for making skin and hair care products. For example, one issue published in 1855 explained how to make elder flower oil for the hair, as well as a hair lotion and rinse for "restoring" the hair. In 1855, the famous international beauty Lola Montez shared her hair care recipes, including the instructions for making a hair rinse, called "Honey Water," in a book called *The Arts of Beauty*.

In Colonial days, enslaved **African Americans** found ways to style their hair in an unfamiliar and harsh environment, using materials that were available. Like other American women, they also mixed oil with eggs to make a hair conditioner. By the 1800s, some of them were selling products to style and condition the hair.

Rebecca Elliott was one of the first successful African American female hair care entrepreneurs. During the 1880s, Elliott sold her line of products, called System of French Hair Care. Based in Indianapolis, Indiana, the company used direct-sales techniques, and Elliott traveled widely to demonstrate her products. Her Nutritive Pomade was designed to add shine and help manage wavy or frizzy hair. The line also included Elliott's Medicated Hair Grower and a straightening cream called Cheveline. Others who achieved great success selling ethnic hair care products included **Annie Minerva Turnbo Pope Malone**, **Madam C. J. Walker**, and **George Ellis Johnson**.

At the turn of the century, **Martha Matilda Harper** also was selling her own products in the chain of salons she founded. Harper stressed her use of natural ingredients for clean, healthy hair and skin.

During the twentieth century, more commercial hair products were available. By the 1920s, styling products were used to style the short **bob** haircuts, which sometimes included distinct curls on the sides of the face. Performer **Josephine Baker**, an American living in France, was one of the first celebrities to endorse a commercial hair gel. Ads for the product explained that Baker used it on her own hair—"pour se bakerfixer les cheveux."

During the mid-1900s, Americans used new products to set their hair into certain styles, and teenagers became a booming sector in the consumer market. Dippity-Do hair gel was especially popular with teenage girls, who used it to set pin curls or applied it to their hair before setting it with rollers. The gel itself came in pink and other colors, with packaging designed to appeal to youth. Dippity-Do gels and sprays are still sold today and are used to hold modern spiked hairstyles, as well as other styles.

Since the 1950s, companies have introduced improved versions of old products as well as new products. One popular new hair product is hair mousse, which debuted in 1983. For the **punk** styles that arrived in that same decade, gels, mousses, glazes, wax, and paint were used to style hair. These products also worked on modified versions of punk styles and other trendy styles that featured spikes, chunks, or shaggy layers. Beginning in the 1990s, products made expressly to combat frizzy hair, such as those from **John Frieda Professional Hair Care, Inc.**, became top sellers.

Men's Products

In modern times, the list of men's hair care products has steadily increased. Early in the twentieth century, many men in Western cultures were reluctant to spend a lot of time on personal grooming, which was seen as "feminine." However, most men had begun **shaving** their faces daily, and companies provided soaps, creams, lotions, and scented waters that men could use during that process. American ads for these products emphasized that using these products was masculine and could give men an edge both professionally and socially.

Most men also used some kind of hair tonic, hair cream, or oil to groom their hair. Many men used petroleum jelly, bear oil, macassar oil, or bay rum. These could be purchased in barbershops, pharmacies, and other places.

Starting in 1929, Brylcreem became one of the best-known, brand-name products in America and Europe. Created in 1928 by the Birmingham County Chemical Company in Britain, the product, first sold as Elite Hair Dressing Cream, was intended to keep hair in place. Brylcreem was the first truly mass-marketed men's hair care product. It was issued to British soldiers as part of their personal care kits during World War II (1939–1945).

Brylcreem ads stressed that just a small amount of product would add shine to a man's hair and keep it neatly in place. During the 1950s and 1960s, ads featured a jingle with the tag line, "Brylcreem, a little dab'll do ya." The product is still available and now comes in three formulations: normal, strong hold, and wet look. According to Information Resources, Inc., a Chicago-based market research company, sales for Brycreem totaled $6.6 million for the fiscal year ending in September 2001. This represented about 1.2 percent of the hairstyling/setting gel/mousse category of hair care products. Another popular brand from the mid-1900s, Vitalis, had $3.4 million in sales that same year.

Until the latter half of the twentieth century, lanolin was a prominent ingredient in hair products. Lanolin and certain other common ingredients sit atop the hair shaft, which can give it a heavy feel and look. Some products felt greasy or waxy on the hair, but that kind of product worked well with the "wet look" **pompadours** and other men's styles of the 1950s. After that look lost favor during the 1960s, companies looked for new formulations that would style and hold the hair but look and feel lighter. They formulated lotions and gels that worked by a process of molecular attraction. Brylcreem went on to develop some gel- and water-based products, and **Gillette** introduced a line called "the dry look."

Today, numerous companies, including **Vidal Sassoon**, Avon, Sexy Hair Concepts, American Crew, **Revlon**, Suave, Estée Lauder, **L'Oreal**, and Paul Mitchell, to name a few, offer hairstyling products designed for men. In 2003, sales of men's hair care products increased 12.4 percent, to reach a total of more than $727 million. The United States ranks as the second-largest market for men's hair care products; Japan, with sales of $1.15 billion in 2003, is first.

See also: Alberto-Culver Company; Beards, Men's; Egypt, Ancient; Greece, Ancient; Hair Removal; Hair Straightening; Hairspray; Hairstyles, Twentieth-Century; Johnson Products; Natural Products; Regency; Renaissance Europe; Roman Empire; Shampoo; Tonics, Hair; Victorian Era; Wigs and Hairpieces

Further Reading: Begoun, Paula, *Don't Go Shopping for Hair Care Products Without Me* (2004); Macdonald, Veronica, "The Hair Care Market," *Happi* magazine, December 2001, http://www.happi.com/current/December021.htm; Riordan, Teresa, *Inventing Beauty* (2004); Rooks, Noliwe M., *Hair Raising* (1996); Walker, Michael, "My Excellent Brylcreem Adventure," *The New York Times Magazine*, October 13, 2001, http://www.ahundredmonkeys.com/nytimes_article3.htm; Worthington, Charles, *The Complete Book of Hairstyling* (2002).

STYLING TOOLS

Throughout history, humans have identified certain objects they can use to groom and style their hair and have fashioned tools expressly for hairstyling. In modern times, people have designed and manufactured an increasing number of sophisticated items for cutting, styling, grooming, and removing hair.

Some simple styling tools came from animals. For example, African women traditionally used porcupine quills to pull apart braided cornrows. People in different places, including Native Americans, found that pairs of shells could be used to pluck hairs. Tortoise shells, whalebone, antlers, and ivory were among the natural materials used to make grooming and decorative **combs**. Boar's hair provided material for handmade hairbrushes.

Along with combs, hairbrushes have existed since prehistoric times. Some historians believe they existed in some form as early as 2.5 million years ago. Early peoples used brushes to make cave paintings and then adapted brushes for other uses, including grooming their hair. Styles and materials changed through the years, especially after the development of vulcanized rubber and plastics. Lyda Newman of New York patented a hairbrush with a removable handle on November 15, 1898. Her version was easier to clean and recessed air chambers in the brush provided ventilation during brushing. Although some brushes are made completely from synthetics today, many people still prefer brushes with wooden handles and natural bristles from boar's heads or other sources. Modern brushes come in various styles and shapes, including some with rounded heads covered completely with bristles.

The tools used for cutting and trimming hair have changed as metalworking technology advanced through the centuries, and new tools, materials, and alloys became available. Early scissors were crude instruments made from bronze or iron without the common pivot and finger openings of modern cutting tools. One example is the *forfex*. Made in ancient Rome, this prototype of shears was composed of two blades on a common metal loop.

During the 1300s, Sheffield, England, became a center for making cutlery. In the mid-1700s, new methods of making harder steel and fusing silver to copper led to better-quality scissors, and the factories that developed during the Industrial Revolution produced them in larger quantities. Stainless steel was developed in Sheffield in 1913, leading to scissors that were more durable and less prone to rust. Other places noted for their fine steel scissors include Premana, Italy, and Solingen, Germany.

Today's **barbers** and hairdressers use an array of tools for cutting, thinning, blending, and layering hair. These tools include different kinds of scissors, razors, and manual and motor-driven clippers and trimmers (also called edgers or taperers).

People also have designed numerous devices to curl, wave, or crimp hair. At certain times and places, such as in **ancient Rome**, eighteenth-century France, and the **Victorian Era**, members of both genders have worn curls. Hot irons date back to ancient times. Devices that look like curling irons have been found in ancient Egyptian tombs. The Greeks made a hollow metal stick called a *calamistrum* that was heated over wood ashes and then used to create curls. The Assyrians used heated iron bars for curling their hair and sometimes their beards. Similar devices were used for more than 1,000 years.

The curling irons and double-wave crimping irons used in the 1800s and early 1900s were heated over the flames of a fireplace or stove. People had trouble judging the exact temperature and timing the process, which could result in singed, damaged, or lost hair. French hairdresser Marcel Grateau designed a curling iron that would crimp hair into the aptly named **Marcel wave**, which remained in fashion for several decades.

After electricity became available, curling irons were safer and easier to use. They evolved into modern, spring-tension, electric curling irons, which are plugged into a socket and reliably maintain a safe, effective temperature for curling strands of hair. The user can time the curling process and achieve more predictable results.

Historic events have influenced the development of new tools and products. For example, during World War II (1939–1945), more steel was diverted to wartime uses, so less was available for curling irons. People found ways to curl the hair without steel rods or curling irons. The Walker Company, founded by **Madam C. J. Walker**, devised a method called "cold curling on pressed hair" that relied on the use of vapor oil rather than a hot metal iron.

To achieve the large **bouffant** and beehive styles worn during the late 1950s and early 1960s, many women used giant hair rollers. Modern manufactured hair rollers were first used in Italy and spread to England and France by the mid-1950s. By 1965, rollers were common hair care equipment, and they were worn overnight as well as in the daytime. In the United States, women and girls even wore them in public while shopping or going to the movies. Frequently, they covered their heads with scarves. The practice became so common that the April 1965 issue of *Time* magazine discussed the etiquette of hair rollers.

As hairstyles became longer and less structured, hair rollers were used in different ways. Some people opted for wash-and-dry hairstyles that could be achieved with a blow-dryer or a blow-dryer used with other tools. People used rollers to smooth out their hair or achieve a wavy or curly look. In addition to earlier rollers made from mesh, plastic and Velcro rollers became available.

The twentieth century brought new materials and mass-production techniques that led to innovative products for creating or maintaining stylish hairdos. They included new types of **hairpins**, electric **hair dryers**, **permanent wave** machines, heated hair rollers, and new types of standard hair rollers. Also available were plastic devices to help people create French braids, French twists, and various other designs in their hair.

See also: Comb, Decorative; Hair Straightening; Harper, Martha Matilda; Joyner, Marjorie Stewart; Roffler, Edmond O.; Shaving; Wigs and Hairpieces

Further Reading: Fisher, Angela, *Africa Adorned* (1984); Mulvey, Kate, and Melissa Richards, *Decades of Beauty* (1998); Panati, Charles, *Extraordinary Origins of Everyday Things* (1987); Riordan, Teresa, *Inventing Beauty* (2004); Rooks, Noliwe, *Hair Raising*

(1996); Vincent, Peter, "A Cut Above," *Sydney Morning Herald*, February 23, 2005, http://moneymanager.smh.com.au/articles/2005/02/22/1108834779883.html.

SUPERSTITIONS

A number of ancient and modern superstitions have involved hair. The idea that hair has some supernatural power may stem from the fact that it grows on the part of the body that contains the thinking brain and is positioned at the top of the body closest to heaven or the sky. Such beliefs also relate to the unique traits of hair, such as the fact that it regenerates itself, continues to grow throughout life, and will survive for centuries after death, even after other body parts have rotted away.

The fact that hair can regenerate itself may explain why it has played a key role in many fertility rites and other spiritual customs. Hair also has been regarded as a sign of virility, in which case cutting it off had a powerful negative effect on men, as exemplified in the biblical story of Samson and Delilah. Certain Native American groups saw hair as a source of strength. The practice of **scalping** one's enemies was linked to the idea that this could remove their strength and power.

Native Americans believed that their enemies could use the hair from their own heads to cast spells on them. As a result, they burned any hair that came out, even the hair that collected on their combs or brushes. Other cultures also suggested burning hairs to prevent bad luck. An old German superstition said that hairs left on a comb should be burned lest a bird use them in its nest, which could cause various health problems, depending on the type of bird. In ancient Persia, people believed that sorcerers could use bits of hair from an intended victim when they were casting their spells.

Superstitions relating to witches arose during the **Middle Ages**. It was said that if someone put a strand from the hair of a witch under the bed, it would turn into a snake.

Certain cultures believed that evil spirits lived in the hair. A superstition based on such a belief held that putting a hat on a bed would lead to an argument or bad luck in the home.

Since **combs** touched the hair, some ancient cultures regarded them as magical objects. Combs also were used to rid the hair of bad spirits or influences, and a comb had specific powers, depending on the material used to make it. Certain gemstones, such as amber, were thought to give a comb even more power against evil. Ancient people noticed that electrical static could occur sometimes when girls or women combed their long hair. They explained these crackling noises as coming from evil spirits. People who encountered those spirits were supposed to use a special talisman comb to get rid of them.

Certain superstitions related to the length and growth of hair. During the late 1800s, some people still claimed that heavy hair would weigh down a person's head and diminish brain functioning. Some men said this was another reason that women should be encouraged to keep their hair very long, as that would prevent them from thinking about subjects that were best reserved for men. Yet another superstition said that cutting bangs would keep the rest of the hair from growing because hair "wants" to be similar in length all over the head. Another superstition said that pulling out a white or gray hair would cause multiple, similarly colored hairs to grow in its place.

A number of cultures passed on superstitions about the times when hair could be cut. One of them said that cutting the hair on Good Friday would prevent headaches during the coming year. Some cultures based the dates for cutting hair on the position of the moon. Even into the **Victorian era**, people continued to plan their haircuts based on certain "lucky" days.

Superstitions about haircutting also dealt with days of the week and often banned haircuts on Sundays. One rhyme about cutting hair and nails went like this:

Cut them on Monday, you cut them for health.
Cut them on Tuesday, you cut them for wealth.
Cut them on Wednesday, you cut them for news.
Cut them on Thursday, a new pair of shoes.
Cut them on Friday, you cut them for sorrow.
Cut them on Saturday, see your true love tomorrow.
Cut them on Sunday, the devil will be with you all the week.

Although people once thought **shaving** would cause hair in that area to grow back more thickly, scientists say this a myth. They claim that the stubble left behind from shaving looks thicker to the eye because of its blunt edge.

See also: Africa; Coming of Age; Egypt, Ancient; Hair Color; India; Literature; Religion and Hair; Scalping; Yoruba

Further Reading: Chambers, Robert, *Book of Days* (2004); Cooper, Wendy, *Hair* (1971); Grimm, Jacob, *German Mythology* (1981); Hiltebeitel, Alf, and Barbara D. Miller, eds. *Hair* (1998); Opie, Iona, and Moira Tatum, eds. *A Dictionary of Superstitions* (1992); Waring, Philippa, *Dictionary of Omens and Superstitions*, Souvenir Press, 1998.

T

TEMPLE, SHIRLEY (1928–)

Regarded as the best-known child star of all time, Shirley Temple was the most photographed person in the world during the 1930s. Millions of girls around the world copied her trademark, curled hairstyle.

Shirley Jane Temple was born in Santa Monica, California, on April 24, 1928. At age three, while attending dance class, she was selected to appear in *War Babies*, which was part of a series of one-reel comedies called *Baby Burlesks*. Between 1932 and 1934, Temple appeared in six films. In 1934, she took on her first major role, in the film *Stand Up and Cheer*.

Temple's plucky personality, dimpled smile, and golden, corkscrew curls delighted and cheered audiences during the difficult years of the Great Depression. The multitalented child could act, sing, and dance. Onscreen, she tap danced with partners like Buddy Ebsen, James Dunn, William "Bojangles" Robinson, and other legendary performers.

Starting in 1935, Temple made movies for Fox Corporation, including *The Little Colonel, Curly Top*, and *The Littlest Rebel* in 1935; *Poor Little Rich Girl, Dimples*, and *Stowaway* in 1936; *Wee Willie Winkie* and *Heidi* in 1937; *Rebecca of Sunnybrook Farm* and *Little Miss Broadway* in 1938; and *The Little Princess* and *Susannah of the Mounties* in 1939.

For three years running, from 1936 to 1938, Temple was the top attraction at the box office. During these years, she earned $1,000 a week, which was a huge salary during the Depression years. When she celebrated her birthday in 1937, fans from around the world sent 135,000 gifts.

During the 1930s, she achieved many distinctions, including being the youngest person ever to appear on the cover of a magazine, the youngest person to receive an Academy Award, and the youngest to be listed in *Who's Who*.

To achieve the famous hairstyle, Temple's mother, Gertrude, would roll her daughter's hair into pin curls each night. She made precisely fifty-six curls each time so that Temple's hair would look the same from one scene to another during filming.

At the height of her popularity, the Ideal Toy Company launched its first Shirley Temple dolls, which featured Temple's hazel eyes, dimpled smile, and trademark, golden curls. The dolls often wore outfits like those that Temple had worn in her films, such as an Alpine dress from *Heidi*, a plaid kilt from *Wee Willie Winkie*, and a red-and-white dotted dress from *Stand Up and Cheer*. Dolls in Temple's image have been manufactured to the present day in different materials and series, including collectible porcelain models.

Shirley Temple with Eddie Cantor at the March of Dimes, January 30, 1934.
Library of Congress

Between 1942 and 1948, Temple made six more films. She was briefly married to actor John Agar, with whom she had a daughter. In 1949, she married Charles Black and retired from filmmaking but appeared on television from 1958 to 1959 to host a series called *Shirley Temple's Storybook*. From 1960 to 1961, she hosted another television program called *Shirley Temple Theater*. She and Charles Black had two children together.

As Shirley Temple Black, she was active in the Republican Party and entered politics. In 1967, she ran unsuccessfully for a seat in Congress. She then served in various cabinet posts.

Temple was a member of the U.S. delegation to the United Nations (1969–1970), was U.S. ambassador to Ghana (1974–1976), and during the administration of President Gerald R. Ford became the first woman in U.S. history to serve as chief of protocol (1976–1977). In 1989, President George Bush appointed her ambassador to Czechoslovakia. Her autobiography, *Child Star*, was published in 1988. In 1999, she was voted eighteenth on the American Film Institute's list of top actresses before 1950, and, in 2002, a monument was erected in her honor on the studio lot at Twentieth Century Fox.

Further Reading: Basinger, Jeanne, *Shirley Temple* (1975); Edwards, Anne, *Shirley Temple: American Princess* (1989); Windeler, Robert, *Shirley Temple* (1976).

TINEA CAPITUS

Tinea capitus—commonly known as ringworm of the scalp—is an infectious condition that can cause scaling and hair loss. It can occur under men's beards as well as on the scalp.

Despite the nickname, it is not caused by a worm. Some ringworm is caused by a fungus called *Microsporum canis*, which is found on dogs and cats. It also may be caused by *Trichophyton tonsurans*, an organism that can spread from one person to another. About 90 percent of all *Trichophyton tonsurans* cases in the United States occur among children who have not yet reached puberty, most of them between the ages of three and nine. People of any age can get tinea capitus, however. Those who are at a higher risk of contracting the fungus include children in daycare centers, swimmers, and people with weakened immune systems.

Symptoms of tinea capitus on the scalp include the formation of pimples that turn into flaky and/or scaly patches. Treatment for this condition includes prescription oral antifungal medication, which may need to be taken for two to four weeks before improvement occurs. In some cases, treatment continues for a few months. If inflammation occurs, a secondary staphylococcus infection may take hold and require additional treatment.

See also: Dandruff

Further Reading: Powell, J., et al., *An Atlas of Hair and Scalp Diseases* (2001); Sinclair, Rodney D., et al., *Handbook of Diseases of the Hair and Scalp* (1999).

TITLE VII

Title VII of the Civil Rights Act of 1964 offers protection to people in the United States from discrimination in the workplace based on race, color, religion, gender, or national origin. In terms of hair, it protects individuals from being discriminated against because of any unchangeable characteristic related to their race, such as hair texture.

Title VII can be extended to other hair-related matters. For instance, it would protect African American men in the workplace who faced a ban against beards if the man had inherited a tendency to pseudofolliculitis barbae (severe skin bumps resulting from shaving). Furthermore, workplaces probably would need to accommodate a person whose religion specifies the wearing of a headscarf or other hair covering or headgear unless this would pose some serious safety hazard or an undue hardship on the business.

People who believe they have been discriminated against on the basis of their hair texture, hairstyle, or preference in facial hair have filed lawsuits based on the Civil Rights Act of 1964. During the late 1960s and early 1970s, for example, some men cited Title VII when they filed suits against employers who banned them from wearing beards or long hair to work.

See also: Laws and Regulations

Further Reading: Civil Rights Act of 1964, http://usinfo.state.gov/usa/infousa/laws/majorlaw/civilr19.htm; Civil Rights Act of 1964, Title VII, http://www.eeoc.gov/policy/vii.html.

TONICS, HAIR

Hair tonics are toiletries applied to the scalp and/or hair for grooming purposes or to improve the condition of the hair. Other kinds of tonics are taken internally, rather than being applied topically, for the purpose of promoting healthy hair. Commercial hair tonics became especially popular in the United States during the nineteenth century and the early part of the twentieth century. Vendors said these substances would grow hair, among other things.

Since ancient times, people have used hair tonics made from a single substance or a mixture of ingredients, often derived from plants. For example, the ancient Egyptians used fir oil, rosemary oil, sweet almond oil, and castor oil as hair tonics. The use of fenugreek seeds to stimulate hair growth also dates back to ancient times and was known in India, among other places. In Africa, people used avocado leaves to make a scalp treatment, and they mixed flowers with olive oil to make scented tonics. Infusions of nettle leaves were popular for making hair tonics in Germany and other European countries. A popular hair tonic in Spain was made by boiling peels from a fruit called quince. Some tonics did not harm the hair and even did some good. Others, such as preparations from the **Elizabethan era** containing sulfuric acid, could damage the hair and scalp.

Native Americans used buffalo and bear fats on their hair, and settlers from Europe also began using these substances. Historians have traced advertisements for bear-oil hair tonics back to 1822. During the 1830s, stores offered bear oil and bear grease for adding shine to the hair, restoring its color, and fighting **hair loss**. Sales of these products, made from the grease of bears living in Canada and the United States, were high. Although fats from cattle and oxen also were promoted as hair tonics, none were as popular as bear oil. Some ads for bear oil claimed that it would prevent and/or cure baldness.

By the mid-1800s, a variety of topical hair tonics were being promoted and sold in the United States and Europe. For example, in England, Sir John E. Erichsen, a surgeon, recommended "stimulating washes, ointments [and] lotions" to his patients, and these were likely to contain copper sulfate, cayenne pepper, and/or Spanish fly (Bundles 2002, 52). As a result, bear oil became less available and less popular, though it was still being sold for use on the hair during the late 1800s. Ads emphasized that the product was pure or that it included a high amount of bear's oil. Analyses of old bottles of "bear oil" show that some products contained little bear oil or none at all.

Despite the claims of their manufacturers, many hair tonics were made from common ingredients with no special value for the hair. Thus, these products could not live up to the extravagant claims that were being made in order to sell them. Since these products were not regulated by law, manufacturers were not required to prove their claims or list ingredients.

People also made their own hair tonics. Recipes for hair tonics appeared in cookbooks and other books, and some recipes were handed down from one generation to the next. A number of these formulas included herbs that were said to improve circulation of the scalp. Popular ingredients included rosemary, nettles, and lavender. Jojoba oil also has traditionally been used. To stimulate hair growth, people in India used macassar oil, which comes from the seeds of a small tree that grows in eastern India. In Russia, burdock seed oil has been popular for many years as a hair tonic. During the late 1800s, European and American men relied on bay rum as a tonic to invigorate their scalp and stimulate hair growth.

Before and after the Civil War, **African American** women made and sold hair tonics and pomades, using recipes that called for plants, herbs, and natural oils. In New England, three African American sisters—Caroline, Cecilia, and Marchita Redmond—ran a successful mail-order business in New England selling Mrs. Putnam's Medicated Hair Tonic. Rebecca Elliott was one of the most successful early African American entrepreneurs, and ads for Elliott's Medicated Hair Grower said it would restore the hair. Barbers also made and sold their own hair tonics as well as tonics made by other people. Athenian Hair Tonic and Good Samaritan Hair Tonic were other popular nineteenth-century brands.

Mail order was another way to obtain hair tonics. During the late 1890s, people could order Princess Tonic Hair Restorer from the Sears, Roebuck catalogue. Advertisements in magazines and newspapers invited people to order various hair tonics. Still, many people made their own tonics based on recipes that were handed down for generations or their own original concoctions.

Starting in the 1800s, companies marketed products especially for African Americans that were labeled as "hair tonics" or "hair growers" but were actually straightening products. Since curly hair did look longer when it was straightened, the products had the effect of visually "growing" the user's hair. One such product, Ozono, came from the Boston Chemical Company, which began marketing this formula in 1875.

The 1900s brought more hair tonics, and many successful companies emerged. At the turn of the century, a patent-medicine company called E. Thomas Lyon heavily advertised its hair tonic, Kaitheron, to African American consumers, saying that the formula would improve the scalp and hair. Mississippi-born Madame Gold S. M. Young began offering hair care services and she patented her Gorine Hair Grower in 1913. This product, advertised as a tonic and conditioner, was part of Young's Gorine line.

One hair tonic business earned nearly $3 million over its thirty-eight-year history. The Seven Sutherland Sisters Hair Grower was advertised at circuses and events where the longhaired sisters performed in concert. Print ads declared, "It's the hair not the hat that makes a woman attractive." When the sisters' father, Fletcher Sutherland, applied for a patent, he listed the ingredients as borax, salt, quinine, cantharides, bay rum, glycerin, rose water, alcohol, and soap. In 1896, a pharmaceutical journal had an analysis conducted and found the following ingredients: 56 percent water of witch hazel, 44 percent bay rum, hydrochloric acid, and trace amounts of magnesia and other salts.

Barbers and hairdressers were among the people most likely to sell their own hair tonics. Some books written for **barbers**, hairdressers, and druggists contained directions for making tonics and other hair care products. An example of a book for professionals was *The Barbers' and Hair-dressers' Private Recipe Book: Embracing Recipes for Hair Producers, Hair Renewers, Tonic Dressings, Hair Oils, Hair Dyes,*

Pomades, which was published in 1868. In 1885, druggist Charles E. Hamlin published *Hamlin's Formulae: Comprising a Collection of Valuable Recipes for the Manufacture of Soda Syrups, Flavoring Extracts, Essences, Lily Whites, Face Washes, Hair Tonics.*

People could also find recipes for hair tonics in magazines and newspapers. For example, a syndicated columnist writing for the *Washington Star* in 1904 advised readers who were losing their hair to wash it thoroughly each month using coal tar soap and to apply a mixture containing sulfate quinine and glycerin, among other ingredients, twice each day.

One of the best-selling hair tonics was Vaseline hair tonic for men, manufactured by Chesebrough Manufacturing Company (later Chesebrough-Ponds). A 1939 ad for the product that appeared in *Life* magazine said that the tonic would "stimulate the circulation, help to relieve excessive dryness" and keep hair "manageable and handsome." During the 1940s, Jeri's Hair Tonic for men was promoted as a way to control dandruff. Starting the 1940s, Vitalis Hair Tonic, from Bristol-Meyers, became extremely popular. A 1950 ad that appeared in *Life* magazine urged men to experience the "60-Second Workout," by massaging their scalp with Vitalis for fifty seconds and then combing it for another ten seconds. According to the ad, Vitalis would stimulate the scalp, prevent dryness, control dandruff flakes, and "help check excessive falling hair." Different formulas for Vitalis hair tonic have been made since then, and the product still is sold today.

Throughout the twentieth century and into the present day, new hair tonics have continued to appear on the market, often claiming that they will improve circulation on the scalp, improve the hair's texture and shine, and even restore lost hair.

See also: Aging and Hair; Hairdressing; Laws and Regulations; Middle Ages; Styling Products: Walker, Madam C. J.

Further Reading: Anderson, Ann, *Snake Oil, Hustlers, and Hambones* (2004); Bundles, A'Lelia Perry, *On Her Own Ground* (2002); Byrd, Ayana, and Lori L. Tharps, *Hair Story* (2002); Fowler, Gene, ed. *Mystic Healers and Medicine Shows* (1997); Gill, Tiffany M., "Civic Beauty," *Enterprise & Society*, December 2004, 583–593.

TOUPEE

A toupee—also spelled "toupet"—is a partial wig used to conceal thinning hair or bald spots on the head. Toupees came into use during the 1700s in Europe. Often, they were used together with wigs. One popular hairstyle of that era involved combing a roll of natural hair above the hairline to blend in with the wig, so wig makers, barbers, and hairdressers sold rolls of artificial hair for that purpose.

> "Hair brings one's self-image into focus; it is vanity's proving ground. Hair is terribly personal, a tangle of mysterious prejudices."
>
> SHANA ALEXANDER (1925–), journalist and author

Other kinds of toupees evolved to cover various parts of the head or to add volume to wigs and hairstyles. These hairpieces were made from the same materials as wigs, including human hair, animal hair, wool, and other fibers. Far more men than women wore toupees.

Before the late twentieth century, many toupees were easy to spot, and they prompted jokes about bad toupees or men who "wore a rug." Some male celebrities have not hidden the fact that they were wearing toupees. Interest in this subject even prompted some people to start Internet sites where viewers are invited to vote on the worst looking celebrity toupee.

As of 2005, a toupee was the most common form of wig worn by men, and toupees were being worn by men around the world. Technology has advanced so that some synthetic fibers strongly resemble human hair. Human and/or synthetic hairs can be fashioned into hairpieces that look much more natural than the toupees of the past. They come in a vast range of colors, textures, and sizes.

Today, people can select from ready-made toupees or order their own custom-made hairpieces, sending a sample of their own hair for this process. Barbers and hairstylists offer services to help people choose, buy, and arrange their hairpieces so that they blend in with existing hair. Stylists also can trim and style a toupee. Usually a toupee is attached to the head with adhesive, and the wearer must be careful when participating in certain sports and other activities.

Numerous wig makers and companies offer these hairpieces, which often are manufactured in Asia. A high-quality toupee can cost more than most wigs—even several thousand dollars. One well-known source of hairpieces is The Hair Club for Men and Women, which operates various hair-related retail services in the United States, Canada, and Australia. People also can buy do-it-yourself kits, complete with videos and instruction manuals, to make their own hairpieces.

See also: Baldness, Voluntary; Hair Loss; Hair Transplant; Wigs and Hairpieces

Further Reading: Love, Toni, *The World of Wigs, Weaves, and Extensions* (2001); Matheson, Whitney, "Toupée or Not Toupée? Is There Really Any Question?" *USA Today*, January 13, 2004, http://www.usatoday.com/life/columnist/popcandy/2004-01-13-pop-candy_x.htm; Scott, Susan Craig, *The Hair Bible* (2003).

TRICHOLOGY

Trichology deals with the scientific study of the hair and scalp, and trichologists work with people who are having problems in these areas. People have been studying hair since ancient times, but trichology as a scientific field began to develop in the early 1900s.

To become a qualified trichologist, a person completes a course of study that is approved by the International Association of Trichologists (in the United States) or the Institute of Trichologists (in the United Kingdom). Such courses cover the anatomy and physiology of the hair and scalp, causes of hair loss, baldness, hair breakage, and scalp problems such as itching and scaling as well as treatments for these problems, including nutrition. One course of study listed the following topics, among many others: alopecia, dandruff, folliculitis, hirsutism, impetigo, lichen planus, neurodermatitis, ringworm, trichotillomania, and hair loss from chemical procedures.

When consulting with clients, trichologists may study the hair microscopically and have it analyzed for its mineral content. Some clients have blood tests to check their nutritional status and determine the functioning of various glands that affect hair growth. As they work with clients, trichologists may use various medical and complementary treatments, including changes in diet, nutritional supplements, or referrals for prescription medicines. They may also suggest changes in the hair care regime and recommend products that are gentler to the hair and scalp.

Since the late twentieth century, new technology has provided new tools for trichologists. Scientists are learning more about hair and its chemical components (which include carbon, nitrogen, hydrogen, phosphorus, chlorine, and sulfur) and chemical bonds. Research has led to sophisticated new tests as well as new hair care products and services.

See also: Allergic Reactions; Allopecia Areata; Dermatology; Hair Colorants

Further Reading: International Association of Trichologists, http://www.trichology.edu.au; Ogle, Robert R., *Atlas of Human Hair* (1998); The Trichological Society, http://www.hairscientists.org/education.htm.

TRICHOPHAGY

Trichophagy is a condition in which people eat hairs that they have pulled from their heads or other parts of the body (a separate hair-pulling disorder called trichotillomania). An estimated 5–18 percent of people with trichotillomania eat their hairs.

This condition can result in health problems, including medical emergencies. Since hairs cannot be broken down and digested, they form balls in the stomach. A build up of these hairs in the gastrointestinal tract can lead to severe medical problems and even life-threatening intestinal blockages. Trichobezoars (clumps of hair) can cause partial obstruction of the intestine and internal bleeding. Physicians have reported discovering trichobezoars that were up to one foot, ten inches wide and four inches thick. If a large obstructive clump is not surgically removed in time, death can occur. Symptoms of trichobezoar build up include loss of appetite, weight loss, abdominal pain, weakness, nausea, vomiting, diarrhea, and constipation.

Besides intestinal obstructions, persistent trichophagy can damage the enamel on a person's teeth. It can also cause problems with teeth and gums if hairs become lodged in these areas for long periods of time.

See also: Trichotillomania

Further Reading: Corsini, Raymond J., *The Dictionary of Psychology* (2001); Doski, J. J., et al., "Duodenal Trichobezoar Caused by Compression of the Superior Mesenteric Artery," *Journal of Pediatric Surgery*, November 30, 1995, 1598–1599; Rudolph, Colin D., et al., *Rudolph's Pediatrics* (2002).

TRICHOTILLOMANIA

Trichotillomania—from the Greek words *thrix* (hair), *tillein* (to pull), and *mania* (madness)—is a condition in which a person repeatedly pulls out hairs over a long period of time, leading to visible hair loss on the scalp. People may also pull hairs from their eyebrows, beards, and/or eyelashes as well as other parts of the body. The condition is called TTM for short.

Trichotillomania is listed as a psychiatric disorder in the *Statistical Manual of Mental Disorders* (DSM IV), which physicians use to diagnose psychiatric conditions.

The exact cause of hair-pulling disorders is not known, but such disorders have been known since ancient times. For instance, the Greek physician Hippocrates (460–377 BCE) wrote about a woman who pulled out her hair during an intense state of grief. In 1889, a French dermatologist, François Henri Hallopeau (1842–1919), wrote about a male patient who had pulled out all of his body hair. Hallopeau thought the condition might have occurred because the patient experienced itching that he hoped would be relieved if he removed the hairs. Hallopeau concluded that there was no cure.

Doctors theorize that people turn to hair-pulling behavior as a way to relieve tension that comes from anxiety, conflict, boredom, or frustration. People with this condition are said to have an impulse control problem or compulsive behavior that they cannot control. Some researchers, however, believe abnormal hair pulling is a neurological disorder that reflects abnormal levels of dopamine and serotonin in the brain, while others have called it a "bad habit." An estimated 2–4 percent of the population suffers from this disorder, which may be triggered or aggravated by stress.

Research has shown that hair-pulling disorders typically first appears around ages eleven to thirteen (early adolescence), though they can begin as early as infancy. While about twice as many women as men have the condition, among people under age six the ratio is three males for every two females. Most people with trichotillomania are between eleven and forty years old, and the peak incidence occurs in females ages eleven to seventeen.

People who suffer from trichotillomania may have other disorders. The most common is depression. Others include anxiety disorders, obsessive-compulsive disorders, alcohol or drug abuse, or eating disorders. In adolescents, attention deficit hyperactivity disorder (ADHD) also may accompany trichotillomania.

Treatment for trichotillomia includes medications and/or psychotherapy. Psychotherapy may include behavioral therapy and/or cognitive therapy. People learn to identify the thoughts and feelings they have at the time they begin to pull their hair and learn to replace these with other thoughts. Treatment may need to continue to prevent relapses. People also use nutritional supplements and relaxation techniques to deal with the anxiety that can trigger their hair-pulling behavior.

The main problems associated with TTM are social and emotional, since hair loss affects a person's appearance and self-concept, and lack of self-control can diminish self-esteem. A hair-pulling disorder can cause problems in relationships when people isolate themselves out of shame or embarrassment. If they believe that nobody else has this problem, they may feel even more alone. Serious physical health problems can occur if the person has a disorder called **trichophagy**, in which they chew and swallow the hairs they pluck from their heads or bodies. About 5–17 percent of the people with TTM also have trichophagy.

Further Reading: Jefferson, James W., and Jeffrey L. Anders, *Trichotillomania, A Guide* (1998); Keuthen, Nancy J., et al., *Help for Hair Pullers* (2001); King, Robert A., et al., "Childhood Trichotillomania," *Journal of the American Academy of Child & Adolescent Psychiatry*, November 1995, 1451–1459; Penzel, Fred, *The Hair-Pulling Problem* (2003).

TWIGGY (1949–)

During the late 1960s, Lesley Hornby, nicknamed "Twiggy" because of her very slim figure, was one of the world's top models and one of the world's first "supermodels." Her short, androgynous haircut set trends and was a key part of the "Carnaby Street" or "mod" look that became popular during the 1960s.

A teenager when she began her modeling career, Twiggy was five feet, seven inches tall and weighed ninety pounds. Originally from Neasdon, a suburb of London, her skinny frame and waif-like manner suited the miniskirts, tall boots, and colorful prints that became fashionable in England during the late 1960s. Leonard, a well-known hair stylist working in the Mayfair section of London, gave Twiggy a very short cut, parted on one side and slicked back behind her ears with styling cream. The haircut plus a meticulous bleaching job reportedly took eight hours. Dark, false-lashed "panda" eyes, which included eye shadow and lashes painted across the lower lids, dominated Twiggy's face.

Twiggy. *Photofest*

In 1966, the *London Daily Express* named Twiggy the "Face of '66," and around the world, young girls imitated her look. The next year, Twiggy was the highest-earning person in England. In addition to her modeling jobs, she received money from her clothing line, agency for singers, and other enterprises. People bought

Twiggy dolls and other Twiggy items, including lunchboxes, coloring books, stockings, and paper dolls.

During the 1970s, Twiggy, who had grown her hair long, focused on her careers as singer and actress. She appeared on Broadway in a revival of a popular 1920s musical, *The Boyfriend*, and won two Golden Globe awards for her performance.

She married American actor Michael Witney in 1977, and they had a daughter in 1978. Witney died of a heart attack five years later. In 1988, Twiggy married British actor Leigh Lawson, and together they moved back to England.

Twiggy has continued to perform on stage and screen. She also has recorded albums and performed in concert. During the 1990s, she hosted her own television show, in which she interviewed various celebrities. She has written two autobiographies: *Twiggy, An Autobiography* (1975) and *Twiggy in Black and White* (1999).

See also: Eyelashes; Hairdressing; Hairstyles, Twentieth-Century; Sassoon, Vidal

Further Reading: Carter, Ernestine, *The Changing World of Fashion* (1977); Stodder, Chris, *Swingin' Chicks of the 60s* (2000); Twiggy, http://www.twiggylawson.co.uk/biography.html; Twiggy, *Twiggy, An Autobiography* (London: Hart & Davis, 1975); Twiggy, *Twiggy in Black and White* (New York: Simon and Schuster, 1977).

U

UNIBROW

The word "unibrow" (sometimes "monobrow") refers to hair located between the eyebrows so that the brows appear to be one unit instead of two separate tufts of hair. A continuing line of hair across the brow is more commonly seen in certain regions, such as the Mediterranean nations of Greece and Turkey. (Observers note, however, that since the unibrow is more acceptable in these countries, it may seem more prevalent because people there may choose not to remove it.) In certain Asian cultures, eyebrows that form a continuous line across the face have been regarded as attractive.

While some cultures accept this look, in most cultures a unibrow is considered unattractive, perhaps because it is unusual, is associated with animals in the ape family, or may be seen as a sign of poor personal grooming. For women in particular, a unibrow has been considered undesirable and unfeminine. Most women, therefore, remove hair that grows between their brows, either on a regular basis by plucking, waxing, or using depilatory creams, or permanently, through electrolysis.

Some individuals have decided to retain their unibrows as a distinctive feature. One of the most famous women to keep her unibrow was Mexican artist Frida Kahlo (born Magdalena Carmen Frieda Kahlo y Calderon, 1907–1954). Kahlo not only kept her unibrow but also accentuated it with makeup. Her unibrow and the hair on her upper lip became signatures for Kahlo's distinctive personal style. Other well-known people who have appeared on lists of celebrities with a unibrow include, tennis player Pete Sampras, Bill Berry, former drummer for the rock music group R.E.M., and Jim Adkins, lead singer for the rock group Jimmy Eat World. Some fictional characters on television have sported a unibrow. They include Baby Gerald and Willie on *The Simpsons* and Bert on *Sesame Street.*

See also: Eyebrows; Hair Removal

Further Reading: Herrera, Hayden, *Frida* (2002); Norris, Michael, "Divining Secrets from Frida Kahlo's Unibrow," *The Pentagram* (Fort Myer), November 1, 2002; Togher, Irene, "Managing the Unibrow," *Sharpman*, December 27, 2000, http://www.sharpman.com/Article.asp?ArticleID=438.

UNILEVER

Unilever is a multinational company that sells numerous personal care products, including several top-selling hair care lines. In 2004, Unilever had sales of approximately $46.93 billion and was operating in eighty countries. Sales in the United

States that year were around $10 billion. The company, which began as Lever & Co., was named Lever Brothers in 1890. Then, in 1930, it was formally founded as Unilever.

William Hesketh Lever started the company in England during the 1880s, offering Sunlight Soap as his first product. Over the next few decades, the Lever company joined with other European companies that were making margarine and other products from fats and oils. Lever also introduced new soap products, including Lifebuoy and Sunlight Flakes (later called Lux Flakes). An innovative household-cleaning product called Vim was introduced in 1904.

The company continued to expand its food products businesses through growth and acquisition. The list of food products grew to include canned foods, ice cream and other frozen foods, tea, meats, and chewing gum. By the 1980s, Unilever was the world's twenty-sixth largest business.

In 1954, Unilever launched its Sunsilk brand of **shampoo**, and within five years, Sunsilk was available in eighteen countries. Today, the Sunsilk hair care line is sold around the world under various names, including Sunsilk, Hazeline, Elidor, Seda, and Sedal. It is the number-one brand of shampoo in Latin America, Asia, and the Middle East, with sales in 2004 of more than £1 billion pounds. In 2003, Unilever added a new line called Sunsilk **Afro**, which offered a one-step hair relaxant and other products. This line has been selling well in **Africa**, where the company held stylist parties and demonstrations during 2004 to help people learn more about the products.

Organics shampoo was launched in Thailand in 1993 and was being sold in more than forty countries within two years. In 1996, Unilever acquired the Helene Curtis hair care line in the United States for $770 million. The Helene Curtis division included the Thermasilk, Finesse, Salon Selectives, and Suave line of hair products. Lever's Lux shampoo is one of the most popular brands in Japan.

As of 2005, Unilever hair care lines, including Sunsilk, Dove, Finesse, Salon Selectives, Suave, and Thermasilk, offered consumers dozens of shampoos, conditioners, and **styling products**, including gels, mousses, pomades, relaxants, and **hairsprays**.

See also: Shampoo; Styling Products; Styling Tools

Further Reading: Alton Press Release, "Helene Curtis and Main Floor Help 'Untangle' Hair Care Advice on the Web," August 14, 2000, http://altonent.com/pressreleases/2000-08-14-helenecurtis.htm; Unilever, "Our History," http://www.unilever.com/ourcompany/aboutunilever/history/default.asp; Unilever, "Unilever Appoints to Senior Level Execs," October 13, 2005, http://www.unileverusa.com/ourcompany/newsandmedia/pressreleases/Unilever_Polk_Jope.asp; Unilever Canada, "Products," http://www.unilever.ca/products/index.asp?navLev=4&PCateId=10&NavId=32; Wang, Christopher, "Coty to buy Unilever's perfume business," *Detroit News*, May 21, 2005, http://www.detnews.com/2005/business/0505/22/biz-188501.htm.

V

VALENTINO, RUDOLPH (1895–1926)

Known as "the Sheik" and the prototypical "Latin lover" of the silent-screen era, actor Rudolph Valentino was regarded as one of the world's most handsome men. His look, including sleek, dark hair, was widely copied around the world. Film historians believe that Valentino paved the way for new generations of dark, sensual-looking actors.

Born Rodolfo Alfonzo Rafaelo Pierre Filibert Guglielmi di Valentine D'Antonguolla in Italy, the future matinee idol planned a career in the navy. When he failed to pass a required physical exam, Valentino left for America and settled in New York City, where he worked in various low-paying jobs.

In 1914, he found work as a dancer. After a well-known dancer named Bonnie Glass asked him to be her new male partner, the duo appeared at Maxim's, a popular New York City nightclub. Valentino went on to dance with other partners and was known for his rendition of the tango. During his years dancing in New York City, he had some walk-on parts in movies that were filmed in New York and New Jersey.

Hoping to expand his film career, Valentino left New York to tour the country as a vaudeville performer. When he arrived in California, he found work in the growing film industry. From 1917 to 1926, Valentino made more than a dozen silent films and gained a reputation for "exotic sensuality" (Lawton 1974, 45). His leading ladies included Gloria Swanson, Vilma Banky, and other top actresses of the day. His most famous roles were in *The Sheik* and *The Four Horsemen of the Apocalypse* in 1921 and *Blood and Sand* in 1922. Some critics said his best performance came in 1926 with *Son of the Sheik*.

Valentino influenced trends in men's hairstyles and grooming. Sales of petroleum jelly and men's hair pomades soared during the 1920s as men emulated the slick, shiny appearance of Valentino's dark hair, which was compared to black patent leather. Some men also wore the kind of sideburns that he wore while playing the matador Juan Gallardo in the film *Blood and Sand*: neatly trimmed sideburns that became gradually broader until they ended just below the ear. Critics, however, said that Valentino looked effeminate rather than ruggedly male. They nicknamed the actor "Vaselino." Also, hoteliers complained that after Valentino reached his late twenties, he left oily stains on pillowcases during overnight visits. Since a bald spot had begun to appear on his head, the actor used black hair paste to hide it.

In 1923, Valentino and his second wife, Russian dancer and set designer Natacha Rambova, promoted a skin care product called Mineralava Beauty Clay

Rudolph Valentino, ca. 1915–1926. *Library of Congress*

during their world dance tour. The next year, a public furor arose when Valentino grew a beard while he was traveling in Europe. When the actor appeared in photographs with his new beard, the Barbers of America Association announced that they would boycott Valentino's films if he did not shave off the beard. Valentino complied.

Despite his immense popularity, fellow actors recall that Valentino was modest, friendly, and easy to work with. Costar Bebe Daniels later commented, "He didn't know what conceit was" (Slide 2002, 90). Alice Terry recalled, "He was always agreeable, tried hard to please everybody" (Slide 2002, 382).

When Valentino died in 1926 of complications following surgery for a perforated ulcer, fans were distraught. Thousands of mourners gathered around the New York funeral parlor where his body lay, and many struggled to get inside. An estimated 100,000 people tried to attend his funeral in Hollywood. For years after his death, a mysterious "woman in black" continued to visit Valentino's grave. Fans even visited the stable where his horse from *The Sheik* was boarded and pulled souvenir hairs from its tail. Years later, author Yvonne V. Sapia used Valentino's mystique as a plot element in her 1991 novel *Valentino's Hair*. In the novel, a Puerto Rican barber who cuts Valentino's hair in 1926 tries to use the hair for its magical powers as an aphrodisiac.

See also: Beards, Men's; Hairstyles, Twentieth-Century; Styling Products; Styling Tools

Further Reading: Everson, William K., *Love in the Film* (1979); Lawton, Richard, *A World of Movies* (1974); Oberfirst, Robert, *Rudolph Valentino* (1962); Slide, Anthony, *Silent Players* (2002).

VAMP *See* Bara, Theda; Hair Color

VICTORIAN ERA (1837–1901)

During the Victorian era, hairstyles were distinctly different from the towering powdered wigs that were popular in Europe during the 1700s. Styles for both men and women changed several times during this historical period, which spanned the long reign of Queen Victoria of England. Generally, the Victorians emphasized a healthy, shining look that reflected an increasing emphasis on cleanliness of hair and body, especially after the 1860s. The use of a hairdresser's services became increasingly common during the late 1800s, and an increasing number of **beauty salons**, including chains of salons, appeared.

Although clothing and most aspects of appearance continued to emphasize gender differences, some hairstyles became popular with both men and women. One such style, the half-shingle, emerged during the 1840s. Hair was cut short on top but left longer around the head. Both genders also wore earlocks, which were curled locks that fell in front of the ear.

Men's Styles

From the 1840s to about 1865, many men wore their hair in a crest shape achieved by brushing the hair either forward or to the back, forming a cowlick or curled lock at the front. This style was worn with either a side or center part. Most men also wore **sideburns**, which became fuller as the century went on. A **mustache** called an imperial was popular during the mid-1800s, as was the spade beard, which fell from the chin in an oblong shape with a soft point at the bottom.

Soap locks were popular with some young men. They cut their hair very short from the back up to the crown but left the side long so that the strands could hang in front of their ears. Some fashionable youths tied these two hanging locks under their chin. This name also referred to a hairstyle worn by members of New York City gangs during the 1800s. They curled a lock of hair and then applied soap to make the hair lie flat.

After 1865, men began wearing their hair shorter, a trend that persisted until around 1890. Hair still was usually parted on the side or the middle but the part extended further from the forehead toward the back of the head. Some men chose to wear a **pompadour**, which required more maintenance than simpler styles. Styles in facial hair favored longer beards along with mutton-chop sideburns. The long and drooping handlebar mustache became popular during the late 1870s and was worn either alone or with a beard.

In contrast, as the nineteenth century came to an end, most fashionable men preferred a clean-shaven face, and sideburns also became smaller. Men who wore beards or mustaches usually kept them small and carefully trimmed, similar to the beards and mustaches worn by Albert, Prince of Wales, and the future King Edward VII. Wax was used to groom mustaches. While men in the eastern United States and settled urban areas tended to follow British fashions, men in the western United States liked the handlebar mustache, often worn without a beard.

During the late 1800s, Victorian men parted their hair either in the center or slightly to the left, and the pompadour remained a favorite style for those who had enough money and leisure to maintain it. Older men tended to prefer the walrus-style mustache.

Men could choose from a growing number of manufactured hair tonics as well as homemade preparations. Many Victorian men continued to use bear oil, which had been used for centuries, while others preferred bay rum. Companies that made these products claimed they would encourage hair growth as well as help to style the hair and hold it in place. Another popular hair care product was macassar oil, which also dated back to the 1700s. So many men used hair oils during the late 1800s that people placed cloth covers called antimacassars on the backs and arms of their furniture to prevent oil stains when people sat down.

A special look for young boys emerged from Francis Hodgson Burnett's popular novel, *Little Lord Fauntleroy*, which was published in 1886. Worn mostly by boys no older than six, the Fauntleroy hairstyle featured long ringlet curls, sometimes tied with hair bows. Long hair had been common on very young boys before Burnett's novel was published, but the book made it more acceptable to curl the hair and delay cutting the hair until boys were ten or even older. Setting these curls in papers each night was a time-consuming process that ended when the curls were finally cut off, a sign that the boy was growing up. Mothers often saved these shorn curls as keepsakes. During the early twentieth century, some mothers continued to prefer long, curled hair on their young sons. Author Thomas Wolfe later wrote about the embarrassment he felt during the 1920s when his mother insisted on keeping his hair styled in long curls until he was nine years old.

Women's Styles

Victorian hairstyles for women aimed to create a sweet, feminine look as well the appearance of an oval or round-shaped face. Hair was considered a primary aspect of a woman's appearance, and long, thick hair was admired. Girls and women spent time each day brushing and grooming their hair. Some historians think the idea of brushing a hundred strokes a day originated at this time, but the purpose of the brushing may have been to get rid of lice nits more than to improve the hair's appearance.

Throughout the 1800s, young girls tended to wear at least part of their hair hanging loose. Many girls wore long "drop curls" that were known as sugar curls or barley curls. Pinning up their hair and wearing longer skirts were signs that a girl had become a young woman, usually around age fifteen or sixteen.

During the early Victorian Era, most women wore their hair parted in the center and pulled back smoothly from the temples toward the back with no bangs. From 1840 to 1860, the topknots that were popular early in the century became smaller and moved further back on the head. Women were combining side curls with a chignon that was worn coiled at the back of their head. Toward mid-century, many women wore their hair in braids pinned neatly at the nape of the neck.

Accessories and ornaments were simpler than those worn a century earlier. In the daytime, many women wore their hair inside a net, secured on each side with a comb or black bow. Women adorned their hair with flowers, foliage, beads, pearls, jeweled bands, and **combs** made from ivory, tortoise shells, faux tortoise shells, or bone.

Chignons became especially popular during the 1860s. To wear this style, women created a roll or knot of hair at the back of the neck. Curls and poufs around the face were popular at mid-century, and these began moving further to the back of the head as the Victoria era continued. Netting, lace, or flowers were common adornments for a chignon.

After the 1860s, the center part remained popular, as did the bun and the chignon. The style called for these to be positioned either very low on the neck or high on the head. Using curling irons or metal curlers, women created ringlets around their faces. Some cut a short fringe of bangs, which might also be curled. One popular style of the 1870s left some hair cascading down the back in ringlets or large loops while the rest was swept up and secured with **hairpins**.

Curls and waves were regarded as attractive and feminine features, and curling irons were often used to achieve that look. Nighttime curlers made of metal also were used to add curls. Styling became easier after French hairdresser Marcel Grateau introduced his new curling iron in 1872, which led to the development of the **Marcel wave**. New types of curling irons caused less damage than the older methods. To crimp their hair, women pulled strands of hair over a hot iron to create a turned-up, wavy effect. **Styling products** included creams designed to keep curls intact during hot or damp weather.

The pompadour gained ground during the 1880s, sometimes with part of the hair hanging down. A special type of wide pompadour known as the **Gibson Girl** hairstyle developed by the 1890s and remained popular for two decades. Women also wore the French twist during these years, sometimes adorned with flowers.

Hairpieces became even more common when pompadours rose in popularity during the late 1880s. To create the wide Gibson Girl hairstyle, women rolled their front hair over a "rat" made from human hair or horse hair. Some added pieces of false hair to the back as well. Women made their own "rats" by saving the hair that came off on their brush each day. They stored loose hair in a ceramic, bronze, or crystal container called a hair receiver. When they had collected enough hair, they wove it or plaited it to make the "rat" that would add volume to their hairstyles.

A substantial amount of the hair used in human hairpieces was gathered from convents in countries with large Catholic populations. Hair also was collected from prisons, where officials required women to wear their hair short for sanitary reasons. Still more was obtained from women who sold their hair to earn money. One memorable scene from Louisa May Alcott's classic novel *Little Women*, set in the 1860s, occurs when the character Jo March sells her long, thick chestnut-colored hair to give her mother money to travel to Washington DC, where her father lies ill in a military hospital.

Hair Color

During the 1800s, dying the hair was still considered daring, and **hair colorants** could endanger a person's health and hair. Even so, hair-coloring recipes were passed among family members and friends, and commercial products were available. Some women used **henna** to add reddish or gold highlights to brown or black hair.

Because of its soft look, gray hair was regarded as becoming during these years, but some women preferred the color of their youth. In *The Arts of Beauty*, published in 1858, the famous dancer and international beauty Lola Montez offered a recipe for coloring gray hair a brown or black color. It contained gallic acid, acetic acid, and tincture of sesqui-chloride of iron.

Hair Art and Jewelry

Art and jewelry made with or from hair became quite popular during Victorian times. **Hair jewelry** included lockets containing the hair of a loved one as well as pieces of jewelry, such as rings or bracelets, made from hair. Queen Victoria fueled this trend, along with the widespread use of mourning jewelry, when she commenced a forty-year period of **mourning** after her husband, Prince Albert, died in 1861. The queen continued to wear black and various pieces of mourning jewelry for the rest of her life. When people met with the queen, they were expected to dress in kind.

In the United States, mourning jewelry commemorating the loss of loved ones became especially popular during the Civil War. Soldiers carried a lock or strand of their sweetheart or wife's hair, often inside a piece of jewelry. Departing soldiers often left locks of their own hair so their loved ones could wear it inside a locket. If the soldier died, the hair was moved to a black mourning locket. Sometimes hair was cut while a person was still alive but near death and then given to relatives who made it into watch chains and other items.

See also: Barbers; Beards, Men's; Comb, Decorative; Hair Art; Hair Net; Hairdressing; Harper, Martha Matilda; Headgear; Memento; Salons, Hair and Beauty; Styling Tools; Tonics, Hair; Wigs and Hairpieces

Further Reading: Boucher, Francois, *20,000 Years of Fashion* (1967); Bryer, Robin, *The History of Hair* (2003); Corson, Richard, *Fashions in Hair* (1965); Gibson, Charles Dana, *The Gibson Girl and Her America* (1969); Hellerstein, Erna O., *Victorian Women* (1981); Montez, Lola, *Arts of Beauty* (1982); University of Virginia: Selected Images from Godey's Lady's Book, http://www.iath.virginia.edu/utc/sentimnt/gallgodyf.html.

VIKINGS

The name "Vikings" is given to the Nordic peoples of Denmark, Norway, and Sweden who lived from about 800 to 1100 CE. Often, the most common image is of longhaired, blond sailors on a Viking ship, ready to explore and conquer, but the Viking era also is known for its art, technology, commercial advances, and other achievements. Historians have studied art, archeological sites, and written accounts to determine how the Vikings dressed and wore their hair.

Contemporary accounts by writers of that era show that the Vikings emphasized cleanliness and careful personal grooming. They bathed more often than most of their medieval counterparts in Europe. During warm weather, people bathed in streams, lakes, and other natural waters as well as in bathhouses. Heated bathhouses were used during the winter. As was true in certain other cultures, people tended to abandon their regular bathing and grooming routines when they were in mourning.

Grooming tools found in Viking grave sites include tweezers, razors, and **combs**. People plucked their eyebrows with tweezers made from antlers, bones, or more commonly, a metal such as iron or silver. Razors for shaving the hair were made from metal.

The Vikings were known for their well-made combs, which they used to groom the hair and to remove dirt and parasites. Combs also were used while washing the hair to enhance the cleansing process. The Vikings made combs from various materials, including animal antlers, wood, whalebone, and elephant ivory. They were formed either in a single piece or as a composite comb; composite combs were more common by the late Viking era. Some combs had teeth on both sides and most had decorative carvings, especially those made for wealthier people. Scientists who have examined the contents of grave sites concluded that Viking women carried their combs in small pouches, along with other small personal goods, while Viking men used a comb case sized to fit the comb. Comb making remained an important industry in Scandinavian countries into modern times.

The Vikings developed distinctive hairstyles and preferences in facial hair. As in many other societies, hairstyles could determine profession and social status. Most Viking men wore their hair close to shoulder length, in a variety of styles. Slaves (called *thralls*) were usually the only males with short hair. Most Viking men wore beards, and the length varied according to personal preference or occupation. Warriors, for example, might choose to wear their hair and beards somewhat shorter for practical reasons. Men in certain regions bleached their hair and sometimes also their beards a saffron yellow color. The bleaching agent contained lye obtained from ashes.

Historical evidence shows that Viking women probably had fewer different hairstyles than men. For unmarried girls, long and loose hair or braids were the most common styles. Married women often wore a bun. Slaves wore their hair shorter than other women to show their status as *thralls*.

Women wore various kinds of headgear for warmth, adornment, or to show marital status. These included cloth fillets, often made from silk with gold or other metallic, brocaded designs. They were similar to the fillets worn by women of that era in France, Germany, and England. Also common were scarves and hoods, mostly simple pieces made from wool, silk, or linen. Married women were most likely to cover their heads, as were Christian women. Non-Christian women might choose not to do so. Artwork shows women with a long "tail" hanging down the neck, which could have been hair tied in a long ponytail or the dangling ends of a cloth scarf. Hair ornaments included rings and pins made from gold, sometimes studded with garnets or other gems.

One well-known Viking saga deals with the hair of Harald, king of Norway, who was known as "Fairhair." Harald wanted to court Gyda, daughter of a king in Hordaland, but she told his representatives that she would not wed a king who ruled such a small kingdom. Harald then resolved that he would conquer all of Norway and announced that he would not cut or even comb his hair until he attained that goal. His blond hair grew quite long, and people began calling him King Harald the Fairhair.

See also: Middle Ages

Further Reading: Brondsted, Johannes, *The Vikings* (1978); Jones, Gwyn, *A History of the Vikings* (2001); Kendrick, T. D., *A History of the Vikings* (1930); Simpson, Jacqueline, *Everyday Life in the Viking Age* (1987); Williams, Mary Wilhelmine, *Social Scandinavia in the Viking Age* (1971).

WALKER, MADAM C. J. (1867–1919)

The child of former slaves, Madam C. J. Walker (born Sarah Breedlove) developed a highly successful business selling ethnic hair care products that provided jobs for thousands of **African Americans** and improved the lives of countless others.

Walker was born Sarah Breedlove on December 23, 1867, in Delta, Louisiana, where her parents worked as sharecroppers. The family was poor and Walker and her siblings worked alongside their parents, who died when Walker was six. She then moved to Vicksburg, Mississippi, with her older sister Louvenia, and they found work as maids. However, her brother-in-law's temper and cruel treatment prompted her to leave at age fourteen to marry Moses ("Jeff") McWilliams. Their daughter, Lelia, was born four years later.

Walker and two-year-old Lelia were left with no means of support after McWilliams died in 1887. They moved to St. Louis, Missouri, where Walker's brothers had become barbers. She worked as a laundress and attended night school to further her education. From her wages of only $1.50 a day, she managed to save some money for Lelia's future schooling, which later included Knoxville College. Recalling these years, Walker said, "When I was a washerwoman, I was considered a good washerwoman and laundress. . . . I got my start by giving myself a start" (Bundles 2002, 68). As a member of the St. Paul African Methodist Episcopal Church and the National Association of Colored Women, she met other women who were building better lives for themselves and their families.

Walker's strong interest in hair care dated back to the 1890s, when she experienced scalp problems and hair loss. Scalp problems were common in those days, but none of the homemade recipes and other treatments she tried provided much help. Around 1900, she began experimenting with formulas for hair care products. Several African American women had succeeded in the hair care business, and during the early 1900s, **Annie Minerva Turnbo Pope Malone** built a particularly successful company called Poro. Walker moved to Denver, Colorado, in 1905, to work as a Poro agent and as a cook while she continued to make hair care formulations.

Finally, she came up with a conditioning salve that worked well on her hair and began offering it to friends. She later said that the formula had come to her in a dream in 1905. It probably contained sulfur, along with herbs and other ingredients. Convinced that her salve had commercial value, she began selling it door-to-door in African American neighborhoods.

From 1894 to 1903, Walker had been married to a man named John Davis. She married her third husband, newspaper sales agent Charles Joseph Walker, in

1906, and then renamed her product Madam Walker's Wonderful Hair Grower. The business expanded as the couple advertised the products, which grew to include cleansers, including a coconut oil shampoo, a salve to treat eczema and ringworm, and a product called Glossine. Used with a heated pressing comb, Glossine was designed to smooth the hair and make it easier to style. By 1908, Walker also offered skin cleansers. A clean scalp and clean hair were fundamental aspects of her "Walker method."

Sales rose as the Walkers started a mail-order business and hired more saleswomen, called Walker agents, to demonstrate and sell their products. Charles Walker thought they should keep the business somewhat small, but Madam Walker disagreed.

Her vision was key to the company's continuing success. She realized that women were eager to earn a good living through their own efforts. In promoting her products, Walker emphasized cleanliness and good grooming as ways to boost pride in one's appearance, leading to greater self-confidence. African American women had lived in a society where white standards of appearance prevailed. As she traveled around the country conducting demonstrations in homes, schools, lodges, and churches, Walker urged women to appreciate their own beauty.

Growing sales enabled Walker to add new offices, training schools, and a factory. In 1903, Walker's daughter, Lelia, had moved to Pittsburgh, Pennsylvania, where she helped her mother expand the business. Walker founded Lelia College there to train beauty operators. A correspondence course for Walker "hair culturists" cost $25. Another change occurred when Indianapolis, Indiana, became the company's headquarters. There, Walker built a hair and manicure salon, another training school, and a large new factory, the Madam C. J. Walker Manufacturing Company, where several thousand African American women made Walker's cleansers, shampoos, salves, pressing oil, and skin care products. In 1912, Walker would tell members of the National Negro Business League, "I am a woman that came from the cotton fields of the South. I was promoted from there to the washtub. Then I was promoted to the cook kitchen and from there I promoted myself into the business of manufacturing hair goods and preparations. . . . I have built my own factory on my own ground . . ." (Bundles 2002, 135–136).

When her company was incorporated in 1911, Walker was the only shareholder and headquarters were still located in Denver. She and Charles Walker were divorced the next year. Afterward, she continued to expand her business, adding new beauty schools around the country and hiring more sales agents and representatives to promote and distribute her products. She also founded Walker beauty salons at which her products were used and sold. When the agents visited customers, they wore crisp white blouses and long dark skirts. They also agreed to keep their hair clean and well groomed using Walker's products.

Walker visited cities in the eastern and southern United States giving speeches about her business and lecturing on hair care techniques and products. Standing nearly six feet tall and dressed in high-fashion clothing, she impressed audiences both with her appearance and her message. Walker's reputation spread

Advertisement showing images of cold cream and hair and complexion products by Madam C. J. Walker. *Library of Congress*

beyond the United States, and she traveled to Central America and the Caribbean, including Costa Rica, Jamaica, Haiti, Panama, and Cuba, to demonstrate and sell Walker products.

Between 1911 and 1919, Walker's business grossed more than $100,000 a year. In 1916, Walker joined her daughter, now called A'Lelia, in the Harlem section of New York City, where they lived in two adjoining homes that the famous black architect Vertner W. Tandy had designed for them in 1913. A luxurious Walker beauty salon was located in this complex. Walker also hired Tandy to design her country mansion, called Villa Lewaro, in Irvington-on-Hudson, New York. Villa Lewaro, which featured a swimming pool and formal gardens, cost about $350,000, an enormous sum in those days. It was located in the same area as the estates of billionaire John D. Rockefeller, the founder of Standard Oil Company, and multimillionaire railroad financier Jay Gould.

The year 1917 was another prosperous time for the business, and Walker earned about $276,000 from business profits and her speaking engagements. People speculated that Walker's own personal fortune had reached at least $1 million, which would have made her one of the first African American millionaires in history and one of the first female self-made millionaires of any race.

Throughout her career, Walker had been donating money and time to causes she believed in, and she had encouraged her employees to take part in community service activities, too. Walker contributed money to various African American schools and churches, the National Association for the Advancement of Colored People, Mary McLeod Bethune's Daytona Normal and Industrial Institute for Negro Girls, the Tuskegee Institute, and a YMCA for African Americans in Indianapolis. In 1917, she joined with other concerned citizens to ask President Woodrow Wilson to support antilynching laws, a cause to which she contributed more than $5,000, and she urged the passage of other laws to advance civil rights. Walker also worked to make sure that African American veterans of World War I received the respect they deserved after serving their country.

Walker employees received special recognition and prizes for their community service work, which was discussed during their training programs. Employees paid dues of about twenty-five cents a month to join the Madam C. J. Walker Hair Culturists Union of America, which offered members insurance policies and other benefits.

In 1919, Walker died at the relatively young age of fifty-one from kidney failure caused by chronic hypertension (high blood pressure). Her estate was valued at $509,000. After her death, Walker's daughter continued to operate the business, followed by her own daughter.

In her will, Walker provided money to continue her charitable work. Her mansion, Villa Lewaro, was later sold, and the proceeds were given to the National Association for the Advancement of Colored People. The mansion became the Annie Poth Home for the Aged. The Madam C. J. Walker Manufacturing Company was sold in 1985 and ceased business operations. The five-story Walker building in Indianapolis, now called the Madam Walker Theater Center, is a national historic landmark. It contains offices and a cultural arts center.

Walker's great-great-granddaughter, A'Lelia Perry Bundles, later wrote a biography about her famous ancestor and campaigned for the 1998 commemorative U.S. postage stamp that was issued in Madam C. J. Walker's honor. Walker has also been inducted into the National Women's Hall of Fame.

See *also*: Hair Straightening; Salons, Hair and Beauty; Styling Products; Styling Tools; Tonics, Hair

Further Reading: Bundles, A'Lelia Perry, *On Her Own Ground* (2002); Indiana Historical Society; Manuscripts and Archives: Madam C. J. Walker Collection, 1910–1980; Peiss, Kathy L., *Hope in a Jar* (1998); The New York Times, "Wealthiest Negress Dead" (obituary) May 26, 1919, http://www.nytimes.com/learning/general/onthisday/bday/1223.html.

WASHINGTON, SARAH SPENCER (1881–1953)

Entrepreneur Sarah Spencer Washington founded a successful business that sold ethnic hair care products. A native of Virginia, Washington excelled in school and graduated from Norfolk Mission College. In 1913, she decided to enter the beauty profession. Despite her family's objections to this career, Washington thought she could succeed in this field. **Madam C. J. Walker** and other **African American** women had built extremely successful hair products businesses. To prepare herself, Washington studied cosmetology in Pennsylvania. Her strong interest in science and product development led her to take additional courses in chemistry at Columbia University in New York City.

In 1916, Washington moved to Atlantic City, New Jersey, where she opened a small beauty parlor two years later using the business name Madame Sarah Spencer Washington. During the day, she worked in her salon; at night, she sold her line of Apex products door-to-door. Under her expert management, the business expanded steadily and employed a growing number of African American women. In addition to providing jobs, Washington used her business profits to improve the lives of other African Americans in the community.

During the Great Depression of the 1930s, Washington saw cosmetology as an important means of economic survival for African American women. Philip Scranton wrote that Washington "urged black women to enroll in her beauty school and 'plan for [their] future by learning a depression-proof business'" (Scranton 2000, 182).

Washington's hair products and salon businesses were so profitable that she was able to build the Apex Manufacturing Company in 1940 for the production of her beauty products. It also included a laboratory. Washington went on to establish Apex News Service, which published a magazine for her agents and beauty salon operators. Her other enterprises included an Apex drugstore in Atlantic City and a chain of eleven beauty and barber schools in other cities.

Washington's beauty schools were especially successful, and that business became franchised, with schools established in twelve states as well as in South Africa and the Caribbean. Approximately 3,000 African Americans graduated from her schools each year and became licensed beauty operators. At its height, the company was graduating 4,000 people per year. In 1946, the business had 200 employees and was worth about $500,000. Washington herself became a millionaire. In 1944, she was able to buy the Brigantine Hotel, which later became the first integrated beachfront property in Atlantic City.

Washington received several awards for her business achievements and community service work. At the World's Fair in 1939, she was recognized as one of

America's most outstanding businesswomen and one of ten top businesswomen in the world. Washington died at age seventy-two on March 23, 1953.

Further Reading: Bundles, A'Lelia Perry, *On Her Own Ground* (2002); Byrd, Ayana D., and Lori L. Tharps, *Hair Story* (2002); Drachman, Virginia G., *Enterprising Women* (2001); Scranton, Philip, ed. *Beauty and Business* (2000); State of New Jersey, "New Jersey's African American Tour Guide," http://www.state.nj.us/travel/pdf_files/afam_tg.pdf.

WATER WAVE

The water wave (also called a finger wave) is a wavy hairstyle that became popular, primarily in Western cultures, during the 1920s and 1930s. **The bob** had replaced long hair, but some women did not like a straight bob. The water wave offered an alternative for women who found a curvier look more flattering. Many of the women who adopted this style had either a **permanent wave** put into their hair or had hair with a natural tendency to curl or wave.

Stylists used standard patterns or came up with their own variations as they created water waves. The traditional way to achieve the style, which is still used today, starts with wet hair (moistened with water and/or styling lotion). Then the hair is set into a series of waves, according to the desired design. These waves are set in place with six to ten curved combs, teeth pointing upward, or they can be secured with clamps or pins. Women may wear a net, scarf, or cloth on their head to keep these combs or pins in place until the hair dries. Then the implements are removed to reveal the wavy style.

See also: Flappers; Marcel Wave

Further Reading: Bryer, Robin, *The History of Hair* (2003); Turudich, Daniela, *Art Deco Hair* (2004).

A woman with a wave hair bob. *Library of Congress*

WIGS AND HAIRPIECES

Short for "periwig," from the French word "*perruque*," a wig is a head covering made from real hair or artificial fibers. Since the beginning of recorded history, men and women have worn wigs for various reasons, including personal adornment, disguise, professional need, concealment of hair loss, social status, or religious observances. Wigs also have been worn for health reasons such as during times when people shaved their heads to control lice or to protect one's head from the elements. Some people wear wigs to change hairstyles or hair colors easily, to save time, or for convenience while traveling. Men may wear wigs as part of crossdressing to look female.

> "A large head of hair adds beauty to a good face, and terror to an ugly one."
>
> LYCURGUS (ca. 800 BCE), Greek political leader

Ancient Times

People in ancient Sumer, Assyria, Egypt, Greece, Rome, and Phoenicia wore wigs for hygienic purposes and to reduce the signs of aging. Wigs also were placed on the heads of the dead before they were buried, and ancient tombs contain wig boxes along with other personal items.

In **ancient Egypt**, members of the higher classes tended to shave their heads and bodies to prevent lice infestations and because this was more comfortable in their hot climate. They disliked wearing a bald head in public, however, so they donned wigs made in various styles and colors, including black, indigo, and bright tones of blue, green, red, yellow, and gold. Before 1150 BCE, black was the favorite color for wigs and was the natural color of the Egyptians' own hair; after that time, colored wigs became more popular.

Women or professional barbers made wigs on their own or in factories, using human and animal hairs, including hair from sheep and horses. These hairs often were combined with plant fibers. Human hair for wigs came from slaves, people who sold their hair, or the heads of dead persons. Wigs made from real hair were more costly, while wigs made from grasses or plant fibers were the least expensive. Egyptians who could not afford a complete wig used hair extensions, which also were sometimes attached to wigs to make them even more luxurious.

A typical wig contained about 300 strands, which were kept in place with a wax-based pomade. To condition their wigs, people used emollients made from plant and animal oils, which increased the life of the wig. They also scented their wigs with flower petals, spices, or perfumed oils.

Styles varied depending on the occasion and the person's gender, age, and social status. Men's wigs generally were smaller than women's. Some wigs were designed with plaits, while others featured curls. One common style featured three sections of hair, two on either side and one down the back.

During the Old Kingdom (ca. 2705–2213 BCE) and Middle Kingdom (ca. 1986–1759 BCE), many wigs featured short hair styled in horizontal rows of overlapping curls, made in either square or triangular shapes. The bangs for these wigs were cut either straight across or given a rounded edge. Wigs in another style were made with long hair that hung down to the shoulders, sometimes with a soft wave or twisted into spiral shapes. Queens and women of the noble classes were allowed to wear a special style called the *goddress*, which had three sections of long hair styled in a special way.

During the New Kingdom, styles shifted to short, simpler hair for a while. Another style featured long wigs with tassels on the ends of hair that was first tied into sections. Wealthy Egyptians added extensions and other ornaments, such as beads, ribbons, and diadems.

In **ancient Greece**, wigs were uncommon, except for actors, who used masks, stage makeup, and wigs onstage. According to Francois Boucher, "Tragic actors wore . . . tall wigs or at least tufts of hair stuck to their masks" (Boucher 1987, 110). Similarly, people in ancient **Japan** and **China** rarely wore wigs except for theatrical performances. Among **Native Americans**, wigs usually were reserved for specific ceremonial occasions because they prized their natural hair. Certain tribes, including the Mandan and Yuma, did wear false hair.

Wigs were worn in ancient Rome. In the early days of the **Roman Empire**, prostitutes were required by law to either bleach their hair or wear blond wigs to show their trade to the public. According to the writings of the Roman historian Juvenal, Messalina, who was the third wife of Emperor Claudius, would hide her dark hair with a blond wig for her nightly visits to Roman brothels. Fair hair became fashionable among upper-class Roman women, and because they bleached their hair or wore blond or red wigs, the earlier law was repealed. Roman women especially favored wigs imported from Germany and Gaul. They also wore black full wigs or added hairpieces of blond or deep black shades to augment their own hair. Some Roman men, including Emperor Caracalla, wore blond wigs, too.

Some wigs were worn to cover damage to the scalp and hair loss caused by harsh bleaching formulas. In *Amores*, the Roman poet Ovid addressed women who faced this kind of situation:

> You alone bear the blame for the loss you feel. Your own hand poured the poisonous lotion on your head. Now the spoils of our triumphant armies will save you; you'll wear braids captured in Germany. But you'll blush every time someone raves about your new look; "I'm upstaged by a wig!" you'll cry. "It's some Sygambrian woman he's praising. I remember when those compliments were truly mine." (Rayor and Batstone, eds., 1995, 105)

Wigs played a role in Roman art. Because fashions in hair began changing so often starting around 200 CE, sculptors began placing marble wigs on their statuary to keep these figures in the current style.

Sixteenth to Eighteenth Centuries

Wigs went out of favor in western countries during the **Middle Ages**. The powerful Roman Catholic Church discouraged their use, urging that people wear simpler and more natural hairstyles. For men, church leaders recommended short, straight hair. King Henry IV of England (r. 1399–1413) banned long hair and wigs at his court. The preference for long hair persisted, however, and by the 1400s, many men wore longer hair as well as curls. Bald men or those with thinning hair had to wear wigs to achieve this look.

During the 1500s, Catholic clergymen became less strict regarding matters of dress, and wigs became more common. Some European women added wigs or artificial hair to the top of their natural hair to create complex hairstyles with plaits and coils. By the end of that century, most upper-class and middle-class European men regarded wigs as another item of clothing for daily wear.

Queen **Elizabeth I** (r. 1558–1603) had more than eighty red wigs of different styles that she wore to enhance and then cover her own hair as it became thin with age. Women in Britain followed suit, wearing wigs made from the hair of peasants or silk threads. Later in her reign, Elizabeth I also wore wigs in shades of blond. Her cousin, Mary Queen of Scots, wore an auburn-colored wig during her later years. This became known when she was beheaded at age forty-four and her wig fell off, revealing short gray hair. When Elizabeth died, an effigy dressed in one of the queen's wigs and her parliamentary robes was placed above her coffin during the funeral procession.

During the early seventeenth century, wigs became extremely fashionable among the French nobility. The style for men at the start of this century called for long hair styled in locks. One lock, hanging lower than the rest, was called the lovelock—a plaited strand with a bow tied to the end. Some men added false hair to achieve this look.

The use of wigs increased after King Louis XIII (r. 1601–1643) began wearing false hair. The king began losing his hair prematurely during his early twenties, as had his ancestors, who included Charles the Bald, who ruled during the eighth century. To please Louis XIII and show their camaraderie, his courtiers also donned wigs—called *perruques* in France—even if they had thick hair.

Early seventeenth-century wigs for men were about shoulder length, with a center part and bangs. They were frizzed or crimped and then curled at the ends, with three sections that fell down the back and on either side. After the middle of the century, more men began tying the two front pieces with bows. Another popular style featured thick curls on the forehead and hair that was arranged in horizontal rows along the sides of the face. Some older men preferred to wear an accessory called a *tour*, which was a round skullcap with hair sewn around it.

Wigs became increasingly popular among the upper classes after the mid-1600s. Under King Louis XIV (reign 1643–1715), forty wig makers were employed at the royal court of Versailles, outside Paris. Early in his reign, the fashion-conscious Sun King disliked wigs and preferred to show off his thick natural brown hair. However, when Louis noticed his own hair thinning, he started wearing wigs in all social situations, as did his courtiers. Some of these men had added false hair to their real hair as it grew thin, then moved on to completely shave their heads and use a full wig. Louis XIV acquired a large wardrobe of wigs for various events and different times of the day. His barber, Binette, was the only person who saw him in his natural bald state. As Louis XIV's reign continued, the simple, curled wigs that resembled hairstyles of earlier decades were replaced with longer, curlier, and more elaborate styles. By the late 1600s, men's wigs were growing taller, along with women's hairstyles.

The increasing use of wigs sparked the beginning of the wig industry. Many barbers became wig makers, which made it easy for them to provide full services, since they could shave male customers and measure them for new wigs. Besides making wigs, wig makers also cleaned and repaired them and refreshed the curls, powder, and fragrances. By 1665, a wig makers guild had been organized and wig makers needed to pay a fee to gain official recognition in their trade. This guild continued to build its power base and tried to control the entire wig industry, forcing independent wig makers out of business.

John Erskine wearing a wig and armor. *Library of Congress*

While the wig industry boomed, the millinery industry experienced changes. New hat designs were required for large, heavy wigs, and many men stopped wearing hats, although rules of etiquette still required them to carry a hat under their arms in public. Louis XIV's brother, the duc D'Orleans, refused to wear any hat, even during a **military** battle, because he did not want to squash his wig.

Milliners also made caps, sometimes quite ornate, for men to wear at home. Since they shaved their heads in order to wear wigs, men used scarves or caps to cover their bald heads at home. Caps for wealthier men were made of imported silk and brocade, featuring scrolls, flowers, vines, trees, and geometric designs. Often the caps had cuffs, which were edged with braid or embroidery.

The cost of wigs depended on their size, design, and materials. Large, natural-hair wigs in shades of blond and brown were most expensive, while black wigs were cheaper because they could be made from less costly materials. Wealthy people who could afford to replace worn-looking wigs sometimes sold their old ones, and poorer citizens bought them secondhand.

Wig fashions spread from France to England when King Charles II returned to reclaim the English throne after having spent time in exile at the French court. He and his cousin, the duke of York, were wearing wigs in the early 1660s. King

Charles II covered his gray hair with long, thick wigs featuring black curls, prompting English gentlemen of the upper and middle classes to adopt similar styles. The English called these hairpieces perukes, or periwigs, which was then shortened to "wig."

Rumors spread about the sources of the hair used in the booming wig trade. Cheap wigs might have contained different materials than those wig makers claimed to their customers. In England, people wondered if wig makers were using the hair of dead victims during the Great Plague that raged during 1665 and 1666. On September 3, 1665, the famous London diarist Samuel Pepys wrote:

> Up, and put on my coloured silk suit, very fine, and my new periwig, bought a good while since, but darst not wear it because the plague was in Westminster when I bought it. And it is a wonder what will be the fashion after the plague is done as to periwigs, for nobody will dare to buy any haire for fear of the infection? That it had been cut off the heads of people dead of the plague. (Pepys 2001, 163)

Wig styles could reveal a person's trade or profession. For instance, English soldiers wore a distinctive style called the *ramillie*, which featured side curls and a pigtail down the back, tied with black ribbon. In courts of law, the judges and barristers (attorneys) had their own particular styles of wigs.

Certain members of English society did not approve of the rise of the wig. Many clergymen, particularly **Puritans** or those representing other reform groups, harshly criticized the new fashion and refused to admit people who were wearing wigs to their places of worship. King Charles II passed an ordinance that banned English clergymen from wearing wigs. In Italy, people in Venice had begun wearing wigs during the mid-1660s, but some political leaders frowned on the practice. In 1668, the Council of Ten banned wigs, but later they came into wide use again.

Wigs increased in size after 1680. From the long, curled styles, wigs changed to a two-pointed design, then to styles that featured three tufts of hair. The latter style, designed by wig maker Sieur Binet, was called a *binette*. France was the center of the wig-making industry, importing hair from various places to make into wigs, many of which were sold abroad.

Eighteenth to Nineteenth Centuries

Though styles changed, wigs remained popular in the eighteenth century, and fashions continued to emerge from France. Eighteenth-century wigs were made from human hair, often obtained from European women, and hair from horses, goats, and yaks.

Early in the century, simpler, more-affordable wigs that were accessible to men beneath the upper classes replaced the expensive, full-bottomed wigs common among seventeenth-century noblemen. Long hair was still the norm for men, and those at court who lacked enough hair used a wig or a hairpiece to create a curled tail at the back.

Men placed their wigs right behind the hairline and then brushed some of their natural hair over the area where the wig met their heads. Rows of curls known as *ailes de pigeon* (pigeon's wings) were styled over the ears. The back could be styled in different ways. With one style called a bag wig, the hair in the back of the head was placed inside a black silk bag. For the *queue*, hair was divided into two plaited pigtails, which were then joined and secured with a ribbon. A variation of this style featured pigtails styled in ringlets instead of plaits. Still another style featured three sections of hair, two on the sides formed into plaited pigtails and the one in the back made into a rolled pigtail.

During the mid-1700s, a new style emerged that involved fewer rows of horizontal curls on the sides, revealing the ears. That style changed again in the 1780s, when curls styled around the head replaced the layers of curls on the side of the head. In the style called the *catogan*, a single pigtail was tied with a bow at the back of the neck. One popular style featured tumbling ringlets tied with bows. Fashionable young Englishmen nicknamed "macaronis" were seen in 1760 wearing tall wigs with curls around the ears. Later in the century, wigs were arranged with even, tight curls.

As the century went on, wigs for both genders became more elaborate and extravagant. These became a status symbol, distinguishing rich from poor. Valuable wigs were often included in wills. Ornate designs showed the high status of a person who could afford such finery, and people competed to see who could wear the most creative and expensive designs. In France, the comtesse de Matignon paid the famous hairdresser Baulard 24,000 livres a year to make her a new headdress every day. Jeweled combs of gold and silver were common accessories for fashionable men.

At the peak of their popularity, wigs became towering masses of hair, rising several feet above the head. Starch was used to keep many of these tall styles in place. Women placed frames and pads on their heads for more height and then placed the wigs on top. Their wigs were further adorned with gemstones, feathers, flowers, fruits, vegetables, garlands, and other trimmings. Some women created entire scenes on their heads—rooms full of miniature furniture, arrangements of small children's toys or musical instruments, gardens, birdcages with real birds inside, and detailed model ships.

Even the poorest people wore wigs if they could afford them. Before the 1700s, sumptuary laws had limited what people of certain classes could wear, even if they had enough money to buy certain items of dress or jewelry. Members of the lower classes wore wigs made from cheaper materials in more modest styles, such as the so-called "bushy" wig with a center part and the Sunday buckle, which had long, tight curls around the bottom. Those who could not afford wigs attempted to wear their natural hair in styles intended to resemble wigs.

Powdered wigs, using starch or Cyprus powder, also became very popular during this century, waning during the late 1700s. Women enjoyed using wig powders in various pastel colors, including pink, violet, and blue, and most were scented. Men tended to use white or gray, and gray became the favored color after the early 1700s. People of lesser means used household flour on their wigs. Since the process could be quite messy, wealthy people designated certain rooms of their homes for wig powdering. People wore special dressing gowns and covered their faces with a paper cone. Women who did not want to repowder their wigs daily wore caps to bed.

Giant wigs posed special problems. Doorways were raised so that people could pass through without knocking off their wigs. Since these wigs were extremely heavy, some people developed sores on their temples from the pressure. Powdered wigs posed special problems outdoors during foul weather. Fire posed another hazard, since some wigs were made from wool, and the animal fats used to style and condition wigs were combustible. It was not considered poor etiquette to groom one's wig in public. However, another rule of etiquette stated that people should not powder or ornament their wigs when visiting a person in court who was in mourning.

In England, powdered wigs were fashionable from about 1720 to the early 1800s. People used flour or starch to tint their wigs a white or gray color. As in France, wealthier people set aside "powder rooms" in their homes for this chore. In 1798, Prime Minister William Pitt pushed for a special tax on wig powder. After Pitt created his powder tax, opponents to the tax stopped using powder on their wigs in protest. A small number of elderly people continued the practice, which ended within a few decades. Powdered wigs remained a tradition for English barristers (attorneys) appearing in court.

Wigs became tied to other economic and political issues. During the mid-1700s, people seemed to be moving away from wigs toward wearing natural hair. In 1765, London wig makers asked the king to pass laws requiring all adult citizens to wear wigs. The king denied this petition. Despite the wig makers' fears, wigs did remain in style for several more decades, through changing styles, and wig making continued to be a profitable trade.

Meanwhile, the custom of wearing wigs had spread throughout Europe and to the American colonies. Fashionable people in Spain, Germany, Portugal, Russia, and other countries tended to follow French styles. In Germany, the count of Bruhl, who lived in Dresden, claimed to own 1,500 wigs.

In eighteenth-century Poland and Russia, wealthy people wore powdered wigs and further displayed their wealth by supplying their servants with powdered wigs as part of their uniforms. During the 1810s, a Russian family named Selivanov retained an enormous household staff that included eighty footmen wearing fancy uniforms and powdered wigs. Wealthy Russians bought their wigs with them during trips to England and France.

On the eve of the **French Revolution**, members of the French royalty and upper-class men and women were wearing fancy clothing and elaborate, powdered wigs. These symbols of an extravagant aristocracy became politically incorrect during the revolution. There were practical concerns as well, since flour sometimes was used to powder wigs, and many people were going hungry for want of bread. Wigs lost favor as supporters of the revolution adopted simpler hairstyles. Nobles who wanted to escape criticism and blend in with other citizens also stopped wearing their wigs.

The trend at the end of the 1700s was for light wigs or partial wigs that were blended into a person's own hair. A number of men in England and France wore wigs placed further back on the head, covered the front section with their own hair, and powdered both the false and natural hair for further concealment.

Colonial America

European settlers brought the custom of wig making to the American colonies. Like their European counterparts, eighteenth-century colonial men tended to wear wigs more than women did. Since people seldom bathed, men frequently shaved their heads to prevent lice infestation and then covered their bald heads with wigs. Wealthy men could afford expensive full wigs for business and social occasions. Poorer farmers and other men of lesser means could not buy expensive wigs, although they often purchased a simple queue. For their occasional visits to town or special occasions, these men attached a queue that matched their hair and tied it with black bows.

Although some colonists purchased European wigs, colonial wig makers began supplying customers who preferred to buy a local product. Wigs were made by barbers and wig makers—sometimes called perruke makers, from the French word *perruque*. Besides ready-made wigs, people could buy a custom-made wig ordered to fit their head sizes and other specifications. High-quality wigs were made from human hair or wool. A top-quality wig could require six people working full-time for nearly a week.

To construct a wig, a wig maker first cleaned, combed, and separated hairs obtained from a hair merchant. Strands of hair were styled and held in place with clay pins while they were boiled, dried, and baked. The wig maker nailed a net frame made from ribbon and cotton or silk net securely to a blockhead, all the while considering the measurements of the customer's head. By carefully weaving and stitching a few strands at a time, the wig maker created rows of hair on the frame. When all the rows were finished, the hair could be curled with rods made from clay. The wig maker finished a piece with scissors, combs, and a curling iron, doing any necessary trimming and then shaping each curl and section of the wig. The wig might be further dressed to the customer's requirements with powder, perfume, and various trims.

Wool wigs were cleaned in a rather unusual way—by baking them inside a hollowed-out loaf of bread. The wig was placed in the opening and baked in a hot oven, where the heat caused the wool fibers to swell. This practice may have led to the use of the term "big wig" to indicate a rich or important person.

As was true in England, men's wigs became controversial in the colonies. During the 1670s, Puritan clergymen urged men not to wear wigs, saying they made men look like women. Not all Puritans agreed, however, and some of them did wear wigs. At Harvard College, the president asked students at this all-male school not to wear wigs, but most of them did.

Wigs also became a status symbol in America. To further demonstrate their wealth, for example, some slave owners on Southern plantations bought wigs or hairpieces for the slaves who worked in their homes.

After the Revolutionary War, the use of wigs died out in the United States as citizens grew increasingly more independent from Europe economically, socially, and politically. The idea of equality and the blurring of class distinctions also influenced fashions.

Twentieth Century and Beyond

After 1800, wigs were not the fashion norm, although hairpieces were used to create the full hairstyles of the **Victorian era** and the pompadours that were popular at the turn of the twentieth century. Women who had lost their hair from aging or disease pinned false curls to their heads or used a wig to replace the lost hair.

Both wigs and hairpieces experienced a strong revival during the 1960s. Women in Western countries wore bouffant hairstyles that some could not achieve without the use of a full wig or hairpieces. The famous Carita sisters, hairstylists in Paris, are credited with popularizing wigs and hairpieces for women in the early 1960s. Fine wigs were made from human hair, usually from Asian countries, for affluent clients.

As demand grew, Dynel and other synthetic fibers became the most common material for mass-produced wigs, which made wigs affordable to more women. Some wigs from this era look stiff and unnatural compared to today's models.

A number of well-known women, especially performers, wore wigs. The singing trio called the Supremes—Diana Ross, Mary Wilson, and Florence Ballard—were known for their glamorous, bouffant styles. Ross, who attained superstar status as she continued her singing and acting career after the Supremes disbanded, wore an array of wigs for her appearances. Pop singer Tina Turner is known for red-toned wigs, styled with spikes or thick, shaggy layers, that contribute to her personal style. Country singer and actress Dolly Parton has worn various bouffant, blond wigs during concerts, acting roles, and other appearances.

Hairpieces called falls and postiches also were popular during the 1960s. Women used these items to add length and height to their hair, especially during the early part of the decade when large bouffants and beehives were in style. Falls and other hairpieces were popular during the late 1960s when long hair became one of the most fashionable looks.

Today, people still wear wigs for personal, professional, or religious reasons. They include actors who require a certain look for a part they are playing, singers, comedians, television journalists, and other people in the public eye as well as average citizens.

Women who lose their hair because of illness or cancer treatments may opt to wear wigs. In recent decades, health insurance companies have agreed to cover the costs of these wigs when women lose their hair because of cancer treatments. State governments also have been asked to waive taxes on the purchase of such wigs. In 1990, state officials in Massachusetts issued a ruling on this matter, stating:

> The Company's sales of wigs prescribed by a physician to persons who have suffered hair loss as a result of chemotherapy are included within the scope and intent of the exemptions provided by Section 6(l). Such sales are therefore exempt from the sales tax. (Kidder, 1990)

Hasidic Jewish women living in Israel, the United States, and other places have traditionally worn wigs to cover their hair after they marry. They may cut or shave off their own hair beneath a wig or leave it alone. Certain other Jewish women allow only their husbands to see their natural hair. Controversies have arisen over the source of hair used in the wigs worn by Hasidic women. In 2004, some religious leaders of ultraorthodox sects said that women should only use synthetic wigs because so many human-hair wigs come from **India**, where the haircutting is part of Hindu religious ceremonies.

Modern Wig Industry

Modern wigs come in numerous styles, colors, sizes, shapes, and materials. People can buy full wigs, half wigs, hairpieces, and extensions. The industry has been thriving since the late twentieth century because of the increased demand for hair extensions as well as traditional full wigs and men's **toupees**.

During the early 1990s, most of the hair used in the U.S. wig and hairpiece industry came from South Korea, but China surpassed Korea in the following decade. Most wigs imported into western countries now come from China, Thailand, and Indonesia. In 2003, 96 percent of the almost 11 tons of hair that were imported to the United States was shipped from China. Not all of this hair originated in China, however. A great deal comes from India, which many experts consider the best source of quality hair. Dealers collect the hair, which is then sent to hair-processing plants. Such plants are located in China, Indonesia, Italy, and other countries.

Artificial fibers also are used to make wigs and hairpieces. New and more natural-looking synthetic fibers were developed during the 1980s, and Japan played a key role in this technology. Since wigs were less popular with women during the 1980s, men's hairpieces were the major product being sold at that time.

Surveys of U.S. wig and hairpiece sales showed that they are more popular with **African Americans** than whites. In the early 1970s, African Americans made up about 12 percent of the U.S. population, but they bought more than 30 percent of the wigs sold in the nation. Many people working in the U.S. wig industry from the 1960s into the 1990s were Korean immigrants, many of whom opened profitable wig shops in African American neighborhoods in Los Angeles and other large cities.

Sales of false hair increased as more African American women began wearing hair extensions, braids, weaves, and curls. Women in Africa also adopted these styles, and by the early 2000s, tons of hair were being shipped to Congo, Nigeria, and other countries.

The foundations used for making wigs also have evolved. Modern monofilament wigs are sewn onto a thin, gauze-like material that is almost transparent. Strands of hair are attached one at a time and hand-knotted, which allows the hairs to move more freely on the wig base, making them easier to style. This process also allows more air to reach the scalp and natural hair, which reduces the build up of heat and perspiration and looks more natural than a wig made on a thicker foundation. Monofilament wigs may contain a small area in the back made from traditional cloth material that helps the wearer to adjust the wig to fit the head.

Celebrities have developed and/or endorsed lines of wigs. They include actresses Eva Gabor and Raquel Welch, singer and actress Dolly Parton, and models Cheryl Tiegs and Beverly Johnson. **Jose Eber** is among the well-known hairstylists who have launched a line of hair extensions, hairpieces, or wigs.

In addition to wigs, companies make products designed for wig care as well as wig stands and other accessories. Wig care accessories include adhesives and tapes used to anchor wigs and hairpieces, cleansing and conditioning products, hairsprays formulated for synthetic hair, and special combs and brushes.

See also: Alopecia Areata; Baldness, Voluntary; Beards, Men's; Elizabethan Era; False Beard; Hair Color; Hair Straightening; Hair Transplant; Hair Weave; Hairdressing; Locks of Love; Mesopotamia; Mustache; Occupations; Regency; Religion and Hair; Renaissance Europe

Further Reading: Arnold, Janet, *Perukes and Periwigs* (1970); Botham, Mary, and L. Sharrad, *Manual of Wigmaking* (1968); Boucher, Francois, *20,000 Years of Fashion* (1987); Chin, Ku Sup, In-Jin Yoon, and David Smith, "Immigrant Small Business and International Economic Linkage," *The International Migration Review*, Summer 1996, http://www.findarticles.com/p/articles/mi_qa3668/is_199607/ai_n8755242; Colonial Williamsburg Foundation Staff, *Wigmaker in Eighteenth-Century Williamsburg* (1959); Corson, Richard, *Fashions in Hair* (1965); Cosgrave, Bronwyn, *The Complete History of Costume & Fashion* (2001); Cox, James Stevens, *Crowning Glory* (1974); Cox, James Stevens, *Hair and Beauty Secrets of the 17th Century* (1977); Fraser, Antonia, *Royal Charles* (1979); Kidder, Stephen W., Commissioner of Revenue, "Sales Taxation of Wigs," Letter Ruling 90-4, August 3, 1990, http://www.dor.state.ma.us/rul_reg/LR/LR_90_4.htm; Montespan, Madame de, *Memoirs of Madame de Montespan* (2002); Pepys, Samuel, with Richard LeGallienne, ed., *The Diary of Samuel Pepys* (2001); Rayor, Diane J., and William W. Batstone, eds., *Latin Lyric and Elegiac Poetry* (1995); Reuters News Service, "Fear of Idolatry Sparks Wig Ban in Irael," *Jerusalem Times*, May 15, 2004; Ribeiro, Aileen, *Fashion in the French Revolution* (1988).

WORLD BEARD AND MOUSTACHE CHAMPIONSHIP

Also known as the Beard Olympics, the World Beard and Moustache Championship competition, which began in 1990 in Germany, is now held every two years in different locations.

At the 2003 event, 123 contestants came from Germany, Switzerland, Norway, Sweden, Italy, Austria, England, the United States, and Hong Kong to compete in Carson City, Nevada. These contestants arrived with a variety of long and short beards as well as braided beards and other styles.

The event has featured seventeen competitive categories. These include eight for moustaches: natural, English, wild West, handlebar, Dali, Fu Manchu, imperial, and freestyle. The partial-beard categories are musketeer, goatee, sideburns, and freestyle. The five full beard categories are natural, full, Garibaldi, Verdi, and freestyle. Rules permit contestants to use certain styling aids—moustache wax, hairspray, hair cream, styling foam, and hair gel—for some categories but not others.

Karl-Heinz Hille of Berlin, Germany, took top honors in the overall best beard category in 2003. His thick, black beard projected beyond both cheeks in an upswept "C" curve.

In October 2005, 243 men from 20 countries competed in Berlin. At this competition, Hille won a gold medal in the Imperial Cheek Beard category. Germans Elmar Weisser took the gold medal in the freestyle full beard category and Max Pankow won in the Dali Moustache category. American Toot Joslin won the top honors in the Sideburns category.

Local communities, states, and countries also hold competitive events or exhibitions for people with facial hair. Alaska, for example, awards prizes for beards at the annual Miners and Trappers Ball held in Anchorage. The Mr. Fur Face award goes to the person whose beard is judged best overall in the competition. Other men can compete for prizes based on the color of their beards: black bear, brown bear, honey bear, polar bear, and red fox. In Italy, the town of Grottaglie holds its annual Beard and Moustache Festival in September.

See also: Beards, Men's; Competitions; Mustache; Shampoo; Shaving; Sideburns; Soul Patch

Further Reading: Markey, Sean, "Whiskers Go Wild at World Beard, Mustache Games," *National Geographic World*, March 25, 2005, http://news.nationalgeographic.com/news/2005/03/0325_050325_beardmustache.html; "World Beard Championship," http://www.worldbeardchampionship.com.

WORTHINGTON, CHARLES (1963–)

British hairdresser Charles Worthington became prominent during the 1980s and is known as one of the world's most creative and influential stylists, as well as for his ability to develop other talented hairdressers. Worthington, who originally trained as an architect, began his hairdressing career in 1986 with a small London salon and staff of three people, himself included. As his reputation grew, Worthington expanded his original business and eventually operated five London salons and another salon in New York City, which later closed. As of 2005, Worthington's London salons were serving more than 2,000 clients each week.

Worthington works with actors, including Jamie Oliver, Mena Suvari, and Jennifer Love-Hewitt, and other celebrities. He often styles the hair of people who are attending important film industry events, such as the Cannes Film Festival, the BAFTA awards, and the Academy awards. He works with celebrities and models featured in top beauty and fashion publications. His honors include London Hairdresser of the Year (1993), British Hairdresser of The Year (twice), and Men's Hairdresser of The Year (1998).

Worthington helped to develop and launch the lines of hair care products that include Dream Hair and Results for Men, and the electrical styling tools that bear his name. Charles Worthington products are sold around the world. Worthington's product line Results, launched in 1995, and was the best-selling designer hair care line in the United Kingdom. He has written several books about hair care and styling techniques.

See also: Salons, Hair and Beauty

Further reading: Fashion UK, "Charles New Hair Results," http://www.widemedia.com/fashionuk/news/2004/06/30/news0003225.html; Worthington, Charles, "About Charles," http://www.cwlondon.com/home/; Worthington, Charles, *The Complete Book of Hairstyling* (2002); Worthington, Charles, et al., *Big Hair Day* (2002); Worthington, Charles, and Carmen Allen, *City Hair* (2002).

YORUBA

During a history that dates back at least 5,000 years, Africa's largest ethnic group, the Yoruba-speaking people of southwestern Nigeria and Benin, have stressed the importance of the head and hair. Among adult Yoruba, Dada and Asante priests both let their hair grow in a natural state, but for others, failure to groom the hair would indicate illness or antisocial behavior. **Hairdressing** traditionally had been a highly respected calling, and people who showed a special talent for hairdressing were urged to develop it. As adult hairdressers, they could gain the title of "master," which meant they cared for the hair of people in their community.

The Yoruba regard the head as the seat of the soul, as shown in this old saying: "One's head is one's creator." Their phrase for "human beings" can be translated as "humanity, the species that grows hair mainly on the head." Special cleansing rituals have been performed to nourish and invigorate the head.

This reverence toward hair began at birth. During the naming ceremony held about one week after birth, a ritual shaving was performed on the baby's head to show that he or she had left the spirit world to join the world of the living. Hair from this ceremony often was kept. Later, it was used for good-luck charms or medicinal preparations.

Some heads were not shaved. Children born with dense, curly, or knotted hair were considered a gift from the gods who would bring their parents good fortune, and they were given the name of Dada. Their hair could be washed and then was left to grow, uncut, forming natural locks. The hair of twins usually was not shaved either, since a multiple birth was regarded as special and sacred. Twins were later given identical hairstyles.

In the present day, parents in these cultures are accustomed to keep their children's hair well groomed. During childhood, boys' heads may be shaved on a regular basis, usually each month. Other styles for boys involve shaving the sides and back but leaving a patch on top (called the *osu*) or leaving a strip (called the *jongori*) extending from the top of the forehead down the back of the head. The sons of noble or wealthy Yoruba wear a style called the *aaso*, featuring three round patches of hair on the front, center, and rear of the scalp. Yet another version of this style is reserved for esteemed hunters and warriors. They have a patch of hair in the center of the head, which is braided into a knot that hangs down the left side. Men often wear a cap containing amulets over this hair.

Throughout their lives, Yoruba males usually shave their heads as well as their facial hair. Some clans wear special hairstyles in which part of the head is shaved and the remaining hair is styled in a way that identifies members of that clan.

The practice of shaving the head changes when Yoruba men reach old age, since gray hair and a beard are respected signs of maturity and wisdom.

In keeping with the Yoruba saying, "The hair adds to a woman's beauty," women carefully groom their hair, which is worn long throughout their lives. Young girls usually wear braids or other designs, and they learn styling techniques at an early age. Later, they wear various styles with a crown-like appearance. Some plaited designs—categorically known as *irun didi*—are extremely intricate and require hours to complete.

Several elaborate Yoruba hairstyles serve as a form of social communication by expressing spiritual beliefs, age, professions, and marital status, among other things. For example, a traditional woman's style called the *agogo* shows that the wearer is married. It features a high crest running from the forehead to the nape of the neck. Unmarried girls wear their hair braided, wrapped, or in other styles that set them apart from married women. They may also wear a style called the *olowu* that is regarded as especially attractive to men.

Spiritual beliefs in Yoruba included hundreds of gods and goddesses, and people wore specific braided styles to show their connection to these beings. Centuries ago, the Sande placed medicinal herbs inside the cleaned-out horns of various animals, such as sheep and antelope, and then braided these objects into their hairstyles. After the Islamic faith became more common in this region, people began substituting *lasimoisia*—amulets filled with scriptures from the Koran.

At death, the head of a Yoruba is again shaved to show that the deceased had left earth to reenter the spirit world. To show respect for the dead, some Yoruba, such as the Akan of Ghana, shave their heads when they are in **mourning**. One ritual involves putting this hair into a pot with a lid made to resemble the deceased. The family takes the pot, which also contains food and cooking utensils, to a specified area on the burial grounds, where they recite a blessing.

Since the 1950s, Western hairstyles have been influencing traditional African ideas about hair and dress, but many traditions remain popular. Some leaders have spoken out against these trends and urged people to carry on their own traditions. For example, officials in the Ivory Coast had a factory cloth printed with traditional women's hairstyles after a local beauty contest showcased contestants with thin bodies and Western hairstyles. This cloth, called *The Hair of Awoulaba*, showed hairstyles worn by women in the Awoulaba beauty pageant, which was organized to showcase "authentic African beauty." One of the criteria for the contest, held in 2000, was thick, black hair. Contestants had fuller figures than are seen in Western pageants, and they wore traditional African hairstyles and clothing. The winner was a forty-one-year-old mother of six children. In 2002, the winner was a thirty-three-year-old mother of four children.

See also: Africa; African Americans; Coming of Age

Further Reading: Arnoldi, Mary Jo, and Christine Mullen Kreamer, *Crowning Achievements* (1995); Bascom, William, *The Yoruba of Southwestern Nigeria* (1969); Byrd, Ayana D., and Lori L. Tharps, *Hair Story* (2002); Houlberg, Marilyn, "Social Hair: Yoruba Hairstyles in Southwestern Nigeria," in *Fabrics of Culture*, ed. Justine M. Cordwell and Ronald A. Schwarz (1979), 349–397; Sieber, Roy, and Frank Herreman, *Hair in African Art and Culture* (2000); Sobotta, Sharon K., "World's Body Perceptions Vary," *University Chronicle*, February 26, 2001, http://www.universitychronicle.com/media/paper231/news/2001/02/26/News/World8217s.Body.Perceptions.Vary-38169.shtml.

YOUNG, MADAME GOLD S. M. *See* Salons, Hair and Beauty; Tonics, Hair

Z

ZOTOS INTERNATIONAL, INC.

Zotos International, Inc., is a leading international producer of hair care products for salons and salon professionals. Zotos is part of the Shiseido International Corporation, which is a subsidiary of Shiseido Co., Ltd., of Tokyo, Japan.

Founded in 1919, Zotos made a significant contribution to the beauty industry in 1933 when it developed a chemical formula for permanent waving. Known as the Mercapton cold wave permanent, this process did not require electricity to deliver a permanent, and it was less apt to damage the hair. Cold waves also gave a longer-lasting result. Zotos became the leading manufacturer of permanent wave products in the beauty industry. In 1960, the company's Moisture Wave was one of the top-selling permanent wave preparations. The cold wave concept is still used today.

In 1972, Zotos continued to refine its permanent wave products and launched new products, including a method for the acid weave. As "big hair" became stylish again during the 1980s, sales of Zotos permanents surged. Zotos continued to launch new products, including many cleansing, conditioning, and styling products made with botanical ingredients.

When Shiseido acquired the company in 1988, Zotos was part of the Stamford, Connecticut-based Conair Corporation. Founded in 1959, Conair specializes in handheld hair dryers and sets of hot rollers. Shiseido is a large global corporation known for its lines of cosmetics, skin care products, and fragrances, and the acquisition of Zotos gave it a major presence in professional hair care markets around the world.

Further acquisitions gave Zotos an even stronger presence in the professional hair care industry. It acquired the North American salon hair care division of Helene Curtis in 1996 and Lamaur's professional products line in 1998. As of May 2005, Helene Curtis ranked number one in sales of hairspray and hair spritz products in the United States and western Europe.

In 2001, Shiseido added a California hair care company, Joico Laboratories, Inc., to the Zotos division. Joico, which was founded in 1975, was known for an ingredient called the Triamine complex. Its line grew to include heavy-duty conditioners and products geared for teenagers. Joico's SPIKER line was designed to help consumers create popular "street looks" for hair. Production of Joico was moved to the Zotos manufacturing plant in Geneva, New York, and that facility was expanded to accommodate this change.

Today, Zotos offers high-end shampoos, conditioners, styling products, permanents, and hair texture and hair coloring products. The corporation, which is based in Darien, Connecticut, also contributes to various charitable organizations, including the humanitarian group AmeriCares, as well as Bread & Roses, which benefits children who are afflicted with the AIDS virus or affected by HIV in their family. Zotos also has donated personal care items to victims or hurricanes and other disasters.

See also: Salons, Hair and Beauty

Further Reading: CCL Press Release, Media Resource Center, "Zotos International Sports a New Look with CCL Container's Trimwave Shape," http://www.cclcontainermedia.com/pr-TrimWave.html; *Happi*, "Hair Care: A Growing Market," December 2004, http://www.happi.com/current/Dec041.htm; *Happi*, "Hairstyle Trends for Spring and Beyond," May 2005, http://www.happi.com/May05Feature1.htm; Kline & Company, Inc.; Zotos International, Inc., "Company History," http://www.zotos.com/company/asp.

Bibliography

BOOKS

Ackerman, Diane. *A Natural History of the Senses*. New York: Vintage Press, 1991.
Adams, David Wallace. *Education for Extinction: American Indians and the Boarding School Experience, 1875–1928*. Lawrence: University of Kansas Press, 1995.
Adamson, Joy. *The Peoples of Kenya*. New York: Harcourt, Brace Jovanovich, 1967.
Alexander, Paul J., ed. *The Ancient World: To 300 AD*. New York: Macmillan, 1963.
Algrant, Christine Pevitt. *Madame de Pompadour, Mistress of France*. New York: Grove Press, 2002.
Allen, David Grayson. *In English Ways: The Movements of Society and the Transferral of English Local Law and Custom to the Massachusetts Bay in the Seventeenth Century*. Chapel Hill: The University of North Carolina Press, 1981.
Allen, Margaret. *Selling Dreams: Inside the Beauty Business*. New York: Simon and Schuster, 1981.
American Academy of Pediatrics. *Caring for Your Baby and Young Child, Birth to Age 5*. New York: Bantam, 1998.
American Medical Association. *The AMA Book of Skin and Hair Care*. Philadelphia: J. B. Lippincott, 1976.
American Mothers Committee, comp. *Mothers of Achievement in American History, 1776–1976*. Tokyo: Charles E. Tuttle Co., Inc., 1976.
Ames-Lewis, Francis, and Mary Rogers, eds. *Concepts of Beauty in Renaissance Art*. London: Ashgate Publishing, 1998.
Amphlett, Hilda. *A History of Fashion on Headgear*. New York: Dover Publications, 2003.
Anand, Margot. *The Kama Sutra of Vatsayana*. Translated by Richard Burton. New York: Modern Library, 2002.
Andelin, Helen. *Fascinating Womanhood*. New York: Bantam, 1965.
Anderson, Ann. *Snake Oil, Hustlers, and Hambones: The American Medicine Show*. Jefferson, NC: McFarland and Co., 2004.
Andrews, Ralph W. *Curtis' American Indians*. Seattle: Superior Publishing, 1962.
Angeloglou, Maggie. *A History of Makeup*. New York: Macmillan, 1970.
Anthony, Katharine. *Marie Antoinette*. New York: Knopf, 1933.
Arkwright, F., ed. *The Memoirs of the Duke de Saint-Simon*. New York: Brentano's, 1918.
Arndt, K. A., et al., eds. *Cutaneous Medicine and Surgery*. Philadelphia: W. B. Saunders, 1996.
Arnold, Janet. *Perukes and Periwigs*. London: HMSO, 1970.
Arnoldi, Mary Jo, and Christine M. Kreamer. *Crowning Achievements: Africans Art of Dressing the Head*. Los Angeles: UCLA Fowler Museum of Cultural History, 1995.
Atwan, Robert, Donald McQuade, and John W. Wright, *Edsels, Luckies, & Frigidaires: Advertising the American Way*. New York: Dell, 1971.

Auboyer, Jeannine. *Daily Life in Ancient India, 200 BC to 700 AD*. New York: Macmillan, 1965.
Auerbach, Nina. *Woman and the Demon: The Life of a Victorian Myth*. Cambridge, MA: Harvard University Press, 1982.
Axtell, James. *The European and the Indian: Essays in the Ethnohistory of Colonial North America*. New York: Oxford University Press, 1981.
Ayscough, Florence. *Chinese Women Yesterday and Today*. New York: Da Capo Press, 1937.
Bachman, Mary. *Collectors Guide to Hair Combs*. Paducah KY: Collector Books, 1998.
Bakalar, Nick, et al. *Wiping Out Head Lice*. New York: Brookhill Books, 1997.
Balsdon, J. P. V. D. *Roman Women: Their History and Habits*. Westport, CT: Greenwood Press, 1962.
Banner, Lois W. *American Beauty*. New York: Knopf, 1983.
———. *In Full Flower: Aging Women, Power, and Sexuality*. New York: Vintage, 1993.
Baran, Robert, and Howard I. Maibach, eds. *Textbook of Cosmetic Dermatology*. New York: Taylor & Francis Group, 1998.
Barlow, Ronald S. *The Vanishing American Barbershop: An Illustrated History of Tonsorial Art, 1860–1960*. El Cajon, CA: Windmill Publishing, 1996.
Bascom, William. *The Yoruba of Southwestern Nigeria*. New York: Holt, Rinehart and Winston, 1969.
Basinger, Jeanine. *Shirley Temple*. New York: Pyramid, 1975.
———. *Silent Stars*. Middletown, CT: Wesleyan University Press, 2000.
Basten, Fred E., with Robert Salvatore and Paul A. Kaufman. *Max Factor's Hollywood: Glamour—Movies—Makeup*. Los Angeles: General Publishing Group, 1995.
Batchelor, John. *Ainu Life and Lore*. Tokyo: Kyobunkwan, 1927.
Baudet, A. L., et al., eds. *The Metabolic Basis of Inherited Disease*. New York: McGraw-Hill, 1989.
Baumann, Leslie. *Cosmetic Dermatology: Principles and Practice*. Columbus, OH: McGraw-Hill Professional, 2002.
Beckwith, John. *Ivory Carvings in Early Medieval England, 700–1200*. London: Arts Council of Great Britain, 1974.
Bede. *Ecclesiastical History of the English People*. rev. ed. New York: Penguin, 1991.
Bedrick, Roy. *The Sense of Smell*. Garden City, NY: Doubleday, 1960.
Beer, Thomas. *Mauve Decade: American Life at the End of the Nineteenth Century*. New York: Vintage, 1926.
Begoun, Paula. *The Beauty Bible*. Seattle: Beginning Press, 1997.
———. *Don't Go to the Cosmetics Counter without Me*. Seattle: Beginning Press, 2003.
———. *Don't Go Shopping for Hair Care Products without Me*. Seattle: Beginning Press, 1995.
———. *Don't Go Shopping for Hair Care Products without Me*. 3rd ed. Seattle: Beginning Press, 2004.
Bell, Jeanenne. *Collector's Encyclopedia of Hairwork Jewelry: Identification & Values*. Paducah, KY: Collector Books, 1998.
Berdan, Frances F. *The Aztecs*. New York: Chelsea House, 1989.
Berg, Charles. *The Unconscious Significance of Hair*. London: Allen & Unwin, 1951.
Bergman, Ron. *The Mustache Gang: The Swaggering Saga of Oakland's A's*. New York: Dell, 1973.
Bernier, Olivier. *Eighteenth-Century Woman*. Garden City, NY: Doubleday, 1982.

Bernstein, Gail Lee, ed. *Recreating Japanese Women, 1600–1945*. Berkeley: University of California Press, 1991.

Bettelheim, Bruno. *The Uses of Enchantment: The Meaning and Importance of Fairy Tales*. New York: Alfred A. Knopf, 1976.

Bibby, Geoffrey. *Four Thousand Years Ago: A World Panorama of Life in the Second Millennium B.C.* New York: Alfred A. Knopf, 1963.

Bickmore, Helen. *Milady's Hair Removal Techniques: A Comprehensive Manual*. Albany, NY: Milady Publishing, 2003.

Bish, Barry. *Body Art Chic; The First Step-by-Step Guide to Body Painting, Temporary Tattoos, Piercing, Hair Design, Nail Art*. London: Trafalgar Square Publishing, 1999.

Blackman, Cally. *The 20s and 30s: Flappers and Vamps*. Portsmouth, NH: Heinemann Educational Books, 2000.

Blackwell, Earl, ed. *Celebrity Register*. New York: Simon and Schuster, 1973.

Blumner, Hugo, and A. Zimmern. *The Home Life of the Ancient Greeks*. New York: Cooper Square Publishers, 1966.

The Body Shop Team. *The Body Shop Book*. New York: Dutton, 1994.

Bonner, Lonnice Brittenum. *Good Hair: For Colored Girls Who Have Considered a Weave When the Chemicals Become Too Ruff*. New York: Three Rivers Press, 1994.

Boot, Adrian, and Chris Salewicz. *Punk: The Illustrated History of a Music Revolution*. Corvallis, OR: Studio Books, 1997.

Bordes, Francois. *The Old Stone Age*. New York: McGraw-Hill, 1968.

Bornoff, Nicholas, et al. *Things Japanese*. Tokyo: Periplus Publishing, 2002.

Boston, Lloyd. *Men of Color: Fashion, History, Fundamentals*. New York: Artisan, 1998.

Botham, Mary, and L. Sharrad. *Manual of Wigmaking*. New York: Funk and Wagnalls, 1968.

Boucher, Francois. *20,000 Years of Fashion: The History of Costume and Personal Adornment*. New York: Harry N. Abrams, 1967.

Bowen, Donna, ed. *Everyday Life in the Muslim Middle East*. Bloomington, IN: Indiana University Press, 2002.

Bradford, Sarah. *America's Queen: Jacqueline Kennedy Onassis*. New York: Penguin, 2001.

Brady, Kathleen. *Lucille: The Life of Lucille Ball*. New York: Watson-Guptill, 2001.

Brain, Ronald. *The Decorated Body*. New York: Harper & Row, 1979.

Brantley, Ben. *The New York Times Book of Broadway: On the Aisle for the Unforgettable Plays of the Last Century*. New York: St. Martin's Press, 2001.

Braund, Kathryn E. Holland. *Deerskins and Duffles*. Omaha: University of Nebraska Press, 1993.

Braunstein, Peter, and Michael William Doyle, eds. *Imagine Nation: The American Counterculture of the 1960s and '70s*. New York: Routledge, 2001.

Bray, Warwick. *Everyday Life of the Aztecs*. New York: Putnam, 1968.

Breasted, James Henry. *Ancient Times: A History of the Early World*. Boston: Ginn, 1944.

Brickell, John. *The Natural History of North Carolina, With an Account of the Trade, Manners, and Customs of the Christian and Indian Inhabitants*. 1737. Murfreesboro, NC: Johnson Publishing, 1968.

Brier, Bob, and Hoyt Hobbs. *Daily Life of the Ancient Egyptians*. Westport, CT: Greenwood Press, 1999.

Brondsted, Johannes. *The Vikings*. New York: Penguin, 1978.

Brooke, Iris. *English Costume From the Early Middle Ages Through the Sixteenth Century*. New York: Dover Publications, 2000.

Brothers Grimm. *The Complete Brothers Grimm Fairy Tales*. New York: Gramercy, 1993.
Brownmiller, Susan. *Femininity*. New York: Linden Press / Simon and Schuster, 1984.
Bryer, Robin. *The History of Hair: Fashion and Fantasy Down the Ages*. London: Philip Wilson Publishers, 2003.
Buchwach, Kenneth A. *Contemporary Hair Transplant Surgery*. New York: Thieme Publishing Group, 1997.
Bundles, A'Lelia Perry. *Madam C. J. Walker*. New York: Chelsea House, 1991.
———. *On Her Own Ground: The Life and Times of Madam C. J. Walker*. New York: Scribner, 2002.
Burstein, Patricia. *Farrah*. New York: Fawcett, 1977.
Burkhardt, Jacob. *The Civilization of the Renaissance in Italy*. New York: Modern Library, 2000.
Burton, Janet E. *Monastic and Religious Orders in Britain, 1000–1300*. London: Cambridge University Press, 1994.
Buskin, Richard. *Blonde Heat: The Sizzling Screen Career of Marilyn Monroe*. Cincinnati, OH: Watson-Guptill, 2001.
Byrd, Ayana D. and Lori Tharps. *Hair Story: Untangling the Roots of Black Hair in America*. New York: St. Martin's Press, 2002.
Cadbury, Deborah. *The Lost King of France: A True Story of Revolution, Revenge, and DNA*. New York: St. Martin's Press, 2002.
Caine, Kenneth W., and Perry Garfinkel. *The Male Body: An Owner's Manual*. Emmaus, PA: Rodale Books, 1996.
Camacho, Francisco M. *Hair and Its Disorders: Biology, Pathology, and Management*. London and New York: Taylor & Francis Group, 2000.
Camden, Carroll. *The Elizabethan Woman: A Panorama of English Womanhood, 1540–1640*. London: Cleaver-Hume, 1952.
Campbell, Mark, Jules Kliot, and Kaethe Kliot. *The Art of Hair Work: Hair Braiding and Jewelry of Sentiment with Catalog of Hair Jewelry*. Berkeley, CA: Lacis Publications, 1989.
Carcopino, Jerome. *Daily Life in Ancient Rome: The People and the City at the Height of the Empire*. New Haven, CT: Yale University Press, 1940.
Carter, Ernestine. *The Changing World of Fashion*. New York: G. P. Putnam's Sons, 1977.
Cassini, Oleg. *A Thousand Days of Magic: Dressing Jacqueline Kennedy for the White House*. New York: Rizzoli, 1995.
Casson, Lionel. *Daily Life in Ancient Rome*. New York: American Heritage, 1975.
Catesby, Mark. *The Natural History of Carolina*. London: Benjamin White, 1996.
Center for the Study of Responsive Law. *Being Beautiful: Deciding for Yourself*. Washington, DC: Center for the Study of Responsive Law, 1986.
Chamberlin, Eric Russell. *Everyday Life in Renaissance Times*. New York: Putnam Publishing Group, 1966.
Chambers, Robert. *Book of Days*. Whitefish, MT: Kessinger Publishing Co., 2004.
Chandler, Kurt. *Shaving Lessons: A Memoir of Father and Son*. San Francisco: Chronicle Books, 2000.
Charles, Ann, and Roger DeAmfrasio. *The History of Hair*. New York: Bonanza Books, 1970.
Chevannes, Barry. *Rastafari: Roots and Ideology*. Syracuse, NY: Syracuse University Press, 1994.

Chubb, Mary. *Nefertiti*. London: Bles, 1954.
Cicero, Marcus T. *The Orations of Marcus Tullius Cicero*. Vol. II. Translated by C. D. Yonge. London: George Bell & Sons, 1917.
———. *Selected Works*. New York: Penguin, 1960.
Clark, Eric. *The Want Makers: The World of Advertising: How They Make You Buy*. London: Penguin, 1988.
Clayton, Peter A. *Chronicle of the Pharaohs: The Reign-By-Reign Record of the Rulers and Dynasties of Ancient Egypt*. New York: Thames & Hudson, 1994.
Coba, Bernard. *Inca Religion and Custom*. Austin: University of Texas Press, 1990.
Coe, Michael D. *The Maya*. 4th ed. New York: Thames & Hudson, 1987.
Cole, Hubert. *Beau Brummell*. New York: Mason / Carter, 1977.
Cole, W. Owen, and Piara Singh Sambhi. *The Sikhs: Their Religious Beliefs and Practices*. London: Routledge & Kegan Paul, 1978.
Collins, Roger. *Early Medieval Europe, 300–1000*. New York: Macmillan, 1999.
Colonial Williamsburg Foundation Staff. *Wigmaker in Eighteenth-Century Williamsburg*. Williamsburg, VA: Colonial Williamsburg Foundation, 1959.
Contenu, Georges. *Everyday Life in Babylon and Assyria*. London: Edward Arnold Publishers, 1954.
Cooley, Arnold J. *The Toilet and Cosmetic Arts in Ancient and Modern Times*. New York: Lenox Hill Publishing, 1970.
Conrad, Barnaby. *The Blonde: A Celebration of the Golden Era from Harlow to Monroe*. San Francisco: Chronicle Books LC, 1991.
Cooper, Wendy. *Hair: Sex, Society, Symbolism*. New York: Stein and Day, 1971.
Cormack, Margaret Lawson. *The Hindu Woman*. New York: Bureau of Publications, Teacher's College, Columbia University, 1953.
Corsini, Raymond J. *The Dictionary of Psychology*. London and New York: Taylor & Francis Group, 2001.
Corson, Richard. *Fashions in Hair: The First Five Thousand Years*. New York: Hastings House, 1965.
———. *Fashions in Hair: The First Five Thousand Years*. 2nd ed. London: Peter Owen Publishers, 2001.
———. *Fashions in Makeup: From Ancient to Modern Times*. New York: Universe Books, 1972.
Cosgrave, Bronwyn. *The Complete History of Costume & Fashion: From Ancient Egypt to the Present Day*. New York: Checkmark Books, 2001.
Cosio, Robyn, with Cynthia Robins, *The Eyebrow*. New York: HarperCollins, 2000.
Coulton, G. G., ed. *Social Life in Britain from the Conquest to the Reformation*. London: Kegan Paul, 2004.
Cox, James Stevens. *An Illustrated History of Hairdressing and Wig Making*. London: B. T. Batsford, Ltd., 1984.
———. *Hair and Beauty Secrets of the 17th Century*. Surrey, England: Toucan Press, 1971.
Craig, Maxine. *Ain't I A Beauty Queen? Black Women, Beauty and the Politics of Race*. New York: Oxford University Press, 2002.
Cronin, Vincent. *Louis and Antoinette*. New York: Crown, 1974.
Crossley, Pamela Kyle. *The Manchus*. Cambridge, MA: Blackwell Publishers, 2002.
Cunliffe, Barry. *The Ancient Celts*. New York: Penguin, 2000.
Daidoji, Yuzan, et al. *Code of the Samurai: A Modern Translation of the Bushido Shoshinsu*. Tokyo: Tuttle Publishing, 1999.

Davidson, Basil. *African Kingdoms*. Alexandria, VA: Time-Life Books, 1966.
Davies, Adrian, and T. A. Davies. *The Quakers in English Society, 1655–1725*. New York: Oxford University Press, 2000.
Decarreaux, Jean. *Monks and Civilization: From the Barbaric Invasions to the Reign of Charlemagne*. Translated by Charlotte Haldane. Garden City, NY: Doubleday, 1964.
DeCastelbajac, Kate. *The Face of the Century: 100 Years of Makeup and Style*. New York: Rizzoli, 1995.
De Courtais, Georgine. *Women's Headdress and Hairstyles in England From AD 600 to the Present Day*. London: B. T. Batsford, 1973.
De la Haye, Amy, et al. *Surfers, Soulies, Skinheads, & Skaters: Subcultural Style from the Forties to the Nineties*. London: Overlook, 1996.
De Saussure, Cesar. *A Foreign View of England in 1725–1729*. Montclair, NJ: Caliban Press, 1995.
Densmore, Frances. *Krakow Indians Use Wild Plants for Food, Medicine, and Crafts*. New York: Dover Publications, 1974.
Diaz, Bernal. *The True History of the Conquest of New Spain*. Reprint of 1860 edition. New York: Penguin, 1963.
Dobson, Jessie. *Barbers and Barber-surgeons of London: A History of the Barbers' and Barber-surgeons Companies*. London: Blackwell Scientific Foundation for the Worshipful Company of Barbers, 1979.
Donoghue, Daniel. *Lady Godiva: A Literary History of the Legend*. Oxford: Blackwell Publishers, 2002.
Douglas, Stephen. *The Redhead Encyclopedia*. Newport Beach, CA: Redheads International, 1996.
Dowling, Colette. *The Cinderella Complex*. New York: Simon and Schuster, 1981.
Doyle, Bernard W. *Comb Making in America*. Salem, MA: Higginson Book Company, 1993.
Doyle, Marian I. *An Illustrated History of Hairstyles, 1830–1930*. Atglen, PA: Schiffer Publishing Co., 2003.
Doyle, William. *The Oxford History of the French Revolution*. New York: Oxford University Press, 2003.
Drachman, Virginia G. *Enterprising Women: 250 Years of American Business*. Chapel Hill: University of North Carolina Press, 2001.
Driver, Godfrey Rolles, and John Charles Miles, eds. *The Babylonian Laws*. 2 vols. London: Oxford University Press, 1952–1955.
Drucker, Philip. *Indians of the Northwest Coast*. Garden City, NY: Natural History Press, 1963.
Dubois, Cora. *The People of Alor*. Minneapolis: University of Minnesota Press, 1944.
Dumenil, Lynn. *The Modern Temper: American Culture and Society in the 1920s*. New York: Hill and Wang, 1995.
Dunbar, Andrew, and Dean Lahn. *Body Piercing*. New York: St. Martin's Press, 1999.
Dutton, Bertha P. *American Indians of the Southwest*. Santa Fe: University of New Mexico Press, 1983.
Dyer, Davis, et al. *Rising Tide: Lessons from 165 Years of Brand-Building at Procter & Gamble*. Boston: Harvard Business School Publishing, 2004.
Eber, Jose. *Beyond Hair: The Ultimate Makeover Book*. New York: Simon & Schuster, 1990.

———. *Shake Your Head, Darling!* New York: Warner Books, 1984.
Editors of Advertising Age. *Procter and Gamble: The House That Ivory Built*. New York: National Textbook Co., 1988.
Edwards, Anne. *Shirley Temple: American Princess*. New York: Penguin, 1989.
Edwards, Audrey, ed. *Essence: 25 Years Celebrating Black Women*. New York: Harry N. Abrams, 1995.
Edwards, Chilperic. *The World's Earliest Laws*. London: Watts & Co., 1934.
Eliade, Mircea, editor in chief. *The Encyclopedia of Religion*. New York: Macmillan, 1987.
Elias, Alan N. *Hirsutism*. Westport, CT: Praeger Publishers, 1983.
Elkin, A. P. *The Australian Aborigines*. New York: American Museum of Natural History / Doubleday, 1964.
Ellingwood, Finley, MD, *The American Materia Medica, and Therapeutics and Pharmacognosy*. Self-published, 1919.
Ellis, Peter Berresford. *Celtic Women*. London: Constable and Company, 1995.
Emerson, Kathy Lynn. *The Writer's Guide to Everyday Life in Renaissance England from 1485–1649*. Cincinnati, OH: Writer's Digest Books, 1996.
Erman, Adolf, and H. M. Tirard. *Life in Ancient Egypt*. New York: Ayer Company, 1940.
Estrin, Norman. *The Cosmetic Industry: Scientific and Regulatory Foundations*. New York: Marcel Drekker, 1984.
Euromonitor International. Cosmetics and Toiletries Company Profile: Henkel. MarketResearch.com, 2003.
Evans, Nekhena. *Hairlocking: Everything You Need to Know: African Dread and Nubian Locks*. 3rd ed. Brooklyn, NY: A & B Publishers Group, 1999.
Everitt, Anthony. *Cicero: The Life and Times of Rome's Greatest Politician*. New York: Random House, 2003.
Everson, William K. *Love in the Film*. Secaucus, NJ: Citadel Press, 1979.
Ewen, Stewart. *PR! A Social History of Spin*. New York: Basic Books, 1996.
Eyman, Scott. *Mary Pickford: America's Sweetheart*. New York: Donald I. Fine Books, 1991.
Fagan, Brian M. *The Aztecs*. New York: Freeman, 1984.
Falkus, Christopher. *The Life and Times of Charles II*. Garden City, NY: Doubleday, 1972.
Fantham, Elaine, et al. *Women in the Classical World*. New York: Oxford University Press, 1994.
Farber, David, and Beth Bailey, *Columbia Guide to America in the 1960s*. New York: Columbia University Press, 2003.
Faris, James C. *Nuba Personal Art*. London: Duckworth, 1972.
Fekkai, Frédéric. *A Year of Style*. New York: Clarkson Potter, 2000.
Ferencz, Benjamin B. *Less Than Slaves*. Boston: Harvard University Press, 1979.
Ferrell, Pamela. *Where Beauty Touches Me: Natural Hair Care & Beauty*. Washington DC: Cornrows and Company, 1995.
Fest, Joachim C. *The Face of the Third Reich*. New York: Da Capo Press, 1970.
Firenzuola, Agnola. *Tales of Firenzuola*. Rome: Italica Press, 1987.
Fisher, Angela. *Africa Adorned*. New York: Harry N. Abrams, 1984.
Fishman, Diane, and Marcia Powell. *Vidal Sassoon: Fifty Years Ahead*. New York: Rizzoli International, 1993.
Fiske, John. *The Dutch and Quaker Colonies in America*. Boston: Houghton Mifflin, 1902.

Fitzgerald, F. Scott. "Bernice Bobs Her Hair." Whitefish, MT: Kessinger Publishing, 2004.
Fitzpatrick, Thomas B. *Color Atlas & Synopsis of Clinical Dermatology*. New York: McGraw-Hill Professional, 2000.
Flaherty, Tina Santi. *What Jackie Taught Us: Lessons from the Remarkable Life of Jacqueline Kennedy Onassis*. New York: Perigee Books, 2004.
Forde, Daryll, ed. *African Worlds*. London: Oxford University Press, 1954.
Foster, G. Allen. *Advertising: Ancient Market Place to Television*. New York: Criterion, 1967.
Fowler, Gene, ed. *Mystic Healers and Medicine Shows: Blazing Trails to Wellness in the Old West and Beyond*. Santa Fe, NM: Ancient City Press, 1997.
Fox, Stephen. *The Mirror Makers: A History of American Advertising and Its Creators*. Champaign–Urbana: University of Illinois Press, 1984.
Frame, Grant. *Rulers of Babylonia*. Toronto: University of Toronto Press, 1995.
Frankfort, Henri. *The Birth of Civilization in the Near East*. Garden City, NY: Doubleday, 1956.
Fraser, Antonia. *Marie Antoinette: The Journey*. New York: Anchor, 2002.
———. *Royal Charles: Charles II and the Restoration*. New York: Knopf, 1979.
Frazier, Gregory, and Beverly Frazier. *The Bath Book*. San Francisco: Troubadour, 1973.
Freedman, Rita. *Beauty Bound*. Lexington, MA: D. C. Heath and Co., 1986.
Freeman, Jo, ed. *Women: A Feminist Perspective*. New York: McGraw-Hill Humanities, 1995.
Frey, Otto Hermann, et al. *The Celts*. New York: Rizzoli, 1991.
Friday, Nancy. *The Power of Beauty*. New York: HarperCollins, 1996.
Gabel, Medard. *Global Inc.: An Atlas of The Multinational Corporation*. New York: New Press, 2003.
Gardner, Jane F. *Women in Roman Law and Society*. Indianapolis: Indiana University Press, 1986.
Garland, Robert. *The Greek Way of Death*. London: Oxbow Books, 1985.
Garrett, Elisabeth Donaghy. *At Home: The American Family 1750–1870*. New York: Harry N. Abrams, 1989.
Gatewood, Willard B. *Aristocrats of Color: The Black Elite, 1880–1920*. Little Rock: University of Arkansas Press, 1990.
Genders, Roy. *Perfume Through the Ages*. New York: G. P. Putnam's Sons, 1972.
Gentry, Tony. *Elvis Presley*. New York: Chelsea House, 1994.
Gibson, Charles Dana. *The Gibson Girl and Her America*. New York: Dover Publications, 1969.
Godfrey, Sheila, et al. *Principles and Practice of Electrical Epilation*. Portsmouth, NH: Butterworth-Heinemann, 1992.
Goldberg, David Joseph. *Laser Hair Removal*. New York and Philadelphia: Taylor & Francis Group, 2000.
Golden, Eve. *Platinum Girl: The Life and Legends of Jean Harlow*. New York: Abbeville Press, 1991.
———. *Vamp: The Rise of Theda Bara*. New York: Emprise Publishers, 1996.
Goldman, Irving. *Ancient Polynesian Society*. Chicago: University of Chicago Press, 1970.
Goodrum, Charles, and Helen Dalrymple. *Advertising in America: The First 200 Years*. New York: Harry N. Abrams, 1990.
Gordon, Michael. *Hair Heroes*. New York: Bumble & Bumble, 2002.

Gottfried, Martin. *Broadway Musicals*. New York: Abraddale / Abrams, 1979.
Gould, George M., and Walter L. Pyle, *Anomalies and Curiosities of Medicine*. Philadelphia: W. B. Saunders, 1896.
Graham, James Walter, et al. *The Palaces of Crete*. Princeton, NJ: Princeton University Press, 1977.
Granger-Taylor, Hero. *The British Museum Book of Ancient Egypt*. London: Thames & Hudson, 1992.
Grant, Michael. *The Ancient Mediterranean*. New York: Penguin Books, 1969.
———. *A Social History of Greece and Rome*. New York: Scribner, 1992.
Green, Monica H., ed. and trans. *The Trotula: A Medieval Compendium of Women's Medicine*. Philadelphia: University of Pennsylvania Press, 2001.
Greenwood-Robinson, Margaret. *Hair Savers for Women: A Complete Guide to Preventing and Treating Hair Loss*. New York: Three Rivers Press, 2000.
Gregory of Tours. *The History of the Franks*. New York: Penguin, 1983.
Grimm, Jacob. *German Mythology 1835*. Frankfurt am Main, Germany: Ullstein, 1981.
Gross, Michael. *Model: The Ugly Business of Beautiful Women*. New York: William Morrow & Co., 1995.
Guilaroff, Stanley. *Crowning Glory: Reflections of Hollywood's Favorite Confidant*. With Cathy Griffin. Los Angeles: General Publishing Group, 1996.
Guiles, Fred L. *The Life and Death of Marilyn Monroe*. Lanham, MD: Scarborough House, 1991.
Haertig, Evelyn. *Antique Combs and Purses*. Carmel, CA: Gallery Graphics Press, 1983.
Hague, Norma. *Combs & Hair Accessories (Antique Pocket Guides)*. Cincinnati, OH: Seven Hills Book Distributors, 1999.
Haig, Diana Reid. *Walks Through Napoleon and Josephine's Paris*. London: Granta, 2004.
Hamill, Dorothy, with Elva Fairmont. *Dorothy Hamill On and Off the Ice*. New York: Knopf, 1983.
Hammond, N. G. L. *The Genius of Alexander the Great*. Chapel Hill: University of North Carolina Press, 1998.
Hampton, Aubrey. *Natural Organic Hair and Skin Care*. Tampa, FL: Organica Press, 1987.
Haney, Lynn. *Naked at the Feast: A Biography of Josephine Baker*. New York: Dodd Mead, 1981.
Hart, C. W. M., and Arnold R. Pilling. *The Tiwi of North Australia*. New York: Holt, Rinehart, and Winston, 1960.
Hashimoto, Sumiko. *Okazaki Collection: Combs and Ornamental Hairpins*. Tokyo: Books Nipan, 1989.
Hatfield, E., and S. Sprecher. *Mirror, Mirror: The Importance of Looks in Everyday Life*. Albany: State University of New York Press, 1986.
Hawkes, Jacquetta, and Leonard Woolley. *Prehistory and the Beginnings of Civilization*. vol. 1. New York: Harper & Row, 1963.
Hebdige, Dick. *Subculture: The Meaning of Style*. New York: Routledge, 1981.
Hecht, Annabel. *Hair Dyes: A Look at Safety and Regulation*. Washington, DC: U.S. Department of Health, Education, and Welfare, 1978.
Heilmeyer, Marina. *The Language of Flowers: Symbols and Myths*. Prestel, Germany: Prestel Publishing Co., 2001.
Hellerstein, Erna O. *Victorian Women: A Documentary Account of Women's Lives in Nineteenth Century England, France and the United States*. Palo Alto, CA: Stanford University Press, 1981.

Helmer, Diana. *Belles of the Ballpark*. Brookfield, CT: The Millbrook Press, 1993.
Hempel, Rose. *The Golden Age of Japan, 794–1192*. New York: Rizzoli, 1983.
Henry, Jules. *Jungle People*. New York: Random House, 1964.
Henshall, Kenneth G. *A History of Japan: From Stone Age to Superpower*. London: Palgrave Macmillan, 2001.
Herrera, Hayden. *Frida: A Biography of Frida Kahlo*. New York: HarperCollins, 2002.
Herzog, Johann Jakob.*The New Schaff-Herzog Encyclopedia of Religious Knowledge: Embracing Biblical, Historical, Doctrinal, and Practical Theology and Biblical, Theological, and Ecclesiastical Biography from the Earliest Times to the Present Day*. vol. 12. New York: Funk and Wagnalls, 1908.
Hewett, Edgar L. *Ancient Life in Mexico and Central America*. New York: Biblo and Tannen Publishers, Inc., 1968.
Hibbert, Christopher. *Cavaliers & Roundheads: The English Civil War, 1642–1649*. Old Tappan, NJ: Macmillan, 1997.
———. *The Days of the French Revolution*. New York: Harper Perennial, 1999.
Higham, Charles. *Lucy: The Life of Lucille Ball*. New York: St. Martin's Press, 1986.
Hilberg, Raul. *The Destruction of European Jews*. New York: Harper & Row, 1961.
Hiltebeitel, Alf, and Barbara D. Miller, eds. *Hair: Its Power and Meaning in Asian Cultures*. Albany: State University of New York Press, 1998.
Hitzig, Gary S., MD. *Help & Hope for Hair Loss: Questions & Answers About Rogaine, Restoration, and Replacement*. New York: Avon Books, 1997.
Hollis, Alfred Claud. *The Masai: Their Language and Folklore*. Oxford: Clarendon Press, 1905.
Holm, Jeanne. *Women in the Military: An Unfinished Revolution*. New York: Ballantine Books, 1992.
Holmes, George. *The Oxford Illustrated History of Italy*. New York: Oxford University Press, 2001.
Honychurch, Penelope N. *Caribbean Wild Plants and Their Uses*. London: Macmillan/ Caribbean, 1986.
Hooks, Bell. *Black Looks: Race and Representation*. Boston: South End Press, 1992.
Horn, Barbara Lee. *The Age of Hair: Evolution and Impact of Broadway's First Rock Musical*. Westport, CT: Greenwood Press, 1991.
Horsting, Ruth, and Rosana Pistolese, *History of Fashions*. New York: John Wiley & Sons, 1970.
Hostetler, John, ed. *Amish Roots: A Treasury of History, Wisdom and Lore*. Baltimore: The Johns Hopkins University Press, 1989.
Houlberg, Marilyn. "Social Hair: Yoruba Hairstyles in Southwestern Nigeria." In *Fabrics of Culture: The Anthropology of Clothing and Adornment* edited by Justine M. Cordwell and Ronald A. Schwarz. The Hague, Netherlands: Mouton Publishers, 1979.
Houston, Mary G. *Medieval Costume in England and France: The 13th, 14th, and 15th Centuries*. New York: Dover Publications, 1996.
Hoxie, Frederick E., ed. *Encyclopedia of North American Indians*. Boston: Houghton Mifflin, 1996.
Hunting, Anthony. *Encyclopedia of Shampoo Ingredients*. Weymouth, England: Micelle Press, 1983.
Hutchens, Alma R. *Indian Herbology of North America*. Boston: Shambhala Publishers, 1991.

Hyman, Rebecca. *The Complete Guide to Wigs and Hairpieces*. New York: Workman, 1968.
ICON Group International, Inc., *The World Market for Hair Nets Made of Any Material and Knitted or Crocheted Hats and Headgear Made of Felt or Other Textile Fabric in the Piece: A 2004 Global Trade Perspective*. San Diego: ICON Group International, Inc., 2003.
ICON Health Publications, *The Official Patient's Sourcebook on Pubic Lice: A Revised and Updated Directory for the Internet Age*. San Diego: ICON Group International, Inc., 2002.
Imwold, Denise, et al., eds. *Anatomica's Body Atlas*. Berkeley, CA: Laurel Glen Publishing Co., 2003.
Innes-Smith, James. *Big Hair*. New York: Bloomsbury, 2003.
Isidore of Seville. *The Letters of Isidore of Seville*. Gordon B. Ford, ed. Amsterdam: A. M. Hakkert, 1970.
James, Peter, and Nick Thorpe. *Ancient Inventions*. New York: Ballantine Books, 1994.
James, Simon. *The World of the Celts*. London: Thames & Hudson, 1993.
James, Sue. *The Diana Look*. New York: Quill, 1984.
Janaway, Alison. *Diana, Her Latest Fashions*. Surrey, England: Greenwich House, 1984.
Jefferson, James W., and Jeffrey L. Anders, *Trichotillomania, A Guide*. Madison, WI: Madison Institute of Medicine, 1998.
Jenkins, Elizabeth. *Elizabeth the Great*. New York: Coward-McCann, 1958.
Jenkins, Ian. *Greek and Roman Life*. Cambridge, MA: Harvard University Press, 1986.
Johnson, Marie, Maria Evans, and Ethel Abrahams. *Ancient Greek Dress*. Chicago: Argonaut, Inc., Publishers, 1964.
Johnson, Wanda, and Barbara Lawson, illus. *The Art of Dreadlocks*. Decatur, GA: Henceforth Publishing Co., 1991.
Johnston, Mary. *Roman Life*. Glenview, IL: Scott, Foresman and Company, 1957.
Jones, Christian R. *Barbershop: History and Antiques*. Atglen, PA: Schiffer Publishing, Ltd., 1999.
Jones, Gwyn. *A History of the Vikings*. New York: Oxford University Press, 2001.
Jones, Jim. *Men's Hairstyles and Beard Designs: Clipper Cutting, Razor Cutting, Blender Shears, Motivation*. Clifton Park, NY: Milady Publishing, 1997.
Jones, C. S., and Henry T. Williams. *Hair Work and Other Ladies' Fancy Work 1876*. New York: H. T. Williams, 2003.
Jorgensen, Anne D'Arcy. *Is There Cancer in Your Hair Dye? The Real Possibilities*. Kettering, OH: Pamphlet Publications, 1982.
Kanfer, Stefan. *Ball of Fire: The Tumultuous Life and Comic Art of Lucille Ball*. New York: Knopf, 2003.
Karr v. Schmidt, 460 F.2d 609 (5th Cir. 1972).
Kendrick, T. D. *A History of the Vikings*. New York: Charles Scribner's Sons, 1930.
Keogh, Pamela Clarke. *Jackie Style*. New York: HarperCollins, 2001.
Kerdel, Francisco A., and Francisco Jimenez-Acosta. *Dermatology: Just the Facts*. New York: McGraw-Hill Professional, 2003.
Kessler-Harris, Alice. *Out to Work: A History of Wage-Earning Women in the United States*. New York: Oxford University Press, 2003.
Keuthen, Nancy J., et al. *Help for Hair Pullers: Understanding and Coping With Trichotillomania*. Oakland, CA: New Harbinger Publications, 2001.
Keville, Kathi. *Herbs, an Illustrated Encyclopedia*. New York: Friedman / Fairfax Publishers, 1995.

Kilbourne, Jean. *Deadly Persuasion: Why Women and Girls Must Fight the Addictive Power of Advertising*. New York: The Free Press, 1999.

Kinzer, Norma. *Put Down and Ripped Off: The American Woman and the Beauty Cult*. New York: Crowell, 1977.

Kintz, Pascal. *Drug Testing in Hair*. Boca Raton, FL: CRC Press, 1996.

Kitch, Carolyn. *The Girl on the Magazine Cover: The Origins of Visual Stereotypes in American Mass Media*. Chapel Hill: University of North Carolina Press, 2001.

Kliot, Jules. *The Art of Hairwork*. Berkeley, CA: Lacis Publications, 1989.

Ko, Dorothy. *Teachers of the Inner Chambers: Women and Culture in Seventeenth-Century China*. Palo Alto, CA: Stanford University Press, 1994.

Kolbenschlag, M. *Kiss Sleeping Beauty Good-Bye*. New York: Doubleday, 1979.

Krenz, Carol. *Audrey Hepburn: A Life in Pictures*. London: Metro Books, 1997.

Krumholz, Phillip L. *A History of Shaving and Razors*. Bartonville, IL: Ad Libs Publishing Co., 1987.

Kuntzman, Gersh. *Hair! Mankind's Historic Quest to End Baldness*. New York: AtRandom, 2001.

Lake, Veronica, with Donald Bain. *Veronica: The Autobiography of Veronica Lake*. New York: Bantam, 1971.

Lakoff, Robin Tomach, and Raquel L. Scherr, *Face Value: The Politics of Beauty*. Boston: Routledge & Kegan Paul, 1984.

Lancaster, Joan C. *Godiva of Coventry*. Coventry, England: Coventry Corp., 1967.

Landau, Elaine. *Living With Albinism*. New York: Franklin Watts, 1998.

Langdon, William Chauncy. *Everyday Things in American Life, 1607–1776*. New York: Scribner, 1937.

Lansdale v. Tyler Junior College 470 F.2d 659 (5th Cir. 1972).

Larkin, Geraldine A. *First You Shave Your Head*. Berkeley, CA: Celestial Arts, 2001.

Larson, Mark. *The Mullet: Hairstyle of the Gods*. New York: Bloomsbury, 2000.

Laubner, Elle. *Fashions of the Roaring '20s*. Lancaster, PA: Schiffer Publishing, Ltd., 2000.

Laver, James. *Dandies*. London: Weidenfeld & Nicholson, 1968.

———. *Taste and Fashion: From the French Revolution to Today*. London: G. G. Harrap & Co., 1937.

Lawhead, Stephen R., and Steve Lawhead. *Byzantium*. New York: Harper Prism, 1997.

Lawner, Lynn. *Lives of the Courtesans*. New York: Rizzoli, 1987.

Lawton, Richard. *A World of Movies: 70 Years of Film History*. New York: Dell, 1974.

Lax, Roger, and Maria Carvainis. *Moustache*. New York: Quick Fox, 1979.

Leaming, Barbara. *Marilyn Monroe*. New York: Crown, 1998.

Leeming, David Adams, and Margaret Adams Leeming, *Dictionary of Creation Myths*. New York: Oxford University Press, 1995.

Lefkowitz, Mary R., and Maureen B. Fant, *Women's Life in Greece and Rome*. Baltimore: The Johns Hopkins University Press, 1982.

Leigh, Michelle Dominique. *The New Beauty: East-West Teachings in the Beauty of Body and Soul*. Tokyo: Kodansha International, 1995.

Lenburg, Jeff. *Peekaboo: The Story of Veronica Lake*. New York: St. Martin's Press, 2001.

Leslie, Anita. *The Marlborough House Set*. Garden City, NY: Doubleday, 1972.

Lester, Katherine Morris, and Bess Viola Oerke. *Accessories of Dress*. Peoria, IL: Charles A. Bennett Publications, 1940.

Lewis, Alfred Allan, and Constance Woodworth. *Miss Elizabeth Arden*. New York: Coward, McCann, & Geoghegan, 1972.

Lindsay, Jack. *The Ancient World: Manners and Morals*. New York: G. P. Putnam's Sons, 1968.
Liversidge, Joan. *Everyday Life in the Roman Empire*. New York: G. P. Putnam's Sons, 1976.
Lizot, Jacques. *Tales of the Yanomami: Daily Life in the Venezuelan Forest*. Cambridge: Cambridge University Press, 1991.
Logan, Rayford, and Michael R. Winston, eds. *Dictionary of American Negro Biography*. New York: Norton, 1982.
Lougee, Carolyn C. *Le Paradis des Femmes: Women, Salons, and Social Stratification in Seventeenth-Century France*. Princeton, NJ: Princeton University Press, 1976.
Love, Robert. *Elvis Presley*. New York: Franklin Watts, 1986.
Love, Toni. *The World of Wigs, Weaves, and Extensions*. Clifton Park, NY: Thomson Delmar Learning, 2001.
Luthi, Ann L. *Sentimental Jewellery*. Princes Risborough, Bucks, England: Shire Publications, 2002.
Macdonald, Anne L. *Feminine Ingenuity: How Women Inventors Changed America*. New York: Ballantine, 1992.
Macgregor, Arthur. *Bone, Antler, Ivory, and Horn: The Technology of Skeletal Materials Since the Roman Period*. New York: Barnes and Noble, 1985.
Majors, Monroe A. *Noted Negro Women: Their Triumphs and Activities*. Freeport, NY: Books for Libraries Press, 1971.
Malagoli, Marisa. *Hairdressing Throughout History*. Milan, Italy: C. E. B. Edicharme, 1984.
Malpass, Michael A. *Daily Life in the Inca Empire*. Westport, CT: Greenwood Press, 1996.
Mandeville, A. Glenn. *Doll Fashion Anthology & Price Guide*. Cumberland, MD: Hobby Horse Press, 1987.
Manos, Paris, and Susan Manos. *The World of Barbie Dolls*. Paducah, KY: Collector Books, 1983.
Marinella, Lucrezia. *The Nobility and Excellence of Women*. Translated by Anne Dunhill. Chicago: University of Chicago Press, 2000.
Mark, Vernice. *The National Beauty Culturists' League History: 1919–1994*. Detroit: Harlo Printing Co., 1994.
Martin, Jeanne Marie. *Complete Candida Yeast Guidebook*. New York: Prima, 2000.
Mastalia, Francesco, and Alfonso Pagano. *Dreads*. New York: Artisan, 1999.
Masters, George, and Norma Lee Browning. *The Masters Way to Beauty*. New York: E. P. Dutton, 1978.
McCracken, Grant. *Big Hair: A Journey into the Transformation of Self*. Woodstock, NY: Overlook Press, 1995.
McCutcheon, Marc. *Everyday Life in the 1800s: A Guide for Writers, Students, and Historians*. Cincinnati, OH: Writer's Digest Books, 2001.
McKeever, Susan. *Ancient Rome*. New York: Dorling Kindersley Publishing, 1995.
McKibben, Gordon. *Cutting Edge: Gillette's Journey to Global Leadership*. Cambridge, MA: Harvard Business School Press, 1997.
Mehta, Narenda. *Indian Head Massage*. Wellingborough, UK: Thorsons Publishers, 2003.
McNeill, Daniel. *The Face: A Natural History*. Boston: Little Brown, 2000.
Melamed, Elissa. *Mirror, Mirror: The Terror of Not Being Young*. New York: Linden Press, 1983.

Men's Shaving Products Research Group. *The 2000–2005 World Outlook for Men's Shaving Products*. New York: ICON Group International, Inc., 2000.

Miczak, Marie Anakee. *Henna's Secret History: The History, Mystery and Folklore of Henna*. Lincoln, NE: Writer's Club Press, 2001.

Miller, Melba. *The Black Is Beautiful Beauty Book*. Englewood Cliffs, NJ: Prentice-Hall, Inc., 1974.

Miller, Stephen G. *Ancient Greek Athletics*. New Haven, CT, and London: Yale University Press, 2004.

Moers, Ellen. *The Dandy: Brummel to Beerbohn*. New York: Viking, 1960.

Montespan, Madame de. *Memoirs of Madame de Montespan, Being the Historic Memoirs of the Court of Louis XIV*. Paris: Grolier Society, 2002.

Morley, John. *Death, Heaven and the Victorians*. Pittsburgh: University of Pittsburgh Press, 1971.

Morella, Joe, and Edward Z. Epstein. *The "It" Girl: The Incredible Story of Clara Bow*. New York: Delacourte, 1976.

Morris, Desmond. *The Naked Ape*. Surrey, England: Delta Publishers, 1999.

Morris, Edwin T. *Fragrance*. New York: Scribner, 1984.

Morris, Ian. *Key Themes in Ancient History: Death-Ritual and Social Structure in Classical Antiquity*. Cambridge: Cambridge University Press, 1992.

Morris, Ivan. *The World of the Shining Prince: Court Life in Ancient Japan*. New York: Knopf, 1964.

Morrow, Willie Lee. *Curly Hair and Black Skin: An Informational Guide for Youth and Adults*. San Diego: Black Publishers of San Diego, 1973.

Mosse, G. I. *Nazi Culture: Intellectual, Cultural and Social Life in the Third Reich*. New York: Schocken Books, 1981.

Muller, Max F., ed. *The Buddhist Suttas: The Sacred Books of the East*. Translated by Rhys T. W. Davids. Whitefish, MT: Kessenger Publishing, 2004.

Muller, Richard W. *Baldness: Its Causes, Its Treatment, and Its Prevention*. New York: E.P. Dutton, 1918.

Mulvaney, Jay. *Jackie: The Clothes of Camelot*. New York: St. Martin's Press, 2001.

Mulvey, Kate, and Melissa Richards. *Decades of Beauty: The Changing Image of Women 1890s–1990s*. New York: Checkmark Books, 1998.

Murray, Venetia. *An Elegant Madness: High Society in Regency England*. New York: Penguin, 2000.

Musil, Alois. *The Manners and Customs of the Rwala Bedoins*. vol. 14. New York: American Geographical Society, 1928.

Nicholas, John, ed., *Illustrations of the Manners and Expenses of Ancient Times in England, in the Fifteenth, Sixteenth, and Seventeenth Century*. Stoughton, MA: Ams Press, 1997.

Normant, Serge, et al. *Femme Fatale: Famous Beauties Then and Now*. New York: Harry Abrams, 2001.

———. *Metamorphosis*. New York: Harry Abrams, 2004.

Norris, Herbert. *Medieval Costume and Fashion*. New York: Dover Publications, 1999.

———. *Tudor Costume and Fashion*. New York: Dover Publications, 1997.

Norwood, O'Tar T., and Richard C. Shiell. *Hair Transplant Surgery*. Springfield, IL: Charles C. Thomas, 1984.

Nunn, Joan. *Fashion in Costume, 1200–2000*. 2nd ed. Chicago: New Amsterdam Books, 2000.

Oberfirst, Robert. *Rudolph Valentino: The Man Behind the Myth*. New York: Citadel, 1962.
O'Donnell, Mark, et al. *Hairspray: The Roots*. New York: Faber & Faber, 2003.
Olsen, Elise A. *Disorders of Hair Growth: Diagnosis and Treatment*. New York: McGraw-Hill Professional, 2003.
Opie, Iona, and Moira Tatum, eds. *A Dictionary of Superstitions*. New York: Oxford University Press, 1992.
Ormsby, O. S., and H. Montgomery. *Diseases of the Skin*. 7th ed. London: Henry Kimpton, 1948.
Oswalt, Wendell. *Alaskan Eskimos*. San Francisco: Chandler, 1967.
Ouidad. *Curl Talk: Everything You Need to Know to Love and Care for Your Curly, Kinky, Wavy, or Frizzy Hair*. New York: Random House, 2002.
Ovid. *The Art of Love*. Translated by Rolfe Humphreys. Bloomington: University of Indiana Press, 1957.
Owen, David. *Hidden Evidence*. London: Quintet Publishing, 2000.
Owen, Nicholas. *Diana, The People's Princess*. Pleasantville, NY: Reader's Digest Press, 1997.
Packard, Vance. *The Hidden Persuaders*. New York: Random House, 1957.
Padmini, Sengupta. *Everyday Life in Ancient India*. Bombay: Oxford University Press, India Branch, 1955.
Panati, Charles. *Extraordinary Origins of Everyday Things*. New York: Harper & Row, 1987.
Papadopoulos, Linda, et al. *Understanding Skin Problems: Acne, Eczema, Psoriasis, and Related Conditions*. New York: John Wiley, 2003.
Paris, Barry. *Louise Brooks, A Biography*. Minneapolis: University of Minnesota Press, 2000.
Parrish, James Robert. *The Fox Girls*. Secaucus, NJ: Castle Books, 1971.
———. *The Paramount Pretties*. Secaucus, NJ: Castle Books, 1972.
Payne, Robert. *Ivan the Terrible*. Lanham, MD: Cooper Square Press, 2002.
Peiss, Kathy. *Hope in a Jar: The Making of America's Beauty Culture*. New York: Metropolitan Books, 1998.
Penzel, Fred. *The Hair-Pulling Problem: A Complete Guide to Trichotillomania*. New York: Oxford University Press, 2003.
Pepys, Samuel. *Diary of Samuel Pepys*. vol. 6. 1665. Edited by William Mathews and Robert Latham. Berkeley: University of California Press, 2000.
———. *The Diary of Samuel Pepys*. Edited by Richard LeGallienne. New York: Modern Library, 2001.
Persadsingh, Neil. *The Hair in Black Women*. Kingston, Jamaica: N. Persadsingh, 2002.
Perutz, Kathrin. *Beyond the Looking Glass*. New York: William Morrow, 1970.
Peterkin, Alan. *One Thousand Beards: A Cultural History of Facial Hair*. Vancouver, BC: Arsenal Press, 2002.
Pevitt, Christine. *Philippe, Duc D'Orleans, Regent of France*. New York: Atlantic Monthly Press, 1997.
Phelps, Shirelle, ed. *Who's Who Among African Americans*. Detroit: Gale Group, 1997.
Phillips, Kathy. *The Vogue Book of Blondes*. New York: Studio, 2000.
Pinfold, Wallace G. *A Closer Shave: Man's Daily Search for Perfection*. New York: Artisan, 1999.
Pitman, Joanna. *On Blondes*. New York: Bloomsbury USA, 2003.
Plitt, Jane R. *Martha Matilda Harper and the American Dream: How One Woman Changed the Face of Modern Business*. Syracuse, NY: Syracuse University Press, 2000.

Plumb, Richard A., and Milton V. Lee. *Ancient and Honorable Barber Profession*. Indianapolis, IL: Barbers, Beauticians and Allied Industries International Association, 1974.

Polykoff, Shirley. *Does She...or Doesn't She?: And How She Did It*. Garden City, NY: Doubleday, 1975.

Potter, Eliza. *A Hairdresser's Experience in High Life*. New York: Oxford University Press, 2001.

Powell, J., et al. *An Atlas of Hair and Scalp Diseases*. London: Taylor & Francis Group, 2001.

Powell, T. G. E. *The Celts*. London: Thames & Hudson, Ltd., 1958.

Powers, John Robert, and Mary Sue Miller. *Secrets of Charm*. Philadelphia: John C. Winston Co., 1954.

Prynne, William. *The Unloveliness of Lovelockes*. 1628. Norwood, NJ: Walter J. Johnson, Inc., 1976.

Quennell, Marjorie. *Everyday Things in Ancient Greece*. London: Batsford, 1954.

Rayor, Diane, and William W. Batstone, eds. *Latin Lyric and Elegiac Poetry: An Anthology of New Translations*. New York: Garland Publishing Co., 1995.

The Research Group/The Hair Dryers Research Group, *The 2000–2005 World Outlook for Hair Dryers*. New York: ICON Group International, Inc., 2000.

Reynolds, Reginald. *Beards: Their Social Standing, Religious Involvements, Decorative Possibilities, and Value in Offence and Defence Through the Ages*. Garden City, NY: Doubleday, 1949.

Ribeiro, Aileen. *Dress and Morality*. Providence, RI: Berg Publishers, 2004.

———. *Fashion in the French Revolution*. New York: Holmes & Meir Publishers, 1988.

Rice, Tamara Talbot. *Everyday Life in Byzantium*. New York: G. P. Putnam's Sons, 1967.

Riordan, Teresa. *Inventing Beauty: A History of the Inventions that Have Made Us Beautiful*. New York: Broadway, 2004.

Roach, Marion. *The Roots of Desire: In Hot Pursuit of the Power, Cult, Myth, and Meaning of Red Hair*. New York: Bloomsbury USA, 2005.

Robbins, Clarence R. *Chemical and Physical Behavior of Human Hair*. 3rd ed. New York: Springer-Verlag, 1994.

Roberts, J. A. G. *A Concise History of China*. Boston: Harvard University Press, 1999.

Robertson, James. *Forensic Examination of Human Hair*. Boca Raton, FL: CRC Press, 1999.

Robinson, C. E. *Everyday Life in Ancient Greece*. Oxford: Clarendon Press, 1933.

Robinson, Julian. *The Quest for Human Beauty: An Illustrated History*. New York: W. W. Norton, 1998.

Robison, Joleen, and Kay Sellers. *Advertising Dolls: Identification & Value Guide*. Paducah, KY: Collector Books, 1980.

Rogozinski, Jan. *A Brief History of the Caribbean: From the Arawok and Carib to the Present*. New York: Plume, 2000.

Romer, John. *Valley of the Kings*. New York: Henry Holt, 1981.

Romm, Sharon. *The Changing Face of Beauty*. St. Louis: Mosby Publishing Company, 1992.

Rook, Arthur. *Textbook of Dermatology*. Mosby-Year Book, 1986.

Rooks, Noliwe M. *Hair Raising: Beauty, Culture, and the African American Woman*. New Brunswick, NJ: Rutgers University Press, 1996.

Rose, Phyllis. *Jazz Cleopatra: Josephine Baker in Her Time*. New York: Doubleday, 1989.

Roszak, B., and T. Roszak, eds. *Masculine/Feminine*. New York: Harper & Row, 1969.
Rowan, A. N. *Of Mice, Models, and Men: A Critical Evaluation of Animal Research*. Albany: State University of New York Press, 1984.
Rowsome, Frank, Jr. *The Verse by the Side of the Road*. New York: Plume Books, 1965.
Rudoy, Marion. *The Complete Book of Men's Hairstyles and Hair Care*. New York: Crown, 1974.
Rudolph, Colin D., et al. *Rudolph's Pediatrics*. East Norwalk, CT: Appleton and Lange, 2003.
Ruiz-Maldonado, Ramon, et al. *Textbook of Pediatric Dermatology*. Philadelphia: Grune & Stratton, 1989.
Sacharov, Allen P. *The Redhead Book: A Book For & About Redheads*. Baltimore: Word of Mouth Press, 1985.
Sagay, Esi. *African Hairstyles: Styles of Yesterday and Today*. Portsmouth, NH: Heinemann Educational Books, 1983.
Saint-Simon, Louis de Rouvray. *The Memoirs of the Duke de Saint-Simon on the Reign of Louis XIV, and the Regency*. Translated by Bayle St. John. London: Dunne, 1901.
Salem, Dorothy C., ed. *African American Women: A Biographical Dictionary*. New York: Taylor & Francis, 1993.
Sanders, Coyne S., and Tom Gilbert. *Desilu: The Story of Desi Arnaz and Lucille Ball*. New York: HarperEntertainment, 1994.
Sanford, L., and M. Donovan. *Women & Self-Esteem*. Garden City, NY: Doubleday, 1984.
Sansom, G. *History of Japan to 1334*. Palo Alto, CA: Stanford University Press, 1958.
Saslow, James M. *The Medici Wedding of 1589*. New Haven, CT: Yale University Press, 1996.
Sassoon, Vidal. *Cutting Hair the Vidal Sassoon Way*. New York: Butterworth Heinemann, 1984.
———. *Sorry I Kept You Waiting, Madam*. New York: Putnam, 1968.
———. *Supercuts*. London: Vidal Sassoon Holdings, Ltd., 1972.
Sassoon, Vidal, and Beverly Sassoon. *A Year of Beauty and Health*. New York: Simon and Schuster, 1976.
Sawyer, Joan, and Roberta Macphee. *Head Lice to Dead Lice*. New York: St. Martin's Press, 1999.
Sayce, A. H. *Babylonians and Assyrians: Life and Customs*. New York: Charles Scribner's Sons, 1899.
Scarce, Jennifer. *Women's Costume of the Near and Middle East*. London: Routledge Curzon Press, 2003.
Schaff, Philip. *History of the Christian Church*. Oak Harbor, WA: Logos Research Systems, Inc., 1997.
Schulz, David A. *Human Sexuality*. Englewood Cliffs, NJ: Prentice-Hall, 1984.
Scobie, G., et al., *The Meaning of Flowers*. San Francisco: Chronicle Books, 1998.
Scott, Susan Craig, and Karen W. Bressler. *The Hair Bible: The Ultimate Guide to Healthy Beautiful Hair Forever*. New York: Atria, 2003.
Scranton, Philip, ed. *Beauty and Business: Commerce, Gender, and Culture in Modern America*. New York: Routledge, 2000.
Segrave, Kerry. *Baldness: A Social History*. Jefferson, NC: McFarland & Co., 1996.
Segraves, Daniel L. *Women's Hair: The Long and Short of It*. Dupo, IL: The Good Word, 1979.

Seitz, Ruth Hoover, and Blair Seitz. *Amish Ways*. Harrisburg, PA: RB Books, 1991.
Severn, Bill. *The Long and Short of It: Five Thousand Years of Fun and Fury Over Hair*. New York: McKay, 1971.
Shai, Avi, Robert Baran, and Howard I. Maibach, *Handbook of Cosmetic Skin Care*. London: Martin Dunitz, 2002.
Shapiro, Marc. *Sarah Jessica Parker*. Toronto, Ontario: ECW Press, 2001.
Shaw, Ian, ed., *The Oxford History of Ancient Egypt*. New York: Oxford University Press, 2002.
Shep, R. L. *Civil War Gentlemen: 1860s Apparel Arts and Uniform*. Mendocino, CA: R. L. Shep, 1995.
———. *Early Victorian Men*. Fort Bragg, CA: R. L. Shep, 2001.
Shirley, David. *The History of Rock and Roll*. New York: Franklin Watts, 1997.
Siculus, Diodorus. *Library of History, Vol. 3, Books 4–8*. Translated by C. H. Oldfather. New York: Harvard University Press, 1992.
Sieber, Roy, and Frank Herreman, eds. *Hair in African Art and Culture*. New York: The Museum of African Art, 2000.
Simon, Diane. *Hair: Public, Political, Extremely Personal*. New York: St. Martin's Press, 2000.
Simon, James. *The World of the Celts*. London and New York: Thames & Hudson, 1993.
Simpson, Jacqueline. *Everyday Life in the Viking Age*. New York: G. P. Putnam's Sons, 1987.
Simpson, James B., comp. *Simpson's Contemporary Quotations*. New York: Crowell, 1981.
———. *Simpson's Contemporary Quotations Revised Edition: Most Notable Quotations 1950 to the Present*. New York: HarperCollins, 1997.
Sinclair, Rodney D., et al. *Handbook of Diseases of the Hair and Scalp*. London: Health Press UK, 1999.
Sivananda, Sri. *All About Hinduism*. Rishikesh, India: Sivananda Literature Research Institute, Divine Life Society, 1977.
Slide, Anthony. *Silent Players: A Biographical and Autobiographical Study of 100 Silent Film Actors and Actresses*. Lexington: University Press of Kentucky, 2002.
Smith, Adelaide. *Modern Beauty Culture*. Englewood Cliffs, NJ: Prentice-Hall, 1934.
Smith, Jessie Carney, ed. *Notable Black American Women*. Detroit: Gale Research, 1992.
Smith, Lacy Baldwin. *Elizabeth Tudor: Portrait of a Queen*. Boston: Little Brown, 1975.
Smith, Richard J. *China's Cultural Heritage, the Qing Dynasty 1644–1912*. Philadelphia: Westview Press, 1994.
Sorbie, Trevor. *Visions in Hair*. London: Thomson Learning, 1998.
Speroff, Leon, and Marc A. Fritz, eds. *Clinical Gynecologic Endocrinology and Infertility*. 6th ed. Philadelphia: Lippincott, Williams and Wilkins, 2004.
Spoto, Donald. *Jacqueline Bouvier Kennedy Onassis: A Life*. New York: St. Martin's Press, 2000.
Starkey, Armstrong. *European-Native American Warfare, 1675–1815*. Norman: University of Oklahoma Press, 1998.
Staten, Vince. *Do Bald Men Get Half-Price Haircuts?: In Search of America's Great Barbershops*. New York: Simon and Schuster, 2002.
Steinman, David, and Samuel S. Epstein, MD. *The Safe Shopper's Bible*. New York: John Wiley, 1995.
Stenn, David. *Bombshell: The Life and Death of Jean Harlow*. Garden City, NY: Doubleday, 1993.

———. *Clara Bow: Runnin' Wild*. Garden City, NY: Doubleday, 1988.
Sterling, Dorothy, ed. *We Are Your Sisters*. New York: W. W. Norton, 1984.
Steinman, David, and Samuel S. Epstein, MD. *The Safe Shopper's Bible*. New York: John Wiley, 1995.
Stodder, Chris. *Swingin' Chicks of the 60s*. San Rafael, CA: CEDCO Publishing, 2000.
Strouhal, Eugen. *Life of the Ancient Egyptians*. Norman: University of Oklahoma Press, 1992.
Stuart, George E., and Gene S. Stuart. *The Mysterious Maya*. Washington, DC: National Geographic Society, 1983.
Sulieman, Susan R., ed. *The Female Body in Western Culture*. Cambridge, MA: Harvard University Press, 1986.
Swaddling, Judith. *The Ancient Olympic Games*. Austin: University of Texas, 2000.
Tapert, Annette, and Diana Edkins. *The Power of Style*. New York: Crown, 1994.
Taylor, Lou. *Mourning Dress: A Costume and Social History*. London: George Allen and Unwin, 1983.
Tedlow, Richard S. *New and Improved: The Story of Mass Marketing in America*. Boston: Harvard University Press, 1990.
Tertullian. *The Apparel of Women*. Whitefish, MT: Kessinger Publishing Co., 2004.
Thomas, Charles. *Celtic Britain*. London: Thames & Hudson, 1996.
Thompson, Wendy, et al. *Alopecia Areata: Understanding and Coping With Hair Loss*. Baltimore: The Johns Hopkins University Press, 2000.
Tobias, Andrew. *Fire and Ice: The Story of Charles Revson—the Man Who Built the Revlon Empire*. New York: William Morrow, 1976.
Trasko, Mary. *Daring Dos: A History of Extraordinary Hair*. New York: Flammarion, 1994.
Treadgold, Warren. *A History of the Byzantine State and Society*. Stanford, CA: Stanford University Press, 1997.
Trout, Lawana Hooper. *The Maya*. New York/Philadelphia: Chelsea House, 1991.
Trusty, L. Sherman. *The Art and Science of Barbering*. Los Angeles: Wolfer Printing Co., 1956.
Turnbull, Colin. *The Forest People*. New York: Simon and Schuster, 1961.
Turnbull, Stephen R. *The Samurai, A Military History*. London: Japan Library, 1977.
Turudich, Daniela. *Art Deco Hair: Hairstyles of the 1920s and 1930s*. Long Beach, CA: Streamline Press, 2003.
———. *1940s Hairstyles*. Long Beach, CA: Streamline Press, 2001.
———. *1960s Hair: Hairstyles for Bouffant Babes and Swingin' Chicks*. Long Beach, CA: Streamline Press, 2003.
Turudich, Daniela, and Laurie G. Welch. *Plucked, Shaved, and Braided: Medieval and Renaissance Beauty and Grooming Practices, 1000–1600*. Long Beach, CA: Streamline Press, 2004.
Tyldesley, Joyce. *Daughters of Isis: Women in Ancient Egypt*. New York: Penguin, 1995.
Uglow, Jennifer S., comp. and ed., *International Dictionary of Women's Biography*. New York: Macmillan, 1985.
U.S. Food and Drug Administration (USFDA). *Hypoallergenic Cosmetics*. December 19, 1994. Revised October 18, 2000. Washington, DC: U.S. Food and Drug Administration (USFDA), Center for Food Safety and Applied Nutrition, Office of Cosmetics, 2000.
Van Deusen, Edmund. *What You Can Do About Baldness*. New York: Stein and Day, 1978.

Van Paassen, Pierre. *A Crown of Fire; The Life and Times of Girolamo Savonarola*. London: Hutchinson, 1961.

Vecellio, Cesare. *Degli habiti antichi et moderni di viverse parti del mondo (The Clothing, Ancient and Modern, of Various Parts of the World)*. Venice: Presso Damian Zamaro, 1590.

Verbov, Julian L. *Superficial Fungal Infections*. Norwell, MA: Macmillan Technical Publishers, 1986.

Vermilye, Jerry. *The Complete Films of Audrey Hepburn*. Secaucus, NJ: Carol Publishing Group, 1995.

Verrill, A. Hyatt. *Perfumes and Spices*. Boston: L. C. Page & Co., 1940.

Vickers, Michael. *The Roman World*. New York: Peter Bedrick Books, 1989.

Vlahos, Olivia. *Body: The Ultimate Symbol*. New York: Lippincott, 1979.

Vossler, Bill. *Burma-Shave: The Rhymes, The Signs, The Times*. St. Cloud, MN: North Star Press of St. Cloud, 1998.

Waardenburg, Petrus Johannes. *Remarkable Facts in Human Albinism and Leukism*. Assen, The Netherlands: Van Gorcum & Co., 1970.

Wade, Carlson. *Health Secrets from the Orient*. New York: Signet, 1973.

Wald, Carol. *Myth America: Picturing Women, 1865–1945*. New York: Pantheon, 1975.

Walden, George. *Who Is a Dandy?* London: Gibson Square Books, Ltd., 2004.

Walker, Juliet E. K. *The History of Black Business in America: Capitalism, Race, Entrepreneurialship*. New York: Twayne, 1998.

Wallace-Hadrill, J. M. *Long-Haired Kings and Other Studies in Frankish History*. Toronto: University of Toronto Press, 1982.

Walton, Buddy. *High Styles: Stories From a World Class Hairdresser*. Lincoln, NE: IUniverse Inc., 2004.

Waring, Philippa. *Dictionary of Omens and Superstitions*. London: Souvenir Press, 1998.

Warner, Marina. *The Dragon Empress: Life and Times of Tz'u-his 1835–1908, Empress Dowager of China*. New York: Macmillan, 1972.

Watkins, Julian Lewis. *The 100 Greatest Advertisements, Who Wrote Them and What They Did*. New York: Dover Publications, 1959.

Waugh, Norah. *The Cut of Women's Clothes, 1600–1930*. London: Faber, 1984.

Weinberg, Norma Pasekoff. *Henna From Head to Toe: Body Decorating, Hair Coloring, Medicinal Uses*. Collingdale, PA: Diane Publishing Co., 1990.

Weir, Alison. *The Life of Elizabeth I*. New York: Random House, 1998.

Weitz, Rose. *Rapunzel's Daughters*. New York: Farrar, Straus and Giroux, 2004.

White, Shane, and Graham J. White. *Stylin': African-American Expressive Culture from Its Beginnings to the Zoot Suit*. Ithaca, NY: Cornell University Press, 1998.

Whitfield, Eileen. *Pickford: The Woman Who Made Hollywood*. Lexington: University of Kentucky Press, 1997.

Williams, Mary Wilhelmine. *Social Scandinavia in the Viking Age*. London: Taylor & Francis Group, 1971.

Williamson, Colin. *Plastics Collecting and Conserving*. Edinburgh: National Museums of Scotland Publishing, 1999.

Willms, Johannes. *Paris Capital of Europe: From the Revolution to the Belle Epoque*. Translated by Eveline L. Kanes. New York: Holmes & Meier, 1997.

Windeler, Robert. *Shirley Temple*. London: W. H. Allen, 1976.

———. *Sweetheart: The Story of Mary Pickford*. Detroit: Thomson Gale, 1974.

Winkler, Susan Swire. *The Paris Shopping Companion*. Nashville, TN: Cumberland House Publishing, 2002.

Woodward, Ian. *Audrey Hepburn*. New York: St. Martin's Press, 1984.
Woog, Adam. *Marilyn Monroe*. San Diego: Lucent Books, 1997.
Worthington, Charles, et al. *Big Hair Day*. London: Carlton Publishing Group, 2002.
———. *City Hair*. London: Carlton Publishing Group, 2002.
———. *The Complete Book of Hairstyling*. Richmond Hill, Ontario: Firefly Books, Ltd., 2002.
Woshner, Mike. *India Rubber and Gutta-Percha in the Civil War Era: An Illustrated History of Rubber & Pre-Plastic Antiques and Militaria*. Alexandria, VA: O'Donnel Publications, 1999.
Wright, Lawrence. *Clean and Decent: The Fascinating History of the Bathroom and the Water Closet, and Sundry Habits, Fashions and Accessories of the Toilet, Principally in Great Britain, France, and America*. New York: Viking, 1960.
Wright, Les, ed. *The Bear Book II*. Binghamton, NY: Haworth Press, 2001.
Wyse, Lois. *Blond Beautiful Blond*. New York: M. Evans, 1980.
Yamamura, Kozo. *The Cambridge History of Japan*. New York: Cambridge University Press, 1993.
Yee, Chiang, *Chinese Childhood*. New York: The John Day Co., 1952.
Zaoui, Miriam, and Eric Malka, *The Art of Shaving*. New York: Clarkson Potter, 2002.
Zdatny, Steven. *Hairstyles and Fashion: A Hairdresser's History of Paris, 1910–1920*. Providence, RI: Berg Publishers, Inc., 1999.

PERIODICALS AND WEB SITES

"Abraham Lincoln in Buffalo: The Legend of the Whiskers." http://www.buffalohistoryworks.com/lincoln/whiskers.htm.
"AHBAI Milestones." http://proudlady.org/about/milestones.html.
Ahrens, Frank. "Why Is This Rat Smiling?" *Washington Post*, August 17, 1995.
Alexander, Brian. "Personal Grooming Down There." *MSNBC News*, April 22, 2004. http://www.msnbc.msn.com/id/4751816.
Alireza, Marianne. "Women of Saudi Arabia." *National Geographic*, October 1987, 422–453.
All-American Girls Professional Baseball League (AAGPBL). http://www.aagpbl.org/history/hist_cs.html#foreword.
All-American Girls Professional Baseball League (AAGPBL) Charm School. http://www.aagpbl.org/league/charm.cfm#beauty.
Allan, Vicky. "A Career to Dye For." *Sunday Herald* (London), May 25, 2003. http://www.sundayherald.com/print34061.
Alton Press Release. "Helene Curtis and Main Floor Help 'Untangle' Hair Care Advice on the Web," August 14, 2000. http://altonent.com/pressreleases/2000-08-14-helenecurtis.htm.
American Academy of Dermatology. http://www.aad.org.
American Beauty Association. "ABBIES," "About the ABA," "Association News," and "Events Calendar." http://www.abbies.org.
American Hair Loss Council. "Causes of Hair Loss." http://www.ahlc.org/causes-m.htm.
American Health and Beauty Aids Institute (AHBAI). "About AHBAI." http://www.ahbai.org.
American National Business Hall of Fame (ANBHF). "Fairfax Cone Ad Samples: 'Toni.'" http://www.anbhf.org/cone_ads.html.

Ashley, Julia, and Dennis L Cates. "Albinism: Educational Techniques for Parents and Teachers," *RE:view* 24 (Fall 1992): 127–133.

Associated Press. "China Bans Ponytails for Youth Soccer," February 26, 2004. www.dailypress.com/broadband/sns-othernews-0226soccerhair,0,219935.story.

———. "French Law Bans Sikh Turbans in School," May 16, 2004. http://web.mid-day.com/news/world/2004/may/83552.htm.

———. "Germany's Henkel to Buy U.S.-Based Dial." MSNBC.com, December 16, 2003. http://www.msnbc.msn.com/id/3717086.

———. "North Korea Tells Men: Be Patriotic and Cut Hair." *MSNBC News*, February 1, 2004. http://www.msnbc.msn.com/id/6894691.

"Aubrey the Company." http://www.aubreyorganics.com.

Badillo, Casandra. *Only My Hairdresser Knows for Sure: Public Perception of Women's Hair in the Dominican Republic.* North American Congress on Latin America (NACLA), vol. 34, no. 6, May 2001.

Belinkskij, Andrej, and Heinrich Harke. "The 'Princess' of Ipatovo." *Archaeology*, March/April 1999. http://www.archaeology.org/9903/newsbriefs/ipatovo.html.

Bara, Theda (biography). http://www.silentladies.com/Pbara1.html.

Bernstein, Michael J. "Locks of Hair Jewelry." *Smithsonian* 6 (12) (1976): 97–100.

Blersch, Stuart. "Victorian Jewelry Made of Hair." *Nineteenth Century* 6 (1) (1980): 42–43.

Book of Discipline of the Ohio Valley Yearly Meeting Religious Society of Friends, 1978. http://www.quaker.org/ovym/friends.htm.

Bradbard, Laura. "On the Teen Scene: Cosmetics and Reality." *FDA Consumer*, May 1994. http://www.cfsan.fda.gov/~dms/cos-teen.html.

Branna, Tom. "Fragrance and African-American Women." *Happi*, July 1997. http://www.happi.com/special/julmain2.htm.

"Burma-Shave in the Fifties." http://www.fiftiesweb.com/burma.htm.

Canning, Christine. "Animal Testing Alternatives: The Quest Continues." *Happi*, February 1997. http://www.happi.com/special/febmain2.html.

———. "Fine Fragrances," *Happi*, November 1996. http://www.happi.com/special/novmain.htm.

Catholic Encyclopedia. "Tonsure." http://www.newadvent.org/cathen/14779a.htm.

Chain Drug Review. "Parker to Promote Nutrisse Hair Color," December 11, 2000. http://static.highbeam.com/c/chaindrugreview/december112000/parkertopromote-nutrissehaircolorbriefarticle/index.html.

Chin, Ku Sup, In-Jin Yoon, and David Smith, "Immigrant Small Business and International Economic Linkage: A Case of the Korean Wig Business in Los Angeles, 1967–1977," *The International Migration Review*, Summer 1996. http://www.findarticles.com/p/articles/mi_qa3668/is_199607/ai_n8755242.

"A Chinese Barber in New York." *Harper's Weekly*, March 10, 1888, 167. Reprint. http://immigrants.harpweek.com/ChineseAmericans/Items/Item124L.htm.

"Civil Rights Act of 1964." http://usinfo.state.gov/usa/infousa/laws/majorlaw/civilr19.htm.

Civil Rights Act of 1964. Title VII. http://www.eeoc.gov/policy/vii.html.

Civilization. "The Golden Age of Big Hair," September/October 1995, 29.

"Classic TV Ads." http://www.roadode.com/classic.htm.

Colwell, Shelley M. "Shape of the Future." *Soap/Cosmetics/Chemical Specialties*, October 1993. http://members.aol.com/lishelley/hair.htm.

Consumer Aerosol Products Council. "Aerosols and the Environment," January 2004. http://www.nocfcs.org/ae.html.

Cosmetic Executive Women. "About CEW," "Achiever Awards," and "Beauty Awards." http://www.cew.org.

Cosmetic, Toiletry, and Fragrance Association (CTFA). "CTFA Annual Report, 2004." http://www.ctfa.org; http://www.cir-safety.org.

Cummings, Bart. "Polykoff Put Herself in User's Shoes." *Advertising Age*, October 1985, 48–51.

Dahlberg, John-Thor. "France Solves Mystery of What Happened to Marie Antoinette's Son." *San Francisco Chronicle*, April 20, 2000.

Damjanov, Milena. "Golden Arches." *TimeOutNY*, November 2, 2000. http://www.timeoutny.com/checkout/267/267.checkout.html.

Daniels, Cora. "Return of the Breck Girl?" *Fortune Small Business*. http://www.fortune.com/fortune/smallbusiness/articles/0,15114,360967,00.html.

De, Aditi. "Trappings for Tresses." *The Hindu* (India), March 17, 2003. http://www.hindu.com/thehindu/mp/2003/03/17/stories/2003031701680300.htm.

Debrohun, Jeri. "Power Dressing in Ancient Greece and Rome." *History Today* 51 (February 2001): 18–25.

Devillers, Carole. "What Future for the Wayana Indians?" *National Geographic*, January 1983, 66–83.

De Witt, Barbara. "The Big Swing: Ponytails Again Turn Heads With Decidedly '90s Blend of Innocence and Seduction." *Daily News* (Los Angeles), May 16, 1996. http://static.highbeam.com/d/dailynewslosangelesca/may161996/thebigswingponytailsagainturnheadswithdecidedly90s/index.html.

Dhakal, Sanjaya. "People at Loss." Spotlight, The National News Magazine, June 8–June 14, 2001, at NepalNews.com. http://www.nepalnews.com.np/contents/englishweekly/spotlight/2001/jun/jun08/national9.htm.

Dial Corporation History. www.dialcorp.com.

Dominus, Susan. "He's Still Hair." *New York Magazine*, May 13, 2002. http://newyorkmetro.com/nymetro/shopping/beauty/features/5999/.

Doski, J. J., et al. "Duodenal Trichobezoar Caused by Compression of the Superior Mesenteric Artery." *Journal of Pediatric Surgery* (November 30, 1995): 1598–1599.

"Dubarry: The Secret of Everlasting Beauty." http://www.dubarryusa.com/main.htm.

Dunn, Carolyn A. "The Ethnic Hair Care Market." *Happi*, April 1997.

Empire Online. " *Hairspray* Remake." March 4, 2004. http://www.empireonline.co.uk/site/news/newsstory.asp?news_id=15653.

Essence. "Sisters Love the Weave," August 1990. http://www.findarticles.com/p/articles/mi_m1264/is_n4_v21/ai_9252025.

Faiola, Anthony. "The Geisha Stylist Who Let Her Hair Down." *Washington Post*, August 17, 2004, C01.

"Famed Asahi Ball Club Celebrates Centennial." *Honolulu Advertiser*, September 12, 2005. http://the.honoluluadvertiser.com/article/2005/Sep/12/ln/FP509120333.html.

"The Feathered-Back Hair Site." http://www.featheredback.com.

"Fekkai, About Frederic." www.fredericfekkai.com.

Foster, Stephen. "If You've Only Got a Moustache" (song lyrics). http://www.stephen-foster-songs.de/Foster12.htm.

Friedman, Steve. "The Importance of Being Farrah." *Mirabella*, March/April 1998, 122–124.

Gabler, Neal. "The Lives They Lived: Edward L. Bernays and Henry C. Rogers; The Fathers of PR." *The New York Times*, December 31, 1995.

Garden, Mary. "Why I Bobbed My Hair." *Pictorial Review*, April 1927, 8.

Geist, William E. "Selling Soap to Children and Hairnets to Women." *The New York Times*, March 27, 1985. http://partners.nytimes.com/books/98/08/16/specials/bernays-selling.html.

Geracimos, Ann. "Hair Peace." *The Washington Times*, March 8, 2004. http://washingtontimes.com/metro/20040317-091612-2002r.htm.

Gill, Tiffany M. "Civic Beauty: Beauty Culturists and the Politics of African American Female Entrepreneurship, 1900–1965." *Enterprise & Society*, December 2004, 583–593.

Gilliard, E. Thomas. "New Guinea's Rare Birds and Stone Age Men," *National Geographic*, April 1953.

Gitter, Elizabeth G. "The Power of Women's Hair in the Victorian Imagination." *PMLA* (journal of the Modern Language Association of America) 99 (1984): 936–953.

Gladwell, Malcolm. "True Colors: Hair Dye and the Hidden History of Postwar America." *The New Yorker*, March 22, 1999.

Good, David L. "Hair Today, Sold Tomorrow." *The Detroit News*, March 29, 2001. http://www.detnews.com/2001/decorating/0103/29/c01-205246.htm.

———. "Collecting Hair." *Maine Antique Digest*, May 2001. http://www.maineantique-digest.com/articles/hair0501.htm.

Goodheart, Herbert E., MD, "Hirsutism." http://www.emedicine.com/derm/topic472.htm.

Gribbin, August. "Five-Nation Team Drafts Working Map of Human Genome." *The Washington Times*, June 26, 2000, 13.

Griffing, George T., MD, "Hirsutism," http://www.emedicine.com/med/topic1017.htm.

Griffith, Susan R. "Salute to Leominster," *Massachusetts Review*, August 13, 1975. http://members.aol.com/Leominster476/History.html.

Haddad, Ann. "New York Loves Lebanese Hair Stylist." *The Daily Star* (Lebanon), May 25, 2004. http://www.dailystar.com.lb/article.asp?edition_id=10&categ_id=4&article_id4344.

Hairspray (the musical). http://www.hairsprayonbroadway.com

Hall, Alice J. "Dazzling Legacy of an Ancient Quest." *National Geographic*, March 1997, 293–311.

Happi. "Another British Invasion?" August 1997. http://www.happi.com/special0196.htm.

Happi. "Happi Breaking News: L'Oréal Uses Catia V5 to Study Hair," October 24, 2002. http://www.happi.com/new/break6.htm.

Happi. "Survey," March 2004, 14.

Harran, Susan, and Jim Harran. "Remembering a Loved One With Mourning Jewelry." *Antique Week*, December 1997. http://www.hairwork.com/remember.htm.

Harris, Joyce Saenz. "Browmania: Celebrity Pluckers, New Products Can Shape Up Your Brows." *Dallas Morning News*, June 4, 2001. http://amarillo.com/cgi-bin/printme.pl.

Healy, Peter. "A Market to Dye For." *Wall Street Journal*, May 27, 2001.

Henkel, John. "A Colorful History," *FDA Consumer*, December 1993.

"Henkel to Acquire Dial" (press release). http://www.henkel.de/int_henkel/channelpress/channel/index.cfm?channel=281%2CPR_2003&picture=157&nav=281&base=2&pageid=281.

"Henkel to Buy Indola Professional Hair Care Company from Alberto-Culver." Cosmetics Design, July 5, 2004. http://cosmeticsdesign.com/news/news-NG.asp?id=51946.

Henson, Melanie. "Baby Care Update." *Happi*, August 2004. http://www.happi.com/current/August041.htm.

Hilton, Lisette. "Skating was Passion, Therapy for Hamill," *ESPN Classic*. http://espn.go.com/classic/biography/s/Hamill_Dorothy.html.

Leominster, Massachusetts. "History." http://members.aol.com/Leominster476/History.html.

Holbrook, Stewart. "The Beard of Joseph Palmer." *The American Scholar*, Autumn 1944, 455–458.

Holmstrom, David. "For the Fashion-Conscious Man, Bald Is Beautiful." *The Christian Science Monitor*, October 21, 1997. http://csmonitor.com/cgi-bin/durableRedirect.pl?/durable/1997/10/21/feat/feat.2.html.

Horowitz, Elliot. "The New World and the Changing Face of Europe." *Sixteenth Century Journal,* XXVIII/4 (1997): 1181–1201.

Howard, Jenni Baden. "The Hair Necessities." *Daily Telegraph* (London), March 15, 2001.

Hudson, Patrick, MD, "Causes of Male Pattern Baldness." http://www.phudson.com.

Hunter, Melissa H., and Peter J. Karek, "Evaluation and Treatment of Women With Hirsutism," *American Family Physician*, June 15, 2003. http://www.aafp.org/afp/20030615/2565.html.

Hyde, Melissa. "The 'Makeup' of the Marquise: Boucher's Portrait of Madame Pompadour at Her Toilette," *The Art Bulletin* 82, September 2000. http://www.findarticles.com/p/articles/mi_m0422/is_3_82/ai_66304031.

Indiana Historical Society. Manuscripts & Archives: Madam C. J. Walker Collection, 1910–1980.

International Association of Trichologists. http://www.trichology.edu.au.

Issues & Views. "Anthony Overton: Born Entrepreneur," Spring 1997. http://www.issues-views.com/index.php/sect/1000/article/1006.

Jacques Dessange. "Hair Care Products" and "History." http://www.jacquesdessange.com.

"Jennifer Aniston." http://www.tvtome.com/tvtome/servlet/PersonDetail/personid-896.

Johns, Brad. "Dyeing to Know." *American Salon*, November 1, 2004. http://www.americansalonmag.com/americansalon/article/articleDetail.jsp?id=129445.

"Johnson, George." Business & Industry Hall of Fame biography. http://www.businessandindustryhalloffame.com/Johnson_George.html.

Johnson, Kate. "Vulvar Folliculitis Often Caused by Waxing, Shaving," *OB-Gyn News*, July 1, 2003.

Kalsi, Jyoti. "Makeover in a Minute." *Gulf News* (Florida), May 8, 2005. http://www.gulf-news.com/Articles/people-places.asp?ArticleID=87461.

Kidder, Stephen W., Massachusetts Commissioner of Revenue. "Sales Taxation of Wigs." Letter Ruling 90-4, August 3, 1990. http://www.dor.state.ma.us/rul_reg/LR/LR_90_4.htm.

King, Robert A., et al., "Childhood Trichotillomania: Clinical Phenomenology, Comorbidity and Family Genetics." *Journal of the American Academy of Child & Adolescent Psychiatry* (November 1995): 1451–1459.

Kraft, Joy. "Hair Care Pros: Clairol Reliable, Not Cutting Edge." *The Cincinnati Enquirer*, May 22, 2001. http://www.enquirer.com/editions/2001/05/22/fin_hair_care_pros.html.

Kuczynski, Alex. "You Paid *How Much* For That Haircut?" *The New York Times*, November 21, 2004, sec. 9.

———. "Trading on Hollywood Magic." *The New York Times*, January 30, 1998, C1, C4.

Kurien, Miriam, and Alexis Petrosa. "Sugar and Spice and Everything Nice: Advertising the Gendered Child and the 1950s and 2003." http://www.trincoll.edu/~mkurien.

Larocca, Amy. "Big Hair." *New York*, March 1, 2003.

Larsen, Polly. "Bonny LeVine Award 2001. (Celebrating Franchising's Success) Martha Matilda Harper." *Franchising World Magazine*, February 2, 2002.

Leigh, Michelle Dominique. "Ageless Beauty." *Natural Health*, July–August 1996, 80–82, 145.

Lewis, Carol. "Clearing Up Cosmetic Confusion." *FDA Consumer*, May–June, 1998.

Leyser, Conrad. "Longhaired Kings and Short-haired Nuns: Power and Gender in Merovingian Gaul." *Medieval World*, March–April 1992.

"Locks of Love: About Us." www.locksoflove.org.

"L'Oreal Company History." www.lorealusa.com.

"L'Oreal USA Products and Brands." www.lorealusa.com.prodbrand/home.

Loyer, Michele. "The Hands That Mold the Hair." *International Herald Tribune*, October 18, 1997, 13.

Macdonald, Veronica. "The Hair Care Market." *Happi*, December 2001. http://www.happi.com/special/Dec011.htm.

"Les Maitresses Royales." http://maitressesroyales.free.fr/fontanges.htm.

"Marine Corps Uniform Regulations." http://www.usmc.mil/directiv.nsf/Pdocuments?openview&count=5000&start=1.

Markey, Sean. "Whiskers Go Wild at World Beard, Mustache Games." *National Geographic World*, March 25, 2005. http://news.nationalgeographic.com/news/2005/03/0325_050325_beardmustache.html.

Markusen, Bruce. "Thirty Years Ago: The Birth of the Mustache Gang." Baseball Museum. http://www.baseballlibrary.com/baseballlibrary/submit/Markusen_Bruce5.stm.

Matheson, Whitney. "Toupée or Not Toupée? Is There Really Any Question?" *USA Today*, January 13, 2004. http://www.usatoday.com/life/columnist/popcandy/2004-01-13-pop-candy_x.htm.

"Max Factor—The Makeup of Makeup Artists." http://www.maxfactor.com/about/about.jsp;jsessionid=pg-prodweb-b03-1d0:4130a378:269d2464fcb793.

"Max Factor Beauty Museum." http://www.seeing-stars.com/Museums/MaxFactor.shtml.

Maybelline. "About Us" and "History." http://www.maybelline.co.uk/about_us/l282l283.htm.

Meadows, Michele. "Hair Dyes and Chemical Relaxers: Use With Caution!" *FDA Consumer,* February 26, 2001.

Miami Herald. "Elvis Hair Sells for Over $100,000," November 16, 2002. http://www.miami.com/mld/miamiherald/4536571.htm.

"Michaeljohn, Salon and Agency." http://www.michaeljohn.co.uk.

Minnick, Mimi. "Breck Girls." *Smithsonian*, January 2000. http://www.smithsonianmag.si.edu/smithsonian/issues00/jan00/breck.html.

———. "Breck Girls Collection." Archives Center of the National Museum of American History. http://americanhistory.si.edu/archives/d7651.htm.

Minor, Christina. "Still Lashing Out." *Herald-Tribune* (Waco, TX), December 6, 2003.

Morago, Greg. "Hairy Problem." *The Journal Gazette* (Fort Wayne, IN), November 27, 2002. http://www.fortwayne.com/mld/journalgazette/4601209.htm.

Moritz, Robert. "A Brief History of Whiskers Starting with God." *GQ*, September 2000, 345–350.

Morrison, Margaret. "Hypoallergenic Cosmetics." *FDA Consumer*, June 1974.

Muhammad, Larry. "Top Rows: Braids are Trendy Coiffure of the Urban Black Male." *The Courier Journal* (Louisville KY), August 27, 2001. http://www.courierjournal.com/features/2001/08/fe20010827.html.

Musser, Mary. "Massachusetts Horn Smiths: A Century of Comb-making 1775–1875." *Old-Time New England* 58: 59–68.

National Cosmetology Association. http://www.ncacares.org.

National Psoriasis Foundation. http://www.psoriasis.org.

Naughton, Julie. "Frizz Pays Dividends for Frieda." *WWD*, November 5, 1999.

New Jersey. "New Jersey's African American Tour Guide." http://www.state.nj.us/travel/pdf_files/afam_tg.pdf.

The New York Times. "George Masters" (obituary), March 7, 1998.

The New York Times. "Martha M. Harper, Pioneer Beautician" (obituary), August 5, 1950, 15.

The New York Times. "The Saga of the Moustache," August 20, 1944.

Newsday. "Joan Bove: 99, Co-Founder of Clairol" (obituary), July 25, 2001.

Norris, Michael. "Divining Secrets from Frida Kahlo's Unibrow." *The Pentagram* (Fort Myer), November 1, 2002.

Ogunnaike, Lola. "Some Hair Is Happy to be Nappy." *The New York Times*, December 27, 1998, Section 9: 1, 3.

Olsen, E. A., et al. "Five Year Follow-Up of Men With Androgenetic Alopecia Treated with Topical Minoxidil." *Journal of the American Academy of Dermatology* (April 1990): 643–646.

Organization for the Advancement of Facial Hair. "About Us" and "History." http://www.ragadio.com/oafh/page2.html.

Page, Jake. "Inside the Sacred Hopi Homeland." *National Geographic*, November 1982, 607–629.

"The Palmer Grave." http://edutel.musenet.org:8042/gravenet/grave_palmer.html.

Parker, Emanuel. "Efforts Made to Stop Sale of Rio Products." *Los Angeles Times*, February 2, 1995.

Parry, Jason. "Milwaukee Mustaches: Rollie Fingers," February 5, 2002. http://www.onmilwaukee.com/articles/print/rollie.html.

Paul Mitchell. "About Us" and "The Story." http://www.paulmitchell.com/intro.asp; http://www.islandconnections.com/edit/mitchell.htm

Peale, Cliff. "Clairol's Potential About to Be Tapped." *The Cincinnati Enquirer*, January 12, 2003.

Pearson, David B. "Stars of the Photoplay, 1916." Silent-Movies.org. http://silentladies.com/indexPhotoplay.html.

Pease, Theresa. "Finding That 'Something Special.'" *Andover Academy Bulletin*. http://www.andover.edu/publications/2000winter_bulletin/special/special.htm.

People for the Ethical Treatment of Animals (PETA). http://www.peta-onlin.org.

Peters, Jacquelin C. "Braids, Cornrows, Dreadlocks, and Hair Wraps: An African Continuum." Paper presented at the 1992 Festival of Michigan Folk Life at Michigan State University, East Lansing, MI. http://accad.osu.edu/~dkrug/367/online/ethnicarts4/r_resources/reading/Peters.asp.

Peterseim, Locke. "Minds, Bodies and Soul Patches." http://espn.go.com/page2/s/closer/020221.html.

Peterson, Barbara Bennett. "Alice Sae Teshima Noda." American National Biography. http:www.anb.org/articles/20/20-01408-article.html.

Pine, Devera. "Hair! From Personal Statement to Personal Problem." *FDA Consumer*, December 1991. http://www.cfsan.fda.gov/~dms/cos-817.html.

Poinsett, Alex. "Unsung Black Business Giants; Pioneer Entrepreneurs Laid Foundations for Today's Enterprises." *Ebony*, March 1990.

Pollack, Richard, MD. "Head Lice: Information and Frequently Asked Questions." Harvard School of Public Health. http://www.hsph.harvard.edu/headlice.html.

Pollak, Margie. "Hair Dye Dilemmas." *FDA Consumer*, April 1993.

Procter and Gamble. "General Information," "History," and "FAQs." http:/www.pg.com.

"Procter and Gamble History." http://www.petragroup.com.jo/history.htm.

Public Broadcasting System (PBS). "Martha Matilda Harper (They Made America)." http://www.pbs.org/wgbh/theymadeamerica/whomade/harper_hi.html.

"Q & A With Manual Diaz, the Wolf Man." http://www.circusfolks.com/circus/interview.html.

Redding, Marie. "Packager of the Year." Cosmetic/Personal Care online, http://www.cpcpkg.com/03/12/PackagerOftheYear.html.

Reilly, Steve. "Bearded Woman Finds Shelter in Punta Gorda." *Sun Herald* (Florida), May 21, 2003. http://www.sun-herald.com/NewsArchive2/052103/tp3ch17.htm?date=052103&story=tp3ch17.htm.

Reuters News Service. "Fear of Idolatry Sparks Wig Ban in Israel." *Jerusalem Times*, May 15, 2004.

"Revlon History." http://www.revlon.com/corporate/corp.

Rickard, Ken. "Facial-Fuzz-Challenged Reflections on the Hip Hirsute Look." *Honolulu Advertiser*, February 17, 2003.

Roffler. "Then and Now." http://www.roffler.com.

Rousseau, Ingrid. "Who, Or What, Killed Napoleon?" *CBS News*, October 30, 2002. http://www.cbsnews.com/stories/2002/10/30/tech/main527531.shtml.

Salon Channel. "NCA Plans Second National Beauty Salon Month." http://salonchannel.com/articles/beauty_salon_month.htm.

Schaff, Philip. "Chapter X: Close of the Middle Ages." *History of the Christian Church, Vol. 6: The Middle Ages.* http://www.ccel.org/ccel/schaff/hcc6.ii.xi.htm.

Schervish, Susan. "Euromonitor: Global Report Market Direction for Makeup and Color Cosmetics." Efficient Collaborative Retail Marketing (ECRM). http://www.ecrm-epps.com/Expose/V3_3/V3_3_A26.asp.

Schrieberg, David, and Sharon Begley, "Children of the Ice." *Newsweek*, November 6, 1995.

Schuck, Jill. "A Curl's Best Friend." *Platinum*, July 2002. http://www.ouidad.com/news_and_events/press_magazines_detail.asp?detail=320&start=92.

Seeger, Anthony. "The Meaning of Body Ornaments: A Suya Example." *Ethnology* (July 1975): 211–224.

Severy, Merle. "The Byzantine Empire, Rome of the East." *National Geographic*, December 1983, 709–721.
Shelton, Karen M. "Jose Eber: The Messenger of Love & Beauty." http://www.hairboutique.com/tips/tip3530.htm.
Shoji, Kaori. "The Mane Attraction." *The Japan Times*, May 25, 2004. http://202.221.217.59/print/features/life2004/fl20040525zg.htm.
Shultz, Harald. "Brazil's Big-Lipped Indians." *National Geographic*. January 1962.
Silverman, Robert Mark. "The Effects of Racism and Racial Discrimination on Minority Business Development: The Case of Black Manufacturers in Chicago's Ethnic Beauty Aids Industry." *Journal of Social History* 31 (1998). http://www.findarticles.com/p/articles/mi_m2005/is_n3_v31/ai_20574140.
Sobotta, Sharon K. "World's Body Perceptions Vary." *University Chronicle*, February 26, 2001. http://www.universitychronicle.com/media/paper231/news/2001/02/26/News/World8217s.Body.Perceptions.Vary-38169.shtml.
Sontag, Susan. "The Double Standard of Aging." *Saturday Review*, September 23, 1972, 29–38.
Spencer, Jim. "Argument Over Dyed Hair is a Tangled Mess."http://www.digitalcity.com/hamptonroads/hampton_issues/main.adp#story.
Stapley, Karen. "Locks of Love." *Desert Dispatch* (Barstow, CA), May 25, 2005. http://www.desertdispatch.com/2005/111702689685478.html.
Stark, Andrew. "What's Natural?" *Wilson Quarterly* 27 (Spring 2003): 1.
Stehlin, Dori. "Cosmetic Allergies." *FDA Consumer*, November 1986. Reprint. http://vm.cfsan.fda.gov/~dms/cos-224.html.
———. "Cosmetic Safety: More Complex Than at First Blush." *FDA Consumer*, November 1991. http://vm.cfsan.fda.gov/~dms/cos-807.html.
Stockinger, Günther. "The Curse of the Hair." *Der Spiegel*, December 31, 2004. http://service.spiegel.de/cache/international/spiegel/0,1518,335660,00.html.
Stokes, Paul. "Pay Out for Man Denied Bar Job Over His Ponytail." *Telegraph.com* (United Kingdom), January 13, 2000. http://www.choisser.com/longhair/telegraph.html.
Stuart, Julia. "Young Blades." *The Independent* (London), January 2003.
Stuller, Jeff. "Cleanliness Has Only Recently Become a Virtue." *Smithsonian*, February 1991, 126–134.
Swiencicki, Mark A. "Consuming Brotherhood: Men's Culture, Style and Recreation as Consumer Culture, 1880–1930," *Journal of Social History* 31 (4) (Summer 1998).
Synnott, A. "Shame and Glory: A Sociology of Hair," *The British Journal of Sociology* 38 (3) (1987): 381–413.
Takashima, Miki. "Black and Beautiful." *Daily Yomiuri* (Japan), November 18, 1999, 7.
Tarshis, Joan. "Dorothy Hamill's Amazing Grace," *Reader's Digest*, January 2001. http://www.rd.com/common/nav/index.jhtml?articleId=9520003.
Taylor, T. B. "Soul Rebels: The Rastafarians and the Free Exercise Clause." *Georgetown Law Journal* 72 (1984): 1605–1635.
Theil, Art. "Like No Other." *Hoop*, April 1998. http://www.nba.com/jordan/hoop_oneforages.html.
Thomas, Karen. "She's Having a Blonde Moment," *USA Today*, October 27, 2003.
Time. "*Time*'s 100 Most Influential Women of the Century," November 1999.
Treman, Irene Castle. "I Bobbed My Hair and Then—." *Ladies Home Journal*, October 1921, 124.

Trichological Society. http://www.hairscientists.org/education.htm.

Turner, Terence S. "Tchikrin: A Central Brazilian Tribe and Its Symbolic Language of Bodily Adornment." *Natural History*, October 1969.

TV Guide. "From Hair to Eternity: Jennifer Aniston, Friends." http://www.tvguide.com/features/hair/jennifer.asp.

Twiggy. http://www.twiggylawson.co.uk/biography.html.

Unilever. "Our History." http://www.unilever.com/ourcompany/aboutunilever/history/default.asp.

Unilever Canada. "Products." http://www.unilever.ca/products/index.asp?navLev=4&PCateId=10&NavId=32.

"United States Navy Uniform Regulations." http://buperscd.technology.navy.mil/bup_updt/508/unireg/toc/tableOfContents.htm.

U.S. Environmental Protection Agency. "Government Ban on Fluorocarbon Gases in Aerosol Products Begins October 15 [1978]," October 15, 1978. http://www.epa.gov/history/topics/ozone/01.htm.

U.S. Food and Drug Administration. "Cosmetic Labeling." *FDA Consumer*, March 26, 2003. http://vm.cfsan.fda.gov/~dms/cos-labl.html.

———. "Decoding the Cosmetic Label." *FDA Consumer*, May 1993. http://vm.cfsan.fda.gov/~dms/cos-labl.html.

Vespa, M. "A Two-Year-Old in False Eyelashes." *Ms.*, September 1976, 61–66.

Vincent, Peter. "A Cut Above." *Sydney Morning Herald*, February 23, 2005. http://moneymanager.smh.com.au/articles/2005/02/22/1108834779883.html.

Wade, Nicholas. "Why Humans and Their Fur Parted Ways," *The New York Times*, August 19, 2003, Section F: 1, 4.

Wadhwani, Anita. "From India to Nashville: The Human Hair Trade Links People a World Apart." *Middle Tennessee News and Information*, March 9, 2003. http://www.tennessean.com/special/hair/archives/03/03/29911318.shtml.

Walker, Michael. "My Excellent Brylcreem Adventure." *The New York Times Magazine*, October 13, 2001. http://www.ahundredmonkeys.com/nytimes_article3.htm.

Weiss, Michael J. "Guys Who Dye—Males' Use of Hair Dye." *American Demographics*, June 1, 1999. http://www.findarticles.com/p/articles/mi_m4021/is_ISSN_0163-4089/ai_54933563.

Wells, Rhona. "The Most Precious Incense." *The Middle East*, September 1993.

Whitaker, Charles. "The Real Josephine Baker: What the Movie Didn't Tell You." *Ebony*, June 1991.

White, Shane, and Graham White, "Slave Hair and African American Culture in the Eighteenth and Nineteenth Centuries." *Journal of Southern History* LXI (1) (February 1995): 45–76.

"World Beard Championship." http://www.worldbeardchampionship.com.

Worley, Kelly. "Joyner Marks a Century of Black Progress." *The Chicago Reporter*, December 1993. http://www.chicagoreporter.com/1993/12-93/1293Joyner-MarksaCenturyofBlackProgress.htm.

Wulff, Jennifer, and Rebecca Paley, "Mane Attraction." *People*, September 13, 2004, 115–116.

Index

Note: Main entry page numbers are indicated by **bold** type; page numbers with photos are indicated by *italic* type.

About the Author

VICTORIA SHERROW is the author of *For Appearance's Sake: The Historical Encyclopedia of Good Looks, Beauty, and Grooming* (2001), *Encyclopedia of Youth and War: Young People as Participants and Victims* (1999), and *Women and the Military: An Encyclopedia* (1996). She is also the 1996 RUSA Outstanding Reference Source award winner.